Toward an Ecology of
Transfiguration

Orthodox Christianity and Contemporary Thought

SERIES EDITORS
George E. Demacopoulos and Aristotle Papanikolaou

This series consists of books that seek to bring Orthodox Christianity into an engagement with contemporary forms of thought. Its goal is to promote (1) historical studies in Orthodox Christianity that are interdisciplinary, employ a variety of methods, and speak to contemporary issues; and (2) constructive theological arguments in conversation with patristic sources and that focus on contemporary questions ranging from the traditional theological and philosophical themes of God and human identity to cultural, political, economic, and ethical concerns. The books in the series explore both the relevancy of Orthodox Christianity to contemporary challenges and the impact of contemporary modes of thought on Orthodox self-understandings.

Toward an Ecology of Transfiguration

Orthodox Christian Perspectives on Environment, Nature, and Creation

EDITED BY
JOHN CHRYSSAVGIS AND
BRUCE V. FOLTZ

FORDHAM UNIVERSITY PRESS
New York • 2013

Copyright © 2013 Fordham University Press

All rights reserved. No part of this publication may be reproduced, stored in a retrieval system, or transmitted in any form or by any means—electronic, mechanical, photocopy, recording, or any other—except for brief quotations in printed reviews, without the prior permission of the publisher.

Fordham University Press has no responsibility for the persistence or accuracy of URLs for external or third-party Internet websites referred to in this publication and does not guarantee that any content on such websites is, or will remain, accurate or appropriate.

Fordham University Press also publishes its books in a variety of electronic formats. Some content that appears in print may not be available in electronic books.

Library of Congress Cataloging-in-Publication Data

Toward an ecology of transfiguration : orthodox Christian perspectives on environment, nature, and creation / edited by John Chryssavgis and Bruce V. Foltz. —First edition
    pages cm— (Orthodox Christianity and contemporary thought)
    Includes bibliographical references and index.
    Summary: "Can Orthodox Christianity offer spiritual resources uniquely suited to the environmental concerns of today? This book makes the case emphatically that it can indeed. In addition to being the first substantial and comprehensive collection of essays, in any language, to address environmental issues from the Orthodox point of view, this volume (with contributions from many of the most influential theologians and philosophers in contemporary world Orthodoxy) will engage a wide audience, in academic as well as popular circles—resonating not only with Orthodox audiences but with all those in search of a fresh approach to environmental theory and ethics that can bring to bear the resources of ancient spirituality, often virtually unknown in the West, on modern challenges and dilemmas"—Provided by publisher.
    ISBN 978-0-8232-5144-5 (hardback)—ISBN 978-0-8232-5145-2 (paper)
    1. Orthodox Eastern Church—Doctrines. 2. Ecology—Religious aspects—Orthodox Eastern Church. 3. Nature—Religious aspects—Orthodox Eastern Church. 4. Creation. 5. Human ecology—Religious aspects—Orthodox Eastern Church. I. Chryssavgis, John. II. Foltz, Bruce V.
    BX323.T69 2013
    261.8'80882819—dc23

2013002532

Printed in the United States of America

15 14 13   5 4 3 2 1

First edition

Contents

Prefatory Letter by Ecumenical Patriarch Bartholomew   xi
Foreword by Bill McKibben   xiii

Introduction. "The Sweetness of Heaven Overflows onto the
Earth": Orthodox Christianity and Environmental Thought   1
   John Chryssavgis and Bruce V. Foltz

I. "KNOWLEDGE UNITED TO GOD": ENVIRONMENT, NATURE, AND CREATION IN PATRISTIC THOUGHT

The *Logoi* of Beings in Greek Patristic Thought   9
   David Bradshaw

Hierarchy and Love in St. Dionysius the Areopagite   23
   Eric D. Perl

The Beauty of the World and Its Significance in St. Gregory
the Theologian   34
   John Anthony McGuckin

Natural Contemplation in St. Maximus the Confessor and
St. Isaac the Syrian   46
   Metropolitan Jonah (Paffhausen)

Man and Cosmos in St. Maximus the Confessor   59
   Andrew Louth

II. "THE HEART THAT RECEIVES": ENVIRONMENT, NATURE, AND CREATION IN TWENTIETH-CENTURY ORTHODOX THOUGHT

Ecology, Theology, and the World 75
Savas Agouridis

Through Creation to the Creator 86
Metropolitan Kallistos (Ware) of Diokleia

Creation as Communion in Contemporary Orthodox Theology 106
Aristotle Papanikolaou

The Theological-Ethical Contributions of Archimandrite Sophrony (Sakharov) to Environmental Issues 121
Perry T. Hamalis

The Cosmology of the Eucharist 131
George Theokritoff

"A 'Tradition' That Never Existed": Orthodox Christianity and the Failure of Environmental History 136
Jurretta Jordan Heckscher

A New Heaven and a New Earth: Orthodox Christian Insights from Theology, Spirituality, and the Sacraments 152
John Chryssavgis

Proprietors or Priests of Creation? 163
Metropolitan John (Zizioulas) of Pergamon

III. "LOVE COMES FROM MEETING GOD": HISTORICAL, THEOLOGICAL, AND PHILOSOPHICAL DIMENSIONS

Sedimentation of Meaning in the Concepts of Nature and the Environment 175
James Carey

Existential versus Regulative Approaches: The Environmental Issue as an Existential and Not a Canonical Problem 186
Christos Yannaras

Nature and Creation: A Comment on the Environmental
Problem from a Philosophical and Theological Standpoint 193
    Nikos Nissiotis

Physis and *Ktisis*: Two Different Ways of Thinking of the World 204
    John Panteleimon Manoussakis

Human Image, World Image: The Renewal of Sacred Cosmology 210
    Philip Sherrard

Environment and Security: Toward a Systemic Crisis
of Humanity? 226
    Costa Carras

Church Walls and Wilderness Boundaries: Defining
the Spaces of Sanctuary 235
    L. Michael Harrington

Orthodoxy and Ecopoetics: The Green World in the Desert Sea 243
    Alfred K. Siewers

Perspectives on Orthodoxy, Evolution, and Ecology 263
    Gayle E. Woloschak

Ecology, Morality, and the Challenges of the Twenty-First
Century: The Earth in the Hands of the Sons of Noah 276
    H. Tristram Engelhardt Jr.

IV. "SWEETNESS OVERFLOWING ONTO THE EARTH": INSIGHTS FROM ORTHODOX SPIRITUALITY

The Fragile Surround 293
    Scott Cairns

Liturgy, Cosmic Worship, and Christian Cosmology 295
    Elizabeth Theokritoff

"All Creation Rejoices in You": Creation in the
Liturgies for the Feasts of the Theotokos 307
    Christina M. Gschwandtner

Traces of Divine Fragrance, Droplets of Divine
Love: On the Beauty of Visible Creation 324
    Bruce V. Foltz

Natural and Supernatural Revelation in Early Irish and
Greek Monastic Thought: A Comparative Approach   337
    Chrysostomos Koutloumousianos

Ecology and Monasticism   348
    Archimandrite Vasileios

The Prophetic Charisma in Pastoral Theology: Asceticism,
Fasting, and the Ecological Crisis   356
    Anestis Keselopoulos

The Spirit of God Moved upon the Face of the
Waters: Orthodox Holiness and the Natural World   365
    Donald Sheehan

APPENDIXES

A. Vespers for the Environment   379
    Translated by Archimandrite Ephrem (Lash)

B. Environment, Nature, and Creation in Orthodox Thought:
   A Bibliography of Texts in English   398
    Compiled by John Chryssavgis and Bruce V. Foltz

C. Glossary   410
    Compiled by Nicholas R. Anton

Notes   415

List of Contributors   469

Index of Names (Classical)   475
Index of Names (Contemporary)   477
General Index   480

Prefatory Letter

It is with particular satisfaction and personal joy that we welcome this publication, being originally the fruit of an innovative conference held from October 25–28, 2007, in California, at the St. Nicholas Ranch and Retreat Center of the Greek Orthodox Metropolis of San Francisco, for the purpose of gathering Orthodox thinkers from a variety of disciplines and range of backgrounds in order to explore scholarly perspectives of our relationship toward the natural environment.

As is well known, this topic has been of urgent concern and spiritual priority to the Ecumenical Patriarchate since at least the mid-1980s and, more especially, during our tenure since 1991. We have spared no effort whatsoever in endeavoring to raise popular awareness—both within the Orthodox Church worldwide as well as within the broader community globally, across religious and disciplinary divides—on the sacredness of material creation, formed out of nothing by our loving Creator and offered to humanity as a sacrament of communion and thanksgiving, but also on the sinful abuse of its natural resources by human beings who, over the centuries, have demonstrated a sense of arrogance and failed to recognize when enough is enough.

Throughout our international conferences with theologians and scientists, our political conversations with world leaders, and our encyclical communications with Orthodox faithful, we have emphasized the liturgical, iconic, and ascetic dimensions of the divine command and human vocation for the prayerful preservation and needful protection of the natural environment. Nevertheless, it has always been our foremost expectation and fervent hope alike that communities throughout the world would gradually assume responsibility for this crucial matter on the regional and parochial but also on the local and personal levels.

In this respect, we appreciate in particular the collective concern of the academic community and welcome with profound pleasure this unique volume edited by Archdeacon John Chryssavgis and Dr. Bruce Foltz, bringing together voices from Orthodox communities throughout the world in perhaps the most comprehensive exploration of environmental theology of our time. It is our sincere and firm conviction that members of the scholastic community are, perhaps in a unique and even unprecedented manner, able to provide invaluable insights and influential incentives to the wider community with regard to the limitless treasures of the philosophical, patristic, and prophetic tradition of our Church.

This volume documents and expands on the effort initiated at the conference in 2007, with the additional participation and inclusion of leading spokespersons on the subject over the last decades. The areas of concentration are as varied as the contributors themselves, spanning such disciplines as theology and epistemology, religion and science, philosophy and poetry, ethics and morality, liturgy and doctrine, phenomenology and technology.

It is our fervent prayer that this book will prove truly beneficial, awakening the conscience and planting seeds in the hearts of numerous people and diverse institutions around the world for many years to come.

☦ ***Bartholomew***
Archbishop of Constantinople–New Rome and Ecumenical Patriarch

Foreword

Bill McKibben

This remarkable volume helps answer a worldly question that's interested me for some years: Why has Bartholomew, the Ecumenical Patriarch and spiritual leader of Orthodox Christians worldwide, been such a standout figure among religious leaders in his call for environmental care? A Western Christian such as myself can establish an ethic of stewardship from the Catholic or Protestant readings of the Bible, but it must be said that most of these churches have been slow at best to embrace the move toward care of creation. Bartholomew, by contrast, was dubbed the "Green Patriarch" in the very first years of his patriarchate and anointed by *Time* as one of the world's hundred most important people precisely for his role in "defining environmentalism as a spiritual responsibility." When we formed 350.org, the first big grassroots climate change campaign, he was uniquely forthright in declaring that "global warming is a sin."

Ignorant of Orthodox theology, I concluded that it must have been some personal tic, perhaps the way a movie star adopts a cause. But as I've listened over the years, journeyed to the island of Halki for an ecological summit, and especially as I've read this volume, I've gotten a clearer sense that his forthright activism is simply an expression of an underlying spiritual tradition with deep connections to the natural world and remarkable gifts to offer to the rest of the world. The notion that the Logos can be seen in every created thing— that the world is in some sense a living museum of divine intent—is scandalously powerful. It undercuts the most alien idea of the Western tradition, of God (and man in his image) apart from the natural world. At war with the natural world, to judge from the results.

But that Orthodox sense of the natural world seems at odds not just with Cartesian secular modernity—it's also at odds with too much of the rest of the church, which has tended to tremble at embracing God's creation for fear it would somehow turn pagan. In fact, scholars have routinely condemned Christianity for its role in aiding and abetting the secular drive to treat the earth as nothing more than a mine to be plundered, a prosaic resource to be used up while we impatiently inhabit this waystation on the road to a better eternal home. If instead the natural world is a gift from God, the possibilities enlarge.

For one thing, it becomes possible to see in the beauty of the world around us a reminder of our need to be recalled to our relationship with the divine. A mountain, not surprisingly, is more effective than an office building in making that connection (from Sinai on, and probably long before). A lake more than a bathtub. In the natural world we are reminded, among other things, that we are small, which is one of God's great gifts to us—but one of the easiest to forget in a world where most surfaces mirror our human might. We can't know God directly, these essays suggest, but we can encounter Him, and perhaps most easily in the larger world around us, with its 24/7 testimony.

"Seeing nature as a divinely written icon, it is possible to praise the Creator and give thanks to Him for this beautiful creation, as the Psalms everywhere enjoin us," the editors write in their Introduction. So: starry night, rosy dawn, deep forest, broad beach, rolling wave, towering cloud. All worth *seeing*, seeing with the soul.

I believe this volume will offer remarkable insight for those of us from allied traditions—it is a generous gift, a pair of corrective lenses through which to view scripture and practice that we've been squinting to try to make sense of. The world, with its rising temperatures, melting ice, acidifying oceans, and ever-more-arid plains, no longer seems something to ignore. Instead it seems something to love, a part of the whole. I am reminded of God's sarcastic taunts in his great speech from the whirlwind at the close of the book of Job, the longest divine soliloquy in either testament, that account of laying the cornerstone of creation when "the morning stars sang together and all the sons of God shouted for joy." That exuberance is in this book, that joy is in this tradition; may we learn, and soon, how to share in it.

What is knowledge? The experience of eternal life.
And what is eternal life? The experience of all things in God.
For love comes from meeting God. Knowledge united to God fulfills every desire. And for the heart that receives it, it is altogether sweetness overflowing onto the earth. Indeed, there is nothing like the sweetness of God.
—*St. Isaac the Syrian*

Introduction. "The Sweetness of Heaven Overflows onto the Earth": Orthodox Christianity and Environmental Thought

John Chryssavgis and Bruce V. Foltz

During the past few decades, the world has witnessed alarming environmental degradation—the threat of anthropogenic climate change, the loss of biodiversity, and the pollution of natural resources—along with the widening gap between rich and poor, as well as the increasing failure to implement environmental policies. We are reminded—in a painful way—of this crisis when we learn of the cruel extinction of flora and fauna and of irresponsible soil degradation and forest clearance, as well as when we endure unacceptable noise, air, and water pollution. Nonetheless, for Orthodox Christian philosophers and theologians, the concern for the environment is not a form of superficial or sentimental love. It is a way of honoring and dignifying the reality of our own creation by the hand and Word of God. It is, as well, a way of respecting "the mourning of the land" (Hosea 41:3) and heeding "the groaning of creation" (Rom. 8:22).

During this same period, one religious leader has notably discerned the signs of the times and called people's attention to this ecological and social situation. The worldwide leader of the Orthodox Churches, His All-Holiness Ecumenical Patriarch Bartholomew, has persistently proclaimed the primacy of spiritual values in determining environmental ethics and action. We are sincerely indebted to him for his spiritual leadership and pioneering initiatives as well as deeply grateful to him for his generosity in providing the foreword to this volume.

Western thought in the modern age has not been kind to the created world. From the exhortations of Galileo and Bacon that we subject it to violent interrogation to Descartes' vision of the natural environment as populated with only seemingly animated robots, from the general Enlightenment concept of nature as a great machine to Hegel's view of the natural world as Spirit in a degraded and paralyzed condition, modern thought has given us a view of nature as something that is, in Max Weber's words, thoroughly "disenchanted"—drained of its power to elicit from us wonder and a sense of transcendence glimmering through and within it. And against the quiet, largely unheeded voice of Gerard Manley Hopkins reminding us that "there lives the dearest freshness deep down things," there is a far louder chorus decrying the very Christian faith that had originally allowed us to see and wonder and give thanks and praise—to approach nature no longer as the lair of treacherous, preternatural powers against which we must ever be wary but instead to see it as the gift of creation, God's initial, glorious revelation to humanity.

Indeed, beginning with Feuerbach and proceeding with Nietzsche, it was said that it was not Western modernity at all but Christianity itself that had silenced nature, subjugating the rich beauty of earth to the ethereal delights of heaven and degrading the earthly to mere matter given over to human control and exploitation. Perhaps the most influential proponent of this view has been Lynn White Jr., himself a Presbyterian layman, who argued that Christianity was singularly responsible for the present environmental crisis. According to White, as early as the thirteenth century the Latin West began to see nature as "a vast reservoir of energies to be tapped and used according to human intentions," and this promoted a violent, "arrogant," and dominating relation toward creation—leading us from seeing ourselves as "part of nature" to being "an exploiter of nature" entitled to exercise a now-characteristic "ruthlessness toward nature."[1]

Yet of those who actually read his essay "On the Historical Roots of Our Ecologic Crisis"—which has been endlessly cited, since its publication in the 1960s, as canonical in environmental literature—few stop to notice that at decisive points in his argument, White explicitly exempts the Christianity of the East from his critique, commending rather than censuring its view of creation:

> In the early Church, and *always in the Greek East*, nature was conceived primarily as *a symbolic system through which God speaks to men*. . . . This view of nature was *essentially artistic rather than scientific*. While Byzantium preserved and copied great numbers of ancient Greek scientific texts, science as we conceive it could scarcely flourish in such an ambiance. However in the Latin West by the early 13th century, natural theology was following a very different bent. It was ceasing to be the

decoding of the physical symbols of God's communication with man and was becoming the effort to understand God's mind by discovering how his creation operates.[2]

White's understanding of Orthodox Christianity here is far from flawless. But his instincts are sound, for he sees that in the Christian East, as was the case in the earliest Christian thought of the patristic era, creation was understood not mechanically but aesthetically; not as an impersonally functioning mechanism but as the personal revelation of a loving Creator, a great gift that is meant to recall us to a relation to God within which alone our authentic happiness can be found; not as a free-standing substance with which to fabricate commodities to satisfy our desires but as an endless love poem being ever written by the Logos through Whom all things are made and meant for us to read and reread, to heed and treasure.

Understood more deeply, Orthodox Christianity holds a set of views that is not entirely absent in Western thought but that have not been grasped in their synergistic integrity outside Eastern lands and that have unhappily remained so thoroughly hidden from Western thought that it has (uncritically) adopted the Feuerbach-Nietzsche-White critique of Christianity as definitive, either abandoning Christianity altogether for the sake of a natural environment clearly in dire straits or else jettisoning much of the Christian tradition in favor of revisionist interpretations that are thought to be more salutary for our relation to the earth. Yet it is the claim of the present collection, taken as a whole, that it is solely on the basis of these very principles that we can embrace and articulate a spirituality that is adequate to the environmental tasks awaiting us.

What are these principles? Stated briefly, they proceed from the recognition—based upon a distinction long ignored or rejected in the Latin West—that while the divine essence (*ousia*) is eternally mysterious and unknowable, the uncreated energies or activity (*energeia*) of God can not only be known but encountered and experienced in this life and in this world, for they are at work everywhere around us. Connected with this is the realization that the Eternal Son of God, the Logos through whom the world is created, is mirrored and expressed in all things—in every leaf and blade of grass—as their inner meaning or depth, their *logoi*, thereby allowing us truly, in Blake's words, to see "Heaven in a wildflower." Hence, once the soul is purified (*katharsis*) through spiritual discipline (*askesis*), our Edenic ability to engage in a seeing of nature (*theoria physike*) can be at least partially restored to us—a discovery made, to some degree, independently in the West by nature poets and naturalists such as Thoreau and Muir. Seeing nature as a divinely written icon, it is possible to praise the Creator and give thanks to Him for this beautiful creation, as the Psalms everywhere enjoin us. In doing so, we serve as a priesthood of creation, fulfilling the task for which we were ourselves created: not to exploit the created world after our own designs but rather to celebrate and consecrate and offer it back to the Creator—"Thine own of Thine own we offer unto Thee on behalf of all and for all," as the Divine Liturgy of the Orthodox Church proclaims. And in this set of theological insights, drawn not from speculative metaphysics but from the lived experience of the holy men and women whom Orthodox Christians recognize as saints—as "spiritual athletes" or "friends of God"—we believe there are principles upon which to build the theology and spirituality of which we, along with the earth that we have despoiled, stand in urgent need.

This collection of articles is the first substantial anthology, in any language, to address environmental issues from the point of view of Orthodox Christianity, and its contributors include many of the most highly respected Orthodox theologians and philosophers in recent decades. Corresponding to the *sobornost* or freedom-within-dialogue that is traditional to Orthodox intellectual life, readers will find here a perhaps surprising diversity and richness of writing styles, of theological and intellectual and methodological concerns, and of approaches to environmental issues. But overall, and especially for those accustomed to current trends in "ecotheology" and environmental philosophy, the reflections on environmental issues presented here will likely be found fresh and distinctive in several important ways:

1. The articles characteristically proceed from lived spirituality rather than religious doctrine, and when theological concepts are introduced, they are understood to be rooted in concrete religious experience.

2. Hence, they are often shaped more by noetic or mystical insight than by analysis and propositional argument, not infrequently employing language whose resonance is poetic.

3. Moreover, they characteristically draw upon the ontological roots of sacramental and liturgical sensibilities to point toward the often tacit, unexamined relations between creation and creator, visible and invisible, heaven and earth.

4. In addition, their approach is oriented cosmically rather than anthropocentrically, regarding the process of salvation or redemption as systemic and ecological in the broadest sense.

5. Finally, they are based upon a theology of Incarnation that looks toward the transfiguration of all creation as the ultimate goal of his-

tory, for which humanity would serve, humbly and contemplatively, as a cosmic priesthood celebrating and consecrating creation, and offering it back to its Creator—thereby addressing, more powerfully than he could have anticipated, Nietzsche's oft-cited challenge that thinking today "be true to the earth."

The compilation itself is organized around a quotation by the great mystic St. Isaac the Syrian:

What is knowledge? The experience of eternal life.
 And what is eternal life? The experience of all things in God.
 For love comes from meeting God. Knowledge united to God fulfills every desire. And for the heart that receives it, it is altogether sweetness overflowing onto the earth. Indeed, there is nothing like the sweetness of God.[3]

Our volume opens with a series of historical reflections in Part I, "'Knowledge United to God': Environment, Nature, and Creation in Patristic Thought," which examines central aspects of the understanding of nature, environment, and creation in the ancient Christianity of the first millennium. Part II, "'The Heart That Receives': Environment, Nature, and Creation in Twentieth-Century Orthodox Thought," shows that these ancient views have far more than antiquarian interest, engaging them with important issues and thinkers of the twentieth century. Part III, "'Love Comes from Meeting God': Historical, Theological, and Philosophical Dimensions," examines a variety of problems in environmental theory by employing the resources developed in the first two sections, exploring the concepts of "nature" and "creation" as competing rubrics for environmental understanding, the phenomenology of sacred space, and historical and ethical issues concerning ecology and environmentalism. Finally, Part IV, "'Sweetness Overflowing onto the Earth': Insights from Orthodox Spirituality," shows how the ideas presented earlier relate to the connection between living spirituality and our experience of the natural world around us.

This collection of essays boasts some of the most important voices within contemporary Orthodox thought both in North America and in Europe—what we feel is an embarrassment of riches featuring some of its most respected hierarchs and its most celebrated scholars, its monks and professors, its clergy and scientists and poets. It will be a rare reader who will not discover treasures here. At the same time, it brings together new and original contributions with articles that have become classics in Orthodox circles yet that are currently unobtainable because they were first printed in small editions. Nor is it univocal in its conclusions, offering a rich display of the diversity of Orthodox thinking. We believe that *Toward an Ecology of Transfiguration: Orthodox Christian Perspectives on Environment, Nature, and Creation* has the potential to become a groundbreaking volume, not just as pointing toward new horizons in environmental thought but as a contribution to the millennial attempt to reconcile East and West, Byzantine and Latin, if not initially as complementary components of a single *ekkelsia*, then at least as dedicated, serious participants in a common and globally critical project of offering to the world hope for the possibility of a viable and salutary future—one for which the reality named by terms such as nature and environment and creation is more than a memory or an aspiration but a living benediction and icon of divine grace. It is a book that we hope will engage a very wide audience in academic as well as more popular circles—not only Orthodox audiences but just as much those who are simply looking for a fresh, provocative approach to environmental thought that brings to bear the resources of ancient spirituality upon modern perplexities.

We are especially honored to include in this anthology the writing of three prophetic figures in the development of an Orthodox sensitivity to the environment. As in many other aspects of his thinking, Nikos Nissiotis (1924–1986) spoke and wrote of creation theology among international and ecumenical circles well before anyone considered its significance. Philip Sherrard (1922–1995) was the first Orthodox theologian to articulate a systematic approach to the ecological crisis, doubtless drawing upon his experience of monasticism and his exposure to the classic texts of the *Philokalia*. And Savas Agouridis (1921–2009), a biblical scholar in Greece, was among the first and few Orthodox theologians in the past century to call into question the conservative approach to the Church Fathers while emphasizing the social depth of the gospel message. Along with articles by these three authors, we are also honored to include an essay by the late Donald Sheehan (1940–2010) of Dartmouth University and the Robert Frost Place.

Feast of the Epiphany 2013

PART

I

"KNOWLEDGE UNITED TO GOD": ENVIRONMENT, NATURE, AND CREATION IN PATRISTIC THOUGHT

THE *LOGOI* OF BEINGS IN GREEK PATRISTIC THOUGHT

David Bradshaw

One of the most intriguing aspects of Greek patristic thought about nature is the concept of the *logoi* of beings. The *logoi* are the "inner essences" of things, the value and significance they have in the eyes of the Creator rather than in our faulty human estimation. To perceive the *logoi* in beings is the act known as *theōria phusikē*, the second of the three stages of the spiritual life distinguished by Evagrius and the tradition that followed him.[1] A full discussion of *theōria phusikē* would require situating it within its role in the ascetic life—as, on the one hand, the outgrowth of *praktikē* (ascetic and moral practice) and, on the other, the gateway to *theologia* (pure or imageless prayer). My aim here is the more modest one of understanding the concept of the *logoi* of beings itself. I wish to identify the philosophical sources of this concept and in the process to notice both some of its pitfalls as well as the promise it offers for Christian thought about nature.

Although the notion of the *logoi* of beings has important biblical resonances, its immediate origin lies in the confluence of two strands within Greek philosophy. The first is Plato's account of the creation of the world in the *Timaeus*. Plato writes that God created the world as an image of the "absolute Living Being" that "contains within itself all the intelligible living beings, just as our world is made up of us and all the other visible things" (30c–d). Each entity in the sensible world is an image of a Form present in the absolute Living Being.[2] The precise identity of the "absolute Living Being" remains rather mysterious, but the salient point for our purposes is that the Forms are here presented not as discrete and unconnected (as they seem to be in Plato's middle dialogues) but as parts of an integral living whole.

Although Plato does not describe the absolute Living Being further, later Platonists, recognizing the needless duplication in positing an intelligible model separate from the creator and taking note that the model is alive, identified it with the content of the divine mind. One of the earliest examples of this approach was the treatise *On the Making of the World* by Philo of Alexandria, the first-century Jew whose works influenced Clement of Alexandria and Origen. Philo presents God as like an architect who first sketches out beforehand in his mind the city he is going to build. This "intelligible cosmos" present within the divine mind contains the "Forms and measures and patterns and seals" of the objects in the sensible world.[3] Notably, Philo refers to the divine mind itself as the Logos. By this he means not a separate *hypostasis*, as in Christian thought, but God himself considered in his rational aspect.[4]

Thus Philo presents a view in which each type of creature is created in accordance with a paradigm existing in the divine Logos. Significantly, the relationship here is between *types* of creatures and their paradigms. There is not a paradigm of each individual—although later Platonists such as Plotinus did posit such individual paradigms in the case of intellectual beings. Another current within ancient philosophy presented a quite different way of understanding the relationship between God and creatures. The Stoics too spoke of the Logos, but in their case Logos is simply a name for God himself, whom they understood as the divine mind or reason that governs the world. Unlike Plato or Philo, however, they thought of God as a material being. They identified the Logos with a particularly ethereal substance called *pneuma* that permeates all things, giving them form and order and directing them in accordance with divine wisdom. Although God creates the world, he is himself part of the world he creates, shaping it from within. Here is how the process is described by Diogenes Laertius:

> God is one and the same with Reason (*nous*), Fate, and Zeus; he is also called by many other names. In the beginning he was by himself; he transformed the whole of substance through air into water, and just as in animal generation the seed has a moist vehicle, so in cosmic moisture God, who is the seminal reason (*spermatikon logon*) of the universe, remains behind in the moisture as such an agent, adapting matter to himself with a view to the next stage of creation.[5]

Diogenes here emphasizes that God as the Logos is present in all things, including water and the other primordial elements. He also describes the Logos as the "seminal reason" of the cosmos. This is not quite the Stoics' most normal way of speaking. Since the Logos is a material substance present in all things, it (or he) can also be understood as divided, and so the Stoics more frequently speak of each thing as having its own *spermatikos logos*. For example, Origen reports that on the Stoic view, "matter receives the *spermatikoi logoi* of the god, retaining them within herself in order to ornament the universe."[6] These *spermatikoi logoi* are the Logos in divided form, distinguished according to the bodies in which they are present as the governing principle of each.[7]

Although the Stoic conception of God as a material being was unacceptable to Christianity, the early Christians drew from Stoicism in many ways. St. Paul famously quotes with approval the Stoic poet Aratus, who describes God as the one in whom "we live and move and have our being" (Acts 17:28). This is a line from Aratus's *Phaenomena*, a poetic description of the constellations and their significance for human life written circa 270 B.C. The full passage reads as follows:

> The sky is our song
> and we begin with Zeus; for men cannot speak
> without giving Him names: the streets are detailed
> with the presence of Zeus, the forums are filled,
> the sea and its harbors are flooded with Zeus,
> and in Him we move and have all our being.
> For we are His children, and He blesses our race
> with beneficent signs, and wakes man to his work,
> directing his mind to the means of his life.[8]

For the Stoics, God as the Logos provides the context for our existence—both the physical context and that of meaning and purpose. Most importantly, he is immediately present to each individual as that individual's *spermatikos logos*. The challenge for Christian thought was to disengage these ideas from their materialistic framework, reinterpreting them within an understanding of creation that was closer to that of Plato and Philo. In so doing, of course, Christian thought was governed by neither the Philonic nor the Stoic conception of the Logos but rather by its own understanding of the Logos as the second person of the Trinity.

The first author to begin drawing these diverse strands together was Origen. In his *Commentary on the Gospel of John*, Origen writes at length about the verse, "In the beginning was the Logos" (John 1:1). He identifies the "beginning" as the divine Wisdom that, according to Proverbs 8, was the first created of all things. As Origen understands it, the verse asserts the identity of the Logos with this divine Wisdom and thus affirms the wisdom of God's creation:

> For I think that just as a house and a ship are built or devised according to the plans of the architect, the house and the ship having as their beginning the plans and thoughts (*logous*) in the craftsman, so all things have come to be according to the thoughts of what will be, which were prefigured by God in wisdom, "For he made all things in wisdom" (Ps. 103:24).⁹

Origen echoes here the description in Philo of God as like an architect who first mentally conceives the city he wishes to build. Yet there are two differences: Origen terms the thoughts in the divine mind *logoi*, and for Origen, the divine Logos in whom these thoughts are present is a separate *hypostasis* from the Father. Indeed, a little later he describes the Logos as "an incorporeal *hypostasis* comprised of the various ideas which embrace the principles (*logous*) of the universe."¹⁰ However, let us note in passing that for Origen the Logos is not consubstantial with the Father; he is instead a creature, as indicated by his identity with the divine Wisdom of Proverbs 8, which Origen also takes to be a creature.¹¹

In affirming the identity of the divine Logos and the divine Wisdom, Origen affirms the fundamental goodness of creation. The significance of this for the divine *logoi* becomes apparent as he comments on the verse, "Behold I say to you, lift up your eyes and see the fields, for they are already white for harvest" (John 4:35). He first observes that the command to "lift up your eyes" admonishes us "to exalt and lift up our thoughts, and to elevate the insight that lies below in a rather sickly condition."¹² To do this one must cease to perform the "works of the flesh" and so attain freedom from the passions. For those who have done so, the white fields that are ready for harvest "are all the things that are perceptible to the senses, including heaven itself and the beings in it." He continues:

> The *logos* of each is clear to those who, by being "transformed into the same image from glory to glory" (II Cor. 3:18), have assumed a likeness to those eyes that have seen how each of the things that have been made was good. For the declaration concerning each of the created things, "God saw that it was good," means this: God perceived good in the *logoi* of each thing, and saw how each of the created things is good in relation to the *logoi* in accordance with which it came to be.¹³

Origen goes on to give as examples the creeping things and sea monsters that God creates in Genesis 1; only in relation to their *logoi*, he says, can these be seen as good. What precisely is the meaning here of *logos*? The English translator of Origen's commentary, Ronald E. Heine, renders it as "purpose." That seems to me partly correct but alone insufficient, for the purpose of each thing exists prior to and independently of the thing itself, whereas the *logoi* Origen describes can be seen *in* the object. Instead I would prefer the term used earlier, "inner essence," where this is understood to include not only the thing's original purpose but also its continuing meaning and significance in God's eyes.[14] The *logos* of an object exists both *prior to* the object, as that in accordance with which it is made, and *in* the object, as its continuing eternal significance. In other words, Origen here combines the transcendence of the Platonic archetype with the immanent presence of the Stoic *spermatikoi logoi*. He does so by understanding the *logoi* as the variegated articulation of the single divine Logos who is also the divine Wisdom; in seeing the *logoi* within creation, one also sees the divine plan and presence that renders all things good.

Another passage from Origen's commentary further clarifies the relationship between the Logos and the *logoi* but at the same time raises some difficulties. It comes as Origen comments on the verse, "You are of this world, I am not of this world" (8:23). Origen infers from this that "there is also another world in which there are things that are not seen . . . a spiritual world on whose appearance and beauty the pure in heart will look, being prepared in advance by beholding it to seek God, so that they may also see him, to the degree that God is disposed by nature to be seen."[15] He then elaborates:

> But you will inquire if, in some sense, the first-born of all creation can be a world, especially insofar as he is the "manifold wisdom" (Eph. 3:10). For by being the *logoi* of absolutely everything according to which all things made by God in wisdom have come to be—as the prophet says, "You made all things in wisdom" (Ps. 103:24)—in himself he would also be a "world" that surpasses the world of sense perception in its diversity and excels it as much as the *logos* (or Logos?) stripped of all the material of the whole world excels the material world. This would be a world constituted, not of matter, but of the participation of the things that have been set in order in the Logos and Wisdom which set matter in order.[16]

Origen here appropriates from Philo the notion of the divine Logos as the intelligible cosmos that constitutes the pattern for the sensible cosmos. In so doing, he also illustrates some of the pitfalls of this idea. He says that "by being the *logoi* of absolutely everything" made by God in wisdom, the Logos constitutes an intelligible cosmos. One has to wonder, then, what if God had chosen not to create or had created a world different from this one—would the Logos thereby be different? Could the Logos *not* be an intelligible world, or could he be a world very different from the one he is now? These questions posed little difficulty for Origen himself because, within Origen's theology, the Logos is a creature.[17] From the standpoint of post-Nicene orthodoxy, however, they present a serious challenge. A passage in a fourth-century follower of Origen, Eusebius of Caesarea, further illustrates the difficulty. He states that the Logos "is called the Word of God because the Almighty has set in him the *logoi* that make and create all things, delivering to him the task of governing all things and steering them by reason and in order."[18] Here the Logos is actually subordinate to the *logoi*, in that they are that which constitute his identity. Plainly such a view is unacceptable for one who believes that the Logos is already the Logos even apart from the act of creation.

The passage in Origen also points to another difficulty, one more directly germane to our present theme. In speaking of how the *logos* "stripped of all the material of the whole world excels the material world," Origen reveals a certain tendency to denigrate the material world in comparison to the *logoi* it contains. This tendency is muted in Origen, for (as we have seen) he also emphasizes the goodness of creation, and even in the present passage it is not clear whether *logos* refers to the rational principles of creation or to the second person of the Trinity. In later Origenists, however, the tendency to denigrate materiality became more apparent. Eusebius, in describing how the Logos "imprints the *logoi* of his own wisdom" on material beings, emphasizes that the Logos is not thereby harmed or "defiled in his own nature."[19] Even more striking in this regard is Evagrius of Pontus, the fourth-century monk who was the first theoretician of monasticism.[20] Evagrius sees the vision of the *logoi* as less a matter of perceiving the divine presence within matter than of *escaping* from matter altogether. Thus we find in his *Gnostic Chapters*:

> The mind that is divested of the passions and sees the *logoi* of beings does not henceforth truly receive the images (*eidōla*) that arrive through the senses; but it is as if another world were created by its knowledge, attracting to it its thought and rejecting far from it the sensible world.[21]

A bit later, he adds:

> The world established in the mind seems difficult to see by day, because the mind is distracted by the senses and by the sensible light that shines; but at night it can be seen, luminously imprinted at the time of prayer.[22]

These passages are typical of a tendency in Evagrius to see the spiritual life as less a matter of apprehending the sensible creation in a new and truer way than of leaving the sensible world behind so as to ascend to the intelligible world that is our true home. It is partly because of this tendency that the writings of Evagrius were condemned at the Fifth Ecumenical Council.[23]

Yet there is another side to Evagrius that ultimately had greater influence. Despite the problematic tendencies of his theoretical works, in his practical works of spiritual guidance Evagrius offered much that was of great value. Several of these continued to circulate in monastic circles, sometimes hidden under the name of more respectable authors, and were eventually incorporated in the *Philokalia*. It is here that we find the classic description of *theōria phusikē* as the contemplation of the *logoi* of beings. For example, in his *On Prayer* (traditionally attributed to St. Nilus) Evagrius writes:

> We pursue the virtues for the sake of the *logoi* of created beings, and these we pursue for the sake of the Logos who gave them their being, and he usually manifests himself in the state of prayer.[24]

This is a succinct description of the three stages of the spiritual life mentioned earlier: first the ascetic practice of the virtues, then the contemplation of the *logoi* of beings, and finally the contemplation of the Logos who is their source. It is helpful to read this statement against its background in Origen, for whom the *logoi* of beings are visible to those who "have assumed a likeness to those eyes that have seen how each of the things that have been made was good." Evagrius makes more explicit than had Origen that to thus see things as God sees them is achieved only through the habitual practice of self-denial, along with related virtues such as forgiveness, obedience, and charity. At the same time, he is also more emphatic than had been Origen that such vision is not the highest stage of the spiritual life. As he cautions a few chapters later:

> Even when the mind does not delay among the simple contemplations of objects, it has not yet attained the place of prayer; for it can remain in the contemplation of objects and be engaged in meditation on their *logoi*, which, even though they involve simple expressions, nevertheless, insofar as they are contemplations of objects, leave their impress and form on the mind and lead it far away from God.[25]

In other words, *theōria phusikē* is not yet *theologia*, the pure "communion of the mind with God."[26] Evagrius thus fixes the contemplation of the *logoi* firmly as a kind of revelation and communion with God—a matter, indeed, of seeing things as God sees them, and to that extent of being deified—that is not yet the highest form of such communion. Nature is theophany, but only because it points beyond itself to its source.

It took centuries for the complex legacy of Origen and Evagrius to be assimilated fully. The first important step in this direction as regards the *logoi* was taken by St. Dionysius the Areopagite.[27] In an important passage of chapter 5 of the *Divine Names*, Dionysius presents a Christian understanding of the Platonic Forms. He first describes how the sun is the source of being, life, and unity for all things, so that in this sense the sun may be said to "pre-contain within itself, in a unity, the causes of the many things that participate in it."[28] He then uses this as an analogy for the causal relationship between God and creatures:

> Much more as regards the cause of the sun and of all things, one must recognize that the paradigms of all beings preexist in a single supersubstantial unity, since it brings forth beings in accordance with the procession of being. And we say that paradigms are the substance-making *logoi* of beings, which preexist in a unified way in God. Theology calls them predeterminations (*prohorismous*) and divine and good acts of will (*thelēmata*) which produce and define the things that are, by which the supersubstantial one predetermined and led forth all beings.[29]

By calling the divine *logoi* acts of will, on the one hand, and paradigms, on the other, Dionysius places them in an important position. As acts of will they are not identical to the *hypostasis* of the Logos nor, obviously enough, to the divine essence or nature. They are acts that God performs and that presumably, in at least some cases, could be different. Yet as paradigms they are not creatures but the models and patterns for creation. Anyone familiar with the essence-energies distinction in Greek patristic theology will recognize here a familiar pattern: the *logoi* are neither the divine essence nor creatures but instead the articulated and active expression of God within the created order. This opens the way to understanding the relationship between them and the Logos not strictly as one of identity but rather as that of person and act.

At the same time, Dionysius also decisively rejected the denigratory attitude toward matter and the senses evident in Origen and Evagrius. In the long discussion of evil in chapter 4 of the *Divine Names*, he denies that matter is intrinsically evil since "it too partakes of order and beauty and form."[30] As for the senses, God is known "in all things and as distinct from all things," so that "of him there is thought and reason and knowledge and touch and sensation," although he also transcends all of these faculties.[31] The sensory apprehension of the divine is fundamental to Dionysius's two treatises on the angelic and ecclesiastical orders, the *Celestial Hierarchy* and *Ecclesiastical Hierarchy*. Near the beginning of the former he explains the role of material and sensible images within the Church:

It would be quite impossible for our intellect to be drawn up to the immaterial imitation and contemplation of the heavenly hierarchies unless, making use of the material guide that is proper to it, it considers visible beauties as images of an invisible loveliness; sensible fragrances as representations of an intelligible largesse; material lights as an icon of the immaterial gift of light; sacred discursive teachings as an icon of the fulfillment of intelligible contemplation; ordered ranks here below as an icon of the harmonious and ordered habit that leads to divine things; and sharing in the most divine Eucharist as an icon of participation in Jesus.[32]

The "material guide that is proper to it" is the Divine Liturgy, including the various rites Dionysius goes on to describe at length in the *Ecclesiastical Hierarchy*. For Dionysius, the Church's worship offers a kind of liturgical education of the senses, one that enables the communicants to enter into and experience directly the true meaning of sensible reality.[33] Plainly, although his focus in these texts is upon liturgy, there is implicit within such a view a reevaluation of the sensible world that has important implications for nature as well.

The fullest exponent of the Dionysian legacy among the later Greek Fathers was St. Maximus the Confessor. Maximus's teaching on the *logoi* has in recent years received extensive attention, so it will be sufficient here to touch upon a few high points.[34] Maximus shares with Dionysius a vivid sense of the interpenetration of the sensible and the intelligible. As he writes in the *Mystagogy* (itself a kind of sequel to Dionysius's *Ecclesiastical Hierarchy*):

> The whole intelligible world seems mystically imprinted on the whole sensible world in symbolic forms, for those who are capable of seeing it, and conversely the whole sensible world subsists within the whole intelligible world, being rendered simple, spiritually and in accordance with intellect, in its rational principles (*logois*). The sensible is in the intelligible in rational principles, and the intelligible is in the sensible in types. And their function is one, "a wheel within a wheel," as says the marvelous seer of extraordinary things, Ezekiel, in speaking, I think, of the two worlds.[35]

"Type" (*tupos*) refers here to the sensible representation of a spiritual reality, as a bishop is a type of Christ or baptism is (according to Romans 6) a type of death and resurrection. In saying that "the intelligible is in the sensible in types," Maximus presents the sensible world as a kind of cosmic liturgy, the earthly enactment of an eternal heavenly drama. Conversely, "the sensible is in the intelligible in rational principles," so that sensible objects have a higher level of existence, one at which their real meaning and purpose is revealed. Just as one cannot understand baptism except as a type of death and resurrection, so one cannot understand sensible objects apart from their *logoi*. The relationship is both semiotic and ontological, for the type both figures or represents the *logos* and constitutes its immediate sensible presence.

Like Dionysius, then, Maximus sees the liturgy of the Church as preeminently manifesting the *logoi* of beings. But he goes beyond Dionysius in a number of ways. One is in synthesizing this theme with the Origenist conception of the identity of the *logoi* with the Logos; as he comments later in the *Mystagogy*, "it is in him [God the Logos] that all the *logoi* of beings both are and subsist as one in an incomprehensible simplicity."[36] This identity is central to his most systematic discussion of the *logoi*, *Ambigua* 7. There he seeks to explain the orthodox meaning of the statement of St. Gregory Nazianzen that "we are a portion of God and have flowed from above."[37] He begins in a straightforwardly Origenist vein:

> If someone . . . were to judge and consider with understanding the Logos according to which things have been made, will he not know that the one Logos is many *logoi*, judged by the indivisible difference among created things and their unconfused identity both in themselves and in relation to one another? He will also know that the many *logoi* are the one Logos, judged by the relation that all bear to Him, who exists in Himself without confusion, God the essential and hypostatic Logos of God the Father.[38]

He goes on to add that the Logos has possessed from all eternity not only the *logoi* of particular beings but also those of universals—angel, man, and so on—and that He now leads particulars and their genera into being at the proper time. It is in this sense that (as stated in Ephesians 1:10) "all things are gathered together in Christ," and so rational beings, at least, may be said to be "a portion of God."[39]

If Maximus were to stop there, he would leave unanswered the question noted in connection with Origen, that of how the identity of the Logos can fail to be defined by that of the *logoi*. His resolution of this difficulty lies simply in noting that, since the Logos embraces the *logoi* from all eternity, He is *always* in full actuality the Creator, whereas creatures necessarily pass from potentiality to act. In this sense the Logos is infinite, whereas creatures are finite, bounded by the *logoi* that define them.[40] He summarizes the difference in a passage that neatly balances the kataphatic and apophatic, both affirming and, in a different sense, denying the identity of the Logos and *logoi*:

The highest, apophatic theology of the Logos being set aside (according to which He is neither spoken nor thought, nor in general is any of the things which are known along with another, since He is supersubstantial and is not participated by anything in any way), the one Logos is many *logoi*, and the many are one. The One is many by the goodly, creative, and sustaining procession of the One into beings; the many are One by the returning and directive uplifting and providence of the many to the One as to an almighty principle, or a center which precontains the principles of the rays that go out from it, and as the gathering together of all things.[41]

At first glance this might seem to be a dual-aspect theory: considered in one way, the Logos is neither spoken nor thought; considered in another, He is the many *logoi*. However, Maximus emphasizes that the one Logos becomes many by His "procession into beings" and that the many are one by the inverse movement of providence. It is crucial that the procession at issue here is a voluntary act, both in the weak sense that it is in accordance with the divine will and in the stronger sense that it is deliberately chosen. Maximus goes on to quote with approval Dionysius's description of the *logoi* as "divine acts of will," a description that (as noted earlier) indicates that each *logos* is specifically and individually intended.[42] The statement that "the one Logos is many *logoi*" must therefore be understood as presupposing the divine decision to create. Given that decision, the *logoi* are the articulated content of the Logos, His manifestation within the created world; thus they are uncreated but have a content that is determined by God's creative intent.

The other issue raised by the Origenist legacy is that of the value of the body and the senses. Although the intrinsic value of matter had been decisively affirmed by Dionysius, it remained for Maximus to apply this understanding to the divine *logoi*. Perhaps the most important text where he does so is *Ambigua* 21, a short treatise that describes how the senses can be "rendered rational" (*logistheisas*) so as to share in the deification of the entire person.[43] Maximus first draws upon the classical hierarchy of the senses to correlate each sense with a corresponding faculty of the soul: sight is an "exemplary image" of intellect (*nous*), hearing of reason (*logos*), smell of spirit (*thumos*), taste of appetite (*epithumia*), and touch of life (*zōē*).[44] In view of this correspondence, the soul, by using the senses properly, can transform both them and itself so as to perceive through them the *logoi* of beings. The passage stating this goal is worth quoting in full:

> If it [the soul] uses the senses properly, discerning by means of its own faculties the manifold *logoi* of beings, and if it succeeds in wisely

transmitting to itself all the visible things in which God is hidden and proclaimed in silence, then by the use of its own free choice it creates a world of spiritual beauty within the understanding. This it does by combining the four general virtues with each other as if they were physical elements, so as to form from them a world completely constructed in a spiritual and intellectual way.[45]

In saying that the soul "creates" (*edēmiourgēse*) a world of spiritual beauty, Maximus does not mean, of course, that the world so perceived is merely an arbitrary fantasy. The soul remains receptive to reality, "transmitting to itself" the visible things in which God lies hidden. The difference is that it now receives these things precisely *as* God-laden rather than merely as physical objects. It does this, in turn, by acquiring the "four general [i.e., classical] virtues," using them as if they were the elements from which it creates this new world.

Maximus goes on to explain the relationship between the four virtues and the five sense/psychic faculty pairs. The "interweaving" of the activity of intellect and reason with sight and hearing produces moral judgment (*phronēsis*), that of spirit with the sense of smell (that is, with the nostril, in which spirit dwells as breath) produces courage, that of the appetitive faculty with taste produces self-control (*sōphrosunē*), and that of the vivifying faculty with touch—and, thereby, with all the objects with which touch has to deal—produces justice. No doubt some of these correspondences are strained, but the underlying point is that the activity of the senses becomes rational to the extent that the soul is present to and directs them, rather than standing apart as a mere passive recipient of their deliverances. The form this engagement takes is that specified by each virtue, so that each sense acquires the habit, under the soul's direction, of being directed as appropriate to its own objects. Although Maximus does not elaborate here, elsewhere he makes it plain that the training he has in mind consists in the whole of the ascetic Christian life, including fasting, prayer, vigils, and liturgical worship, as well as the active practice of virtues such as patience, forgiveness, and hospitality.[46]

Finally, Maximus explains how the union of these virtues leads to transformed perception. The synthesis of moral judgment with justice produces wisdom (*sophia*), the more comprehensive form of the specific understanding that the lower virtues manifest, and that of courage and self-control produces meekness (*praotēs*), "the complete immovability of the incensive and appetitive aspects [of the soul] with regard to what is contrary to nature," for which another name is dispassion (*apatheia*). The union of wisdom and dispassion, in turn, produces the highest of the virtues and the one that alone is "productive of deification," charity (*agapē*). When all of these virtues are present, the soul, with its senses now operating in accordance with reason, apprehends the *logoi* of beings:

> Thus the soul . . . apprehends sensible things in a profitable way through the senses, since it has assimilated the spiritual *logoi* that are in them, and appropriates the senses themselves, now rendered rational (*logistheisas*) through the abundance of reason (*logos*) which they contain, using them as intelligent vehicles of its own faculties. . . . And God embraces the whole of the soul, together with the body natural to it, and renders them like Him in due proportion.[47]

Here it is precisely the innate affinity between the soul, the senses that have been rendered rational, and the *logoi* present within natural beings that enables the soul to apprehend such beings as they truly are.

In summary, it would seem that for Maximus there are two fundamental forms of the education of the senses: liturgical (discussed above all in the *Mystagogy*) and ascetical (discussed in *Ambigua* 21). Each provides the essential context for the other, for without regular practices of self-denial and obedience, liturgical worship is little more than a form of aesthetic enjoyment, and without liturgical worship, asceticism is merely what St. Paul (coining a marvelous word) calls "will-worship," *ethelothrēskeia* (Col. 2:23). Indeed, one might go so far as to say that for Maximus asceticism is intrinsically liturgical and liturgy is intrinsically ascetic, inasmuch as both are expressions of the same underlying ethos. It is only through *both* forms of practice, undertaken habitually and with a good will, that the senses can be purified so as to become capable of perceiving the *logoi* of beings.

This is, for us in the modern world, a hard saying. Modern science has had from the beginning an orientation that is fundamentally antiascetic, in that it presupposes that there is no connection between one's ability to understand reality and one's moral character or the state of one's soul. For the same reason, it has had little to do with liturgy or worship in any form—save perhaps for the early modern idea that science would enable us to read the "Book of Nature" written by the Creator, a belief soon discarded in the Enlightenment.[48] Nonetheless, despite its spiritual aridity, we tend to assume that science provides the deepest insight possible into nature and that it is to be valued and even reverenced on that account. Surely anyone who holds that nature is the product of a purposeful Creator must consider such a view to be deeply misguided. Generally speaking, the most important thing one can know about *any* purposeful work is not simply its "what" (of what it is made, how it works, and so on) but its "why," its purpose and meaning. And this will be especially true when the one who made it is the source of being itself, and the purposes and meanings he imparts are definitive for reality.

The concept of the *logoi* of beings opens up the possibility of knowing nature in an entirely different way, one far more consonant with its true place within a theistic worldview. If such a possibility seems alien to most of us today—including, I suspect, most Christians—the reason probably has much to do with the extent to which modernity itself is both antiascetic and antiliturgical. These tendencies are so pervasive and so deeply ingrained that for the most part we are scarcely aware of them. Yet despite the grip that modernity has upon our imaginations, innumerable causes, from ecological catastrophe to the triviality of consumer culture, have led many today to ask: are we bound always to be modern? Does not the possibility lie open, even today, of recovering a more holistic sense of who we are and of our place within nature? If that is truly what we seek, then we may find that the teaching of the Greek Fathers, alien though it is, opens precisely the door for which we have been searching.

Hierarchy and Love in St. Dionysius the Areopagite

Eric D. Perl

The idea that human beings, as rational, as persons, made "in the image and likeness of God," are radically set apart from and above all lesser beings is often pointed to, with some justice, as one of the major sources of today's degradation of the natural environment. In its extreme form, that idea implies that subhuman beings have no intrinsic purpose or value, and exist only for humans to use for our own ends. Consider, for example, the following statement, taken from a discussion of human cloning:

> The cloning of sheep, supercow, chicken and pigs poses no ethical problems because given their nature, they are meant for food, and the more they increase and multiply the better. The only objection to animal cloning is that . . . it has paved the way to human cloning. . . . The cloning of a human poses serious ethical and religious questions, for unlike sheep, a human clone is supposed to be a "person," i.e. a being endowed with self consciousness, intellect and will; a being who is an *end in se* and never to be treated like a means to some other end, a being that is spirit in matter, an *imago Dei* entitled to human dignity and fundamental freedoms because of the divine spark in him/her.[1]

This is, perhaps, an extreme formulation, but some version of this view is often attributed to traditional Christianity or to the so-called Judeo-Christian tradition, and, regrettably, has also been espoused by some Orthodox Christians. I propose to present the fifth- or sixth-century Church Father who wrote under the name of St. Dionysius the Areopagite as a witness against this position within the Orthodox tradition. This may seem an odd choice: after all, it is well known that it was Dionysius who coined the word "hierarchy" (*hierarchia*), which has today become a four-letter word connoting domination and exploitation on the part of the superior and envy and a thirst for empowerment on the part of the inferior. Indeed, it is precisely the idea of man's hierarchical superiority to other beings that is often held to promote his exploitation of them and thus to be a chief if not the sole cause of today's "ecological crisis." In fact, however, hierarchy as Dionysius understands it implies precisely the reverse: continuity rather than opposition between higher and lower orders of beings and beneficent and grateful love rather than domination and subservience as the relation between them.

Although Dionysius uses his neologism *hierarchia* only with reference to the angelic and ecclesiastical orders, he explicitly understands the whole of reality as a structure of higher and lower, greater and lesser, superordinate and subordinate beings (*On Divine Names* IV.4, 697C; IV.7, 704B; IV.8, 704D; IV.10, 708A; IV.12, 709D; IV.15, 713AB; V.3, 817AB).[2] Indeed, it is in *On Divine Names*, which offers a philosophical account of reality as a whole, rather than in *On the Celestial Hierarchy* and *On the Ecclesiastical Hierarchy*, that he most fully develops the metaphysical principles of hierarchy. Here he consistently recognizes five principal levels of beings: angels, humans, irrational animals, plants, and nonliving things (DN I.5, 593D; IV.4, 700B; V.1, 816B; V.3, 817AB). This sequence is based on the classical tradition and, indeed, on common sense. First there is the basic distinction of "animal, vegetable, or mineral," that is (in the reverse order), those beings that merely exist, those that are living, and those that have some form of conscious awareness. The last group is then subdivided into those whose characteristic modes of consciousness are sense perception, discursive reason, and intellection, respectively, that is, irrational animals, humans, and angels.

It is vital to recognize that God, for Dionysius, does not stand above the angels at the peak of this hierarchy as if he were merely the "highest" being. God is "beyond being" (*hyperousios*), that is, not any being, even the highest, because a being, for Dionysius, means something knowable, something comprehensible, something distinct, determinate, finite, and therefore something created. God, therefore, is not any member of the totality of beings, even the "first" or "highest," but is rather the source or cause of that totality. The Godhead "is cause of all beings, but itself nothing, as transcending all things in a manner beyond being" (DN I.5, 593C). God is "nothing" in that he is not any being, not one of the things-that-are,[3] and is the "cause" of all things in that he is present to all things as the constitutive determinations or perfections in virtue of which they are what they are and so are beings. Thus he is, for example, "the life of living things and being of beings" (DN I.3, 589C). He is the cause of living things in that in all living things he is the life by which they are living; he is the cause of beings in that in all beings he is the being by which they are beings: God "neither was nor will be nor came to be nor comes to be nor will come to be; rather, he is not. But he is being to beings [*autos esti to einai tois ousi*]" (DN V.4, 817D). But since a thing is made to be itself, and so to be, by all the determinations or perfections that it has, it follows that not only being and life but all the perfections of all things are God-in-them, making them to be by making them what they are, so that God is not only being in beings and life in living things but "all things in all things [*ta panta en pasi*]" (DN I.7, 596C).[4] Hence God is not any one being but "all beings and none of beings" (DN I.6, 596C), or, better, "all things in all things and nothing in any" (DN VII.3, 872A). He is all things in all things, in that the whole content of any being and thus the whole being itself is God-in-it in the differentiated way that constitutes it as that being, and he is nothing in any, in that he is not himself any one being distinguished from others as one member within the whole. Consequently, God is at once and identically transcendent and immanent: transcendent, in that he is not any being, not included within the whole of reality as any member thereof; immanent in that he is immediately present to all things as their constitutive determinations and thus as the whole of what they are. God, therefore, does not stand at the head of the hierarchy of beings but rather transcends and permeates that entire hierarchy. "The goodness of the Godhead which is beyond all things extends from the highest and most venerable realities to the last, and is still above all, the higher not outstripping its excellence nor the lower going beyond its containment" (DN IV.4, 697C).

God is immediately present to all things, then, in the manner appropriate to each: in nonliving things he is present as being, in living things he is present as life, in conscious things he is present as wisdom, that is, conscious awareness.

> The divine name of the Good, manifesting the whole processions of the cause of all things, is extended both to beings and to non-beings [i.e., formless matter], and is above beings and above non-beings. That of being is extended to all beings and is above all beings. That of life is extended to all living things and is above living things. That of wisdom is extended to all intellectual and rational and sensitive beings and is above all these things. (DN V.1, 816B)

This must not be taken to mean that the higher levels lack the characteristic perfections of the lower, as though plants participate in God as life rather than as being and animals participate in him as wisdom rather than as being and life. Rather, the higher orders possess the perfections of the lower ones in an eminent way. Living things, in possessing life, also possess being, and conscious things, in possessing wisdom, also possess being and life.

> But since the divine intellects [i.e., angels] also are [in a way] above other beings, and live [in a way] above the other living things, and think and know [in a way] above sense and reason . . . they are nearer to the Good, participating in it in an eminent way, and receiving from it more and greater gifts; likewise rational beings excel sensitive ones, having more by the eminence of reason, and the latter [excel other living things] by sensation, and [living things excel mere beings] by life. And . . . the things which participate more in the one and infinitely-giving God are closer to him and more divine than the rest. (DN V.3, 817B)

As this indicates, all of these perfections—intellect, reason, sense, life, and being—are in fact higher and lower modes of participation in God, or of God's presence in beings. In plants, for instance, life is not superadded to being but is rather the higher mode of being proper to living things as distinct from inanimate ones.[5] Consciousness, in animals, is not superadded to being and life but is the higher mode of being and life proper to them as conscious beings. At the highest level, therefore, intellection, the characteristic perfection of the angels, is the highest mode not only of consciousness but of life and of being. Conversely, if life is a higher mode of being and consciousness a higher mode of life, then the life of plants is their lesser mode of what in animals is consciousness, and the mere being of inanimate things is a still lesser, weaker mode of what in animals and plants is consciousness and life. What Dionysius says of the ranks of angels in fact applies throughout all levels of reality: "Just as the first [i.e., the higher ranks] possess eminently the holy-befitting properties of the lower, so the later possess those of the earlier, not in the same way, but in a lesser way" (*On the Celestial Hierarchy* XII.2, 293B).[6] The proper perfections of different kinds of beings, therefore, are higher and lower modes of the same divine presence that constitutes the whole of reality.

Hence, as Dionysius says, all things participate in God analogously, that is, in the manner appropriate to each. "The Good is altogether not uncommunicated to any of beings, but shines forth the ray beyond being, established remainingly in itself, by illuminations analogous to each of beings" (DN I.2, 588CD; see also DN IV.1, 693B). These analogous "illuminations" are, precisely, the constitutive perfections of the different ranks of beings. They are "analogous" or "proportional" in that being is to a stone, as life is to a plant, as sense is to an animal, as reason is to a human, as intellection is to an angel: its proper way of being, of being good, of participating in God. In the hierarchy of beings, then, we find not discontinuity, as though each level were characterized by perfections totally different from the others, but rather an articulated continuum of higher and lower modes of the same divine presence that constitutes all things. Nothing is absolutely devoid of life and thought: living, for a plant, is its lesser mode of thinking, and merely existing, for a stone, is its lesser mode of thinking and living. Mere being, we may say, *is* life and thought, in the mode in which these are found in stones, and intellection *is* being and life, in the mode in which these are found in angels.

It follows, therefore, that all things at all levels, the least speck of dust no less than the greatest of the seraphim, are theophanies, the immediate manifestation and presence of God, in stronger and weaker ways, and consequently that the utterly transcendent, inaccessible God can and must be seen and known in all things.

> God is known both through knowledge and through unknowing. And of him there is both intellection and reason and knowledge and touching and sense-perception and opinion and imagination and name and all other things; and he is neither thought nor spoken nor named. And he is not any of beings, nor is he known in any of beings. And he is all things in all things and nothing in any, and he is known to all from all and to none from any. (DN VII.3, 872A)

To deny this, indeed, would be not to take seriously the idea of creation, the absolute dependence and derivation of all things from God. God's creative activity, which is God himself, extends to all things, and this activity is his beneficent, providential love for all things, not humans and angels alone:

> The cause of all things, through excess of goodness, loves all things, makes all things, perfects all things, sustains all things, reverts all things; and the divine love is good, of good, through the good. For love, the very benefactor of beings, pre-existing in excess in the Good, did not permit it to remain unproductive in itself, but moved it to productive action, in the excess which is generative of all things. (DN IV.10, 708AB)

God's ecstatic love for all things, then, is his creative presence in them, so that he is productively and providentially present throughout the whole of reality:

> The very cause of all things, by the beautiful and good love of all things, through excess of erotic goodness, becomes out of himself in his providences toward all beings, and is as it were enticed by goodness and affection and love and is led down, from above all things and beyond all things, to in all things, according to an ecstatic power beyond being, without going out from himself. (DN IV.13, 712AB)

The hierarchical structure of reality, therefore, rather than separating the lower orders of beings from God, is the very way in which he is present to all things. All things participate directly in God precisely in and by occupying their proper places within the hierarchical order of the whole.

Likewise, the creative presence of God throughout the whole of reality implies not only that God loves all things but also that all things—not rational and intellectual beings alone—love God. Since all things depend on God, all things need and desire him as the Good in virtue of which they exist. Hence God, as Goodness, is not only the source from which all things come but also the end toward which all things return. "Every being is from the Beautiful and Good and in the Beautiful and Good and is reverted to the Beautiful and Good" (DN IV.10, 705D), and again, "By all things . . . the Beautiful and Good is desired and loved and cherished . . . and all things, by desiring the Beautiful and Good, do and wish all things that they do and wish" (DN IV.10, 708A). The most fundamental activity of any being is to be, and any "other" activities, such as living and thinking, are not additional to this but are modes or specifications of the activity of being. The very being of all things, then, is their love for God, their striving or tending toward him as their end. No being can be without loving God, and the failure of this love is the deficiency of being itself, in which evil consists. As Dionysius says of the demons,

> They are not altogether without a share in the Good, insofar as they are and live and think, and, in short, there is some motion of desire in them. But they are said to be evil through being weak in their activity according to nature. Evil for them, then, is a turning away and going from the things proper to them, and a missing of aim and imperfection and lack of power, and a weakness and flight and falling away from the power that preserves the perfection in them. (DN IV.23, 725B)

And again, "They desire the Good, insofar as they desire to be and to live and to think. And insofar as they do not desire the Good, they desire that which is not. And this is not desire, but a missing of genuine desire" (DN IV.34, 733D). To the extent that any being fails to love God, it is failing to exercise its proper nature, to be in the way that is proper to it, and so to that extent failing to be.

But the love for God which is the being of all things is realized in many different ways, in accordance with the hierarchical structure of reality:

It is the Good . . . from which all things originate and are, as brought forth from an all-perfect cause; and in which all things are held together, as preserved and held fast in an all-powerful foundation; and to which all things are reverted as each to its own proper limit; and which all things desire: the intellectual and rational cognitively, the sensitive sensitively, those without a share in sensation by the natural motion of vital desire, and those which are not living and are merely beings merely by their fitness for existential participation. (DN IV.4, 700AB; cf. DN I.5, 593D)

The proper activity that constitutes each thing as what it is, which is that thing's distinctive mode of being, is its way of loving or returning to God. A stone in merely existing as a stone—that is, in being heavy, hard, and brittle, in exercising the proper perfections that make it a stone—a plant in living, an animal in living sensitively, a human in living rationally, an angel in living intellectually—in short, each thing simply in being what it is, that is, in being in its proper way, is loving God, the Good, in its proper way, participating in him as the distinct mode of goodness and being in virtue of which it exists.

In this vision of reality permeated and constituted by divine goodness and love, we find an understanding of hierarchy that does not reductively view the lower levels as merely in the service of the higher. It is not the case that, as has sometimes been said, "Nature is ordered to man, and man is ordered to God," as might be the case if God merely stood at the summit of the hierarchy of beings. Rather, all things are ordered to God, each in its own proper way. All things, therefore, have their own proper, intrinsic ends or perfections, their modes of being, of activity, which are their ways of loving God and the ways in which God is manifest in them. As Dionysius says in his account of evil, "This is evil, in intellects and souls and bodies"—in other words, at any level of reality—"the weakness and falling away from the possession of their proper goods" (DN IV.27, 728D). Likewise, in his discussion of the divine names "salvation" or "preservation" (*soteria*) and "redemption" (*apolytrosis*), he remarks, "Since one might hymn . . . this salvation as redeeming all beings, by the goodness which is salvific of all things, from the falling away from their proper goods . . . therefore the theologians also name it 'redemption' . . ." (DN VIII.9, 897AB). It is striking and significant that

Dionysius here expressly extends divine salvation and redemption not to humans alone but to all things. Just as God loves all things and all things love God, so all things have their own proper goods from which they may fall and to which they must be restored.

But the love of all beings for God, the proper perfections of all things, do not occur in isolation. Since each being's participation in God lies in its fulfilling its proper place within the hierarchical structure of the whole, it follows that this participation consists in its rightly relating to other beings, above, below, and coordinate with it in that structure. Each thing exercises its proper activities, which are its way of participating in God, not in isolation, but in relation to other beings. It is not accidental, therefore, that Dionysius's principal presentations of hierarchy in *On Divine Names* occur precisely in the context of his discussion of divine goodness and love. The love of all things for God is realized in their love for each other, according to the proper rank of each: "By all things, then, the Beautiful and Good is desired and loved and cherished, and through it and for its sake also the lesser love the greater revertively, and those of the same kind [love] their coordinates communally, and the greater [love] the lesser providentially . . . and all things, by desiring the Beautiful and Good, do and wish all things that they do and wish" (DN IV.10, 708A). Not only do all things proceed from and return to God, but also, among beings, the higher love, or proceed to, the lower, and the lower love or return to the higher. That is to say, the lower love the higher receptively, as in need of the good that they receive from the higher order (thus Dionysius sometimes refers to the subordinate as "the more needy," e.g., DN IV.8, 704D–705A), and the higher love the lower not exploitatively but beneficently, donatively, passing on to them the goods that they themselves have received.

For every being, therefore, its providential and receptive love for other beings, its giving to those below it and receiving from those above it, is its own immediate participation in God, as love itself.

> Perfection for each of those appointed in hierarchy is to be led up according to its proper analogy to the imitation of God, and . . . to become a co-operator [*sunergon*] of God and to show the divine activity revealed in itself as far as possible. As, since the order of hierarchy is that some are purified and others purify, some are illumined and others illumine, some are perfected and others perfect, the imitation of God is adapted to each in a certain mode. (CH III.2, 165B)

"Imitation," here, means not extrinsic copying but participation, the presence of the archetype in the image: the hierarchically ordered love of beings for one another is "the divine activity" itself at work in each of them. As Dionysius says, "The angel is an image [*eikon*] of God, a manifestation of the unmanifest light, a pure mirror, most transparent, unblemished, undefiled, spotless, receiving whole . . . the bloom of the good-stamped deiformity, and unmixedly shining back in itself, as far as it can, the goodness of the silence in the sanctuary" (DN IV.22, 724B). And since all things are, in lesser ways, what angels are most fully, this is true, in analogically appropriate ways, not only of angels but of all things. We can thus imagine the whole of reality as a series of vessels, each of which can be filled from above only in ceaselessly emptying itself into those below, and God as the overflowing love that runs through and fills them all.[7] Better still, we may use Dionysius's own imagery: "The purpose of hierarchy, then, is likeness and union with God as far as possible . . . making the members of his dancing company divine images, clear and spotless mirrors, receptive of the original light and thearchic ray and sacredly filled with the granted radiance, and ungrudgingly flaring it up again to the next, according to the thearchic ordinances" (CH III.2, 165A). Here Dionysius likens the hierarchy of beings to an array of mirrors, all at once receiving and passing on the divine light, so that the same light, which is God himself, is present throughout the entire structure by means of the structure itself.

The love of all things for God, then, which is their being and the presence of God in them, is realized in their providential and receptive love for one another within the hierarchy of creation. This is the very opposite of the conventional concept of hierarchy based on domination, exploitation, and subservience. Here, the higher love the lower providentially, with a view not to their own good but to that of the subordinate. Indeed, since to be is to be a mirror, which gives in receiving and receives in giving, to receive from the higher and provide for the lower is the very meaning of occupying a given place in the order of the whole. To be higher *is* to give; to be lower *is* to receive. The higher any being is, the more—not the less!—it is in the service of, or, in Dionysius's terms, providentially proceeds to, all that is below it. Dionysius's understanding of hierarchy could thus be read as a metaphysical commentary on Matthew 20:25–27: "'You know that the rulers of the Gentiles lord it over them, and their great men exercise authority over them. It shall not be so among you; but whoever would be great among you must be your servant, and whoever would be first among you must be your slave.'"

It would, of course, be anachronistic to expect Dionysius to develop the implications of such a hierarchical ontology for man's relation to the non-human environment. Hence it remains for us to draw them out. First, and perhaps most important of all, we must recognize the insight that a truly transcendent God is not separated from the world, but, on the contrary, is present throughout all things. From this Dionysian point of view, we can have no sympathy with the widespread notion that the Christian idea of God entails the desacralization or dedivinization of nature. On the contrary, the recognition of a transcendent creator God is not a denial but an affirmation of the sacredness of all things. Precisely because God, as creator, is radically transcendent, not any being but the "cause" by which all beings are beings, it follows that all reality, all that is, is nothing but the presence and manifestation of God and as such is sacred. The mistaken interpretation of transcendence as separation, and the consequent stripping of divinity from nature in the name of divine transcendence, has been one of the major sources, in later medieval and modern times, of the tendency to reduce the world to a meaningless field for human manipulation and exploitation. But if God were merely separate, set apart from the world, he would be merely another determinate being, one member of a larger totality, and thus not truly transcendent. Precisely in that he is transcendent, not included within the whole of reality as any member of it, he is not separated but present throughout all things.[8] From this it follows that all being is sacramental and incarnational in nature: the whole of reality is theophany. Consequently, to see beings as they truly are, we must learn to find the inaccessible God in all things: "He is all things in all things and nothing in any, and he is known to all from all and to none from any."

In turn, then, it follows that there is no absolute line, although there is a difference of hierarchical order, between humans and lesser beings. If being and life are lesser modes of thought, and if the proper activities of all things are their love for God, then not humans alone but all beings, including animals, plants, and minerals, are sacramental theophanies that, in their own analogous ways, think, live, and love. Such a vision of the world as a hierarchical continuum must be set in opposition to the more conventional modern religious view that tends to deny any share of reason, spirit, or love to natural things, accepting the modern, mechanistic view of nonhuman nature. It is this view, setting the natural over against both the human and the divine, which is largely responsible for the human domination and destruction of nature. Finally, man's hierarchical superiority to other beings implies not a right to exploit them but, on the contrary, a responsibility of service and beneficent love for them. The understanding that all beings have their own proper goods must condition the ways in which we treat and make use of lower members of the hierarchy of creation. If all beings have their own intrinsic ends, then nothing is merely a "thing," mere raw material for human projects, having its meaning, purpose, and value only in serving our ends.

Nothing is merely "meant for food." Rather, we must recognize and respect the intrinsic nature of all beings, which is the mode of God's presence in them, and fit our treatment of them to this nature. If we use them, as indeed we do and must, we must distinguish between exploitation and respectful use, finding a mode of use that does not deny but respects and works with, not against, the nature of what is used, which is that being's mode of participating in God.

This may seem a very modest conclusion, offering no precise prescriptions as to what we may or may not do. But what matters most is that the opposing ontological comportment, which sets both man and God apart from nature and denies any sacredness, any intrinsic meaning, value, or participation in God to nonhuman nature, is to a large extent the source of our environmental problems. If we can correct our ontological stance, finding God in all things in the manner appropriate to each, coming to see all reality as a hierarchical structure of theophanies pervaded by the divine light, we will not be able to regard anything as a "mere thing," an object to be manipulated for our own ends. Hence this sacramental vision of reality finds itself lived out in ascesis. Asceticism is often misunderstood as a "Manichean" or "gnostic" contempt for nature. But in fact, it is sensual indulgence that expresses such contempt, treating the world as merely something to be exploited for our own gratification. The ascetic life, on the other hand, is life in a sacred world, in which all beings are regarded with respect and hence not reductionistically exploited. Traditional asceticism thus responds to the "ecological crisis" not merely or even primarily in the immediate practical sense of reducing our "footprint" on the world but, far more profoundly, in an ontological sense, by recognizing in all reality the presence and manifestation of God, who is "all things in all things and nothing in any."

The Beauty of the World and Its Significance in St. Gregory the Theologian

John Anthony McGuckin

This paper sets out to consider some of the ways one of the most eminent of the Greek Fathers spoke about the loveliness of the world and to examine what motives lay behind his rhetorical celebration of Cosmic beauty in that much-deliberated elegance of the chosen word. In this instance, Gregory of Nazianzus (329–390; known in the Eastern Christian world always as "The Theologian"), like many of the other Fathers who represented a moderate Origenian tradition, followed a longstanding and commonly adopted Platonic axiom of the day that "Only like can know, and be known by, like."[1] This is the positive side of Plato's ideas on correspondence and empathy, less commented on than his negative concept of *mimesis* as a poor shadow of a shadow,[2] perhaps, but more fundamental in the philosopher's psychological epistemology and in the later religious understandings of the principle of human empathy with the Ideal Transcendent that grew from late Platonic and early Christian readings of the former's *Symposium* and *Timaeus*. To see the beautiful requires an eye with some capacity to understand it. There has to be some ontological correspondence there on which to posit this empathy, this inherent understanding.

To develop this correspondence theory of divine connectivity to itself, early Christianity supplied what was not there in Plato. It took the notion of the creation of the world as having within it the "Divine Image" (*eikon*), and through the exegesis of variations in the creation account in Genesis, developed a distinction the ancient texts hinted at in terms of God making humanity "in his own image and likeness" (Gen. 1:26). Here the two key terms were *eikon* and *homoiosis*. Christian theorists among the Greek Fathers, largely following Origen of Alexandria,[3] the initiator of this connection, attributed the element of divine image to refer specifically to divine *Logos*, what Plato would have referred to as the Demiurgic principle at work in the structuring of being. The "Likeness" was the inner soul (not *Psyche* for the Greek Fathers but *Nous*) or the spiritual force of consciousness present in the world order: that movement of ascent toward awareness in all its degrees,[4] which for the Christians was preeminently present as the "goal" (*telos*) of the created order in the form of the species of angelic and human *noes*, which we may translate as "spiritual intelligences."

Noetic awareness is thus understood as the highest form of created existence. At this level it reflects its archetype and foundation, the Divine Logos who patterned it after himself. At this juncture we may perhaps see that Plato's negative view of *mimesis* as misleading and innately falsifying was consistently rejected among the Greek Christian philosophers, who argued to the contrary that it was taken up at an ontological level and accounted for all experience of the divine as beauty and order. The experience of beauty in the world was thus to Noetic Intelligence an epiphany of the underlying energy of the Logos who had made the world, to this end alone—that noetic intelligences would see his epiphany within it and glorify the maker through a rational ethical life aimed at divine communion. The apprehension of beauty became, in short, a matter of divine epiphany: what the Greek Fathers would also called *Doxa*, the glorification of the Logos as *fundamentum* of all being, by the only *loci* of the created order who could appreciate its meaning, namely, illuminated noetic intelligences. Evagrius of Pontus and Maximus Confessor, with their doctrines of the *logoi* (revelatory principles) hidden within the world order, are perhaps the most explicit continuators of this master theme from Origen. It became, after him, the root of both the mainstream Christian soteriology (the incarnation of the Logos within the world order for the cause of saving it) and the Church's mystical theory (union with the Logos being the soul's yearning for restored communion and its primal *raison d'être*). Gregory the Theologian represents both themes before they became, perhaps, more separated after the fifth-century Christological disputes, diverging into early Christian dogmatic and ascetical literature.

The trajectory of this argument demonstrates how Beauty, therefore, became not only an ontological concept in the hands of the Greek Fathers but also an ethical and social construct, with a profundity that it has, perhaps, lacked within other systems where aesthetics tended for the most part to remain an accidental and peripheral category. Without an understanding of its *fundamentum* and its ethical *telos* (end or goal)[5], the appreciation of what is beautiful about the world lacks existential force. It is something we observe all too clearly in the way that aesthetical approaches are often appealed to in ecological *apologia*,[6] but they generally lack the force (what the ancients would call *energeia*) of practical, even moral, conviction. Some of the supreme argumentation behind the need to respect the world's fabric (its primal beauty) is thus degraded in much modern consciousness because the concept of beauty has itself been degraded in thought, widely desacralized, and listed as a peripheral (an *accidental* category in Aristotle's terminology, not a substantive), and this not because the concept no longer applies but more because its *energeia* has diminished along with the dwindling perception of its intrinsic holiness (or what some would describe as its sacrality). This, in turn, is because of the lack of empathy between like and like. In other words, using ancient patristic terms, once the observer no longer sees the sacral connection between the observing self and the observed order of the Cosmos (namely, the *logos* behind the connection between sentient and insentient life forms, which is the substructure and the "value" of consciousness, that is, its valency, *eudaimonia*, *phronesis*, or purpose, *telos*), then there can be no moral empathy. This principle of empathy in ancient philosophy was very significant to the ancient Christian writers who spoke on Cosmic beauty and who stood in the intellectual tradition of Origen,[7] often adapting him considerably,[8] just as he himself habitually adapted Plato, a significant influence nonetheless.[9]

Many of the Greek Fathers were trained rhetoricians in the classical style and knew, from both their aesthetical training and their philosophy, that *cosmos* was a Greek word with two meanings: "Beauty" and "World." Cosmology in their hands, therefore, was often a deliberate theological fusing of aesthetic and cosmological-metaphysical categories that we moderns have, generally, philosophically separated out from their ancient dense weave, not always having a macroscheme with which to harmonize them any longer. But while pulling out the old weave is well and good, sometimes it weakens the fabric of coherence. The semantic pun inherent in *cosmos* lives on among us, nevertheless, in the way we still use the Greek to signify aspects of beauty in the term "cosmetic." Sadly, this is only skin deep, in common parlance.

The rhetoricians among the Fathers of the Church also knew—and played on the related pun as often as they could—that the term for "word" (*logos*) simultaneously meant "scheme of thought" (or rationale) as well as "inner system of coherence" (*raison d'être*). Based as it is upon the consonance between Logos (as Word of God and Incarnate revelation) as inner meaning in the Creation, and small-case *logos* (*qua* rationale) being the principle of ordered beauty in the environment that speaks to the soul of the inner significance of its making (*logos qua raison d'être*, or the fingerprints of the Maker, as it were), the aesthetic doctrine of the Fathers is an ancient, deep-seated, quintessentially Christian response to problems facing men and women today in coming to terms with Cosmic degradation. It is an old earth-wisdom of a transcendentalist type, which has rarely been understood, hardly ever been commented upon, and deserves more exposure as the "mainstream" Christian reflection on the subject (a kind of doctrine of ecological chastity in a promiscuous environment of discourse) than many of the critics of Christianity have wished to allow, preferring to foist upon the ancient wisdom a Johnny-come-lately doctrine of work ethic that is alleged to be willing to enslave all things to the venal principle of wealth accumulation. Yet the Greek Fathers were old before the Industrial Revolution was dreamed of. And was it not the foundational text of Christianity, the Gospel *logia* of Jesus, that made a classic response to that capitalist builder of bigger and bigger barns, who thought all should be subordinated to the process of growing wealth, addressing to him that simple adjudication: "What a fool you are!" (Lk. 12:20)?

Here let us allow the ancient sages of the Christian movement to speak for the religion on the terms of aesthetic theory in relation to the loveliness of the world, and let us see what harmony can be derived from them that can still resonate for us. We choose as our *exemplum* perhaps the greatest rhetorician of the Eastern Christian tradition: St. Gregory the Theologian.[10] Gregory has many passages concerned with aesthetic theory. By and large, he advanced an interesting artistic theory of discernment (*diakrisis*) that deliberately set out to attempt a reconciliation between one of the great divides of ancient thought: namely, whether poetry was capable of being considered a philosophical art or whether it was hopelessly fictive. Aristotelian sympathizers in antiquity had wanted to moderate Plato's dismissive attitude to poets as liars and falsifiers, as exemplified in his banning all of them from his ideal Republic. The intellectual conflict is not entirely dead even now. In ecological terms it is akin, I think, to the argument over whether religious insight can lend any useful voices. Do Gaia advocates, for example, have anything scientifically relevant to say, or are they hopelessly confusing the argument with imported mythological terms? For that matter, have Christians anything to add to the ecology debate that might convince someone who may not otherwise subscribe to the general axioms of the religion?

Gregory posits an interesting synthesis between the two philosophical positions about poetry. The Greek term here is *poiesis*, and we pause, if only briefly, to note once more an inherent pun: since the word does not just signify poetic art but the generic concept of creativity, the act of making, and to that extent the art of seeing what it is that has been made and presented before one's eyes. We may thus see a symbolic connection to ecological theory insofar as an interpretation of the world through the category or value of beauty thus emerges as an act of literary appreciation or at least as a poetic act of understanding the "text" of reality (the word itself means "weave"). Gregory lends his voice to seeing a poetic instinct in a commentator as akin to the ancient (archaic) Greek understanding of *afflatus spiritus*, that divine rapture that allowed an enthusiast to rhapsodize (in poetry, oratory, or temple hymns) about the beauty of the world, or that of human beings or gods, as a testimony not only to human insight but also to divine seizure. The word *enthousiasmos* derives from the Greek for "being taken by the god," and in this case the god was Apollo, Master of the Muses and the source of enlightened insight and art. Gregory, though a Christian, is well aware of all these resonances and assonances; he intends to speak to a wide audience of cultured Hellenes, not merely to his Christian friends, and both Christian and pagan would find common ground in this syntax of broad cultured appeal.

Gregory argues in many of his extensive poems, for example, and specifically in *Oration* 27, that only a person of culture and ascetical restraint can hope to be able to claim the insight of truth, the wider picture of deeper things that eludes those who merely work on the surface, never advancing to the *logoi* of matters, the manner in which all things cohere. Only those who are specifically and technically "inspired" can see the deeper truth, he argues, for the truth of matters is something that is so profound it transcends mere logical capacity to catalogue it (the Greek for which is *logos*, and so he slips in his pun once more). The specifically Christian part of Gregory's argument is that Christ is the real Apollo, the true substance behind the pagan myth. It is Christ the Logos's Spirit, given to the seers and sages of the world in each generation, that allows for insight to be thickened with wisdom and truth to emerge as more than mere logic. To his wider audience, deliberately meant to include cultured pagans (devotees of Apollo), he is making the point that the correct interpretation of reality demands a transcendental quality.

In his poetry he argues the case that the Christian artist is *par excellence* the bearer and herald of the Spirit: that same Spirit of God who, in the Hebrew Scriptures, is said to have raised up all manner of craft and culture among ancient Israel (Ex. 31:3). In his own case he applies the typology of thought to himself first and foremost. It was an age when Christianity was much conflicted internally over issues we have now come to synopsize as the "Arian crisis." Gregory makes an audacious claim (for postmodern ears), but one he soberly buttresses from his aesthetic theory: those wishing to learn what is authentic, as opposed to erroneous, Christianity need to listen to him, not to other voices of the day, for his voice carries the power of someone who perceives beauty alive in the world, and its élan thereby demonstrates him to be a herald of the Spirit (we might today say "prophet") while its absence proves others (he has in mind specific opponents such as Aetius and Eunomius, logicians by trade) to be mythmakers. Gregory himself was a writer who deliberately set out to knock down Plato's relegation of the understanding of beauty to the sidelines. This was chiefly why he deliberately elected to write extensively in poetic form, thus contradicting the Platonic presupposition that the poet had no place in the Ideal Republic.[11]

This appeal to "inspired perception" is important in terms of the wider structure of the argument. Several central premises are being philosophically advanced: that true analysis of the proper balance of the world order demands a cultured and artistic appreciation of beauty, that the true world order is greater than a simple attempt to catalogue it taxonomically, that it has to be approached artistically and acclaimed enthusiastically if it is to be an accurate translation (*metaphrasis*) or comment (*exegesis*) on reality, and that only those who demonstrate such transcendent appreciation are qualified to act as leaders and shapers of the dialogue about reality.

A similar set of themes can be noticed in some of the poems themselves, where Gregory often treats of aesthetic terms more directly. From only a few examples out of his large corpus I shall select some of the references to the ecstatic view of the world's beauty that Gregory often speaks about.[12] Our first instance comes from a poem entitled "An Evening Prayer."[13] From the mid-second century at least, it has been the Christian custom to celebrate the onset of twilight (that moment called the "light of eventide") by the threefold action of lighting household oil lamps, offering incense to the divine glory, and saying a psalm or singing a hymn. The offering of actual lights was a widespread practice, so much so that the office was actually called "The Service of Lamplighting" (*Lucernarium*). The first such "evening hymn" (the *Phos Hilaron*) calls Christ himself the "gladsome light." Gregory begins his own verse with a similar sentiment:

> Now it is time to bless you my Christ, the Word of God,
> Light of Light without beginning,
> Steward of the Spirit
> And of that threefold light that runs to one sole glory.

He then immediately passes on to the core of the poem, which is to celebrate the beauties of the *cosmos* (he is well aware of the pun) as an elaboration of aesthetic theory that underscores the manner in which humanity's spiritual awareness rises out from materiality as the priest of this "order" of being.

> You it is who set darkness free,
> And you who brought forth light,
> That you might make all things in light.
> You set fast unstable matter, forming it into a world
> And that good order we now have.
> You enlightened the human mind
>   with reason and with wisdom
> And thereby placed an *Eikon* here below
> Of that great brightness which is above,
> That Man may see the light by light
> And thus become entirely light.

What we see here, quite explicitly, is what for me stands as the quintessential patristic contribution to ecological thought: that the perception of the beauty of the world is a sacred and priestly matter that is the core rationale of why things exist at all.[14]

In Gregory's hands, and he is typical in this of all the major Greek Fathers, the beauty exists in order to "enlighten" the eyes of noetic intelligence. Enlightenment in turn produces doxology. Doxology leads the creaturely noetic intelligence into Deification (*theopoiesis*) or deep unity with the divine transcendent. Far from there being a profound chasm between materiality and the divine transcendent (a presupposition of much late medieval Western Christian thought, which erected high barriers between the created order and the divine transcendent), the whole structure of this way of thinking presumes the closest of relational bonds between the *cosmos* and the divine immanence.[15] The bridge is human noetic enlightenment. When the human mind acts as priestly "bearer of witness" to the beauty of God in the world, then by its adding of appreciative value to the wonder of the order of existing things that it sees, it thus acts as priest on behalf of all reality: both animate and inanimate matter. All has the potential to be lifted up in the song of glory that is the creation and given ontological stability and meaning in its relation to the divine.

For Gregory, the proper starting point of the acclamation of the world's beauty is this almost ecstatic experience of enthrallment with wonder. In this following poem entitled "Hymn to the Godhead,"[16] he begins with the paradox of the eloquence of apophatic wonderment:

> You stand high above all existent things.
> What other way could we rightly begin to sing of you?
> How can words chant your praise
> When no word can ever speak of you?
> How can the mind consider you
> When no thought can ever grasp you?

But this is an oratorical play on the paradox, for he immediately goes on to say that the very speechless nature of the divinity is itself the cause for confession. *Apophasis* demands *kataphasis*. God's unknowability is the spur to all creation's desire to seek him, and the longing is built into the fabric of being, a fabric that quintessentially demands interpretation (*exegesis*):

> You alone are unutterable
> From the time you created all things that can be spoken of.
> You alone are unknowable
> From the time you created all things that can be known.
> All things cry out about you
>   those which speak, and those which cannot think;
> For there is one longing, one yearning,
> That all things have for you. (Rom. 8:22–23)

The seeing of the glory, however, is reserved for those who are able, in priestly and prophetic charism, to see through the *species* (appearance of reality) to the *fundamentum* (the core):

> All things pray to you, that comprehend your plan,
> And offer you a silent hymn.
> In you, the One, all things abide
> And to you all things endlessly converge
> Who are the end and goal of all.
> You are One, and All, and None of these.
> You who bear all names,
> How shall I ever name you?

Gregory the Poet elegantly balances the themes of silence before transcendence, with awed response (in words) to the beauty witnessed. The world, in short, because it is the "poem" (*poesis*) of God, becomes the sacrament of God's presence: a holy thing in itself but serving the immense task of being the source of enlightenment for a high transcendence: a destiny that is placed within the fabric of being but energized only for those who "see" it through the gate of beauty in revelation.

The same idea is supplied once more in this litany-type song entitled "Grant Immortal Monarch,"[17] deliberately written in a style allusive of the Homeric hymns:

> Grant, Immortal Monarch,
> That we may hymn you.
> Grant that we may sing of you
> Our Ruler and Lord.
> Through whom derives the hymn

Through whom the praise
Through whom the chorus of angels
Through whom the endless ages
Through whom the light of Sun
Through whom the course of Moon
Through whom the great beauty of stars
Through whom noble man was made
So that, as creature of reason, he might see the deity.

We can raise up a last instance of citation from his "Hymn of Glory to the Trinity."[18] I shall cite it in full, because it so classically illustrates the patristic theme of celebrating the beauties of the world in order to chart out the curve of the "Ascent of Man": from creature within a beautiful environment (a rational animal celebrating beauty) to transcendent *illuminatus* who is given noetic life by the Divine Spirit who makes the *cosmos*, precisely in order to rise up as the one earthly form and species that gives praise to God intellectively and thus acts as priest of a wider cosmos that in parts can neither feel nor articulate rational insight:

Glory to God the Father
And to the Son who reigns over all.
Glory to the Spirit, All-Holy,
To whom praise is fitting.
This is the Single God, the Trinity,
Who created all things that are;
Who filled the heavens with spiritual beings,
The land with earthly creatures,
The oceans, rivers, springs,
With all aquatic living things.
Out of his own Spirit he gives life
to all that lives (Ps. 104:30; Jn. 6:63)
So that all created life can sing out praise
To the wisdom of the Maker;
That single cause of their existence,
Their continuing subsistence.
But more than all other things,
And in all things,
Rational nature must sing out
That he is the Great King, Good Father.
And so, my Father, grant to me
In spirit and in soul, in heart and voice,
In purity of heart (Mt. 5:8)
To give you the glory. Amen.

I would like, as a conclusion, to end with Gregory's prose poem in his twenty-eighth *Oration*, which was one of the most widely read pieces of Christian antiquity after its lifting up by the Fathers of the Council of Chalcedon in 451 as "definitive" Christian teaching on divine transcendence. It forms the second of a series of perorations designed to elaborate the Christian doctrine of the Trinity, known since ancient times as the "Five Theological Orations."[19] At the end of a long and closely argued debate with opponents who wanted to argue for the priority of scientific logic in world analysis, Gregory restates his master theme that the best way to make deep statements about even deeper realities is to fall back on poetry as the best method of discourse and to realize that everything related to such profundity bears a tentative character relative to the mental and spiritual acuity of the "one who sees and speaks." In other words, there is not, in this world, a single given reality that can be taxonomically ordered and exhausted by any single given method of analysis, but rather insight into reality is gifted in the degree of the perspicacity of the one who sees. The Fathers would call this a prophetic and priestly charism; on a wider ecumenical front we might also describe it as a poetic and spiritual insight into truth. Accordingly, Gregory argues, discourse about deep mysteries ought to be equally tentative and never leave its preference for silence in the face of transcendent things. To meet his opponents' protests that this is simply obscurantism, he turns, at the end of his speech, to a challenge back to them. If logic can tell us all that needs to be known about the divine order, why is it that the present order of things, so apparently quantifiable and subordinate to investigation, retains a plethora of mysteries that exceed the capacity of even the most refined intelligence? If this basic world order that lies before us is profoundly mysterious at its core (and the experience of beauty opens this truth out to the percipient observer), then a fortiori the nature and acts of God exceed our capacity to grasp or exhaust them.

To elaborate this argument, Gregory pours out some extraordinarily gracious *encomia* of the beauty of the world. In a sense he is deliberately doing this to stress the paradox of beauty: what is ineffable can only be spoken of by a priestly, prophetic, and poetic mind. But this speaking of the truth of the world order is highly difficult, because it is a high poetic art, demanding an interpreter *hierophant* who is working at the limit of his or her capacities. Gregory wishes to take us, in the issue of exegeting the beauties of the world, to the very threshold of articulated meaning itself:

> The truth then, and the whole World, is full of difficulty and obscurity; especially since we set out to complete this labor with so small an

instrument, for with simple human wisdom we pursue the knowledge of the Self-Existent; and this because we cannot separate this wisdom from our senses which tend to meander with us, and lead us into error when we struggle to search after things which really can only be grasped by the intellect. For we are simply unable to meet bare realities with bare intellect so as to approximate a little more closely to the truth, and to mould the mind by its concepts. Let us make clear at once that the subject of God is more difficult to come at to the extent that it is more perfect than any other, and is open to more objections, and the solutions of them are exceedingly laborious.[20]

This is his climactic peroration after a long series of elegant rhapsodies on the beauties of the world order that he finds the human mind cannot adequately speak about. Once again, this is clearly a sardonic rhetorical ploy. If his logician opponents are able to explain all things about the world technologically, he suggests, it is only because their explanations are banal and superficial. He himself, however, will show that all cannot be explained, but this preference for *apophasis* (turning away from speech) will actually celebrate those beauties of a world order that tower over us even in our human capacities, precisely because they are meant to lead us onward to an understanding of our transcendent capacities as intelligent, insightful, and deified *Noes*. His irony lies in the fact that, asking his audience to resist the claim that "anyone" can interpret the world (as technological datum), he does so in such a brilliantly poetic manner as to hold his listeners spellbound, ready to confess at the end of his speech (loud applause was expected by the orator in antiquity) that Gregory, at least, was a true priest of the confession of existential mystery. His words advocating apophatic reflection, therefore, were worth a thousand other words that bore no insight into the meaning of the world as a mysterious and beautiful sacrament of transcendence. The answer he is offering to his hearers that evening in Constantinople in 380 is that the interpretation of cosmic order is not gained by making an exhaustive taxonomy of the Cosmos but rather by entering poetically into its sacramentality and in stilling the desire to control the data, finding a deeper and broader truth that satisfies the desire to know with the perception of a truth that exceeds our ability to grasp it and that in that transcendent "excess" demonstrates its own authenticity despite our logic and perhaps even apart from it.

To sum up: for many of the most philosophically subtle of the Greek Fathers, and for Gregory in particular, what the world is, in its beauty and mystery, is a sacrament that sings out silently but whose song can only be heard by a trained ear. To have that ear, to hear that song, is to be a priest of cosmic beauty. The priestly task is at one and the same moment a confession of the deepest levels of existential reality and also the discovery of the principles (*logoi*) of the heart of human identity as transcendent mystery.

NATURAL CONTEMPLATION IN ST. MAXIMUS THE CONFESSOR AND ST. ISAAC THE SYRIAN

Metropolitan Jonah (Paffhausen)

When someone reaches insights into creation on the path of his ascetic life, then he is raised up above having prayer set for him within a boundary: for it is superfluous from then onwards for him to put a boundary to prayer by means of (fixed) times or the Hours; his situation has gone beyond its being a case of his praying and giving praise when he (so) wants. From here onwards he finds the senses continuously stilled and the thoughts bound fast with the bonds of wonder; he is continually filled with a vision replete with the praise that takes place without the tongue's movement. Sometimes, again, while prayer remains for its part, the intellect is taken away from it as if into heaven, and tears fall like fountains of water, involuntarily soaking the whole face. All this time such a person is serene, still, and filled with wonder-filled vision. Very often he will not be allowed even to pray: this in truth is the (state of) cessation above prayer when he remains continually in amazement at God's work of creation—like people who are crazed by wine, (for) this is "the wine which causes a person's heart to rejoice" (Isaac, II: XXV, §1–5, p. 151).[1]

Introduction

Natural contemplation, *theoria physike*, is an essential category in Orthodox spiritual terminology for the relationship of man with the environment. Natural contemplation is a stage in spiritual growth wherein the soul of a person has been cleansed of the effects of the passions and has returned to the natural state of human being, of human nature as it was created to be. Thus a person who has purified himself and been illumined with grace will have a unique perspective on how to live in the created world, one informed by his enlightened perception. This perception in a state of natural contemplation is a transcendence of conceptual categories and their inherent dualism. It is, rather, a unitary experience of the synergy of all created beings with the Creator, of which one is a part rather than a subjective observer. Not only will the spiritually mature Christian have a profoundly different perspective and experience; he will seek to live according to that vision and draw others into it.

In other words, the whole creation comes to be perceived as a Mystery of God, a sacramental experience of communion. In the words of St. Isaac, "The world has become mingled with God, and creation and Creator have become one! Praise to You for Your inscrutable purpose: truly this mystery is vast" (II: V, §18, p. 14). The created world itself is sanctified and must be treated as something holy because it has been recapitulated in Jesus Christ (Eph. 1:10).

Consciousness

Many of the terms used in contemporary Orthodox spirituality and theology are Greek, such as *nous*, *theoria*, and others. While these have very specific meanings in their original contexts and various other meanings that developed over the course of the centuries, we need to look at how we are using them and at what our own cultural and linguistic predilections do to those concepts. As contemporary Westerners, we tend to make all these things into concrete objects or processes, rationally definable and describable. Thus *nous* must designate a thing, a part of the soul, which has a specific function. *Theoria* must mean some kind of spiritual vision that has objective content experienced subjectively. We want concrete existent "things," which can be quantified and objectified. This, I would suggest, is because of the inherent dualism in our language and culture, which structurally categorizes everything by drawing distinctions. This is inescapable, on one level. And its definitions are misleading, if not wrong.

We must go beyond the concrete language and understand that these terms—*nous*, *theoria*, contemplation, vision, etc.—can only be comprehended and perceived as aspects of consciousness or awareness; they are not "things" or stages. The *nous* can best be thought of as a center of consciousness, with its faculty of attention. *Theoria*, contemplation or vision, is a state of consciousness of the *nous* that transcends rational objective awareness or any conceptual forms. As St. Isaac says:

> But sometimes they designate as contemplation (*theoria*) what they elsewhere call "spiritual prayer"; or sometimes they term it as "knowledge" (*gnosis*) or "revelations of spiritual things." . . .
>
> Precise terms can only be established for earthly matters; for matters concerning the New World this is not possible: all there is a single straightforward awareness which goes beyond all names, signs, depictions, colors, forms, and invented terms. For this reason, once the soul's awareness has been raised up above this circle (Is. 40:22) of the visible world, the Fathers employ whatever designation they like concerning this awareness, since no one knows what the exact names should be. But [we employ such terms] in order that the soul's thoughts may have something to hold on to . . . . (Isaac *Syriac Fathers* disc. XXII, 257–258)[2]

Natural contemplation is about a state of consciousness that is attained through ascetic discipline. It is not a practice in the mind of St. Isaac. It is rather the fruit of grace in a person purified from the effects/reactions to passions, so that he sees with both the eyes of the body as well as of the soul (*nous*).

In St. Maximus, natural contemplation is a spiritual practice, the contemplation of creatures:

> When the intellect is absorbed in the contemplation of things visible, it searches out either the natural principles of these things or the spiritual principles which they reflect, or else it seeks their original cause.
>
> When the intellect is absorbed in the contemplation of things invisible, it seeks their natural principles, the cause of their generation and whatever follows from this, as well as the providential order and judgment which relates to them. (Max. 1 *Love* §98, §99, p. 64)[3]

This is not a scientific investigation using rational principles and concepts as to the origins of creatures or what they consist of. Rather, it is a spiritual perception of created beings in relation to God and other beings, a chain of dependent origination, and their harmony with the rest of the created world. Noetic attention is focused on the material world, and together with the senses and rational mind it perceives the divine Presence, Will, and glory through the material world.

> When the intellect practices the virtues correctly, it advances in moral understanding. When it practices contemplation, it advances in spiritual knowledge. The first leads the spiritual contestant to discriminate between virtue and vice; the second leads the participant to the inner qualities of incorporeal and corporeal things. Finally the intellect is

granted the grace of theology when, carried on the wings of love beyond these two former stages, it is taken up into God and with the help of the Holy Spirit discerns—as far as this is possible for the human intellect—the qualities of God. (Max. 2 *Love* §26, p. 69)

Thus ascending through the virtues to discrimination and then to contemplation of the inner principles of created beings, angelic and material, one ascends by grace into the realm of theology. The attention first is on oneself, in the practice of the virtues; then on the created world, conjoining sensory perception with noetic; and finally, the attention is focused on God in love. Purification is necessary first, however, lest the attention be drawn back to the passions through entertaining conceptual images that evoke passionate reactions.

Until you have been completely purified from the passions you should not engage in natural contemplation through the images of sensible things; for until then such images are able to mould your intellect so that it conforms to passion. An intellect which, fed by the senses, dwells in imagination on the visible aspects of sensible things becomes the creator of impure passions, for it is not able to advance through contemplation to those intelligible realities cognate with it. (Max. 2 *Var Texts* §75, p. 204)

If the imagination seizes on conceptual images, especially those that are charged with emotional energy, it will prevent the ascent into contemplation, and a person will remain in the imaginal realm. This is a state of delusion and is very dangerous. The path to contemplation and spiritual vision demands the cutting off of meditation on conceptual forms and images of sensible things until such time as those images no longer evoke a reaction. Otherwise, the content of meditation will simply be imaginations.

Via Negativa

Spiritual vision, *theoria*, can only be attained by the process of purification from egocentric passions, enlightenment by grace, and the transcendence of rational understanding. It is the ascetic way and the way of apophatic ascent beyond conceptual categories. Then and only then can a person have the detachment necessary for clear vision of God and of the creation. It demands a life of discipline.

Discipline performed by the body in stillness purifies the body of the [unclean] matter within it. But the discipline of the mind humbles the soul, filters out her crass notions of things that perish, and draws her from the state where the thoughts are passionately engrossed to the state where they are moved by her divine vision. This divine vision brings her close to the nakedness of the intellect which is called immaterial *theoria*. And this is the spiritual discipline. For it lifts up the understanding from earthly things, brings it close to the spirit's pristine *theoria*, and presents it to God through the divine vision of that unutterable pristine glory (and this is a movement of the intuitions of His nature's majesty) and separates it from this world and the awareness thereof . . .

The bodily discipline that is pleasing to God is called bodily labors which are done for the purging of our flesh with the practice of virtue through visible deeds, by which the impurity of the flesh is filtered out. Noetic discipline is: a work of the heart carried on without pause in pondering upon judgment, that is, upon God's righteousness and the judgments He has decreed; unceasing prayer of the heart, mindfulness of the providence and care of God active in this world particularly and universally at once; and a watching for the secret passions, lest you encounter any of them in the secret and spiritual realm. This work of the heart is called the noetic discipline. By the work of this discipline, which is also called the righteous activity of the soul, the heart is refined and is separated from communion with life that is both ephemeral and contrary to nature. Because of this fineness and separation, she begins to be moved at all times by an understanding (*theoria*) of sensory things which were created for the body's use and growth and through whose ministry, vigor is given to the four elements in the body.

But spiritual discipline is an activity apart from the senses. This is the discipline written about by the Fathers, namely that whenever the intellects of the saints receive hypostatic *theoria*, then even the body's grossness is taken away, and from thenceforward their vision becomes spiritual. Now "hypostatic *theoria*" refers to the created state of man's primordial nature. And from this hypostatic vision a man is easily moved and led up to what is called unitary knowledge which is, in plain terms, awestruck wonder at God. This is the state of the majestical way of life (discipline) [Gr: good things to come], which is granted in the freedom of immortal life in existence after the resurrection. There human nature never ceases from its awestruck wonder at God, and entertains no thought at all concerning created beings . . . (Isaac, I: 43, p. 213–214).[4]

The Mind of the Fathers and Reading the Scriptures

There is a lot of talk about the "mind of the Fathers"—the phrase of Fr. Georges Florovsky. The ascetic way of negation, through self-discipline and self-emptying, is the way of the Fathers. No academic studies or discipline can bring about natural contemplation, much less *theologia*; only prayer and fasting, hesychast contemplation in silence, the liturgical discipline, and the holy mysteries.

What is the "mind of the Fathers"? Certainly they were very well educated in philosophy, history, literature, and the classics. They were mostly from the upper classes, the educated and clerical elite, or sons of bishops like the Cappadocians. There were a few exceptions to this rule, such as Symeon the New Theologian. But their formation was not only intellectual and cultural. It was the formation of monks, founded on repentance and pursued through discipleship to a spiritual father in the context of obedience. The Fathers were mostly monks who had renounced the world, even if they were bishops and served in the imperial court. Their lives were focused on the process of spiritual ascent through repentance and asceticism. They were steeped in the Scriptures, many having memorized them completely. The Scriptures were the basis of their prayers, both liturgical and private. But the real means of interpretation was their spiritual vision: natural contemplation. As St. Maximus says:

> Interpretation of the outward form of Scripture according to the norms of sense-perception must be superseded, for it clearly promotes the passions as well as proclivity towards what is temporal and transient. That is to say, we must destroy the impassioned activity of the senses with regard to sensible objects, as if destroying the children and grandchildren of Saul (cf. 2 Sam. 21:1–9); and we must do this by ascending to the heights of natural contemplation through a mystical interpretation of divine utterances, if in any way we desire to be filled with divine grace.
>
> When the Law is understood only according to the letter, it is hostile to the truth, as the Jews were, and as is anyone else who possesses their mentality. For such a person limits the Law's power merely to the letter, and does not advance to natural contemplation, which reveals the spiritual knowledge hidden mystically in the letter; for this contemplation mediates between figurative representations of the truth and the truth itself, and leads its adepts away from the first towards the second. On the contrary, he rejects natural contemplation altogether and so excludes himself from initiation into divine realities. Those who

diligently aspire to a vision of these realities must therefore destroy the outward and evanescent interpretation of the Law, subject to time and change; and they must do this by means of natural contemplation, having ascended to the heights of spiritual knowledge. (Max. 5 *Var Texts* §36, §s37, p. 269)

The Fathers, while knowing the Scriptures, did not use them mainly for argument. They did do this, and their interpretations are the basis for later study. The primary use of the Scriptures, however, was as a basis for meditation. This was called *lectio divina* in the West, but the basic practice was common to the whole Church. They did not so much analyze the text but prayed it, integrated it into their consciousness, minds and hearts. They did not subject the text to critical dissection but used it anagogically: to ascend to the Word through the words. They used it as a jumping-off point for contemplation, turning the words over and over until silence seizes the mind and a spiritual vision imparts a superrational understanding of the Word. Thus the reading of the Scriptures becomes a means of communion. The analysis and interpretation of the Scriptures—literal, moral, typological, allegorical—came as secondary, using these conceptual tools.

> Sometimes biblical verses themselves will grow sweet in the mouth, and a simple phrase of prayer is repeated innumerable times, without one having had enough of it and wanting to pass on to another. And sometimes out of prayer contemplation (*theoria*) is born: this cuts prayer off from the lips, and the person who beholds this is like a corpse without soul in wonder. We call this the faculty of "vision in prayer"; it does not consist in any image or portrayable form, as foolish people say. This contemplation in prayer also has its degrees and different gifts, but up to this point it is still prayer, for thought has not yet passed into the state when there is non-prayer—for there is something even more excellent than prayer. For the movements of the tongue and of the heart during prayer act as the keys; what comes after these is the actual entry into the treasury: from this point onward mouth and tongue become still, as so the heart—the treasurer to the thoughts; the mind—the governor of the senses; and the bold spirit—that swift bird; along with all the means and uses they possess . . .
>
> Moving inwards from purity of prayer, once one has passed this boundary, the mind has no prayer, no movement, no tears, no authority, no freedom, no requests, no desire, no longing for anything that is hoped for in this world or the world to come. For this reason, after pure prayer there is no longer any prayer: all the various stirrings of prayer

convey the mind up to that point through their free authority; that is why struggle is involved in prayer. But beyond the boundary, there exists wonder, not prayer. From that point onwards the mind ceases from prayer; there is the capacity to see, but the mind is not praying at all. (Isaac *Syriac Fathers* disc. XXII, 253–254)[5]

The goal of spiritual ascent is conscious communion with the Father in the Son by the Holy Spirit: to be united in the *hypostasis* of the Logos by the grace of the Spirit and thus know God as Father. This is true theology, *theologia*, and it can only be fulfilled by renouncing all conceptual forms and categories and becoming enlightened by the Spirit. It can only be accessed through contemplation, beyond prayer.

The pursuit of intellectual studies in theology without this ascetic foundation, the purification from egocentric passions and contemplative practice, was unthinkable. Now, however, it is the norm. Academic theology thus has become a conceptual game, another realm of philosophy. True philosophy has always meant the ascetic life, leading one beyond the conceptual and rational to the realm of spiritual vision, natural contemplation, and *theologia*.

> Many simple people imagine that the philosophers' form of meditation is a (fore)taste of this converse that conveys the beauties of all of God's mysteries. The blessed bishop Basil speaks of this in a letter of his brother, where he makes a distinction between this perception of creation which the saints receive—that is, the ladder of the intellect of which the blessed Evagrius spoke, and the being raised up above all ordinary vision—and the perception of the philosophers.
>
> "There is," he says, "a converse which opens up the door so that we can peer down into knowledge of created being, and not up into spiritual mysteries." He is calling the philosophers' knowledge "downwards knowledge," for he says, even those who are subject to the passions can know this kind of knowledge; this perception which the saints receive through their intellect as a result of grace, however, he calls, "knowledge of the spiritual mysteries above" (Isaac, II: XXV, §7–8, pp. 153–154).

Dispassion

The ascetic process of repentance progresses from renunciation of external behaviors to watchfulness over thoughts and control of internal reactions. From there, it moves to remembrance of God—awakening of spiritual awareness or noetic consciousness—and into the realm of mystical prayer. This growth demands constant self-denial, bringing the will under the control of the rational mind. Then one's whole being, senses, and consciousness become reintegrated by grace through the perception of God's Presence and synergy with the divine will through obedience. This first stage of ascetic activity is called *praktike*, the process of purification by grace through self-denial. It leads one to illumination, and with it natural contemplation. Finally, through continued practice, the body and soul are deified and behold the spiritual *theoria* of true *theologia*.

> When a man's intellect is constantly with God, his desire grows beyond all measure into an intense longing for God and his incensiveness is completely transformed into divine love. For by continual participation in the divine radiance his intellect becomes totally filled with light; and when it has reintegrated its passable aspect, it redirects this aspect towards God, as we have said, filling it with an incomprehensible and intense longing for Him and with unceasing love, thus drawing it entirely away from worldly things to the divine. (Max. 2 *Love* §48, p. 73)

Natural contemplation presupposes a mind that has been freed from the passions: *apatheia* or dispassion. This does not mean that one is free from thoughts and impulses but that they are under control. It means that when conceptual images, memories, thoughts, or *logismoi* occur, they are not "charged" with emotional energy that unconsciously motivates one to act. And if they are, one has enough self-control to dismiss them. This is the fruit of obedience and watchfulness, so that no passionate reactions are accepted or indulged. The way to this is constant revelation of thoughts to the spiritual father (or mother) and, especially, by learning to still the mind in silent prayer. Silent prayer without impassioned conceptual images is already a taste of dispassion, according to St. Maximus the Confessor:

> The first type of dispassion is complete abstention from the actual committing of sin, and it may be found in those beginning the spiritual way. The second is the complete rejection in the mind of all assent to evil thought; this is found in those who have achieved an intelligent participation in virtue. The third is the complete quiescence of passionate desire; this is found in those who contemplate noetically the inner essences of visible things through their outer forms. The fourth type of dispassion is the complete purging even of passion-free images; this is found in those who have made their intellect a pure, transparent mirror of God through spiritual knowledge and contemplation. If then you

have cleansed yourself from the committing of acts prompted by the passions, have freed yourself from mental assent to them, have put a stop to the stimulation of passionate desire, and have purged your intellect of even the passion-free images of what were once objects of the passions, you have attained the four general types of dispassion. You have emerged from the realm of matter and material things, and have entered the sphere of intelligible realities, noetic, tranquil and divine. (Max. 3 *Var Texts* §51, p. 222)

The battle with *logismoi* is the focal point in this process. This is also the battle with the ego, which itself is both the source and creation of one's thoughts. The constant effort to cut off passionate thoughts and reactions cuts off the ego and brings the will into submission to the mind. The point is to keep the rational mind watchful, to guard against impassioned thoughts, so that the heart can pray. This is what the Fathers call "the descent of the mind into the heart." This is the beginning of pure prayer.

Prayer's purity or lack of purity consists in the following. If, at the times when the mind invites one of these stirrings we have specified to offer a sacrifice, it mingles in this sacrifice some alien thought or distraction, then it is called impure . . .

But when the mind is longingly involved with one of these stirrings—this depends on the urgency of the matter at the time of supplication, and is the result of its great eagerness—the gaze of its stirring is drawn by the eye of faith inside the veil of the heart, and the entries of the soul are thereby fenced off, keeping out those alien thoughts . . . . (Isaac *Syriac Fathers* disc. XXII, 256)

From this state of awareness undisturbed by *logismoi* or any conceptual images, with senses enlivened and deified by grace, the purified mind beholds the creation and is aware of God permeating the whole cosmos. It is a perception that transcends subject-object, even subject-subject. It is rather a perception in God—not seeing God in all things but rather seeing all things in God. This perception is essentially nondual, nonconceptual, and participatory. This natural contemplation is the actualization of communion, participation in the "*nous* of Christ." The deeper one goes, the less one is conscious of his own subjectivity, because in a state of pure awareness there is no object, all is in God, and God is radiant through all created beings. He is the sight and the subject, the ground of being and life of all. He is the unity of all creation. "All things were created through Him and for Him, and in Him all things consist" (Col. 1).

> Faith is knowledge that cannot be rationally demonstrated. If such knowledge cannot be rationally demonstrated, then faith is a supernatural relationship through which, in an unknowable and so indemonstrable manner, we are united with God in a union which is beyond intellection.
>
> When the intellect is in direct union with God, that quality in it by virtue of which it apprehends and is apprehended is completely in abeyance. As soon as it activates this quality by apprehending something sequent to God, it experiences doubt and severs the union which is beyond intellection. So long as the intellect is joined to God in this union, and has passed beyond nature and become god by participation, it will have transposed the law of its nature as though shifting an immovable mountain. (Max. 2 *Var Texts* §12, §13, p. 190)

Union with God, nondual awareness in God, is the state of the life to come. It is the state of deification in which spiritual vision, knowledge, and love converge. What draws them together is attention. Attention is not a matter of the will; rather, it is a faculty of the *nous* and operates in synergy with God's energy and will. The greater the state of one's purification, the greater the synergy, until God is the only subject in a unity of being by grace.

> But once the Spirit's activity starts to reign over the intellect—the orderer of senses and thoughts—then the inborn, natural free choice is removed, and the intellect is then itself guided, and no longer guides.... It does not direct the stirring in the mind in the way it wants, but a captive state reigns over what is endowed by nature at that time, guiding it in a direction of which it is not aware. For a person no longer has a will at that time, and does not even know whether he is in a body or without a body, as Scripture testifies. (Isaac *Syriac Fathers* disc. XXII, 259)

Or, as St. Maximus writes:

> Two states of pure prayer are exalted above all others. One is to be found in those who have not advanced beyond the practice of the virtues, the other in those leading the contemplative life. The first is engendered in the soul by fear of God and firm hope in Him, the second by an intense longing for God and by total purification. The sign of the first is that the intellect, abandoning all conceptual images of the world, concentrates itself and prays without distraction or disturbance as if God Himself were present, as indeed He is. The sign of the second is that at the very onset of prayer the intellect is so ravished by the di-

vine and infinite light that it is aware neither of itself nor of any other created thing, but only of Him who through love has activated such radiance in it. It is then that, being made aware of God's qualities, it receives clear and distinct reflections of Him. (Max. 2 *Love* §6, pp. 65–66)

The purified and enlightened man sees himself no longer outside of God and nature but rather as an integral part. Through the enlightened perception of natural contemplation, he sees all things as a whole, not in a subjective way. All things form a unity in diversity and multiplicity, including himself. Thus he can exercise his role within the creation as opposed to trying to dominate and control it. Like St. Isaac, his heart burns with love for all creation, visible and invisible, even the reptiles, bugs, and demons. The deified man lives on earth as Adam and Eve in Eden—in harmony with all created things and in synergy with God.

And what is a merciful heart? It is the heart burning for the sake of all creation, for men, for birds, for animals, for demons, and for every created thing; and by the recollection of them the eyes of a merciful man pour forth abundant tears. By the strong and vehement mercy which grips his heart and by his great compassion his heart is humbled and he cannot bear to hear or to see any injury or slight sorrow in creation. For this reason he offers up tearful prayer continually even for irrational beasts, for the enemies of the truth, and for those who harm him, that they be protected and receive mercy. And in like manner he even prays for the family of reptiles because of the great compassion that burns without measure in his heart in the likeness of God. (Isaac, I: §71, pp. 344–345)

We may not be able to do much about global warming and ecological destruction, save to console ourselves with the idea that we have "done our bit" in recycling and reducing carbon emissions. But what we can do is to bring forth Christians who not only see clearly but who perceive the creation as an image and mystery of God and who can lead others into that vision as well. Then, living in the midst of the creation, man will fulfill the role for which he was created: to offer the creation back to God in thanksgiving, as its priest, exercising dominion and care for all creatures in synergy with Divine love.

Let us take refuge in the Lord,
And ascend a little to the place
Where thoughts dry up

And stirrings vanish,
Where memories fade away
And the passions die,
Where human nature become serene
And is transformed
As it stands in the other world.
> *(Isaac, II: X: §28, p. 47)*

MAN AND COSMOS IN ST. MAXIMUS THE CONFESSOR

Andrew Louth

I want to do something more in this paper[1] than simply expound the teaching of St. Maximus the Confessor, for the subject—Man and Cosmos—is not some arcane bit of teaching from late antiquity, like, for instance, St. Maximus's understanding of the links between the passions and the various internal organs of the human body—liver, kidneys, etc.—though even with such teaching we may have more to learn than we might think at first sight. Rather, the subject of Man and the Cosmos is still something that deeply concerns us, perhaps even more so now that man seems to have some purchase over the earth, at least, so that the question of his responsibility for the world has become a pressing issue. It is not just interesting to know what Maximus thought about our subject; we need to try to reinterpret his ideas in the light of what we now know about the cosmos through the advances of modern science. For Maximus, like the other Fathers of the Church, took for granted the scientific wisdom of his day and readily made use of it. He would, I think, be very surprised if in our day people appealed to his authority to resist what has nowadays become scientific wisdom. We need, then, both to explore carefully Maximus's own conceptions and then try to relate them to the very different cosmology that we take for granted today.

The first and largest part of this paper focuses on St. Maximus the Confessor, a seventh-century monk widely regarded as the greatest of all Byzantine theologians.[2] It is because of the profundity and richness of his vision that I have chosen to speak of him. It will perhaps be useful to begin by briefly sketching his life. Born in 580, probably in Constantinople, Maximus seems to have served in the imperial court after the accession of Emperor Heraklios the Great in 610. Within a few years he abandoned this secular career and became a monk, initially in monasteries near Constantinople and then, after the Persian invasion of Asia Minor and the siege of Constantinople in 626, in exile, mostly, it seems, in North Africa. He defended the Orthodox teaching affirmed at the Council of Chalcedon, nearly two hundred years earlier, of Christ as one divine person existing in two natures, human and divine, against imperial attempts at ecumenical compromise and so angered the imperial court that he was eventually arrested, tried, deprived of his tongue and right hand (the instruments of his "heresy"), and exiled to Lazica, in Georgia, where death soon followed in 662. His cosmic theological vision is expressed in writings addressed mainly to fellow monks, mostly before his struggle against the imperial court, though the same principles underlie both his cosmic vision and his understanding of the Incarnation.

We shall consider Maximus's vision of the cosmos under three headings: first, his idea of the analogy between the cosmos and the human person, the idea of macrocosm and microcosm; second, his notion of what he called the *logoi* of creation; and third, Maximus's idea of the "divisions of nature," to use the term made famous by the ninth-century Irish monk and scholar John Scotus Eriugena, who translated into Latin several of St. Maximus's works and who called his own great synthesis of ideas, largely drawn from Maximus, *On the Division of Nature* (*De Divisione Naturae*).

Macrocosm/Microcosm

Let me begin by quoting some words from one of St. Maximus's most profound commentators from the century just concluded, the Romanian theologian Fr. Dumitru Stăniloae, who died in 1993. At the very beginning of his *Orthodox Dogmatic Theology*, the first volume of which has been translated into English as *The Experience of God*, he has this to say:

> Some of the Fathers of the Church have said that man is a microcosm, a world which sums up in itself the larger world. St. Maximus the Confessor remarked that the more correct way would be to consider man as a macrocosm, because he is called to comprehend the whole world within himself as one capable of comprehending it without losing himself, for he is distinct from the world. Therefore, man effects a unity greater than the world exterior to himself, whereas, on the contrary, the world, as cosmos, as nature, cannot contain man fully within itself without losing him, that is, without losing in this way the most important reality, that part which, more than all others, gives reality its meaning.

The idea that man is called to become the world writ large has a more precise expression, however, in the term "macro-anthropos." The term conveys the fact that, in the strictest sense, the world is called to be humanized entirely, that is, to bear the entire stamp of the human, to become pan-human, making real through that stamp a need which is implicit in the world's own meaning: to become, in its entirety, a humanized cosmos, in a way that the human being is not called to become, nor can ever fully become, even at the farthest limit of his attachment to the world where he is completely identified with it, a "cosmicized" man. The destiny of the cosmos is found in man, not man's destiny in the cosmos. This is shown not only by the fact that the cosmos is the object of human consciousness and knowledge (not the reverse) but also by the fact that the entire cosmos serves human existence in a practical way.[3]

This sums up more clearly than St. Maximus himself ever does the core of his understanding of the analogy between the universe and the human person. The idea of the human as microcosm is, of course, an old one, and in drawing on it Maximus would not have been thought to be saying anything exceptional. Let us note that the ideas Maximus draws on—philosophical, anthropological, cosmological, medical—would not have seemed strange to his contemporaries; his use of them, however, would have seemed striking, if not actually strange. As I have already said, if we are going to learn from Maximus, we shall have to think through his ideas again, using concepts that are contemporary to us, just as he used concepts that were contemporary to him. If we simply attempt to revive ancient cosmology, we shall probably lose Maximus in the process. And the way Fr. Stăniloae restates the insight of St. Maximus seems to me a step in the right direction. Because of the position of the human in the cosmos—ultimately, because the human is created in the image of God—the human person is a bond of the cosmos, or, looked at another way, the human person is priest of the cosmos. It is through the human that the cosmos relates to God; it is in the human that the cosmos finds its meaning. But conversely, if the human fails to fulfill such a priestly, interpretative, relating role, then that failure is not just a personal, individual failing; it is a failing with cosmic consequences. We are becoming dimly aware of this as we realize how human behavior that fails to recognize the integrity of God's creation, its inherent value, its inherent beauty, and treats it as simply so much material to be consumed—how such behavior is more than simply self-destructive or destructive of human society but threatens the ordered beauty of the cosmos itself. St. Maximus goes further: fallen human activity threatens the very *meaning* of the cosmos, insofar as that meaning is perceived by and articulated through the human person. The cosmos ceases to be an ordered, beautiful structure—an idea implicit in the very word *cosmos*, which in Greek suggests something ordered and beautiful—and becomes obscure, dark, dangerous, at least to humans—a forest of symbols no longer clearly disclosing the divine but difficult to interpret and easily misunderstood. The perfect fit, as it were, between unfallen humanity and the cosmos becomes awkward, ill-fitting, painful, and mutually harmful.

This is one way in which Maximus understands the coherence of the universe—a sort of coinherence between the human and the cosmos, more than simply a sympathy between all the different parts of the cosmos—though that is implied, too—but a sympathetic togetherness that is focused on the human person, for good or ill.

Logoi of Creation

The next theme is that of the *logoi* of creation.[4] The very word *logos* causes problems: it is a very special word in Greek. Theodor Haecker, the lay Austrian Catholic theologian who died at the end of the Second World War, once suggested that in every language there are one or two untranslatable words—he called them *Herzwörter*, heart-words—in which is concentrated something of the genius of the language. In Latin, it is *res*, usually translated "thing"; in German, *Wesen*, "essence"; in French, *raison*, "reason"; in English, *sense*. In Greek it is, he suggested, *logos*.[5] It can be translated, according to context, as word, reason, principle, meaning, but this fragments the connotation of the Greek word, which holds all these meanings together. There is a lot that could be said about the history of the word *logos* in Greek thought, but I shall simply dwell on its use in Greek Christian thought. The universe was created by God, through his Logos, which is identical with the second person of the Trinity, the Son of the Father. To say that the universe is created by the Logos entails that the universe has a meaning, both as a whole and in each of its parts. That "meaning" is *logos*: everything that exists has its own *logos*, and that *logos* is derived from God the Logos. As St. Maximus is fond of saying: "the one Logos is the many *logoi*," and also "the many *logoi* are the One Logos." To have meaning, *logos*, is to participate in the Logos of God. Behind this lurks the Platonic idea that everything that exists exists by participating in its form, or idea, which is characterized by its definition; the Greek for definition (in this sense) is, again, *logos*. These Platonic forms, or *logoi*, to call them by what defines them, are eternal. Between Plato and St. Maximus much water had flowed down the history of ideas, and for Maximus, because the world has been created by God through his Logos, it can no longer be regarded as a pale reflection of eternal reality, as with Plato's world. The created world has value, meaning, beauty, in itself: because God is the supreme craftsman, his creation is supremely lovely. The beauty and meaning is found in the *logoi*: so the *logoi*, in one sense at least, are created; they belong to the created order. In another sense they are uncreated, because they are, as it were, God's thoughts, or intentions, or, to use the words Maximus borrows from the early sixth-century thinker who wrote under the name of Dionysius the Areopagite, "divine predeterminations and wills."[6] So the *logos* of a created being means what it is, what defines its nature—Maximus speaks of the *logos tês physeôs*, meaning or definition or principle of nature—but this means what God intends it to be, what he wills, what he predetermines. This final point needs to be underlined: the divine *logoi* are expressions of the divine will. Here we find perhaps the most important point at which Maximus, building on his Christian predecessors, advances beyond Plato. For Plato, beings participate in the Forms; for Maximus, created beings participate in God through the *logoi*, but these *logoi* must also be seen as expressing God's will and intention for each created being and for the cosmos as a whole. There is a dynamism about Maximus's understanding of God's relationship to the cosmos through the *logoi*, a dynamism lacking in Plato; the cosmos itself is moving toward fulfillment, and that fulfillment is ultimately found in union with God, by whom it had received being. This opens out into an aspect of Maximus's thought of which we can only catch glimpses: on the one hand, these *logoi* are inviolable, they may be obscured by the Fall, but they cannot be distorted—"nothing that is natural is opposed to God."[7] But on the other hand, these *logoi* are not static, certainly not if we take into account that they represent God's will for each creature. Maximus assumes that natures are fixed—all his contemporaries did—but his thought is open to the idea of evolution, say, as a way of expressing God's providence, and certainly in the case of human beings, who possess rational freedom, the meaning of each human *logos* is expressed through what he calls *logoi* of providence and judgment, by which God's providential intention is expressed through a working together with free human actions (*synergeia*).

But to understand Maximus properly, we have to add something else that we have already begun to adumbrate. For if human beings are created in the image of God, and if it is the Logos of God that communicates the divine nature, that displays God's image, then this means that human beings are fashioned after the Logos of God, something manifest in the fact that human beings are *logikos*, the adjective from *logos*, usually translated as "rational" but really connoting something much broader and deeper. One could say that human beings, as *logikos*, are capable of discerning meaning, maybe even conferring meaning (is that the implication of the story of Adam naming the animals?): it certainly includes free will, which Maximus designates by the Greek word *autexousia*, which means fundamentally "authority over oneself." Because human beings participate in the divine Logos, they are *logikos* and are therefore capable of discerning meaning, that is, *logos*: they are capable of discerning the *logoi* of creation, the whole depth of meaning that can be found in creation in all its manifold splendor. This understanding of the cosmos he calls *physike theoria*, natural contemplation. But alas, because of the Fall, human beings can no longer fulfill their role as priest and interpreter of creation: they fail to achieve understanding, and the limpid meaning of the cosmos becomes dark obscurity. What is needed is for the Logos himself, the Son of God, to assume rational humanity and to renew the human function as bond of the cosmos from within, so to speak. That is the purpose of the Incarnation: through being born of Mary, the Mother of God, the Logos of God lives through human existence from within, renewing it in the course of his life, finally confronting the ultimate meaninglessness of death, and giving it meaning in the resurrection. But that is only part, though the biggest part, of the story, for this renewal worked by the Incarnate Word of God has to be appropriated by all those who are baptized into the death and resurrection of Christ, and this appropriation takes place through participation in the sacramental life of the Church and through the ascetic struggle of the Christian life, the overcoming of vices and growing in virtue. This has the implication that the personal life of struggle against temptation and growing in virtue is not simply a personal matter, what Michel Foucault has called *souci de soi*, care for the self; it is a matter of cosmic significance, for such ascetic struggle restores the human capacity of being priest of nature, interpreter of the cosmos. This is true for Maximus in various ways, but one that is immediately relevant here is that through ascetic struggle the Christian attains a state of serenity, and one of the fruits of that serenity is being able to discern the *logoi* of creation: to see the cosmos as God intended it, to have restored our capacity for spiritual sight.

Maximus, in fact, relates this idea of the Logos and the *logoi* of creation to two other ways in which Logos and *logoi* are bound together: that is, to the idea of the historical Incarnation of the Logos, who, as human, spoke to his fellow human beings in words, *logoi*, and to the revelation of the Logos in the words, *logoi*, of Scripture. This is sometimes called by interpreters Maximus's doctrine of the three incarnations, for he speaks of each of these relationships of Logos and *logoi* in terms of incarnation, or embodiment. All three are examples of the Word making himself understood through words: through the creative principles of the cosmos; through the words of the Incarnate One, especially his parables, in which he expressed deep mysteries in simple terms; through the words of Scripture, which again clothe divine mysteries in words that can be understood. Maximus in the second of his *Theological Centuries* puts it like this:

> The Logos of God is called flesh not only inasmuch as He became incarnate, but in another sense as well. . . . When he draws near to men who cannot with the naked intellect come into contact with intelligible realities in the naked state, He selects things which are familiar to them, combining together various stories, symbols, parables and dark sayings; and in this way he becomes flesh. Thus at our first encounter our intellect comes into contact not with the naked Logos but with the incarnate Logos, that is, with various sayings and stories. . . . For the Logos becomes flesh in each of the recorded sayings.[8]

In all these cases there is a double movement: the movement of the Word of God toward us and our movement toward Him of understanding. This answering movement of understanding involves more than an expansion of our knowledge (though it does not exclude that): the understanding gained here involves an inner transformation—requiring personal effort, personal asceticism—that opens us up to what we know (or the One whom we know), so that it is through *participation* that our understanding is deepened. How far such participation can go—Maximus certainly speaks of it in terms of union with God and even deification or *theosis*, "becoming God"—is a natural question to raise here. For Maximus, this participation in God through the *logoi* (and therefore through the Logos himself) remains creaturely participation and only takes place through grace: however deeply one comes to participate in God, one remains a creature, and that movement of participation, or deification, is only possible in response to God's prior movement toward us in incarnation (in any of its forms).

But the point of mentioning participation in this context is less to raise such questions than to draw attention to the kind of understanding attained through participation in God through the *logoi*. Just as we can only understand Scripture if we let it call into question the smallness of our ideas and the narrowness of our desires, so we can only understand the *logoi* of the cosmos if we renounce any attempt on our part to understand the world as material for human exploitation and seek to see it as expressive of the Logos of God. Maximus's doctrine of the *logoi* of creation is not simply a way of expressing the immanence of the divine will but is also a way of finding a place for human understanding of that will as expressed in creation—a way of human understanding that has its own ascetic demands of patience and objectivity.

Division of Nature

The notion of the division of nature is again a traditional theme: one can find some of its roots in Plato, with his division between the world of the intellect and the world of the senses, but Maximus's most significant predecessor is St. Gregory of Nyssa, one of the so-called Cappadocian Fathers, who lived during the latter half of the fourth century. For Gregory, the most fundamental division in reality is that between uncreated and created reality—between God the Blessed Trinity, who is alone uncreated, and the whole created order, which is created out of nothing. The recognition of this profound gulf between God and creation has a paradoxical effect: on the one hand, it stresses the utter transcendence of God, but on the other hand it means that *within the created order* nothing is nearer or further away from God by virtue of the constitution of its being. As the other Cappadocian Gregory said, the most exalted archangel is, in metaphysical terms, no closer to God than the "low, heavy compound" of our human nature: God transcends all creatures infinitely.[9] More immediately, this means that the human person, composed of soul and body, does not consist of one part close to God—the soul—and one part remote from God—the body: both in body and soul the human person is equally close to and remote from God. That is at the level of being, but for human beings there is another level, and that is the level of what we make of our being, the level of what Maximus sometimes calls "mode of existence," *tropos hyparxeos*, the way we are, which is the result of the life we have led, the decisions we have made—ultimately, it is the level of the depth or shallowness of our love. Through love we can become close to God; through love—or rather failure in loving—we confirm the distance from God that exists as a result of the Fall. But Maximus, like many thinkers, sees love as fundamentally a unitive force: it draws beings together, sometimes in a violent possessive way, sometimes in a healing and reconciling way. It is this context that Maximus develops the idea of "divisions of nature." In one place (*Ambiguum* 41) it is developed like this:

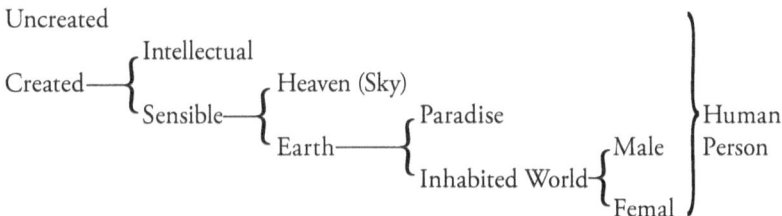

All of these divisions are contained within the human person—even, in some sense, the division between uncreated and created, given that the destiny of the human person is deification. As Maximus puts it:

> For humanity clearly has the power of naturally uniting at the mean point of each division since it is related to the extremities of each division in its own parts. . . . For this reason the human person was introduced last among beings, as a kind of natural bond mediating between the universal extremes through their proper parts, and leading into unity in itself those things that are naturally set apart from one another by a great interval.[10]

Maximus goes on to show how the human person can embrace all these divisions in his own nature: what emerges is a picture of the spiritual life in which each stage consists of transcending these divisions, one by one. However, this work of human mediation has been frustrated by the Fall, and Maximus shows, especially in *Ambiguum* 41, how through the life, death, and resurrection of the Incarnate Word the human task of mediation has been recapitulated, so that, through the life of ascetic struggle and contemplation, the cosmic function of humankind once again becomes a possibility. These divisions are not resolved by the work of mediation but are embraced or transcended: the divisions remain, but as evidence of the manifold nature of the created order—they do not divide so much as relate. However, in the fallen cosmos—which is the world we know, since the reconciliation achieved by Christ has not been fully appropriated—these divisions are gulfs of separation and incomprehension. The first we encounter is the divide between the sexes, all too often experienced as a massive fault line in human relationships, and the last of these divisions—that between uncreated and created—is called by Maximus ignorance: ultimately an "unknowing" in which God is known in a way that transcends the operation of the intellect but that all too often simply becomes an experience of the universe as godless and abandoned.[11] When, however, humanity fulfils its mediatorial role, then humanity itself leads the whole created order into union with the uncreated life of the Godhead—to deification.

Deification, or *theosis*, which we have already mentioned a couple of times, is a key term in Maximus's theology.[12] Briefly, it means the way in which the uncreated God is to share with the cosmos, through humankind, all his divine qualities, save the inalienable quality of being uncreated. As with the notion of deity itself, deification is best approached *apophatically*, that is, by denying what it does not mean. It expresses the *unlimited* parameters of human and cosmic participation in the divine: the goal of a diaphanous openness by humankind and the whole of creation to God's will and presence, and in particular it includes the insistence that the ultimate purpose of the cosmos is something inherent in God's act of creation itself, with the consequence that a theological understanding of creaturely reality is not limited to considering the restoration of God's purpose to a fallen and fragmented cosmos but looks beyond that to the ultimate transfiguration of the cosmos, intended from the beginning, a transfiguration in which, in St. Paul's words, God "will be all in all" (1 Cor. 15:28, cf. Eph. 1:23).[13] It is this point that is most important here, namely, that the goal of deification is not limited to the human but is the destiny of the whole cosmos.[14] St. Maximus's divisions of nature may seem to us quaint, but his idea that within the manifold that is the created order there are divisions that can either, when transcended, express the richness and beauty of the created order or, alternatively, cause gulfs of incomprehension, darkness, and pain seems to me an insight of continuing relevance.

Conclusions

What I have tried to show in my exposition of Maximus's cosmic vision is the way in which his doctrine of the *logoi* not only speaks of God's intimate involvement in the cosmos but also of the central role played by humankind, as microcosm, both reflecting the cosmos in itself and in its capacity to *interpret* the cosmos. How much of this can we, in the twenty-first century, still *think*? I say "think," because it seems to me it is not so much a matter of accepting certain ideas but of thinking in a certain way. We must recall what we noticed at the beginning, that St. Maximus expressed his cosmic vision using ideas that he shared with his contemporaries, both Christian and non-Christian, even if he interpreted these ideas in ways that went beyond what many of his contemporaries would have thought. For Maximus and his contemporaries the cosmos was conceived of with the earth at the center (most thought of it as a sphere; the "flat earth" idea, though espoused by some Byzantine Christians, notably, Cosmos Indicopleustes, the traveler to the Indies, was not generally accepted in intellectual circles),[15] surrounded by the planets that moved round the earth in cycles that could be represented by spheres, the whole surrounded by the sphere of the fixed stars. It was not very old either: estimates varied, but Maximus probably thought that the cosmos had been created something like six thousand years before his time. And it had all been there—from humans to earthworms, stars to stones—for virtually all of that time.

The way in which Maximus understood the *logoi* of creation and the mediatorial role of the human in such a cosmos is not difficult to *imagine*. If we are to retain something of Maximus's vision, then we have a good deal of rethinking to do. The universe, as we conceive it, is immensely large both in time and space. The human presence in the cosmos seems correspondingly minute—and not just minute but apparently peripheral. We live on the planet of a not very distinguished star, in one galaxy among many, and we have only been on the scene for what seems an unimaginably tiny moment when set against the timescale of the universe.

One of the first in Western history to grasp something of the significance of this was the mathematician Blaise Pascal. I find in his reaction to the realization of this the beginnings of a way in which we might attempt to rethink something of Maximus's vision. "*Le silence éternel de ces espaces infinis m'effraie*" ("the eternal silence of these infinite spaces fills me with fear").[16] What kind of fear? Philippe Sellier, in his note to this passage, points to parallels in Augustine (on Psalm 145: "You look to the heavens, and are greatly afraid, you think of the whole earth and tremble") and to Pascal's longer treatment of this theme a little earlier in this section and draws what seems to me the only valid conclusion: that it is fear or awe at the magnitude of the cosmos, not an inward intimation of failing faith. The infinity of the universe opened up by science (though it is not a literal infinity, as Pascal thought, only something unimaginably vast) surely only deepens our sense of wonder, compared with what our forefathers felt when they surveyed their rather cozy universe. It only reinforces that characteristic of the thought of the Greek Fathers that has been so appealing over the last century: its emphasis on apophaticism, on the silent denial of our concepts before the ineffable greatness of God.

Pascal's further steps seem to me even more significant. We tremble before the vastness of the universe; in contrast, our humanity seems something puny.

> Man is only a reed, more frail than nature, but he is a thinking reed. It does not need the whole universe to wipe him out: a breath, a drop of water, is enough to kill him. But when the universe wipes him out,

man will still be nobler than what kills him, since he knows that he dies and knows the advantage the universe has over him. The universe knows nothing.[17]

This is what Fr. Stăniloae meant in the quotation with which we began: that rather than thinking of the human as a microcosm, it would be more illuminating to think of the universe as a "macro-anthropos," for man can comprehend something of the cosmos, whereas the cosmos comprehends nothing of the human. In an earlier consideration of the "thinking reed," "*roseau pensant*," Pascal had reflected:

> It is not at all in space that I must seek my dignity, but in the ordering of my thought. I would have no advantage at all in possessing the earth. By space the universe embraces me and swallows me up like a point, but by thought I understand it.[18]

Thought—*logos*: this it is that secures humankind its position in the universe, not any physical position at the center of the cosmos. In fact, the Fathers recognize this, for although they did see man as the culmination of creation, living on the earth at the center of the cosmos, it is his participation in *logos* that marks out his true dignity.[19] It seems to me that Pascal's reflection here converges on modern ideas about the anthropic principle. And it seems to me that we can take these reflections further. Maximus sees the universe given meaning by the *logoi* through which creatures participate in God. Science sees the universe as governed by laws to which we humans can give mathematical expression. But for all the impersonal objectivity of mathematics, it is only humans that can know it and understand it. The same seems to be true at the other end of the scale: for instance, the discovery of how all living beings are structured by DNA. Again, it is only to reason that these complex codes can yield any meaning, despite the tendency of some to anthropomorphize and speak, for example, of the "selfish gene."

All this suggests that much of the vision of St. Maximus can be rethought in terms of current science. But why bother? Why attempt to rethink in terms of such ancient modes of thought? Briefly, I would respond thus. Over the last few centuries, science has vastly expanded our understanding of the development of the cosmos, the history of life on this planet, and the details of the structures of living beings. But in so doing, there has been lost a sense of the whole, of the interrelationship between the vast and the tiny, the technical and the meaningful. A monument to this lost coherence might be found in a work like Robert Burton's *Anatomy of Melancholy*, which still preserved the ancient sense of the coherence of all things, from the stars to the humors, in his terms. It is this loss that, I suspect, lies behind the attraction of a host of modern fashions, such as New Age religion, the revival of paganism, alternative medicine, even ecological concerns: all of these bear witness to the loss of a sense of relationship and coherence. Maximus's vision holds together both a confidence in reason and a sense of the coherence of the whole, and it does this, at one level at least, by having a rich sense of what is meant by reason or *logos*: not a mere calculating cleverness, a facility for getting results, but a way of making sense that is ultimately participation in the wisdom of the Creator. More than that, Maximus's vision is more than an intellectual theory. One work that brings together many of the ideas outlined above is his brief exposition of the Christian Eucharistic liturgy, the *Mystagogia*. In that work, the healing power flowing from the Incarnation and made effective in personal asceticism is given a cosmic dimension not through ideas but through the celebration of the Divine Liturgy, in a symbolism that Maximus shows illuminates everything from the mysteries of the Trinitarian Godhead itself, through the glories of the cosmos, to the hidden depths of the human soul. It is this sense of coherence revealed in a profound coinherence of everything in God through the Logos, who is the many *logoi*, that the vision of St. Maximus may help us recover.

PART II

"The Heart That Receives": Environment, Nature, and Creation in Twentieth-Century Orthodox Thought

Ecology, Theology, and the World

Savas Agouridis

The church today, confronted by the ecological revolution, is in danger of suffering just as it did during the technological and other revolutions.[1] It is in danger of being entirely unprepared, since the effective preparation for radical changes in human thought and behavior is neither an easy nor simple process. It demands serious theological adaptation and large-scale upheaval within the church body, and this requires rigorous struggle and considerable sacrifice.

Christians and theologians entered the new technological and ecological age as the "accused." The ecological movement targeted the unbridled exploitation of natural resources and the unrestrained economic development of nations in the northern hemisphere, along with an absence of any ideological restraints or reins. This polemical attitude of the environmentalists was expressed, at least in the religious domain, predominantly as an assault against Christianity: not only did Christianity fail to prevent the irrational stance of the Western world in relation to nature, but in fact it promoted it. It was natural for this critique to affect Christian theological thought. Thus, for instance, in his essay "The Historical Roots of the Ecological Crisis,"[2] Lynn White denounces Judeo-Christian anthropocentric principles as supporting Western aggression against nature. Some theologians generally accepted this censure; others rejected it. Of course, it is true that all Christians, both Eastern and Western, embrace some degree of distance or detachment of God from nature and humanity or of humanity from God and nature. This teaching is especially prevalent in Protestant thought of the seventeenth and eighteenth centuries; however, it was also emphasized by Protestant neo-orthodoxy in our own times.

Anthropocentric Genesis

Indeed, upon reading the book of Genesis about the accounts of creation,[3] as introductions to the history of Adam's creation and fall in the paradise of Eden, we observe the following:

> 1. God subdues nature, and especially the waters, subjecting them to a certain order so that everything might be configured for the survival of humanity on the earth. Thus, we have an anthropocentric perception of nature.
> 2. Adam is created according to the image and likeness of the Creator, thereby representing divine domination and authority over creation. "Lord over creation and rule over the fish of the sea. . . . Behold, I have given you all forms of vegetation and trees" (Gen. 1:27–30). Moreover, the power of humanity over the animal world is evident in the scene where Adam gives names to all creatures (Gen. 2:19).

This account is overall characterized by an anthropocentric inclination, despite that God remains the "Lord" of the world, and, as a result, there is no room or license for any arrogance over or abuse of nature. This picture is slightly complicated afterward, when God adopts nature for punishment against human beings with the stubborn labor of the farmer and the birth pangs of the mother, as well as the great flood. Nevertheless, beyond all this, nature itself ultimately competes against God in human experience, when people worship "creation instead of the Creator" (Rom. 1:25). Consequently, nature too is now subjected to "vainglory" and "corruption"—not voluntarily, as in the case of Adam and Eve, "but through the one that subdues," whatever this phrase may actually mean. Nature "groans and travails" with humanity in the struggle for liberation and reconciliation; at the same time, like humanity, nature lives "in the expectation of being freed from the slavery of corruption to the freedom of glory of the children of God" (Rom. 8:20–22). What is apparent from the above considerations as a whole is the dynamic relationship between God, humanity, and the world. However, despite the unmistakable anthropocentric overtones of this system of thought, we cannot blame Christianity alone for the ecological crisis of our day.

Still, the criticism of ecologists against religion in general and against Christianity in particular is surely crucial inasmuch as, within the human experience of God, religion has underlined the upward direction of mysticism, displacing the center of human interest away from the natural and social environment. One might even dare to propose that, to the degree that humankind's relationship with nature and society becomes problematic or negative, the human drive for mystical union with God becomes more frantic and fierce. Human devotion to God thus proportionately became the reverse of human dedication to nature and society.

Of course, biblical theologians of every Christian confession are aware that, for the religion of the Old Testament and early Christianity, fervent faith in God and in divine providence for the world hardly prevented the development of a horizontal and eschatological dimension of the human religious experience or a "service" to the world and the intense hope for social change and natural preservation—in accordance with "a new earth and a new heaven" (Rev. 21:1). The truth is, as Oscar Cullmann observes, that this horizontal dimension gradually shifted from the center to the margin, and simultaneously theology stressed the Greek Platonist aspect of the individual dimension.[4]

Theological Viewpoints

Many theologians respond to the ecological challenge in a positive manner, genuinely searching for points of correspondence and connection with environmentalists. Others feel more comfortable with ecological issues, convinced that the Christian tradition reveals an ambiguous environmental position: on the one hand the upward movement toward God described above, but on the other hand an ecological orientation based on the cooperation of the divine and human factors in relation to nature.[5] Roman Catholic theologians explore tradition to discover someone that can serve as a patron saint of a contemporary Christian ecological system. Santmire proposes St. Augustine of Hippo, who speaks of God as the essential Good that satisfies the human soul while at the same time giving prominence in his later writings to the good of God as expressed through creation. Thus, while Augustine originally attributes exclusive priority to the individual's union with God (*unio mystica*), in his later works the fundamental glorification of humanity lies not so much in union with God but in the communal life of the saints (*vita socialis sanctorum*). However, the conclusion drawn by someone reading these views of Santmire is that any worldly spirituality in Augustine probably misinterprets his theological and spiritual intention.

The worldview of St. Francis of Assisi differed greatly in this respect. Francis has become the refuge for Christian environmentalists. All of his biographers, particularly the more recent ones, make mention of the "nature mysticism" of the saint. Francis combines ingredients from medieval ascetic spirituality and hagiology: primeval elements of a mysticism of nature, an extraordinary familiarity with every part and particle of creation, and a sense of the goodness of nature. Some contemporary biographers emphasize that this saint reflects an outburst of positive religious reaction toward nature from within a medieval asceticism, which otherwise presents an ambivalent attitude toward the natural world. Others, of course, refer to an emotional if romantic approach to life. I will circumvent all these opinions because the characteristic vision of Francis that seems most appealing to me is described by Leonardo Boff, for whom the saint's respect for the created world is rooted in a more stringent form of asceticism. Francis originally tested his life in communion with the poor (whom he called the *minores*) and associated his love for human beings with his love for created nature. Boff's observation is especially relevant for many of the ascetics of the Eastern Church. Many of the ascetics in the Orthodox Christian tradition would—out of frustration against a powerful institutional Church that only grew wealthier over time—escape to the desert in order to achieve salvation. There, paradoxically, they discovered a form of affinity with and empathy for nature, both animate and inanimate; it was an essential solidarity with and theological connection to the rest of creation. It is now time for this subject to be the object of more scholarly research; some doctoral dissertations should be written on this topic in our theological schools.

Boff particularly highlights the awareness of "iffness" in the lives of ascetics like Francis. The source and foundation of their being lies not so much within—but rather outside of—themselves. This is why they recognize how "poor" humanity is. Only the genuinely *expropriatus*—or estranged, namely the one who literally possesses nothing—can be "brother" (or, as Francis would say, *frater*) to all being, to human beings and created nature alike.

Francis's dependence on contemporaneous Islamic Sufi models is underlined by Idries Shah.[6] Nonetheless, what is important here is that authentic parallels of nature mysticism are also encountered in Muslim asceticism, which most probably borrowed heavily from Christian ascetics.

To this point, I have mentioned certain basic problems related to ecology and theology as well as certain theological efforts to reconcile the two. However, all of this cannot properly be appreciated unless we take into serious consideration the thrust of ecological philosophy, which comes to the conclusion about the immediate necessity today for an "endocosmic" form of asceticism. More specifically, "Deep Ecology"—which blends science and philosophy—is centered on the concept of "biocentric equality," namely on the notion that recognizes equal rights for every being, living or dead, on our planet. Accordingly, so it is claimed, all people and all things achieve their self-realization within a broader self-realization of the world. The goal of deep ecology is the preservation of an environmental harmony and balance as well as the protection of the particularity of the diverse forms of being within nature, which includes the continuation of the uniqueness of all civilizations and the creation within the field of economy of "standards" for vital needs and quality of life. These standards will contribute to a restrained (or sustained) economic development where the excess of affluent nations is applied to the poverty of the "third world" as a manifestation of balance. The complexity of these demands constitutes the essence of a "contemporary asceticism," which must be adopted by everyone in order for our planet and us to survive. Since everything in nature is intimately interconnected and inseparably interdependent, everything is equally "sacred"; nothing is superior to anything else. This ecological school of thought truly facilitates a vision of life as a "whole," but it may be more suited to the worldview of East Asian peoples and religions.

Nevertheless, other ecological schools of thought propose more moderate beliefs, which are based on a philosophy or worldview that is generally more consonant with the Greek and Judeo-Christian tradition, inasmuch as it admits the superiority and at the same time the immense responsibility of humanity for the preservation of the ecosystem on our planet. The contemporary "asceticism" suggested by this school of thought as an antidote for the ecological crisis is unrelated to the renunciation of sex but pertains rather to the formation within us of an instinct to enjoy life without destroying nature or hurting our fellow human beings.

This form of "ascesis," however, proves to be very difficult and invariably encounters numerous stumbling blocks established by greater secular interests that are at stake. To overcome these barriers of the "greater interests," it is crucial to promulgate the scientific data regarding our relationship with the environment, natural and social alike, as well as to promote more publicly the awareness of the visible and invisible biological and spiritual connection that binds us to the world around. Ultimately, all ecologists emphasize the respect that is due all forms of life, all cultural differences, all the particular values they represent, and a new quality of life, instead of respect derived from per capita income and economic survival.

Eschatological Asceticism

The problem facing theologians is that all environmentalists, irrespective of their school of thought, are "biocentrically" and not theologically oriented. From my study of the subject, any theological response to the issue must, on the one hand, be somehow grounded on Christian tradition and, on the other hand, include certain elements from the contemporary science of ecology.

Both of these factors are equally indispensable. In any case, Christianity has survived and advanced in this way throughout history—namely, by emphasizing certain elements from within its tradition while simultaneously assimilating other elements external to it. And in referring here to traditional elements of Christianity, I am not simply alluding to specific aspects of Christian ascetic practice but also to the closely related eschatological theological tradition of the Church. Indeed, it should be made clear that I am referring to an extreme aspect of the eschatological dimensions of Christian life, which can be identified with the nature mysticism of St. Francis and with an intimate—that is to say, free from any aversion or mutual hostility—connection with nature, as experienced by many ascetics of the Eastern Church. Still, we must be careful to avoid any vague generalization or even any exaggeration of these connections. Perhaps we might more moderately and accurately formulate this worldview in the following manner: The horizontal Semitic eschatological perspective curiously makes its appearance within early Christian asceticism despite that the overall theological orientation of the time leaned in the direction of a Platonist dimension, which implied a renunciation of the world and history.

This is valid for both Eastern and Western Christianity. Yet it would be a serious error not to accept the real significance of the fact that many ascetics, who lived far from the world in the desert, experienced so intensely and vividly the foretaste of the heavenly Kingdom that they also experienced their environment as transfigured—or, at least, as participating in an advanced stage of transfiguration. In their case, they believed that the predictions of the prophets about the peaceful coexistence of the lamb, the lion, and the ox were being revealed before their very eyes. They saw the world around them as reconciled—or, at least, as advancing toward reconciliation. We might recall some of these prophetic exaltations:

> The wolf shall live with the lamb, the leopard shall lie down with the kid, the calf and the lion and the fatling together, and a little child shall lead them. The cow and the bear shall graze, their young shall lie down together; and the lion shall eat straw like the ox. The nursing child shall play over the hole of the asp, and the weaned child shall put its hand on the adder's den. They will not hurt or destroy on all my holy mountain; for the earth will be full of the knowledge of the Lord as the waters cover the sea. (Isaiah 11:6–9)
>
> The wolf and the lamb shall feed together, the lion shall eat straw like the ox. . . . They shall not hurt or destroy on all my holy mountain. (Isaiah 65:25)

I will make for you a covenant on that day with the wild animals, the birds of the air, and the creeping things of the ground; and I will abolish the bow, and the sword, and war from the land; and I will make you lie down in safety. (Hosea 2:18)

I will make with them a covenant of peace and banish wild animals from the land, so that they may live in the wild and sleep in the woods securely. I will make them and the region around my hill a blessing; and I will send down the showers in their season; they shall be showers of blessing. The trees of the field shall yield their fruit, and the earth shall yield its increase. They shall be secure on their soil; and they shall know that I am the Lord, when I break the bars of their yoke, and save them from the hands of those who enslaved them. They shall no more be plunder for the nations, nor shall the animals of the land devour them; they shall live in safety, and no one shall make them afraid. I will provide for them a splendid vegetation so that they shall no more be consumed with hunger in the land, and no longer suffer the insults of the nations. They shall know that I, the Lord their God, am with them, and that they, the house of Israel, are my people, says the Lord God. You are my sheep, the sheep of my pasture; and I am your God, says the Lord God. (Ezekiel 34:25–31)

These prophetic images about "the end times" and the relationship between human beings and the natural world are sometimes experienced and expressed in asceticism in the form of a foretaste of the end to the modern relationship of enmity and hostility.

From all the above, it is clear that eschatology must return from the marginal importance it was attributed by medieval theology to the center of the Christian worldview, just as it was in the primitive Christian community. This is precisely why the sacraments of the Church—including baptism, chrismation, the Eucharist, and repentance—are essentially permeated by the eschatological theology of the early Church. Despite the way in which certain subsequent periods interpreted the meaning of the Church's literature and practice, the eschatological perspective of the world and history introduces a horizontal—in addition to the vertical—dimension to theological thought. By continuously and ardently beholding the future through repentance and conversion, it is also capable of appreciating the worldly and ephemeral through the lens of preserving as well as transforming God's creation in the light of the heavenly Kingdom. Within such a theology, God is not only "the one who was and is" but also "the one who is yet to come" (Rev. 1:4).

Combined with the Christian respect for the small, the frail, the poor, and everything nontitanic or nongigantic, this eschatological perspective regarding the transfiguration of the world can establish a sure and sincere cooperation with the ecological movement. The motto of the universal youth revolt of the 1960s, namely that "small is beautiful," could wonderfully articulate an ecological as well as a Christian purpose. The modern giants of technology, consumerism, and warfare lead to the depletion of the rich natural resources of our planet, to destructive pollution, and to the danger of nuclear holocaust, as well as to the fatal imitation of the rich North by the undeveloped South. Time is running out. In previous centuries, asceticism was the choice of a small group of spiritual people in the Church. Today, beyond the traditional form of monasticism, contemporary asceticism is a matter of catechetical instruction and Christian ethics for all people, since humanity itself is now contributing to the destruction of the world and the annihilation of our species. Of course, even with regard to this new form of asceticism, things are not quite as simple as they appear. What is required is the cultivation of a new awareness of the world, a new sensitivity that regards the world as a gift and as a promise offered by God to His children, a new outlook that considers the world as an object of love for God and humanity alike. This is not a new form of idealism or romanticism, since the world is both a gift and a promise in the sense that it provides the space within which the world can survive and be transformed within the Church. We are called to advance toward this new eschatological asceticism while also assimilating certain elements from modern environmental science.

This is a new way of thinking, which for Christians may imply a fulfillment, classification, or even improvement of certain traditional elements. This new way of thinking moves dialogically between the "part" and the "whole," commencing from the part we know as the "self." This new way of thinking rejects the division of the world into individual systems, the separation of our self from inanimate matter and the remaining animate organisms with a view to estranging us from them. It recognizes that each part of the world has its own value in relation to the proper operation of the whole. Thus, all states of being, all forms of existence in the world, have *privileges and rights*. Such a recognition inevitably and immediately contradicts contemporary utilitarianism with regard to a worldview defined solely by the benefits of one of its parts, namely humanity. Previous worldviews would often erroneously perceive humanity as being the whole (*pars pro toto*).

It is unacceptable for some to respond that, by increasing our concern toward the world, such a way of thinking will decrease our love for God. History has proven that humanity has not loved God primarily by loving itself.

The dialogue between theology and ecology removes our thought from ourselves and directs it toward other creatures and to the journey of us all toward the encounter of "the one who is yet to come." It is in the exclusive inversion toward ourselves and our self, as if we were the sole proprietors of the world, that we lose sight of and lose God Himself. Surely this is not an easy task, especially since our very churches are historical institutions so focused on themselves and their history, manifestations of the *pars pro toto*.

Assimilation at All Times and in All Places

There is no reason, however, for concern. All that is required is careful attention to the way in which theology and Christian ethics ought to assimilate elements of contemporary scientific research and thought. Although it may come as a surprise to some, Christianity survived historically as a religion of syncretism. This syncretistic dimension was the force that enabled it to assimilate various elements at all times and in all places; it proved one of the most successful secrets of Christianity.[7] Let us consider, for example, the way in which early Christianity assimilated material from Hellenistic philosophy on the subject of "self-sufficiency," which is naturally related to the emphasis of modern ecology in the domain of sustaining or restraining one's vital needs for survival.

In his address *To the Greeks*, Tatian (120–180) observes that Diogenes was self-content to dwell in a tiny barrel and was modestly proud of his self-sufficiency.[8] The virtue of self-sufficiency was undoubtedly the reaction of the Cynics to the Hellenistic and Roman tendency toward plutocracy. Furthermore, in his treatise entitled *Instructor*, Clement of Alexandria (150–215) notes that the mother of frugality and simplicity is justice, and their nurturer and nurse is self-sufficiency.[9] Similarly, in his commentary on 1 Tim. 6:6, St. John Chrysostom (347–407) remarks that the greatest resource is godliness with self-sufficiency—not so much when one has money but rather when one does not.

It is within the context of such Cynic and Stoic philosophy that we should also interpret the first accounts in the New Testament regarding self-sufficiency:

> God is able to provide you with every blessing in abundance, so that by always having enough of everything, you may share abundantly in every good work. (2 Cor. 9:8)
>
> Of course, there is great gain in godliness combined with contentment. (1 Tim. 6:6)

This is precisely how contemporary biblical scholars construe these passages. They regard the concept of wealth in these texts, as well as in the teachings of Jesus, neither as a privilege nor as an opportunity but rather as dangerous. The traps encountered by the soul as it amasses wealth are so great that they cannot guarantee the virtue of charity or the goal of salvation.[10] This understanding of wealth is not only shared by Christianity and Stoicism but also by the history of religions in general.[11]

There are a host of ideas, principles, and institutions in Christianity that relate to this kind of assimilation of external contributions. Some of these are emphasized and assume a critical role in the Christian teaching; others are clear borrowings embraced in their entirety. This holds true not only for the early Christian community but also throughout the history of Christian thought. It is helpful, for example, to recall the struggle of the Church to accept and finally assimilate the system of Copernicus, the urban revolution, or other modern scientific theories about evolution. Christianity even assumes a different outlook in various regions of the world where it prevails. Indeed, the power of Christianity perhaps lies in the fact that it is able to adapt better than any other religion without losing any of its essential characteristics. From its very nature, Christianity is comprehensive, alive, and versatile as a religion. Or, rather, since it is identified with life itself, Christianity can maintain its identity as it passes through the diverse stages of life from infancy to adolescence and then to maturity.

We have already referred to the concept of self-sufficiency in relation to the contemporary emphasis and demands of ecological thinkers about human survival needs. Nonetheless, this does not mean that this concept is easy for modern Christians to embrace or reproduce. In fact, with regard to the daily practical life of Christians, this is perhaps one of the most difficult concepts to adopt and adapt. To paraphrase the words of the German biblical theologian Gerd Theissen about the eschatological challenge of God, the pressing or stressing of self-sufficiency can genuinely lead Christians to repentance; it can certainly oblige them to remove the last mask of hypocrisy that remains. One will readily ascertain how difficult any adaptation of Christian ethics proves before the social and commercial demands of modern life simply by reading Christian reactions to questions, for instance, about the relationship between labor and capital, both in European and American circles.

Let me offer another example. Much like previous generations, my own generation was raised—from an ethical and a Christian perspective—with an understanding about the struggle or "battle to be waged against the flesh." The defining literature on the subject was the *Unseen Warfare* by St.

Nikodemus of the Holy Mountain.[12] There is no need to argue this extensively, but this kind of asceticism sometimes expresses a masochistic aversion to human nature—beginning with oneself and extending to other human beings and the world in general—in the name of love toward God. The Church never formally subscribed to such asceticism, yet often it would promote or reinforce it in one way or another. What would it mean today for such a mentality if our worldview is challenged not to be absorbed or consumed into itself but rather to be attracted or drawn to more universal interests, even cosmic concerns? Our worldview must undergo a painful, albeit mandatory reorientation to the rights of other beings and all creation, animate and inanimate. In brief, we could describe the situation as follows: we must endure "poverty" in order for others and the whole of creation to regain the place they deserve in the world. This way of thinking must be developed theologically along principles derived from the Christian tradition, whether from a theology of liberation or anywhere else, irrespective of the label. The "battle waged against the flesh" is crucial for humanity not to be subjected to its instincts. There is no question about this. However, we must not commit the same error here of *pars pro toto*. Humanity must—first and foremost, primarily and principally—"wage battle" against its individuality, namely its class identity, its racial and ethnic selfishness, and whatever else feeds its existence unfairly and unjustly to the detriment or at the expense of others, whether human or other beings.

After all, the "battle waged against the flesh" wastes a great deal of human vigor in a one-sided direction, particularly against sex; whereas, if this warfare is directed properly and comprehensively, it is capable of shaping a new era of contemporary Christian "asceticism" for all people, married and celibate alike, both clergy and lay. Moreover, the celibate monks and nuns, who generally bear lesser burdens, could—in accordance with tradition—assume initiative and leadership in this new struggle. However, in order to achieve this, we require much faith and informed minds not only in regard to the Christian tradition but also about the contemporary challenges and demands of science and of life itself.

Through Creation to the Creator
Metropolitan Kallistos (Ware) of Diokleia

Hurt not the earth, neither the sea, nor the trees.
—*Revelation 7:3*

The saints embrace the whole world with their love.
—*St. Silouan the Athonite (1938)*

I
"Love the Trees"

On the Holy Mountain of Athos, the monks sometimes put up beside the forest paths special signposts offering encouragement or warning to the pilgrim as he passes. One such notice used to give me particular pleasure. Its message was brief and clear: "Love the trees."

Fr. Amphilochios (d. 1970), the geronta or "elder" on the island of Patmos when I first stayed there, would have been in full agreement. "Do you know," he said, "that God gave us one more commandment, which is not recorded in Scripture? It is the commandment 'love the trees.'" Whoever does not love trees, so he believed, does not love God. "When you plant a tree," he insisted, "you plant hope, you plant peace, you plant love, and you will receive God's blessing." An ecologist long before ecology had become fashionable, when hearing confessions of the local farmers he used to assign to them as penance the task of planting a tree. During the long summer drought, he himself went round the island watering the young trees. His example and influence have transformed Patmos: photographs of the hillside near the Cave of the Apocalypse, taken at the start of the twentieth century, show bare and barren slopes; today there is a thick and flourishing wood.[1]

Fr. Amphilochios was by no means the first spiritual teacher in the modern Greek tradition to recognize the importance of trees. Two centuries earlier, the Athonite monk St. Kosmas the Aetolian, martyred in 1779, used to plant trees as he traveled around Greece on his missionary journeys, and in one of his "prophecies" he stated, "People will remain poor, because they have no love for trees."[2] We can see that prophecy fulfilled today in all too many parts of the world. Another saying attributed to him—not in this instance about trees—is equally applicable to the present age: "The time will come when the devil puts himself inside a box and starts shouting; and his horns will stick out from the roof-tiles."[3] That often comes to my mind as I survey the skyline in London, with its serried ranks of television masts.

"Love the trees." Why should we do so? Is there indeed a connection between love of trees and love of God? How far is it true that a failure to reverence and honor our natural environment—animals, trees, earth, fire, air, and water—is also, in an immediate and soul-destroying way, a failure to reverence and honor the living God?

Let us begin with two visions of a tree.

The World as Sacrament; or, A Tale of Two Trees

Have we not known, each of us, certain moments when we have started with sudden amazement at the lines before us on the printed page, words of poetry or prose that, once read, have forever remained luminous in our memory? One such moment happened to me at the age of eighteen as I was reading that magical anthology by Walter de la Mare, *Behold, This Dreamer*, and came across a passage from the book of Edward Carpenter (1844–1929), *Pagan and Christian Creeds*. "Has any one of us ever seen a tree?" asks Carpenter, and he answers, "I certainly do not think that I have—except most superficially." He continues:

> That very penetrating observer and naturalist, Henry David Thoreau, tells us that he would often make an appointment to visit a certain tree, miles away—but what he saw when he got there, he does not say. Walt Whitman, also a keen observer . . . mentions that, in a dream trance he actually once saw "his favorite trees step out and promenade up, down and around, very curiously." Once the present writer seemed to have a

partial vision of a tree. It was a beech, standing somewhat isolated, and still leafless in quite early Spring. Suddenly, I was aware of its skyward-reaching arms and up-turned finger-tips, as if some vivid life (or electricity) was streaming through them far into the spaces of heaven, and of its roots plunged in the earth and drawing the same energies from below. The day was quite still and there was no movement in the branches, but in that moment the tree was no longer a separate or separable organism, but a vast being ramifying far into space, sharing and uniting the life of Earth and Sky, and full of most amazing activity.[4]

Two things above all are noteworthy in Edward Carpenter's "partial vision." First, the tree is alive, vibrant with what he calls "energies" or "electricity"; it is "full of most amazing activity." Second, the tree is cosmic in its dimensions: it is not "a separate or separable organism" but is "vast" and all-embracing in its scope, "ramifying far into space . . . uniting the life of Earth and Sky."

Here is a vision of joyful wonder, inspired by an underlying sense of mystery. The tree has become a symbol pointing beyond itself, a sacrament that embodies some deep secret at the heart of the universe. The same sense of wonder and mystery—of the symbolic and sacramental character of the world—is strikingly manifest in *Peaks and Lamas*, the masterwork of that spiritual mountaineer Marco Pallis.

Yet there are at the same time certain limitations in Carpenter's tree vision. The mystery to which the tree points is not spelled out by him in specifically personal terms. He makes no attempt to ascend through the creation to the Creator. There is nothing directly theistic about his vision, no reference to God or to Jesus Christ.

Let us turn to a second tree vision, which is by contrast explicitly personal and theophanic:

> Moses was keeping the flock of his father-in-law Jethro, the priest of Midian; he led his flock beyond the wilderness, and came to Horeb, the mountain of God. There the angel of the Lord appeared to him in a flame of fire out of a bush; he looked, and the bush was blazing, yet it was not consumed. Then Moses said, "I must turn aside and look at this great sight, and see why the bush is not burned up." When the Lord saw that he had turned aside to see, God called to him out of the bush, "Moses, Moses!" And he said, "Here I am." Then He said, "Come no closer! Remove the sandals from your feet, for the place on which you are standing is holy ground." He said further, "I am the God of your Father,

the God of Abraham, the God of Isaac, and the God of Jacob." And Moses hid his face, for he was afraid to look at God. (Ex. 3:1–6)

Comparing the experience of Moses with that of Carpenter, we observe three things: in the first place, the vision described in Exodus reaches out beyond the realm of the impersonal. The burning bush at Horeb acts as the locus of an interpersonal encounter, of a meeting face to face, of a dialogue between two subjects. God calls out to Moses by name, "Moses, Moses!" and Moses responds, "Here I am."

"Through the creation to the Creator": in and through the tree he beholds, Moses enters into communion with the living God. Nor is this all. On the interpretation accepted by the Orthodox Church, the personal encounter is to be understood in more specific terms. Moses does not simply meet God, but he meets Christ.

All the theophanies in the Old Testament are manifestations not of God the Father—Whom "no one has ever seen" (John 1:18)—but of the preincarnate Christ, God the eternal Logos. Visitors to St. Mark's in Venice will recall that in the mosaics depicting the story of Genesis 1, the face of God the Creator bears unmistakably the lineaments of Christ. In the same way, when Isaiah sees God enthroned in the temple, "high and lifted up" (Isaiah 6:1), and when Ezekiel sees in the midst of the wheels and of the four living creatures "something that seemed like a human form" (Ezekiel 1:26), it is Christ the Logos whom they both behold.

In the second place, God does not only appear to Moses but also issues a practical command to him: "Remove the sandals from your feet." According to Greek Fathers such as St. Gregory of Nyssa, sandals or shoes—being made from the skins of dead animals—are something lifeless, inert, dead, and earthly, and they symbolize the heaviness, weariness, and mortality that assail our human nature as a result of the Fall.[5] "Remove your sandals," then, may be understood to signify: strip off from yourself the deadness of familiarity and boredom; free yourself from the lifelessness of the trivial, the mechanical, the repetitive; wake up, open your eyes, cleanse the doors of your perception, look and see!

And what, in the third place, happens to us when in this manner we strip off the dead skins of boredom and triviality? At once we realize the truth of God's next words to Moses: "The place on which you are standing is holy ground." Set free from spiritual deadness, awakening from sleep, opening our eyes both outwardly and inwardly, we look upon the world around us in a different way. Everything appears to us, as it did to the infant Traherne, "new and strange . . . inexpressibly rare, and delightful, and beautiful."[6] We experience everything as vital and living, and we discover the truth of William Blake's *dictum*, "Every thing that lives is Holy."[7]

So we enter the dimensions of sacred space and sacred time. We discern the great within the small, the extraordinary within the ordinary, "a world in a grain of sand . . . and eternity in an hour," to quote Blake once more. *This* place where I am, *this* tree, *this* animal, *this* person to whom I am speaking, *this* moment of time through which I am living: each is holy, each is unique and unrepeatable, and each is therefore infinite in value.

Combining Edward Carpenter's living tree, uniting earth and heaven, and the burning bush of Moses, we can see emerging a precise and distinctive conception of the universe. Nature is sacred. The world is a sacrament of the divine presence, a means of communion with God. The environment consists not in dead matter but in living relationship. The entire cosmos is one vast burning bush permeated by the fire of divine power and glory:

> Earth's crammed with heaven,
> and every common bush afire with God;
> but only he who sees, takes off his shoes,
> the rest sit round it and pluck blackberries.[8]

Certainly there is nothing in itself wrong about plucking blackberries. But as we enjoy the fruits of the earth, let us also look beyond our own immediate pleasure and discern the deeper mystery that surrounds us on every side.

Essence and Energies, Logos and Logoi

Does such an approach lead us to pantheism? Not necessarily. As a Christian in the tradition of Eastern Orthodoxy, I cannot accept any worldview that identifies God with the universe, and for that reason I cannot be a pantheist. But I find no difficulty in endorsing panentheism—that is to say, the position that affirms not "God is everything and everything is God" but "God is *in* everything and everything is *in* God." God, in other words, is both immanent and transcendent: present in all things. He is at the same time above and beyond them all. It is necessary to emphasize simultaneously both halves of the paradox beloved of the poet Charles Williams: "This also is Thou; neither is this Thou."[9]

Upholding this "panentheistic" standpoint, the great Byzantine theologian St. Gregory Palamas (1296–1359) safeguarded the otherness-yet-nearness of the Eternal by making a distinction-in-unity between God's essence and His energies. In His essence, God is infinitely transcendent, radically unknowable, utterly beyond all created being, beyond all understanding and all participation from the human side. But, in His energies, God is inexhaustibly immanent, the core of everything, the heart of its heart, closer to the heart of each thing than is that thing's very own heart. These divine energies, according to the Palamite teaching, are not an intermediary between God and the world, not a created gift that He bestows upon us, but they are God Himself in action, and each uncreated energy is God in His indivisible totality, not a part of Him but the whole.

By virtue of this essence-energies distinction, Palamas is able to affirm without self-contradiction:

> Those who are counted worthy enjoy union with God the cause of all. . . . He remains wholly within Himself and yet dwells wholly within us, making us share not in His nature but in His glory and radiance.[10]

In this way, God is both revealed and hidden—revealed in His energies, hidden in His essence:

> Somehow He manifests Himself in His totality, and yet he does not manifest Himself; we apprehend Him with our intellect, and yet we do not apprehend Him; we participate in Him, and yet He remains beyond all participation.[11]

Such is the antinomic stance of the true panentheist:

> God both is and is not; He is everywhere and nowhere; He has many names and He cannot be named; He is ever-moving and He is immovable; and, in short, He is everything and nothing.[12]

What St. Gregory Palamas seeks to express through the essence-energies distinction St. Maximus the Confessor (d. 662) indicates by speaking in terms of Logos and *logoi*, even though the specific concerns of Maximus and the context in which he is writing are not altogether identical with those of Palamas. According to Maximus, Christ the Creator-Logos has implanted in each created thing a characteristic *logos*, a "thought" or "word," which is the divine presence in that thing, God's intention for it, the inner essence of that thing, which makes it to be distinctively itself and at the same time draws it toward God. By virtue of these indwelling *logoi*, each created thing is not just an object but a personal word addressed to us by the Creator. The divine Logos, the Second Person of the Trinity, the Wisdom and the Providence of God, constitutes at once the source and the end of the particular *logoi* and in this fashion acts as an all-embracing and unifying cosmic presence.

Anticipating Palamas, Maximus speaks of these *logoi* as "energies,"[13] and at the same time he likens them to birds in the branches of a tree:

> The Logos of God is like a grain of mustard seed: before cultivation it looks extremely small, but when cultivated in the right way it grows so large that the highest principles (*logoi*) of both sensible and intelligible creation come like birds to revive themselves in it. For the principles or inner essences (*logoi*) of all things are embraced by the Logos, but the Logos is not embraced by any thing.[14]

According to the interpretation of Maximus, then, the cosmic tree is Christ the Creator-Logos, and the birds in the branches are the *logoi* of you and me and all the created things. The Logos embraces all the *logoi* but is not Himself embraced or circumscribed by them. Here Maximus seeks—as does Palamas in his use of the essence-energies distinction—to safeguard the double truth of God's transcendence and His immanence.

Whether we speak, as St. Maximus does, of the indwelling *logoi* or prefer to use the Palamite word "energies"—and we can of course choose to employ both terms—our basic meaning and intention remain the same. All nature is theophanic. Each created person and thing is a point of encounter with "the Beyond That is in our midst," to use Dietrich Bonhoeffer's phrase. We are to see God in everything and everything in God. Wherever we are and whatever we are doing, we can ascend through the creation to the Creator.

After listening to our two Eastern witnesses, Maximus and Palamas, let us also hear a Western prophet, St. Hildegard of Bingen (1098–1179), who is equally definite about the panentheistic character of the universe. In *The Book of Divine Works* she affirms that "all living creatures are, so to speak, sparks from the radiation of God's brilliance, and these sparks emerge from God like the rays of the sun."[15] Elsewhere in the same treatise she records the remarkable words addressed to her by the Holy Spirit:

> I, the highest and fiery power, have kindled every living spark and I have breathed out nothing that can die. . . . I am . . . the fiery life of the divine essence—I flame above the beauty of the fields; I shine in the waters; in the sun, the moon and the stars, I burn. And by means of the airy wind, I stir everything into quickness with a certain invisible life which sustains all. For the air lives in its green power and its blossoming; the waters flow as if they were alive. Even the sun is alive in its own light. . . . I, the fiery power, lie hidden in these things and they blaze from Me, just as man is continually moved by his breath, and as the fire contains the

nimble flame. All these things live in their own essence and are without death, since I am Life. . . . I am the whole of life—life was not torn from stones; it did not bud from branches; nor is it rooted in the generative power of the male. Rather, every living thing is rooted in Me.[16]

The approach adopted by Palamas, Maximus, and Hildegard has two important consequences for our understanding of God's creative power. First, when we speak of God creating the world, we are to envisage this not as a single act in the past but as a continuing presence here and now, and in that sense it is legitimate to speak in terms of *continual creation*. Second, and closely linked with the first point, we should think of God as creating the world not, as it were, from the outside but *from within*.

In the first place, when it is said, "In the beginning, God created the heavens and the earth" (Gen. 1:1), the word "beginning" is not to be interpreted in a temporal sense. Creation is not a once-for-all event happening in the remote past, an initial act that constitutes a chronological starting point. It is not a past event but a present relationship. We are to think and to speak not in the past but in the present tense; we are to say not "God *made* the world, once upon a time, long ago" but "God *is making* the world, and you and me in it, here and now, at this moment and always." "In the beginning" (*en arche*), then, does not signify, "God started it all off, billions of years ago, and since then He has left things to keep going by their own momentum." It means, on the contrary, that God is at each and every instant the constant and unceasing *arche*, the source, principle, cause, and sustainer of all that exists. It means that if God did not continue to exert His creative will at every split second of time, the universe would immediately collapse into the void of non-being. Without the active and uninterrupted presence of Christ the Creator-Logos throughout the cosmos, nothing would exist for a single moment.

Second, it follows from this that Christ as Creator-Logos is to be envisaged not as on the outside but as on the inside of everything. It is a frequent fault of religious writers that they speak of the created universe as if it were an artifact of a Maker Who has, so to speak, produced it from without. God the Creator becomes the celestial clockmaker Who sets the cosmic process in motion, winding up the clock but then leaving it to continue ticking on its own. This will not do. It is important to avoid such images as the divine architect, builder, or engineer and to speak rather in terms of indwelling (without thereby excluding the dimension of divine transcendence). Creation is not something upon which God acts from the outside but something through which he expresses Himself from within. Transcendent, He is also immanent; above and beyond creation, He is also its true inwardness, its "within."

Double Vision

If we adopt the sacramental understanding of the world implied in our "tale of two trees," we shall gradually find that our contemplation of nature is marked above all by two qualities: distinctiveness and transparency.

Distinctiveness: If we are to see the world as sacrament, then this signifies that, first of all, we are to discover the distinctive and peculiar flavor of each created thing. We are to perceive and to value each thing in and for itself, viewing that thing in sharp relief, appreciating what in the Zen tradition is called the special "Ah!" of each thing, its "is-ness" or *haeccitas*. The point is vividly expressed by Gerard Manley Hopkins:

> As kingfishers catch fire, dragonflies draw flame . . . each mortal thing does one thing and the same . . . Selves—goes itself; myself it speaks and spells; crying What I do is me: for that I came.[17]

To see nature as sacred is, in the first instance, to recognize how each thing "selves" and "speaks *myself.*" We are to perceive each kingfisher, each frog, each human face, each blade of grass in its uniqueness. Each is to be real for us, each is to be immediate. We are to explore the variety and the particularity of creation—what St. Paul calls the "glory" of each thing: "There is one glory of the sun, and another of the moon, and another glory of the stars; indeed, star differs from star in glory" (1 Cor. 15:41).

Transparency: Having evoked and savored the particular "is-ness" of each thing, we can then take a second step: we can look within and beyond each thing and discover in and through it the divine presence. After perceiving each kingfisher, each frog, each human face, each blade of grass in its uniqueness, in its full reality and immediacy, we are then to treat each as a means of communion with God and so to ascend through the creation to the Creator. For it is impossible to make sense of the world unless we also look beyond the world; the world only acquires its true meaning when seen as the reflection of a reality that transcends it.

The first step, then, is to love the world for itself, in terms of its own consistency and integrity. The second step is to allow the world to become pellucid, so that it reveals to us the indwelling Creator-Logos. In this way we acquire Blake's "double vision":

> For double the vision my Eyes do see, and a double vision is always with me. . . . May God us keep, from Single vision and Newton's sleep![18]

It is vital not to attempt the second step without previously embarking upon the first. We need to recognize the solidity of the world before we can discern its transparency; we need to rejoice in the abundant variety of creation before we ascertain how all things find their unity in God. Moreover, the second level, that of theophanic transparency, does not in any way cancel out the first level, that of particularity and distinctiveness. We do not cease to value the "is-ness" of each thing because we also apprehend the divine presence within it. On the contrary, by a strange paradox the more a thing becomes transparent, the more it is seen as uniquely itself. Blake was right to speak precisely of *double* vision; the "second sight" that God confers upon us does not obliterate but enhances our "first sight." Created nature is never more beautiful than when it acts as an envoy or icon of the uncreated Beauty.

Never should it be imagined that this ascent through the creation to the Creator is easily accomplished in a casual and automatic way. If we are to see God in all things and all things in God, this requires persistence, courage, imagination. In the words of the prophet Isaiah, "Truly You are a God Who hides Himself" (Isaiah 45:15). When we played hide-and-seek as children, did it not sometimes happen that we concealed ourselves in a marvelously secret spot, but then to our disappointment nobody bothered to come look for us? After waiting for a long time, we came out crestfallen from our hiding place, only to find that the others had all gone home. As the Hasidic master Rabbi Barukh of Mezbizh observes, we disappoint God in exactly the same way. "I hide," God says in sorrow, "but no one wants to seek Me."[19]

This, then, is God's word to us through His creation: Explore!

II

The Human Presence: Priest of the Creation

Thus far we have been considering what the Greek Fathers termed "physics" (*physike*), that is to say, natural contemplation or the contemplation of nature. Our human vocation, however, is not only to contemplate the creation but also to act within it. We do not merely gaze with double vision; there is work for us to do. Adam in Paradise did not simply wander through the groves and avenues, admiring the view like an eighteenth-century English gentleman; the Creator set him in the garden of Eden "to till it and to look after it" (Gen. 2:15). How, then, shall we define our active human role within this sacred and sacramental universe?

This brings us to a further question: What kind of an animal is man? What is it that, without separating us from the other animals, yet serves to distinguish us from them? I say "without separating," because several of the characteristics that we commonly choose to designate as uniquely human turn out to be present, at any rate in a less developed form, in many of the other animals. For example, many animals think, in the sense that, when confronted with an obstacle, they puzzle over it until they work out a solution. Many animals have a memory, recalling the past with fear or joy: a horse, separated from its human owners for weeks or years, on meeting them again will show alarm or happiness, depending on the treatment it has once received. Some animals form lifelong monogamous unions and show grief—or something very similar to it—when they lose their partner, and so on. Yet, despite all this, can we not identify a specifically *human* vocation set before us?

Five definitions of the human animal, each expressing part of the truth, will help us in our enquiry.

1. The human animal is an animal that *laughs* and *weeps*. Essential to our humanity is a sense of humor and also a sense of tragedy. If so, we may well weep over what we are doing to the other animals and to the earth that feeds both them and us!

2. The human animal, according to the Stoic philosopher Chrysippus (c. 207 B.C.), is a *logical* or *rational* animal, *logikon zoon*,[20] an animal endowed with self-awareness, an animal that speaks and thinks in an articulate and sequential manner. This is certainly a significant element in the truth about our humanness, but it is far from being the whole truth. I am more than my reasoning brain, very much more. Indeed, the narrow concentration upon rational self-awareness that has dominated the Western philosophical tradition from Descartes onward—*Cogito, ergo sum*, "I think, therefore I am"—is one of the factors that has directly contributed to the present ecological crisis.

3. The human animal, states Aristotle, (c. 322 B.C.), is a *political* animal, *politikon zoon*.[21] This comes closer to the heart of the matter, provided that the word "political" is understood—as it is by Aristotle himself—in its original and wider sense: the human animal is by nature communal, created for interpersonal relationship, and so is uniquely suited to live in a *polis*, in a city, in an ordered an organized society. Made as we are in the image of the Trinity—in the image of a God who is reciprocal love—we express our humanness through mutual coinherence, "dying in each other's life, living each other's death," to quote Charles Williams once more.[22] The basic principle of the city, as Williams reminds us, is "the doctrine that no man lives to himself or indeed *from* himself"; its life is "unexclusive," and its proper and typical features are "substitution" and "the exchange of pardon."[23] "What is the characteristic of any City? Exchange between citizens."[24]

How disastrously has the symbolism of the city altered in the past half-century! What in so much European literature is an image of protection, reassurance, and glory—"I saw the holy city, the new Jerusalem, coming down out of heaven from God . . . the city is pure gold, clear as glass" (Rev. 21:2, 18)—has now become an image of selfishness, danger, and corruption. One of the gravest aspects of the present degradation of the environment is precisely urban pollution in all its varying forms. Yet at the same time we are conscious as never before of our interdependence as "political" animals. The slogan "One world or none" is no less true for having become a commonplace.

4. To speak of the human animal as political is to emphasize the horizontal dimension: our relationship, that is to say, as humans with the other members of our own kind. But complementing the horizontal dimension there is also the vertical axis: our relationship with God. It is this fourth characteristic of human personhood to which St. Gregory of Nazianzus (d. c. 390) draws attention when he describes the human being not as *politikon zoon* but as *zoon theoumenon*, "an animal that is being deified."[25] Made in God's image, as humans we are capable of sharing in the divine life, of becoming "partakers of the divine nature" (2 Pet. 1:4). On the Orthodox Christian understanding of the human personhood, the line of demarcation between creature and Creator is never abolished, yet, as humans fashioned in the divine image, as living icons of the transcendent God, we have the possibility of becoming like God, of attaining *theosis*, "deification" or "divinization." In this context Christ quotes the worlds of Psalm 81 [82]:6: "Is it not written in your law, 'I said, you are gods'? . . . Those to whom the word of God came were called 'gods'; and the scripture cannot be annulled" (John 10:34–35).

As "an animal that is being deified," then, our human vocation is self-transcendence and unification. We are called by God's grace to reach out beyond space into infinity, beyond time into eternity. It is our task to mediate between the created world and the Uncreated. As icons of God, we have the capacity to unite earth and heaven and thus "to make of the earth something heavenly," in the words of the Hasidic teacher Rabbi Hanokh.[26]

This unifying role is exactly illustrated in the etymology of the words for the human person in Greek and Latin. The Greek word *anthropos* is connected with the verb *anarthrein*, meaning "to look up"; unlike most of the other animals, humans stand upright, with their eyes toward heaven and their gaze directed toward the stars. In Latin, on the other hand, the words *homo* and *humanus* are linked to the noun *humus*, "earth."[27] Such, then, is the human being: an animal that looks up to heaven, an animal endowed with a conscience, with a sense of the numinous, an animal capable of mystical union with the Divine, but at the same time an animal with its feet set firmly on the ground, an animal with a physical body, an animal that eats and drinks, that expresses interpersonal love through sexual union in "one flesh" (Gen. 2:24; Matt. 19:5).

Heavenly yet earthly, spiritual yet material, we human persons are each a microcosm, and, as microcosm, it is our high privilege to act as mediator. Our human task, as St. John Chrysostom (c. 407) expresses it, is to be *syndesmos* and *gephyra*, the "bond" and "bridge" of God's creation.[28] Uniting earth and heaven, making earth heavenly and heaven earthly, we reveal the spirit-bearing potentialities of all material things, and we disclose and render manifest the divine presence at the heart of all creation. Such was the task assigned to the First Adam in Paradise, and such—after the Fall of the First Adam—is the task eventually fulfilled by the Second Adam Christ, through His incarnation, transfiguration, crucifixion, and resurrection.

5. How precisely do we human animals exercise this unifying and mediatorial role? The answer: through thankfulness, doxology, Eucharist, offering. This brings us to a fifth characteristic of the human animal: it is a *Eucharistic animal*, an animal capable of gratitude, endowed with the power to bless God for the creation, an animal that can offer the world back to the Creator in thanksgiving.

Fr. Alexander Schmemann (1921–1983) illustrates this aspect of human personhood by referring to the opening part of the evening service of Vespers. In the Orthodox Christian understanding of time, as in that of Judaism, the new day begins not at midnight or at dawn but at sunset. "There was evening and there was morning, the first day" (Gen. 1:5): the evening comes before the morning. By the same token, the church year in Orthodox Christianity begins not in midwinter on January 1 nor in spring on March 25 but at the start of autumn on September 1; once more, there is a parallel with Judaism. Thus Vespers is not an epilogue or conclusion, but it is the first act of the prayer in the new day.

How, then, do we commence our daily cycle of prayer? Vespers starts with the reading or singing of Psalm 103 [104], which is a hymn of cosmic praise:

> Bless the Lord, O my soul. Blessed art Thou, O God.
> O Lord, my God, Thou art exceeding glorious:
> Thou art clothed with majesty and honor . . .
> O Lord how manifold are Thy works: in wisdom hast Thou made them all.
> The earth is full of Thy riches: so is the great and wide sea also . . .
> I will sing unto the Lord as long as I live:
> I will praise my God while I have my being.

In this way, writes Fr. Alexander, the daily vesperal service "begins at the beginning":

It begins at the *beginning*, and this means in the "rediscovery," in adoration and thanksgiving, of the world as God's creation. The Church takes us, as it were, to that first evening on which man, called by God to life, opened his eyes and saw what God in His love was giving to him, saw all the beauty, all the glory of the temple in which he was standing, and rendered thanks to God. And in this thanksgiving he *became himself*. . . . If the Church is *in Christ*, its initial act is always this act of thanksgiving, of returning the world to God.[29]

Here, then, is the fifth aspect of our human personhood. In thanksgiving we *become ourselves*. Without gratitude we are not human but subhuman or, rather, antihuman. Only in the attitude of offering and blessing do we attain authentic personhood.

Using this fivefold delineation of the human animal, we can now attempt to specify our responsibility as humans toward the world around us. Our human vocation, briefly expressed, is to be *priest* of the creation. As logical animals possessed of self-awareness and free choice—and at the same time as *Eucharistic* animals who are *being deified*—it is our supreme privilege, consciously and gratefully, to offer the created world back to God the Creator. This distinctively human function is precisely indicated just before the *Epiclesis* or Invocation of the Holy Spirit in the Divine Liturgy, when the celebrant elevates the gifts of bread and wine, saying; "Thine own from Thine own we offer to Thee, in all things and for all things."

"Priest of the creation" and "offerer": what do these two terms signify?

First, we say in the Liturgy, "Thine own from Thine own." What we offer to God is nothing else than what He Himself has given to us. Unless God had first conferred the world upon us as a free gift, we could make no offering at all. The offering is His rather than ours; without Him our hands would be empty. Indeed, in the Divine Liturgy it is Christ Himself who is the true Offerer, the unique High priest; we, the ordained ministers and the people present at the Eucharist, can only act as priest by virtue of our unity with Him. He alone is Celebrant in the true sense; we are no more than concelebrants with him. Indeed, not only is this true of the primary act of offering that is made in what Charles Williams called "the Operation of the Mass," but it applies to every act of offering throughout the whole of human life.

Second, in the Divine Liturgy we say not "I offer" but "we offer." As offerers, whether in the Eucharist or in other ways, we do not act alone but in union with our fellow humans. As *political* animals, our thanksgiving is social and corporate. Whenever we offer, we are acting as persons in relationship: in John Donne's words, "No man is an Island, entire of itself."

This corporate character of our humanness, as we have already emphasized, is more important today than ever before. Unless we can learn to share the world, we shall destroy the world and ourselves in it. "One world or none."

Third, when we offer, we are ourselves part of what we offer. As cosmic priests, we stand within nature, not above it. In Kathleen Raine's words:

> Seas, trees and voices cry,
> "Nature is your nature."

Fourth, we are offerers rather than rulers or even stewards. The language of ruling and also sometimes of stewardship can easily be misinterpreted to signify arbitrary control and exploitation, as if the creation were our exclusive property rather than a gift that we hold in trust for the Creator.[30] All too often we Christians have tragically misapplied God's words to the newly created Adam, "Fill the earth and subdue it; and have dominion . . . over every living thing" (Gen. 1:28). Let us remember that dominion does not signify domination. And let us remember also that this dominion is given to us specifically because we are made in the divine image. It is therefore a dominion that we exercise in obedience to Christ and in imitation of His own example. Since He said, "My power is made perfect in weakness" (2 Cor. 12:9), since He exercised His power by "emptying" Himself and accepting death on the Cross (Phil. 2:7-8), it follows that our dominion within the realm of nature is essentially kenotic, after the divine example, a dominion of humble love, compassion, and self-sacrifice. "Love the trees."

Christianity has much to learn here from the Taoist understanding of nature, with its ideal of harmony rather than hegemony, of balance and equilibrium rather than control and mastery. According to Taoism, perfect action is to act without acting, to cooperate with the norms and rhythms of nature rather than to impose our own will upon it. In the words of Chuang Tzu, as rendered by Thomas Merton, "In the age when life on earth was full . . . rulers were simply the highest branches on the tree, and the people were like deer in the woods."[31]

Of course, the same ideal of balance and harmony is also to be found in the Christian tradition. A friend of mine has the ability—which some might think harmless enough and even somewhat entertaining—of imitating birdcalls in such a way that the birds themselves reply. Once he was doing this while walking through the woods of Mount Athos in the company of a monk. After a time the monk said, "Please stop doing that." "All right, I'll stop," my friend answered, "but what's wrong?" The monk replied, "You are disturbing the natural order."

Yet even though we humans are called to cooperate with nature rather than to control it, at the same time God has given us the ability to alter and refashion the world. This brings us to a fifth point. As rational or "logical" animals endowed with self-awareness, we humans do not offer the world back to God simply in the form in which we received it, but through the work of our hands we transform that which we offer. At the Eucharist, we offer to God the fruits of the earth not in their initial state but reshaped through our human skills; we bring to the altar not grains of wheat but bread, not bunches of grapes but wine. And so it is throughout all human life.

It is true that, here as elsewhere, there is no absolute line of division between us humans and the other animals. Beavers build dams, bees construct honeycombs. But on the whole the other animals simply live in the world, glorifying God through their instinctive actions, whereas we humans consciously reshape our environment, glorifying God through art and technology. Once on a journey through France, attracted by the picture of a squirrel on the front of a bottle, I bought a liqueur made from nuts. This led me to reflect: squirrels collect nuts, they bury them underground, they forget where they have put them, they quarrel (just as if they were humans) about the ownership of their nutty stores—but one thing they cannot do is make a liqueur out of nuts. That is a distinctively human activity. (In fact, the liqueur was somewhat disagreeable; I would have far preferred to eat the original nuts.)

As humans, then, we modify and refashion the creation. The world is not only a gift but a task. In the words of the Romanian theologian Dumitru Staniloae (1903–1993), "Man puts the seal of his understanding and of his intelligent work onto creation, thereby humanizing it and giving it humanized back to God. He actualizes the world's potentialities."[32] Formed in the image of God the Creator, we are in J. R. R. Tolkien's phrase "sub-creators," appointed not only to preserve but to transfigure.

Through our power of self-awareness and through this ability to alter and restructure the world, we humans are able to give creation a tongue, rendering it eloquent in praise of God. As the Dalai Lama said at the interfaith meeting in Assisi, "The universe has no voice, and the universe needs to speak. We are the voice of the universe." It is through us humans that the heavens declare the glory of God (cf. Ps. 18 [19]:1), through us that the moon and the stars, the rocks, trees, flowers, and animals, give Him praise and worship.[33] In his book *Byzantine Aesthetics*, Fr. Gervase Matthew develops this point with particular reference to liturgical worship and iconography, but what he says can be applied more widely to all forms of craftsmanship and agriculture:

Because Man is body he shares in the material world around him, which passes within him through his sense perceptions. Because Man is Mind he belongs to the world of higher reality and pure spirit. Because he is both, he is in Cyril of Alexandria's phrase "God's crowned image"; he can mould and manipulate the material and render it articulate. The sound in a Byzantine hymn, the gestures in a liturgy, the bricks in a church, the cubes in a mosaic are matter made articulate in the Divine praise.[34]

Cosmic Metanoia

Because the human person is in this way both microcosm and mediator, unifying the creation and offering it back to God in thanksgiving—because, more particularly, we humans have the ability consciously and by deliberate choice to modify and refashion the world—there is imposed upon us a grace and daunting responsibility. The fact that we are made in the divine image and so endowed with freedom—creators after the image of God the Creator—carries with it a terrible risk. We can use our creative power both for good and for evil. We can illumine and transfigure, but equally we can pollute and destroy. The effects of the misuse of our human creativity are too obvious to need emphasizing, for the tragic evidence of what we choose to call the "ecological crisis" is all around us.

Yet in fact the crisis is not first and foremost an ecological crisis. The fundamental difficulty lies not outside but inside ourselves, not in the ecosystem but in the human heart. The present-day crisis, that is to say, is primarily a crisis not concerning the environment but concerning the way we ourselves think. What is the reason why we humans are treating our planet in an inhuman, intolerable way? It is because we look at things in an inhuman and alienated fashion. And we look at things in this manner because that is basically how we look at ourselves. As Philip Sherrard, among others, has rightly insisted,[35] this means that we have to change our *world-image*, and this in turn means that we have to change our *self-image*. Until we do that, our conservation projects, however well intentioned, will prove ultimately ineffective, for we shall be dealing only with the symptoms and not with the cause.

The basic problem, therefore, in the present "ecological crisis" is not technological miscalculation but human sin. A solution cannot come simply through the development of greater technical skills. It will come solely through repentance, through cosmic *metanoia*—understanding the world in its literal sense, which is "change of mind." We need a new way of thinking, a complete reversal of perspective, a radical alteration in our self-image. Lectures and international conferences may indeed play a useful part in awakening our conscience, but what is required on a far more profound level is a baptism of tears.

In this *metanoia*, this revolutionary "change of mind," three things in particular are necessary. I shall give them their Greek names, as found in that basic work of Orthodox spirituality, *The Philokalia*.

> 1. As our starting point, we need *nepsis*. This is a basic concept in Orthodox spirituality and has a wide range of related meanings. It signifies sobriety, vigilance, wakefulness, alertness, inner clarity. The neptic person is recollected, mindful, attentive, truly present in the place where he or she is, gathered into the "here" and "now," practicing the sacrament of the immediate moment. To be neptic is to be like Moses before the burning bush; it is to remove our sandals and to recognize that the place where we are standing is holy ground.
>
> 2. Next we need *sophrosyne*, "chastity," understood not merely in a sexual sense (although this is certainly included) but in its deeper meaning of wholeness and integrity. On this more profound level, chastity is part of married life no less than of monasticism. Chastity signifies the overcoming of self-indulgence and permissiveness, the metamorphosis of lust into love, the purging away of a false eroticism so that a God-given *eros* may take its place. There can be no transformation of the cosmos without *eros*, and no true *eros* without chastity.
>
> 3. We also need *enkrateia*, "self-restraint," voluntary self-limitation in our consumption of food and natural resources. This means in the first instance that we each strive to make a distinction between what I *want* and what I *need*. Only through self-denial, through fasting, through the willingness to forgo and to say "no" will we rediscover our true place in the universe. Greed and avarice render the world opaque, turning all things to dust and ashes; generosity and unselfishness render the world transparent, turning all things into a sacrament of communion with one another and with God.

Here precisely we touch upon a crucial aspect of our cosmic *metanoia*. Let us not for one moment imagine that the ecological crisis can be resolved simply through sentimental expressions of regret. What is asked from us is costly self-discipline, sacrificial forbearance, an inner martyrdom—in a word, Cross-bearing. And this brings me to a third tree vision to be set beside the two with which I began. It is from a sermon attributed to St. John Chrysostom and appointed to be used during Holy Week on Great or Good

Friday. From the same series comes the Paschal homily read in the Orthodox Church at the Easter midnight service, beginning with the words, "If any is devout and a lover of God . . ."[36] The Great Friday homily, although less familiar, is no less powerful:

> This Tree is my eternal salvation. It is my nourishment and my banquet. Amidst its roots I cast my own roots deep; beneath its boughs I grow and expand; as it sighs around me in the breeze I am nourished with delight. Flying from the burning heat, I have pitched my tent in its shadow, and have found a resting-place of dewy freshness. I flower with its flowers; its fruits bring perfect joy. . . . This tree is sweet food for my hunger, a spring of water for my thirst; it is clothing for my nakedness; its leaves are the breath of life . . . this is my strait path, my narrow way; this is Jacob's ladder, on which the angels pass up and down, while the Lord in very truth stands at its head. This Tree, vast as heaven itself, rises from earth to the skies, a plan immortal, set firm in the midst between heaven and earth, base of everything that exists, foundation of the universe, support of the whole inhabited world, binding-force of all creation, holding in oneness the complexity of human nature. . . . With its foot resting firmly on the earth, it towers to the topmost skies, and spans with all-embracing arms in boundless gulf of space between.

Gradually, as the sermon progresses, we begin to realize that this Cosmic Tree is nothing else than the Tree of the Cross on which Jesus Christ was lifted up and crucified:

> He was wholly in all things and everywhere, filling everything with Himself, stripped naked for battle against the powers of the air. . . . When the great Jesus breathed forth His divine spirit, saying, "Father, into Thy hands I commend my spirit" (Luke 23:46), all things shuddered and were shaken in the earthquake, reeling from fear; but His divine spirit ascended, giving life and animation and strength to all. Creation stood firm once more, as this divine extension and crucifixion unfolded and spread everywhere, penetrating all things, through all and in all. O Thou who art alone among the alone, Paradise Thy soul, and the earth Thy blood. For the Indivisible has been divided, so that all things might be saved.[37]

The renewal of the planet Earth and the ecological salvation of the human race can come about in one way and in one way only: through the Tree of the Cross. Only through Cross-bearing, through the denial of our selfishness, through what the Divine Liturgy of St. Basil calls "life-creating death" shall we be able to rediscover the wonder and beauty of the world. What is needed, to quote the late Ecumenical Patriarch Dimitrios, is a "Eucharistic and ascetic spirit,"[38] a spirit of thankful and self-denying love. "Love the trees": love is the only true answer to our ecological crisis, for we cannot save what we do not love. But there is no genuine love without costly self-sacrifice.

No More Time

During September 1995, I was on the island of Patmos. I was taking part in the festivities marking the nineteen-hundredth anniversary (according to the traditional dating) of the coming of St. John to Patmos, where he is believed to have written the last book of the Bible, the Apocalypse or Revelation. One of the events connected with the celebrations was an international conference on "Revelation and the Environment." Throughout the different sessions that I attended, continually there rang in my ears the warning of the angel of the Apocalypse, "There will be no more time" (Rev. 10:6), no more postponement or delay. In all our ecological work, never for one instant let us lose our sense of urgency. In many respects we are already too late: irreversible damage has been done in the last thirty years. In very truth, there is no more time.

There is a story told of three young devils who were completing their training in hell. Immediately before their dispatch to earth, they appeared before the chief devil for their concluding examination. Turning to the first of the three, he asked: "What will you tell them when you go up to earth?" "I shall tell them that there is no God," the first devil replied. "That's not much use," said the examining devil, "they've been told that many times before. The trouble is that too many of them know Him personally." He turned to the second devil. "And what will you tell them?" he enquired. "I shall say that there is no hell," the second responded. "Ah," said the old devil, "that's more ingenious. But unfortunately it won't work. Too many of them are living in hell already." Finally he asked the third, "What will you say?" And the third answered, "I shall tell them that there is no hurry." "Excellent!" exclaimed the chief demon. "Go up immediately and set to work."

That is surely an anecdote with an ecological application.

CREATION AS COMMUNION IN CONTEMPORARY ORTHODOX THEOLOGY

Aristotle Papanikolaou

This paper will critically compare the creation theologies of Sergius Bulgakov, Vladimir Lossky, and John Zizioulas. I offer this critical comparison of the three most influential trajectories in contemporary Orthodox theology to discern whether, in fact, contemporary Orthodox theology has anything to offer to the wider, global discussion of Orthodoxy's response to questions and concerns about the environment.

In previous work,[1] I have argued that, their differences notwithstanding, contemporary Orthodox theologians ground their theology in one fundamental principle: the realism of divine-human communion. The realism of divine-human communion affirms that God exists so as to be free, as love, to create and unite Godself with what is other than God—creation. From the point of view of creation, the realism of divine-human communion means that creation exists so as to be in communion with God. Bulgakov's, Lossky's, and Zizioulas's agreement on this fundamental axiom does not necessarily lead to similar conclusions on their theologies of the Trinity, especially on the relation of apophaticism and the importance of the concept of the divine energies to the doctrine of the Trinity. In similar fashion, I will demonstrate that the principle of the realism of divine-human communion shapes the theologies of creation for these theologians, but this shared starting point does not prevent the emergence of fundamental differences in their creation theologies.

Sergius Bulgakov

The key to understanding Bulgakov's theology of creation is his trinitarian theology, and the key to understanding his trinitarian theology is to decipher, literally, what he means by Sophia, which, in my estimation, has been the chief stumbling block to appreciating Bulgakov's work fully. The question that must be posed to Bulgakov is the following: why is the concept of Sophia necessary for theology?

Sophia, for Bulgakov, is entailed in the logic of the patristic affirmation that the Father, Son, and Holy Spirit are *homoousios*. In both the Latin and Greek forms of trinitarian theology, the *homoousios* was interpreted in terms of the attributes common to the Father, Son, and Holy Spirit and as what constituted the unity of the Godhead. While Bulgakov does not necessarily dispute these understandings of the *homoousios*, they do not fully account for the God-world relation. It is a particular understanding of the God-world relation in terms of communion that leads Bulgakov to claim that a further theological unpacking of the *homoousios* is needed. He states that "the dogma of consubstantiality, which safeguards the unity of the Holy Trinity, thus remains a sealed book so far as we are concerned—for in a religious sense it has been neither assimilated nor unfolded."[2] For Bulgakov, the unfolding of the *homoousios* leads logically to Sophia.

The key to understanding the link between *homoousios* and Sophia in Bulgakov lies in his notion of the self-revelation of God. The relation between the Father and the Son is the self-revelation of the Father in the Son. This self-revelation, however, is only complete in the Holy Spirit, who unites the Father and the Son. Bulgakov identifies the Father as "the transcendent principle within the Holy Trinity . . . the divine subject, the subject which manifests itself in the predicate . . . intelligence contemplating itself, the source of being and love, that love which cannot but diffuse itself,"[3] "Divine Depth and Mystery, the Divine Subject of self-revelation."[4] It seems that Bulgakov is saying that if one were to bracket the self-revelation of God in the Son and in the Spirit, the Father is Absolute Spirit, which cannot even be called God, since the latter is a relative term. This Absolute Spirit is an unknowable, impenetrable mystery. It is in the self-revelation of the Father in the Son that the Father transcends this transcendence, or reveals his transcendence as immanence, and is immanent as revealed.

The Son, thus, is the Image of the Father, the Word of the Father in which is contained all words; the "objective self-revelation"[5] of the Father, the Truth of the Father, and, as such, the divine content. As Bulgakov puts it, "the Son surrenders Himself as the *Word of all and about All* to the Divine world; He serves the self-revealing Divinity, and He posits Himself as the *content* of this self-revelation."[6] Bracketing now the person of the Holy Spirit, the Father knows the Son as the Image of the Father, and the Son knows the Father as that of which he is the perfect image. The relationship is one of mutual mirroring, but this mirroring is not yet the accomplished self-revelation of God. Such a revelation is not a self-revelation unless it is actualized, and this actualization is accomplished in the person of the Holy Spirit, who is the love that unites Father and the Son: the Father loves all that is revealed in the Son, and the Son returns this love kenotically as the hypostatic image of the Father. As Bulgakov explains, "this dyadic relation of the Father and the Son can in no wise exhaust the self-definition of the Absolute Spirit, however, for it is characterized not only by self-revelation as self-consciousness, as being in truth, but also by self-revelation as self-life, as being in beauty, as the living out of its proper content."[7]

According to Bulgakov, the self-revelation of the Father is not complete until the content that is revealed in the Son is actualized as life by the Holy Spirit. In this sense, the Holy Spirit, for Bulgakov, is the "spirit of truth" and

> relates not to the content, but to the special form and to the divine hypostases in which this content is manifested.... In himself he constitutes this transparency, for he is Love. And as such the Holy Spirit represents the principle of the quickening spiritual reality within the Holy Trinity, the reality and the life of the Word of Truth. The reality of Truth is Beauty ... the Word becomes adorned by beauty, because the Holy Spirit abides in him. The Holy Spirit who abides in the Son, manifests him to the Father in beauty.... In the divine self-revelation ... the Holy Spirit represents the principle of reality. He transforms the world of ideas into a living and real essence.[8]

Insofar as the Holy Spirit is the form of the content revealed in the Son, the Holy Spirit is identified with the glory of God. The Trinity is thus the self-revelation of God to Godself, specifically the self-revelation of the Father mediated through Godself, the revealing hypostases of the Son and the Holy Spirit, the Word and Glory of God, respectively.

Where does Sophia fit into all this? In the end, Sophia is identified with *ousia* in Bulgakov's system. This may sound ordinary, except that Sophia is not simply an attribute possessed by all the persons of the Trinity. Sophia is, quite simply, the *ousia* of God hypostatized in the trihypostatic self-revelation of God, but, as such, it is no longer simply *ousia*. Bracketing the self-revelation of the Father in the Son and the Spirit, Bulgakov argues that the Father remains "in himself undisclosed"; as undisclosed, he adds that

> the divine Sophia abides in the Father primarily as Ousia, the undisclosed depth of his nature ... his Ousia abides within him, unrevealed, in the capacity of Sophia. This relationship may be expressed by

the following formula: Sophia so far as the *hypostasis* of the Father is concerned, connotes predominantly Ousia—prior to its own revelation as Sophia.[9]

Only in the self-revelation of God in the Son and the Holy Spirit is all that God *is* revealed; it is only in this self-revelation that all that God is *is*; that is, there is an identification in Bulgakov between the self-revelation of God and the fullness of God's existence. In this fullness of God's existence, *ousia* is no longer an apophatic concept indicative of impenetrable mystery and transcendence of the Absolute; *ousia* is Sophia. Sophia, then, for Bulgakov is God's being as the self-revelation of the Father in the Son and the Holy Spirit. As Bulgakov himself states, "Sophia is Ousia as revealed,"[10] or "Sophia is the revelation of the Son and the Holy Spirit, without separation and without confusion,"[11] or "Divine Sophia is God's *exhaustive* self-revelation, the fullness of divinity, and therefore has absolute content."[12]

At this point, however, it is still not quite clear why the concept of Sophia is necessary for trinitarian theology and, thus, what Bulgakov really means to signify with Sophia. Although Sophia is identified with the *ousia* of God, Bulgakov seems to be arguing that, as hypostatized in the trinitarian relations, *ousia* is no longer what simply signifies the common attributes or what accounts for the unity of God as Trinity. As hypostatized, it is the very being of God as trinitarian self-revelation. As the very being of God it must necessarily, Bulgakov argues, refer to God's relation to the world and not simply to the intratrinitarian relations. Why is this the case? Because, for Bulgakov, the self-revelation of God in the Logos and the Holy Spirit is the revelation of all that God is, and included in all that God *is* is God's relation to creation and humanity. Let me be clear: Bulgakov is not arguing for the eternity of a creation that is restricted by time and space. If, however, all theology is grounded in the premise that God has revealed Godself as Creator and Redeemer, it is impossible for Bulgakov to conceive the thinking of God that does not include God existing as eternally relating to creation in some way. Thus, God's self-revelation as the revelation of all that God *is* is also God's being as love and, thus, as freedom to create and redeem what is not God, and, thus, as eternally relating to creation. For those who would argue that Bulgakov is making creation constitutive of the being of God, Bulgakov explicitly denies this charge. To think the being of God in such a way that brackets creation would be to try to determine God's relation to the world in terms of deliberation and volition, which is incoherent for Bulgakov, especially if God's being is the all in all. For Bulgakov, it is impossible to conceive of God's being as not already existing as an eternal relation to creation, even if that means that God is not compelled to realize this creation in time and space.

Sophia, then, refers to the being of God as existing as this eternal relation to creation; as the self-revelation of all that God is, which is the God who is from eternity freedom and love toward creation; as the *ousia* hypostatized, which is "more" than simply the unity of God or common attributes but the very being of God and, as such, as God's eternal relation to creation. It is for this reason that Bulgakov argues that

> the *Divine Sophia* is nothing other than *God's nature*, His ousia, not only in the sense of power and depth, but also in the sense of self-revealing content, in the sense of All-unity. . . . Sophia is the Pleroma, the Divine world, existent in God and for God, eternal and uncreated, in which God lives in the Holy Trinity. And in itself this Divine world contains all that the Holy Trinity reveals about itself and in itself; it is the Image of God in God Himself. . . . It is the real and fully realized divine Idea, the idea of all ideas, actualized as Beauty in ideal images of beauty.

Bulgakov then links Sophia with that famous Russian theological term *sobornost*: Sophia is the "cosmic *sobornost* of concrete all-unity in divine love."[13]

As the all-unity, Sophia is also identified with another famous Russian theological term, *bogochelovechestvo*, which is probably untranslatable but has been rendered as God-manhood, the humanity of God, or divine-humanity. The term divine-humanity signifies in a more concrete way that God's being as trinitarian is always already an eternal communion with humanity, and this always already eternal communion with humanity becomes the foundation for God's creation of the *anthropos* as the image of God and of the incarnation of the Logos in Jesus. Creation in time and space is essentially a repetition of the being of God, which includes the self-revelation of the Father in the Son through the Holy Spirit. Bulgakov distinguishes between the divine Sophia and the creaturely Sophia, with the divine Sophia being the foundation for the becoming of the world in time and space. As the soul of the world in time and space, it is the creaturely Sophia, the power of the world in its becoming toward union with the divine Sophia, which is divinization for Bulgakov—the unity of the divine and creaturely Sophia. Divine-humanity is an especially important concept in this scheme for Bulgakov, since it is in and through humanity that the world is divinizable. Even though Sophia is about God's relation to the world, it is identified with divine-humanity for Bulgakov because it is in and through humanity that the world is divinizable. As Bulgakov explains, the central point from which sophiology proceeds is that of the relation between *God* and *the world*, or, what is practically the same thing between *God* and *humanity*. In other words we are faced with the question of the meaning and significance of Divine-humanity—not only insofar as it concerns the God-human, the incarnate Logos, but precisely insofar as it applies to the theandric union between God and the whole of the creaturely world, through humanity and in humanity. Within Christianity itself there is a neverending struggle between the two extreme positions of dualism and monism, in a constant search for truth, which can only be found in the synthesis of Divine-humanity. . . . The dogma of Divine-humanity is precisely the main theme of sophiology, which in fact represents nothing but its full dogmatic elucidation.[14]

In essence, what Bulgakov is saying is that if the world, the not-God, is capable of communion with God, then the world is already, in some way, in God, which means that the world is also, in some way, divine. As Bulgakov states, "this is not pantheism, but panentheism," and, in his mind, this is the only way to account for a Christian panentheism.

Vladimir Lossky

For Lossky, all theology begins with the Incarnation, the realization of divine-human communion in Christ. The Incarnation itself, as the instantiation of divine-human communion, demands that theology be apophatic. Apophaticism for Lossky is not simply defining God in terms of what God is not. The heart of apophaticism is the affirmation of the seemingly contradictory notion of God as simultaneously transcendent and immanent to creation. Apophaticism, in one sense, affirms the transcendence of God—God is Other than creation and exceeds all attempts to express God in language, symbols, or reason. In another sense, however, God's transcendence is such that God is free, a freedom that is realized as love, to unite what is Other than God with Godself. God's transcendence is not simply the affirmation of a cold, distant God but a God who makes Godself available for communion. A theology of creation must be consistent with these fundamental affirmations about God as transcendent and immanent to creation, and if it is to do so, such a theology must be antinomic; that is, it must exceed any simple binary form of human logic and necessarily express two contradictory but equally true affirmations. Apophaticism, then, for Lossky, is theology understood as a lived experience of union with God made possible by the Incarnation. The very expression of this lived union must be antinomic, that is, can only be expressed in statements that are seemingly contradictory but true. Antinomic expressions disrupt any complacent knowledge of God that grounds itself in human reason, and they keep the theologian, seeking knowledge of God, moving in the right direction through the performance of ascetical practices, which are really the only means for a true knowledge of God as personal union.

The principle of the realism of divine-human communion is what grounds two central concepts for Lossky's theology of creation: creation *ex nihilo* and the essence/energies distinction. Put another way, for Lossky the realism of divine-human communion necessarily leads to these concepts as adequate expressions of a theology of creation. Creation *ex nihilo*, for Lossky, expresses the fact that creation is not necessary and utterly dependent on the freedom and will of God. Creation *ex nihilo*, however, is also required for affirming a created Other that is capable of a non-necessary communion with God. A non-necessary communion with God is one realized in freedom and love, but such a communion is not possible if creation is eternally present with the divine in either a material or ideal form. Lossky's concern with an eternal world is not so much about power but about love; an eternal world or a necessary creation limits, most of all, God's freedom to love, to risk Godself in creation by creating what refuses God's love.

A logical consequence of affirming creation *ex nihilo* is the distinction between the essence and will of God. The essence of God is eternal, while creation itself is a product of God's will by which God relates to creation both in terms of creating and redeeming. The essence/will distinction is a further affirmation that creation itself is not God, is Other than God, is not necessary, and, hence, a result of God's freedom. The essence/will distinction still does not capture all that can be said about a creation that is a result of God's *loving* will. God wills out of love to create what is Other than God, and this created Other exists by virtue of its relation to this loving will of God. Put another way, God creates the created Other in communion and for communion with God. This always already existing participation as communion with God in and through creation is expressed most adequately in the essence/energies distinction, which, for Lossky, finds its most developed and coherent formulation in Dionysius the Areopagite. The essence of God signifies what is Other to creation, utterly transcendent and unknowable; the energies signify the activity of God in and through which the created Other realizes a real communion with the divine without being God, that is, the divine essence.

It is through the essence/energies distinction that Lossky interprets the divine *logoi* or the divine ideas, especially in the work of Dionysius and Maximus the Confessor. The logical consequence of a non-necessary creation based on God's free, loving will is the identification of the "divine ideas" with the energies rather than the essence of God. If the essence/will distinction within God is meant to express the transcendence of God vis-à-vis creation, between the necessary and non-necessary, then the idea of creation must also be a product of God's will. God is bound by no necessity to create, not even the idea to create. The identification of the divine ideas with the will of God is meant to preserve God's freedom to create. Lossky thus rejects any identification of the divine ideas with the divine essence, one that he sees in different ways in both neoscholasticism and Bulgakov's sophiology. To equate the divine ideas with the inner life of God either disparages the created world and deprives it "of its original character as the unconditioned work of the creative Wisdom," or, creation itself is introduced into the inner life of God, thus becoming determinative of God's very being.[15] In the first case, creation loses its uniqueness, its otherness insofar as being derivative of God's essence; in the second place, God's otherness is lost as creation forms part of the very being of God. In both cases, a communion of love and freedom is precluded.

Identified with the divine energies rather than with the divine essence, the divine ideas are not simply static replicas of created realities. Rather than serving as models for replication, the divine ideas intend creation toward a particular end. "The divine ideas are inseparable from the creative intention."[16] This intention of God for creation is communion in God's love. Thus "they no longer constitute a 'hinterworld,' but the very depth of the creature, its method of participation in divine energy, *its vocation to the highest love.*"[17] Their purpose is to "determine the different modes according to which created beings participate in the creative energies."[18] Created existence is an image of the divine, but it is an image that participates in the divine. The ideas determine the mode of participation, that is, the degree and extent of participation in the uncreated energies. The different modes of participation are what accounts for the diversity of created existence. As image, a created thing reflects the uncreated light of the energies the more it corresponds to its divine idea, that is, the more it participates in the uncreated energies according to the mode intended by the divine ideas. This understanding of the divine ideas shapes Lossky's understanding of analogy, which he defines as the particular capacity of a created being to participate in God.

Of all the divine names, the one that most encapsulates God's relation to creation is, not surprisingly, love. Love signifies the ekstatic character of

God's relation to creation, insofar as God goes outside of Godself to effect the created Other; love also signifies a God-world relation based on freedom, which makes possible a rejection of God's love but is also the condition for the possibility of a real divine-human communion. Love in the created order is more than an intention to create on God's part; it is *the* divine energy that creates and stirs creation toward its final end, which is love. In a poignant summary written early in his career, Lossky says:

> The two ways in theology correspond to the way of divine love by which God proceeds outside of himself, creating all in order to be manifest in all, and returning all created beings to the divine union by the love that God inspires in them. In this "eternal circle" of divine Love, God appears as Love, proceeding outside of his essence and creating all things by his energies, and as Beloved, remaining united in himself in his procession, in whom no thing can participate even though he is present in all things [*imparticipable même en participations*]. As Love, God gives proportionally his infinity to created beings, in defining their "analogies" (ideas); as Beloved, he produces in created beings the love that is the analogy of the will of beings, making them desire union in the divine energies, according to the pre-established mode for each being.[19]

In God's relation to the created order one discerns in Lossky's thought a type of metaphysics of love. Love is the beginning, middle, and end of creation. The primacy of this name flows naturally from the uncreated/created distinction; only the love of God can create an "other" outside Godself, which is created being. It is also the soteriological principle of union that constitutes love as the metaphysical principle of creation.[20] Knowledge cannot bridge the gap between the created and the uncreated. Mind, in that it is created, cannot transcend the created. Union requires a leap beyond the created toward the uncreated. In that God's love is ecstatic in going forth from Godself to create an other, this very ecstatic love is at work in creation, allowing creation to transcend its own limits, even those of mind, in order to unite with the uncreated. This ecstatic love of God is the very life source of all creation and the gift that grants to creation the capacity for its own ecstatic love toward God.[21]

The revelation of Christ reveals that God is both transcendent and immanent to the world. God is *hyper*essence, nonbeing, ontologically other than creation, but immanent through God's uncreated energies. God is most present in creation through God's love, which is the beginning, middle, and end of created existence. Thus, in relation to creation the Incarnation reveals a God who is nonbeing, essence and energies, essence and will. It reveals more, however, in declaring God to be Trinity.[22]

John Zizioulas

Zizioulas's starting point is also the realism of divine-human communion, but the revelation of this communion is not so much the fact of the Incarnation as much as the early Christian experience of the Eucharist, even if the experience of the divine in the Eucharist is itself grounded in the life of Christ.

Like Lossky, Zizioulas affirms that the principle of the realism of divine-human communion demands the affirmation that God created *ex nihilo*. This assertion, for Zizioulas, constitutes the first leavening of Greek cosmology by the Fathers of the Church en route to an articulation of a trinitarian theology of personhood. Also like Lossky, the affirmation of creation *ex nihilo* is less about asserting God's transcendence or absolute freedom and more about the conditions necessary for a real communion with the divine. For Zizioulas, communion implies difference; communion is the overcoming of division for the sake of difference. For there to be a communion between the uncreated and the created based on freedom and love, then the created must be "Other" to the Uncreated, with its own integrity. Creation *ex nihilo* is the only way in which creation itself can exist in such a way so as to be capable for communion with the noncreated, with what is "Other" to creation, that is, God. This is the way to make sense of the following remark by Zizioulas:

> Now it is all too easy to admit *on a doctrinal level* that for Christians things are different because the world was created *ex nihilo*. But I venture to suggest that unless we admit *on a philosophical level* that personhood is not secondary to being, that the mode of existence of being is not secondary to its "substance" but *itself primary* and constitutive of it, it is impossible to make sense of the doctrine of creation *ex nihilo*.[23]

For Zizioulas, divine-human communion is a realization of personhood, and the precondition for personhood is creation *ex nihilo*.

There is a negative consequence, however, to creation *ex nihilo*, one that is absent in both Bulgakov and Lossky and that explains what Zizioulas means by admitting "on a philosophical level that personhood is not secondary to being." Creation as created *ex nihilo* is inherently marked by finitude, which means for Zizioulas that it is inherently marked by death. In itself, creation is surrounded by nothing and tends toward annihilation of itself, which is death. There are glimmers of striving to transcend these limitations in an effort to realize a personal, irreplaceable, eternal uniqueness, which is how Zizioulas defines personhood, but in the end, all these attempts are ultimately tragic insofar as death is inherent to finite existence. As Zizioulas states: "If we take the world as a 'whole,' as an entity in itself, which we *can* do if we regard it, as we do, as *finite* and as *other* than God.... All this means that creation *taken in itself*... constitutes an entity surrounded and conditioned by *nothing*: It came from nothing and will return to nothing."[24] The idea of creation in itself "surrounded and conditioned by nothing" plays a very central role in Zizioulas's theological system. In terms of his trinitarian theology, one cannot fully understand his controversial claims about the monarchy of the Father without going back to the concept of creation *ex nihilo*. If creation itself is surrounded by nothing, then its longing for freedom from the limitations of its own nature can only be secured through a communion with what is not created, that is, the divine. But if freedom is defined for created being as a freedom from the limitations and necessity of nature, by what Zizioulas calls the "given," and if this freedom is realized through a communion with the divine, then God's very existence must also be such so as not to be bound by necessity. The monarchy of the Father, for Zizioulas, is meant to express the theological claim that God is not bound by the necessity of essence but freely constitutes the divine being as trinitarian. This form of freedom within the divine life is necessary for created being if it is to have any hope to free itself from the necessity of death inherent in created existence. The basic axiom for Zizioulas is that God cannot give what God does not have, and if God is bound by the necessities of God's essence, if God is to be strictly identified with God's essence, then so must created existence: both are bound by the "given." So, philosophically, the priority of a relational ontology is indicated by the longing for freedom from the *nothing* that surrounds created existence that is realized in communion with what is other than created existence; theologically, this human longing for communion with the divine, a communion that overcomes the division between the created and the uncreated for the sake of difference, that is, personal uniqueness, is only possible if God exists in such a way so as to be free to be in communion with what is not God; in other words, God must exist as a trinity of persons whose communion is grounded in the monarchy of the Father.

For Zizioulas, this longing for personal uniqueness through communion is accomplished in the *hypostasis* of Christ. Being persons is an event of union in the *hypostasis* of Christ. To exist in the *hypostasis* of Christ is to share in the eternal relation that the Son has with the Father. It is to be constituted as a unique, irreplaceable being through a relation of love and freedom that exists in the Father-Son relation; it is a freedom from the annihilation that surrounds created existence.

This personal uniqueness is not limited to human beings but is possible for all created things, though human beings function as the mediators of this personal uniqueness to all created things. Human beings, according to Zizioulas, have the capacity to function as priests of creation, whereby they bring all of creation into relation to God in the person of Jesus Christ and in so doing render all created things as unique and irreplaceable.

Toward a Trinitarian Theology of Creation

One of the most interesting points of comparison between Bulgakov, Lossky, and Zizioulas is their understanding of the principle of *creation ex nihilo*. Lossky and Zizioulas share the claim that the Christian understanding of creation *ex nihilo* is not strictly about securing God's transcendence or absolute freedom; it is also the necessary precondition for a communion of love and freedom between the uncreated and the created. This communion is not made available simply to human beings but to all created realities as mediated through human beings. Communion, for both theologians, consists of relations based on difference, but it is a difference that does not degenerate into division but that constitutes that difference as particularity, uniqueness, and irreducibility, that is, as "Other," in and through freedom realized as love. Bulgakov does not deny *creation ex nihilo* but clearly understands it in a way different from Lossky and Zizioulas. Although he is often misunderstood as positing a Platonic form of eternal creation, such is not the case. Bulgakov is arguing that if the Trinity-as-Sophia is the self-revelation of God to Godself, then it is impossible from our standpoint to think how that self-revelation does not entail all that God is in relation to creation. This "all that God is in relation to creation" is eternal; thus, there is an eternal aspect to creation. There is something else at stake in this discussion for Bulgakov: if theology does not admit this relation of creation to God's trinitarian being, then there is no way, according to Bulgakov, to account for how the not-God can be in communion with God. Creation itself must contain a divine principle, Sophia, if it is to have any hope of union with the uncreated. On this point, Zizioulas and Bulgakov appear to be on opposite sides of the fence, with Zizioulas affirming an understanding of creation surrounded by nothingness and Bulgakov emphasizing the divine principle in creation. For Bulgakov, the mediating principle between God and creation is Sophia; for Zizioulas, it is the *hypostasis* of the Logos. Lossky stands somewhere in between in identifying this mediating principle with the uncreated divine energies, which are always present throughout creation and which realize the divine ideas, the latter of which, however, are created and not eternal.

These theologians also agree that created realities are personalized in communion with the divine. They do not, however, talk about that communion in the same way, and it is in the way they talk about communion that we can discern the more substantial differences between their theologies, differences that have implications for an Orthodox theology of creation. For Lossky, each created reality participates in the divine according to the degree and mode determined by the divine ideas, which are identified with the divine energies. Lossky would add that the degree and mode of the tree's participation in the divine ultimately depends on how humans relate to the divine. Although for Bulgakov, the point of contact between the divine and the created is Sophia, he shares with Lossky the affirmation that creation is already, in some way, participating in God. The realization of the creaturely Sophia ultimately depends on how humans relate to the divine. In similar fashion, humans function for Zizioulas as priests of creation, personalizing all of creation in offering it to God for communion. Curiously absent from Zizioulas is the centrality of the concept of divine energies for understanding this personalization.[25] Zizioulas argues that the essence/energies distinction is "essentially nothing other than a device created by the Greek Fathers to safeguard the absolute transcendence of God without alienating Him from the world."[26] More recently, Zizioulas has amplified that

> "maximizing" the role of divine energies may obscure the decisive significance of personhood for the God-world relationship—and this is, in fact, the case with many modern Orthodox theologians. It is extremely important not to forget or overlook the fact that the God-world relationship is primarily *hypostatic*, that is, in and through *one person* of the Trinity and not through an aspect of God's being that belongs to all three of the Trinitarian Persons, such as the divine energies.[27]

Although Zizioulas may not reject the essence/energies distinction outright, nowhere in his theological writings does he integrate the distinction into his theology in such a way as to attribute a soteriological significance to the notion of divine energies. The primary soteriological category for Zizioulas is not energies but *hypostasis*, since all of creation is personalized in the *hypostasis* of Christ by being incorporated into the Body of Christ in the Eucharist. One question that this critical comparison raises is whether or not the concept of divine energies is as central to Orthodox theology, and in particular to an Orthodox theology of creation, as is often assumed. It certainly is not central to Zizioulas's theology, nor to Bulgakov's.

There are, however, some troubling aspects to Zizioulas's creation theology, and these may or may not be related to his rejection of any meaningful soteriological significance to the essence/energies distinction. Zizioulas's creation theology is built upon a series of dualisms: uncreated/created, freedom/necessity, *hypostasis*/nature.[28] This compels him to talk about creation in such a way that creation seems to hang over an abyss of nothingness. Put another way, there seems to be a chasm between creation and the Creator. The impression is that the two are so ontologically distinct that, once created, creation appears to be devoid of divine presence. Zizioulas's theological system and, as we saw, even his trinitarian theology seem to rely on an emphasis, perhaps an overemphasis, on the logic of finitude, by which the createdness of creation is contrasted with God's eternal being. If God's being is what is eternal, then creation is finite, corrupt, and surrounded by death. This set of dualisms tends to forget that creation is indeed the creation of *God*; that is, it is God's creation. As such, there is not a clear sense in Zizioulas on how creation as God's creation is always already relating and participating in God's life, even when annihilation of creation is a possibility. It is one thing to say that annihilation is possible for creation and quite another to say that creation is surrounded by nothing; the latter implies that creation, once created, is completely devoid of God's presence, a position that is dangerously close to nominalism, in spite of Zizioulas's own intentions.

To be fair to Zizioulas, he is not a nominalist, since the uncreated-created divide is bridgeable hypostatically in Christ. He also will make claims that disavow any notion that creation is completely devoid of God's presence: "'Energy,' by being *uncreated*, involves in history and creation the very being of God. . . . For 'energy,' that is God's love towards creation, stems from his very being and is not to be dissociated from it."[29] But these statements come into tension with the rigid set of dualisms upon which his theology of personhood and his trinitarian theology is grounded. If the God-world relation is understood hypostatically for Zizioulas, but if Zizioulas also allows for an understanding of God as creator in terms of the divine energies, it is not at all clear how it all comes together in a coherent manner for him. Perhaps Zizioulas can learn something from Lossky and Bulgakov, who with the concepts of divine energies or Sophia avoid any rigid set of dualisms, so much so that their own tendency is opposite of Zizioulas, with Bulgakov endorsing an eternal aspect to creation and Lossky appearing to affirm the notion of the *apokatastasis*, or the idea that all creation in the end will be saved: "But though creation is contingent in its origin and began to exist, it will never cease to be; death and destruction will not involve a return to non-being, for 'the word of the Lord endureth forever' (1 Pet. 1, 25), and the divine will is unchangeable."[30]

One of Zizioulas's greatest contributions to theology, one he in part owes to Lossky, is the recovery of the soteriological and existential significance of the trinitarian category of *hypostasis*. *Hypostasis* cannot simply mean that which differentiates the persons of the Trinity; the *hypostasis* of Christ is that in and through which we are saved, in and through we are brought into communion with the divine. Theology needs, however, a more positive understanding of created nature if it is to coherently talk about God's creation and salvation of the world. I think the real challenge for Orthodox theology in the future is to bring Bulgakov, Lossky, and Zizioulas together into a synthesis, meaning to find a way to relate coherently Zizioulas's own trinitarian theology of personhood with the traditional Orthodox distinction between essence and energies, together with Bulgakov's concept of Sophia. Such a synthesis, I think, would be especially fruitful for an Orthodox theology of creation.

The Theological-Ethical Contributions of Archimandrite Sophrony (Sakharov) to Environmental Issues

Perry T. Hamalis

The subject of environmental issues and Orthodox Christianity does not, typically, bring to mind the names of Fr. Sophrony (Sakharov) or his mentor in the spiritual life, St. Silouan the Athonite. Indeed, even those who knew Elder Sophrony personally or who are familiar with his writing would likely not identify "the environment" as a subject on which he had something unique or especially significant to offer. Monasticism, the "person," repentance, prayer, or the spiritual life more broadly, yes—but environmental ethics, no. Having said this, however, we should note, first, that St. Silouan's teachings have been cited within such landmark documents as the Ecumenical Patriarchate's 1990 statement *Orthodoxy and the Ecological Crisis*,[1] and, second, that thinkers including Jean-Claude Larchet, Metropolitans Kallistos Ware, and John Zizioulas have included some analysis of St. Silouan's views on the animal and plant world within the context of more general works on the saint's teachings.[2] In what follows, I will argue that Fr. Sophrony's theological-ethical vision includes teachings that contribute in important ways to Orthodoxy's engagement with environmental issues. More specifically, by drawing from both Fr. Sophrony's published writings and from material collected through interviews with members of the monastic community at Essex,[3] I will defend the claim that it is his understanding of the meaning of the human person that holds together Fr. Sophrony's normative teachings about the nonhuman sphere of creation. I will discuss four areas where Fr. Sophrony's most significant teachings seem to lie: (1) his account (inspired by St. Silouan) of the status of nonhuman and human life, (2) his postlapsarian anthropology, (3) his conservation mindset, and (4) his teachings on hypostatic prayer. But first, I will begin with a brief biographical note.

Fr. Sophrony: Biography and the Influence of St. Silouan

Fr. Sophrony was born Sergei Symeonivich Sakharov in 1896 to Russian Orthodox parents living in Moscow. From the time of his childhood, Fr. Sophrony was inclined to contemplate metaphysical questions of death, meaning, and eternity.[4] His unquenchable pursuit of the eternal manifested itself in multiple ways. He studied painting at Moscow's Academy of Arts and at the National School of Painting, Sculpture, and Architecture, seeking meaning through artistic expression. He also dedicated between seven and eight intense years to Far Eastern transcendental meditation—something he lamented later in his life.[5] Fr. Sophrony left Russia in 1921 and, after brief stays in Italy and Germany, settled in Paris. Here he enjoyed some success as an artist, exhibiting his paintings in two prestigious Parisian salons. Having returned to the Orthodox faith in 1924 and still on a quest for God, he enrolled at St. Sergius Orthodox Theological Institute, where he met and was influenced by Sergei Bulgakov and Nicholas Berdyaev. The academic study of theology, however, did not satisfy Fr. Sophrony's thirst for the divine, and in 1925 he departed from France for the peninsula of Mt. Athos, where he was to spend the next twenty-two years of his life as a member of the Russian Orthodox Monastery of St. Panteleimon. It was there in 1930 that he met Staretz Silouan, the man who would shape his spiritual life and teachings most profoundly and whose holiness was officially recognized through canonization by the Ecumenical Patriarchate in 1987. For eight years, the monk Sophrony pursued God under the direct counsel of Staretz Silouan, and Silouan, in turn, revealed to Sophrony the details and the wisdom of his spiritual experience. After Silouan's death in 1938, Fr. Sophrony left the communal monastic life for the Athonite wilderness. He was ordained a priest and served as confessor to several Athonite communities. In 1947, Fr. Sophrony returned to France, in part so that he could edit and publish the writings and teachings of his beloved elder.[6] While there, he became a trusted friend of Vladimir Lossky and coedited the periodical *Messager de l'Exarchat du Patriarche Russe en Europe Occidentale*. Prohibited by his deteriorating health from returning to Athos, and at the request of several spiritual children who had gathered around him in Paris, Fr. Sophrony established the community of St. John the Baptist in Essex, England, where today over forty monks and nuns coexist in prayer, realizing concretely the theological-ethical vision he articulated. It was on July 11, 1993, at the monastery he had cofounded thirty-four years prior, that Fr. Sophrony reposed peacefully. Since then, there has been a steady interest in his theological-ethical writings among Orthodox and non-Orthodox, academics and nonacademics, in the East and the West.[7]

An assessment of Fr. Sophrony's environmental teachings properly begins with a brief consideration of St. Silouan's normative views on the subject. Fr. Sophrony insisted that his first book was strictly a rearticulation of what his elder had entrusted to him. He was—in his language—a mere "postman" delivering the words he had received.[8] While as scholars we might question the possibility of such pure hermeneutics, the point remains: from Fr. Sophrony's perspective, Silouan's teachings were authoritative, inerrant, saving words. "Throughout my time with Blessed Staretz Silouan," he writes, "I never for an instant doubted that his words were the 'words of life eternal.'"[9] Elsewhere he states, "I am not conscious of the slightest resistance to the Staretz' teaching, feeling in my heart that his is the *final* word."[10] While several outstanding voices within Orthodoxy influenced Fr. Sophrony's ethical vision, none affected him as decisively or as unequivocally as St. Silouan.[11]

The Leaf: An Image of Nonhuman and Human Life

St. Silouan's contribution to environmental thought is neither systematic nor detailed. It does, however, reflect a central emphasis on the human person and his or her salvation in a way that clearly continues in Fr. Sophrony's normative vision. Let me note briefly two dimensions of St. Silouan's environmental teachings that carry over in this way, linking them through the image of a leaf.

Fr. Sophrony writes that he witnessed in St. Silouan "an astonishingly harmonious conjunction of seemingly incompatible extremes,"[12] and this was certainly true in Silouan's teachings pertaining to plant and animal life. In a well-known passage, Fr. Sophrony recounts:

> I remember once walking with [the Staretz] from the monastery to [a hermit's hut]. We carried walking-sticks, usual in mountainous regions. On each side of the path there were clumps of tall wild grass. With the idea of not letting the path get overgrown I hit out with my stick at one of the stalks. . . . The Staretz thought this rough of me and shook his head [disapprovingly]. . . . I understood, and felt ashamed of myself.[13]

In his own writings, St. Silouan expands on this point. "The Spirit of God," he writes, "teaches the soul to love every living thing so that she would have no harm come to even a green leaf on a tree, or trample underfoot a flower of the field."[14] On the one hand, then, St. Silouan both exhibits and calls for a profound sensitivity toward all living things, regardless of species. He is a "preservationist" in a deep and broad sense and to an extent not frequently witnessed among Christian thinkers writing on such themes. For him, the Spirit of God seeks the preservation of *all* life and seeks a response of loving respect toward all living things from *every* human person. Consider another passage from St. Silouan's notebook:

> Once I needlessly killed a fly. The poor thing crawled on the ground, hurt and mangled, and for three whole days I wept over my cruelty to a living creature.... [Another time,] it happened that some bats bred on the balcony of the storeroom where I was, and I poured boiling water over them, and once again I shed many tears on this account and since then I have never harmed any living creature.[15]

What Fr. Sophrony takes from these accounts is a radical preservationist attitude toward nonhuman life, one that would seem to lie beyond the reproach of even the most devout environmentalist. Yet what is also clear is that the emphasis here is not merely on the intrinsic value of leaves, flies, or bats but rather encompasses the effect of human responses to nonhuman life upon the spiritual condition and salvation of persons. That is, St. Silouan and Fr. Sophrony seem to be calling for a response within each human being akin to that of a caretaker, a shepherd, or even a priest. To harm *needlessly* part of God's nonhuman creation is to betray this high calling, causing God's Spirit to withdraw. In addition, to understand truly the significance of this betrayal leads to the kind of weeping St. Silouan described above.[16]

The other side of this "radical preservationism" is where the "harmonious conjunction of seemingly incompatible extremes" noted earlier becomes apparent. Put simply, St. Silouan unapologetically prioritizes human persons over nonhuman creation. As an Orthodox monk, he ate moderate portions of vegetables and seafood, harvested hay, and chopped trees for firewood,[17] and there was no dilemma in doing so. Furthermore, St. Silouan writes explicitly against overattachments to animals. In a passage that has scandalized many readers, he states, "There are people who attach themselves to animals, and stroke and fondle and talk to them.... It is silly to do this. Feed animals and cattle, and do not beat them—in this consists man's duty of kindness towards them; but to become attached, to love, caress and talk to them—that is folly for the soul."[18] According to Fr. Sophrony, the Staretz considered such responses toward animals (so common and often extreme among pet owners in our society) to be "a perversion of the order established by God and contrary to the [normative] state of man (cf. Gen 2:20)."[19] Yet here again St. Silouan's core soteriological concern becomes apparent. It is not that genuine caring relationships with animals, including pets, are wrong but rather that extreme anthropomorphisms, he contends, imply a dangerous attachment to earthly things and a distorted prioritization that draws one's mind away from the love of God and neighbor,[20] away from the greatest divine commandment which is—in Fr. Sophrony's view—itself God's uncreated, saving energy.[21]

What seems to be at work, then, is a fundamental difference in status and value between human and nonhuman life in both St. Silouan's and Fr. Sophrony's teachings, and this brings us back to the image of the leaf, but with a significantly different meaning this time. Fr. Sophrony uses a wonderful variety of terms and analogies in order to express the mystery of the human person and the unity of humanity. Because of their Trinitarian grounding, he prefers theological terms like "human *hypostasis*," "*persona-hypostasis*," and "hypostatic principle in man."[22] In several works one finds him invoking such terms to make bold claims about divine-human commensurability, stating, for example, "mankind is one being but multi-hypostatic, just as God is One Being in Three Persons."[23] In other contexts, however, Fr. Sophrony appeals to biological images and describes the entire human race as a "single organism" and—as I have been hinting—as a leafy tree.[24] Consider the following passage from one of Fr. Sophrony's addresses to the monastic community in Essex:

> "Love thy neighbor as thyself." It was given to me to understand this commandment in the form of a gigantic tree, of cosmic dimensions, whose root is Adam. Myself, I am only a little leaf on a branch of this tree. But the tree is not foreign to me; it is the basis of my being. I belong to it. To pray for the whole world is to pray for this tree in its totality, with its milliards of leaves.[25]

For Fr. Sophrony, every human being is a leaf that has grown out of the root of Adam, and, as such, each human person remains ontologically united both to that root *and* to every other leaf on the tree. We will return to the idea of prayer for the "whole Adam" below, but for now two other points should be made that carry environmental implications. First, this extraordinary emphasis on humanity's ontological unity levels a sharp critique upon all forms of individualism. Notwithstanding personal distinctiveness, all of humanity—every human being born in history—is ontologically united. There are so many ethical ramifications stemming from this single, very simple teaching that one would be hard pressed to overstate its significance.

While I will return to this point below, for now we should note that this anthropological claim sheds important light on the meaning of a saving word or spiritual counsel Fr. Sophrony received from St. Silouan and repeated frequently: *"Our brother is our life."*[26] No one is a Christian alone, and no one's spiritual development can occur in a mode detached from other human beings.

The tree image is also important because Fr. Sophrony makes it very clear in other passages that while human beings are like leaves on a tree of the total Adam, organically connected with one another, we are also fundamentally different from actual leaves and from all of the nonhuman creation in a most important way: *among God's creatures we alone are hypostatic.* Flies, bats, and leaves, dogs, cats, and trees are to be respected and should not be harmed unnecessarily, but, since they are not hypostatic beings—not beings created in the divine image—their value remains relative to the earthly realm. To be overly attached to them is to be overly attached to the world. In *His Life Is Mine*, Fr. Sophrony writes, "As the image and likeness of the Absolute, man is conscious that in his spirit he transcends every other form of natural being."[27] And in *On Prayer*, he makes it clear that only hypostatic beings exist in the realm of eternity.[28] Unlike the love of animals or other nonhypostatic creatures, there is no proper limit on love directed to a person—whether divine or human, for to love one's neighbor is to ascend to the eternal realm and, thus, fulfill one's divine purpose. Fr. Sophrony writes:

> [The true ascetic] does not deny the reality and value of the creation. All he does is not to regard it as absolute, not to deify it or consider it an end and a value in itself. God did not create the world in order that He Himself might live the life of the creature. He created it in order to associate man with His own Divine Life. And when man does not arrive at deification, which cannot be achieved without his own collaboration, the very meaning of his existence disappears.[29]

So here, once again, Fr. Sophrony's environmental teaching about the status of the natural world traces back to his understanding of the meaning and salvation of the human person.

The Fall, the Hypostatis, and the Environment

In a rich passage from *His Life Is Mine*, Fr. Sophrony articulates a series of claims about the fallen human condition. He writes:

In the person of the first Adam, all mankind suffered a fearful catastrophe, an alienation which is the root of all alienations. The body was wounded, the skeleton smashed, the countenance—the image of God—distorted. Succeeding generations have added many another injury and broken bone to the wounds of the first created man. The whole human corpus is sick.[30]

Here we see the graphic flipside of Fr. Sophrony's teaching on the unity of humanity. Yes, each human person remains *homoousios* with every other, but the Fall has effected a fragmentation and infection within the "total Adam's" body. Returning to his tree image, we might say that, according to Fr. Sophrony, the leaves began turning brown—or became diseased—when our forefathers sinned, but we have not fallen off the branches. The point that seems environmentally significant, however, comes toward the end of the passage, where Fr. Sophrony writes, "Succeeding generations have added many another injury and broken bone to the wounds of the first created man." Similarly, in another work he writes, "I inherited the terrible *fall of Adam*, the fall made worse by his sons down the ages; the fall which I aggravate every day of my life."[31] Fr. Sophrony's point here seems to be that, while the Fall carries certain unchanging, perennial consequences, it also carries cumulative and distinctively contemporary effects. In other words, the fallen human condition changes, to some extent, with time. Typically, it gets worse. Here again the basis for Fr. Sophrony's view seems to be his teaching on the ontological unity of humanity. Since a shared—albeit fragmented—nature unites all of humanity, it makes sense that the sins of each human being *and each generation* affect the commonly held and transmitted nature.[32]

When I began reflecting on the topic of environmental ethics within Fr. Sophrony's teachings, it was exactly this point about the postlapsarian condition, including dimensions that are historically and culturally determined, that first came to my mind. When Fr. Sophrony discusses such dimensions, most of them do not refer directly to the environment, but some do. One example he notes pertains to our modern views on science. "Contemporary science," he states, "has developed considerably in the domain of mastering the forces of nature. But what a result! The Creator of nature has each time been ousted more and more from the world and the human conscience."[33] For Fr. Sophrony, the fact that people are born today into a culture that views technology as we do and seeks to master nature through science as we do is a distinctive part of our generation's inherited fallen condition. While he emphasizes the significance of changes in human attitudes for properly diagnosing the fallen condition, it seems appropriate to extend this insight to the health of the natural world as well. Environmentally, things are getting worse—this much we know. I believe that Fr. Sophrony's account of postlapsarian anthropology can provide a theological rubric for thinking about how each human being's sins against the natural world and each generation's contributions to the sickness that permeates all creation are appropriated and passed on. Once more we see that it is his understanding of the meaning and the salvation of the human person that directs Fr. Sophrony's environmental ethics.

"The Sweat of My Brother": Conservation in Hypostatic Perspective

Perhaps one of the most profound contributions Fr. Sophrony makes to environmental issues came out only in the context of semistructured interviews I held with various members of the monastic community in Essex and pertains directly to the way he lived. Fr. Sophrony was a conservationist before "being green" became fashionable. He cared deeply about the trees on the monastery property and personally selected and oversaw the planting of different varieties on the grounds. One monastic shared with me a conversation held with him about whether or not to plant a new oak tree, given that we do not know how much time remains before Christ's Second Coming. When this monastic replied by saying, "Yes, Father, I believe it is a sign of hope for the world to plant it," he responded with a smile and said, "I'm glad you said that!"

What I heard most from the monks and nuns I interviewed, however, was that Fr. Sophrony was adamant about not wasting energy or goods. Lights, for instance, should never be on if no one is in the room. During the 1970s, as part of a conservation campaign, the British government issued stickers that could be placed around a light switch and that read, "Switch off, Save it!" Fr. Sophrony enthusiastically applied these stickers to switches throughout the monastery (and there are a few that remain up today). Similarly, to save energy and water, Fr. Sophrony would boil a full pot for tea and then pour whatever he did not use immediately into a large thermos in order to avoid having to reheat the pot. Furthermore, when the large thermos was half empty, he would pour the remaining water into a smaller thermos to keep it hot enough, thus refraining from using more gas or electricity. One monk told me that at meals Fr. Sophrony would never put more water into his glass than what he could drink, and he would never leave a drop in his glass or food on his plate. Another member of the community recalled that, in his sermons on the miraculous feeding with the loaves and fish (cf. Lk. 9:10–18; Mt. 14:13–21; Mk. 6:32–44; Jn. 6:1–14), Fr. Sophrony often focused on Jesus's instruction to "Gather up the fragments left over, that nothing may be lost," offering a conservationist interpretation of the pericope. With respect to recycling, Fr. Sophrony insisted on reusing items long before such efforts became popular. When he received a letter in the mail, for example, he would cut the envelopes and use them for note taking and even for cards in the library cataloging system. To this day, members of the Community of St. John the Baptist often repurpose used envelopes for personal correspondence.

Were these aversions to "wasting" merely a reflection of Fr. Sophrony's upbringing? Was he strictly concerned about saving the monastery's limited funds? When this question arose, the answer I received was a profound expression of Fr. Sophrony's ethical vision. Yes, I was told, Fr. Sophrony was quite careful with the community's financial resources, but this was not what drove his behavior. Was it, then, his loving respect for the natural world? This, too, motivated him, I was told; however, it also was not the primary factor. What, then, was left? "Fr. Sophrony was so keen about this issue," I was told, "because he did not want to waste his brother's sweat." For Fr. Sophrony, to toss away an empty envelope meant that the human labor that went into producing that envelope was not fully respected. In addition, it meant that more work would be created for his brother, who would have to collect and dispose of the trash he generated and would have to make more notepaper to meet demand. In Fr. Sophrony's view, wasting natural resources indicated—first of all—*a lack of neighbor love*, a lack of sensitivity to the human sweat and sacrifice that go into producing goods. And, in his words, "acquiring this Love is the ultimate purpose of Christian asceticism."[34] For Fr. Sophrony, therefore, one's conservationist/ascetic relationship to nonhuman creation shapes and reflects one's hypostatic relationships with one's neighbor and with God. Waste not, for "our brother is our life." Again, it is the meaning and salvation of the human person that grounds Fr. Sophrony's environmental insights.

The Aim: Hypostatic Prayer and the Royal Priesthood

The final environmental contribution I want to note from Fr. Sophrony brings us back to the opening section on what sets human persons apart from the rest of the created world. While Fr. Sophrony was not opposed to socially conscious governmental policies—indeed, he applauded some such efforts—he gave priority to prayer. "Prayer is more important than any other activity, whether social or political, in the field of science or the arts."[35] Much insightful material has been written on the topic of "prayer for the Total Adam" in St. Silouan, what Fr. Sophrony also refers to as hypostatic prayer,

Gethsemane prayer, and liturgical prayer, and an extended discussion lies beyond our present scope.[36] Nonetheless, we should at least note that this highest of human activities encompasses not only all our fellow human beings since the beginning of history—not only each of the "milliards of leaves" on the great tree of Adam—but also the whole of nonhuman creation.[37] It is an activity possible only because of the hypostatic principle within human beings, which enables an enlargement of one's heart to cosmic proportions[38] and through which man becomes "the connecting principle between God and the rest of creation."[39] For Fr. Sophrony, hypostatic prayer is the highest expression of environmental stewardship, precisely because it both sanctifies nonhuman creation and fulfills the human person's most distinctive—and dignified—capacity. Hypostatic prayer is also an activity that Fr. Sophrony equates with the universal human calling to the "royal priesthood" (cf. 1 Pet. 2:9).[40] It reflects every human person's Eucharistic role and responsibility as a member of the body of Christ. Actualizing this highest capacity, he contends, effects a restoration and healing both within that great tree and between humanity and all other living things.[41] Hypostatic prayer, finally, is a pure expression of love, a love that participates in and imitates Christ's infinite love for us and for the world He created.

Conclusion

Neither St. Silouan nor Fr. Sophrony ever authored a systematic work on environmental ethics. Nor were either of them engaged in properly political activities with the aim of shaping public policy. They were, instead, Orthodox monks living out their calling to love God and neighbor. However, I have argued that Fr. Sophrony's written and unwritten teachings nonetheless carry important insights for critical reflection on one of the most acute social problems of our time, the condition of the natural world, and I have sought to demonstrate that for Fr. Sophrony this problem is at its core both anthropological and soteriological. Through his claims regarding the value and interconnectedness of creation, his insight into the link between environmental destruction and the current generation's fallen condition, his strict conservationism, and his affirmation of hypostatic prayer as humanity's highest calling, Fr. Sophrony enriches our understanding of environmental issues and reminds us that a hermeneutical key for examining these issues is Orthodox Christianity's theology of the person. As thinkers and church leaders continue to harvest Orthodoxy's abundant theological and ascetical tradition for resources relevant to environmental ethics, the example and teachings of Archimandrite Sophrony merit our ongoing attention.

The Cosmology of the Eucharist
George Theokritoff

A grain of wheat falls to the earth and decomposes, and is then raised with manifold increase by the spirit of God, who contains all things; by wisdom it is then used by human beings, receives the Word of God and becomes the Eucharist, which is the Body and Blood of Christ. In the same way our bodies, being nourished by it, will be deposited in the earth and decompose there, and then rise at their appointed time, as the Word of God grants them resurrection to the glory of God.
—*St. Irenaeus*, Against Heresies, *V 2, 3 (trans. E. Theokritoff)*

Here, in a statement that focuses on the work of God in the Eucharist, St. Irenaeus summarizes the essence of the Cosmology of the Eucharist in a seemingly simple yet profound statement. What I propose to do here is to approach this Cosmology from a different perspective, drawing on what we know of the workings of the Cosmos. We could usefully start by asking the questions "What is bread?" and "What is wine?"

It needs hardly to be said that bread is made of flour, yeast (or leaven), and water, and wine by the fermentation of grape juice. What is produced by wheat (Irenaeus's "grain of wheat") and by the vine is transformed by human labor ("used by human beings"). But this is not the only intervention of human labor: the wheat is sown ("a grain of wheat falls to the earth") and then germinates, grows, bears ears of wheat ("raised with manifold increase by the Spirit of God"), and finally reaped, threshed, and the grains ground to give flour. Similarly, vines have to be planted and grafted. They then grow and bear fruit ("raised with manifold increase by the Spirit of God"), and finally the grapes are gathered and pressed. In this, we see the synergy of the transformative power of God with human labor.

> We too should wonder and give thanks,
> that from the dry stalk of wheat there comes ample bread,
> that from the vine stalk there flows wine,
> that from each tree, all kinds of varied delights—
> this too is a great wonder, as great as the miracle at Cana.[1]

In the wheat and in the vine, and at Cana, there is the same key element in the transformation: water. The third question, then, is "What is water?" An essential constituent of all living things, water also has a vital role at every stage, every transformation, in the preparation of the elements of the Eucharist. Both the wheat in the fields and the vines on the hillsides utilize water and carbon dioxide as well as the energy of sunlight in photosynthesis. But it is important to be aware that plants also obtain nutrients from the soil.

And so we come to the fourth question: "What is soil?" Most soils consist of two components. The first is minerals derived from weathering of the bedrock, which is broken down into smaller pieces by the action of frost, tree roots, and burrowing animals. Once in smaller pieces, the increased surface area enhances the chemical alteration of the bedrock. Here, naturally occurring acids (carbonic, nitric, nitrous, and those produced by plant roots) and the activity of microorganisms play important roles in the release, from the minerals that make up the bedrock, of nutrients, in a water-soluble form that can be utilized by plants. The second component is an organic material called humus. This is of great importance because it retains soil moisture, thereby binding the soil and inhibiting loss by erosion. It is made up mostly of plant debris, such as the leaf litter that accumulates in the woods. But in itself leaf litter is of little use to plants because the nutrients in it are locked up in complex molecules, which must be broken down into simple molecules that plants can utilize. This is done by decomposers: nonphotosynthetic microorganisms such as bacteria and fungi. Thus, the decomposers obtain their own energy and nutrients. In the larger context, the working of the decomposers is of profound importance in the functioning of the biosphere because it completes the cycling of nutrients and energy.

Up to this point, we have noted the contributions of the sun, the atmosphere (carbon dioxide, water, oxides of nitrogen), the hydrosphere (water), the solid earth (mineral nutrients such as potassium and calcium), plants, decomposers, and human labor. All are made of matter derived from our planet, the Earth. And so we come to the fifth question: "What is matter?"

The two lightest elements, hydrogen and helium, which predominate in the stars, are by far the most abundant elements in the Cosmos. But the heavier elements (for example, carbon, phosphorous, nitrogen, sulfur) are the product of the death of generations of stars. The temperatures and pressures that develop in some kinds of dying stars convert the lighter elements into the heavier, which are then flung out as dust into the surrounding space when the star explodes. Eventually, under the influence of gravity and the pressure of light, the dispersed heavier elements are either incorporated into new stars, going through the cycle again, or cluster into bodies called planets. The Earth and everything on it, including our bodies and blood, as well as the Eucharistic bread and wine, are cosmic in origin. In taking flesh and blood from his Holy Mother, the Eternal Word of God clothed himself in his own creation, the Cosmos. Thus Christ's words, "This is my body; this is my blood," have a profound literal sense in that the matter making up the Eucharistic bread and wine—and that making up the flesh and blood taken from his Holy Mother—share the same cosmic origin.[2]

The entire Cosmos thus participates by representation in the preparation of the matter used by the Church sacramentally and in other ways. And it in this fashion that the entire cosmos offers its praise. With specific reference to the Eucharist, the wheat and the grapes are the offering of the community that is the Cosmos, the offering of the dust clouds in space, the stars, the Earth and other planets, of bacteria and fungi, of plants and animals. This offering is transformed into bread and wine by human labor and skill, and it *receives the Word of God and becomes the Eucharist*, an offering to God by man, the priest of the Cosmos. Man depends on the Cosmos for the matter that makes up his and her body and for the matter that is used sacramentally; reciprocally, the Cosmos depends on Man to complete its own offering. Thus the seventh-century saint Leontius of Cyprus wrote:

> Through heaven and earth and sea, through wood and stone, through relics and church buildings, and the Cross, and angels and men—through all creation, visible and invisible, I offer veneration to the Creator and master and Maker of all things. For creation does not venerate the Maker directly and by itself, but it is through me that the heavens declare the glory of God; through me the moon worships God, through me the stars glorify him, through me the waters and showers of rain, the dew and all creation, venerate God and give him glory.[3]

In the Eucharist we offer, in this piece of bread and in this cup of wine, the entire Cosmos and every living creature including ourselves—everything from the tiniest particles of matter to the farthest reaches of space, as well as the fruits of human labor in all places and all times.[4] We thus come to see that the Eucharist is central to the Cosmos. And it is the Eucharist that enables us to recognize more clearly that the Cosmos is transparent to Christ, who shines through all matter.

The late Protopresbyter Alexander Schmemann has reminded us that the Eucharist may best be understood as a journey or procession.[5] If we are to consider the local Eucharist, one celebrated in a given place and at a given time, we might state that the procession starts in the gathering of the local community and at the table of preparation. In the light of what has been written above, we might opt at a deeper level for an arbitrary spot in the cycle leading up to the fruiting of the grains of wheat and grapes. This spot might be, for instance, the working of decomposers. But the arbitrary nature of the choice points beyond, to include the whole creation. If this is accepted, the beginning of the Procession of the Cosmic Eucharist, of which the local Eucharist is the full local manifestation,[6] is in Creation—"*In the beginning.*" Christ is the lamb slain from the foundation of the world.

It is worth noting that we have now arrived at a corrective to contemporary neopagan attempts to grasp a holistic worldview of creation. In one way or another, they venerate the cycles of nature and see the "meaning" of creation in itself. In contrast, Christians find the meaning of creation in the uncreated Word of God, through Whom all things were made, and they recognize the cycles of nature as the ongoing work of God in the Cosmos. In this connection, it is worth noting that in the second half of St. Irenaeus's statement ("In the same way . . . the glory of God"), he shows us a parallel in the life, death, and resurrection of man. Taken from the Earth, nourished by the Eucharist, man returns in death to the Earth, where, like the grain of wheat, he decomposes. The Word of God then grants him resurrection to the glory of God. It is through the Eucharist, in which we offer the fruits of corruption (the work of decomposers) and receive them back as the fruits of incorruption, that we escape the cycle of life and decay. Father John Jillions, in a somewhat different context, stated that Christ's disciples "tasted of the banquet of immortality that transforms the corruption of the tomb [of Lazarus] into the blessing of Cana [the new wine of the Kingdom]."[7]

Questions are raised here that are beyond the scope of this paper: Just what do we mean by corruption? Is corruption just one thing? Can some form of what we call corruption be an essential step in the process of renewal?

Apart from a few details, nothing has been added to what is implied in St. Irenaeus's understanding of the Cosmology of the Eucharist. But I am suggesting that the preceding discussion, albeit couched in terms that would be quite unfamiliar to St. Irenaeus and his contemporaries, nevertheless underlines the church's understanding of the Cosmology of the Eucharist. It points to Creation as a sacrament, a means of communion, a gift from God for us "to till and keep," but certainly not a commodity to be abused. It also helps us to perceive more clearly Christ, the Wisdom and Word of God, who comes to us in bread and wine, present in every element of creation and at work in all its processes.

"A 'Tradition' That Never Existed": Orthodox Christianity and the Failures of Environmental History

Jurretta Jordan Heckscher

A particular understanding of historical Christianity's approach to nature is now accepted in the academic study of environmental history (here defined to mean any account of the man-nature relationship that engages the realm of history) and among the general public throughout much of the world. The present paper explores this understanding with particular reference to English-language scholarship, to demonstrate that it depends on a failure to integrate or, often, even acknowledge Orthodox Christian history, and to argue an imperative for historians, ethicists, theologians, environmentalists, religious leaders, and members of the general public to come to terms with that neglected Orthodox history, whether or not they are Orthodox or even Christian themselves.

The White Thesis

Any discussion of historical Christianity's approach to nature must begin with Lynn White Jr., a medieval historian and professing Christian whose article "The Historical Roots of Our Ecologic Crisis" appeared in the journal *Science* on March 10, 1967.[1] Its lasting importance lies in its argument for the particular, and particularly pernicious, impact of Christian belief on the natural world. Christianity, White claims, "bears a huge burden of guilt" for the contemporary environmental crisis, because in Christian belief the natural world has no other purpose than to serve man's needs. "Especially in its Western form, Christianity is the most anthropocentric religion the world has seen," for in it "man shares, in great measure, God's transcendence of nature. Christianity . . . not only established a dualism of man and nature but also insisted that it is God's will that man exploit nature for his proper ends."[2]

White cautions that he is painting with a broad brush. He notes that the differing approaches of Eastern and Western Christianity meant that "the implications of Christianity for the conquest of nature would emerge more easily in the Western atmosphere," because the Greek East saw nature "primarily as a symbolic system through which God speaks to man," an "essentially artistic" approach that precluded the development of modern science and technology. In the modern West, science and technology were "cast in a matrix of Christian theology" and have exploited nature in accordance with it. "Since the roots of our trouble are so largely religious," White concludes, "the remedy must also be essentially religious, whether we call it that or not." He discerns no hope for a reform of Western Christian attitudes in those of the Christian East. Instead, hope rests in the unique legacy St. Francis of Assisi and in Christianity's fundamental revision: we must "find a new religion, or rethink our old one."[3]

The Evidence of History

The effect of White's essay—of what may be called the White thesis—was immediate, immense, and enduring. Within five years of its publication, "The Historical Roots of Our Ecologic Crisis" was being hailed as "a modern classic" and recognized as "an article of faith for many conservationists, ecologists, economists, and even theologians."[4] Much of its power lay in its sharpening and clarifying suppositions already embedded in historical analysis. The critique of Christianity's anthropocentric indifference to nature extends at least as far back as Ludwig Feuerbach and Max Weber.[5] By 1954, the young Paul Shepard could note that viewing nature as benevolent "might be contrasted to the orthodox Christian viewpoint that nature is evil or at best features isolated symbols of divinity."[6] In fact, White's was merely the most influential of several similar contemporaneous critiques of Christianity.[7]

Among historians, perhaps inevitably, White's bold analysis has been modified by a set of widely accepted criticisms. Large-scale human destruction of the natural environment has occurred in many non-Christian cultures; indeed, destructive environmental interventions on at least a limited scale may well be the human norm. Christianity is not alone among major religious traditions in its attenuation of nature, and in comparative perspective the relationship between a culture's religious affinity for nature and its disturbance of the natural environment is far from clear. Definitive conclusions about the influence of a religion's official teachings cannot be drawn without knowledge of how those teachings were understood and enacted—or disregarded—in ordinary believers' lives. It is also difficult, if not impossible, to assess the relative influence of religion on human behavior among complementary or competing historical forces such as economics, technological development, and material opportunity.[8]

If, however, few environmental historians would now endorse without significant qualification White's claim that Christianity is uniquely responsible for the global environmental crisis, his account of Christianity's historical indifference and even hostility to the natural world has become academic orthodoxy. It endures despite an outpouring of scholarship arguing that it greatly oversimplifies the complexity of Western Christian attitudes toward nature and, in particular, that it fails to account for Christianity's traditional understanding of man's vocation as nature's steward.[9] In this view, the injunctions of Genesis 1:28 to subdue the earth and have dominion over nature are less a license for exploitation than a scriptural foundation for responsible stewardship.

Yet as Henryk Skolimowski notes, such rebuttals to White have come mainly, though not wholly, from "Christian theologians and clergymen," and they "help but little when the Bible can still be seen as ecologically insensitive."[10] This apparent insensitivity is formidably reinforced by historical and contemporary evidence: White's condemnation of Christianity persists among environmental historians because in large measure it appears to be true. Nowhere else in the world, for example, have traditional ecologies, both human and nonhuman, been more drastically transformed in so short a time as they were in the Americas following the European invasions, and it is abundantly clear that Christian antipathy to wild nature provided a sanction quite consciously invoked. A Michigan senator spoke for his culture when he wrote in 1830, "There can be no doubt . . . that the Creator intended the earth should be reclaimed from a state of nature and cultivated."[11] The advance of Christianity across the hemisphere can be mapped exactly to the spread of ecological impoverishment and environmental degradation.

Such attitudes persist among many American Evangelical Protestants, a dynamic segment of the U.S. population that has made the term "Christian" synonymous with its own membership and its membership synonymous with the Republican Party. Despite some recent stirrings of dissent, a hallmark of Evangelical identity has long been hostility to the environmental movement and denial of the scientific evidence for environmental crisis. "Environmentalism . . . promotes its own worldview and its own doctrines of God, creation, humanity, sin, and salvation," warns the Evangelical-led Cornwall Alliance for the Stewardship of Creation. "And those doctrines aren't Biblical." Countless Evangelicals agree. Climate change is "a flat-out lie," declared Norman Dennison of Corydon, Indiana, in 2010. "I read my Bible.... He [God] made this earth for us to utilize."[12] Inevitably, environmental historians have taken note of the fact that "the most robust form of western Christianity today . . . is, in the main, implacably opposed to environmentalist aspirations."[13]

The Scholars' Consensus

Because the scholarly response has complicated but not undermined its central claims about Christian belief, then, and because its claims find continuing reinforcement in some of the most vocal quarters of contemporary Christianity, the White thesis now defines the depiction of Christianity in the literature of environmental history. With or—more often—without explicit citation, it persists as a set of interlocking propositions almost endlessly exemplified in current scholarship:

1. *Christianity has been relentlessly anthropocentric, concerned only with the human relationship with God while affirming humanity's radical separation from and superiority to the rest of creation.* As Jack Turner concludes, "we believe our species is separate from and superior to other species; we are, as we say, God's children, and the rest of creation is, and should be, subject to our whims. This is the heritage of Christianity." "Christianity, in its official pronouncements particularly," writes David Drew, "has continually emphasized the gulf between humans and the remainder of creation. This mental distancing in Western thinking has continued to the present day."[14]

2. *The Christian focus on human salvation has entailed a pervasive otherworldliness, a focus on Heaven and a denigration of the Earth and its nonhuman inhabitants, animate and otherwise.* "The essence of the Christian [worldview]," according to Gilbert LaFrenière, "is its virtually obsessive preoccupation with an otherworldly, transcendental reality which it considers to be inordinately superior to the things of the secular world." Christianity "hastened the death of ecological awareness," writes Paul Harrison. "The present world became a transit hall to the next, a human threshing ground where grain is divided from worthless chaff. God and soul are separate from matter, not inherent in it." "Christians' aspirations were fixed on heaven," agrees Roderick Nash. "The earth was . . . a kind of halfway house of trial and testing from which one was released at death."[15]

3. *Christianity's primary commitment to the spiritual world likewise entails a profound and dualistic disdain for the flesh, for the human body, for matter itself, as mere impediments to be transcended and discarded on the soul's journey*

toward eternity with a transcendent God. "Christian ideals of salvation subordinated the 'unimportant' earthly world of nature and material life to the immaterial celestial world beyond the earth," writes Val Plumwood. "The mainstream Christian viewpoint," explains David Spangler, is "that only humans have souls and that the nonhuman world is of little spiritual consequence and can be used as we wish." Frederic Bender goes further: "Christianity framed Earth, nature, human embodiment, sexuality, and everything else of the physical world as evil."[16]

4. *The paramount Christian teaching about man's proper relationship to nature is the injunctions in Genesis 1:28 to have dominion over and subdue the earth—and dominion is essentially indistinguishable from domination.* "The Judeo-Christian tradition . . . stressed humankind's right to dominate and subdue the natural world (Genesis 1:26–9)," notes Stephen Mosley. Since the advent of Christianity, says Charles Redman, "individuals have claimed that it is God's will that they multiply freely and exploit nature. . . . A consistent theme in [Christian] religious teachings . . . is human dominance over nature."[17]

Anthropocentrism, otherworldliness, dualism, domination: these, then, academic environmental history tells us, are what Christianity has offered the natural world, and the result has both fueled the present global environmental crisis and rendered Christianity all but impotent to address it. Thus can the historian Donald Worster, in his authoritative history of ecological ideas, confine his account of Christian attitudes to a restatement of White's analysis, and thus can the ecological philosopher Paul Shepard, near the end of his life, dismiss the Christian heritage with erudite contempt:

> One could pick any number of Christian blue-noses, from popes to puritans and apostles to saints, who wanted nothing to do with nature and who were disgusted to think they were part of it. The best that can be said about Christianity from an ecological viewpoint is that the Roman church, in its evangelical lust for souls, is a leaky ship. Locally it can allow reconciliation of its own dogma with "pagan" cults, as when the Yucatán Indians were Christianized by permitting the continued worship of limestone sinks, or *cenotes*, making the Church truly catholic. Similar blending may be seen in eccentrics like St. Francis or Wendell Berry, who voice a "tradition" that never existed.[18]

The Problem of Orthodox Christianity

The problem, of course, is that however approximate for the Christian West, this account of Christianity cannot possibly be reconciled with Orthodox

Christian history. The ordinary Orthodox churchgoer, familiar with the practices of centuries-old liturgy and customary piety, will find the account puzzling; the scholar of that ancient and vital tradition, whose existence Shepard denies, will find it distorted almost past recognition.

A systematic exposition of historical Orthodoxy's approach to nature is of course beyond the scope of this discussion, but no such exposition is necessary to demonstrate the fallaciousness of the accepted account of Christian environmental attitudes with regard to Orthodox Christianity. On the contrary, it is possible to do so simply by citing a few passages from a handful of standard works about Orthodox history and theology that were widely available in English by 1980 and have remained so ever since. These works would be among the first encountered by any reader, let alone scholar, seeking a basic understanding of Orthodox historical belief. They are Vladimir Lossky's *The Mystical Theology of the Eastern Church* (1957), Timothy (later Kallistos) Ware's *The Orthodox Church* (1963; rev. ed. 1997), Nicolas Zernov's *The Russians and Their Church* (3rd ed. 1978), and Kallistos Ware's *The Orthodox Way* (1979; rev. ed. 1995).[19]

No assumption that Christianity is exclusively anthropocentric, for example, can be reconciled with a statement such as Ware's that in Orthodox Christian teaching man's "own salvation involves also the reconciliation and transfiguration of the whole animate and inanimate creation around him—its deliverance 'from the bondage of corruption' and entry 'into the glorious liberty of the children of God' (Rom. 8:21). In the 'new earth' of the Age to come," Ware explains, "there is surely a place not only for man but for the animals: in and through man, they too will share in immortality, and so will rocks, trees and plants, fire and water."[20] Thus in traditional Russian Orthodox popular culture, according to Zernov, "salvation was conceived not so much in terms of the forgiveness of the sins of the individual, as a part of a healing and sanctifying process which aimed at the transfiguration of men, of beasts and plants, and of the whole cosmos."[21]

Likewise, all these works confound any notion of Christian otherworldliness with evidence of Orthodoxy's central belief in the interpenetration of the earthly and heavenly realms. "All things are permeated and maintained in being by the uncreated energies of God, and so all things are a theophany that mediates his presence," writes Ware. "God is above and beyond all things, yet as Creator he is also within all things—'panentheism,' not pantheism. . . . To contemplate nature, then, . . . is to discover, not so much through our discursive reason as through our spiritual intellect, that the whole universe is a cosmic Burning Bush, filled with the divine Fire yet not consumed."[22] He quotes the great fourteenth-century Greek theologian St. Gregory Palamas:

"He [God] is everywhere and nowhere, he is everything and nothing."[23] "The world," explains Lossky, "created in order that it might be deified, is dynamic, tending always towards its final end. . . . The creation . . . can have no other end than deification. . . . Created beings have the faculty of being assimilated to God because such was the very object of their creation."[24]

This vocation of all things, including the natural world, to union with God is the meaning of the holy icons, Orthodoxy's most distinctive physical emblems. Thus Zernov explains that icons (*obraza* in Russian)

> were, for the Russians, not merely paintings. They were dynamic manifestations of man's spiritual power to redeem creation through beauty and art. The colors and lines of the *obraza* were not meant to imitate nature; the artists aimed at demonstrating that men, animals and plants, and the whole cosmos could be rescued from their present state of degradation and restored to their proper "Image." The *obraza* were pledges of the coming victory of a redeemed creation over the fallen one. . . . concrete example[s] of matter restored to its original harmony and beauty, and serving as a vehicle of the Spirit.[25]

Such an understanding renders dualism an impossibility, and these works illuminate the degree to which the last great theological crisis in Orthodox history—the Iconoclast controversy of the eighth and ninth centuries—turned on the question of the potential holiness of matter and settled it once and for all. In finally and fully condemning the Iconoclasts, Ware explains, the Orthodox Church affirmed that

> God took a material body [in the Incarnation], thereby proving that matter can be redeemed: "The word made flesh has deified the flesh," said John of Damascus. God has "deified" matter, making it "spirit-bearing"; and if flesh became a vehicle of the Spirit, then so—though in a different way—can wood and paint. The Orthodox doctrine of icons is bound up with the Orthodox belief that the whole of God's creation, material as well as spiritual, is to be redeemed and glorified.[26]

Far from being an esoteric or merely historical issue, the proclamation of the doctrine of icons by the Seventh Ecumenical Council in 843 is known today as the Triumph of Orthodoxy. It is continuously affirmed by the presence of icons in every Orthodox church and home and is solemnly commemorated every year on the first Sunday in Lent—a day known to the faithful as Orthodoxy Sunday. By such means does the Orthodox Church proclaim, as Lossky explains, its central conviction that "the entire universe is called to enter within the Church, to become the Church of Christ, that it may be transformed after the consummation of the ages, into the eternal Kingdom of God."[27]

In expounding the Orthodox understanding of nature, accordingly, none of these works alludes to Genesis 1:28 or to the possibility that nature's vocation is dominance by man. Instead, as Ware notes, Orthodoxy's "idea of cosmic redemption is based, like the Orthodox doctrine of the human body and the Orthodox doctrine of icons, upon a right understanding of the Incarnation: Christ took flesh—something from the material order—and so has made possible the redemption and metamorphosis of all creation—not merely the immaterial, but the physical."[28] Orthodoxy's great texts for understanding man's right relation to the natural world are therefore not in Genesis but in the Gospels and the Epistles that illuminate them. Lossky, like Ware, cites one of the most important of these in a passage that sums up the place of nature in the vision of the historical Orthodox Church:

> Man is not a being isolated from the rest of creation; by his very nature he is bound up with the whole of the universe, and St. Paul bears witness that the whole of creation awaits the future glory which will be revealed in the sons of God (Rom. 8:18–22). This cosmic awareness has never been absent from Eastern spirituality, and is given expression in theology as well as in liturgical poetry, in iconography, and, perhaps above all, in the ascetical writings of the masters of the spiritual life of the Eastern Church. . . . In his way to union with God, man in no way leaves creatures aside, but gathers together in his love the whole cosmos disordered by sin, that it may at last be transfigured by grace.[29]

The Failures of Environmental History

Even a cursory glance, then, at the standard introductory works on Orthodox history and theology published in English before or shortly after White's essay suffices to demonstrate that Orthodoxy contradicts the accepted academic view of historical Christianity's approach to the environment. So it is hardly surprising that the pervasive influence of the White thesis, both among those who accept it and those who contest it, has involved a striking neglect of the Eastern Orthodox Christian vision of nature. In the more than four decades since White wrote, the widespread omission of all but the most superficial treatment of Orthodoxy from accounts of historical Christian attitudes toward nature is nothing short of remarkable. It is also indefensible, whether or not one has the least regard for Orthodoxy as a vision of truth.

In many instances, Orthodoxy is simply ignored, as works of environmental history make generalizations about "Christianity" that are irreconcilable with a knowledge of Eastern Christianity or anthologize Christian approaches to nature, past or present, without acknowledging the Orthodox tradition. This difficulty arises both in works where Christianity is a central concern and in more general studies.

Thus, to take a handful of examples, an article that attempts to set forth "The One Body of Christian Environmentalism" by drawing on "six core [Christian] traditions" completely ignores Orthodoxy; Peter Hay's authoritative *Main Currents in Western Environmental Thought* fails to mention Orthodoxy in its extensive discussion of Christian attitudes toward nature; a work subtitled *An Ecumenical Approach to the Environmental Crisis* is ecumenical enough to embrace Protestantism, Catholicism, Judaism, and such recent spiritual movements as Goddess feminism—but not Orthodoxy, which it ignores; an anthology of essays "that seeks to answer the question 'What has Christianity to offer to the current debate on the environment?'" includes no Orthodox answers; the volume on *Attitudes to Nature* in the series Themes in Religious Studies has an appropriately lengthy chapter on Christianity that never mentions the Orthodox Church; and remarkably, even a work titled *Nature Reborn: The Ecological and Cosmic Promise of Christian Theology* nowhere acknowledges the existence of the Orthodox tradition.[30]

Compounding the problem of neglect is a persistent carelessness of terminology: the inveterate tendency of writers on the history of Christian ecology to use the terms "Christian" or "Christianity" when what they obviously mean is "Western Christian" or "Western Christianity." The historical overview in Michael Northcott's *The Environment and Christian Ethics* is typical in this respect, devoting some forty pages to an analysis of "Christian" developments that in fact pertains to Western Christian developments alone. Such arrogant synecdoche effectively erases Orthodoxy from Christian history, yet the reader cognizant of the Christian East who so much as glances at this literature soon learns to make her silent corrections habitual.[31]

In justice, it must be acknowledged that almost since the time of White's essay some treatments of Christianity's environmental history have accurately integrated Orthodox history. In 1975, the Anglican theologian A. M. Allchin wrote eloquently of the early Orthodox understanding of the natural world. A 1980 work by a group of scholars at Calvin College, Michigan, included a concise and sensitive summary of the Orthodox approach to nature. A 1990 anthology of "contemporary approaches to ecological theology" included an essay by the Oriental Orthodox scholar Paulos Mar Gregorios.[32] And more recent years have seen an increasing number of works that fully and perceptively integrate Orthodoxy's historical understanding: Charles Cummings's *Eco-Spirituality*, James A. Nash's *Loving Nature*, Duncan Reid's "The End of Matter," Denis Edwards's *Ecology at the Heart of Faith*, and Willis Jenkins's *Ecologies of Grace* notable among them.[33] These are grounds for hope.

For the most part, however, even where Orthodox belief is acknowledged, it is not addressed with the adequacy and integration that would permit it to inform the reader's understanding of Christianity as a whole. Typically, the only significant Orthodox history consists of brief discussions of some of the Eastern Fathers, occasionally accompanied by the desert ascetics, before the author moves on to focus exclusively on developments in the Western Church. The result is almost formulaic, a ritual bow to the East before the Western story can unfold. H. Paul Santmire's influential and otherwise valuable study *The Travail of Nature: The Ambiguous Ecological Promise of Christian Theology* is unfortunately representative. Santmire provides a chapter on the Classical world, followed by twenty-three pages on Irenaeus and Origen—and then devotes the rest of his 274-page account exclusively to the Christian West; the "Christian theology" of his title knows nothing of the Christian East. Similarly, Robin Attfield titles one historical survey "Christian Attitudes to Nature" but evinces no consciousness of Orthodox history after the Patristic era.[34] One would scarcely discern from such treatments that Orthodoxy is a living faith with a highly developed, integral, and historically continuous theology of nature.

What is the explanation for this scholarly neglect? Doubtless it lies partly in the sort of laziness that Susan Bratton describes: a tendency "to rely on a few well-known texts . . . and to dwell on the best-known figures and groups," resulting in "a historiography that dabbles in the most accessible literatures and then summarizes information from widely disjunct sources and eras."[35] To this explanation one must surely add, here as in so many other realms, the long, tragic shadow of the Great Schism as well as the proportionally marginal, culturally introverted, institutionally fragmented, and ethnically segregated situation of the contemporary Orthodox Church in nearly all parts of the world outside its historical homelands. One might wish but can scarcely expect that a society where Orthodoxy goes almost unnoticed will produce scholarship where it is otherwise.

The Consequences of Neglect

Demonstrably, then, the neglect of Orthodoxy is real and persistent. Yet the question must be asked: does it matter? Unfortunate though it may be, why is environmental history's neglect of Orthodox Christianity important?

At the most straightforward level, integrating Orthodoxy into Christianity's environmental history is simply a matter of accuracy. To speak of the Christian understanding of nature without including the Orthodox Christian understanding of nature is to misrepresent that history by obscuring its breadth and complexity. It is also to misrepresent the beliefs of the Undivided Church of the First Millennium, the common heritage of all Christians—and therefore very much a part of the intellectual heritage of the Western world and the cultures transformed by its imperial reach.

It can nevertheless be argued that the neglect of Orthodoxy in the annals of environmental history is a small thing, because the Christian East has for so long been numerically inferior to the Christian West and because relative to Western Christianity, Orthodoxy has had so little influence on global environmental developments. To argue thus, however, is to miss a fundamental point. The portion of the White thesis that remains most vital is not its claim that Christianity is primarily responsible for the contemporary environmental crisis, a claim that (as we have seen) few historians would now make unqualified and to which the Orthodox Church is indeed almost irrelevant. It is, rather, its claim that Christianity is at best indifferent if not actually inimical to the natural world and thus singularly ill equipped to address the environmental crisis. And to the debate on that claim Orthodox Christian history is not only relevant but transformative.

The integration of Orthodox Christian history into the debate over historical Christian approaches to nature demonstrates that Christianity is not the problem; Western Christianity is, or certain mutations within it that have deformed it from its source. Orthodox history proves that there is nothing inherent in the Christian vision, nothing essential to Christianity, that is hostile to nature or conducive to its abuse. If traditional Christianity is to be rejected or excluded from the spiritual inheritance marshaled against global environmental catastrophe, it must be on other grounds. On the contrary, the Orthodox experience suggests that Christianity carries at its heart a profoundly ecological vision of sacrificial love for the cosmos, of sacred and potentially divinized materiality, and of embodied—indeed, enearthed—divinity. It calls the natural world into eternal love and names its degradation a sin, a moral enormity that defies the will of God and the very purpose for which both man and nature were made.[36]

This Orthodox history matters particularly, moreover, because the story of Christianity's vision of nature now accepted in academic writings has become the story accepted by the general public also, at least throughout much of the English-speaking world. No longer is it merely in academia that "the claim that Christianity is ecologically bankrupt is widely assumed to be a self-evident fact." Instead, there now exists also a widespread "popular characterization of Christianity as an anti-ecological religion."[37] The White thesis, unnamed and unrecognized as such, has long since escaped the confines of historians' discourse to become a commonplace of contemporary culture.

This development is particularly evident among environmentalists, or "greens." White's article was reprinted in "the first major manifesto" of the environmental movement, the 1970 *Environmental Handbook*.[38] By the 1990s, Wendell Berry could write that "the culpability of Christianity in the destruction of the natural world, and the uselessness of Christianity to any effort to correct that destruction, are now established clichés of the [environmental] movement."[39] Such assumptions continue to flourish.[40] This, too, is why the neglect of Orthodoxy in environmental history matters: it means that those working most intensively to address the global environmental crisis are likely to believe traditional Christianity complicit in its development and irrelevant if not antithetical to its solution.

The Crisis of the Western Church

To a remarkable degree, absent awareness of the Orthodox example, such has also been the conclusion of Christians themselves. What, after all, has been the Western Christian response to environmental crisis in the years since White wrote? Apart from the widespread antipathy to environmental concerns among certain Evangelical Protestants, it has taken three forms.

In the first place, in Western societies historically identified with Christianity, the decades since the 1960s have witnessed a proliferation of radical semi-Christian, counter-Christian, and even anti-Christian faiths and philosophies such as ecofeminism, neopaganism, "geopaganism," and even Deep Ecology. These are notable for their formative rejection of traditional Christianity on explicitly ecological grounds. Inasmuch as many of their participants come from Christian backgrounds—and as Christianity's supposed ecological weakness forms an essential component of their foundational identities—these movements must be seen as Christian heresies, in a technically descriptive rather than evaluative use of that term. Their worldviews are both dependent on elements incompatible with orthodox Christianity and consciously shaped in corrective opposition to it.[41]

The character of these movements as Christian heresies fueled in part by environmental anguish becomes clearer when one recognizes that they are merely the end of a continuum that includes fundamental ecological critiques of Christianity by those still within the Church. Here is the second widespread Western Christian response to the global environmental crisis.

One thinks of Thomas Berry, who argues the imperative for "a new type of religious orientation" toward a "sense of the sacred character of the natural world as our primary revelation of the divine"; or of Matthew Fox, who urges Christianity to replace its "Fall/redemption" theology with an Earth-centered "creation spirituality" and the vision of a universal "Cosmic Christ"; of Gordon Kaufman, who calls on Christians to "conceive of God, humanity, and their relationship to each other in a way different from that found in traditional Christian thinking, a way that will facilitate . . . an ecological ethic"; or of Sallie McFague, who advocates an "encompassing agenda . . . to deconstruct and reconstruct the central symbols of the Jewish and Christian traditions," a "paradigm shift" to "a cosmocentric rather than anthropocentric focus" for Christian faith.[42]

The radicalism of such projects is evident in their language; they call for central elements of Christian belief to be discarded and replaced. It is striking, however, that similarly radical language pervades even the third and least radical of the widespread Western Christian responses to the global environmental crisis: the efforts within the churches to recover and freshly emphasize stewardship toward nature and other minor aspects of the Christian tradition that run counter to the destructive tendencies identified in the White thesis. Chastened by its claims and by the like conclusions of their own researches, many Western Christian bodies have begun to supplement and even replace their traditional theological and pastoral foci with unprecedented attention to and advocacy of the ideals of stewardship, "ecojustice," and "creation care."[43] This so-called greening of the churches is a vital movement arising from much sincere and often creative soul searching. Yet its character as a new direction for Western Christianity, not the reaffirmation of an older vision, is clear in the language its advocates use to describe it. "If the Christian church is to make a positive contribution" to solving the ecological crisis, Santmire argued in 1970, "many things within the sphere of the church's own life and thought must be corrected and reformed."[44] In the decades since, a host of Western Christian writers have spoken likewise, hailing an "ecological reformation of Christianity" involving "ecotheological reinterpretations of doctrine," "the basis of a new Christian reformation," "a new Christian theology," "a new Christianity" that is "the transformation of the tradition in which we now stand," "the Catholic tradition . . . reinterpreted, revised," "attempts to reformulate the Christian tradition," "the disclosure of a new paradigm for theological thought."[45] Implicit in all such language is the White thesis and its legacy: the conviction that the main body of Christian tradition is inadequate to address the ecological predicament and must be fundamentally reformed.

This, then, is the most important and far-reaching reason why the neglect of Orthodox Christianity in environmental history matters, and matters greatly. It has meant that Western Christians—the majority of Christians on Earth—are as ignorant as secular academics, environmentalists, and the general public of the Orthodox vision of nature beloved, redeemed, and transfigured into eternal life that is the heritage of all Christians from the Undivided Church—and that Orthodoxy has carried forward undiminished to the present hour. Such neglect has allowed the global environmental crisis to precipitate a crisis in Christian faith and self-understanding, a crisis met by the deliberate abandonment of tradition rather than its renewal and replenishment from ancient and vital roots. For the greening of the churches, however devotedly engaged, has been the grafting upon old vines of alien shoots: in the words of a Roman Catholic writer, "the Church is not leading the way but seeking to legitimize, appropriate, and refine cultural and philosophical trends originating outside itself.... There is no 'environmental ethic' simply waiting to be drawn forth from scripture or tradition."[46] Here again is Paul Shepard's claim, made in this instance by a distinguished Christian writer, that a Christianity alive to the spiritual importance of nature is "a 'tradition' that never existed." The failure of environmental historians to identify and integrate the Orthodox heritage has silenced vast reaches of the Christian past, stifling much of the holy wisdom that might yet recall the Earth and its peoples from the brink of human catastrophe and ecological death.

The Reintegration of Orthodoxy

To bring that wisdom forth anew is therefore a great and urgent task for Orthodox Christians. The moment is at hand, for in the face of such immense threats as climate change, even secular commentators acknowledge the role of faith: "the need for an unselfish love of nature," writes Joachim Radkau, "and thus for a quasi-religious foundation to the affection for the natural world—is greater than ever before in history."[47] Orthodoxy sees the whole of history in the light of the Age to Come, the Kingdom of God, the Paschal "day without evening." History is ultimately inseparable from eschatology. Something similar might be said, ironically, of the secular discipline of environmental history, where in our own time the *telos* of impending catastrophe rips away history's illusion that it can be anything other than the delineation of the particular dimensions within which humanity may still construct its fate. By countenancing a Christianity that understands nature to be seeded already with eternity, quickened by a God "who is everywhere present and fills all things," environmental history may yet help enable humankind to reshape the future out of a sacred past.[48]

If this be a uniquely Orthodox vocation to the contemporary world, there is heartening evidence that many within the Orthodox Church both recognize and embrace it. Foremost among them has been the current Ecumenical Patriarch, Bartholomew I, justly hailed as "the Green Patriarch" for his role as Christianity's most important voice on the environment, as well as his immediate predecessor, Demetrios I, who in 1989 established September 1—the first day of the ecclesiastical year—as the Day of the Protection of the Environment.[49] Increasingly, other Orthodox hierarchs and theological writers have also illuminated the Orthodox understanding of nature for a wide and growing audience.[50] Meanwhile, formal Orthodox participation in ecumenical activities such as the U.S. National Council of Churches of Christ, the World Council of Churches, and official rapprochements with the Vatican have furnished unsurpassed opportunities to communicate Orthodoxy's ecological understanding. The results are clear: in numerous ways, from the demonstrable influence of Patriarch Bartholomew to the increasingly frequent and well-informed acknowledgment of Orthodoxy in recent ecological publications, planetary crisis has galvanized an often-insular Church to fresh encounter with a suffering world.[51]

In embracing this work, we Orthodox can at last refute the false image of Christianity upheld by the White thesis in its manifestations both popular and academic—and can permit the crisis of the Earth to be a means of healing revelation, enabling others to glimpse, perhaps for the first time, the inexhaustible love of Christ for all that He has made. Against the charge of antimaterialism, let us offer to the Earth and our brothers and sisters the Resurrection of the body, the radical materialism of St. John of Damascus, the true asceticism of monastic silences, and the theology of the icon that proclaims the whole of matter suffused with the unspeakable amplitude of the Energies of God. Against dominion as domination, let us offer St. Seraphim of Sarov and St. Herman of Spruce Island and their bear companions, Elder Isidore of Gethsemane Skete singing psalms to the frogs, Fr. Gelasios of Simonopetra and his ministry to cats, Elder Amphilochios of Patmos and his proclamation that one who does not love the trees does not love God, and St. Silouan the Athonite in his exquisite tenderness for "the little leaf."[52] Against narrow biblicalism, let us offer the Tradition that created the Bible, with its liturgies of water, fire, bread, incense, architecture, song, flowers, oil, kneeling, fruit, and the baptism of all the waters of the Earth by the very body of the Son of God. Against the charge of anthropocentrism, let us offer the poetry of love that fills the great "Akathist of Thanksgiving, in Praise of

God's Creation," singing to Christ: "How beautiful art Thou in the triumph of spring when all creatures arise! And in thousands of harmonious ways joyfully cry unto Thee. . . . The whole Earth, Thy bride, awaiteth her Eternal Bridegroom."[53]

Nor must we forget what we can learn from heretics and from the self-declared enemies of faith: that if we are to baptize our culture as Christ taught us to baptize all cultures and as the Spirit led us in the gift of Pentecost, if we are to baptize our postmodern, post-Christian global milieu as St. Innocent and St. Herman sanctified indigenous Alaska, then we cannot flee the world but must embrace it in its wounded longing, finding in its disease its stifled hunger for the *eros* of Christ. And so let us offer to the ecofeminists and the Deep Ecologists and the neopagans and the enraged atheist environmentalists and all who suffer at the suffering of nature our humility, our repentance, the passionate love of all creation that Dostoevsky imaged in the figure of Fr. Zossima and that St. Isaac the Syrian imaged in the radiance of his tears—and the sense of the Divine Beauty in the Earth, *kata panta kai dia panta*, that has already, we know of a certainty, remade the world.[54]

A NEW HEAVEN AND A NEW EARTH: ORTHODOX CHRISTIAN INSIGHTS FROM THEOLOGY, SPIRITUALITY, AND THE SACRAMENTS

John Chryssavgis

Theological and Historical Context

Contributing to the ecumenical statement by the National Council of Churches on the environment, published in the form of an open letter in 2005 and entitled "God's Earth is Sacred: An Open Letter to Church and Society in the United States" (http://www/nccusa.org/news.14.02.05theologicalstatement.html), was a natural response for me as an Orthodox theologian. Ecumenical Patriarch Bartholomew has long assumed an active leadership in this field, placing ecological issues at the center of his ministry. This article examines some of his initiatives, while exploring some of the biblical and theological insights that continue to shape his ecological vision. It also presents a spiritual and sacramental interpretation of the "guiding norms for church and society" proposed by the open letter of the NCCUSA, particularly the affirmation of justice and humility, generosity and frugality, solidarity and compassion.

Setting the Scene

In considering the theological foundation for an ecological consciousness, I sometimes find it useful to journey back to the story of creation. Whenever we think of the Genesis account of creation, we tend to ignore our connection to the environment. Perhaps it is our natural reaction—or perhaps it is a sign of arrogance—but we often overemphasize our creation "in the image of God" (Gen. 1:26) and overlook our creation from "the dust of the ground" (Gen. 2:7). Yet our "heavenliness" should not overshadow our "earthliness."

Most people forget that we human beings did not even get a day to ourselves in Genesis; we shared the sixth day with the creeping and crawling things of the world (Gen. 1:24–26). There is a binding unity and continuity that we share with all of God's creation; it is helpful to recall this truth.

Of course, in more recent years we have been painfully reminded of this truth when we learn of the extinction of flora and fauna, witness soil degradation and forest clearance, and suffer from the effects of air and water pollution. However, our urgent concern for the environment does not result from any superficial threat or even some sentimental romanticism. Rather, it arises from our effort to honor and dignify God's creation. It is a way of paying attention to "the mourning of the land" (Hosea 41:3) and "the groaning of creation" (Rom. 8:22).

This is the reason why the Ecumenical Patriarchate has organized, among other initiatives, a number of international and interdisciplinary symposia over the last decade: ones in the Aegean Sea (1995) and the Black Sea (1997), along the Danube River (1999) and in the Adriatic Sea (2002), in the Baltic Sea (2003), on the Amazon River (2006), and on the Mississippi River (2009). Like the air that we breathe, water is a source of life; if defiled, the very essence of our existence is threatened. Tragically, however, we appear to be caught up in selfish lifestyles that repeatedly ignore the constraints of nature, constraints neither deniable nor negotiable. There will be some things that we learn about our planet's capacity for survival that we will discover only when things are beyond the point of no return.

Initiatives and Activities of the Ecumenical Patriarchate

The environmental initiatives of the Ecumenical Patriarchate date back to the mid-1980s with the third session of the Pre-Synodal Pan-Orthodox Conference held in Chambésy (October 28–November 6, 1986). Representatives at this meeting expressed concern for the abuse of the natural environment, especially as this appears in more affluent Western societies. The meeting also underlined the harm of war, racism, and inequality on human societies and the environment. The emphasis was on leaving a better world for future generations. Several inter-Orthodox meetings followed on the subject of "Justice, Peace, and the Integrity of Creation": the first of three consultations was held in Sofia, Bulgaria (1987). A third inter-Orthodox consultation was held in Minsk, Belarus (1989), while an environmental program was also piloted in Ormylia, Greece (1990).

The second—and perhaps most significant—of these consultations was held in Patmos, Greece (1988), to mark the nine-hundredth anniversary of the historic Monastery of St. John the Theologian. The then Ecumenical

Patriarch, Dimitrios, assigned Metropolitan John (Zizioulas) of Pergamon as Patriarchal representative to this conference, entitled "Revelation and the Future of Humanity" and organized jointly by the Patriarchate and the Greek Ministry of Cultural Affairs in cooperation with the local civil authorities. One of the primary recommendations of this conference was that the Ecumenical Patriarchate should designate one day each year for the protection of the natural environment. This conference proved a catalyst for subsequent Patriarchal initiatives on the environment.

In 1989, Patriarch Dimitrios, the immediate predecessor of Patriarch Bartholomew, his closest adviser, published the first encyclical letter on the environment. Dimitrios was known for his meekness, and it was fitting that during his tenure the worldwide Orthodox Church was invited to dedicate a day of prayer for the protection of the environment, which human beings have treated so harshly. This encyclical, proclaimed on the occasion of the first day of the new ecclesiastical calendar, formally established September 1 as a day for all Orthodox Christians within the jurisdiction of the Ecumenical Patriarchate to offer prayers for the preservation of the natural creation. A similar encyclical is published annually on the first day of September.

In 1990, the foremost hymnographer on Mount Athos, Monk Gerasimos Mikrayiannanites, was commissioned by the Ecumenical Patriarchate to compose a service of supplication for the environment. The Orthodox Church has traditionally prayed for the environment. Whereas, however, in the past, Orthodox faithful prayed to be delivered from natural calamities, the Ecumenical Patriarch now called Orthodox Christians to pray that the planet may be delivered from the abusive and destructive acts of human beings.

A month after his election in 1991, the present Ecumenical Patriarch, Bartholomew, convened an ecological gathering entitled "Living in the Creation of the Lord." That convention on the island of Crete was officially opened by Prince Philip, the Duke of Edinburgh and International Chairman of the WWF. In the following year, Patriarch Bartholomew called an unprecedented meeting of all Orthodox Patriarchs and Primates in Istanbul, submitting a historical expression of unity in theological vision and pastoral concern. The Ecumenical Patriarch again introduced the topic of the protection of the natural environment, inviting all the Orthodox leaders to inform their churches about the critical significance of this issue for our times. The official Message of the Orthodox Primates endorsed September 1 as a day of pan-Orthodox prayer for the environment.

In the summer of 1992, the Duke of Edinburgh visited the Ecumenical Patriarchate for an environmental convocation at the Theological School of

Halki. In November 1993, the Ecumenical Patriarch returned the visit, meeting with the Duke at Buckingham Palace, where they sealed a friendship of common purpose and active cooperation for the preservation of the environment. In June 1994, an ecological seminar was convened at the historic Theological School of Halki, the first of five successive annual summer seminars on diverse aspects of the environment: "Environment and Religious Education" (June 1994), "Environment and Ethics" (June 1995), "Environment and Communications" (July 1996), "Environment and Justice" (June 1997), and "Environment and Poverty" (June 1998). These seminars, the first held at such a level in any Orthodox Church context, were designed to promote environmental awareness and action, engaging leading theologians, environmentalists, scientists, civil servants, and especially students. Participants from all over the world represented the major Christian confessions and world religions.

Convinced that any appreciation of the environmental concerns of our times must occur in dialogue with other Christian confessions, other religious faiths, and the scientific disciplines, in 1994 Patriarch Bartholomew established the Religious and Scientific Committee. He was convinced that, as we share the earth, so do we share the responsibility for our pollution of the earth and the obligation to find tangible ways of healing the natural environment. This ecumenical and interdisciplinary committee is chaired by Metropolitan John of Pergamon, formerly a visiting professor of theology at King's College, London, and currently a professor at the University of Thessalonika. To date, as already mentioned, the Religious and Scientific Committee has hosted six international, interdisciplinary, and interreligious symposia to reflect on the fate of the rivers and seas and to force the pace of religious debate on the natural environment. These symposia have gathered leading scientists, environmentalists, and journalists as well as senior policymakers and representatives of the world's main religious faiths in an effort to draw global attention to the plight of the rivers and seas of the world. Once again, participants meet in plenary, workshop, and briefing sessions, hearing a variety of speakers on various environmental and ethical themes. Delegates also visit key environmental sites in the particular region of the symposium.

Orthodox Theology: Three Ways of Perceiving the World

One of the hymns of the Orthodox Church chanted on the Feast of the Epiphany (January 6, marking the Baptism of Jesus Christ in the River Jordan), a feast of renewal and regeneration for the entire world, eloquently articulates this tragedy: "I have become the defilement of the air, the land, and the water."

How, then, are we to restore within ourselves a sense of wonder before God's creation? Our theology presents us with three helpful ways:

icons (namely, the way we perceive creation);
liturgy (namely, the way we celebrate creation); and
asceticism (namely, the way we respect creation).

The Iconic Vision of Nature

A sense of the holy in nature implies that everything that breathes praises God (Ps. 150:6); the entire world is a "burning bush of God's energies," as Gregory Palamas claimed in the fourteenth century. When our heart is sensitive, then "our eyes are opened to discern the beauty of created things" (Abba Isaac the Syrian, seventh century). Seeing clearly is precisely what icons teach us to do. The world of the icon offers new insights into reality. It reveals the eternal dimension in everything that we experience. Our age, it may be said, is characterized by a sense of self-centeredness toward the natural world, by a lack of awareness of the beyond. We appear to be inexorably trapped within the confines of our individual concerns. We have broken the sacred covenant between our selves and our world.

Well, the icon restores; it reconciles. The icon reminds us of another way of living and offers a corrective to the culture that we have created, which gives value only to the here and now. The icon reveals the inner vision of all, the world as created and as intended by God. Very often, it is said, the first image attempted by an iconographer is that of the Transfiguration of Christ on Mt. Tabor. This is precisely because the iconographer struggles to hold together this world and the next, to transfigure this world in light of the next. For, by disconnecting this world from heaven, we have in fact desacralized both. The icon articulates with theological conviction our faith in the heavenly kingdom. It does away with any objective distance between this world and the next, between material and spiritual, between body and soul, time and eternity, creation and divinity. The icon speaks in this world the language of the age to come.

This is why the doctrine of the Divine Incarnation is at the very heart of iconography. For, in the icon of Jesus Christ, the uncreated God assumes a creaturely face, a beauty that is "exceeding" (Ps. 44:2), a "beauty that can save the world" (Fyodor Dostoevsky). And in Orthodox icons, faces—whether of Christ or of the saints—are always frontal; two eyes always gaze back at the beholder. The heart becomes—as the desert father would describe it in the fourth century—"all eyes," eternally receptive of divine grace. Christ is in our midst, here, Emmanuel (Matt. 1:23). Profile signifies sin; it implies a rupture in communication. "I see" means that "I am seen," which in turn means that I am in communion. This is the powerful experience of the invisible and the immortal, a passing over—a Passover, or *Pascha*—to another way of seeing and "a different way of living," as our Easter hymns proclaim.

Indeed, the entire world is an icon, a door opening up to this new reality. Everything in this world becomes a seed. "Nothing is a vacuum in the face of God," wrote Irenaeus of Lyons in the wake of the apostolic era; "everything is a sign of God." Thus, in icons, rivers have a human form; so, too, do the sun and the moon and the stars and the waters. All of them assume human faces; all of them acquire a personal dimension—just like people; just like God.

The Liturgy of Nature

What an icon does with matter, the liturgy does with time. If we are guilty of relentless waste, it is perhaps because we have lost the spirit of worship. We are no longer respectful pilgrims on this earth; we have been reduced to mere tourists. Our original sin lies in our prideful refusal to receive the world as a sacrament of communion.

By liturgical, however, I do not mean ritual. I mean dynamic movement. This world is a never-ending movement toward the kingdom. It is profoundly and intimately related to the heavenly kingdom. This means that what we do on earth matters for what we believe about heaven. The way we relate to other people on earth reflects the way we pray to God in heaven. And, by extension, we respond to nature with the same sensitivity and the same tenderness with which we respond to human beings. We have learned not to treat people like things, because they are created "in the image of God." We must now learn not to treat even things like mere things, because they contain the very trace of God.

Liturgy, then, is precisely a commemoration of this innate connection between God and people and things. It is a celebration of the sense of communion; it is a dance of life. When we recognize this interdependence of all persons and all things—this "cosmic liturgy," as Maximus the Confessor described it in the seventh century—then we will begin to resolve the environmental crisis. For, then we will have acquired, as St. Isaac the Syrian noted in the same century, "A merciful heart burning with love for all of creation—for humans, birds, beasts, and demons—for all God's creatures."

The world in its entirety comprises an integral part of the liturgy. God is praised by trees and birds, glorified by the stars and moon (Ps. 18:2), worshiped by sea and sand. There is a dimension of art and music in the world. This means, however, that whenever we reduce our spirituality to ourselves and our own interests, we forget that the liturgy implores God for the renewal of the whole polluted cosmos. And whenever we narrow life to our own concerns and desires, we neglect our vocation to raise creation into the kingdom.

The Way of the Ascetics

Of course, this world does not always feel or even look like heaven; a quick glance at the suffering inflicted through wars is sufficient to bring us to our senses. Nonetheless, St. Paul writes, "Through Christ, God was pleased to reconcile to himself all things, whether on earth or in heaven, by making peace through the blood of his cross" (Col. 1:20). Reference to "the blood of the cross" is a clear indication of the cost involved. There is a price to pay for our wasting. Only a spirit of asceticism can lead to a spirit of gratitude and love, to the rediscovery of wonder and beauty in our relationship with the world. So the ascetic way is a way of liberation. The ascetic is one who is free, uncontrolled by attitudes that abuse the world, characterized by self-restraint, as well as the ability to say "no" or "enough." The goal of asceticism is moderation, not repression. Its content is positive, not negative: it looks to service, not selfishness; to reconciliation, not renunciation. Without asceticism, none of us is authentically human.

Consider one example of asceticism in our tradition, namely fasting. We fast from dairy and meat products for half the year, almost as if to reconcile one half of the year with the other, secular time with the time of the kingdom. What does fasting imply? To fast is to learn to give and not simply to give up. It is not to deny but, in fact, to offer; it is learning to share, to connect with human beings and the natural world. Fasting means breaking down barriers with my neighbor and my world: recognizing in others' faces, icons, and in the earth the face of God. Ultimately, to fast is to love, to see clearly, to restore the original beauty of the world. To fast is to move away from what I want to what the world needs. It is to liberate creation from control and compulsion. Fasting is to value everything for itself and not simply for ourselves. It is to be filled with a sense of goodness, of God-liness. It is to see all things in God and God in all things.

Orthodox Practice: Three Models of Caring for the Earth

Now, if our ecological prayer is to move from the distant periphery of an abstract theology to the center stage of practical living, if our spirituality is to become "incarnate," then there are three complementary models that are proposed—and have been tested—by the Orthodox tradition.

The Biblical Model

According to this model, the Church is called to be in solidarity with the weakest parts of the Body of Christ. It must stand for the most vulnerable, the helpless or voiceless elements of this world, which according to St. Paul "groan in travail, awaiting their liberation from the children of God" (Rom. 8:22). This implies a kind of cosmic "liberation theology": "One member cannot say to another, 'I have no need of you.' On the contrary, those members that seem to be weaker are indispensable . . . and our less respectable members are treated with great respect" (1 Cor. 12:20–25).

The earth, too, is a member of our body, a part of our flesh, inseparable from our history and our destiny. In the same way as the God of Israel once heard the cry of the poor and the oppressed (Ex. 3 and Jonah 4), God also hears the silent cry of the earth. This is the biblical covenant, God's promise to the people of Israel: God listens to the world; God attends to the world; God tends to the smallest details of this earth.

The Ascetic Model

In the second model, we might think of the three R's of the ascetic life: renunciation, repentance, and responsibility.

Renunciation is an ancient response—indeed, it is pre-Christian; the ancient Greek philosophers recommended a simple lifestyle. It is also a universal response—indeed, it is even non-Christian; Aboriginal and Indian peoples know this very well. As we have seen, renunciation is a way of learning to share. Therefore, it has social consequences; it reminds us to use material goods respectfully. Renunciation is about living simply and about simply living.

Repentance is a return to a God-given life "according to nature," as the Church Fathers would say. In repentance, we confess that we have sinned—the open letter by the National Council of Churches cites the definition by His All-Holiness Ecumenical Patriarch Bartholomew of the abuse of the natural environment as sin. Moreover, in all humility, we must confess that we do not share, that we are self-centered, that we in fact abuse the resources of the earth. Through repentance, we recognize that we have fallen short of our vocation "to serve and preserve the earth" (Gen. 2:15).

Responsibility is our challenge, our choice. Having renounced whatever clutters our mind and our life, and after repenting of our wastefulness, we can direct our lives in love and reverence toward creation and Creator.

The Sacramental Model

And—at least in the Orthodox Christian practice—we achieve this through the sacraments, which have an undeniable and indelible environmental seal. Unfortunately, the sacraments are often reduced to ritual observances. Yet communion is much more than a way of pious inspiration or individual reward. It is the imperative to share. It is crucial, then, that we recall the sacramental dimension of the world, recognizing that nothing is merely secular or profane. Everything is created by God and embraced by God. God is—and is within—the very constitution of our world. If God were withdrawn from the world, the world would collapse. Before Vespers each evening, we recite the Ninth Hour and recall our vocation to realize the presence of God "at every hour and every moment, both in heaven and on earth, indeed in all places of his dominion" (Ps. 103:22). Such is the depth of a sacramental worldview.

Orthodox Christians in fact prefer to speak of "mystery" rather than "sacrament," the latter of which tends to imply the acquisition of something "objective." Traditionally, it is said that there are seven mysteries or sacraments. Yet this categorization is neither completely true nor always helpful. The Orthodox Church has never limited itself to seven sacraments, preferring to speak of every moment and aspect of life as being sacramental—from birth through death. Indeed, the funeral service was once also classified as a sacrament in Orthodox liturgical practice. So the sacraments do not work in some magical manner; rather, they function "mystically," silently permeating the hearts and lives of those who choose to be open to the possibility of encounter with God—like the flow of blood in the human body.

Let us consider the mysteries.

In the sacramental way, Baptism becomes more than merely a formal initiation to some exclusive or closed community. Baptism is a re-creation of humanity and the world in the light of Christ. Through the water of Baptism, we are immersed into the death and resurrection of Christ (Rom. 14:8), being "planted together" (Rom. 6:5) forever with Christ. In a world where water is so carelessly wasted and polluted, the sacrament of Baptism highlights the profound connection between the Spirit of God brooding over "the face of the world," as in the first moments of Genesis, and the entire universe. The living water of the living God is able to renew and sanctify all of creation.

The sacrament of Chrismation is more than a confirmation of our personal membership in the Body of Christ. It recognizes "the seal of the gift of the Holy Spirit" in all human beings, in all corners of the world, and in all elements of the universe. We are, therefore, called to recognize the face of God in the face of each person as well as in the face of the natural world. The word "chrismation" derives from the Greek *chrisma*, which means anointing; the "anointed one" is the "Christ" or the "Messiah" (in Hebrew). Our goal is to be "in Christ" and Christ-like, anointing and healing the entire world.

The sacrament of the Eucharist is of course pregnant with endless possibilities for deepening communion. It is an invitation to conform to the Body of Christ. The Eucharist is not a spiritual reward for rigorous ascetic discipline. Rather, it challenges individuals and communities to work for a just society where basic food and water are plentiful for all and where everyone has enough.

The sacrament of Confession provides more than simply an opportunity to express remorse for the removal of guilt. Forgiveness provides the grace and space "for giving," for sharing. It focuses attention on others and on God's creation—not only on ourselves. It is a way of reintegration into the Body of Christ. But it is also a reintegration into the body of society and the world.

In Marriage, a couple is invited to experience and celebrate communion despite the pain of brokenness, separation, and isolation. How unfortunate it is that this sacrament has been conveniently reduced to a social contract, somehow introducing a romanticized urban lifestyle in Western society. In its spiritual sense, marriage is primarily the experience of the cross, the other side of the coin that we call ascesis. As such, it is the desire for unity between Creator and creation, God and humanity, body and soul, time and eternity, heaven and earth.

Holy Unction is a healing sacrament. In the Orthodox practice, it is celebrated throughout life as the outpouring of "the oil of gladness" on the scars of the soul and the wounds of the world. It aims at healing the breach or brokenness between body and soul, mending the shattered parts of the heart and the earth while reconciling heaven with all of God's creation.

Finally, the sacrament of Ordination is not a formal declaration of the exclusive rights granted to the hierarchy. Priesthood is the royal vocation of all people. Through ordination, the Body of Christ receives new expression and renewed vitality. The whole world becomes a cathedral; every person is ordained for the kingdom, and no place is unhallowed. When we discern the presence of God in everyone and in every place, then we can rejoice and celebrate the fullness of life.

Conclusion

The ultimate image of sacramental communion in the Orthodox Church is represented in color through the icon depicting the hospitality of Abraham and Sarah welcoming three strangers in the desert of Palestine. It is an icon of the communion between the three persons of the Trinity. The story is related in Genesis 18 of Abraham sitting under the oak trees of Mamre: "The Lord appeared to Abraham by the oaks of Mamre, as he sat at the entrance of his tent in the heat of the day" (Gen. 18:1). If we pay close attention to the biblical narrative, not only do the oaks provide refreshing shade for the Patriarch of Israel, but they are the occasion for divine revelation. By analogy, not only do the trees of the world provide sustenance for humankind in diverse ways, but they reflect the very presence of God. Cutting them down implies eliminating the divine presence from our lives. Indeed, the Hebrew interpretation of this text implies that the oak trees themselves—just as the visitors who appeared at the same time—actually reveal God. Indeed, it was not until Abraham recognized the presence of God in the trees (namely, in creation, or *adamah*) that he was also able to recognize God in his visitors (namely, in human beings, or *adam*). Creation, just like the human beings who appeared in the form of angels, is itself the manifestation of God in the world.

The crisis that we are facing in our world is not primarily ecological. It is a crisis concerning the way we envisage or imagine the world. We are treating our planet in an inhuman, godless manner precisely because we fail to see it as a gift inherited from above; it is our obligation to receive, respect, and in turn hand on this gift to future generations. Therefore, before we can effectively deal with problems of our environment, we must change the way we perceive the world. Otherwise, we are simply dealing with symptoms, not with their causes. We require a new worldview if we are to desire "a new heaven and a new earth" (Rev. 21:1). This is our calling; indeed, this is God's command. It would be advisable to hear and heed it now. As His All-Holiness Ecumenical Patriarch Bartholomew declared jointly with the late Pope John Paul II in Venice in 2002: "It is not too late. God's world has incredible healing powers. Within a single generation, we could steer the earth toward our children's future. Let that generation start now, with God's help and blessing."

Proprietors or Priests of Creation?

Metropolitan John (Zizioulas) of Pergamon

I

The development of ecological awareness and sensitivity in the last years has led to the use of various models of speaking about the relation of the human being to nature.[1] The prevailing model is that of *steward*: the human being is the steward of creation. This terminology has become widespread not only among secular ecologists but also among religious ones, and especially among the latter. We encounter it in almost every reference by theologians to the ecological problem. The idea of stewardship is a useful one mainly from the point of view of what it intends to exclude, namely, that the human being is the lord and proprietor of creation. Such an understanding of the human being as a proprietor of creation found support in modern times mainly in two areas: the anthropology of the Enlightenment and Western, particularly Protestant, theology.

The Enlightenment found its typical representatives in this respect in such thinkers as Descartes, Francis Bacon, and even Kant. In the words of Descartes, the development of science would make human beings *maîtres et possesseurs de la nature*, and Francis Bacon in an almost brutal way invites humanity to treat nature as its "slave." Kant, on the other hand, understood humanity's relationship to nature as that of a "judge" whose function is to exercise rational and moral judgment on nature, directing it in accordance with what the human being considers to be right or wrong, good or bad for it.

Protestant theology, on the other hand, particularly in the Calvinist tradition, did its best to exploit the biblical verse "Subdue and have dominion over the earth" (Gen. 1:28) in order to promote, directly or indirectly, capitalist views of work and economy, as Max Weber has demonstrated so clearly. Without such religious ideas, the appearance of the ecological crisis would probably be difficult to explain historically.

The replacement of the model of proprietor and possessor with that of steward of creation may be useful in order to exclude the undoubtedly unacceptable view that the human being is the lord of creation or may behave as such a lord. Ecologists recognized this and adopted the model of stewardship. However, a closer examination of this model would reveal to us its limitations and disadvantages from the ecological viewpoint.

1. Stewardship implies a *managerial* approach to nature. The Greek word *oikonomos*, which stands behind the notion of steward, points to the capacity of the human being to "manage" a given "property" and make "use" of it, albeit within the limits of what has been "entrusted" to humanity. In this sense stewardship resembles what the English mean by the function of a "trustee." A utilitarian implication in the relation of the human being to nature seems to underlie this model. Equally significant is the underlying conception of nature as a "thing" and an "object" to be managed, arranged, rearranged, distributed, etc. by the human being.

2. Stewardship suggests a *conservatist* attitude to nature. The steward is the "guardian" of what is given to him or her, called to conserve it, albeit, as we have just noted, while managing it. This conservatist approach to our relation to nature seems to overlook two important truths. On the one hand, the human being is not called only to "guard" but also to "cultivate" nature, that is, to improve its capacities and help it grow and bring forth fruit. On the other hand, human intervention has already reached such proportions that it would be unrealistic and futile to speak of sheer conservation of the environment. Certain parts of the environment may still be capable of conservation, but other parts have undergone irrevocable changes, and any attempt to preserve them would be unrealistic and in some cases even undesirable.

Thus, the idea of stewardship, much as it is useful to indicate our objection to the view that the human being is the lord and proprietor of creation—a view that accounts historically to a considerable degree for the appearance of the ecological crisis—has its own limitations and would appear to be problematic from the ecological point of view. It may be, therefore, necessary to complement it with another model, namely with what we may describe as *the priest of creation*. Such a model seems to emerge naturally from the Patristic and liturgical tradition of the Orthodox Church, but its existential meaning is universal. The word "priest" is part of religious language, and for this reason it may appear to have a significance limited only to religious people. We shall try to show that this is not so. But to do that we must first clarify our anthropological presuppositions. We cannot tackle the idea of what man—in the sense of *anthropos*, that is, both male and female—is. (From now on we shall use the word "man" in this sense and not in its gendered usage.)

II

What is the being that we call "man"? It is not only theology that tries to answer this question but also science and philosophy. Although each of these three disciplines has something different to say, they cannot but also have something common about this matter. Otherwise there would be no common ground and, therefore, no possibility of a dialogue between them.

For science—and for biology in particular—the human being is very closely connected with what we call animals; he or she is another animal. This view has prevailed in biology ever since Darwin produced his theory of evolution. Although this may sound rather disturbing to theologians, we must bear in mind, as we will see below, that it is important for all of us to remember this connection of the human being with the rest of the animals. Biology approaches the human being as another animal with higher qualities than those of the rest of the animals but with many things in common as well, including intelligence and consciousness. Attributes such as these used to be attached exclusively to human beings in the past. But for biological scientists today, the human being is, in a certain sense, basically an animal.

Philosophy tries to give a different view of the human being. Although it admits that the human being is an animal, it distinguishes man from the animals in one important way. In the past, philosophers made this distinction by saying that humans were specially characterized by intelligence or rationality. However, ever since Darwin showed that intelligence can also be found in other animals and that the difference is a matter of degree and not of kind, philosophy no longer insists on rationality as the special characteristic of man.

The difference seems now to lie in the fact that whereas other animals adjust to the given world—and sometimes they manage that very well, much better than the human being—the human being wants to create its own world, to use the existing world in order to make something specifically human out of it. This is why the human being produces tools of its own, which are used to exploit nature. But more significantly, it treats nature as a raw material from which it creates new realities, as is evident particularly in the case of art. Only the human being can see a tree, for example, and make another tree out of that, a tree which is "his" or "her" tree, bearing the personal seal of the person who painted it. Thus it is creativity that characterizes the human being, and this we cannot find in the animals. Man is a creative being. This is very important, as we will see later, for ecology as well.

In his attempt to be creative and to create his own world, man is normally frustrated, because he tends and wishes to create, as God does, out of nothing and to be fully free from what is given to him as his environment, his "world." It is because the human being has this tendency to use the natural world for his own purposes that he can be both good and bad for creation. The human being can exploit creation in such a way as to subject it to himself and in this way make the natural environment suffer under his dominion.

All this indicates that what distinguishes the human being from the animals is freedom expressed as creativity, as the free creation of something new. There are two ideas here to remember that will be very important for our subject. The first we draw from biological science, and that is that the human being is organically and inseparably linked with the natural world, particularly with the animals. The second is that although he is united with the rest of creation, man tends to rise above creation and make use of it in a free way, either by creating something new or sometimes by simply destroying what is "given" to him.

With these thoughts from science and philosophy in mind, let us now ask what theology thinks the human being is. For theology, the human being is not only related to the rest of creation but also to another factor, one that science does not want to introduce and that philosophy sometimes does but very often does not—namely, God. For theology, God is crucial in order to know what the human being is. The human being must emerge as something different, as a different identity with regard to the animals, with regard to the rest of creation, and also with regard to God. Thus man is a link between God and the world. This is what is expressed in theological terms through the idea of the "image and likeness of God."

In the Bible, when man was created, God said: "Let us now create man in our image and likeness." What does that mean? What does it mean that the human being is an image of God? This has been discussed throughout the centuries, and I will not bother you with all this complex discussion. Instead, I will simply mention that one of the elements that the Fathers saw as expressing this "image of God" in man is rationality (*logos*), that man is a *logikon zoon* ("rational living being"), and that it is through his rationality that he reflects the being of God in creation. However, *logos* or "rationality" had a particular meaning at that time, and it had mainly to do with the capacity of the human being to collect what is diversified and even fragmented in this world and make a unified and harmonious world (*cosmos*) out of that. Rationality was not, as it came to be understood later, simply a capacity to reason with one's mind. Instead, as the ancient Greeks thought of *logos*, it is man's capacity to achieve the unity of the world and to make a *cosmos* out of it. Man has the capacity to unite the world.

There is also another element that was stressed by the Fathers as expressing the "image of God." This is what Gregory of Nyssa calls the *autexousion*—the freedom of the human being. The animals do not have a *logos* in the sense of acquiring a universal grasp of reality, nor do they have freedom from the laws of nature; the human being has to some extent both of these things, and that is very important for him in order to be, as we shall see, the priest of creation. Another aspect of the image of God in man—or rather, another aspect of what man is or represents for theology, particularly Orthodox and Patristic theology—is that man is the "prince of creation" and the microcosm of the whole of creation. One of the Fathers who wrote in the seventh century, St. Maximus the Confessor, developed this idea in particular, namely that in the human being we have the whole world present, a sort of microcosm of the whole universe. Because the human being has this organic link with creation and at the same time the drive to unite creation and to be free from the laws of nature, he can act as the "priest of creation."

III

The priest is the one who freely, as himself an organic part of it, takes the world in his hands to refer it to God and who, in return, brings God's blessing to what he refers to God. Through this act, creation is brought into communion with God himself. This is the essence of priesthood, and it is only the human being who can do it, namely, unite the world in his hands in order to refer it to God so that it can be united with God and thus saved and fulfilled. This is so because, as we said earlier, only the human being is united with creation while being able to transcend it through freedom.

This role of the human being, as the priest of creation, is absolutely necessary for creation itself, because without this reference of creation to God the whole created universe will die. It will die because it is a finite universe, as most scientists accept today. This is theologically a very fundamental belief: the world was not always there but came into being at some point and, for this reason, will "naturally" have an end and come into nonbeing one day.

Therefore, the only way to protect the world from its finitude, which is inherent in its nature, is to bring it into relation with God. This is because God is the only infinite, immortal being, and it is only by relating to him that the world can overcome its natural finitude and its natural mortality.

In other words, when God created the world finite and therefore subject by nature to death and mortality, he wanted this world to live forever and to be united with him—that is, to be in communion with him. It is precisely for this reason that God created the human being. This underlines the significance of man as the priest of creation who would unite the world and relate it to God so that it may live forever.

Now, the human being did not perform this function, and here lies for theology the root of the ecological problem. The human being was tempted to make himself the ultimate point of reference, that is, God. By replacing God with himself—that is, with a finite created being—man condemned the world to finitude, mortality, decay, and death. In other words, the human being rejected his role as the priest of creation by making himself God in creation.

This is what we call in theology the "Fall of man." When this occurred, God did not want the world to die and brought about a way of restoring this lost communion between himself and creation. The Incarnation of the Son of God was precisely about this. Christ is the one who came in order to do what Adam did not do, namely, to be the priest of creation. Through his death and resurrection, Christ aimed precisely at this unity and communion of the whole of creation with God, at the reference of creation back to God again. It is for this reason that Christ is called the "second Adam" or the "last Adam" and that his work is seen as the "recapitulation" (*anakephalaiosis*) of all that exists, that is, of the entire creation.

Now it is this role, which Christ performed personally through his cross and resurrection, that he assigned to his Church, which is his Body. The Church is there precisely to act as the priest of creation who unites the world and refers it back to God, bringing it into communion with him. This takes place in the Church particularly through the sacraments.

The meaning of the sacraments, for example that of baptism, is that through it the attitude of the fallen Adam is reversed. Man dies to his claim to be God in creation and instead recognizes God as its Lord. Through the path of asceticism, the Church educates man to sacrifice his own will and his self-centeredness and subject himself freely to the will of God, thus showing that man has reversed the attitude of the first Adam. Finally, through the Eucharist, the Church proclaims and realizes precisely this priestly function of humanity. The Eucharist consists in taking elements from the natural world, the bread and the wine that represent the created material world, and bringing them into the hands of the human being, the hands of Christ who is the man *par excellence* and the priest of creation, in order to refer them to God.

At this point, it is important to remember—especially those of us who belong to the Orthodox Church and are familiar with the Orthodox Liturgy—that the central point in our Liturgy is when the priest exclaims: "Thine of Thine own we offer unto Thee." This means precisely that the world, the creation, is recognized as belonging to God and is referred back to him. It is precisely the reversal of Adam's attitude, who took the world as his own and referred it to himself. In the Eucharist, the Church does precisely the opposite: the world belongs to God, and we refer it back to its Creator through the priestly action of Christ as the real and true man, the head of the Body of the Church.

IV

Let us now look briefly at the ecological significance of all this.

1. The understanding of the human being as priest rather than steward of creation means that the role of man in creation is neither passive (conservationist) nor managerial, that is, "economic." (The notion of "economy" is deeply linked with that of management, that is, the idea of arranging things according to and for the sake of *expediency* not only in political but also in ecclesiastical language.) The human being is related to nature not *functionally*, as the idea of stewardship would suggest, but *ontologically*: by being the steward of creation the human being relates to nature by what he *does*, whereas by being the priest of creation he relates to nature by what he *is*. The implications of this distinction are very significant. In the case of stewardship our attitude to nature is determined by ethics and morality: if we destroy nature we disobey and transgress a certain law, we become immoral and unethical. In the case of priesthood, in destroying nature we simply *cease to be*; the consequences of ecological sin are not moral but existential. Ecology is in this way a matter of our *esse*, not of our *bene esse*. Our ecological concern becomes in this way far more powerful and efficient than in employing the model of stewardship.

2. The idea of priest of creation gives to ecology a *cultural* dimension. The word "culture" must be taken in its deepest meaning, which is the elevation of an otherwise transitory and ephemeral entity to something of lasting and even eternal value. When an artist creates, he or she wishes to bring about something of eternal value and significance. The priest is in this sense an

artist: he takes the material world in his hands (the bread and the wine, for example, in the case of the Eucharist, which are perishable by nature) and lifts it up to acquire eternal divine meaning. In such an approach the entire *raison d'être* of ecology undergoes a profound change. We do not ask people to respect the environment simply for negative reasons, such as the fear of destruction, etc.—this would be an ecology based on fear. We ask people to take a *positive* view of ecology, something like an attitude of *love* toward nature. As priests rather than stewards we *embrace* nature instead of managing it, and although this may sound romantic and sentimental, its deeper meaning is, as we stated above, ontological, since this "embracing" of nature amounts to our very being, to our existence.

3. Such a cultural dimension of ecology implies that the protection of nature is not contrary to the *development* of nature. The human being is the priest of creation in the sense that the material world he takes in his hands is *transformed* into something better than what it is *naturally*. Nature must be improved through human intervention; it is not to be preserved as it is. In the Eucharist we do not offer to God simply grain or wheat and grapes but bread and wine: natural elements developed and transformed through human labor, in our hands. Ecology is not preservation but development. The model of priest is in this sense far more suggestive and rich than that of steward. It does not, however, bring us back to the model of proprietor, since in the case of priesthood the development of nature through the intermediary of human hands does not end up with the human being and its interests but is referred to God.

Ecology and development have always been, as we all know, two terms that require some kind of reconciliation. (There is always the fear among developing countries that ecology has been "invented" as a means of keeping them underdeveloped.) This is indeed the case if the development of nature has as its ultimate purpose the satisfaction of human needs. But in a priestly approach to nature we develop it not to satisfy our needs as human beings but *because nature itself* stands in need of development through us *in order to fulfill its own being* and acquire a meaning it would not otherwise have. In other words, there is a development of nature that treats it as *raw material for production* and distribution, and there is a development that treats nature as an entity that must be developed *for its own sake*. In the latter case, although the human being is not passive, simply preserving or sustaining nature, he is developing nature with respect for its, and not his, interests, taking care of its fragility and its "groaning in travail," to remember St. Paul's moving expression in Romans 8.

V

I have tried to describe the model of priest of creation in its ecological significance. I hope I have shown some of the advantages that this model may have for ecology compared with other models, especially that of stewardship. I am fully aware that the way things are going with regard to ecology, none of these models would save us. I nevertheless think that the moralistic approach to the ecological problems expressed through such words as "responsibility" has to be complemented with a cultural approach. Our ecological crisis is attributable not so much to a wrong ethic as to a bad ethos; it is a *cultural* problem. In our Western culture we did everything to desacralize life, to fill our societies with legislators, moralists, and thinkers, and we undermined the fact that the human being is also, or rather primarily, a *liturgical* being faced from the moment of birth with a world that he or she must treat either as a sacred gift or as raw material for exploitation and use. We are all born priests, and unless we remain so throughout our lives we are bound to suffer the ecological consequences we are now experiencing. We must allow the idea of priest of creation to reenter our culture and affect our ethos. An ethic that is not rooted in ethos is of little use to ecology.

PART
III

"Love Comes from Meeting God": Historical, Theological, and Philosophical Dimensions

Sedimentation of Meaning in the Concepts of Nature and the Environment

James Carey

One of the concerns of present-day philosophy is the problem identified by Edmund Husserl as "sedimentation." In the history of human thought, a concept emerges that captures an insight or a new way of looking at things. This concept contains a certain density of meaning for those who first come up with it, label it with a name, and incorporate it into their discourse. The term is then communicated in writing to later generations. What was at first grasped actively and with insight is received more and more passively, and with decreasing insight, as a taken-for-granted inheritance. In time, sedimentation occurs—sedimentation not only of the meaning of the concept but also of its problematic character, which did not go unnoticed by those who first came up with the concept. Contemporary discourse, including academic discourse conducted at a relatively high level of sophistication, is saturated with concepts that are employed so thoughtlessly that it is virtually tyrannized by a hand-me-down inheritance that is not adequately understood or even thought much about. A few examples of such concepts are those named by the following terms and expressions: "rights," which in the singular originally meant what is just but is now used in the plural to name an assemblage of entitlements that one is presumably born with simply by virtue of being human; the "unconscious mind," an expression almost as problematic as the oxymoronic "unconscious consciousness"; "culture," which originally named the cultivation of the intellect and imagination and an attendant refinement of outlook and taste but is now used in the plural to designate whatever habits, practices, or so-called lifestyles any particular group of people, however barbaric or rebarbarized, share in common; "number," which originally designated a multitude of units of whatever kind, but always a definite amount, and certainly not a mere symbol to operate on, as some today hold it to be; "science," which originally meant knowledge, particularly demonstrative knowledge, but today means only natural science and those disciplines that imitate, not to say ape, its special methodology.[1]

Instances of such concepts, the original meaning of which has become sedimented across time, can be multiplied. Philosophical, historical, and etymological research into their origins is necessary if we are to avoid having our thought dominated by inherited assumptions that we have not scrutinized and made our own. In this way, inquiry into the history of philosophy, which is where the most important concepts typically emerge, can have a liberating effect, one without any historicist presuppositions, least of all anything as questionable as "progress," which, we note, is another concept whose meaning has become sedimented.[2]

Occasionally, sedimentation occurs when a rather simple concept gets progressively invested with a meaning, ostensibly richer, that it did not originally have. To take just one example, "gravity," which literally meant nothing more than weight or heaviness, has become the name of an invisible, not to say occult, pull that one body exercises on another across empty space, a force we can measure without being able to explain adequately or even define. And this kind of sedimentation is happening, I submit, to the concept of the "environment." The word itself, which is French in origin, means literally what "circuits around," and fifty years ago it was used in close accordance with its etymology to mean just what happens to surround us. Today, the term seems to mean something deeper, though it is not entirely clear what this deeper something is. In some quarters, the word "environment" is routinely capitalized, as though it named a kind of deity for our time: nonjudgmental, immanent, and indifferent to the moral worth of our lives. We are supposed to respect the environment, as though, like us, it too were somehow endowed with fundamental rights that should not be violated. How the environment—again, literally the surroundings—has come to be something that we are to treat with respect, perhaps with something like reverence, is a question well worth exploring. But it is not the theme of this essay. Instead, I want to inquire into the origin and sense of a venerable, two-and-three-quarter-millennia-old concept, one that the concept of the environment seems to be slowly replacing: the concept of nature.

The Greek word for nature is *physis*, from which we get our word "physics." The root of this word is *phy-*, which refers primarily to growing, especially to the growing of plants: the Greek word for plant is *phyton*, that which grows. The first appearance of the word *physis* is in the *Odyssey*. Odysseus is recounting his adventure with the witch Circe. He hears that his men have been bewitched by her and turned into swine. And so he sets out to find a way to free them from her spell. On his way to Circe's abode, he is met by Hermes, the messenger of Zeus. Hermes tells Odysseus about a medicine, a *pharmakon*, that will render him immune to Circe's charms and spells. The medicine is a plant called *moly*, a strange word that is, interestingly, cognate with *mūlam*, a word in another Indo-European language, Sanskrit, that means root.[3] Odysseus says that Hermes uprooted the *moly* plant and showed him the *nature* of it. The *physis*, the nature of the plant, is its growing. This passage from the *Odyssey* is particularly interesting because we see that, in its first appearance in Western thought, nature is presented as something the gods know about but that they do not make and for which they are not responsible in any way. Nature is presented as a kind of limit to divine power. Because Odysseus does not say what he does with the *moly* plant after Hermes shows him its nature, Homer may wish us to think that the only thing Odysseus does with the plant is simply to know that it *has* a nature, to *know* that there is something that is not art, neither human art nor divine art, and deeper, more primal, than either. This interpretation receives support from Circe's words when she fails to charm Odysseus. She exclaims in something like horror that he has a mind (*nous*) that will not be charmed.[4]

In the post-Homeric development of Greek philosophy, nature is a central theme, arguably *the* central theme. Nature is understood to be the principle of impersonal and immanent organization of the world. Nature is contrasted not only with art of any kind but with law (*nomos*) of every kind, including allegedly divine law. It has been argued, persuasively I think, that the discovery of nature in this sense—if discovery rather than invention is what it should be called—inaugurates philosophy as the nonreligious, arguably antireligious, attempt to comprehend the world in its own terms, in terms of its inner constitution rather than in terms of an ultimate, transcendent, divine, originating cause. The meaning of nature in Greek philosophy broadens out far beyond mere growing. Nature becomes a synonym for the being, or rather the essence, of anything that happens to be.[5] This extension seems to be latent in Indo-European languages. *Physis* is, as others have noted, cognate with the third and fourth principle parts of the Latin word for "to be": *sum, esse, fui, futurus*, and so it is cognate with our word "future" as well. There is even strong reason to suspect an etymological connection with the Sanskrit verbal root, √*bhū*, which means "to be."[6]

Aristotle is the Greek philosopher who wrote most extensively and most influentially about nature. His *Physics* attempts to consider nature from every angle. And Aristotle has a theology. He teaches that there is first mover, which he calls both "god" and "the intellect." Aristotle's first mover, however, does not get things moving at some point way back in time. Much less does he create the cosmos or anything else.[7] Whatever he is responsible for, there is a residuum that he is not responsible for. The first mover, according to Aristotle, is simply the ultimate cause of motion at any instant, including right now. Whatever particular motion is taking place, the first mover is ultimately responsible for it, and for all intervening motions, at the very moment when this particular motion is taking place. The causality of the first mover is simultaneous with the motion of the thing being moved. For Aristotle, there are actually a number of unmoved movers. He needs a number of them to account for the number of irreducibly distinct circular motions that, by hypothesis, underlie the actual motions that can be observed, over time, in the heavens.[8] But among these unmoved movers one is the supreme, the unmoved mover of the outermost sphere of the fixed stars. One cannot be certain, however, whether Aristotle is thinking only of *this* unmoved mover or of *every* unmoved mover when he calls him, or it, "god" and describes his activity as thought thinking itself or as intellect understanding itself (*noēsis noēseōs*).[9]

Be that as it may, Aristotle is emphatic that the unmoved mover moves only as an object of desire. Its perfect activity stimulates those secondary intellects that catch sight of it—primarily the heavenly bodies themselves, which Aristotle treats as incorruptible, luminous, and intelligent—to a circularly moving imitation of the unmoved mover's perfectly reposeful activity. Aristotle's god does not voluntarily bring the cosmos into being, *ex nihilo* or otherwise, for the cosmos is eternal. Nor does he providentially oversee it. Aristotle's god is indeed a principle without which the cosmos would not have the orderly character it has. But he is a principle by virtue of being imitated. In that way he is responsible for the form that the cosmos has as well as for the particular forms that are found in the cosmos and thus for its overall and detailed organization. On the other hand, Aristotle's god is in no sense responsible for the material constituent (*hylē*) of the world. And, as Aristotle makes quite clear, his god thinks of, and can think of, nothing but himself—from which we infer that he does not know that there is a world beneath him.[10] The first mover does not even know that he is the first mover, for then he would have to know something of the moved, and he does not. Most importantly, Aristotle's god does not know about nor take interest in man's moral strivings. He is as indifferent to man's moral strivings as is *physis* itself.

In early modern philosophy, which defines itself largely in opposition to the rational theology of the Middle Ages, the concept of nature is detached from any relation to the divine. The earlier meaning of this concept, as we see it in Homer and in pre-Socratic philosophy, is, however, not simply restored. Though no longer understood as dependent on god, nature gets interpreted by a number of philosophers as dependent on man, on the constitutive activity of human consciousness. This is the interpretation advanced by Kant, for whom the human mind, functioning not at the individual and personal level but as transcendental subjectivity, prescribes laws a priori to nature.[11]

Before Kant, Bacon announced that we must put nature on the rack and torture her to find out what will enable us to relieve the human estate. Descartes goes beyond the mere torture of nature and advertises the fruit of his method as rendering us the masters and possessors not just of this or that natural thing but of nature itself. An extreme instance of the project to master nature would be the attempt to alter the nature of man technologically—as could very well happen in genetic engineering. The contemporary environmentalist movement, whatever one may think of the forms it assumes and the alternative theologies that it occasionally gives rise to, is driven in part by reservations about the specifically modern *hybris* that would so transform the world, remake and subordinate it to human will.

Of course, the West is heir not only to Greek philosophy but to the Bible as well. Orthodox Christianity, which is often called Eastern Orthodoxy, belongs to the West. Like Roman Catholicism, it too incorporates concepts from Greek philosophy into its theology. Orthodox Christianity and Roman Catholicism, in spite of the thousand-year-old schism, have vastly more in common with each other than either has with, say, Hinduism, Buddhism, or any of the other major Eastern religions. Orthodox Christianity may well be the most Eastern part of the West. It is not the most Western part of the East.

Now, it has been said that there is no Hebrew word that can be adequately translated as "nature." But that is because the concept of nature is ambiguous. On the one hand, "nature" names, as Aristotle puts it, what happens always or for the most part.[12] That is, nature is the way things happen not just in Athens and not just in Jerusalem but everywhere, at least for the most part. It is inconceivable that nature in this sense, that is, as typical regularity, was not known by the ancient Hebrews, if for no other reason than that they could not have experienced miracles or wonders *as* wonders had they not experienced them as exceptions to how things happen for the most part.

On the other hand, nature, boldly conceived by some philosophers as the this-worldly order, self-generating, self-sufficient, immanent, eternal, and exceptionless, is most definitely foreign to the Bible, foreign to the

New Testament as well as the Old. Whether this bolder conception is present, if only implicitly, in Aristotle's philosophy is not clear. But his definition of nature as a "ruling principle (*arche*) of motion and rest," his comparison of nature to a "doctor healing himself,"[13] his insistence that the world is eternal, and his theology of a totally hands-off divinity anticipate the bolder understanding of nature that, though suggested as early as the *Odyssey*, gets explicitly worked out in the West only in early modernity, by Spinoza. Spinoza masks the antitheological character of his teaching with his well-known identification of nature with God. But Spinoza's intelligent contemporaries, his intelligent supporters as well as his intelligent opponents, grasped the antitheological, indeed atheistic, implications of his pantheism much more firmly than did later generations.

When we turn to the Bible, we see right away, in the very opening chapter of Genesis, what Spinoza was taking issue with. On the third day of creation we are told that God commanded the earth to sprout grass.[14] We are struck by the fact that the command was directed not to something previously nonexistent and ordering it to be, like the light. The command was directed to something that had already been created and was already existing, namely, the earth. But the command was directed to the earth to do something it would not otherwise have done or have been able to do on its own, namely, to sprout grass. For there were as yet no seeds in the earth. The original sprouting of grass was the result of divine art, as was the case also a bit later on when we are told that God planted a garden in Eden. And all planting, whether divine or human, is the work of art: planting gardens is something that neither the earth nor gardens do of their own accord. Yet once the earth is commanded to sprout grass, and once the garden is planted, further growth does happen naturally, assuming, of course, the right kind of soil, adequate water, and so forth. And this happens not just in one nation and under one divine law but all over the earth. In this example, we find nature, *physis*—literally, to repeat, growing—the very process that Hermes showed to Odysseus. But, whereas we find nature in the *Odyssey* as existing independently of the gods, we find nature in the Bible as existing only under the command of God. And, because nature exists only under the command of God, He can interrupt the natural order, as it appears at His own sweet will. But if He were to interrupt it all the time, His miracles, His wonders, would not be experienced as such.

From the perspective of the Bible, and looking beyond the particular example of the growing of plants, we can say the existence of any finite being, of any creature, and of the world itself as the totality of finite beings is already a miracle. For no finite thing, the world included, *is* by virtue of *what* it is. In the language of the rational theology of Scholasticism, no finite thing (*ens*) and no finite person has being (*esse*) as its very essence or even as a part of its essence. Only God properly has the name, "I am who am." To be sure, because so many finite beings *are* and *have been* for as long as we have been, we get used to their being as we get used to ours. We tend to forget that it is something of a miracle that they and we are at all. The existence of finite beings in their way of being always or for the most part, in their nature, is indeed a miracle according to the Bible. But the intraworldly wonders are a different kind of miracle because they are interruptions of the natural order by the same divine will that also miraculously sustains it.

So, granted that there is no Hebrew word for nature, we nonetheless do find nature in the Bible, though not as Spinoza and other philosophers understood it. We find nature there only as how things are *for the most part*. We do not find unqualified necessity within the world, and we do not find that the world itself is necessary without qualification. In those later parts of the Old Testament written in Greek we find the word *physis*. For example, in the "Wisdom of Solomon" the narrator, who attributes his wisdom as an answer to his prayers and a gift from God,[15] says that through this wisdom he is able to know among other things "the natures of living things (*physeis zōōn*) and the furies of wild beasts, the force of winds and the reasonings of men, the differences of plants and the powers of roots (*dynameis ridzōn*), whatever things are secret as well as manifest."[16] This knowledge of natures, however, is by no means knowledge of an immanent order that exists on its own, independent of God's power and providence.[17] From the perspective of the "Wisdom of Solomon," if nature is like "a doctor healing himself," it is only because God has, by his divine, creative art, made nature this way. And he can unmake it, if he so chooses. It may be, as some have suggested, that this late book in the Bible was written with some awareness of Greek philosophy. If so, it was also written as a response to Greek philosophy and as a correction to the tendency in Greek philosophy to regard nature, rather than a personal and all-creating deity, as *the* ultimate principle.

In the New Testament, the word *physis* and its derivatives or relatives occur several times. Three famous passages are of particular interest to us. In the "Epistle to the Romans," St. Paul writes, "For whenever the nations not having the law [Paul means the revealed law] do by nature (*physei*) the things of the law, they, though, not having the law are a law to themselves, who show the work of the law written in their hearts, their conscience (*syneidēsis*) bearing witness."[18] St. Paul's claim here is that man according to his nature, that is, according to what he *is*, has some knowledge of right and wrong, a knowledge that his fall did not entirely obliterate. Man has a conscience.

Here *physis* is not restricted to the "physical." It has the broader sense of essence, as it also had in the writings of Aristotle.[19]

In another passage, somewhat earlier in the same epistle, St. Paul faults women who "changed the natural use (*hēn physikēn chrēsin*) into what is contrary to nature (*tēn para physin*)."[20] Here *physis* is invoked as a norm, established by God, but in principle intelligible to anyone who is not the victim of willful self-deception. We note in passing, but still with an eye on this passage, that nothing could be more unnatural, more contrary to nature on any understanding of nature, than abortion: if abortion is not contrary to nature, nothing is contrary to nature. Abortion is not, however, contrary to the environment. One cannot help but suspect that part of the contemporary appeal of the concept of the environment is that it offers little or no support for obligations holding *within* the human sphere. Invested with a quasi-sacred character, however, the concept of the environment does generate obligations of humans to the nonhuman sphere *surrounding* us.

The third New Testament passage of interest to us is one that serves as a basis for the Orthodox conception of *theōsis*. St. Peter writes of good things given us by God, whereby we might become "sharers of the divine nature" (*theias koinonoi physeōs*).[21] Here we encounter a notion of nature that not only transcends the physical as matter but also transcends the immaterial essence of finite beings. Even God has a nature, albeit an infinite nature, and participating in it is our progressive, ultimate, but never fully consummated vocation, our very *raison d'être*.

Given that the word *physis* is used in the New Testament in an altogether intelligible way, philosophy cannot simply invoke the concept of nature uncritically in its critique of biblical religion. To be sure, the bolder conception of nature not simply as essence and norm, or as experienced regularity, the typical way of things, but as self-generating, self-sufficient, immanent, eternal, and exceptionless is as alien to the New Testament as it is to the Old. But nature conceived in the latter way can only be inferred from experience. And the inference, like any empirical generalization, is not airtight. Not in the least.

As is well known, the Greek word *ousia* (essence or being), which is employed in, and is indispensable to, the Nicene Creed, is a term of Greek philosophical provenance that does not occur in the Bible. *Physis* is also a term of Greek philosophical provenance but one that does, as we have seen, appear in the Bible, though it is employed there in a restricted sense. The most significant employment of this term in the language and theology of the Church occurs in the definition of the Fourth Ecumenical Council, in Chalcedon, where "one and the same Christ, the only begotten Son and Lord" is confessed "in two natures (*en duo physesin,* Latin: *in duabis naturis*) . . . and in one person and one *hypostasis.*"[22] This definition places Christ in a class by Himself. We know of nothing else in the world that has two natures. For the nature of a thing defines what it is.

Now if God and man, or divine nature and human nature, were contradictory opposites, the Chalcedonian definition would not be declaring a superrational mystery but a subrational absurdity, a relationship one could mindlessly and in imitation of piety utter but that one could not really believe in, inasmuch as, like a square circle, it could not be conceived at all, neither mystically nor rationally. But God and man are not contradictory opposites. Their relation is not entirely reducible to that of creator and creature. For man is the creature who is uniquely created in the image of God. God and man are related as original and image. And in this way the Chalcedonian definition declares something that, though transcending anything human reason could come up with on its own, something that could only be revealed, does not demand the complete foreswearing of our reason, which is after all part of our human nature, arguably the very part wherein the image and likeness of God is found. We humans can be said, figuratively though not literally, to be God's sheep. But even speaking figuratively, it must be added at once, that we are his *rational* sheep.

The Church Fathers do not disagree with Aristotle that man is by nature—that is, according to his very essence—a rational animal. This philosophical definition can be understood as the philosophic analogue, if not anticipation, of the revealed truth that man is uniquely made in the image and likeness of God. The expression "rational sheep" is a metaphor stressing both the need for a humility appropriate to our finitude and the loftiness of our vocation in *theōsis*. We are not literally rational sheep, because sheep are not rational—not the way we are. Similarly, Christ is only metaphorically called "the Lamb of God." He is not the offspring of a ram and an ewe. It suffices to think in this connection of the Orthodox refusal to depict Christ in the icons as a lamb, as he is frequently depicted in the religious art of the Latin West. Such a depiction—a confusion of metaphor with reality—not only inadvertently blasphemes our Lord; it levels the distinction between man and the other creatures, downplaying the central claim of Christianity that God, in the Person of the Son, ennobles human nature, itself already an image of divine nature, by assuming human nature in his Incarnation, by redeeming human nature in his passion and resurrection, and, in his ascension, by taking human nature, including human flesh, albeit glorified, all the way to the right hand of the Father, for all time. It is human nature, human flesh—not the nature of a sheep, or a tree, or a river, or a mountain, or a star—that, in the person of the Son, has been incorporated into the life of the Trinity. And this incorporation prepares the way both for our own *bodily* resurrection and for our own *theōsis*, mysterious and paradoxical as this may seem.

The concept of nature is one of the richest and at the same time one of the most problematic components of our intellectual heritage. The Church Fathers, aware that the concept of nature was problematic, did not take it over uncritically but purged it of its specifically pagan character. Their theological appropriation of the concept of nature consisted in using it in the sense of essence. The nature of man is what pertains to the essence of man, and the nature of God is what pertains to the essence of God. And Christ, uniquely, has, and will for all eternity have, two natures. Nature does not, for the Church Fathers, mean what it meant to Homer, nor does it mean all of what it meant for Aristotle.

The concept of nature has become almost completely sedimented in our time. Today nature is most often held to be just the totality of things that are, apart from man: bushes, birds, bees, bears, mountains, waterfalls, rivers, oceans, and so forth. Understood this way, the concept of nature gets reduced to and replaced by that of the environment, whatever is around man but not man himself. The extreme consequence of this view can be found in so-called Deep Ecology, according to which man, so far from being in the image of God, is a mistake, a freak of nature. To be sure, man emerges out of nature. For the Deep Ecologists there is no other source from which he could emerge. But man's aggressive comportment toward nature, his determination to master and possess it, to remake it in his own image—all this stamps him as a uniquely malignant force in nature. The notions of conservation and stewardship are as inappropriate as mastery and possession. They are offensive manifestations of the speciesism that leads man to misconstrue himself as the pinnacle of creation. Way out on the fringe of Deep Ecology, at its uttermost limits, some go so far as to say that it would be best if man had never been. If man cannot accept his circumscribed place on the earth, it would be best if he were to become extinct.

This view of things is manifestly idolatrous: it elevates the visible world above both man and the invisible God in whose image he is made. But this view is not neopagan, for the pagans understood man to be very much a part of nature. Deep Ecology is like a parody of the biblical proclamation. Man is in the world but not of it—though not because he alone among worldly things is the image of God's eternal glory, even though he bears the wounds of sin. Man is in the world but not of it because he is a monster.

One can anticipate, as a reaction against Deep Ecology, a neo-Gnosticism that will claim that it is the physical world, including man's body, that is the monster. The only thing of real worth in the world is the human spirit, which is imprisoned within the body. Deep Ecology and its contradictory opposite, Gnosticism, both view man as essentially homeless because neither has come to terms with the concept of nature. For both, nature is reduced to all that is not man, to what surrounds man, to the environment literally.

It should go without saying that some aspects of environmentalism are altogether sensible and should be uncontroversial, conservation and stewardship in particular. If we destroy the resources we need for our own survival, we will destroy ourselves and our progeny. If we disfigure the world around us, we will be unable to contemplate instances of beauty that are not the products of human art but that induce us to reflect on the possibility of a divine artisan as their ultimate source. As the environment is elevated above the human beings it surrounds, however, and as our dependence on it is stressed while our dependence on God is more and more widely denied, the environment comes to assume the aspect of a god. Man, after all, is determined to revere *something*.

The Church Fathers, who came to terms with the concept of nature and employed it, appropriately refined, in their theological writings, would surely have rejected the more extreme versions of environmentalism. In particular, they would have rejected, indeed anathematized, Deep Ecology, its implicit pantheology and its explicit morality, just as unequivocally as they rejected Gnosticism—precisely because they had a balanced understanding of the natural order of the world and the unique place of human nature within it. I would urge Orthodox bishops and theologians, as they contemplate incorporating "the environment" and cognate words into the liturgical and theological language of the Church, to scrutinize the concept they refer to as soberly, cautiously, and critically as the Church Fathers centuries before them scrutinized the concept of nature.

Existential versus Regulative Approaches: The Environmental Issue as an Existential and Not a Canonical Problem

Christos Yannaras

The Apocalypse of St. John has been regarded as the supreme symbol of the decisive cultural shift that occurred with the advent of Christianity: a shift from *nature* to *history*.[1] The problem of the environment—the violation of nature, its unrestrained exploitation by the human race—is judged to be a necessary consequence of the priority that Christianity gave to history, subordinating nature to an eschatological perspective that entailed its final disappearance for the sake of an eagerly awaited spiritual "Kingdom."

We are speaking of a cultural shift because Christianity was preceded by ancient Greece. To the Greeks, the idea of the historicity of nature was unknown. The problem of a beginning in time and a predetermined end did not arise. Nature constituted the fullness of *being*: a beautiful structure of harmony and order that rendered it a *cosmo-cosmema*, an ordered ornament. A perfect universe, harmoniously arranged, with a given absolute rationality, it even encompassed the reality of God, who constituted a part of its general seemliness. Given that the world was eternal, it could not have any goal other than itself. It could only *be*. And the greatest thing that human beings could attain was to *contemplate* and to *imitate* the perfection of the cosmos. Knowledge of the cosmos, *episteme*, was identified with virtue, the serene *prudence* that came from participating in the universal "common mind" or *logos*. The collective imitation of the harmony of the cosmos formed "the microcosm of the city," the common effort of *political life*, which did not differ from the art of the composer or the painter, since it aimed at the same imitation of the laws of the rationality that beautified the universe. What was of the first importance to the Greeks was not *becoming* or *the necessary*, was not potentiality and will, but *being* and its rational plenitude.

Modern Europe saw the appearance of Christianity—chiefly through the eyes of Hegel, Fichte, and Schelling—as a radical break in the Greek view of nature. The God of the Judeo-Christian tradition is outside the cosmos. He himself creates the cosmos, giving it a specific temporal beginning and directing it toward a preordained end. Now it is history that has priority, not nature; the *becoming* of nature, not the *being* of nature. This historicity of nature is at the outset devalued because it is dominated by the consequence of the Fall and sin of humanity. Human beings are called upon to participate in history—in God's plan for the salvation of humanity—and they succeed in the measure in which they are liberated from nature and the necessity of the laws of the Fall, which held sway over nature. In this perspective, the book of the Apocalypse of St. John was interpreted as a radical and final condemnation of nature, since the expected eschatological "Kingdom" is announced as a nightmare of physical destruction and the collapse of the entire universe. Thus the world is presented as a simple episode in a *history* that essentially undermines and finally destroys it. The expression "this world" becomes synonymous with the expression "this age" and signifies a particular historical period, an age that is inimical and contrary to the "age that is to come" of the Kingdom of God.

Was the Christian view of nature in reality so radically contrary to the Greek view? Let us put this question to one side for the moment, for I should like to address the second vital shift in our encounter within nature, which has been accomplished within the framework of our modern attitudes, our contemporary culture.

This culture was founded by the philosophy of the Enlightenment on a polemical opposition to metaphysics. The opposition expressed a historical need, after the painful medieval experience of centuries, over the course of which metaphysics was transformed into a dominant ideology of an integral character. The opposition of our modern culture to metaphysics—the shedding of religious integralism—appeared as an enthusiastic affirmation of nature and the potentialities of nature. It was concerned above all with the knowledge of physical reality, not with its metaphysical supports. It was concerned with humanity not as people as the creation and in image of God but as physical entities, physical individuals. It was concerned with enhancing the value of physical existence and life not with a morality supported by threats of eternal punishment but with conformity to the rationality of nature, a "Natural Law" that would guarantee the *rights* of every physical individual.

The nature-centered shift, however, that modern culture has enshrined did not entail a return to the ancient Greek interpretation of the world as a measure of rational harmony and plenitude—even though such a return was pursued by the humanists of the West, who worshipped everything Greek. Certainly the character of the only assured interpretation of reality was attributed to nature; the measure and axis of its rational reality was only individual human subjectivity. The rational self-awareness of the human subject was regarded as the only foundation of reality that could not be shaken by doubt.

The nature-centered shift of our modern culture has proved to be anthropocentric, not cosmocentric. Western European man discovered the universe of objective existents with youthful enthusiasm, but as master and proprietor. "I understand means I possess," wrote the young Hegel in his *Early Theological Writings* (*Theologische Jugendschriften*). The individual understanding decodes the rationality of nature and intervenes in its powers to draw out a result useful and beneficial to man. Nature in the modern view is a useful object, and knowledge, *episteme*, is authority.

In this way the concept and imperative of *progress* is introduced for the first time into human history. This no longer has any relationship with the Christian interpretation of the development of history toward a final end of apocalyptic fulfillment. Progress is now the constant extension of the mastery of the human powers of production in the whole of nature. Progress is measured by indicators of productivity and ease of consumption; the economy subordinates politics and every social dynamic and proves to be the exclusive factor and only criterion of social "development."

Res extensa/res cogitans: the antithetical distinction between man and nature was set out by Descartes, who guided medieval scholastic thought to its unforeseen but inevitable consequences. Kant will also interiorize even the objective external world in the subjective reason: "Outside myself nothing exists except within my own discernment." One step further, and Hegel will see in the human tool a "meta-physics" and in technology a "materialized metaphysics." He will announce that "we are much closer to the spirit when we make a tool than when we give birth to a child." And in absolute accord with the idealist Hegel, the materialist Marx will assert that "the history of industry is the open book of the essential powers of man, the human psychology which is perceived experimentally."

From these theoretical opinions to the practice of the violation of nature by technology is but a small step. That is why it seems at least paradoxical that we seek a solution to the problems of the environment today by relying on the guidelines set by the culture of "modernity" that has led, with an iron inevitability, to the destruction of the natural environment that now threatens us.

Let us return to the questions we left in abeyance. Was the Christian view of nature in reality so antithetical to the Greek view? Is the Apocalypse of St. John a triumph of history over nature, the proclamation of the final denigration and destruction of nature for the sake of the Messianic Kingdom?

Both questions pose problems of interpretation of the relation and differences between Hellenism and Christianity, and together with these a problem of criteria for understanding the symbolism of the Apocalypse. Hermeneutic differences are not always exhausted on the theoretical level: they can lead also to total transformations of cultures, as happened in Europe in the eleventh century. In that period, the Greco-Roman world (the Byzantine world, as we would say today) understood its relationship with Christianity in a manner very different from the way in which the Germanic peoples of Central and Western Europe understood their relationship both with the Greek and with the Christian tradition.

In the history of philosophy, hermeneutic problems become insoluble if we overlook the discontinuity brought about by that critical rupture in the development of European civilization we call the "Great Migration of Peoples," that is to say, if we overlook the fact that from the end of the fourth century until the sixth century A.D. the greater part of Europe was subjected to a cultural reversal that was literally tragic in comparison with its Greco-Roman past. The new tribes that migrated and established themselves in Europe at that time—Franks, Goths, Huns, Vandals, Burgundians, Normans—were on a markedly low, if not downright primitive, cultural level.

Their first civilizing step was their conversion to Christianity. But what could conversion mean to peoples who had not even the elementary presuppositions of education for the understanding of the Greek philosophical forms in which Christian experience was expressed? It was inevitable that they would adapt the understanding of Christianity to the level of their own criteria and needs.

In every situation of cultural backwardness in history, the interpretation of the existent and the pragmatic—which endows with meaning the relations between human beings and nature, their fellow human beings and God—becomes a schematic simplification, usually strongly polarized between distinctions of "good" and "evil," and is consequently juristic and legal. A characteristic example in Judaic history, for example, is the decline of the Talmudic tradition into pharisaic legalism, or, in the later Hellenistic period, the transmutation of Platonic dualism into Manichean Gnosticism.

For this historical assertion to be properly supported with evidence, a special monograph would be needed. Here it is only put forward as a proposal offering a criterion for interpreting the differences distinguishing the Greco-Roman from the medieval Western European version of relations between Hellenism and Christianity. This second version, the medieval Western European, was inherited for the most part by the modern world. In his study of Nietzsche, Heidegger demonstrated clearly the inevitable continuity (*Kontinuität*) of the metaphysics of the Western Middle Ages for the theistic and atheistic systems of modern times.

Here it is worth touching briefly on some basic theses of the Greco-Roman version of relations between Hellenism and Christianity, particularly on what concerns the problem of nature and history, which are directly localized in the Apocalypse of St. John.

Certainly, Christianity denies the eternity of the world. But is this element fundamental in the treating of ancient Greek cosmology? When the problem of a beginning and an end of the world is not posed, the property of the eternal (the "ever advancing") relates mainly to the ubiquitous rationality with which the world, independently of time and period, is offered to the vision-contemplation of the human person.

The fundamental distinguishing mark of ancient Greek cosmology is not the eternity of the world but the recognition of a universal common rational principle (*xynos logos*) that articulates, structures, and governs physical or natural reality. This *logos* forms the universe into a cosmos—an ordered harmony and beauty. The *logos*-mode of participation in being distinguishes the *essences* of existents, shapes the variety of *forms*, formulates the *laws* of the order and harmony, of the coexistence and movement of beings. The *logos*-form is the "lover" of matter, the motive (the appetitive aspect) that urges matter to the movement that gives it form, to the *entelechy* of endowment with form.

This *logical* composition and function of the world is neither denied nor destroyed by Christianity. Christianity only interprets it, revealing the uninterpreted gaps of ancient Greek ontology. The *logos* that brings together, constructs, and governs the universe is not an independent given that ends up as blind fate. It is the personal energy of a creating Person, the created result of an uncreated transcendent First Principle. Uncreated and therefore timeless and infinite—that is the existence of God; created and therefore temporal and finite—that is the nature of the world.

The human personal existence, however, of the painter, the sculptor, the composer is of a different essence from that of painting, sculpture, and song. And just as painting, sculpture, and song do not cease to be a *logos* revelatory of the personal otherness and freedom of the creator-artist, so too the world, in spite of its *essential* difference from God, does not cease to be a *logos* revelatory of his Person.

This is a supreme measure of, as we would say today, the ecological attitude of humanity toward nature: for the Christian, nature is not an impersonal and neutral object, even though created by some Supreme Being. Nature is the artifact of a personal God-Logos that reveals in every fold the personal otherness of the creative energy of its maker. The term "natural contemplation" in the Christian vocabulary refers to the result of ascetic self-transcendence, the ascetic achievement of our transcending our egocentric, acquisitive, and exploitative priorities, and our living our relationship with the world in the way we live our relationship with a painted, sculptured, musical, or any other work of art.

The human person is called not to a one-sided contemplation of the world but to a personal relationship with the *logos* of the cosmos, because this *logos* is called to a communion of life with the Creator of the world. The use of the world—food, clothing, tools—is in one way or another a life-giving prerequisite for humanity. This use, however, which serves the daily survival of the created human being, can bring about a relationship of communion with God. The appropriation of nature by the human person in order that he should exist not in the manner of created nature but in the manner of relationship, of loving communion, is the mode of existence of the Uncreated. For "God is love" (1 John 4:16).

This is the sense of *Eucharist*, which constitutes and forms the Church and gives meaning to the practice of the Christian life. In the Eucharist, Christians receive nature, the cosmos, as food in a direct way—as bread and wine, two kinds of food that encapsulate the things necessary for the sustenance of human life. They receive them *with Thanksgiving* as gifts of God, and this receiving constitutes a communion of human beings with God, a cosmic flesh of divine communion. In every Eucharist, Christians communicate the flesh of the incarnate Logos, the Logos who became flesh within History as the first fruit of the power of created nature to exist in the mode of the fullness of life of the Uncreated.

The "ecology" of the Christian Church is the endowment of the world with meaning through the Eucharist and the eucharistic use of the world. This use, however, is not an existential necessity: it constantly takes risks in the existential adventure of the *freedom* of the human person. The book of the Apocalypse uses a striking poetic iconography to picture this current adventure and its eschatological goal, which is ceaselessly fulfilled and is intended to be accomplished not only as the destruction of nature and end of time but as the restoration of nature and time in a fulfilling communion of life with created and uncreated being, in a universal Eucharist.

The way out from today's ecological blind alleys cannot be accomplished as long as our culture remains tied to the anthropocentric utilitarianism of the modern world and to its medieval religious roots. A different reading of the Apocalypse of John is indispensable for the formation of a view of the relations between *nature* and *history* that will lead to new criteria with respect to the way the world is either used or abused.

Nature and Creation: A Comment on the Environmental Problem from a Philosophical and Theological Standpoint

Nikos Nissiotis

I

Philosophical thinking has been in large part anthropocentric, in a peculiar way: it has regarded man as the center of creation on the basis of his intellect and, more specifically, of rational thought.[1] In this way, philosophy has been the foundation for the intellectual culture and the particular technological culture known as rationalistic; it is given a practical application in science, and it presumes and encourages a unique and dominant position for man vis-à-vis all other living and material beings and natural phenomena. It is the same rationalism that investigates the essence of truth, that investigates the nature and essence of matter in the same way on the basis of consistent questions, and that proceeds to explain the relationships between objects in mathematical terms, and this same rationalism ends up giving all this a practical application through engineering and exploiting nature in a scientific and methodical fashion. Despite the positivism of science and its indifference to metaphysical problems, it is natural that this science, being the outcome of an idealistic philosophy in which matter was not given its proper place, should inspire a subconscious inclination toward human dominance in the material world. Although this "dominion" is not wrong as a tendency, it nevertheless gives rise to the dangers that we see today when it is insatiable and uncontrolled—when it lacks any ethical restraint.

In spite of its rationalistic and spiritualizing basis, classical Greek philosophy managed to achieve a balanced relationship between spirit and matter and inspire admiration and wonder for creation. There was indeed an absolute priority of value given to spirit as compared with matter, chiefly in the works of Plato, yet this did not lead people to devalue material creation utterly or suck it dry—as has happened with the idealism of modern times, which has maintained extreme and one-sided interpretations of Plato. Furthermore, Aristotelian philosophy, by presupposing Platonism and avoiding the extremes of an idealistic interpretation of it, provided an extraordinary balance for philosophy throughout the ages. Matter is not something that simply exists but it is what exists as matter, that is, the possibility of existence from essence to form via movement, which is the essence of existent things. There is a correspondence, a coherence, and a sufficient intimate and indissoluble relationship naturally provided between spirit-intellect on the one hand and material reality and material objects on the other, a relationship on which all sciences have to be predicated. Medieval and modern Western European philosophy was grounded on these classical presuppositions, yet because of the interposition of a false, spiritualistic Christian worldview, it veered off into a purely anthropocentric rationalistic monism; spirit was given absolute priority over matter, and in consequence nature was regarded as material to be exploited, serving only to further material and technological progress. The being, the essence of things was fragmented; it was looked at in the context not of the relationship between being and things but only of the ability of the human spirit to observe things as material and inanimate, to classify them into series and evaluate them on the basis of their properties in order to produce a work of benefit to technological progress. So instead of the relationship between spirit and matter, what inevitably crept in was engineering and, at the end of our era, the supermachine of electrical engineering—the machine of reflex "thoughts," which is a technical substitute for both spirit and matter, combining the two, participating in both, and fashioning a new relationship between them. Thus anthropocentrism and spiritualizing philosophy led to the domination of the machine in the service of man's absolute dominance in nature. When this philosophical aberration began (for example, with Descartes' methodological doubt of all things, on the grounds that they were presented to the reason tainted by the "evil spirit," a taint that only the human intellect escapes because it discovers that it is unable to doubt only the Absolute, meaning the God of idealism), no one perhaps imagined that it would result in a rupture of the proper relationship between spirit and matter, humans and nature, and even the creation of the *deus ex machina* outside that relationship, a powerless god indifferent to the magnitude of the respect that man should have for material nature. To be sure, there was no shortage of reactions against this idealistic anthropocentrism. But neither vulgar materialism nor scientific materialism—nor even romanticism—restored the right relationship between spirit and matter. On the contrary, the former, perhaps involuntarily, expedited the material draining of nature in the industrial age and exalted the absolute superiority of mass humanity over creation, in the end not accepting any metaphysical or higher purpose in creation. As for romanticism, this reacted emotionally to the beauty of creation, which it extolled, so despite transcending rationalism and the mechanistic spirit, it was unable to check the devaluation of material nature because of its own boundless anthropocentricity. Thus it aided still further the self-deception of unbridled idealistic anthropocentrism. The results of the philosophical aberration regarding the meaning and above all the practical application of anthropocentrism in creation, and the scientific aberration that went with it, are noted today by ecology. We realize, in retrospect alas, that the right relationship between man and nature has been broken and that in this relationship nature is simply regarded as something like an exterior shell or like an interior power resource to be exploited by man. No longer is there the required respect for nature as creation; there is not the wonder or even the relationship of love and care that comes from these. For this reason, in parallel with the revolution in relations between man and nature there is also a more profound devaluation of the relationship between the sexes. In the various kinds of blatant pornography we see today, which speak for modern man and satisfy him more than in any previous age, the relationship between man and woman is one of exploitation, the purpose of which is subjective pleasure. Here, too, matter is "separated" from its essence, from the person. In the eyes of the opposite sex, the human being has a body but does not constitute a composite and indissoluble personality. Real love, respect, and deeper admiration recede before the immediate and highly ephemeral exploitation of the purely material substance. Today's crisis in the relationship between the sexes reflects the crisis in the relationship between nature and humanity in a technological age.

II

Furthermore, we should accept the necessity of self-criticism also within Christian theology. This too has in many cases unwittingly served the erroneous view of matter and consequently of nature through an anthropocentric idealism, because it has maintained that man was a purely spiritual being. More specifically, one can mention misunderstandings of Scripture, mistaken theological positions, and misapplications of Christian ethics and wrongful pursuit of the Christian ideal through such ethics. Here are some examples of these three categories:

1. Since God's command is explicitly expressed in Genesis (1:28) in the terms "be fruitful and multiply and fill the earth and subdue it," this was misinterpreted in such a way that man's dominion was understood as permitting or instigating the exploitation of nature at whatever cost, so as to achieve material domination by force. But that is not what this passage means. On the one hand, this command signifies overcoming the dangers that came from nature at a certain historical period when man's life was under threat from the animal kingdom (as is shown by the second half of the verse, "and have dominion over all the beasts and every creeping thing"). On the other hand, the primary meaning here is that God as Creator is represented by man, who looks after His creation, as is also apparent from other verses of the Old Testament, such as the beautiful scene in Genesis where God as Creator calls Adam, in an anthropomorphic fashion, to name the animals in Paradise (Gen. 2:20). In Hebrew tradition, giving a name was equivalent to bringing into being (as the children take the name of the father when they are born); in other words, it is a sign of dominion, love, and care according to the prototype of God the Creator and in no case a sign of subjection and unthinking exploitation.

2. Related to the previous example is the fact that man was created "in the image of God" (Gen. 1:27) and the one-sided understanding of this that prevailed mainly as a result of theological scholasticism in its various forms, according to which the above phrase should be understood as referring to the nature of man's spiritual and rational substance only—a notion that has fostered the imbalance in the understanding of man as an indissoluble unity of spirit and body.

3. Another misunderstanding has to do with the use of a special ascetic discipline in order to achieve the high ideal of Christian life. This asceticism has been regarded as an aversion to everything material, denying the bodily value of the person and reacting against the tendencies and appetites of our fleshly substance. This again is why monastic life has been regarded as antimaterial and antinature and as contributing to the disruption of the normal relationship between spirit and matter or nature, with the result that the latter is treated with disdain. Yet this Christian ethic that aspires to perfection does not mean at all that matter is disdained. The true "spirit-bearer" does not maltreat the body or nature but looks after them and respects them. Especially in these days of inordinate exploitation of both the body and nature, this ethic demonstrates the way in which man should restrain his greedy appetites toward nature and also how he is to show himself more connected with nature, as God has created him to be. St. Francis of Assisi is an example of self-restraint, sobriety, and "naturalness" as well as love and respect for cre-

ation. His frugality is expressed in his loving care for the nature around him and his concern for the birds and animals that live with him in the most unaffected and natural way.

III

Theological self-criticism in regard to the excesses of Christian idealism is able to lead to a positive vision of material nature and a theological evaluation of it. It will then become clear to any conscientious scholar what the actual, true Christian notion of the value of matter is, based on Scripture and the theological tradition. For of all religions, the Christian faith, when of course it is rightly interpreted and applied without eccentricities, inspires the purest and most profoundly positive evaluation of nature, one far removed from any sort of magic or idolatry.

The basic presupposition for such an attitude is the fact of the Incarnation, which is the central axis of Christian faith. Scripture describes it as the central event of creation and of history. It is the Evangelist John who shows this most clearly, speaking of the Creative Word of God through whom "all things were made," the Word who is the light and life of the whole Creation (Jn. 1:1–5), and of whom he declares that "the Word was made flesh" (1:14). The flesh here assures us of the value of material substance and of the whole creation. All things in creation acquire substance, meaning, and purpose as material and bodily since, as Paul writes, all things whether visible or invisible "hold together in Him" (Col. 1:17). The Logos, the Word of God, is not simply an idea, a theoretical principle. He becomes a material, personal being; He partakes in the very material of His creation. The Incarnation, the central fact of our faith, does not permit a division of man into two, with absolute priority given to the spirit or intellect. Faith knows nothing of the rights of philosophical dualism in anthropology and will never recognize them. Man is spirit and matter, body and soul united. There is no human existence without material substance. Even the resurrection of the dead will be bodily. Man is body, as he is also spirit. There is no priority in value or ontological gradation between the two. We must not confuse the concept of "bodily," which refers to the material substance, with that of "natural" (*psychikos*), which refers to the carnal mind (compare 1 Cor. 2:14). The former is given by God from our creation; the latter is a deviation from the way we were created. It is characteristic that in the case of the deviation, Scripture does not use the terms "material" or "bodily" but mainly the term *psychikos*, which signifies a wrong use of material things or of the body and in general something antithetical to the order of the spiritual-material creation. Only with the presupposition of the fact of the Incarnation does one understand how and why the whole Bible, the Old Testament and the New, presents an unbreakable bond between man and nature and indeed in many cases an intimate identification of the two. Again, one appreciates why care for nature appears very frequently in its texts, and the beauty and harmony of nature is used as a means to express hymns of glory to the Creator. Many examples of such an attitude could be quoted, but we shall confine ourselves to a few simply in order to call this attitude to mind. In Deuteronomy, God commands the protection of trees (20:19–20), and later on it is mentioned there that one of the main reasons for the command about keeping the Sabbath is the need for the animals to rest. Man is the steward and keeper of the garden of Eden—in other words, the biblical prototype of nature before it revolted (Gen. 2:15)—and is in an unbreakable relationship with the animals and plants, since he himself had named them in God's presence, and this action of his forever binds together Creator, man, and created things. But the greatest fact after the Incarnation, which has easily been overlooked by idealist philosophy and theology—which has not, in other words, had any influence that could check their tendency toward pure idealism—is the process of creation as set out in the first two chapters of Genesis. Life, organic nature, is presented as "coming forth" out of inorganic material nature ("let the waters bring forth swarms of living creatures," Gen. 1:20), as if foretelling in this way an everlasting identification between the two and meaning that the dividing line between them is still not clearly distinguished. The first organic life emerges from matter by means of the Word of God, who later, at the Incarnation, participates in it. In the making of man, the connection between matter and life is clearer; God is presented in human terms as "taking dust from the earth" (Gen. 2:7) to create man. These points, as they are presented in story form and symbolically in Scripture, are of great importance for the fundamental significance of matter, especially of earth, water, and air, for the first appearance of life and the existence of man. Creation, as it is described symbolically and as it should be interpreted theologically according to the Christian worldview, should constantly be teaching the relationship of identity between nature and organic life: it is an inseparable unity of the dynamic and, further, creative relationship between God, nature, and man. Despite this, apologetic theology, chiefly in the modern West, has been excessively disturbed by the spread of the theory of evolution, according to which man is regarded physiologically as the final offspring of the animal kingdom. This theology has reacted fanatically less because it is scientifically convinced that the theory is untrue than because it considers that man's dignity as a creature specially created by God is being diminished. The fact that man is so closely related physiologically to the most highly evolved species in the animal kingdom was regarded as blasphemous. Misguided theological idealism, ignoring the relationship between material-animal and human nature existing from creation, opposed the theory of evolution from a position that was "spiritualizing" rather than scientific or theological. The reaction against this theory had more of a psychological than a theological basis. Evolution is an affront to man as he is seen from the lofty view of a one-sided and defective anthropology that places him in splendid isolation vis-à-vis creation, which according to this anthropology is merely the inanimate, material stage for the history of man, who enjoys sole dominance. What creates the problem is not so much that man's especially exalted place in creation is maintained—which is quite proper on the basis of the Christian worldview—but that the other forms of life and of nature are devalued and belittled, ending up as mere inanimate materials for exploitation and existing only for the sake of man's material prosperity. The latter position should not be presented as a logical consequence of the former. This has destructive consequences today for contemporary man's moral attitude toward nature and the environment, an attitude quite literally opposite to the Christian view of the whole creation, which maintains the moral obligation for man to show respect and loving devotion to nature and the environment.

IV

This philosophical and theological critique is essential today in the face of the threat of environmental pollution caused by man's indifferent and shabby attitude toward nature, and it opens the way for scholars to make a better evaluation of nature from a philosophical and theological point of view. Beyond the basic points for the positive evaluation of matter from the theological angle we have set out above, we now understand why Scripture avoids speaking of creation (*demiourgia*), nature, or matter. These terms occur in mythology, philosophy, astrology, and nature religions and are laden with connotations at variance with the Christian view of the created world. In place of these terms, the Bible uses the term *ktisis* (creation).[2]

In summary, and on the basis of many New Testament passages, we can observe that three concepts are denoted by the term *ktisis*. First, there is the notion of creation as a whole, including matter, the soil, plants, the animal kingdom, and man, fully interrelated and coexisting. Second, there is the notion of creation as a whole not merely as an outward, material, natural surface or as an inner material structure but as an organic whole with substance, existence, and purpose. This is put very well by one of the foremost writers of the patristic tradition, St. John of Damascus, when he says that creation should be conceived of "not in terms of place but in terms of essence" and that God operates by "volitional thought."[3] Third, we have the notion of the care of the Creator who out of love, which is His essence, and in wisdom creates through the Word a higher purpose, which is the happiness of every creature. Then all things find their fullness, their basis, their true substance and being through their personal relationship with God in creation itself, since the creative Word by His Incarnation participates in creation naturally, materially, and historically. This is why the verb *ktizo*, "create," is used in Scripture in this sense: "in Him [that is, Christ as Word or Principle of creation] all things were created" (Col. 1:16). A closer study of the New Testament from this perspective shows that the meaning of nature as creation, *ktisis*, requires the use of the term in the three main stages of the creative, revelatory, and saving work of God in Trinity. We will again use some of the many relevant passages to show how the term *ktisis* is used in the above sense in the three fundamental operations of the Creator: (1) the revelation of His work through nature, (2) the Holy Spirit's work of renewal in nature, and (3) the work of redemption, which embraces nature and man at the same time, in unbreakable relationship.

1. Nature, when seen rightly as creation, *ktisis*, provides our best means of apprehending the creative energy of the personal God and also His *hypostasis*, as He acts out of love and with wisdom. St. Paul finds those who do not believe in Christ even before His coming without excuse, because through idolatry and nature religion they have replaced God with His own creation in order to satisfy their own appetites and desires. In the Epistle to the Romans he writes, "for God has shown it to them. Ever since the creation (*ktisis*) of the world His invisible nature, namely, His eternal power and deity, has been clearly perceived in the things that have been made" (Rom. 1:19-20). What is of interest here is that deliberate blindness to nature as God's Creation brings with it not only idolatry but also disruption in relations between the sexes, as Paul explains further on, because a wrong estimation of nature and matter and the failure to give it the honor and care proper to it as God's creation is directly reflected in every one of man's personal relationships, particularly in all sexual relations. Bold as it may be, one may justifiably conclude that from an ethical point of view, deviations in this area of personal life are connected with an unethical attitude toward nature. It is, for instance, a form of sexual abuse when in today's technological age nature is sucked completely dry without any restraints. It is a form of fornication when the natural energy that man supposedly "acquires" is misused. Nature as God's creation is offered to us for legitimate use and not for abuse. Man

does not have rights of "acquisition" over nature as creation; he is simply a guest on earth for a short period of time.

2. Nature, regarded as creation, *ktisis*, is presented in Scripture as an organism undergoing renewal. This is a consequence of the basic thesis that all things have been created through the Word of God, and hence all things are subject to His work of renewal through the Holy Spirit. Theological self-criticism should reveal to us that on this point, too, ethics understands this work of renewal in an entirely individual and anthropocentric sense. St. Paul, however, seems to insist that this work of renewal concerns man first and foremost, certainly, but its meaning and its reality is universal and encompasses "all things." In the Second Epistle to the Corinthians (5:17) we read, "if anyone is in Christ, he is a new creation; the old has passed away, behold, all things have been made new." Creation in its entirety, "all things," are made new together with the renewal of man in Christ. New Creation means the re-creation of all things through their dynamic relationship with the Creative Word, in other words, a relationship not only with God but also with nature as His Creation. Creation in this case, that is, nature as matter, is presented as a living organism that develops and is renewed together with man through his genuine re-creative cooperation in the creative work of God. The moral responsibility that stems from the above notion of renewal and the obligation under which it places everyone, particularly scientists, is enormous, because by their work they participate in God's work of renewal, when this is understood in all its breadth and not in the context of a narrow individual morality.

3. Finally, nature regarded as creation receives its highest recognition when it is presented in Scripture as participating in the Creator's work of redemption. In relation to this central question of Christian theology and in his most important letter, the Epistle to the Romans, St. Paul makes nature as creation the center of interest and places it squarely in relationship with man. Nature as creation bears the marks of man's revolt against the Creator and suffers with him deeply as a living organism: "For we know that the whole creation has been groaning in travail until now" (Rom. 8:22). The phraseology calls to mind motherhood, the woman who suffers the pangs of childbirth. It is in this state that creation dynamically awaits its deliverance ("For the creation waits with eager longing for the revealing of the sons of God," Rom. 8:20) and as a creature of God hopes for the same liberation as do humans: "in hope that the creation itself will be set free from its bondage to decay and obtain the glorious liberty of the children of God" (Rom. 8:21). This passage is among the most beautiful in Scripture and among the most profound. Surely nowhere in world literature has nature as creation received

a more exalted evaluation. Here there is no romanticism or idealism. We have a sober description of the grandeur of creation, which follows or rather is joined to the drama of its history, its fall and salvation; of suffering, pain, natural and spiritual evil, decay and death and at the same time hope in a new life that is renewed, as is that of the "children of God." Indeed, this gives the ultimate recognition to nature as creation.

V

It becomes clear now that modern man has an obligation to pay particular attention to his attitude toward material nature, on the basis of Christian faith and theological thought. Matter has a unique value. And this should not be said only of the sources of energy, of deposits, metals, fuels, or foodstuffs, nor again, romantically, of flowers, beautiful scenery, or the wonders of nature. Rather, we must say this of matter in general, even in its lowest form: soil, mud, sand, rocks. This is where the value, the power of life is to be found. We do not protect the environment because it is beautiful and useful but because it is material that belongs to creation, because it is a creative organism, something forever unique, and because we identify ourselves with a profound material and spiritual-ethical relationship leading to a right coexistence and cooperation. Cultivating the land in the right way, having a right understanding of the body, and maintaining the proper attitude toward matter in its manifold forms are all reflected in the cultivation of healthy bodies and characters. The matter of nature participates in the spirit of the New Creation. Our natural environment is the chosen place where the personal being undergoing renewal has breathing space within creation. For this reason, environmental pollution is equivalent to sterilizing the sources of spiritual uplift. The affront to nature as creation leads to rejection of the basic precondition for making higher humanism a reality. The unthinking exploitation of matter until it is sucked dry and the pollution of the material world spell the beginning of the end for a civilization that has not managed to grasp or instill the proper meaning of creation and of the existence of life.

In consequence, it is a primary obligation for the intellectual disciplines today and especially for philosophical theology, together with other scientists and on the basis of the disturbing information that they provide, to take part in the effort to change modern man's attitude and mentality in regard to nature and the environment. After the brief philosophical and theological critique above, it has become apparent what honor and respect for the material nature of the environment and of man is inspired by the Christian faith. Perhaps I might add here that as to the Orthodox tradition of the Eastern

Church, the positive view of matter becomes very clear in hymnography and sacramental symbolism. One needs to go deeply into the meaning of sanctified material nature through the prayers and hymns of certain services, such as those for the feast of Theophany, in order to understand the central place occupied by the material world and man in God's work of taking care of creation as a whole and raising it up. Furthermore, we must not forget that water is the means of our cleansing, spiritual and physical, when we are totally immersed in it at baptism as in the tomb of Christ. It is bread and wine, as representative elements of material nature, that become the Body and Blood of the incarnate Word of God the Creator, the Founder and Builder, and oil becomes chrism and the means of healing by the grace of the Holy Spirit. There is in Orthodoxy a prominent symbolic-actual use of matter and a sanctification of matter that can lead to a deep respect for nature, if these conclusions are applied consistently in the realm of environmental science. When properly understood, the sacramental-symbolic life of our Church does not present simply a use of matter but endlessly testifies to the profound existential relationship between God, Nature, and Man in an indissoluble connection and to the interdependence of material and spiritual life. One might justly dare to apply to Orthodoxy, anti-idealistic and antiromantic as it is, the term "divine-materialism"—not in a pantheistic sense but in the sense that the Creator has taken up nature as a creation constantly being renewed through the energies of the Holy Spirit and as the supreme place, time, and means for the relationship between God and man to become a reality.

PHYSIS AND *KTISIS*: TWO DIFFERENT WAYS OF THINKING OF THE WORLD

John Panteleimon Manoussakis

> . . . so that creation, too, may be saved
> through incorporation in the human being.
> —*Metropolitan John of Pergamon,* Communion and Otherness

My purpose in this paper is to offer some thoughts by means of an elucidation of this statement by Metropolitan John (Zizioulas) of Pergamon, a pioneer in environmental theology. What does it mean that creation will be saved through incorporation in the human being? How are we to understand this incorporation of the world in the human person? Before addressing these questions, perhaps a few words are in order about the world itself. What is the world? Usually, we know what we mean by this term without the need for further explanation or definition. The world, one could say, is everything that is "out there" and "around" us, people and things that we encounter in our everyday lives. Yet we understand that the world is not any of these things separately, nor is it all these things together. Simply put, the world is neither a thing nor a collection of things. Phenomenologically speaking, the world is not a phenomenon but the horizon within which phenomena appear.

The "natural" attitude of man toward the surrounding world is to find himself *in* it. The first concept of the world is that man is *in* it. This understanding seems to reveal a certain image of the world as a container, as an extension that stretches to immeasurable lengths. Here we already have the modern understanding of the world in terms of *space*. Against such a view of the world, we could contrast our everyday being-in-the-world: the totality of lived experiences that make the world more than a space, that make it our *place*. Although that first understanding of the world as space seemed natural, in fact we never live by it; it is an understanding that can be reached only once we have detached ourselves from our experience of the world as place. What we called a minute ago a "natural" attitude is really unnatural, for it can be formulated only through an artificial stance of disentanglement from our relations with the world, but the world is nothing other than precisely this entanglement. We are always involved in the world in such a way that there is no world without or apart from these involvements. It is man (our affairs) that makes the world worldly, that is, more than a container in which man finds himself as a fish finds itself in an aquarium.

Current environmental talk, however, invites us to take precisely such a stance, to consider the world apart from our human affairs—to consider the world-in-itself. This would be, however, a meaningless notion. Here belongs the perplexity or rather the confusion between anthropomorphism and anthropocentrism; according to environmental theories, it is the latter that should be blamed for the damage inflicted upon the environment. A more nuanced distinction between the two models is necessary.

Let us approach the same idea from a different angle: we talked earlier about space and place. These terms are not theological, although the distinction that differentiates them is. That distinction is introduced by Christian thought as between created and uncreated order. Please note that this distinction is absent from classical thought, and it has been eclipsed in modern times (although it is this distinction that enables the inception of modernity, with the critique of John Philoponus on Aristotle).[1] Thus modernity never thinks or takes into account the difference upon which it is itself constituted. Modernity, in a way, becomes forgetful of its own birthplace. The image of a spatially understood world denies such a distinction by substituting it with what is human (man) and nonhuman (natural). Aristotle's philosophy operates precisely on such terms by distinguishing between what is from man (that is, *techne*) and what is independent of human craftsmanship (that is, *physei*).[2] The very concept of *physis* makes sense only within such a scheme. *But physis is not ktisis.*[3] The concept of creation, or *ktisis*, on the other hand, places man together with the rest of creation indistinguishably—creation is man and world thought together; thus, the world becomes man's place.

By emphasizing the question of the subject's identity ("Who am I?"), philosophy neglected the subject's locality ("Where am I?"). No wonder, then, that the philosophical subject remains either a-topic or u-topic. It is my body that localizes me to a particular place (and thus co-constitutes my particularity), and it is through my body that I am related to the world. Our understanding of the world as place (instead of space) aims at giving back the subject his or her body and making him or her topical again.

In the Christian tradition, the world is always thought of not apart from man but together with man (as man is never thought of apart from the world). As, for St. Maximus, man cannot be saved apart from the world (that is, the world is the ladder that man needs to employ in order to reach his salvation, a ladder that, unlike Wittgenstein's, he never kicks away once he has reached his destination),[4] so the world, we could say, cannot be "saved" apart from man.[5] Indeed, for the Church Fathers, the purpose of the world was man; that is why man is the *macrocosm* of the cosmos. Today we think precisely on opposite terms, so much so that it is difficult for us to understand how it is possible for man to be "larger," so to speak, than the universe. For us today the universe is larger than man (note again the concept of the world as space) and therefore, if an analogy is to be established between the two, then we can understand only man as the *microcosm* of the universe. But if for a moment we stop thinking in spatial terms, then man encompasses the whole world, for man, in contemplating the world, recognizes its order (therefore its cosmic and "cosmetic" beauty) and provides, or rather bestows in his priestly function, this order upon the world.[6]

In all this, man's contemplation of the world is ultimately man's contemplation of himself. It should not disturb us that for the Christian thinker there is absolutely no fundamental distinction between humans and their world, for to think of the one often means to think of the other. It is actually only once separation between man and world is introduced that "ethically" man can undertake and even justify the world's exploitation.

Once the world is separated from man (and by man) and is set up against him as that which is *not* him, that is, as nature, only then can man desire its subjugation to his power, that is, to his *techne* (as craftsmanship and technology). It was only once nature was placed against man that man could reflect himself within it, like one who contemplates his image on the surface of a mirror. This moment constitutes the inception of anthropomorphism (one could trace it back in Kant's *Critique of Judgment* and the subsequent development of German idealism). Man "recognizes" in nature (perhaps "projects" might be a better term) his own characteristics. What are these characteristics? Man sees nature as another self, that is, as a producer, a manufacturer. And this gives him the license to treat nature as an extension of his workshop—only larger, better, seemingly inexhaustible.

I want to draw this distinction, crucial in my opinion, between these two attitudes, to underscore that any form of anthropomorphism can never be the solution to the environmental problem, insofar as it is its very cause. Unfortunately and paradoxically, the theoretical discourse of proenvironmental policies falls prey to that mistake on both scores: encouraging the separation between man and the world (by inviting us to think of the world independently of man) and by suggesting solutions that imitate the anthropomorphic paradigm. In other words, it is not enough to emphasize nature's natural character—for such was the thinking that led to nature's destruction.

There are two forms that the belief in nature's naturalism can take. The first is the one with which any student of ancient philosophy is familiar. Nature is simply what keeps flowing out of a primordial source. Nature is also that primordial source itself that remains "hidden" (Heraclitus). In this conception, nature prohibits any idea of creation, for it is itself its own origin—or, rather, the lack of origin (*Abgrund*). Several ideas find their birthplace in this image of the aboriginal flowing of nature (*physis*): for example, nature's anarchy and thus eternity, nature's emanation, and nature's divinity. In all these ideas the prevailing thought is that of nature's *necessity*. For classical thought, *physis* exists necessarily. Its necessary character scorns man's contingency. Ultimately, no matter how much effort man puts into leaving his marks on earth, his efforts are as vain as a child's sandcastle by the seashore—nature, like the great unlimited ocean, will wash it away. But nature's necessity also takes the form of a barrier or a border against which man's freedom is to be measured. Thus man can affirm his freedom only by changing, rearranging what is given. And what is given in this case is nothing other than matter (*hyle*). Man, then, assumes the role of imposing form on the formless matter or reforming what already comes with some natural form. Thus "formless" clay is enformed as pottery, wood becomes furniture, etc. Of course, this form-ing of *hyle* is far from being an innocent process—it is violent through and through, amounting to a destruction of nature.

Here it needs to be said that man cannot cease from destroying nature without ceasing also from being essentially human. This is an unavoidable truth and a challenge for our efforts. If the answer to the environmental crisis is to have humans living in "perfect harmony" with their environment, we should recognize that what we ask from humans is nothing less than becoming like the rest of the animals on our planet. Indeed, we admire the capacity of other animal species to exist by inflicting none or very little damage to their natural environment. Animal adaptability to the environment seems resourceful and successful. But their success lies only on one principle: the acceptance of what is given as given. There is, however, a price to be paid for this success: *freedom*.

Ancient naturalism, thus, sees in nature a plethora of capabilities. The premodern man called them gods. He recognized in the erupting volcano Hephaestus's workshop, in the earthquakes Poseidon's anger; thousands of nymphs inhabited trees, wells, and rivers. In this pandemonium man recognizes only one polymorphous divinity, that of nature. Modern man takes pride in his reason, which does not afford him such a childish spectacle. A more careful look, however, would reveal that modernity has simply substituted one form of paganism for another. Nature is still infested with gods, only now they do not assume mythical figures and names but technical terminology that determines their functions. The belief in nature's functionality is another form of naturalism, one in which man once again worships only one polymorphous divinity, that of technology.

By a way of conclusion, I would like to draw some final remarks:

1. Creation and Personhood: the world as creation is the work of a person—the Creator—and for a person—man (what I elaborated elsewhere as a fourth reduction *ad personam* and *pro persona*).[7] Ultimately, the world makes sense only once inscribed within this nexus of personal relationships.[8] In theological parlance, we would say that creation is *hypostatic*.

2. The necessity of *physis* versus the freedom of *ktisis*: *ktisis* is characterized by the fact that someone decides freely to bring it forth—to create it. And even more, to create it *ex nihilo*. The *ex nihilo* doctrine underscores that nothing is presupposed or given as a condition for the creation of the world—*not even nothing*.[9] The nothing of creation is the pledge of its freedom. *Ktisis* is freely created and freely given to man—man, on the other hand, is also free to accept or not accept this gift. In a way, only *ktisis* is destructible—*physis* cannot be destroyed because it is necessary.

3. Creation is saved only through Christ: when the Logos assumes human nature, He also takes up along with it the entire creation, for all previous developments in the evolution of the species are included in the human flesh. It is, therefore, the incarnation of the Logos that saves creation. That means that creation too has been incorporated into the person of Christ, and thus a theology of the environment is ultimately part of Christology. In addition, God's saving of His creation is now specified as taking place through Christ—and *not* through or by the uncreated energies.[10] Thus, our duty toward creation is also defined as making this Christic character of creation more apparent and visible. It would suffice if man were able simply to recognize the Christic character of creation. Here a risk is avoided: man cannot save the world, nor can man presume that he can save the world, for this is only the work of Christ. The overzealous activism of some environmental organizations assumes two incompatible positions for a Christian. First, that

we, through our actions, can save the creation. That means that we do not believe that Christ can and has already saved creation;[11] this is, after all, the same creation that was created *through* Him. Second, we feel the need to assume this salvific role ourselves, to pose, that is, as the saviors of the world. But this was, precisely, the attitude that led us to the present crisis.

HUMAN IMAGE, WORLD IMAGE: THE RENEWAL OF SACRED COSMOLOGY

Philip Sherrard

Human Image, World Image

One thing we no longer need to be told is that we are in the throes of a crisis of the most appalling dimensions.[1] We tend to call this crisis the ecological crisis, and this is a fair description insofar as its effects are manifest above all in the ecological sphere. For here the message is quite clear: our entire way of life is humanly and environmentally suicidal, and unless we change it radically there is no way in which we can avoid cosmic catastrophe. Without such change, the whole adventure of civilization will come to an end during the lifetime of many now living.

Unhappily, we do not yet appear to have realized the urgency of the need for such a change, and in spite of everything we continue to blunder on along our present path of devastation in a kind of blindfolded nightmare enacted with all the inevitability of a Greek tragedy, planning to extend our empire of sterilized artificiality and specialist methodology even further; advancing even further into the computerized or electronic wilderness; devising bigger and better banking systems; manipulating the natural reproductive processes of plants, animals, and human beings; saturating our soils and crops with high-powered chemicals and a variety of poisons no sane community would allow out of a closely guarded laboratory; stripping the world of what is left of its forests at a speed that defies belief or understanding; and behaving generally in a manner that, even if we had deliberately programmed it, could not be more propitious to our own annihilation and to that of the world about us. It is as if we are in the grip of some monstrous collective psychosis, as if in truth a huge death wish hangs over the whole so-called civilized world.

In the ecological sphere the message is, as I said, unambiguously clear, however much we may continue to ignore it. Yet although the effects of our contemporary crisis are most evident in this sphere, the crisis itself is not first of all an ecological crisis. It is not first of all a crisis concerning our environment. It is first of all a crisis concerning the way we think. We are treating our planet in an inhuman, god-forsaken manner because we see things in an inhuman, god-forsaken way. And we see things in this way because that basically is how we see ourselves.

This is the first thing about which we have to be absolutely clear if we are even to begin to find a way out of the hells of self-mutilation to which we have condemned ourselves. How we see the world depends above all upon how we see ourselves. Our model of the universe—our world picture or world image—is based upon the model we have of ourselves, upon our own self-image. When we look at the world, what we see is a reflection of our own mind, of our own mode of consciousness. Our perception of a tree, a mountain, a face, an animal, or a bird is a reflection of our idea of who we think we are. What we experience in these things is not so much the reality or nature of these things in themselves as simply what our own limitations, spiritual, psychological, and physical, permit us to experience of them. Our capacity to perceive and experience is stereotyped according to how we have molded our own image and likeness.

This means that before we can effectively deal with the ecological problem, we have to change our world image, and this in its turn means that we have to change our self-image. Unless our own evaluation of ourselves and of what constitutes the true nature of our being changes, the way we treat the world about us will not change either. And unless that happens, conservation theory and practice, however well intentioned and necessary, will not touch the heart of the problem. They will at best represent an effort to deal with what in the end are symptoms, not causes.

I do not in the least want to belittle such efforts, which often are heroic, lonely, and incredible, against all odds. One of the terrible temptations we face is that of thinking that the problem is so big that nothing we can do on an individual scale can possibly have any effect: we must leave it to the authorities, to the governments, to the experts.

That is a fatal attitude. Every single gesture made, however pathetic it may seem, counts and may have incalculable consequences. Thought not accompanied by corresponding practice soon becomes sterile. Yet at the same time practice springing from incorrectly based thought easily becomes counterproductive, because practice deals above all with symptoms. Causes are rooted in the way we think, and it is because of this that our crisis is first of all a question of our self-image and our worldview.

This is the crux of our situation. The industrial and technological inferno we have produced around us and by means of which we are now devastating our world is not something that has come about accidentally. On the contrary, it is the direct consequence of our allowing ourselves to be dominated by a certain paradigm of thought—embracing a certain human image and a certain world image—to such a degree that it now determines virtually all our mental attitudes and all our actions, public and private.

It is a paradigm of thought that impels us to look upon ourselves as little more than two-legged animals whose destiny and needs can best be fulfilled through the pursuit of social, political, and economic self-interest. And to correspond with this self-image we have invented a worldview in which nature is seen as an impersonal commodity, a soulless source of food, raw materials, wealth, power, and so on, which we think we are quite entitled to experiment with, exploit, remodel, and generally abuse by means of any scientific and mechanical technique we can devise and produce, in order to satisfy and deploy this self-interest. Having in our own minds desanctified ourselves, we have desanctified nature, too, in our own minds: we have removed it from the suzerainty of the divine and have assumed that we are its overlords and that it is our thrall, subject to our will. In short, under the aegis of this self-image and worldview we have succeeded in converting ourselves into the most depraved and depraving of all creatures upon the earth.

This self-image and worldview have their origin in a loss of memory, in a forgetfulness of who we are, and in our fall to a level of ignorance and stupidity that threatens the survival of our race. By an inescapable logic inherent in this origin we are impelled to proceed along a course each step of which is marked by our fall into ever deeper ignorance of our own nature and consequently into ever deeper ignorance of the nature of everything else as well.

So long as we persist in this course, we are doomed to advance blindly and at an ever-increasing pace toward total loss of identity, total loss of control, and eventually to total self-destruction. And nothing can stop this process except a complete reversal of direction, a complete change in the way we look at ourselves and so in the way we look at the world about us. Without that change, we will simply continue to add fuel to our own funeral pyre.

Can we make this reversal, this complete change? I think the answer to that is that no one can stop us doing so except ourselves. No one can stop us from changing our own self-image and consequently our worldview except ourselves.

The question—the only real question—is what self-image and worldview are we to put in the place of the bankrupt stereotypes, the unensouled fictions, which have taken us over?

Here a certain act of recollection is needed. I said that the self-image and worldview that now dominate us have their origin in a loss of memory, in our forgetfulness of who we are. What do I mean by this?

In the great creative cultures of the world, human beings do not regard themselves as two-legged animals, descended from the apes, whose needs and satisfactions can be achieved through pursuing social, political, and economic self-interest in the material world and as though their life was confined to a material space-time dimension. On the contrary, they think of themselves first and foremost as descended from the gods, or from God, and as heirs to eternity, with a destiny that goes far beyond politics, society, economics, or anything that can be fulfilled in terms of the material world or by satisfying their mortal and physical desires and needs. They think of themselves as sacred beings, even as semidivine beings, not in their own right but because they are created in the divine image, in the image of God, of a transcendent more-than-human form of consciousness. They come from a divine source, and the divine world is their birthright, their true home.

In the same way, in the great creative cultures of the world, human beings do not look upon what we call the outer world, the world of nature, as a mere chance association of atoms or whatever, or as something impersonal, soulless, and inanimate, which they are entitled to manipulate, master, exploit, and generally to tamper and mess about with in order to gratify their greeds and their power lusts. They look upon nature, too, as a divine creation, as full of a hidden wisdom as they themselves are, as full of a personal, sensitive soul-life or psychic life as they themselves are. They recognize and acknowledge in nature, too, a sacred reality, a divine invisible presence made visible. They sense that every part of the earth—of the whole cosmos—is sacred. Every leaf, every grain of sand or soil, every bird, animal, and star, the air and every insect is holy, in sync with their life, their memory and experience. The sap that courses through the trees is as sacred as life blood—is one with their own life blood. Forests, mountains, lakes, fields, seas, the great plains, and even the deserts are not "resources" for exploitation; they are a way of life. They may trade in the gifts they offer—in precious stones and spices, in corn and cattle. They may in ignorance be excessive in their demands on them, in grazing their flocks or in felling too many trees. But they do not deliberately *trade* in *nature itself* or at the expense of nature. They do not and could not (*not* simply because they lack the technical knowhow) deliberately blast its guts out through testing their atom bombs; savage its skies with the din and stench of airplanes and spacecraft; poison its rivers, its lakes, its seas, its underground waters through spilling chemicals into them or through the leaching of toxic wastes; or rape it in any of the thousands of ways in which we are now raping it.

And when I say "could not," I do not mean this in any sentimental sense. It is an interdiction rooted in the profoundest depths of their understanding of things. If nature is the creation of God or the manifestation of Supreme Wisdom and Harmony, it follows not only that it is the expression of a divine order and disposition but also that this order and disposition are the best that are possible, given the conditions under which or within which nature is created or made manifest. Consequently, for us to imagine that we can improve it or remove the imperfections inherent in it by interfering with it, remodeling it, transforming it, and so on, through ways that involve disrupting or perverting its God-given order and disposition as well as the organic processes that are part and parcel of them, is sheer folly and impertinence: it is to imagine that we can outstrip and improve on the wisdom of Wisdom Absolute. Inevitably, therefore, any attempt on our part to interfere in it or to remodel it can only debase, canker, corrupt, and vitiate the conditions in which we have to live our life on earth. Over the last few centuries we have so effectively demonstrated the truth of this that we should not need any further convincing as to the rightness of the understanding in which it is rooted.

In spite of this, such an understanding, and the sense of the sacredness of both man and nature, as well as the awe and reverence that they inspire, are often characterized nowadays as primitive or as based on superstition, regarded as belonging to the prescientific age and as something promoted only by those who have failed, for whatever reason, to move into the twenty-first century. To maintain that theories of biological evolution, whether in a Darwinian or post-Darwinian form, are misconceived and that human beings, far from being descended from the apes, only develop apelike propensities and features when they pervert their human nature and become subhuman or antihuman is still to invite ridicule. To insist that we can obtain no genuine knowledge of the physical world unless we first attain a knowledge of spiritual or metaphysical realities is to provoke the accusation of obscurantism, if not plain dottiness: we tend to take it for granted that not only is it perfectly possible to obtain a knowledge of the physical world without any reference whatsoever to the idea of a God, or a Creator, or of any underlying transtemporal and transspatial metaphysical reality but also that we positively must *not* allow any such idea to determine either the methods we employ in our search for knowledge or the substance of what we put forward as knowledge. We can and must examine visible nature (*natura naturata*) as though it were independent of the invisible metaphysical nature (*natura naturans*) from which it derives and in which it is rooted. We can and must explain natural phenomena as though they were independent of the realm of the supranatural. We can and must explain them merely in terms of the laws of physics and chemistry, without any reference to *natura naturans* or to the realm of the supranatural. Such is the level to which the human intelligence has degenerated in its pursuit of the goals that typify our modern world.

And this in spite of the fact that—to limit ourselves to the European tradition alone—there is no major philosopher, from Plato to Berdyaev, and no major poet, from Homer to Yeats, who has not explicitly or implicitly affirmed the kind of cosmology that we now tend to ridicule, repudiate, or ignore. One of the great unresolved psychological enigmas of the modern Western world is the question of what or who has persuaded us to accept as virtually axiomatic a self-view and a worldview that demand that we reject out of hand the wisdom and vision of our major philosophers and poets in order to imprison our thought and our very selves in the materialist, mechanical, and dogmatic torture chamber devised by purely quantitative and third-rate scientific minds.

In this connection there is one particular fallacy from which we must free ourselves, and this is the idea that contemporary scientific theories and the descriptions that go with them are somehow neutral, or value free, and do not presuppose the submission of the human mind to a set of assumptions or dogmas in the way that is said to be demanded by adherence to a religious faith. This idea is, indeed, still propagated and even believed by many modern scientists themselves. On it is based the claim that scientific descriptions of things are objective descriptions. It is not that these scientists deny that there are, or may be, values. It is that insofar as they are scientists they claim to operate independently of value judgments and to be engaged in what they like to call purely disinterested scientific research.

This is one of the most insidious of the fallacies of which we still tend to be the victims. Even people who maintain that they are fighting for a new philosophy of ecological values, such as Henryk Skolimowski,[2] repeat it as though it were beyond dispute. In fact, far from being beyond dispute, it represents a total lie. Every thought, every observation, every judgment, every description whether of the modern scientist or of anyone else is soaked in a priori, preconceived, built-in value judgments, assumptions, and dogmas at least as rigid, if not more rigid (because they are so often unconsciously embraced), than those of any explicitly religious system. The very nature of human thought is such that it cannot operate independently of value judgments, assumptions, and dogmas. Even the assertion that it could do so constitutes a value judgment and implies a whole philosophy, whether we are aware of it or not.

Alongside this fallacy and closely allied to it is another fallacy of which we still tend to be the victims. This is the notion—already alluded to—not that modern science is value free or that it is the only possible science but that it is valid in relation to that limited aspect of things—namely, that aspect of them which is material or phenomenal and extended in time and space—that it sets out to study. This notion is not intended to deny that there is or may be another aspect of things—an aspect spiritual and eternal and unextended in time and space—that can also be studied in its own right and could be said to constitute the sphere of spiritual knowledge or of a spiritual science. It simply involves the claim that there are two levels of reality; that each level can be studied apart from, and without reference to, the other; and that the knowledge gained as a result of studying the one level is just as valid in its own terms as the knowledge gained as a result of studying the other level.

This way of envisaging things is a fallacy because the primary determinant of the knowledge—or what we assume to be the knowledge—that we form of things is not the particular level of reality to which this knowledge is said to apply. Its primary determinant is the level or mode of consciousness of which this knowledge is the expression. This is to say that it is not so much that there are different levels of reality to perceive and experience, the one inner and spiritual and the other outer and material, each with an independent science that corresponds to it. It is that there are different levels or modes of consciousness in man through which he perceives and experiences, so that what he perceives and experiences will depend first of all on the level or mode of consciousness active within him and not on the level of reality that he happens to be studying.

There are not two sciences, the one concerned with the material and outward aspect of things extended in time and space and the other with their spiritual and eternal dimension, unextended in time and space. There is only one science. But there are two dominant modes of consciousness in man: his ego consciousness, which is his lowest mode of consciousness, corresponding as it does to what is most inhuman and satanic in him, and his angelic or spiritual consciousness, which is his higher mode of consciousness. Of course, there are endless permutations between these two modes, depending on whether the consciousness gravitates more to the one or to the other.

The higher or spiritual consciousness perceives and experiences things as they are in themselves, inner and outer, spiritual and material, metaphysical and physical interpenetrating and forming a single unsundered and unsunderable reality. The profane or ego consciousness cannot perceive and experience things as they are. It can perceive and experience only what its own opacity permits it to perceive and experience, and that is not the reality of things but things emasculated of their reality. There cannot be a science of things—of phenomena—that ignores the reality of phenomena, that by virtue of which they are what they are. There cannot be a valid science of the physical aspect of things alone, for the simple reason that the notion that things possess an outer physical aspect apart from their inner spiritual dimension is an illusory notion.

For if we could perceive and experience with the full clarity of our higher or spiritual consciousness, we would be able to see and understand that no visible thing—nothing belonging to the world of phenomena—possesses existence or being in its own right. We would see and understand that apart from its inner and spiritual dimension and identity it possesses no reality whatsoever, whether physical, material, or substantial, and that the notion that it does so is merely an illusion or distortion inherent as such in the viewpoint of the ego consciousness. In no way is it possible to separate physics from metaphysics, and insofar as we think it is possible we simply confirm the inanity of our thought.

Thus insofar as modern science presupposes the notion that we can obtain a knowledge of phenomena apart from, and without reference to, a prior knowledge of their inner and spiritual dimension, it is based totally upon the ego consciousness, or—which comes to the same thing—it is still in servitude to a dualism that opposes mind and matter, subject and object, the knower and what is to be known—a dualism that represents a total distortion of reality. This means it is tainted with the inhuman and satanic characteristics in man of which this consciousness is the vehicle. That is why its application, in technological or other forms, is liable to be fraught with consequences that are equally inhuman and satanic, whether with regard to our own being or with regard to the natural physical world.

That, too, is why every extension of the empire and influence of our contemporary secular scientific mentality has gone and continues to go hand in hand with a corresponding and increased erosion in us of the sense of the sacred. In fact, we do not have any respect, let alone reverence, for the world of nature because we do not fundamentally have any respect, let alone reverence, for ourselves. It is because we have lost the sense of our own reality that we have lost the sense of every other reality as well. It is because we cripple and mutilate ourselves that we cripple and mutilate everything else as well. Our contemporary crisis is really our own depravity writ large.

So the only real answer to this crisis is to stop depraving ourselves. It is to recover a sense of our true identity and dignity, of our self-image as sacred beings, as immortal beings. A false self-view breeds a false worldview, and together they breed our nemesis and the nemesis of the world. Once we repossess a sense of our own holiness, we will recover the sense of the holiness of the world about us as well, and we will then act toward the world about us with the awe and humility that we should possess when we enter a sacred shrine, a temple of love and beauty in which we worship and adore. Only in this way will we once again become aware that our destiny and the destiny of nature are one and the same. Only in this way can we restore a cosmic harmony. If we do not take this way out, then that is that, for there is no other way out. To fail here is to fail irrevocably: there can be no escaping our inhuman genocide. Without a sense of the holy—that everything that lives is holy—and without humility toward the whole—toward man, nature, and *toward what is beyond both man and nature*, their transcendent source and origin—we will simply proceed headlong along the course to self-destruction to which we are now committed, to that nemesis which is our own choosing and for which we are entirely responsible.

All this means that if we are to confront our contemporary crisis in a way that goes to its roots, our task is twofold. We have first to get absolutely clear in our minds—to identify coherently and unquestionably—the paradigm of thought that underlies and determines our present self-image and worldview. Unless we first do this we are liable to become victims of a kind of doublethink attacking the symptoms while remaining subject to the causes that produce the symptoms. And it is all the more important for us to do it because we have tended to forget what the assumptions and presuppositions that characterize this paradigm are: they are so deeply embedded beneath the ramparts of our ordinary thought processes that we are unaware that they do in fact underlie and determine these processes.

Second, we have to try to recover or rediscover the vision of man and nature—or, rather, the theoanthropocosmic vision—that will make it possible for us to perceive and hence to experience both ourselves and the world we live in as the sacred realities that they are, because unless we do recover a sense of their sacredness that is based upon a coherent understanding of why they are sacred, our attempts to reaffirm this quality in them may be debilitated by what in the end is little more than sentimental prejudice.

The Death and Resurrection of Sacred Cosmology

This vision of a sacred cosmology—one that affirms both a sacred human image and a sacred world image—is rooted in the understanding that the creation of the world is not a gratuitous extra. It is the expression of divine life with all the power of necessity, with all the absolute freedom and spontaneity of God's Being. God *qua* God is Creator and Creator *qua* Creator is God: creation is intrinsic to His very life; it is the inner landscape of His own Being, God making Himself visible to Himself and simultaneously making Himself visible to us. It is in some sense His very self.[3]

Creation, then, is God making Himself visible, or knowable, to Himself. It is God revealing Himself to Himself. That is the initial motive of creation: the desire of God to reveal Himself and to know Himself in beings through being known by them. Being, or Mind, as a subject, issues from Its own formless, unmanifest state in order to possess a means whereby it can know its own subjectivity, as a mirror in which it sees Its own face. It is the desire of the God who is "beyond being," who is not—the *theos agnostos*—unknown and unaffirmed, not only to know Himself and to affirm Himself but also to be known and affirmed. What we are talking about here is not a process of emanation in the neo-Platonic sense. What is in question is what one might call grades of revelation, or a process whereby God establishes within Himself a descending hierarchy, each level of which represents not only a further stage of differentiation but also an increasing degree of subordination and concretization.

Three main degrees or phases in this process of self-revelation may be distinguished. The first is that phase whereby the unknown God reveals Himself to Himself in making Himself conscious of the latent potentialities of His own Being. The second is that whereby this ideal, impersonal, formless, and abstract content of the divine Intelligence—of the divine Logos—is differentiated in specific individuated forms, forms possessing a figure, a pattern, a body, although this is still in an immaterial state. These forms constitute the world of the uncreated spiritual energies, of the divine Images or Ideas or of what—since they represent differentiation within the Logos—Christian authors often refer to as *logoi* and that we for the rest of this chapter will designate as Image-archetypes, since they are the divine archetypes of everything that exists in the visible and sensible world.[4] This world of the Image-archetypes is an intermediary world between the world of pure formless intelligible realities and the visible world. And the third phase in this theophanic process is that whereby these Image-archetypes manifest themselves in the forms of particular, individuated concrete beings.

What it is important to emphasize is that though each phase or degree in this process is distinct, each is inseparable from the other two, and that though here they are presented as successive phases, they all occur in total simultaneity, in divine instantaneousness. There is no question of any lapse or hiatus between them, whether spatial or temporal, for they occur prior to space and time, even though some of their effects have a spatial or temporal character. The three are simply phases or "moments" in a single divine act through which God *reveals* Himself to Himself through all eternity.

The first phase—that whereby God becomes conscious of His own latent Intelligence content—is accomplished in the world of ultimate mystery. This in Christian terms is the world of the Trinity, the world of the three Persons, or hypostases, of God, and of the relations between them, and the theophany that is there accomplished is that through which the potentialities and virtualities concealed in the unknownness of the Father are emancipated from this unknownness in the divine Logos, the Image of the Father. If creation is God's self-revelation, it follows that in Himself—in the totally unmanifest depths of His Being—inhere the potentialities of everything in which when manifest He sees and recognizes Himself. These potentialities are His divine Names, and although these Names cannot be said to be identical with the Godhead, they are not different from it, since they denote what are present in the Godhead from all eternity. And because the name is identical with the thing named, the multiple divine Names are God Himself, and He is one.[5]

In eternity—in pre-eternity—before God brought us into existence, we are beings embraced by Him, in His Being, and our own beings are individuations of His Being—of the states and potentialities of God. We appear in Him. We are not simply *with* Him, because we are His very own Being, the Being that He is. We are His organs, the individuations of His Names. The divine Name creates my being, and reciprocally my being posits it in the very same act as that in which it posits me. Yet at the same time, our action of positing God is really God positing Himself in us: it is not ourselves who create the form in which we represent God—for our autonomy is a fiction. We are images of an Image maker, icons of an Iconographer. We are each the action of a divine Name, the expression of its intention and its will, the form in which its action and influx are manifest. We each of us have no action but our receptivity: insofar as we receive God, God manifests Himself in us.

In the same way, every existential being is the visible form of a particular divine Name—is the being of a particular divine Name—while the divine Name constitutes the particular quality or the essential identity of the being that is its visible form. The totality of the divine Name is the Name together with the being in which it is manifest. The Name and the being in which it is manifest constitute a bi-unity—the one inseparable from the other.

Thus each created thing is also a concretization of divine Being and is embraced by this Being. All created beings possess not only Being but also the consciousness that goes with Being. Already there is life and consciousness in the most humble and elementary natural forms, however blunt and dim their revelation may be. There is always a minimum of image quality in such forms—they are already images of Life and Reality—even though they do not reveal so well or know so well that they are such images. It is the privilege of the higher created forms—of human beings in particular—to reveal this Life and Reality more fully and to be more conscious of their image quality. But the ascent up the ladder of created forms from the lowest to the highest marks only a growing complexity in the formal presentation of Life and Reality, just as the descent down the ladder marks an increasing degree of concretization within divine Being. But they do not mark anything else. The difference is one of complexity and concretization, not of kind. It is a matter not of quantity but of quality. Even the lowest forms—those with the minimum degree of complexity—are already complete revelations of Life, complete revelations of divine Being. There cannot be any scission in Life and Being itself—only the material aspect of things can be multiplied by being sliced up.

The divine Names, then, achieve their meaning and full reality only through and for the beings that are their epiphanic forms—the forms in which they are manifest. This manifestation in forms is itself represented, we said, by two phases, the immaterial and the material. The immaterial phase is that through which the divine Names are individuated in forms that possess figure, pattern, and body, although these lack the materiality of figures, patterns, and bodies in the sensible world. These forms constitute the world of the *logoi* or Image-archetypes, the archetypes of everything that exists in the sensible world. These Image-archetypes might in their turn also be said to constitute the inner consciousness of all created beings, their Inner self-awareness and identity, what makes them what they are and nothing else.[6]

These Image-archetypes—the divine inner reality of everything—are not abstract. They are fully living; they are life itself in all its pulsating actuality and compulsion. They are the unmanifest divine Names, latent in the Father and emancipated from their unknownness in the Logos, now given vitality and beauty. If the Logos is the Image of the Father, this world of Image-archetypes is the image of this Image, its objective self-revelation or its self-determination, life giving and life fulfilling. In this way it is also the revelation of the Holy Spirit, for the Holy Spirit is the principle of quickening spiritual reality within the Trinity, the reality and life and beauty of the Logos of Truth.

It is the Holy Spirit that transforms the ideal, abstract Intelligence content of the Logos into a world vibrating with the life of God: there is an Annunciation in the Trinity as well as a terrestrial Annunciation—a divine *fiat* in God Himself in relation to His own Being—and this is executed by the Holy Spirit. And it is through this Annunciation and *fiat* in God Himself that their life-giving, life-fulfilling qualities—the life of Truth in all its transparency and beauty—are bestowed on the celestial Image-archetypes, so that they, too, become the self-revelation of the Deity, the garment of God, the divine Glory that the heavens declare.[7]

Thus not only are these Image-archetypes not abstract on their own level. They are not abstract either in relation to the third phase of divine self-revelation, which concerns the concrete realities of the visible, sensible world. Concrete existence is the living manifestation or realization of the Image-archetypes. It is not something added to them but is inherent in them. They exist concretely in things in the visible world or, rather, things in the visible world represent their temporal and spatial determinations. The invisible spiritual presence and the visible form of this presence compose an indissoluble bi-unity, with no falling away or seduction from the noumenal to the phenomenal. Just as the Image-archetypes are the personal living God—rooted in the personal triune Godhead—so the created world, too, is the personal living God, rooted in the same Godhead. The visible universe is the living Body of God. It is the temple of the living God.

It is at this point that we return to the theme that, as I said at the beginning of this chapter, is intimately and indissolubly wedded to the theme of creation, namely, the theme of Incarnation. For what we have been describing in these phases of divine self-revelation represents no less than the eternal process according to which the divine Logos is embodied. Assuredly, what is here in question is not so much the historical and individual Incarnation of the Logos in Jesus of Nazareth as His cosmic Incarnation. But the two are mutually supporting, and the understanding of the one illuminates the understanding of the other. In fact, one might say that the historical and individual Incarnation and its formal interpretation are a kind of concentrated and paradigmatic recapitulation of the cosmic Incarnation.

For what we are trying to clarify here is the theandric significance of the world, and the theandric mystery is unfolded most synoptically and unambiguously in the historical Incarnation. That is why the doctrine of creation is linked inseparably with Christology—the doctrine of the relationship of the two natures, divine and human, in Christ—and cannot properly be understood apart from Christology.

The Council of Chalcedon described the relationship between the divine and human natures in the God-man, although it did so only in negative terms: it declared that the two natures are united in Christ inseparably and unconfusedly. Created nature can never not be distinct from the divine nature, though it is important to stress that this distinction is not with respect to the source of its being but only with respect to the particular mode in which it manifests that being. This being is God's Being, and what is meant when it is said that in the God-man the divine and the human are united inseparably is that there is an interpenetration of this Being and the created element of the human. There is a symbiosis between them, even though the two partners of the union are not equal.

This, in brief, is the theandric mystery,[8] and since this mystery, consummated in Christ, is the model according to which we can understand the relationship between the divine and the human as such—for Christ's human nature is universal—and in individual human beings in particular, we can see how the potentiality in each human being for transfiguration and divinization rests upon definite and explicit ontological ground—on a potentiality intrinsic to human nature, on an inherent capacity to be divinized.

Yet this same theandric mystery is the model that applies not only with reference to our understanding of the true nature and potentiality of individual human beings; it applies also with reference to our understanding of the true nature and potentiality of each created being, down to the most humble and elementary. "And the Logos became flesh."[9] But flesh here (*sarx*) can be taken to signify not only the flesh of the human body; it can be taken to signify all matter, all physical nature. All matter, all physical nature, is the Body of Christ.

God-manhood in its accomplishment presupposes the union of the divine and human natures in the one *hypostasis* of the Logos. But the interpenetration of the divine and the human in Christ corresponds precisely to the interpenetration of the particular divine Image-archetype (*logos*) and the created aspects of the natural form in which it is manifested. Christ, the divine Logos, embraces and recapitulates all the Image-archetypes of which He is the active subject and that are immanent in Him, and each creature is an individual manifestation of a single Image-archetype that, again, is immanent in its active subject, Christ. Because I am the manifestation of a divine Image-archetype in which I inhere, my true subject is Christ, for Christ is the subject of that archetype; my true self is the ego of my originating Source.

The manifesting Logos includes within Himself the whole world of the Image-archetypes, and thus every created being is a manifestation of the Logos. The relationship between the Logos and His Image-archetypes (a relationship that subsumes the creaturely aspect or determination of each particular Image-archetype) constitutes the ground of the relationship between the divine and the creaturely in every created existence, and as that relationship is one of union (though not of identity), so it is also one of union (though not of identity) in every created existence. As all creation is grounded ontologically in the world of the Image-archetypes and is their manifestation, so all creation is the Body of Christ, the Incarnation of the Logos.[10]

It is this, too, that links the doctrine of creation not only to Christology but also to the doctrine of the Trinity. In fact, it shows how all three doctrines are inextricably intertwined and how the understanding of any one of them must be deficient unless it is set within the context of the other two. For the Image-archetypes are, as we saw, the joint revelation of the Logos and the Holy Spirit, who together disclose the unknown Father. This, we said, is because the Image-archetypes are the image of the Logos, His objective self-revelation or self-determination. Correlatively, it is the Holy Spirit who transforms the abstract, impersonal Intelligence-content of the Logos into life-giving and life-fulfilling personal forms, forms possessing a figure, a pattern, a body, irradiated with the beauty of God. One could say that the Image-archetypes that are the self-expression of the Logos are given birth through the agency of the Holy Spirit.

Thus the Image-archetypes disclose both the Logos and the Holy Spirit together and simultaneously. Yet since the created dimension of each Image-archetype is subsumed within the Image-archetype itself, this dimension, too, discloses both Persons together: it is an example of God-creaturehood in exactly the same way as Christ is the prototype of God-manhood. It, too, and all creation with it, is an unfolding of the theandric mystery. It, too, and all creation with it, is a disclosure of divine personality.

This is to say that the Image-archetypes, together with their spatiotemporal endorsement, are themselves types of divine manhood or divine creaturehood. That is why just as is the case for individual human beings, so for each created form in the natural world its potentiality for transfiguration and divinization rests upon definite and explicit ontological ground—on a potentiality intrinsic to it, on an inherent capacity to be divinized. And it is upon exactly this same ground that is based the reality of the promise that "God may be all in all"[11]—the promise that God may become all in all *within* the creaturely existence of this universe.

We are now in a position to see more clearly the significance of what I emphasized briefly above, namely that the generation of the Logos, the Son and Image of the Father, is linked inseparably to the cosmogonic act, the act of creation. We have seen how the Logos as abstract and impersonal Intelligence content is given living and personal form through the Holy Spirit in the still immaterial Image-archetypes. This means that on the one side there is potential Sonship—the unexpressed, impersonal Logos-Intelligence—while on the other side there are the forms in which personal Sonship is actually realized, the forms of the living Image-archetypes, though these two phases or "moments" in the generation of the Son are simultaneous, take place in instantaneity.

There is thus generation of the Son prior to creation. But since the single simple act of this generation of the Son includes the generation of that aspect of Sonship which is given character and personality in the world of the Image-archetypes, it follows that this act of generation includes within it and finds its full expression in the act of creation, in and through the manifestation of the forms of the created world. For all the concrete, visible forms of created things are subsumed in the Image-archetypes, are but their spatio-temporal effects, or prolongations, or counterparts.

Thus the generation of the Son is at once both generation prior to creation and simultaneously generation in creation. Generation and creation are linked inseparably: they are distinct yet inseparable "moments" or aspects of a single creative act, and there can be no Sonship without simultaneously the unfolding of the living forms of created existence.

Environment and Security: Toward a Systemic Crisis of Humanity?

Costa Carras

This paper is based on two fundamental observations.[1] First, environmental causes might not only be at the root of social and ethnic conflict—as a result, for instance, of shortages of water and power—but might also provide opportunities for different groups to work together in order to avoid serious crises or indeed catastrophes that may appear otherwise impossible to overcome without broad international collaboration. Second, we need to form a view of likely long-term developments, of our response to date, and, in consequence, of what remains to be done to meet the outstanding challenges.

In beginning such a broad discussion of environmental problems, there is no way to evade the question of whether we shall be able to avoid a future collapse of systemic proportions. This debate involves two more specific questions. The first asks how long it will take the international community as a whole to comprehend the danger to which humanity as a whole is currently subjecting itself; the second, and even more interesting, question asks whether the very pace of the changes involved (climatic, economic, political, and technological) may not turn out to be so rapid that events slip out of human control and become unmanageable. Over the centuries, the human species has created rationally structured societies based on law, on principles of sound administration, on science, on technology, and on markets. Will it, however, prove possible for human beings not just to adjust but to adjust *with the speed, adequacy, and continuity* that will be required to meet the environmental challenges the future holds?

In such discussions, optimistic predictions are sometimes made, especially at moments of heightened international sensitivity regarding some specific ecological problem, such as during the period of worldwide concern regarding the hole in the ozone layer, which led to the 1987 Protocol of Montreal. The writer tends to agree with the more pessimistic observers, although admittedly he is not as pessimistic in 2008 as he had been twenty years earlier. The reasons for pessimism are, however, clear. For one thing, it is evident enough that the world's political leadership (chiefly, but not solely, the leaderships of the United States, China, and India) has lost much valuable time in coming to grips with the problem. More time has been lost, in fact, than is usually believed to be the case, given that climate change has been moving more rapidly than had been assumed until the most recent estimates revealed the true picture. Furthermore, this already difficult situation is further complicated by a more recent development, which is independent of and parallel to the ecological crisis. This development is that a substantial segment of the Islamic world is no longer opposed only to certain policies being promoted by Great Powers but also to their fundamental values with respect to the organization of human communities and activities.

When the first petroleum crisis broke out in 1973, there was already opposition to specific Great Power policies but not as yet to their fundamental values. Today things are different. There are far more existential differences, even if this does not cancel the evident fact that the prototype of a consumption-based society, clearly of U.S. parentage and carrying all the attendant environmental implications, continues to be quite as popular among those who proclaim such existential differences as among those who do not. The critical point, however, is that it has become more difficult for humankind to face the environmental crisis as a united body than it would have been even twenty years ago, because there is another major issue that distracts our attention and impairs our unity, creating an alternative central focus for political action and thought.

There are also reasons for relative optimism compared with twenty years ago. The 1988 meeting on Religion and the Environment, which Elliniki Etairia (Society for Environment and Cultural Heritage) organized on Patmos, opened the way for a constant and consistent expression of acute concern regarding environmental problems by the Ecumenical Patriarchate. Doubtless, many will consider this a matter of minor importance in the larger picture. It is, however, significant that in just five years, between 1988 and 1993, a renewed theology of creation and of the human being as the priest of creation became predominant in the Orthodox Church. Thanks to the active pastoral and theological commitment of Bartholomew, Ecumenical Patriarch since 1991, and the theological writings of John, Metropolitan of Pergamon, this approach has become well known and has exercised great influence throughout the Christian world, though one cannot but note that this hopeful development has been far more noticeable to date internationally than within the Greek-speaking world.

No one will dare question the importance of the second development. The protection of the environment has gradually been raised to the position of a dominant ideology, and indeed of an ideology with religious overtones, inside one of the world's major economic and social groupings, namely the European Union. This development has affected almost all of the major language groups that make up Europe. It would be fair to assert that a common positive attitude to the environment regarding a sense of urgency in relation to environmental issues, together with the common market and rather more than the common currency (which does not include many EU countries), represents the most important set of policy values that makes up the contemporary identity of the European Union as a whole.

This has indeed proven a critical development, especially since one basic fact in relation to the ecological crisis is precisely that it cannot be resolved by the use of "classical" elements of military power. The obverse of that observation remains, however, equally accurate: the resolution of the ecological crisis we face may indeed be delayed or even indeed made impossible if governments give priority to military conflicts and increased defense expenditures as opposed to the need to resolve the fundamental environmental challenges of our age. For not only can military superiority not meet this specific challenge, but it can no longer even be considered the most significant element of power, given the structural changes being gradually brought to the world as a result of the clear emergence of critical environmental risks.

To give a specific example, the United States is currently the world's sole "giant," having, in principle, a hegemonic role in the world political order after the collapse of Soviet communism in the 1990s. The United States has, however, made a series of serious mistakes over the last decade. It underestimated the scale of the world environmental crisis. It has handled its relationships with Russia clumsily and with the Islamic world very poorly indeed. Its most fundamental error, however, has been to have committed a huge proportion of its resources to secure a massive superiority in military armaments, a superiority without precedent in history, at precisely the moment when military superiority in itself is becoming less adequate than ever before for the resolution of the most substantial international threats. This same error of judgment has led the United States to attempt military solutions to problems that could best be resolved chiefly by nonmilitary means.

The subject of this article is certainly not U.S. policy but rather the world environmental crisis. Yet it is important not to underestimate the role of each specific international actor in relation to this crisis. The United States, from "sole giant" on the international scene, is already closer to becoming "first among equals" and perhaps even to becoming a "wounded giant." It remains a fundamental reality, however, that the environmental issue cannot be resolved without the active contribution of the United States, as has been amply demonstrated over the last fifteen years. It is important in this respect that the United States retains three basic advantages, all more significant than military superiority, and these advantages will prove of critical significance for any constructive resolution of environmental dangers. Their system of technological research and development, soundly based on the existence of outstanding universities and research centers, is one. The U.S. economic and entrepreneurial culture, an inherited asset they carefully sustain, is another. It is based on a traditional culture of risk taking and the willingness to accept rapid and widespread application of radically innovative ideas. Finally, together with Britain, Australia, Canada, and New Zealand, the United States forms part of the central core of the English-speaking world, whose dominance of the flow of information in our world today is even greater than the U.S. dominance of the international military balance. In consequence, ideological trends can pass equally not just from the United States to the European Union but from the European Union to the United States through scientific dialogue in the English-speaking and, more generally, English-language world. Just one example of this is the Stern Report, which persuaded an important segment of the U.S. political and economic leadership that, contrary to the impression prevalent for many years, delay in the resolution of the environmental problem, particularly climate change, will cause greater economic damage than its timely confrontation.

It follows that we live in a world where the resolution of the problem of climate change, to take the most obvious example, requires the contribution of many countries, including the United States, the EU nations, Russia, Japan, China, India, and doubtless other emergent countries, so that the overall reduction required in energy consumption and in emissions of greenhouse gases is achieved through coordinated and parallel action. It remains true, however, that in consequence of their dominant position in the formulation of the global political and economic policy agenda, the United States and the European Union have an even more critical role to play. Here lies the reason for my relatively greater optimism in recent years. The scientific and technological leadership of the English-speaking world (to a high degree) and its business and media leadership (to a substantial degree) now appear determined to give the environmental crisis its proper priority.

Thus it is indeed possible to find evidence that would justify a relative optimism, despite the tragic loss of valuable time over the last two decades. It is, however, essential to emphasize also those elements in the situation that continue to give rise to deep and justified pessimism. Such pessimism can in any event represent an important motivating force, which perhaps will move us to confront more effectively the inescapable challenges that certainly lie before us. And this is because the appearance of a deep divide between a substantial segment of the Islamic world and the major world powers, to which reference has already been made, is not the only complicating element in the situation. There is also, and more substantively, the centuries-old and still today all too evident "success" of the Western world as a critical factor in its likely future failure.

What do I mean by such a seemingly paradoxical statement? The Western world has been impressively successful over several centuries, and spectacularly so since World War II, both in achieving economic growth and in the creation of open societies whose values and educational systems encourage and stimulate further economic growth. Both through world markets and through world information networks, these achievements have become available to all other societies. Some are unwilling; others are willing but not able to adopt the relevant systems and patterns of organization, growth, and consumption. Some, however—more obviously China, India, Southeast Asia, and Latin America—are proving capable of doing so. Their impressive success, and indeed with almost unparalleled rates of growth at that, is setting the world an example of the classic dilemma of an "impossible trinity." In simpler language, it appears impossible to ensure simultaneously:

> First, that all Chinese, Indians, and other nations today in their position should achieve a standard and style of living equivalent to that of North Americans and Europeans today;
>
> Second, that North Americans and Europeans should continue to live as today, emitting greenhouse gases at our present rate;
>
> Third, that catastrophic climate change to our planet be avoided.

It is clear that the very nature of Western economic market and information networks makes the first result, the dramatic increase of the economic standard of living in other societies around the world, inevitable. Indeed, from the traditional point of view of Western societies, it is eminently desirable.

If the third consequence, namely catastrophic climate change, is to be avoided, it is the second point where something has to give, or, in other words, where there needs to be a radical change. We need to achieve a rapid and dramatic alteration in our manner of life, which will also provide us with the necessary moral authority to persuade Chinese, Indians, and all the other peoples of the world to follow our example, a moral authority that they today, with very good reason, deny us. The poorer countries, indeed, as for instance the fishermen of western Africa destroyed by EU fishing regulations or cotton cultivators everywhere in the developing world threatened by subsidies in developed countries, can accurately speak not of being set an example to be followed but one to be avoided at any cost.

Now at last it may be possible to appreciate the basic reason for the pessimism I have consistently felt, which provides simultaneously the fundamental reason for immediate and specific changes. It is very easy to make a logical case for radical change; it is exceedingly difficult to persuade people who are riding on a wave of success to implement it. The case for pessimism is strengthened by the harsh fact that it is not realistic to anticipate that technological innovation of itself will provide a timely resolution of our problem. Most certainly it will provide some proportion of the necessary response—and an increasing proportion as the years pass—but it will be an indeterminate proportion of the necessary response, and the overall nature and extent of this response no one can predict in specific detail.

In the meantime, so long as the developed world adheres to an irrational faith that we shall be saved by some future technological miracle, the rest of the world will feel itself justified in holding back, despite all the persuasive arguments for the need to move forward more rapidly with meaningful initiatives. As the timescale becomes shorter, so also it becomes clearer that technological innovation remains a necessary but already clearly insufficient element for resolving our problem.

What, then, must be done? Four needs are clearly apparent, which lead to a fifth, the most fundamental of all.

First, the inclusion of environmental costs in prices, through their timely and radical reform, which would include a system of emission trading permits and a wide-ranging environmental fiscal reform. This will inevitably differ in detail from country to country, but the common element will be a reduction in the tax burden on human labor and an increase in taxation on scarce primary resources and, even more so, on pollutants and emissions. It goes without saying that such an environmental fiscal reform will be of decisive significance in encouraging the development of new and environmentally friendly technologies.

Second, the avoidance of military conflict to the highest degree possible and, in particular, the avoidance of breaches to international legality. This last point is the more critical, as it will provide a sound basis for the various Great Power alliances to focus their separate but combinable energies on the major issue facing humankind within a framework of respect for the gradually evolving body of international law.

Third, a very substantial transfer of resources and technical expertise from the wealthier to the poorer countries on the planet, combining assistance in environmental education and health with support for certain major public works. Some of these are already clearly essential and will in the future become even more necessary in order to mitigate the unavoidable consequences of climate change already under way, as for instance in many river deltas and other coastal regions of Asia and Africa, Bangladesh and Egypt being two examples, or certain regions endangered by desertification, for example in the sub-Saharan region of Africa. Other major works are likely to prove necessary in order to prevent the occurrence of further climate change, examples being the rainforests of the Amazon and Southeast Asia. Both will be necessary to help reduce, since they cannot eliminate, the destabilizing effect of mass migratory movements, movements that are already beginning to occur but are likely to become far more intense and increasingly destabilizing both within and between nation-states.

Fourth, the encouragement of alternative lifestyles differentiated from the "lifestyle" cult of individual conspicuous consumption so intensely and effectively promulgated by the Western media and Western advertising since World War II. Starting from the purposeful promotion of environmental education in schools, which must certainly become compulsory, this would involve the encouragement both of the new ways of life that have already emerged, or that will do so in response to anticipated and unanticipated environmental and economic crises, and of certain traditional ways of life, though by no means all. The reason for this is that certain traditional ways of life place a positive value on simplicity and restraint while also encouraging an ethical and other-directed rather than a hedonistic and egocentric approach to the creation of wealth. Furthermore, they place emphasis on consistency between ideals and practice in the life of every person, that is to say, on personal integrity, something a world removed from the results-oriented utilitarianism that inevitably ignores both integrity and consistency as fundamental values but has increasingly dominated Western societies in recent decades.

In other words, we need a combination of the radically new and the traditional in order to reverse the current "lifestyle" fashion, a lifestyle that is dangerously at variance with the direction in which our world needs to go if we wish to avoid the worst. The more successful the Western world proves in making internal changes, the more persuasive its message will prove in the world at large, and the more likely, therefore, the world as a whole will be successful in its response to a challenge both environmental and existential for humankind.

Simply to set out these four aims indicates very clearly that they require, as a prior condition, a fifth change. This is a further substantial change of public opinion in the open, liberal, and, to a considerable degree, democratic societies that make up the Western world. If we look back only twenty-five years, the obstacles to such a change may appear titanic, or even insurmountable. Titanic they may well be, but not insurmountable, at least for those of us whose memories go further back in time. It does, however, require political and social leadership of an exceptionally high order, both in public and civil society. Above all, it requires an acknowledgment that, in some fields at least, our societies as a whole have gone seriously astray.

One of many examples can be illustrated through the comparative emphasis given to some current physical phenomena. A great deal of publicity is consistently given to the serious possibility of the melting of the Greenland ice sheet. This would indeed be a most serious development, because if it occurs a huge increase in the sea level, of about seven meters, would follow. Yet far less publicity is given to a gradual process that is already well under way, namely, the gradual melting of the Himalayan glaciers. Both these developments are indeed serious, but while the first will bring disaster if certain limits are surpassed, the second is already increasing the danger of serious flooding and reducing the flow of water to the most densely populated regions on our planet. From the point of view of the happiness of human beings—but also from the point of view of global security—the results of such an unfortunate development for the huge populations that live around the rivers Indus, Ganges, Brahmaputra, Mekong, Yangtze, and Yellow are the most immediately significant of all. The problem can indeed be described as local in the broadest sense of that word. It is, however, a problem that is impossible to solve locally; it can only be solved on the planetary level. Effectively, this demands a generally or, at the least, broadly accepted agreement on dramatic reductions in greenhouse gas emissions, most obviously in the developed world, which translates into a revolution in the structure of the economy and in our way of life.

The environmental crisis has effectively canceled any thought that one might achieve some "separate security" for the Western or perhaps the developed world. Such a concept, "separate security," until recently quite attractive in traditional terms, is becoming an impossibility in a situation of environmental crisis. Faced with such a crisis, we are obliged to revise radically our approaches, which were based on the classical concept of *raison d'état* and largely elaborated in very different times and in relation to other problems, as for instance the classical rivalries of great powers or the Cold War. A human observer may admire an F-16 as it cuts its way through the sky, releases missiles of indescribable power, destroys its enemy, and defends the state. The Himalayan glacier, however, remains stoically unimpressed. The challenge is of a quite different scale. In the last resort, the security of human beings will be determined not in separate groups but as a whole.

To conclude, the environmental crisis alters the very concept of security itself. In the past, security referred to situations where military strength was the dominant consideration and provided—or, at least, that was the hope and reasonable expectation—a local solution. Today military strength lies, rather, at the end of a long list of desiderata, and the only solution to the environmental crisis is at a planetary level. On this new list of priorities—economic structures; technological developments; the effectiveness of international cooperation; the influence of the older forms of media and of the new, such as the Internet; the values and way of life of each society; education; information flows; and the timely elaboration of a new existential stance toward life among the peoples of the world—are far more critical elements for achieving security than what has traditionally been described as security itself.

Church Walls and Wilderness Boundaries: Defining the Spaces of Sanctuary

L. Michael Harrington

Most of us know Sequoia-King's Canyon only as a national park, which part of it has been since 1890, but nearly all of it became a federally designated wilderness area in 1984 under the California Wilderness Act, and it is one of the largest wilderness areas in the continental United States. When I use the term "wilderness," I mean only such federally designated wilderness areas. The 1964 Wilderness Act defines them as areas "where the earth and its community of life are untrammeled by man, where man himself is a visitor who does not remain."[1] This definition has provoked a number of questions over the years, not the least of which is: what does it mean to be "a visitor who does not remain"? In what sense can we be visitors? We may remove all human bodies from a piece of land, but can we ever remove all human influence? Will we ever be able to stop shaping the migration of plant and animal species, suppressing and setting fires, as well as changing the climate? And then there is the problem of whether even defining the land as wilderness is itself a form of influence, a form of remaining on the land.

Thomas Birch, in his well-known 1990 article "The Incarceration of Wilderness: Wilderness Areas as Prisons," claims that the defining of wilderness is indeed a form of influence and that it is malevolent.[2] Here I will be working with the argument he develops, without pretending to follow it at every point. We ought to begin by distinguishing two different forms of definition, which are used rather indiscriminately by Birch. There is first of all the literal demarcation of boundaries on the land, as, for instance, in the original mapping out of the seven hundred thousand or so acres to be designated as wilderness within the Sequoia-King's Canyon National Park. Second, there is the regulation of what goes on within those boundaries once they have been established. The Wilderness Act, for example, mandates that wilderness areas be "administered for the use and enjoyment of the American people in such manner as will leave them unimpaired for future use and enjoyment as wilderness." Both forms of definition are subject to Birch's general principle of critique: "by definition," he says, "wildness is intractable to definition, is indefinite."[3] We can easily see how wildness resists the literal demarcation of its boundaries by considering virtually any example of a wild thing. Cougars, oak trees, streams, wildfires—all of them spread without concern for the boundaries drawn up by human institutions. The literal demarcation of boundaries around wildness is then simply impossible. The regulation of wildness is also doomed to failure, but it has the additional pernicious effect of destroying wildness wherever it finds it, even if the regulation seeks only to grant wild creatures the right to continue to be wild. As Birch says, granting rights "presupposes the existence and the maintenance of a position of power from which to do the granting."[4] We do not give wildness its freedom but rather reinforce our position of power over it when we speak about the rights of nature.[5] We subject it to our laws and reduce it to a value or a resource—in other words, something not wild at all.[6] Once wildness is eliminated through this regulation, then the so-called wilderness area can be designated. The literal demarcation of its boundaries is simply a means to the end of subjecting wildness to human law. Within the wilderness boundary, the cougar is a resource; outside the boundary, it is a threat. In neither case does the cougar remain wild. "Managing wildness," as Birch says, "is contradictory."[7]

Birch's analysis of our imprisonment of wildness focuses on wilderness areas, but he intends it also to apply to all Western sacred spaces. Western culture, he says, "is committed to cordoning off sacred space, to separating it as other, effectively keeping it out of the center of our practical lives, and keeping us out of it and thus safe from its subversive effect."[8] The historical source of this claim lies in the ancient Greek concept of the *temenos*, from which we get our English word "temple." The *temenos* is the sacred precinct, and in its very etymology it indicates that it is separated from everything around it: *temenos* derives from *temno*, meaning "to cut off." It is all too easy to think of an example that highlights the corrosive effect of this concept: an urban church, whose members commute by car from the suburbs on Sunday, disappear inside to perform their weekly rite and then get back into their cars, seeing the neighborhood around the church only through their windows. They define a space where the divine can manifest itself, and they keep it far, far away from the place where they actually dwell. Such a situation is destructive in two ways: it condemns the neighborhood surrounding the *temenos* to neglect, and it attempts to restrict the otherness of the god worshipped within the *temenos* by defining boundaries for it. The bizarre consequence is that the neighborhood surrounding the church becomes the truly other—a place of crime and poverty that the city tries to regulate or control without success—while the interior of the church is tamed. The habitually repeated actions of the liturgical rite become familiar and provide the kind of comfort we take in something that is no longer any different from what we are.

Although I chose this example because it suits Birch's argument, it also suggests a weakness in his conception of otherness. Birch tends to see otherness as opposed to identity or familiarity, as in the case of the poor urban neighborhood. But what if the church's members lived in the surrounding neighborhood? And what if they did not seek to confine the sacred within its walls? Perhaps the sacred would then present itself as different from the familiar without being opposed to the familiar. The ancient Greeks seem to have found such an otherness in their *temenos*. The Late Antique rhetorician Libanius, for instance, points out that Greek temples have an intimate relationship with their surroundings. He says:

> the temples are the very life of the countryside; around them are built houses and villages, in their shadow a succession of generations have been born up until the present day. It is in those temples that farmers have placed their hopes for themselves and their wives and children, for their oxen and for the ground they have sown or planted. A country region whose temple has been destroyed . . . is lost, because the despairing villagers no longer have the will to work.[9]

Libanius here defines the temple not in relation to what goes on inside it but outside it. The temple acts on the one hand as a kind of insurance. The farmers need a certain kind of weather for their crops to grow, and they offer sacrifices to the gods to ensure this kind of weather. But Libanius suggests that the temple has an even stronger relation to the ordinary activities of the villagers and farmers. It is their very *life*, not just in the sense of ensuring their livelihood but also in the sense of grounding the meaning of the actions they perform.[10] What gives the villagers the will to work? Not only the confidence that the gods will ensure that their labor bears fruit but also the confidence that they are doing the work that belongs to them, as one of the "generations" that have grown up in the shadow of the temple. In other words, their identity and not just their livelihood is grounded in the temple.

It is by cutting itself off from the ordinary activity of laboring that the *temenos* is able to ground the meaning of that activity. Grain may be offered to the gods in the *temenos*, but it is not grown there. Children may be consecrated in the *temenos*, but they are not born there. The boundary of the temple provides a sanctuary by isolating some actions, such as offering and consecration, and excluding others.[11] In the period of Late Antiquity, this boundary became generally less porous, as more and more of the sacred acts took place within walls rather than outside them. The altar of the Greek temple had once been positioned outside its walls; in Late Antiquity it began more and more to be hidden within the walls, just as the Christian altar had been from the beginning.[12] The period of mutual persecution by Hellenes and Christians meant that no sacrifice was safe in the open air. But the enclosure of activity within walls, whether those of the Greek temple or the Christian church, is not merely a historical accident brought on by the fear of persecution. An enclosure provides something—a sanctuary—that a mere statue of Hermes on the roadside does not. The statue of Hermes can remind the traveler of his or her place in the world. But it has no capacity to isolate the contemplation of Hermes and to exclude the noise and dust of life on the road. The same goes for the icons of the Christians. Any home may contain an image of Christ or the saints, but in the church, the activity of contemplation is made exemplary by the exclusion of all the other necessary and pleasurable activities that take place within the home.[13] The veneration directed to the image in the home is grounded in the exemplary veneration shared within the walls of the church.

This consideration of the church brings us to the specific case of Orthodox Christianity. Rather than present a primer on Orthodox theology, I will simply present four passages from the Church's early thinkers that, taken together, build a concise and coherent Orthodox vision of otherness, the icon, and the space of the church. We will see that in these passages the divine otherness is different from but not opposed to human familiarity. Two of the passages are from the fifth- or sixth-century liturgical commentator Dionysius the Areopagite, and two are from the eighth- and ninth-century iconophile Theodore the Studite. About our contemplation of the divine, Dionysius says: "we cannot be raised up to intelligible contemplation without mediation. We need elevations that we are at home with, that are natural to us."[14] "At home with" literally translates the Greek *oikeion*, according to its derivation from *oikos*, meaning "house." Human beings, or at least the majority of us, are not capable of directly contemplating anything that is not visible. We need a means of contemplation that we can be "at home with," that is familiar, even though the divine itself is not. What is most familiar to us is the bodily—what we can sense. But if the body is to be more than just familiar, if it is to become a means of contemplation, then it must become charged with the divine otherness, or, to use a more Dionysian term, the divine *hyperousiotes*.

This charging of bodies with otherness cannot happen without a space, first and foremost because the contemplation of a body requires the spatial differentiation of the eye from the body that it sees. Since not every space is amenable to the act of contemplation, we also require space of a certain kind, an exemplary space established for the contemplation of bodies as symbols rather than the use of them as tools. The liturgy provides this space. As Dionysius says: "the divine rite of the liturgy—even if it has a unified, simple, and enfolded principle—is multiplied out of love for humanity into a sacred diversity of symbols and makes space for all the hierarchic iconography."[15] Throughout his writings, Dionysius uses the term *philanthropos*, or "out of love for humanity," to refer to the Incarnation of Christ. So when he says here that the liturgy spatially diversifies itself "out of love for humanity," he hints that the actions and icons of the liturgy, by becoming symbolic, reflect the act of Incarnation. Theodore the Studite says this explicitly of the Church's icons, saying: "One of the Trinity has entered human nature, becoming like us. For this reason, he is depicted in icons, and the unseen is seen."[16] The unseen can be seen in the icons of the church because the act of incarnation has already bound together the unseen and the seen in the cosmos at large.

Finally, and perhaps most crucially for our purposes, Theodore argues that the entry of the divinity into a spatially and temporally defined body does not mean that the divinity itself is defined. "Understand," Theodore says of Christ, "that he remains uncircumscribed in being circumscribed."[17] I could equally have quoted Dionysius here, who says of Christ that he "is hidden even after his manifestation, or, to put it more divinely, even *in* his manifestation. And this mystery of Jesus in himself is hidden, and no word or mind can extract it. When spoken, it remains unsayable; when understood, it remains unknowable."[18] So I have cheated a little here, presenting five passages instead of four. But this last point is worth hearing twice. Christ's presence within a spatially and temporally defined human body does not confine his divinity. He has feet, but he walks on water; he is born, but he is born from a virgin. These miraculous activities are significant for Dionysius not because of what they accomplish in their immediate context. Christ's walking on water is not significant because it gets him to his boat without soaking him. It is significant because, whether in the gospel narrative or in an icon, it steers *us* from what is manifest in Christ to what is not manifest, from his humanity to his divinity.[19] In other words, the miraculous character of the activity plays the same role as the sanctuary space in which liturgical activities are performed. It serves to draw the mind of the observer away from the ordinary significance of the body and toward the divine. If this vision of Dionysius and Theodore is tenable, then we may indeed encounter otherness in a way that is different from but not opposed to the familiar. The divine *hyperousiotes* or otherness is not violated when it is contemplated visibly, through the icons and sacraments, within the space of the church.

Now what, we may ask, does any of this have to do with wilderness? In what sense does wilderness share the activity of the church, such that our understanding of otherness within the church can offer an insight into the nature of wilderness? At first, we may be struck only by the absurdity of trying to compare the two. The church building makes a space for the icons, and the icons are first of Christ and then of the saints. Through these images, we contemplate the life of their originals. If we crudely apply the same structure to the wilderness area, we get an absurd result. The wilderness area makes a space for wild plants, animals, and features of the landscape. These plants, animals, rocks, and rivers take the place of the icons in the church. Are we then to treat an oak tree as an image of a saint? Or are we to treat the oak tree itself as a saint to be venerated and supplicated? Here the analogy breaks down, at least if we wish to maintain anything like Christianity as it is now practiced. We will have to develop the analogy of wilderness and church again, a little less crudely. For the church and the wilderness area are not strictly parallel in structure. To begin with the obvious, the church building is the work of human hands, and the wilderness is not. Likewise, the icons are the work of human hands, and the plants, animals, rocks, and rivers of the wilderness area are not. Yet it is not the case that we make no images of these wild creatures. We depict them in an entire genre of art: the landscape painting. Here we find a third term, one necessary if we are adequately to compare the church and the wilderness area. Again we find an obvious dissimilarity—the icon returns our gaze; the landscape painting does not. So there is a confrontation, perhaps even a dialogue, between our gaze and the gaze of the icon that does not at first seem possible with the landscape painting. Yet we cannot say that there is no gaze in the landscape painting, even though no eyes are depicted there. For the landscape has already been arranged according to a gaze, and the viewer of the painting is invited to take on that gaze. We may engage in a dialogue with this gaze, just as with the gaze of the icon. The painter Thomas Moran, for instance, invites us to see the Yosemite Valley with a certain gaze, one that we may resist, or accept, or struggle to accept.

We can now see the true parallel between the church and the wilderness. The icon and the landscape painting are both images of images. The icon is an image of the body of Christ, which is itself the manifestation of the divine otherness. The landscape painting is an image of the wild land, itself a manifestation of the divine otherness, but as perceived according to a certain gaze. The church clears a space for the contemplation of the icons; the wilderness area clears a space not for the landscape painting but for contemplation of the wild land itself according to the gaze adopted in the painting. We do not venerate the wild land as directly as we would an image of a saint, because the gaze that draws our veneration in this case is shared between us and the landscape we see.

And so the wilderness is both more and less than the church. It is more because it puts us in contact with the direct manifestation of the divine otherness, as though the embodied Christ were to walk into the nave of the church. But it is less, because its framing is much less distinct. At first, we do not know how to look at it. Landscape paintings teach us a gaze with which to see wilderness, just as icons teach us how to see Christ. If, today, we no longer need the paintings of Thomas Moran, Frederic Church, and Albert Bierstadt to teach us the gaze with which we may see the sublimity of mountainous terrain, that is only because we have thoroughly absorbed their lesson, so that we are already ready to experience, for instance, the Sierra Nevada mountains that shape so much of the Sequoia-King's Canyon wilderness area.[20]

In conclusion, and as a guide to our discussion, let me summarize both what I have done and left undone in this presentation. I have tried to make three points. First, as many others have shown, the 1964 Wilderness Act is misleading when it defines wilderness as an area "where man is a visitor who does not remain." It is possible to remove all human bodies from an area but not to remove human influence, which manifests itself in the very demarcation of the wilderness boundaries. Second, the act of demarcation does not destroy the wildness of the wilderness area any more than the enclosing of liturgical rites within walls destroys the divine otherness. Just as the divine otherness manifests itself with a defined form in a defined space, so the wildness of the wilderness area manifests itself to us only because we have defined a space for its appearance. Third, the tradition of Orthodox Christianity is helpful in understanding how otherness manifests itself to us, whether in wilderness or liturgical rites, because of its special emphasis on the icon, in which the otherness of God enters the familiarity of visible form without being reduced to the familiar.[21] Finally, let me point out two important themes that I have not discussed. First, I have not provided any argument in support of the claims made by Dionysius and Theodore. I have simply presented, for instance, Theodore's bald statement that the divine "remains uncircumscribed in being circumscribed." It remains for us to think through the arguments of Dionysius and Theodore in the changed context and exigencies of our own times. Second, I have not addressed the problem of the porous border between wilderness and cultivated land. Just as the otherness that we experience in the church has a life that extends beyond it, so the cougar of the wilderness area may sometimes cross its boundary. How we treat the cougar in that circumstance has a great deal to say about whether we treat our wilderness areas as prisons or sanctuaries.

Orthodoxy and Ecopoetics: The Green World in the Desert Sea

Alfred K. Siewers

The early Irish story *Tochmarc Étaíne* ("The Wooing of Étaín"), c. 800, describes a spiritual realm that is entered through portals in Neolithic mounds in the landscape, but also in other texts through islands, springs, or encounters in the countryside itself. This "Otherworld," a framework for a number of early Christian Irish and Welsh texts, is always present but not visible to mortals because of Adam's sin, according to the story. The otherworldly figure Mider tells his rediscovered wife of that realm when he sings:

> Bé Find will you go with me
> to a strange land where there is harmony?
> Hair there like primrose,
> color of snow on a smooth body;
> neither mine nor yours there;
> white tooth, dark brow;
> the troop of our hosts gladdens the eye—
> color of foxglove on each cheek.
> As flowers of the plain, pink each neck,
> blackbird's eggs, joy of eye;
> though Mag Fáil be fair to see,
> it is desolate after experiencing Mag Már;
> though fair be the ale of Inis Fáil,
> more confounding that of Tír Már.
> Miraculous of lands, the land of which I tell:
> youth not leading to ancientness there.
> Warm, sweet currents over the land,
> choicest of mead and wine;
> outstanding human beings, not disfigured,

procreation without sin or illegality.
We see each one on every side,
And no one sees us;
the shadow of Adam's sin
prevents our being reckoned right.[1]

Likewise, the perhaps late eighth-century story *Immram Brain*, "The Voyage of Bran," tells of a spiritual realm under the sea, teeming with life that engages the human Bran. It too mingles native tradition with a biblical sense of Paradise. The sea god sings of it to Bran:

> An extraordinary beauty it is for Bran
> In his coracle across the clear sea:
> but to me in my chariot from a distance
> It is a flowery plain on which he rides about.
> What is clear sea for the prowed skiff in which Bran is,
> That is a delightful plain full of flowers
> To me in a chariot of two wheels.
> Bran sees multiplicitous waves beating across the clear sea:
> I myself see in Mag Mon
> Red-headed flowers without blemish.
> Sea-horses glisten in summer
> As far as glances of Bran's eye traverse:
> Blossoms pour forth a stream of honey
> In the land of Manannán son of Ler.
> The sparkle of the expanses that you go over,
> The brightness of the sea, on which you row about,
> Yellow and blue-grey-green are spread out,
> It is earth that is great.
> Speckled salmon leap from the womb
> Of the shining sea, on which you look;
> They are calves, beautifully colored lambs
> At peace without strife . . .
> The expanse of the plain, the number of the host,
> Beauties shining with bright quality,
> A fair stream of silver, stairs of gold,
> Bring a welcome at every great feast.
> A pleasant game, most delightful,
> They play in fair contention,
> Men and gentle women under a bush,
> Without sin, without crime.
> Along the top of a wood has floated
> Your coracle across ridges,
> There is a beautiful wood with fruit

Under the prow of your little boat.
A wood with blossom and fruit,
On which is the vine's true fragrance,
A wood without decay, without defect,
On which are leaves of golden hue.
We are from the beginning of creation
Without age, without decay of earth-freshness.
We do not expect weakness from decline.
The sin has not come to us.[2]

Both poems differ from the common allegorical trope in Old English poetry (and much Western literature) identifying the sea and wild natural places generally with demonic forces of alienation. The portrayal of nature in a number of early Irish texts (and in Welsh texts influenced by them) as embedded within a spiritual "overlay landscape" articulates the physical environment as an unobjectifiable process rather than a presence or concept to be grasped and possessed. There is no conceptual grid or matrix, as in the cosmos of Dante's later *Commedia*, but a direct engagement of the spiritual with actual geography. In highlighting the distinctiveness of such early Irish material in the heritage of Western European culture, the medievalist Jennifer Neville observes: "For the Old English poet, the representation of the natural world helps to create the context of helplessness and alienation that motivates the seeking of God. For the Irish poet, the representation of the natural world creates the context of wonder and joy that surrounds the seeking of God."[3]

Behind a distinctive early Irish poetics of nature lies a broader cultural genealogy from monastic literary centers around the Irish Sea, involving a non-Augustinian patristic praxis of nature best known today in Orthodox Christianity. In Atlantic Insular literature, the early Irish poetic approach to nature noted by Neville, evident in the so-called Celtic Otherworld of stories such as *Tochmarc Étaíne* and *Immram Brain* later morphed into the "green world" trope of early English literature,[4] which in turn influenced portrayals of nature in modern Romanticism and fantasy. An approach to this trope of overlay landscape from the standpoint of ecocriticism or environmental literary studies—which melds the setting and context of narratives to articulate the relation between symbolism and the physical world—reveals an ecopoetics[5] of this "green world" that is subversive of late medieval and modern instrumentalist views of nature. Such a rereading of this Celtic and Anglophone "green world" literary tradition suggests a submerged history of Orthodox ecopoetics. It also may help further develop qualitative approaches to issues of meaning and value in environmental studies, by highlighting the overlooked legacy of Christian contributions to ecological thinking, policy, and practice.

Early Irish literary culture, predominant in the first post-Roman flowering of Christianity in the British Isles, often expressed the non-Augustinian view of nature summarized above by Neville. St. John Cassian's writings, transmitting his encounters in the Eastern Mediterranean with desert ascetics, provided analogues to the kind of early Irish environmental poetics that Neville describes. Cassian's emphasis on synergy between the "natural" or corporeal human being (including its contexts in Creation) and divine grace, evidenced in his Thirteenth Conference, contrasted with Augustine's emphasis on original sin and predestined grace, which morphed in Latin tradition into the created grace of Thomas Aquinas and a more allegorical and objective sense of nature as analogic rather than energized. The literary culture emerging from the later conversion of the Anglo-Saxons, with its greater cultural orientation toward the continental Christianity of the Frankish imperium, came to privilege the Augustinian approach, which is especially seen in the allegorical treatment of nature as evil in *Beowulf*.[6] The dyadic cosmological emphases of Western Augustinianism, symbolized by what became the Trinitarian doctrine of the *filioque* based on the *De Trinitate*, further helped shape objectifying models of symbolism and semiotics by juxtaposing a melded Father and Son acting instrumentally upon a Holy Spirit associated with the workings of grace in the natural world.[7]

In contrast, the ninth-century Hiberno-Latin philosopher John Scottus Eriugena in his *Periphyseon* expressed a theophanic and dynamic view of physical creation, and divine energies entering into it, to culminate a distinctive tradition of early Hiberno-Latin hexameral studies.[8] Eriugena's work derived significantly from Greek patristic writers, especially the Christian Dionysius and St. Maximus the Confessor, but also melded Cappadocian, Augustinian, and Irish cultural sensibilities. It reflected the developing Orthodox doctrine of the uncreated energies as distinct from the essence of God but engaging with human experience in Creation through the redemption provided by Christ. The *Periphyseon*, like the original text of the Irish Stowe Missal, did not favor the more dyadic Latin model of the Trinity, which had been particularly enforced by Anglo-Saxon and Frankish ecclesiastical regimes. Both key early Hiberno-Latin sources opted for the more relational triadic model of the original Nicene-Constantinopolitan Creed, in which the Holy Spirit (and all its associations with grace flowing into the natural world) proceeded more conciliarly on its own from the Father, rather than being more marginalized and instrumentalized by a fused Father-Son. While not all early Irish sources rejected the *filioque*, there seems to have been a significant affinity in formative aspects of early Irish asceticism for non-Augustinian cosmology and semiotics generally.

In the literary works that emerged from early Irish monasticism, the Otherworld, as a literary realm engaging a spiritual realm with actual geography, was set in a pre-Christian past that often reflected biblical notions of Paradise. The Otherworld trope emerges in works such as the Irish Ulster Cycle, the Welsh *Mabinogi*, and Welsh mythic Taliesin poems (that Welsh material probably having been influenced by Irish texts from the era of Eriugena).[9] Of this literary spiritual Otherworld entwined with geography, the Celticist Marie-Louise Sjoestedt wrote:

> A discussion of the mythological world of the Celts encounters at once a peculiar difficulty, namely, that when seeking to approach it you find that you are already within. We are accustomed to distinguish the supernatural from the natural. . . . The Celts knew nothing of this, if we are entitled to judge their attitude from Irish tradition. Here there is continuity, in space and in time, between what we call our world and the other world—or worlds. Some peoples, such as the Romans, think of their myths historically; the Irish think of their history mythologically; and so, too, of their geography.[10]

This outlook, with its analogues to non-Augustinian patristic views of nature, formed the origins of what the literary critic Northrop Frye famously called the "green world" of English literature. Of the "green world" Frye wrote that "the conception of a second world bursts the boundaries of Menandrine comedy" yet without "eternal forms or divine revelation" in any Dantean or Scholastic sense, involving instead "a wonderful contrapuntal intermingling of two orders of existence."[11] In the process, for Frye "the green world suggests an original golden age which the normal world has usurped and which makes us wonder if it is not the normal world that is the real Saturnalia," making "each world seem unreal when seen by light of the other."[12] Frye's "green world" (which he traced in Elizabethan literature) can be traced back to foundational writers in the late fourteenth century such as Chaucer, drawing on "Celtic" themes when working to invent a new "native" vernacular literature.

The Desert as Sea

Ideas formative of ascetic practice and teachings in the literary-exegetical culture of early Ireland encouraged an understanding of the world as sparkling with divine energies, to use the Romanian Orthodox scholar Dimitru

Staniloae's modern terminology of the uncreated energies in nature as "the sparkle of creation."[13] One influential early Christian ascetic image involved describing the physical desert of Egypt, Sinai, and Palestine, a haven for early monastics developing the Orthodox tradition of monasticism, as a spiritual sea.[14] This was picked up in early Irish Sea cultures, and it influenced their development of the Otherworld trope, as in the view of the sea in *Immram Brain*, probably adapting native pre-Christian traditions as typological in the process. Early Irish monastics used the Latin term *desertum* to describe both the sea and island and remote terrestrial Insular monastic refuges.[15]

St. Athanasius the Great's fourth-century account of *The Life of St. Antony* describes Antony's paradigmatic response to the desert or wilderness:

> And immediately there were shown to him Saracens who were about to travel that route. . . . After journeying three days and three nights in their company, he came to a very high hill. Below the hill there was water—perfectly clear, sweet, and quite cold, and beyond there were plains, and a few untended date palms. Then Antony, as if stirred by God, fell in love with the place, for this was the place the one who had spoken with him at the riverbank had designated. . . . Even the Saracens themselves, perceiving the zeal of Antony, would make it a point to travel that way and would joyfully bring loaves to him. . . . At first, however, when the beasts in the wilderness came for water, they often would damage his crop and his planting. But gently capturing one of the beasts, he said to all of them, "Why do you hurt me, when I do you no injury? Leave, and in the name of the Lord do not come near here any longer" . . . and thereafter many [people seeking wisdom and healing] visited him.[16]

In the account, Antony called the atmosphere of this "wilderness" refuge as essential to an ascetic as the sea for fish: "Just as fish perish when they lie exposed for a while on the dry land . . . we must rush back to the mountain [in the desert], like fish to the sea—so that we might not, by remaining among you, forget the things within us."[17]

In addition to the image of the desert as sea, St. Ephrem the Syrian in the fourth century also described Paradise as a hollow mountain. In Ephrem's model (as in the seventh-century Hiberno-Latin *De Ordine Creaturarum*), Paradise is above earth and (as in all-embracing Otherworld motifs of Celtic narratives) encompasses it in a hollow, otherworldly mountain. St. Gregory of Nyssa, a source for Eriugena, held similar views. To Gregory and Ephrem, Paradise was a place of which only the foothills had been touched by the Flood, whose inhabitants "dance on the sea's surface."[18] Within this perspective we may also place the Irish tradition of St. Brendan building his boat on a mountain before setting out to sea and to the land of promise (a kind of homage-in-reverse to Noah's ark landing on top of a mountain). Augustine, by significant contrast, used the image of the hollow mountain to describe human pride blocking spiritual harbor and rest.[19]

Symbolic imagery of the dynamic relationship of divine energies with physical geography (such as the literary Otherworld) expressed an iconographic sense of landscape as an embodied practice or performance of personal relationship. This iconographic sensibility (evident in different ways in Byzantine and early Christian Irish imagery) involved an engagement of art with audience that occurred in the "space between" subject and object, thus creating a sense of encounter between two subjects within a landscape rather than inside the human self. Likewise, Eriugena in his cosmology iconographically related the firmament in Genesis to the basic four elements interacting with primordial causes[20] that he associated with the divine energies or *logoi* of St. Maximus. Eriugena also identified those causes with the aerial waters dynamically above the firmament but also flowing around the earth. Eriugena's cosmic vision expressed a personal sense of pansemiotics (or a personally meaningful cosmos) related to his reading of Maximus, for whom the Greek *logos*, a term also associated with Christ, had a range of meanings beyond "word" that included harmony, purpose, reason, story, and discourse, identified also with energy. This interactive sense of cosmology found a physical corollary in the ever-moving environment of Ireland's archipelago: a melding of sea, land, and clouds rather than a static, vertically layered cosmology-allegory. Early Irish textual exegesis of the six days in Genesis described the interactive principal winds of Creation and their governing harmonies (analogous to *logoi*) entwined around the earth, using terminology related also to the Irish description of ascetic-penitential martyrdom, which sometimes involved physical immersion in that mix of water and winds of the sea, whether in exile-pilgrimage (following one of the steps in St. John Climacus's *The Ladder of Divine Ascent*) or prayer such as that described of St. Columba.[21]

Augustine in his *Confessions* allegorically described the firmament as scripture separating heaven and earth. But the Irish model encouraged a positive sense of the sea as a geographic image or icon of the energies spanning the aerial and earthly waters, sometimes describing the sea itself as spiritual "desert." Eriugena described clouds, integrally related to the sea in Irish landscape, as images of theophanies of divine energies in the created world as well as of the synergy of potential participation by holy ascetics on earth in those energies through *theosis*.[22] Both the Irish St. Columba and

Eriugena similarly compared the depths of the sea to the mystery of the Trinity, a sea of divinity known only through energies interacting with human experience, not through any sense of essence.[23] Direct echoes of this can be seen in explicitly Christian terms in famous early Irish accounts of the voyage of St. Brendan, mirroring themes and contexts of the retrospectively pre-Christian setting of *Immram Brain*, still known today worldwide from the medievalist J. R. R. Tolkien's use of the sea as an image of interactive immortality set in an ancient earth.

The use of color itself in early Irish Sea exegesis and ascetic writing paralleled often vivid descriptions of Irish and Welsh Otherworld narratives, which were more mosaic-like or iconographic than naturalistic in effect. Both types of writing suggest patristic and Orthodox analogues for an iconographic sense of the natural world, akin to the "color theology" of Orthodox icons. The famous early Irish colors of martyrdom involved a color term, *glas*, often identified with the sea, and indeed probably best defined in English as "the color of sky in water" or of the dynamic sea. This term for a certain brightness or sparkle (relatable to the divine energies) was used for the principal wind associated with the sea and the Otherworld-related direction of the Southwest as well as for otherworldly, shiny metal, and vegetative descriptions—perhaps comparable to the kind of golden infusing background-yet-foreground light of Byzantine icons. *Glas* also was the color of ascetic-penitential martyrdom and seems to have been associated with cosmic patristic imagery of sky, clouds, and aerial waters as well as with early Irish practices of praying in water associated probably with baptism.

An Alaskan Orthodox priest, Fr. Michael Oleksa, has noted similar connections between an iconographic Native Alaskan view of the physical world and that of the Russian Orthodox Alaskan mission. The cosmically semiotic *logoi* of the Logos (associated with the divine energies as articulated by St. Maximus and others) formed an important connecting point with native views of *inua* in the physical world.[24] Similarly, in the Book of Kells, an Irish Sea illuminated gospel book (c. 800), words and images including decorative patterns from pre-Christian Neolithic mounds (featured in other texts as Otherworld portals) meld into inverse or stereoscopic perspectives similar to prototypes in the iconodulic Christian "color theology" of Word thickening into Image.[25]

Patristic Ecosemiotics

The literal relation of stone art patterns in the Irish landscape (on manmade structures that nonetheless had melded into the environment beyond any modern culture-nature binary) to written text in the gospel book of Kells typifies an approach to symbolism paralleled in Orthodox tradition. While Augustine's semiotics, related to his Trinitarian formula, encouraged a dyadic structure of symbolism and cosmos (based on an arbitrary objectification of both), the Orthodox doctrine of the energies as expressed also in early Irish Christian culture involved a triadic emphasis on a symbol formed from an entwinement of sign, symbolic, and "real world" contexts.[26] This foreshadows in certain respects current interest in the environmental-related triadic semiosis described by Charles S. Peirce rather than the interiorized dyadic view of sign in Ferdinand de Saussure's theory, which remains more in the dyadic Western Augustinian tradition.[27] Julia Kristeva describes this difference in cultural semiotics in relation to the different formulation of the Trinity in East and West.[28] Likewise, in their views of the body and the Eucharist, early medieval Christian ascetic practices of subjectivity in Ireland, as in Byzantium, apparently differed from the more individualized and binarized mind-body views later developed in Catholic Scholasticism and translated partly into modern philosophy.[29] In many ways, that distinctiveness can be summed up in the cosmological differences between the Scholastic interiorized conceptualization of *analogia*, based in a grid of meaning binarized from physicality, and the Orthodox experiential and embodied sense of *energeia*.[30]

The "overlay landscape" of the Otherworld trope expresses this difference by contrast with both the more allegorized landscape of *Beowulf* and often with Old English poetry generally. Routes of the "Cattle Raid of Cooley" are still traceable (and now marked for tourists) on the landscape of north-central Ireland, as are places in many other early Irish Sea Otherworld stories, including the Four Branches of the Welsh *Mabinogi*.[31] In fact, the Four Branches, like many early Irish Otherworld texts, reflect also direct elements of patristic themes, perhaps even more explicitly, given their composition probably at a native monastic community, asserting a traditional native Christian learning in resistance to cultural change at the time of the Norman Conquest. As I have noted elsewhere, the Four Branches reflect (and extend cosmically) the exegetical tetrarch of St. Gregory the Dialogist, in his relating of the four creatures of Ezekiel to the four gospel writer-evangelists, to four Christian virtues, and to four phases of the life of Christ on earth, drawing on Insular themes dating back to Eriugena's era.

One thematic link to native traditions in such landscape narratives was the image of the sovereignty goddess, or goddess of the land, often identified with the Otherworld as in *Immram Brain*'s description of that spiritual realm as "the land of women." In the name and description of St. Brigit as "mother of Christ" (tradition giving her a symbolic role in helping to nurse Jesus) some scholars see early Irish writers making a typological link between the sovereignty goddess (one of whose names was Brig) and the Theotokos, to whom Insular evidence shows an early and particular devotion. Byzantine iconography of the Theotokos, sometimes identified with the earth, as bestowing sovereignty on emperors, highlights this potential typological parallel, which would have been in line with other complex parallels with classical mythology in the era. In this sense, the Irish Christian Otherworld takes on elements of a kind of cosmic feminine associated with the Theotokos's role as both in a sense containing Creation, her womb having contained the Creator God, but also in another sense being contained by Christ as Lord God of Creation—thus exemplifying a kind of double-folded cosmic landscape exemplified in Orthodox iconography by the Theotokos of the Sign and by traditions of Christ as Sophia or Wisdom and the Church associated with earthly grace from Russia and Byzantium.[32] Chaucer's work makes this connection by identifying terms for "elvishness," otherworldiness in the sense of the Celtic Otherworld, explicitly with both the natural world and the Otherworld: The fairy queen in "The Wife of Bath's Tale," the iconographic Constance associated with the sea in "The Man of Law's Tale," and the poetry of the text itself in the prologue to "The Tale of Sir Thopas." On a secular level, the modern practice of ecocriticism, in foregrounding the background of narrative and then looking at the reciprocal relation of text and context, can be said to partake symbolically in this type of overlay-landscape experience, with which ecofeminist writings engage in sometimes valorizing a "natural" femaleness at odds with other modern feminist thought.

In any case, in this relation of the feminine to a divinely energized natural landscape, early Irish literary culture distinctively regarded women not in a rigidly theologically binarized hierarchy beneath men extended to the natural world, as in Catholic Scholasticism. It did not emphasize an abstraction of the Theotokos apart from women generally (as in the later West) in its early distinctive reverence for her.[33] The theme of the powerful "fairy queen," adapted from this early literature's sovereignty goddess, informed Chaucer's "The Wife of Bath's Tale," together the Celtic-Christianity-themed "The Man of Law's Tale." Both were pivotal to his *Canterbury Tales* in offering cosmic marriage as an answer to the excesses of both courtly love and bawdy sensuality in the opening tales. And in Spenser's *The Faerie Queene*, the title character serves as a kind of shadow of the Theotokos obscured in Protestant English culture.

An Enduring but Dynamic Literary Tradition

While early Irish Christian literary centers at monastic communities were oriented outward toward physical creation—and indeed, like small cities included beyond the celibate community lay people engaged in degrees of asceticism, including families—the central image of the desert sea in that earlier era of Christianity became superseded in the High Middle Ages by a central metaphor of the Gothic cathedral, with its interiorized cosmos and vertical rather than horizontal orientation. This shift was also reflected in the move toward more centralized monastic orders in the West, with the cloister as focus. But the "green world" literary tradition resisted or presented alternatives to these transitions. The Celticist John Carey in a recent study has shown how the Otherworld landscape ethos of early Irish narratives influenced not only early Welsh literature but the larger Arthurian literature of Europe, in particular the symbol of the Holy Grail that encapsulates it.[34] In trying to seize the Grail or equivalent treasure from feminine otherworldly keepers, would-be male heroes bring cataclysmic disaster down upon their land. In engaging with the treasure respectfully, they in effect engage in cosmic marriage with the land (embodied, again, in a feminine sovereignty figure). The symbol of the Grail associated with these early Irish Sea overlay landscapes and with their later continuation in the Arthurian cycle itself probably had associations with early notions of the Eucharist as more a community than an individualized experience (stimulated, perhaps, by Western contact during the Crusades with Byzantine liturgy) and a sense of the passing of that definition of the Eucharist as a mystery in the face of the more objectified sacrament of the high-medieval West.[35]

Writing from within the early Irish monastic tradition, while translating and interpreting Greek patristic writers alongside Augustine, Eriugena described Nature as consisting of both being and nonbeing, the hidden and the appearing. In Latin Scholasticism, developing from tendencies in Augustine, nonbeing came to be identified with evil. Evil in Scholasticism came to be labeled as natural but necessarily an illusory parallel to essential nature.[36] So a sense of overlay landscape became demonized. The supernatural good became more and more a separate, if constrained, category of reality apart from the natural. Miracles came to be considered, in the view of Aquinas and others, not results from rational occurrences but objectified insertions of supernatural archetypes in God's essence and distanced from Creation. It was the beginning of a disenchantment of the world, paralleling the era of the Crusades.

As the Otherworld trope was adapted by early English literature, it often signaled a kind of narrative resistance against such trends in Western culture. The overlay-landscape trope in Middle English literature functions as a kind of imaginative "push back" against Scholasticism and feudalism in the late medieval West as well, paradoxically part of an effort to reimagine a new alternative type of Christian community life related to older native traditions, in opposition to the failing Anglo-Norman regime. In the same way, the earlier Welsh *Mabinogi* could be read as an alternative native landscape of Christian iconography, resisting the feudal matrix of the Domesday Book being imposed by the Normans upon Wales, with its new, nonindigenous monastic system and Scholasticism.

Middle English works such as the anonymous *Sir Gawain and the Green Knight* and Geoffrey Chaucer's *The Canterbury Tales*, as well as Thomas Malory's return of the continental Arthurian tradition back into an Insular fantasy-history frame, forged the English "green world" literary tradition from earlier influences. Both Chaucer and the Gawain poet drew heavily on earlier Irish Sea motifs of the overlay landscape, Chaucer by shaping an otherworld of stories interwoven with an actual geography in *The Canterbury Tales* and the anonymous author of *Sir Gawain and the Green Knight* by relating a fantasy realm identified with both nature and magic to actual landscape as well. They did so at a time of cultural upheaval in the wake of the Black Death, reflecting a felt need for experiential aspects of faith related to a retrospectively viewed, earlier Insular "age of saints" with a magical multiplex landscape. Chaucer's probable exposure to Irish traditions of the Otherworld connected with an apparent desire to reimagine an experiential native Christianity in the pre-Norman and pre-Scholastic era, expressed in "The Man of Law's Tale." The medievalist Rory McTurk suggests that Chaucer's overlay-landscape framework for *The Canterbury Tales* as a whole echoed the popular Irish narrative *Acallam na Senórach* ("Tales of the Elders"), which melded Otherworld landscape narratives with St. Patrick's missionary travels around Ireland. McTurk argues that Chaucer's proto–iambic pentameter verse found its model in Irish tradition as well, even as its beats also echo Old English patterns blended with continental syllabic style.[37]

The famous opening of the General Prologue to *The Canterbury Tales* sets up the work's overlay landscape from the start:

> Whan that Aprill with his shoures soote
> The droghte of March hath perced to the roote,
> And bathed every veine in swich licour
> Of which vertu engendred is the flour,
> Whan Zephirus eek with his sweete breeth
> Inspired hath in every holt and heeth
> The tender croppes, and the yonge sonne
> Hath in the Ram his halve course yronne,
> And smale fowles maken melodye,
> That slepen al the night with open eye,

> So priketh hem nature in hir corages,
> Than longen folk to goon on pilgrimages,
> And palmeres for to seken straunge strondes,
> To ferne halwes, kouthe in sundry londes;
> And specially from every shires ende
> Of Engelond to Caunterbury they wende,
> The holy blissful martyr for to seke
> That hem hath holpen whan that they were seeke.[38]

Here we have nature in motion and a text that is a map of a journey on earth, very different from the motion and journey of that other great medieval pilgrimage poem, Dante's *Commedia*, written a few generations earlier in Italy in the Catholic Scholastic tradition. In Chaucer's *Canterbury Tales* the landscape is less allegorical and less virtual and also, taking the work as a whole, seemingly incomplete, ever in process. It is nonetheless an overlay landscape draped across the physical geography of countryside from commercial London to a supposedly spiritual Canterbury that, however, is never reached, the journey ending apparently in "The Parson's Tale" and Chaucer's retraction. We can trace the route of the pilgrims along an old Roman road, from the center of English metropolitan commerce in the waning days of the Anglo-Norman feudal regime into a province and provincial seat (Kent and Canterbury) whose names derive from an old Celtic British people, to which the papal mission from St. Gregory the Dialogist came in the days before the Norman Conquest and found remnants of earlier British Christianity. There is already implied in the "map" of the story from the start an antifeudal and anticolonial movement celebratory of natural landscape and language and of an earlier age of "saints and scholars" in the islands, along with its invocation of Thomas Beckett as an icon of the claims of the spiritual against the feudal state. The landscape, unlike that of Dante's great work, is not ultimately all about the author's textual avatar. It is about a rollicking Christian multilogue in the countryside of many voices, including the nonhuman, in which Chaucer's persona is one among many parodied for the foolishness of binarized subjectivity and objectification, a Bakhtinian echo of Orthodox traditions of *sobornost* and conciliarity.[39]

This psychology of the poem arguably projects an environmental experience out-of-text and into multiple contexts, at odds with a developing Western sense of discrete individualism symbolized by the growing power of the pope. The medievalist A. Kent Hieatt noted Chaucer's use of myth to engage experientially or entrap the reader in a kind of empathy aimed against objectification of others or of one's self.[40] We see this in the rogue's gallery of figures in the General Prologue and their tales, which follow from the opening quoted above. But *The Canterbury Tales* as experiential landscape can also be read as ecopoesis, encouraging a transpersonal engagement of the human with the physical environment, evoking an empathy in line with recent work in mind science on how human beings realize themselves more ecologically rather than in a discrete individualistic or "genocentric" way.[41]

Let us briefly consider the world as described in *The Canterbury Tales'* opening lines and subsequent connecting stories. We have the cycle of seasons and stars, the time of nature. We have the social time and cycles of mortality and festival of human beings. We have the created eternity of the saints. And we have, in the "pricking of corages" by Nature, the poetic intimation of the movement of theophanies and divine energies, or manifestations in the physical world, that are everlasting and beyond even eternity, as in the familiar example for medievals of how the hearts of Jesus' students burned within them when taught by the *logoi* of the Lord, unknown to them, on the road to Emmaus. For Chaucer, as mentioned in the *Parlement of Fowles*, Nature is the "vicar of the Almightie Lord," a figure whom Spenser developed in *The Faerie Queene* (in emulation of Chaucer) as shining forth divine energies with mention of the Transfiguration—probably influenced, as the Orthodox literary scholar Harold Weatherby suggests, by the poet's exposure to Greek patristic studies while at newly Protestant Cambridge.[42] One way of translating "so priketh hem nature in hir corages" into modern English involves using "sparkles" for "priketh," reminiscent of Staniloae's already mentioned description of the divine energies in nature in Eastern Christian theology as the "sparkle in creation." Here, poetically, we also see an echo of the four modes of time and nontime of Eastern patristic asceticism, reflected from the origins of early literary monasticism around the Irish Sea engaged with native traditions, rather than the eternal present of Augustinian-derived Scholasticism glimpsed in Dante's work.[43] Chaucer's opening suggests layering of social human time, seasonal cycles of the nonhuman natural world, the eternity of holy saints who yet are still part of Creation, and also perhaps a suggestion of the uncreated divine energies— a layering common to the earlier Irish Sea Otherworld trope. All of these modes are entwined in the landscape of the text on the road to Canterbury, in a cloud of overlapping stories and voices ending in ascetic repentance with "The Parson's Tale," rather than a more individualized and triumphal completed passage from hell to heaven.

We also see adaptations of the Otherworld emerge in another famous foundational English poem contemporary to *The Canterbury Tales*, the anonymous *Sir Gawain and the Green Knight*, involving a similar sense of overlay landscape. In that poem, Sir Gawain's travels are across a mapped geography of Britain into Wales and ultimately to a Green Chapel that scholars link to folklore about specific sites near the poet's presumed location (based on linguistic evidence) in northwestern England. And so we also have an overlay of imaginative fantasy with actual terrain and an accompanying subversion of idealized individuality, in the case of the Gawain poet in terms of the deconstruction of Gawain's individualistic knightly character in dialogue with the Otherworld. The *Gawain* poem, written near the Welsh border, features a distinctive combination of plot motifs—of yearly ritual combat and an otherworldly temptress—known from earlier Irish and Welsh sources, as well as a corrupted probable borrowing of the name of the poem's anti-hero Lord Bercilak from an early Irish story. By the end of the poem, the reader can experience a questioning of which world is more real—that of the supposedly historical Arthurian-metropolitan court, whose geography is unclear, or the clearer geography of the Otherworld overlay landscape of the Green Knight, whose message to Sir Gawain, delivered on behalf of a "goddess" of the land, seems to urge the chivalric star to become more grounded and "real" and less ideally objectifying of both himself and of others. The prick of blood is a reminder of the knight's corporeal humanity in common with other people, engaged with a natural landscape that threatens the artificiality of the feudal Arthurian court, but which ultimately becomes its healer, and also connects with symbolism of the Feast of the Circumcision of Christ.

While the convention of the changing seasons seen in Chaucer's opening is a commonplace, he as usual reworks sources, probably including an Italian text on the destruction of Troy and, in structure (together with the native Otherworld paradigm), Boccaccio's *Decameron*. But the remix stands distinctively within the storytelling mode of Europe's Atlantic archipelago. Thus, unlike the opening's likely adapted source about Troy, springtime culminates in *The Canterbury Tales* not in war but in experiential penitential redemption, in an actual countryside of which the audience forms a physical part. This is akin to the combined punning references to the dynamic Sabbaoth ("Lord of hosts" and "Sabbath's rest") at the end of Spenser's *Faerie Queene*—a poetic intersection of immanence and transcendence "inhabiting the earth."[44]

The "Green World" Today

In Chaucer's opening to the General Prologue, the mention of the zodiac in particular, the Ram in his half course, together with the juices of spring that seem to be flowing through all, all suggest Jeffrey J. Cohen's comparison of medieval notions of astrology and the bodily humors to the postmodern environmental notion of "bodies without organs."[45] That term for nonorganismic bodies comes from the writings of Deleuze and Guattari, and it evokes virtual realities that in their "geophilosophy" embody a kind of ecological connectivity, spanning physical immanence and bodily cultural effects—potentially a kind of ecosemiosphere, or culture of nature, based on information-energy familiar also from ecosemiotics and recent scientific theorizing, overriding Western binaries of subject and object.[46] Although within a secular framework antithetical to Christianity in its ethical nihilism, the geophilosophy or ecosophy of Deleuze and Guattari nonetheless provides, as the philosopher Peter Hallward notes, a contemporary vocabulary for describing in current environmental terms Eriugena's theophanic experience of nature, and thus the effect of experiencing Creation itself as an archipelago in desert and early Irish Sea Christian traditions.[47] Eriugena uses clouds as an image of the theophanic effect of divine energies. He describes these clouds as engaging human imagination in synergy with those energies for an holistic salvation through *theosis* that includes the cosmic component of a return of Creation to God.[48]

In light of early Irish monastic traditions, Europe's Atlantic archipelago itself could be considered such a Christian "body without organs" or, in more patristically related terminology, an iconographic landscape of theophanic energies in Creation. In his essay "Desert Islands," Gilles Deleuze discusses how the geological "double movement" of islands, both pulling away and recreating themselves, parallels human engagement with them imaginatively: is an archipelago sea or land primarily, imagined or physical?[49] A collective cultural imagination, through rites and mythology, in Deleuze's view could produce imaginary identity with islands in a way that "geography and the imagination would be one."[50] Later he and Félix Guattari discussed how the northeastern Atlantic archipelago in particular involved "a plane of immanence as a movable and moving ground ... an archipelagian world where [inhabitants] are happy to pitch their tents from island to island and over the sea ... nomadizing the old Greek earth, broken up, fractalized, and extended to the entire universe."[51] In such a geocultural archipelago, they argue, the landscape sees, much as an icon in effect looks out at its venerator in Byzantine tradition, an effect paralleled in art and culture derivative of the early Irish Sea zone, in which landscape looks out on us (and we, in a sense, look out from within it) rather than cueing us to internalize and objectify it.

Such was the Insular literary "overlay landscape," which grew from narratives of a desert asceticism that came to the islands in search of a desert that was spiritual sea, an archipelago that in the post-Roman period was constituted culturally as both deserted by Rome and as a monastic desert, paralleling Deleuze's secular sense of desert islands but with the infinite difference from an Orthodox perspective of the added overlay of divine energies. Adomnán's late eighth-century Hiberno-Latin *Vita S. Columbae*, for example, refers to a spiritual pilgrim wishing to find a *desertum* in the ocean off Scotland.[52] Examples of such earlier melding of geography and imagination include the Otherworld sea in *Immram Brain*, the early Irish tropes of the colors of the winds and colors of martyrdom, Eriugena's image of the sea as theophanic,[53] and even early Ireland's decentered social and ecclesiastical networks as a dynamic cultural landscape.

If landscape as postmodern "body without organs" in Deleuzean secular and ecosophic terms can involve an immanent "rhizomic" or entwined grassroot sense of symbiotic ecoregion and culture-region (or atmosphere) such as the archipelago itself, it lacks the simultaneous transcendent "arboreal" overlay of immanent divine energies in patristic cosmology symbolized by the Tree of Life in Orthodox Christian tradition. The symbol of the Tree of Life as the Logos or Christ, advanced by St. Maximus, St. John of Damascus, and other Church Fathers, together with Eriguena (and typed by traditions of cosmic and sacred trees in Celtic, Germanic, and Norse literary traditions of northwestern Europe including the Otherworld/"green world" literary tradition), affords a creative meeting of rhizomic and arboreal cosmologies, reaching into multiple dimensions and "worlds" of God's earth, symbolically exemplifying in real terms of the Holy Cross the notion of cosmic overlay landscape in the Incarnation itself. The Old English poem *The Dream of the Rood* apparently emerged from a Celtic border area of Northumbria not far from St. Ninian's early sub-Roman monastic foundation, as suggested by an eighth-century carved cross at Ruthwell. The latter's runic analogue to part of the poem suggests Irish influence in its sculptural context literally inscribed on the landscape. It exemplifies in its devotion to the Cross as also a living tree (alternately and simultaneously bejeweled and triumphant, yet bloodied, and identified with Christ) this multiplex sense of physical experience and incarnational divinity in a traditional Christian context. Creation weeps at the Crucifixion of Christ. The poem echoes Byzantine hymnology.[54] It suggests the Cross as realized symbol of the Otherworld's typological overlay landscape.

During the later Middle Ages and into the Elizabethan period, the growth of what Frye called the "green world" trope, with its more exclusively forest focus, can be traced in the Arthurian "forest of adventure," emerging from the peninsular Forest of Broceliande in Celtic Brittany and the identification of vanishing woods in England with royal preserves, which in the Robin Hood legends encouraged creative subversion of controlled feudal landscapes in a forest Otherworld. Thomas Malory's apparent scrapes with the law indicate how his rehistoricization of the Arthurian overlay landscape in Britain reimagined remaining forests as a symbol for the contested space of royal authority during the Wars of the Roses. And entering the Elizabethan period, the increased cutting down of forests in England and the remaining woodlands in Ireland, together with reports of huge woodlands in the Americas, all increased the prominence of forest as a framework for overlay landscape—still paralleling the sea, in a secular transatlantic analogy to how Eurasian forests became the desert of the "Northern Thebaid" in Russian Orthodoxy.

The continued influence of early Irish Sea traditions and a new infusion of Greek patristic influence during the dawn of the Protestant Reformation in England both figure prominently in Spenser's "green world" masterwork, *The Faerie Queene*. Among other telling analogues with Eastern Christian theology and practice, probably transmitted through Spenser's circle at Cambridge through its study of Greek patristics as well as Spenser's interest in Irish tradition, Weatherby cites the appearance of Nature (modeled explicitly on Chaucer's figure) on Mount Arlo in southern Ireland.[55] This scene forms part of a mythic fantasy landscape woven by the poet directly onto his Irish neighborhood while echoing Eastern doctrines of uncreated energies or light in relation to the Transfiguration of Christ:

> . . . when she on *Arlo* sat,
> Her garment was so bright and wondrous sheene,
> That my fraile wit cannot deuize to what
> It to compare, nor finde like stuff to that,
> As those three sacred *Saints*, though else most wise,
> Yet on mount *Thabor* quite their wits forgat,
> When they their glorious Lord in strange disguise
> Transfigur'd sawe; his garments so did daze their eyes.[56]

Nor did filaments linking the "green world" trope to Orthodox theology end with Spenser. The latter's "wandering wood" became an important influence on James Fenimore Cooper's "Leatherstocking Tales," a formational American fantasy landscape of the vanishing Eastern woodlands and the first protoenvironmental novelistic project in America. Cooper's otherworldly "desert in the sea" is the great forest, with its watery vista at Cooperstown on his fictionally named Lake Glimmerglass overlaying present-day Lake Otsego, the headwaters of the Susquehanna River. Cooper's romanticized noble Indians parallel Tolkien's Elves, though he did draw heavily on early American Moravian Christian accounts of mainly peaceful engagements with Indian culture in the Susquehanna region. The Moravians shared the Orthodox formula for the Trinity, with its triadic (nondyadic) emphasis, and like other Pietist faiths were influenced by the Macarian Homilies of the early Christian desert. The cycle presents the Moravians as the spiritual guides of its hero Natty Bumppo. Cooper, whose family had a strong background in Quakerism (whose sense of "inner light" itself offers an indirect analogue to the Orthodox energy doctrine), presented a romanticized view of both Indians and forest landscape at odds with the skeptical and racist approach of Mark Twain. The difference can be seen in comparing their characters Chingachgook and Injun Joe. Despite the success of Twain's satirizing of Cooper, it would be Cooper's fantasy "green world" cycle that helped inspire early American conservationist leaders such as Theodore Roosevelt with its vision of ecological community, however ultimately pessimistic.

The *longue durée* of the overlay-landscape tradition in literature emerging from Europe's Atlantic islands, and its relation to Orthodox theology, remains part of a submerged history of Christian culture. As John McWhorter's writings on the history of the English language show, the English language itself is an archipelagic "magnificent bastard tongue" whose deep structure includes hidden elements, palimpsests if you will, from native Celtic languages in the islands, underlying several of the most common patterns of English speech, all from an impress left more than a millennium ago.[57] Likewise in the long view of things, the overlay landscape or Otherworld/"green world" trope has a far pedigree tracing back to a Christianity engaging native cultures, while its continued reinvention, persistence, and popularity suggest a lacuna in Western spiritual worldviews, in terms of an unfulfilled need for experiential grounding of human beings in its larger and ultimately spiritual ecology and ethology, liturgically and ascetically, in uncreated energies of the Triune God opened to us fully by the Incarnate Word, the Creator God become human on earth, in Orthodox Christian tradition.

When the pioneering ecocritic Lawrence Buell sat down to write criteria for ecocentric literature, that is, literature whose narrative lends itself to a secular ecocritical reading that focuses on setting within larger cosmic contexts, he identified four parameters: (1) that it features a "nonhuman environment" as a presence that suggests "human history is implicated in natural history," (2) in which "the human interest is not understood to be the only legitimate interest," (3) "human accountability to the environment is part of the text's ethical orientation," while expressing (4) "some sense of the environment as a process rather than as a constant."[58] The Otherworld/"green world" trope can be read, in a patristic context, as offering a cultural typology for teachings of the Church and the gospels while in a sense meeting

Buell's criteria with "environment" and "nature" defined in terms of *ktisis* and *cosmos*, in relation to Orthodox *energeia* rather than Scholastic *analogia*. *The Lord of the Rings*, one of the most popular modern books with an ecological message in the Insular Otherworld/"green world" tradition of overlay landscape, illustrates this. The Hobbit heroes of the cycle learn "their" Shire is not really theirs, as the Elves tell them near Woody End. When Frodo ends his journey by sailing out over the Western sea, he is replicating (like C. S. Lewis's Reepicheep the Mouse in *The Voyage of the Dawn Treader*) early Irish Sea narratives of the desert "ocean of divinity," to use a phrase from Eriugena.[59] If the green world has become fairyland, it is, as Tolkien noted,[60] a type of a larger fairytale come true in the gospel's "moral of all stories" (to use St. Nicholas Velimirovich's phrase),[61] or the *logoi* of the Logos in St. Maximus's terminology,[62] a reminder of a deeper spiritual meaning of the Greek roots of the neologism *ecology* as "the story of home."

Perspectives on Orthodoxy, Evolution, and Ecology

Gayle E. Woloschak

Ecology in the Modern Context

The goal of this paper is to establish two claims: first, that ancient Christianity is not based on concepts that permit humans to "abuse" nature and the environment, and second, that ecology and evolution as scientific disciplines are tightly linked and that a failure to recognize one or the other as valid will have significant societal impact. These views are synergistic: a harmonious relationship between humanity and nature can be founded upon the ancient teachings of the Church as much as upon the views of contemporary science.

Today, the environmental crisis has come to play a critical role in public debate both in the political arena and in academic circles. One aspect of these discourses has been the blame that many non-Christians and even Christians have placed at the feet of Christianity for the existence of ecological problems. Many, including Sallie McFague and Elizabeth Johnson,[1] have expressed the view that the ecological crisis is the direct result of an anthropocentric worldview that has led to an exploitative attitude toward the world and environment. According to this perspective, human beings are the center of the world, and the entire world is at their disposal to use in any way necessary to make humans more comfortable. This kind of anthropocentrism is often attributed to the influence of Christianity.

The ecological problem has proved to be a means of polarizing society in the United States. On one side of the argument are those that support the use of nature solely for human gain, with no inclination toward conservation, protection, or even a slowing down of the pace of the exploitation of environmental resources. On the other side of the spectrum are the broad scientific community and a large component of the ecological movement itself. In taking the opposite view, they have often blamed Christians for environmental exploitation. This has been based partially on the statements of certain Christian contemporaries and partially on their belief that Christianity propounds an anthropocentric view of the world that can be (mis)interpreted as prescribing the use of all creation solely for the selfish purposes of humanity. This has even led some ecological conservatives to challenge such purportedly anthropocentric views of Christianity (and in fact anthropocentrism in all religions), stating that all of life is equal on earth and that any tendency toward anthropocentrism should be met with condemnation. These criticisms raise two questions as central to the issue: (1) is Christianity of necessity anthropocentric, and (2) is the idea that Christianity supports the abuse of creation solely for human gain an ancient, and thus original, idea within Christianity?

First, we must consider the anthropocentric status of Christianity. Christianity is by definition Christ centered, and because Christ became Man, humans become a central focus of Christianity. Certainly, the creation stories in Genesis point to a human-centered creation; when God creates the world, only human beings are made "in the image and according to the likeness" of God. Most of the early Church Fathers do not turn away from a view of humanity as in some way a special part of creation, although as will be pointed out later, this involves a humanity that lives in harmony with creation as a steward of all things. An anthropocentric view of the world, then, probably cannot be avoided in Orthodoxy, and it is consistent with the Church Fathers. Nevertheless, a human-centered creation is not necessarily a human-exclusive creation, which leads to the second issue raised above.

The view that Christianity by nature permits the "use" (which allows the possibility of abuse) of the earth in order to serve humanity's needs is another component of the modern critique of Christianity by environmentalists. Many believe that this has been a component of Christianity since the beginning and that it has led over the centuries to a continual exploitation of the environment that has, in turn, led to the current environmental crisis. Often, ecological problems are placed squarely at the feet of Christianity, along with the call to usher in a post-Christian era in order to save the environment from Christian teachings. I want to maintain, however, that any Christianity that warrants the name cannot be exploitative of the environment and that exploitation is not a teaching of the ancient faith but rather is a recent innovation. Instead of promoting an abuse of the earth, the ancient Christian faith emphasized a correct relationship between humans and nature. Teachings and writings in the early Church Fathers that support a harmonious relationship between human beings and nature point to an older Christian perspective that was lost during the Westernization of Christianity. This view does not remove the anthropocentric view of creation, but at the same time it points to the need for a proper relationship between humanity and nature as one of priesthood, of dominion (rather than domination), and of love.

Clear signs of early "proenvironmental" thinking abound in ancient Church Fathers, St. Maximus the Confessor, for example. Raising awareness of this may perhaps aid in removing both Christianity as such along with a false understanding of anthropocentrism from the list of "issues" in the environmental debate and allow a joint proenvironment action of Christians with others who accept traditional doctrine and who desire the preservation of creation. In addition to St. Maximus, there are other ancient Fathers (such as Dionysius the Aeropagite and St. Gregory of Nyssa) that can be called upon as witnesses of the early church attitude, an attitude that includes anthropocentrism but only as understood within a harmonious relationship between humanity and nature.

Radu Bordeianu examined the writings of St. Maximus and the ecological movement in an article that puts forth the idea that St. Maximus's writings had relevance for environmental protection.[2] In particular, he focused on St. Maximus's theology of the *logoi* and his ideas about movement in creation, where all of creation moves toward its origin, a message strongly ecological in its intention. His view is that St. Maximus considers that Adam was unfaithful in his responsibility to be a true priest of creation; part of this is based in an inability to connect the five divisions within the world. These tensions or divisions Thunberg defines as created and uncreated, intelligible and sensible, heaven and earth, paradise and the inhabited world, and male and female.[3] Bordeianu notes that sin made Adam incapable of fulfilling his role of priest of creation but that Christ the New Adam restores that role to its proper place.

This proper role as priest(s) of creation places humans as a bond of creation to God: as the part of creation that can offer praise and sacrifice to God. Each human being must serve as a priest uniting all things to one another and to God. Human beings are the parts of creation that are both spiritual and earthly, feet on the ground, head turned up to heaven, and thus in prayer humanity can be mediator, protector, and unifier.[4] Von Balthasar, reflecting on St. Maximus's writings, similarly points out that not only is humanity the mediator of creation but that "if the Church is a '*world*,' the world is also a cosmic Church whose '*nave*' is sensible creation and whose '*choir*' is the world of intelligible realities."[5] This puts humanity at the center of creation, which remains consistent with an anthropocentric view of creation, but at the same time this points to the responsibility that humanity has for creation. It provides a more balanced approach to humanity's relationship to creation than either of the polarizing perspectives mentioned above (exploitation versus ecologically antianthropocentric tendencies).

The ideas expressed by the early Fathers of the Church who universally supported an anthropocentric view of creation point to the fact that the "abuse" of the environment is not inherent to the anthropocentric model. On the contrary, because exploitation is incompatible with humanity's priesthood, abuse of the rest of creation removes the title of "man as a center of creation" from those who commit this perversion of the divine plan. The anthropocentrism of the early Church Fathers is not the same as the idea of humans as the only important part of creation, the literalist view with which anthropocentrism is equated today.

Ecology and Evolution Defined

Ecology is the scientific study of the distribution of life and how both the distribution and the abundance of individual life forms are affected by the interactions of organisms with their environment. The term is derived from the Greek words *oikos*, meaning household, and *logos*, here meaning knowledge or study. It is, then, the study of the human "household" (the earth and its environment), and the way in which interaction with the environment plays a role in the survival and development of living organisms has become the context of modern ecological study. The environment within which an organism lives includes physical factors, such as sunlight and climate, that comprise the habitat of the species. In sharing the same biotope with the rest of its own population as well as with the populations of other species, an organism is a part of a wider biological community. The term "ecology" was first used by Ernst Haeckel in 1866 to describe "the comprehensive science of the relationship between the organism and its environment." It is highly interdisciplinary, with interactions among fields including geology, geography, biology, population dynamics, and statistics. Eugenius Warming (1841–1924) is considered to be the founder of the field of ecology as a separate discipline of biology.

Biological evolution is most simply defined as descent with modification. Evolution as a biological theory was first proposed by Charles Darwin, a British naturalist who explained that species develop over time and that they have developed from a common origin. His two most important works are *On the Origin of the Species*, first published in 1859, and *The Descent of Man, and Selection in Relation to Sex*, published in 1871.[6] The major tenets proposed by Darwin and accepted by the mainstream scientific community today are that there is a common ancestry for all of life on earth, that species develop through variations in form (now known to be the result of inheritable mutations), and that natural selection determines variation and drives speciation. At the time, Darwin's books were controversial both from the public viewpoint and from a religious perspective. Influenced by the Church of England, the British scientific establishment reacted against these works at the time, although this softened into an uneasy acceptance over the following decades. Eventually, even the Roman Catholic Church took a proevolution perspective, in part through the work of such noted scholars as Teilhard de Chardin and others, and these views were supported by several recent popes.

Evolution was originally presented as a scientific theory, a logically self-consistent model describing the behavior of a natural phenomenon originating in and supported by observable facts. Like all other scientific theories (such as the theory of gravity and the theory of relativity), evolutionary theory is formulated, developed, and evaluated according to the scientific method, which seeks to explain phenomena in the material (but not the spiritual) realm. The scientific method, which is used to test a scientific theory, is not radically different from a rational attitude that is used in many aspects of everyday life; for example, the fire inspector attempting to uncover the cause of a fire and the detective trying to solve a crime both use approaches similar to the scientific method.[7]

The scientific method is characterized by several major features: (1) it uses an objective approach, where the goal is to observe events as they are without falsifying them; (2) the results (if produced experimentally) must be reproducible in a broad sense in laboratories anywhere in the world; (3) there is an interplay of inductive reasoning (from specific observations and experiments) and deductive reasoning (reasoning from theories to account for specific experimental results); and (4) the objective of the work is to develop broad laws that become part of humanity's understanding of natural laws (such as the theory of gravity developed by Isaac Newton). The definition of a scientific theory, which is generally considered to be a paradigm that is proven or assumed to be true, is in marked contrast to a dogma, which is a principle that is merely proclaimed as true. It is at the core of science to strive for openness to change; this is imposed on it by the utilization of the scientific method. Thus science is required to refrain from making dogmatic claims and must rely instead upon hypotheses, which are assumptions used as the basis for investigation or argument and which can be tested. These hypotheses when all lined up together should support their originating theory.

The Link between Ecology and Evolution

The link between ecology and evolution has long been recognized in academic circles; many universities have a single department of evolution and ecology, and studies in one discipline generally require coursework in the other. They are usually viewed as two different sides of organism-environment interaction, with evolution studying the interaction from the perspective of the population over time and ecology examining this same interaction from the perspective of the environment over time. There are numerous examples of how environment affects evolution and how organisms affect environment. The following examples view humans as a species in its interaction with the environment.

Perhaps one of the simplest examples of the interplay of biological environment and life is evident in the Great Chinese Famine, which occurred between 1958 and 1962. In China at the time, there was a poor crop yield in the cooperative farms. The Chinese government blamed the sparrows for the famine, believing they were eating up all the food crops, and as a result an organized and massive destruction of sparrows was undertaken. However, the sparrows had kept the locust population in check because they feed on insects, and as a result of the near extinction of sparrows in 1958, the locust population massively increased, destroying the crops at a high rate. This exacerbated the famine and caused a large loss of human life. There had been a balance between locusts and sparrows, but once the sparrows were removed from the ecosystem by humans, the locusts, with their natural predator missing, could feed on the crops unchecked.[8]

An example that illustrates the role of environment in evolution is the example of sickle cell anemia and its relationship to malaria in humans. The sickle cell disease is caused by a single mutation in both copies of the beta globin gene, which encodes a protein that transports oxygen in red blood cells. The genetic mutation is a change in a single DNA nucleotide that results in an atypical hemoglobin molecule called hemoglobin S, which can distort red blood cells into a sickle, or crescent, shape. People with one healthy and one hemoglobin S gene have normally shaped discoid red blood cells. However, such red blood cells are resistant to malaria, which is endemic in Africa and areas of the Mediterranean and had existed in southern parts of the United States as well. People that have two copies of the hemoglobin S gene die early of complications from sickle cell anemia, and in regions where malaria is found people with two copies of the healthy version of the gene die of malaria. In the present-day United States, Western Europe, and other areas where malaria is not found, there is no advantage to having a copy of the hemoglobin S gene in the genome; it is only in areas where malaria is endemic that having one (but only one) of the sickle cell genes is actually useful. When the gene is taken out of its environmental context (regions where malaria is endemic), it loses its benefit.

These two examples illustrate the interaction between environment and evolution on the human species and demonstrate how difficult it is to understand one without the other. Rejection of the ideas of evolution, then, can lead to a misunderstanding of the relationship between organisms and their environment and may contribute to an ambivalent attitude toward environmental concerns. Antievolution sentiment may then grow into antienvironmental attitudes. In general, Orthodox Christians do not accept an invariably literal understanding of scripture and therefore need not have a problem with the concept of evolution. One modern Orthodox scholar who dealt extensively with the topic of evolution, nature, and theology is Fr. Sergius Bulgakov.

Causality and Bulgakov

The concepts of eternity and the creation of time are also linked with questions about causality. Much of early science was oriented toward understanding the creative activity of God, and it was the general belief that understanding nature would lead to a greater understanding of its Creator. Mendel, a monk of the Roman Catholic Church, pursued genetics as a way of understanding nature and thereby gain insight into God's creation. Galileo studied the heavens to gain a better understanding the One who created the universe. These early scientific perspectives were linked to the "two-book" model for understanding science and religion—with the "book of nature" and "the book of scripture" being two different approaches of understanding God and His creation. God was seen as the source of all causality, and creation was a reflection of God's action in the universe. Modern science has distanced itself from any concept of a Creator, focusing instead on understanding intermediate causes or "subcausalities." Nevertheless, we are still driven to search for the causes of events. Tolstoy in *War and Peace* acknowledged this when he wrote: "The human intellect cannot grasp the full range of causes that lie behind any phenomenon. But the need to discover causes is deeply ingrained in the spirit of man."[9] This drive to find causes is found in all areas of investigation—history, where we try to uncover the cause of events in hopes of not repeating mistakes; psychology, where we hope to find the cause of mental disorders and thereby cure the patient; medicine, where we hope to find the underlying cause of disease and give the appropriate therapy. The overall goal of science is to provide useful models of material reality, and this is naturally driven by the cause-effect relationship.

Scientists look at bacteria and viruses as causes of infectious diseases, psychological trauma as causes of mental disorders, and so forth, but they no longer attribute any aspect of this to God. While many people have complained that science is wrong because it does not consider God as a cause, in fact, science studies the material world and not the spiritual world. Science attempts to be objective, with the goal of providing a language and approach that is unified among all scientists and allows for communication across the globe and even across disciplines. When a biologist in Chicago and a biologist in Japan are talking about a particular response to radiation, they both know what it takes to define that response and whether the appropriate criteria have been met to establish that it is in fact a response to radiation. When journal papers are being peer reviewed for publication, often the comments on the paper will be similar regardless of whether the reviewer is from Germany or Canada.

While many feel confused or even angered by the fact that scientists can discuss creation without putting God into the story, these same people do not understand that there is sometimes humility in not discussing God. There is a limit to what science can define, and that limit is based on the objective scientific approach of performing hypothesis-driven experimentation on the material world alone. God is not subject to such testing, and therefore whenever the scientist would be bringing God into the discussion, it would be based not on scientific experimentation but rather on his or her personal belief system. This belief system is not amenable to scientific experimentation but rather is based on personal faith and experience. If scientists were to put God into their scientific results, one wonders what the basis for this would be and what criteria would be used for including some pieces of faith-based information and not others. In fact, it could be argued that much of the animosity in the science-religion discussion is based on scientists overstepping their bounds and delving into faith-based concerns.

A recent conference, "Beyond Belief,"[10] held by scientists to discuss the science-religion interface demonstrated how challenging it is to find a middle ground between believing and nonbelieving scientists. The misleading aspect of this discussion occurs when prestigious scientists such as Stephen Hawking or Richard Dawkins take strong stands against religion, leading one to conclude that they are doing this based on scientific evidence rather than their own personal beliefs. The issues of causality understood from a scientific perspective and as approached from a theological perspective become confused. As modern science finds scientific causes and pushes the cause of events (for example, the beginning of cosmos) further and further from God, God appears to be smaller, and one wonders whether God is even there at all.

One early proponent of "God as the cause" was Thomas Aquinas, who argued that God is the Primary Cause of all things:

> There must be found in the nature of things one first immovable Being, a primary cause, necessarily existing, not created; existing the most widely, good, even the best possible; the first ruler through the intellect, the ultimate end of all things, which is God.[11]

This argument of Aquinas has become a hallmark for the Western Church in identifying the relationship of God and Creation with God as the Primary Cause and other causes as being secondary. At first examination, this statement of God as the Primary Cause of all seems well founded in reasoning and understanding, and in fact God could be posited as the Primary Cause of all things, with science examining secondary causes. This, however, may lead to erroneous conclusions.

Drawing upon the insights of patristic Christianity, Sergius Bulgakov takes this perspective to task, arguing that "The One Who Causes" is not a proper designation for God.[12] He bases this on how we understand the word "cause." When humans cause things to happen, we think of these as "cause-effect" relationships: for example, turning the key in the car ignition causes it to start, or exposure to influenza virus causes the person to develop the flu. This is not the proper way to think of God's relationship with the world. Bulgakov argues that the proper description of God's relationship to the world is that of Creator and creation, and this is not the same as "The One Who Causes." If human creativity somehow entails a microrelation to God's creativity and creative activity, then perhaps we can understand God as Creator through considering the creative acts of humans rather than considering causative facts.

A comparison of cause-effect actions with creative actions shows that these are actually quite different. Creativity is often considered to be a mental activity that involves the generation of new ideas or new concepts, although there is great difficulty in defining it and its features. The source of creativity has been attributed to a variety of different processes (social environment, cognitive processes, divine intervention, serendipity, etc.) and is usually multidimensional in nature. Creativity is not something that can be dictated or even defined, nor is it something that can be legislated, such as:

"Today I will be creative." This is much different from a cause-effect relationship where the end result can be easily attributed to a specific action. A person can easily say "I will make an X" and proceed to do it if it involves no inspiration, but such is not the case with creation and creative thinking. While a person can indicate that they will design a particular experiment or a particular building at a given time, the inspiration for a creative component to that work cannot be dictated and may come when least expected, or it may never come. Thus, we often hear people claim that their best ideas (creative moments) happen in the shower or when they first wake up in the morning. If one then extrapolates from human experience with creativity, it becomes clear that creativity and cause and effect are very different things.

Bulgakov provides a critique of certain aspects of Western theology, including arguments against the doctrine of first and second causes. He prefers instead a concept of "co-imagedness," in which the creatures contain the living image of the Creator, and he argues that the world does not have a cause since it was created and that God is not the cause of the world but rather is the world's Creator and Provider. In this sense, the world becomes a correlative unity understood by its connection with its Creator rather than an autonomous and unrelated entity. We can also easily understand this stance from our own creative experiences—things we caused to be made are much less important to us than those we created by drawing upon our inspiration, our originality. Such latter things we are proud of, and we want to be measured by them—in some way, they are us ourselves. There is another meaning to be had from the word originality—when we create and are the origin of a creation, we are truly original. God as Origin of all is infinitely more than a cause. Bulgakov reasons that the proper relationship of the Creator and creation is expressed as an icon:

> In general, the idea of the Creator and creation does not need to be translated into the language of mechanical causality, for it has another category, its proper one, that of co-imagedness, since the creature contains the living image of the Creator and is correlated with Him.... The world does not have a cause, since it is created; and God is not the cause of the world and not a cause in the world, but its Creator and Provider. God's creative act is not the mechanical causation through Himself of the world's being, but His going out of Himself in creation.[13]

This co-imagedness fits well with the Genesis context of humans being made in the image and according to the likeness of God. Humans bear the imprint of their Creator, and therefore they are icons of God. We acknowledge this liturgically by censing the people during all liturgical services, censing the image of God in each person.

Bulgakov is one of the few Orthodox theologians to have addressed questions of the interaction of God and the world by taking into consideration modern scientific thinking about evolution. There are also several others who have addressed the issue of the interface of science and religion in contemporary Orthodox thought.[14] They too have used a theological approach to addressing questions of environment, anthropology, and creation, and while much of their thinking touches directly on evolutionary biology and its meaning in a religious context, they have not had this topic as their major goal. While Bulgakov's writings are often tangential to this topic, he has also specifically examined the theory of evolution and its implications for Orthodoxy. His book *The Bride of the Lamb* tackles the issue of the creation of the world "out of nothing" and uses this as an opportunity to introduce his view of Sophianicity[15] and its role in God's relationship to humanity and to the world.

Bulgakov deals with a variety of problematic questions for the "science and religion" discussion. Was there a time when God was not Creator? Bulgakov considers that the power of creation is so integrated into the Godhead that God cannot fail to be the Creator, and thus God cannot be understood as separated from Creation. God never began being Creator because God is Creator eternally. God's interaction with the world is predominantly creative, not mechanical. Creation is an ongoing process that has not ended and will not end. Bulgakov sees this as being consonant with views of evolution where the life continues to be changed, and hence created, even now.

How can one understand the eternity of creation and the temporality of its being? Is there a beginning of time? Bulgakov considers that eternity is accessible to creatures only through temporality and the overcoming of temporality. He notes that the symbolism of the six days of creation places the creation of time itself only on the fourth day, that is, after the fullness of already existing creaturely life has been implanted. Time exists for humanity, who, by nature, has consciousness and knowledge of time. The world was not created in time—time was created in the world, but this creation was supratemporal, not extratemporal. Bulgakov states: "Even if one could seek the *beginning* of creation, it would have to be perceived not outside, not in time or in space, but inside, in the character of creaturely being, and in the last analysis, in divine being."[16]

To what extent is humanity God's creation? Bulgakov's view is that humanity is created by God's call into being in some cosmic sense but that there is also an extent (paradoxically) to which humanity is its own creator brought about by the freedom of choice given to humanity by God. Human freedom comes with a creative power that is capable of self-determination, while humans are considered "noncreaturely-creaturely beings, created and self-creating," intended to become a god by grace or even a created god. This is balanced by each person's personal acceptance of universal sin, which can be different from one person to another, a concept that Bulgakov favors over traditional views of original sin. Furthermore, this position is tightly bound to his understanding of evolution.

What does acceptance of evolution mean for our understanding of an original Edenic state of humanity on earth? Bulgakov notes that an evolutionary outlook on human origins is diametrically opposed to any view of an original state of humanity that is associated with Eden and a perfect life. This point is expounded in detail as the contrast between the language of empirical history and metahistorical events is described. Bulgakov considers the idea that, while evolution takes place as a series of apparently capricious events, there is an inner progression of creation that allows for the actualization in time of a prior reality that is beyond creation. While evolution defines the "how" of creation, the "what" of creation is defined by this inner progression that reflects a different reality, a reality that existed before this reality, a reality that humans "remember" as an Edenic state and as God's garden. So, just as God is always a Creator, the extratemporal creation that God has always created is always the goal and the memory of the material creation, its Eden. Bulgakov states: "although man is phylogenetically connected with the animal world by his animal nature, his origin is not merely an evolutionary achievement, but an express and new divine creative act that is *outside* the evolutionary process. It is something *new* in creation."[17] The appearance of a godlike spirit in humanity is a mystery that is not understood empirically, and evolution does not attempt to define when or how this spirit first appeared in humans or humanlike creatures, nor is it supposed to.

Concluding Thoughts

The work of Bulgakov demonstrates one way in which the approach of ancient Christian thought can offer us powerful insights into the natural environment, especially with respect to contemporary debates and considerations. It also shows how Christian "anthropocentrism" need not be harmful to the environment. As science and technology become more prominent and as concerns about ecological and technological problems loom, the early Church Fathers can be used as promising guides for understanding humanity's proper relationship with nature, and this relationship is best understood as mediator, priest, contemplator, and unifier, all of which help us strive for unity with God, a goal for which we were created but for which we must struggle. This is based upon a worldview that is anthropocentric but not anthropoexclusive, and it must seek for harmony with nature in order to be consistent with the teachings of the ancient Christian Church. Further, evolution and ecology are tightly linked, and separation of the two only leads to an inadequate understanding of nature and an inappropriate orientation toward the environment. Evolution as a concept should be acceptable to Orthodox Christians, particularly in light of the fact that the Orthodox generally do not accept a literal understanding of Genesis. Acceptance of evolution, ecology, and the ancient faith tradition should all facilitate a more balanced relationship of humanity with the world that surrounds us.

Ecology, Morality, and the Challenges of the Twenty-First Century: The Earth in the Hands of the Sons of Noah

H. Tristram Engelhardt Jr.

Environmental Ethics: Ambiguities Concerning What Is at Stake

Orthodox Christianity can tell us about how to go to heaven but not how the heavens go. The Church does not possess special sensible, empirical, scientific knowledge (although this can be the case in the instance of great ascetics, true theologians) that can inform us about whether and how much global warming can be attributed to the presence of humans, what the implications of those changes are, what specifically should be done to ameliorate adverse changes, or about a host of other sensible-empirical issues that bear on particular policy choices regarding the environment. The Church does not serve as a general source of sensible-empirical knowledge that can guide policy choices through criticizing empirical scientific claims. Nor does the Church have knowledge about how prudently to weigh competing policy options, insofar as these are embedded in different empirical data sets. The Church, however, can join scientists, philosophers of science, and wise policymakers in reminding us about the uncertainty of scientific claims and about the need always to act with prudence and caution. In environmental policy, as with all empirically driven policy choices, there are good grounds for caution with regard to apodictic statements. The role of the Church is to bring us in right worship and right belief through repentance so that we may be purified, illumined by God, and brought into union with Him.

Concerning the environment, and more generally with respect to developing environmental policy, there is uncertainty about all the empirical data that can be invoked to change and frame policy. One might note the extent to which many earlier policy recommendations failed to anticipate the current downward trend in population growth throughout the world.[1] Previous secular prophets of the future have at best had a mixed record. This point is multivalent. The uncertainty regarding predictions with respect to the environment reflects not only the uncertainty of all sensible empirical claims but also the special complexity of environmental studies and their attempts to predict the future. Environmental studies must take account, for example, of a wide range of variables, including fluctuations in the amount of energy emitted by the sun. On the face of the complexities and uncertainties involved, one would expect that precise predictions would generally be difficult, if not impossible. The articulation of a concrete environmental ethics must begin with a recognition of the finitude of human sensible empirical knowledge.

Given that all policy recommendations are also shaped by background moral and political commitments,[2] it must also be recognized that policy recommendations depend on the framing of the moral, cultural, and political presuppositions, and on the special agenda of those who commission studies and reports as well as oversee their production and interpretation. The overlay of moral and policy agendas in the framings of scientific findings in the case of reflections on matters ecological is illustrated by what has come to be termed "Climategate," which shaped disputes regarding the possible influence of the agendas of particular scientists and research groups involved in the reporting of findings regarding the environment.[3] When science is tied to a commitment to particular policy objectives, there is a tendency to accept findings as facts that will support one's position regarding the nature of environmental change and thus regarding what counts as prudent environmental public policy. Empirical disagreements are often framed within disparate views of appropriate environmental policy. Reflections regarding the likely future of the environment are nested in controversy.[4] Nevertheless, defenders of particular positions in scientific and policy debates often fail to nest their findings within sufficiently qualifying, cautionary statements. It is in response to the lack of such caution on the part of Albert Gore's statements that his co–Nobel Laureate John Christy remarked that nature "is so complex, and so the uncertainties are great, and then to hear someone [Gore] speak with such certainty and such confidence about what the climate is going to do is—well, I suppose I could be kind and say, it's annoying to me."[5] Scientists, especially applied scientists and advocates of particular policies advanced on the basis of empirical findings, are well advised to nest their claims within qualifications that recognize the uncertainties of empirical knowledge, the complexity of empirical reality, and the possible distorting force of antecedent moral and political commitments.[6]

Against this background of controversy and contention, this essay focuses primarily on what Orthodox Christianity can bring to the articulation of an environmental ethic. To do this, first a general theological background is sketched, then some salient empirical and moral ambiguities are noted, and then finally some general theological constraints and norms bearing on environmental ethics are elaborated. Throughout, the emphasis is on recalling the prime focus of Orthodox theology, which falls on rightly loving, worshipping, and believing in God and, in the light of that rightly ordered love of God, loving one's neighbor. Within these constraints, Orthodox Christianity leaves a considerable space within which one is left to determine prudent choices. The essay concludes with the recognition that we must first pursue the kingdom of heaven, not the realization of the environmentalist kingdom. Only then can we rightly approach the task of caring for the environment, and then likely only through repentance for the ways in which we will always fall short of a rightful dominion over nature.

The Theological Background

In approaching our state of uncertainty about empirically sensible claims, we must note that the core truths of Orthodox Christian theology are generally not propositions about sensible-empirical facts of the matter.[7] The truth about which Orthodox theology is competent is that of God and God's relationship to us as well as to reality in general. Orthodox theology concerns God and His relation to creation and creation's proper relationship to God.[8] As a consequence, Orthodox Christianity provides little clear, direct, and specific guidance regarding a range of environmental issues. Orthodox theology does in general tell us about what it means to love God with all our hearts, souls, and minds and about how rightly to love our neighbor as ourselves. It does this by informing us about what behavior in general to avoid and about that behavior in which we ought to engage, especially about how to live in repentance. One can as a consequence derive some content for environmental ethics from the obligations of humans not to harm other humans or not wantonly to harm animals, but the guidance is unlikely by itself to be enough to supply sufficient concrete content for affirming a particular, concrete, environmental policy as the Orthodox policy. Orthodox Christianity does give some specific guidance about how to relate to our neighbor, such as not to murder, commit abortion, steal, as well as regarding the importance of feeding the poor and forgiving injuries. The difficulty is that, although some alterations of the environment may be instruments of murder and theft, in most cases matters are much more ambiguous. In addition, it is often unclear what changes in the environment will lead to what kinds of harms or benefits for whom and when.

One may nevertheless be tempted to derive a substantive environmental ethic from Scripture, as from the passage in Genesis (2:15) where God put Adam "in the garden of Eden to work it and to take care of it." One might then attempt to unpack from this circumstance a general but nevertheless content-full environmental ethic. However, matters are much more complicated than such a temptation to ground an environmental ethic might suggest. To begin with, Orthodox Christianity's contemporary, normative relationship to nature is not that of Adam in paradise. It is that of Adam after the Fall—indeed, that of Noah after the Flood (Gen. 9:1–7). A consequence of this state of affairs is that the ways in which great ascetics and monastics have in general lived in relationship with nature cannot directly provide guidance for those living outside of a monastic life. The norms for nonmonastics are different from those that bind monastics. Consider, for example, Canon 51 of the eighty-five Apostolic Canons:

> If any Bishop, or Presbyter, or Deacon, or anyone at all on the sacerdotal list, abstains from marriage, or meat, or wine, not as a matter of mortification, but out of an abhorrence thereof, forgetting that all things are exceedingly good, and that God made man male and female, and blasphemously misrepresenting God's work of creation, either let him mend his ways or let him be deposed from office and expelled from the Church. Let a layman be treated similarly.[9]

The canon indicates that the norms for those who have not taken on the monastic ascetic life are not the norms for life in paradise, where Adam and Eve were vegetarians, nor norms for the quasi-angelic life of the world to come, in which humans will not marry (Matt. 22:30). They are norms for those who live in the world that God blesses for the sons of Noah after the Flood.

Environmental ethics is set first within the condition of Adam after the Fall, when nature is no longer in harmony with man. As God states the matter, "Cursed is the ground because of you; through painful toil you will eat of it all the days of your life. It will produce thorns and thistles for you . . ." (Gen. 3:17–18). However, and crucially, as already noted, conditions change further when the sons of Noah after the Flood are no longer vegetarians and are blessed to kill and eat animals. The contemporary normative relationship of humans to nature is not the special relationship of Adam in the Garden of Eden, although the paradigmatic relationship of men to the world has never simply been that of a gardener. After all, the blessing upon Adam and Eve when God creates them extends beyond just gardening. Adam and Eve are called to

> "Be fruitful and increase in number; fill the earth and subdue it. Rule over the fish of the sea and the birds of the air and over every living creature that moves on the ground." [In this passage] God said, "I give you every seed-bearing plant on the face of the whole earth and every tree that has fruit with seed in it. They will be yours for food. And to all the beasts of the earth and all the birds of the air and all the creatures that move on the ground—everything that has the breath of life in it—I give every green plant for food." And it was so. (Gen. 1:28–30)

Even before the flood, man is to subdue the earth and to fill it with humans, such that man is implicitly blessed to change the environment through his presence. This commission is expanded after the Flood. After the Flood, the authority of man was robustly amplified: he was given a new relationship with nature, for God blesses Noah and his sons by declaring, "The fear and dread of you will fall upon all the beasts of the earth and all the birds of the air, upon every creature that moves along the ground, and upon all the fish of the sea; they are given into your hands. Everything that lives and moves will be food for you. Just as I gave you the green plants, I now give you everything" (Gen. 9:2–3). The sons of Noah are no longer the gardeners of plants but the hunters and consumers of animals. The relation of the sons of Noah to nature in comparison to that of Adam and Eve in Paradise is one of robust dominion. St. John Chrysostom in his commentary describes this relationship as one of "control, authority, and enjoyment."[10] The dominion of Noah and his sons is surely a dominion set within the restraints of particular obligations, but it is a substantial dominion nonetheless. The question is the substance and content of this dominion and the character of the constraining obligations that limit and direct that dominion.[11]

In exploring how to think about obligations regarding the environment in light of Orthodox Christian theological insights about the authority and obligations of the sons of Noah, one must bear in mind that Orthodox Christianity is focused first and foremost on orienting us rightly to God and to love of our fellow man and only at best secondarily on preserving the environment as we now find it. Background to the reflections in this essay is the widespread but not universal secular view that significant environmental changes are occurring consequent upon various forms of pollution and environmental pressures attributable to the presence of humans.[12] For the purpose of this paper, this view regarding environmental change is taken for granted. Nevertheless, as with all empirical matters, as already noted, there are controversies about what exactly is transpiring, about the implications of what is occurring, whatever that may be, and about what interventions are merited in response to what is taking place, whatever that may be. This paper locates considerations regarding the environment within the context of what Orthodox Christianity knows as well as within what it means prudently to choose among policy alternatives when those alternatives depend on findings that have a heavy political and moral overlay. In locating the challenge of making prudent empirical and moral decisions regarding the environment within the insights of Orthodox Christian theology, one must not lose sight of the circumstance that one is not called to love the environment as we now find it with all one's heart, nor to love this environment as one is called to love one's neighbor.

Environmental Ethics and Environmental Policy: A Brief Review of Some of the Challenges

Cardinal ambiguities beset the articulation of an environmental ethics and the justification of a defensible and appropriate environmental policy, even when ethics and policy are informed by Orthodox Christian theology. First, choices regarding environmental policy generally fall in an area that does not benefit from concrete theological guidance. There is no set of right- or wrong-making conditions embedded in Orthodox Christian theology that would per se forbid particular uses of nature apart from prohibitions such as against bestiality (Lev. 18:23, 20:15–16), the profligate wasting of resources, causing pain to animals without sufficient reason, as well as injunctions to care for one's animals (Deut. 25:24, Prov. 12:10), etc. Humans for centuries have felled forests to plant fields, built canals to divert rivers, and used wood and coal to warm their houses (thus polluting the air of cities), all without remonstrations from the Church. Even God Himself cleared the land of Israel from wild beasts (Lev. 26:6). People have likely always recognized that such undertakings involve tradeoffs between costs and benefits flowing from different changes to the environment. There are no clear standards in Orthodox Christianity or in the resources of secular moral philosophy to determine how precisely one ought to compare possible costs and benefits flowing from different changes to the environment. For example, more productive fields have always meant fewer virgin forests and untilled plains. Orthodox Christianity's concerns for the welfare of man have always trumped concerns to keep nature as it was before humans entered. There appears to be no precise formula for determining how one should balance an interest in the welfare of humans with an interest in keeping some virgin forest.

Beyond the question of how to balance changing the environment in order to benefit humans with keeping some wilderness areas somewhat as specially protected large-scale parks (for example, as wilderness areas), there is the question of how to balance obligations to humans with interests in preserving particular species. For example, is it clearly sinful to ban DDT in order to avoid risks to animals such as to condors, knowing that this will most likely lead to the death of millions of children in malaria-infested parts of the world?[13] On the face of it, the consideration would appear to go strongly in favor of children and against the welfare of condors. But is it necessarily clearly sinful to ban DDT? The answer may not be fully clear. However, since there are no overriding obligations to the environment as there are strong obligations to aid poor children, an environmental ethic must prefer children to condors.

Aside from a few instances, Orthodox Christian theology appears devoid of a basis for definitively resolving most disputes about how appropriately to compare many of the costs and benefits to humans associated with different policy approaches to environmental change. How should one compare harms and benefits, and for whom? For example, there is the challenge of determining how one ought to compare the loss of agricultural productivity in one area of the world (presuming compensation to the landowners) with an increase in agricultural productivity in other parts of the world, especially when such changes are combined with a general decrease in poverty in the world. Such disputes, like most policy disputes regarding the engagement of science and technology where there is a significant moral and political overlay, involve competing accounts about how responsibly to compare different costs and benefits as well as how prudently to act in a circumstance of epistemic uncertainty. Orthodox Christianity does not give concrete guidance about how to make such empirical determinations in environmental science, environmental policy, or for that matter regarding ordinary medical treatment (for example, about exactly how certain one ought to be, as an Orthodox Christian physician, about a diagnosis before initiating a particular treatment). Within certain general constraints, Orthodox Christianity does not advise us on how to rank values and harms in the composition of an account of human flourishing, as is illustrated by the diversity of the lives lived by Orthodox saints: great hermits, holy emperors, fools for Christ's sake, ascetic patriarchs, and holy warriors.

This general point requires special emphasis. Many controversies in environmental ethics combine controversies concerning empirical assessments of the probability, extent, and character of harms and benefits associated with particular forms of environmental change with unclarities regarding the probability, extent, and character of the benefits and harms associated with interventions directed to ameliorating adverse environmental changes. Such determinations always depend on empirical circumstances. Policies established on their basis often lead to unanticipated outcomes. For example, consider the question of whether the putatively environmentally friendly policy of diluting gasoline with ethanol on balance benefits or harms persons, or for that matter the environment, whatever "benefit or harm to the environment" might mean apart from reference to man. Any answer is difficult because one must consider the impact on the poor from driving up corn prices, which increases result from the use of corn in the production of ethanol, versus any benefit attributable to decreasing the use of traditional gasoline. As the demand for corn for ethanol production increases, the cost of many basic food staples increases, likely leading in some circumstances to increased marginal death rates. Moreover, agricultural patterns are also changed because of growing more corn, leading to further environmental consequences.[14] Even the establishment of recycling programs cannot be presumed innocent of unintended adverse environmental consequences; for example, the establishment of recycling programs involves more truck-producing exhaust fumes because of picking up and delivering recyclables.

The force of these reflections is that hasty, inadequately considered attempts to address environmental problems, like hasty medical attempts to address the suffering of patients, often cause more harms than benefits. If one simply rushes to "do something" to aid a patient in distress before one is sufficiently clear about the diagnosis and about what treatment will achieve more benefit than harm, one is likely to affect the patient adversely. The challenge is that one must compare the various consequences of deciding to intervene with a particular "proenvironment" policy versus the various consequences of deciding not to intervene. Uncertainties regarding outcomes, as well as unclarities about the proper balancing of risks and benefits to different persons involved in competing policy options, make the nature of appropriate choices in areas of such empirical uncertainty not only difficult but often highly controversial. There is no bright line from Orthodox theology showing how one ought a priori to compare the benefits and harms at stake, let alone frame a concrete environmental policy.

The case of ethanol-enriched gasoline and its impact on the poor illustrates a major challenge. There is always the problem of determining who is helped or harmed, in what way, and how much by environmental changes. Just as the choice to use aspirin to control pain will entail the consequence that some will die of untoward outcomes from this therapy, so, too, any environmental policy will help some and harm others. Global warming, for example, will be of benefit to some populations while it will harm others.[15] One must take into consideration and compare the likelihood and character of the effects of global warming on rising sea levels, for instance, with respect to morbidity and mortality outcomes for particular populations that do not move from high-risk areas versus the morbidity and mortality risks to the poor elsewhere without further industrial development (not to mention the benefit for some areas of having longer growing seasons). One must take into consideration that the poor cannot quit poverty without economic development and that risks to the poor may be associated with constraints on the world economy from environment-friendly regulations. That is, one must consider what impact exacting more regulations against environmental pollution will likely have on the poor in different areas of the world in comparison to the possible harms from environmental changes. Poverty, after all, is a clear predictor of increased morbidity and mortality.[16] In this regard, one must be careful in developing global critiques of our contemporary consumer culture, in that any abrupt departure from our current consumer culture will likely have an adverse impact on the status of the poor.[17] The problem is how to decide which populations will be at risk, to what extent, and for what harms as a result of imposing or not imposing new, putatively environment-friendly policies. Orthodox theology does not provide clear guidance about how to determine whom to benefit or harm through environmental policy choices.

The challenges are further compounded by the difficulty of having to compare benefits and harms to current generations with benefits and harms to future generations. As one attempts to assess harms to future generations from not intervening to slow global warming, one must determine how to discount those possible harms, given the opacity of the future. The choice of a discount rate with respect to future harms will surely be controversial but nonetheless necessary. Among other things, one can never make predictions of future occurrences with absolute certainty. One must instead weight a future occurrence at something less than 100 percent of its full positive or negative value. Indeed, one must discount the significance of future harms by some percent for every year in the future its occurrence is thought to lie. In making such assessments, one will need to ask whether it will help those in the future more if one invests in technologies to counteract the warming attributable to pollution rather than to limit pollution directly. That is, one will need to consider and critically to compare diverse ways of responding to the challenges from an environment that is changing because of global warming. One approach is to devise various interventions that will lower the amount of pollutants that are held to be causing global warming, either by changing technology so as to produce less of the harmful pollutants or instead by developing technologies to remove those pollutants from the air.[18] Quite another approach is to engage in technological interventions in the environment in order to counterbalance the causes of global warming.[19] Since an important concern for Orthodox Christians is caring for the poor, one will need properly to discount possible benefits to future generations in order appropriately to take into account how advantaging future generations may disadvantage the current poor by slowing technological development. One will need in particular to assess which current environment-polluting technologies tend to decrease poverty and by decreasing poverty decrease morbidity and mortality risks among the poor.

What We Do Know as Orthodox Christians That Is Relevant to Environmental Ethics

There are important exceptions to the limited ability of Orthodox theology to give substantive moral guidance regarding the fashioning of actual environmental policy in response to ecological changes. At least six observations can establish some side constraints on environmental policy choices in terms of recognizing that an acceptable environmental ethic must affirm the presence of man and come to terms with the consequences that man's presence brings. In particular, an Orthodox Christian environmental ethic must relativize concerns for the environment so that love of the environment does not diminish or overshadow love for God and man. Theological considerations must nest environmental concerns within broader and normatively prior concerns about obligations to God and man. An authentic Orthodox Christian environmental ethic will have a character quite different from that framed by the heterodox and by the secular. Most particularly, an Orthodox Christian environmental ethic will exclude Deep Ecological commitments that bring into question man's dominion over nature or regard negatively the imprint of man's presence on the environment.

First, there is scriptural basis for recognizing that the environment has properly and rightly been changed by humans as a result of obeying the Divine injunction to increase, multiply, and fill the earth (Gen. 1:28). In assessing the relation of humans to the environment, one must begin with acknowledging that there is a fundamental appropriateness to those environmental and ecological changes consequent on the very presence of large human populations. The ecological systems of the world will never be the same, given the presence of humans, and this is in itself neither wrong nor bad. This state of affairs, as has already been observed, is at least indirectly blessed by God in the command "God blessed them and said to them, 'be fruitful and increase in number; fill the earth and subdue it; and have dominion over the fish of the sea and over the birds of the air and over every living thing that moves upon the earth'" (Gen. 1:28), and then again "be fruitful and increase in number and fill the earth" (Gen. 9:1), and then again "be fruitful and increase in number and multiply on the earth and increase upon it" (Gen. 9:7). The world with its ecological systems absent man cannot be the norm for the proper state of the environment and its ecological systems. Rather, the norm is the world with its ecological systems altered because of the presence and dominion of man, especially the dominion of the sons of Noah. All else being equal, it is good that the environment be altered for the benefit of man's presence. Environmentalist concerns for ecological systems that do not recognize this appropriate man-centeredness in environmental ethics are fundamentally perverse.

Second, there is a strong obligation not to transform one's environmental concerns into an all-consuming project. What St. Basil says in warning concerning all-consuming uses of medicine engaged to prolong life also applies to all-consuming concerns to preserve the environment with its ecological systems as we currently find them. St. Basil forbids "whatever requires an undue amount of thought or trouble or involves a large expenditure of effort and causes our whole life to revolve, as it were, around solicitude for the flesh."[20] An all-consuming engagement in environmentalism occurs when one becomes more invested in maintaining the environment with its ecological systems as we now find them than with discharging the two great commandments to love God and love one's neighbor (Matt. 2:22–36). These considerations are not advanced as an argument against environmental concerns and interventions when they are clearly aimed at protecting one's neighbor against known or likely risks attributable to environmental changes. It is rather to recognize that there can be a temptation to be more concerned with keeping the environment and ecological systems as we now find them than with worshipping God and with feeding the poor. Even from a secular moral point of view, the attempt to keep the environment with its ecological systems as they now exist, in a world where environments with their ecological systems are always dynamically in flux and are constantly changing, is at the very least a dubious project, if not foundationally misguided. Those who focus overzealously on preserving the environment and its ecological systems as they now exist run the risk of being more concerned for the pursuit of preserving a very particular environment than for the pursuit of the kingdom of heaven.

Third, it is important to note that the inclination to approach the contemporary environment and its ecological systems as a quasi-idol is often the result of an immanent displacement of transcendent concerns. In such circumstances, the rituals of recycling can become secular substitutes for the ascetic rhythms and commitments of the traditional Christian life. An immanent displacement of proper transcendent concerns occurs when a transcendent moral commitment is recast in favor of an immanent, moral preoccupation, as when the evil of abortion is no longer recognized and instead access to abortion is embraced as a basic human right, even though abortion for sex selection is condemned with quasi-religious zeal. Under such circumstances, one has lost sight of the primary object of moral concern, namely, the prohibition of abortion, which is rooted in a religiously grounded insight, and has substituted instead a prohibition against abortion when undertaken on sexist grounds. The centrality of the prohibition against abortion is lost sight of and obscured, while an at best secondary issue is given central place. Similarly, zeal for the environment can take on a quasi-religious valence, substituting for the pursuit of the kingdom of heaven, as in the case of Deep Ecologists, who want to pursue the preservation of the environment or indeed its restoration as it would have been without the presence of a multitude of humans.[21] Such zeal for the environment, along with a quasi-religious engagement in activities to preserve the current environment, obscures the circumstance that there is no commandment to keep the environment and its ecological systems as they currently exist but that there is an injunction not to harm the poor. The world and its environment have been given to man to populate and thereby change. When the preservation of the current environment with its ecological systems as they now exist becomes an overriding goal pursued as a matter of ultimate concern, then there has been an immanent displacement of transcendent concerns and obligations. The unique commitment and zeal that one ought to show for the pursuit of the kingdom of heaven, for the Creator, is displaced by a concern for creation, for the environmental kingdom of this earth as we now find it. Among the contributions that Orthodox Christianity can make to the better appreciation of environmental ethics and the articulation of appropriate environmental policy is the relativization of interests in the environment in light of the overriding interest one should have in discharging the two great commandments to love God and love one's neighbor (Matt. 2:22–36). A rightly directed focus on God and neighbor can prevent a displacement of transcendent concerns for God into an inordinate concern for the environment. Such idolization of the environment has its most radical expression in Deep Ecological views that privilege the environment as it would have been in the absence of man.[22]

Fourth, Orthodox Christian theology can remind us that the holiest part of the world is not pristine nature, surely not nature untouched by humans, but where the Orthodox assemble in Liturgy. We worship not primarily in forests (Isaiah 1:29) but in temples made by man. Moreover, God did not take on nature; God became a man. He took on humanity so that men, not nature, can become gods by grace. It is humans who are called to *theosis*, not nature. Nature indeed can be approached by man as an icon, as a window to God. However, nature will not be transformed as man is to be transformed by the uncreated energies of God. The result is that the pagans' worship of nature as sacred has been radically denied by holy saints who cut down groves sacred to pagans[23] and who felled other natural objects revered by the pagans, thus indicating by implication the dangers inherent in some of the dimensions of our contemporary culture's concern to preserve the environment with its ecological systems as they now happen to be. We look not to the restoration of a prehuman wilderness but to a new Earth with a New Jerusalem, the restored holy city (Rev. 21:1–2). The focus is on the holy city.

Fifth, it is crucial that environmentalism not be used to defend distorted preoccupations with self-realization and self-satisfaction. For example, if out of a desire for a comfortable middle-class life, if not a desire for luxury, husbands and wives limit their offspring to two or three children or even less, all under the guise of protecting the environment, even in the face of a general decrease in reproductive rates, a distortion of obligation has occurred. Justifying small families on the basis of environmental concerns, especially in the case of Orthodox, shows a deformation of moral commitment that privileges the environment over the obligation to raise devout Orthodox for the kingdom of God. It is usually much easier to be zealous about the environment than to shoulder the burdens of raising a large family. This point bears most importantly against those who are Orthodox, for surely the world desperately needs the presence of more Orthodox children who can enlarge the presence of the Church and convert an increasingly secular global culture. In the developed world, given the usual obligations to raise Orthodox children, right-believing and right-worshipping Christians rarely have a justification for limiting their families to two or three children. This state of affairs presents itself as an egregious consequence of an ethos of luxury that nevertheless is often cloaked in a supposed commitment to environmentalism.

Finally, the Orthodox Church can help all place their use of the environment, like the use of all that is in the power of humans, within a life of right worship and rightly directed asceticism. When one attempts to live less engaged in the passions and distractions of overconsumption, one must do so out of love first for God and then for man, not simply out of love for the environment. As always, the issue is not merely what one does but how and why one does it. What one does and does not do with regard to the environment must be placed within a life of rightly directed worship, fasting, and almsgiving aimed toward a wholehearted love of God and one's neighbor. All concrete choices will need to be made prudently while prayerfully recognizing that their consequences will always to some extent be unclear and will often unintentionally be harmful to the innocent. Any attempt to articulate an Orthodox Christian environmentalism must be undertaken with humility within an authentically Orthodox way of life. The focus must always be God centered. For instance, the choice to drive on Sunday, even if it is an environment-polluting drive, if it is undertaken to attend church and be able to take Communion, has a character quite different from the same drive undertaken to observe the spectacle of a sports event. The significance of actual choices regarding the environment and the propriety of those choices are usually highly contextually determined. Faced with the ambiguities of this broken world, one is left prayerfully and prudently to choose the best one can.

Remembering What Orthodox Theology Is About: Pursuing First the Kingdom of Heaven, Not the Preservation of the Environment as We Now Find It or as It Was Before Man

This paper's reflections have been directed to locating concerns for the environment within the Orthodox Christian recognition of the priority of God and man over nature. Many of those who direct their energies to the preservation of the environment and its ecological systems as we currently find them do so absent an appreciation of the presence and power of the sovereign God and the dominion over nature He has given to man. They regard the cosmos and the environment as if it all came from nowhere and goes to ultimately nowhere, for no discernable ultimate purpose. Absent a recognition of God, there is also a depriviliging of man and his place in nature. Also, absent a recognition of God as the source and ultimate meaning of all, there is a danger that the environment as we find it will become for many a surrogate god and that environmentalism and environmental ethics will become a surrogate religion replete with its own secular rituals. Orthodox Christian theology relativizes all worldly commitments, including commitments to the environment, in light of the ultimate source and goal of everything: the Trinity. This is not to discount the Christian obligation to use nature wisely and even to recognize nature as an icon through which we can look and see God. This is not to affirm the profligate wasting of resources or careless harm to the environment. Nevertheless, concerns for the environment must be nested within an all-encompassing commitment to the Orthodox Christian way of life. In the face of empirical uncertainty, Christians are called to act prudently and with faith in a loving God Who is Lord of the environment. As always and as with all human commitment, concerns for the protection of the environmental kingdom of this world must be understood in terms of a rightly directed pursuit of the kingdom of heaven.

PART

IV

"Sweetness Overflowing onto the Earth": Insights from Orthodox Spirituality

The Fragile Surround

Scott Cairns

Availing space in which we live and move,
    and chance to glimpse the trembling import of
    our late, suspected being—and, well, yes,
the opening occasion of a guess
that, when we're after meaning, more is always
    likelier to please than the common taste
    of less with which our eager suppositions
are in the main rewarded. I'm thinking such
lacunae as this cove may lend us all their
    latent agency each and every time
    we enter, willing to attend the puzzle,
leaning in to ambiguity, aloof
to any fear accompanying what bit
    we witness in the local, endless, fraught
    fragility of every passing scene.

Keep up. I, too, had chance occasion, once,
to lean, to choose between two such modes of travel—
    that of knowing, clearly, what I meant to see
    and, on the other hand, not so sure, but eager
for the roads' divergences to obtain
to something skirting illumination.
    If I sigh now, it's not so much for me
    as for the prospect of a road constructed
as we go, bearing both our burdens and
ourselves, always just ahead, and bearing on.

And sure, we're hoping to proceed, to *get*
somewhere, and much of our attention speeds ahead.
   My point, I now suppose, has more to do
   with honoring the road itself, the ragged,
dust-glazed bracken by the side, and giving
each attendant host its due—the roebuck,
   woodchuck, turtle, and the toad, the hawk
   the raucous jay or raven yammering,
the fleet and near-angelic wren and chickadee,
the modest beetle, humble bee, blind ant.

LITURGY, COSMIC WORSHIP, AND CHRISTIAN COSMOLOGY

Elizabeth Theokritoff

Introduction

Hearing "liturgy" and "cosmology" in the same breath is unlikely to strike anyone as odd. We are all familiar with the term "cosmic liturgy" felicitously used (so far as I know, coined) by Hans Urs von Balthasar to describe Maximus's vision of the world. Here "liturgy" seems to be used as an analogy for the way the cosmos functions in relation to its Creator. It is a very fertile analogy and one used quite extensively by a number of contemporary Orthodox, especially by monastic writers.[1] But it is often not clear how exactly this cosmic vision relates to liturgy in a literal sense, worship celebrated by humans. Or, to frame the question in another way, how liturgical practice contributes to our understanding of cosmology. Cosmological approaches characterized as liturgical, and still more those characterized as Eucharistic, often focus (quite understandably) more on man's role in the cosmos than on the cosmos itself. Is that the most we can ever talk about, or can we go further? That is the question we will explore here.

Public Worship and Mystical Experience

There are a number of passages in the liturgical texts where we hear explicitly about the cosmos, the nonhuman visible creation. In earlier usage, these included the anaphora (most notably that of the Liturgy of St. James). In contemporary usage, we find more promising sources in vespers and matins. The material comes largely from psalms used in various ways—whether read entire, quarried for verses, or alluded to in hymnography. (In fact, the complexion of Christian worship starts to look very different once one recognizes the extent to which prayers and hymns are intended to be supplementary to the Psalms; when the Psalms are cut back, the whole balance of worship is distorted. This is certainly true of expressions of cosmic worship.) But we must also mention the insight into cosmology from the Song of the Three Children, heard by most of us only once a year, on Holy Saturday, but almost invariably echoed in the eighth ode of the canon.

It becomes immediately apparent that the cosmological picture given in worship differs from that commonly expressed in patristic homilies or treatises. In the latter, we certainly hear about the wonders of nature and its usefulness to man, but there is little to suggest that it might have its own "relationship" to God. Liturgy, however, is about worship, so it is perhaps not surprising that liturgical cosmology depicts nature as involved in worship or, at least, response to God. The clouds drop gladness, the mountains skip, every breath praises the Lord.

But what weight are we to give to expressions of this sort? Surely, we may say, liturgical texts are poetry; surely such literary figures, personifications of the elements and so forth, are not meant to be taken literally. We might indeed want to allow that these variants of the pathetic fallacy express a genuinely cosmic dimension to human affairs: man's relationship with God has consequences for the whole of creation. But still, surely, the language in which they are expressed is entirely metaphorical?

The language of creation rejoicing and singing is unquestionably metaphorical. That is to say, however, that it is *not* an allegory or a fable; it is saying something about the nature and behavior of created things, but in terms that do not quite fit. In fact, it is almost impossible to avoid metaphor when talking about the experience of creatures very different from ourselves: this does not mean that the experience is a figment of our imagination but rather that it is not fully accessible to us.

Take, for example, a fairly obvious case where one might speak of creation offering praise: birdsong. The Elder Porphyrios writes enthusiastically about a nightingale in a deserted spot, singing its heart out in praise of God.[2] On the other hand, one can imagine a disciple of Prof. Richard Dawkins pouring contempt on such fanciful silliness: what the nightingale is *really* doing, we shall be told, is ensuring that it can pass on its genes. Probably there is an element of truth in both explanations, but it should be noted that one is no more literal than the other as an account of the bird's intentions. For a nightingale to have a concept of genes is hardly more probable than for it to have a concept of God. So the relevant question about praise from all creation is not "Isn't it metaphorical?" but "What is it a metaphor *for*?"

LITURGY, COSMIC WORSHIP, CHRISTIAN COSMOLOGY

We can try to approach this question in the following way. There is another area of the Church's tradition where we encounter praise from all creation, and that is mystical experience. We find a considerable body of experience over the centuries in which people perceive the heavens and stars and trees glorifying God; or the grasses praising the Lord, as St. Nectarios did; or indeed the frogs singing matins, as in the Athonite story.

Now, mystical experience is by definition something not accessible to most of us most of the time. It does not correspond to our ordinary perception of reality. So it is tempting to slip into thinking that not only the process of experiencing but also the thing experienced is somehow a private reality, subjective and not repeatable. I am not talking about dismissing such experiences as hallucination or delusion but rather about assuming that the person reporting them has been granted this particular vision with a special meaning, perhaps symbolic, addressed to him or her. (As with Peter's vision in Acts 10: we recognize this as a revelation from God but do not conclude from it that there is a mystical blanket full of nonkosher animals and reptiles invisibly suspended between heaven and earth.)

What I want to suggest is that the vision of cosmic praise so often associated with mystical experience is an objective reality, however different it may be from the way we normally perceive the behavior of the elements, the earth, and other creatures. It is the capacity for perception, not its object, that is different in mystical experience. (To use a mundane analogy, the world perceived by, for example, a bat, is no less objectively real than the world perceived by us, although if we were able to compare notes with the bat, it might be hard to believe that it was in fact describing the "ordinary" world around us.) And I would further suggest that there is a way in which the gathered church as a whole becomes privy to the reality "mystically" perceived: this reality is recorded in the liturgical texts.

It might be objected that there is another obvious explanation for the parallels between the images used in liturgical texts and the perceptions in mystical experiences: that liturgy provides the language, the "grammar," for making sense of the experience. This is undoubtedly true, but it does not entitle us to assume that the grammar is arbitrary. We can just as well assume that there is a circular process of mutual reinforcement: liturgy provides a grammar for apprehending cosmic worship, and the liturgical expressions of cosmic worship endure because they are affirmed by experience.

A few texts have come down to us that suggest that experiences of cosmic praise do indeed correspond to an objective reality. And what is interesting is that they come out of a context of worship. There is the strange text from the *Apostolic Tradition* of Hippolytus, which gives the following rationale for

Christians to pray at midnight: "because at this hour all creation pauses for a moment in order to praise the Lord; the stars and forests and waters stop in their tracks, and at this hour the whole host of angels that minister to Him join with the spirits of the righteous in praising God."[3] Striking is the fact that *all* ranks of creatures, not just rational ones, literally praise the Lord. But what is odd, and to my knowledge unique, is the idea that they *pause from* their usual activity in order to do so. We may compare a text in the *Apostolic Constitutions* that speaks of creatures—the "choir of stars," animals, and trees—in their characteristic habit and activity as "indicating," "pointing to," or even in the case of the heavens "knowing" Him who is the source of that activity. But the conclusion is similar to Hippolytus: "every man should send up a hymn from his very soul to You, through Christ, in the name of all the rest, since by Your appointment he rules over them."[4]

By far the most dramatic account of cosmic praise in a liturgical setting is a story attributed to Anastasius of Sinai. It relates how one year, when the Liturgy for Pentecost was being celebrated on Mt. Sinai, the mountains responded with "Holy, Holy, Holy" and kept this up for half an hour.[5] It was audible, he explains, only to those with ears to hear—which leaves open the possibility that the remarkable event was not the mountains' praise *per se* but the humans' perception of it.

Taken alone, a story such as this might seem a slim basis on which to argue for a realistic interpretation of liturgical references to creation's praise. But it does not stand alone. Remembering the importance of the psalms among liturgical texts that speak of creation's worship, it is instructive to hear what Gregory of Nyssa has to say about the heavens "telling the glory of God" (Ps. 18) and the praise offered by all creation in Ps. 148: that the harmonious interaction of various elements in the universe, the interplay of stability and motion, form a musical harmony that constitutes a hymn to the power that sustains the universe. The classical idea of the music of the spheres, we might say. But he continues: "It was *because David had been a hearer of this hymnody* that he said in one of the Psalms that all the powers of heaven praise the Lord, as well as the light of the stars . . . and everything in creation."[6]

Gregory obviously does not think that these Psalms are just poetic imagery. He thinks that they are a record of experience accessible to the *nous* when it goes beyond the fleshly senses and is raised on high. We will probably not take this as a definitive statement of what the psalmist himself actually heard. But it does lead us to wonder very seriously what Gregory had heard, and indeed all those other often nameless Fathers who were responsible for the shaping of our worship.

As I was drawing these thoughts together, I came across an account that confirmed in a remarkable way the direction in which other evidence seemed to be pointing. This is the description of the vision experienced by Elder Aimilianos of Simonopetra, as recounted by the monk Maximos of Simonopetra.[7] It is a nighttime vision in which everything was filled with light, the stars came down and united themselves with earth, and everything was praying the Jesus Prayer. In this state, the Elder somehow found himself celebrating the Liturgy, as the light moved from his surroundings to his heart. "The Liturgy ended, but the song that had begun in his heart was endless. In his ecstasy, he saw that heaven and earth sing this prayer without ceasing, and that the monk truly lives only when he is animated by it" (23). Fr. Maximos connects this account with the Elder's own comments on Psalms 18:2 and 150, on the mystical "speeches and words" that fill the world so that you hear a single voice that speaks about God, and on the ascent of the mind to the summit of the spiritual mountain whence we call on plants, birds, rivers, and seas to praise the Lord (22 n. 11). We get a very clear picture of the confluence and congruence of the direct experience of a contemporary writer with insights from Fathers who have gone before us (such as Gregory of Nyssa) and the experience of the Church embedded in liturgy (the Psalms).

What is most striking about this account is what Fr. Maximos calls its "deeply ecclesial character" (24). It is not a "private" mystical experience. The personal experience opens out into the Divine Liturgy: it bears a direct relation to the worship of the whole Church. It is "a kind of matins service, in which creation literally responds to the call of the Psalmist" in the Lauds psalms (25). But might we not also put this the other way round? Surely there is a sense in which matins and other services set out as a matter of "public" record the hidden reality of the created order, which only a few experience at first hand.

Praise from Creation in Liturgical Usage

What does liturgical worship disclose to us about this reality? Fundamentally, it reveals the context of our own worship. There is a consistent theme that keeps recurring: creation consists of three "estates" of worshippers, namely the angelic powers, things visible, and us.[8] We see this pattern in many anaphora prayers and other prayers both ancient and current.[9] In more traditional language, it is a tripartite choir: we note the regularity with which the stars in particular are described as a "choir."[10]

The ancient inclusion of both of the nonhuman "estates" in the anaphora prayer is significant. The anaphora is the point at which we are exhorted to raise our hearts "on high"—to aspire, in other words, to the state in which one perceives the worship of all creation. Accordingly, the anaphora prayer speaks of the reality perceived in this state, the usually unseen and unheard context within which we offer our own thanks and praise. There is no doubt that one element of this context draws on a vision, the "victory hymn" of the seraphim revealed to Isaiah, so it may not be so farfetched to associate the worship offered by visible things with other revelations experienced down the ages. This picture of total cosmic praise is characteristically summed up by Cyril of Jerusalem, evidently having in mind an anaphora close to James:

> After this we commemorate heaven and earth and sea, the sun and moon, the stars and all creation rational and irrational, visible and invisible, angels, archangels, virtues, dominions, principalities, powers, thrones, and the cherubim with many faces, in effect saying in David's words, "Magnify the Lord with me." We also commemorate the seraphim whom Isaiah saw in the Holy Spirit.[11]

It is rather disappointing that the Liturgy of St. John Chrysostom seems to be the one in which the visible part of the "choir" has dropped out entirely. Or has it? There may be a vestige of a different perspective on it in Migne's text of the commentary on the Liturgy by Germanos of Constantinople. According to this text, the people take up the thrice-holy hymn in place not only of the seraphim but also of the creatures with four faces (Rev. 4:6–8). More clearly than Isaiah's vision, the depiction of the heavenly liturgy in Revelation points to the heavenly powers worshipping *in concert with* the whole of the visible creation,[12] different categories of creature being represented by the different faces. The commentator sees an allusion to this in the four participles applied to the hymn: the eagle is "singing", the ox is "shouting," the lion is "crying aloud," and the man is "saying" the words of the hymn.[13] I note that this reference to the vision in Revelation appears only in the "corrupt medieval text"[14] used by Migne. For our purposes, however, it does not much matter whether the connection goes back to Germanos himself. The point of interest is that someone before the modern period seems to have found it odd to have an anaphora prayer with no reference to praise from all creation—odd enough that the anomaly needed to be rectified.

All Things Are Your Servants

Does the praise from visible creation fare any better in the Liturgy of St. Basil? Certainly it is very muted compared to what we find in St. James, but it is present in another form: *all things are Your servants*. This might seem an altogether more humdrum statement. But against the backdrop of every creature of reason and understanding worshipping and glorifying—and praise from angels, archangels, etc.—it does appear to be just a more pedestrian way of expressing the same idea. The connection between "service" and "worship" is elaborated (slightly) in the Alexandrian Liturgy of St. Gregory the Theologian: "Things visible worship You, all of them fulfilling Your word."[15] Again, some light is shed on "service" by the Blessing of Waters prayer "Great are You," also attributed to St. Basil:[16] "The sun sings Your praises; the moon glorifies You; the stars supplicate before You; the light obeys You; the deeps are afraid at Your presence, the fountains are Your servants." I would hazard a guess that most of the verbs here are chosen more for variety's sake than to indicate a real difference in relationship (though there are obviously strong precedents for the waters fearing the Lord). Praise and worship on the part of visible creation is not an activity distinct from faithfully doing what it was created to do, but it may express a more profound understanding of what this amounts to.

It is worth pausing a moment to look at the character of creation's "service" with the help of the Blessing of Waters prayer.

1. First of all, the language of visible creation as "servants"—like that of creation as "worshippers"—puts it, as it were, on a level with us. If other creatures serve our needs, they do so by God's grace. On the one hand, this means that they are answerable to their Maker, not to human creatures; they have a *raison d'être* beyond our convenience. One might recall Chrysostom's comments on Ps. 148, where he points out how much space is devoted to natural phenomena that are inconvenient to us—the fire and hail and so forth, which do God's word and are there for His use.[17]

2. On the other hand, creation as God's "servants" carries an obvious antipagan message: the awe and veneration occasioned by natural phenomena and the power they have, whether beneficial or terrifying, should be directed to their Maker and not to the creatures themselves.

3. A further point is that creatures' "service" to God is manifested in equal measure by the natural behavior of the elements—the sea remains walled about with sand—and by obedience to instructions "contrary to their nature."[18] The latter is expressed in the prayer through a series of water miracles from the Old Testament, including the fire

and water in Elijah's sacrifice that confounded the worshippers of Baal—note again how the visible creation contradicts paganism.

"I Respect Inanimate Things"

In speaking of the three estates of creatures praising the Lord, it should be noted in what order they usually come: the bodiless powers, visible things, then humans. This follows the sequence of creation. (In the Lity verse for Theophany, above, we saw the order of humans and the elements reversed—perhaps because salvation involves not simply repeating the pattern of creation but reversing the pattern of the Fall.) But the usual order suggests that when we call on all creation to join us in praising the Lord, we are expressing a joy that exceeds our own capacity to articulate fully—but we are not teaching other creatures to do something that is novel to them. It is more a matter of recognizing that we are now working *with* them in acknowledging our common Creator, not against them.

Perhaps the best example of this is the Song of the Three Children. The sequence of creatures called on to praise the Lord is the familiar one: humans come last. This is particularly striking in the use of this ode on Holy Saturday, originally timed to coincide with the entry into the church of the newly baptized—the latest group of humans to rejoin the choir of creatures who praise the Lord and exalt Him above all for ever. Fr. Ephrem (Lash) has remarked that greeting the newly baptized with the story of the three youths would have been particularly apposite in the pagan world of the early Church,[19] and the relationship between liberation from paganism and the choir of creatures praising the true God is clearly a very close one. After all, what is the basic error in paganism? It lies not at all in the idea that the visible cosmos has a place in worship or even that it has an inner spiritual reality: the problem is that the cosmic component has been slotted in in the wrong position and back to front. Creation is not the *object* but the *offerer* of worship; its "spiritual nature" is not an end in itself but is fulfilled in drawing us to its Maker. Creation is a pointer, and the pagan is like the dog or cat who responds to a pointing finger by sniffing the finger with great interest.

Although the Song of the Three Children underlies the eighth ode of the canon, it has to be said that most canons show scant interest in the theme of praise from nonhuman creation. Some of the exceptions are interesting, however. The second canon for the Birth of the Mother of God (September 8) is quite explicit that "every creature offers a hymn to its Author and Creator," combining this affirmation with some of the stock phrases used to describe God's power in creation: "Who covers His chambers with waters, who sets the sand as a bound to the sea and encompasses the universe: the sun sings Your praises, the moon gives You glory . . ." (*eirmos*). The second canon for Christmas has a colorful description of the visible creation's embarrassment at the misunderstanding to which it has been subjected. Having finally extricated itself from "the disgrace of being deified in error," it fears that its praise will be inglorious because it has become corruptible (as a result of man's Fall). But it is actually rare in liturgical texts to find the suggestion that the changes visited on creation as a result of man's sin have impaired creation's own relationship with God.

The darkening of human *perception* as a result of sin does, however, complicate one of the visible world's most vital tasks: that of leading us to God by its own witness to His wonders and glory. This task is a recurrent theme in our worship. Perhaps its classic expression is Ps. 18:2, "The heavens are telling the glory of God . . ." This appears as a verse at Christmas, doubtless in reference to the star that brought the Magi: "Using a great star as its mouth, heaven shouted out the presence on earth of Him who ineffably became poor for our sake" (December 23, First Canon 7.2).

Verses from the same psalm appear at Pentecost, and we perhaps too readily assume that they are used there as an allegory for the words of the Apostles, which have gone out "to the ends of the earth." While that is undoubtedly one of the allusions, it may not be the whole story. We notice that the *prokeimenon* from Ps. 18 is balanced by alleluia verses from Ps. 32, "By the word of the Lord were the heavens established [and by the Spirit of His mouth all their power]" (v. 6), reminding us that the Spirit does not operate only through humans. Furthermore, when Ps. 18 appears in the third antiphon at Pentecost, it includes v. 4 (". . . their words are not heard")—surely more applicable to the literal heavens than to the Apostles. It is also worth noting that on the second day of the Holy Spirit, we hear in the Apostle reading that "ever since the creation of the world his invisible nature . . . has been clearly perceived in the things that have been made" (Rom. 1:20). It is too superficial to say that Ps. 18 at Pentecost is purely an allegory for the preaching of the Apostles. Rather, it shows how the Apostles and the visible creation are working in tandem: heaven and earth provide the framework within which the Apostles bear witness and present them with a paradigm for their preaching.

In festal services celebrating aspects of Christ's coming, the same pattern is repeated: creation takes the lead in recognizing the Lord. At Christ's baptism, it is the waters that signal that a theophany is taking place: "The sea saw it and fled; the Jordan turned back" (Ps. 113:3). In expressing fear of God as in praising Him, the sequence is the same. Some hymns point to a parallel between the waters and the angels: "The waters saw You, O God . . . and were afraid; for the cherubim cannot lift their eyes upon Your glory . . ." (*stikh.* 2). Another hymn puts words in the Jordan's mouth, saying, "John bears witness with me [note the order!] and cries, Behold the Lamb of God" (Hour 6.3). Indeed, according to the first canon for the feast, John justifies his reluctance to baptize Christ by appealing to the example of Sinai shrouded in smoke, the Red Sea which parted and the Jordan, which had on occasion turned back before God's servants: "Endowed with an understanding soul and honored with the power of reason, I yet respect the things that have no soul. . . . For if I baptize You, I shall have as my accusers the mountain that smoked with fire, the sea which fled on either side, and this same Jordan which turned back" (First Canon 4.3).

But, we might wonder, is this not an example of creation leading man in the wrong direction? Not according to a yet more imaginative hymnographer, who provides a sequel to the above conversation in which the Jordan asks, "Why do you hesitate to baptize my [*sic*] Lord? . . . He has sanctified all creation; let Him sanctify me also and the nature of waters, since for this He has been made manifest" (January 2, Vespers, *Apostikha* 4). We are here invited to consider that the creation may not only guide fallen man to recognize his Lord but also have a surer instinct for His purposes.

"The Wisdom Observed in Creation Is a Word"

Imaginary conversations between the River Jordan and John the Baptist raise the question: what does all this really amount to? We may accept that liturgical references to the visible creation, both the more and the less fanciful, are conveying some sort of truth, but what sort, exactly? Are we talking about an inner reality to visible creation or about the spiritual effect creation has on us? To put it another way, do creation's "words" have any existence apart from a human observer?

St. John Chrysostom helpfully points out apropos of Ps. 148 that there are three ways in which creatures can be said to glorify God: through words, through appearance, and through life and actions.[20] Visible creation, he says, uses the second method: it tells God's glory through its beauty, its vastness, its usefulness, etc., and these qualities lead the observer to praise and bless its Maker. A similar understanding appears in other Fathers. "The wisdom observed in creation is a 'word,' albeit not articulated," says Gregory of Nyssa;[21] the artistry manifest in created things serves as a word to those who are knowledgeable about the natural world. And what does this word say? According to St. Basil, the wisdom manifest in the cosmos as good as shouts out through visible things that they have their origin from God, that they have not come into being on their own. But then he goes on, "This wisdom calls silently upon its Creator and Lord, so that through it you may ascend to insight concerning Him who alone is wise."[22]

Some of these remarks might suggest that when all is said and done, this is just the argument from design decked out in poetic language. But Basil's conclusion alerts us that he has in mind something rather more profound. There is, of course, truth in the more careful and literal explanations of how creation "glorifies" God through our understanding of it, but they do not exhaust the subject. It would be a mistake to try to enlist them in any sort of reductionist "nothing but"-ery, such as "when we talk about visible things praising God, it is *just a way of saying* that the natural world inspires *us* to praise its Creator." It is a long ascent "to insight concerning Him who alone is wise." We start by apprehending that there is much more to the visible world than meets the eye. Then, somewhere along the way, we realize that there is also much more than meets the reasoning brain, which draws inferences about the Creator. The "words" of creation really are addressed to its Creator, not just to us. Our conscious response does not *create* cosmic worship, yet it plays a crucial part in the total "symphony." If we want a metaphor for our own role in cosmic worship, we might say that the nonhuman creation "speaks" in a sort of "vacuum of consciousness"; our conscious response fills that vacuum with a medium that allows creation's own "word" of praise to resonate.

What is the basis for claiming this? One approach is to look at the cycle of daily worship. To return to Elder Aimilianos—I recall the recordings of a vigil from the monastery of Ormylia, which he founded. It does not begin with vespers. It does not quite begin even with the *semandron* calling the nuns to vespers but with a few seconds of birdsong and then the *semandron* amid the birdsong. The natural world glorifying its Creator: the human response in worship. Then vespers, as we know, begins with the psalm of creation (Ps. 103)—a very down-to-earth psalmic treatment of the created world. The various creatures are not praising the Lord; they are obeying Him, or waiting on Him for food, or depending on Him for life and death. Or in some cases they are just being, and our description of them is in itself an act of praise. Here is a classic example of human praise to God for the wisdom manifest in the workings of nature. "In wisdom You have made all things" celebrates the "passive glorifying" on the part of the visible creation.

Then we come to matins: to the "praises we offer *together with all Your creatures.*"[23] This phrase in one of the priest's prayers might refer only to the "powers endowed with speech and reason" who have just been mentioned;

on the other hand, the prayer does go on to say that "every breath and created being sings Your ineffable glory." So perhaps this prayer really does point us forward to the praise not only *for* but *with* all creation, which is recalled in the eighth ode of the canon and most spectacularly in the Lauds Psalms.

This cosmic praise is meant to prepare us to "be on high": to offer our own specifically human worship and so join the choir of all creatures that worship. As we have said, the part played in this choir by visible creation is scarcely mentioned in the anaphoras commonly used today. We may rediscover it if we look beyond the texts to the physical material of the Eucharistic offering and the input they have required from the rest of creation, but that is another story.[24]

Conclusion

In the liturgical texts—as I have suggested above—we affirm an inward reality to visible things that is experienced directly by only a few of our holy Fathers and Mothers (though perhaps more of them than we realize). But liturgy in turn gives us the possibility of growing into that experience so that it becomes our own. Liturgical experience teaches us an "inner vision of the world," as Archimandrite Vasileios writes,[25] but this vision is not some extraordinary, supranatural state. It is an apprehension of "the basic unity ... between the initial origin, the present-day organization and the eschatological reality of all things, which is God who is the cause and end of all."[26] Such an inner vision is what enables us to hold together the growth of plants or the formation and decay of stars with the transformation of matter into Christ. We are talking about an awareness of the Godwardness of all things, an ability to perceive their service, their everyday activity, as a hymn of praise. "We have seen the true light"—as Fr. Vasileios continues—"reflected from the whole of the transfigured world."[27]

I believe that this throws light—I use the expression advisedly—on the point that St. Maximus maintains about the analogy between visible and invisible creation. It is not just that we can and should perceive things invisible through the visible world, as we hear in Rom. 1:20; there is also a "spiritual knowledge and understanding" of visible things through the invisible.[28] The heavens really *are* telling the glory of God: this is not something that we read into nature. We proclaim this truth liturgically, and that is a first step toward perceiving its reality in the world around us.

"ALL CREATION REJOICES IN YOU": CREATION IN THE LITURGIES FOR THE FEASTS OF THE THEOTOKOS

Christina M. Gschwandtner

Introduction

Transfiguration is at the very core of Orthodox liturgy. It is well known that the notion of *theosis* as the transfiguring and deifying of believers is the central redemptive thrust of Eastern theology. This belief and goal is expressed and made real in liturgical practice. Yet such transfiguring does not apply only to the human person. Rather, the liturgy takes up and transforms all of creation, including the very space and time in which it takes place.[1] Increasingly, Orthodox scholars are recognizing the potential of this insight for the ecological debate. In fact, a phrase from the Eucharistic action of the liturgy is used most often to confirm Orthodox valuing of all creation: "Thine own of Thine own, we offer unto Thee, on behalf of all and for all." Patriarch Bartholomew I, the Ecumenical Patriarch, uses this phrase to point to the ecological potential of Orthodox faith:

> In the bread and wine of the Eucharist, as priests standing before the altar of the world, we offer creation back to the Creator in the context of a mutual relationship to Him and to each other. We celebrate the beauty of creation and consecrate the life of the world, returning it to God with thanks. We share the world in joy as a living mystical communion with the Divine. Thus we offer the fullness of creation at the Eucharist, and receive it back as a blessing, as the living presence of God.[2]

His many addresses and activities on behalf of environmental action have earned him the title "Green Patriarch."[3] Other Orthodox thinkers have taken up this challenge and explored further how Orthodox faith might express concern for creation and the environment.[4] In this discussion, the human function as offering the entire creation to God Eucharistically is frequently cited as the central Orthodox insight.[5] Yet rarely do authors go beyond these more general statements to show how Orthodox liturgy more generally might support or give rise to an ecological theology or to injunctions for ecological action. The greater ecological potential of the Liturgy remains unexplored.

Yet the Eastern Liturgy has a great wealth of images, statements, and actions that can inform a more ecologically conscious worldview, namely one that sees nonhuman creation as valuable and as a real partner in sharing the planet, instead of as a resource to be exploited in purely utilitarian fashion for our own benefit. And while a "cosmic" role of human beings is occasionally indicated in the Liturgy, it is far from being the only way in which an examination of the Liturgy can contribute to the conversation. Rather, close attention to liturgical texts and practices shows all of creation as sacred and hallowed by the Spirit, as affected by sin, as redeemed in Christ, and as a full participant in the worship of God (and possibly even in deification). While the liturgy itself does not develop all of these themes in a systematic theological fashion, its wealth of images and affirmations provides sufficient material for making such theological statements explicit and developing their ecological implications.[6] The most obvious liturgical locus for developing theological statements with ecological intent is probably the service of Theophany. It has indeed been used as an example repeatedly, and although it has not been explicated and interpreted as fully as it deserves, certainly more attention has been focused on it than on any other liturgical service in the Eastern tradition.[7] Let me therefore analyze liturgical texts that have not yet received any such attention, namely the services celebrating the feasts of the Theotokos.[8]

The Feasts of the Theotokos

As is true of Orthodox iconography and theology more generally, feasts of the Theotokos usually focus on the Incarnation. There are very few statements about Mary in Orthodox theology that constitute theological Marian reflection disconnected from her role in the Incarnation. Jaroslav Pelikan points out the great role Mary plays even within the regular Liturgy.[9] He examines in detail the various phrases of the Sunday morning Liturgy that mention the Theotokos and shows that veneration of the Theotokos is not in competition with worship of Christ but that she is honored as the first of saints who has become holy, even as we are to live holy Christian lives as well. Joseph Nasrallah, a Roman Catholic thinker who has analyzed Mary's place in the Byzantine liturgy, also examines the "ordinary" Liturgy celebrated every Sunday morning, highlighting various antiphons used within this liturgy.[10] He then goes on to consider briefly fourteen feasts and commemorations of the Theotokos, pointing out that the church year begins with a commemoration of the Theotokos on September 1 and ends with a similar feast of her on August 31.[11] Her feasts therefore frame the church year. Although Nasrallah cites only isolated portions of these feasts and commemorations, and his primary point in this treatment is to justify the immaculate conception, almost all of the texts he cites refer to creation in some way.[12] He begins his treatment of the role of the Theotokos in the Liturgy by emphasizing, as we have seen above, that for the Eastern tradition the Liturgy is the place where the new heaven and earth are present, where all creatures assemble around their creator.[13] In a reflection on Mary's place in the liturgy, Paul Doncoeur similarly points out that "creation can have no other end than the glory of God" and that this is expressed within the liturgy.[14] Redemption means to restore to the cosmos this voice that has been silenced by the fall of Satan and Adam. He claims that the feasts of the Theotokos show Mary in particular as the one who most fully performs this glorification of God in her life and song and draws all of creation (including the angels) into the praise of liturgical worship.[15] It is also interesting that nature is particularly associated with Marian feasts in other ways. In some areas, imprisoned birds are freed on the Feast of the Annunciation to signify the freedom and restoration of creation begun at this inception of the Incarnation.[16] At the Feast of the Dormition in August, flowers are often blessed.[17] It seems that the larger creation is not a peripheral theme in these feasts.

Three different aspects of creation can be detected within the liturgies of these feasts and can be read as making important contributions for an ecological theology: (a) the intimate connection between creation and redemption in the texts, (b) the strong emphasis on the participation of "all of creation" in rejoicing over the incarnation, and (c) the implication that the Incarnation has cosmic significance and is accomplished for all of creation. It would also be possible to consider the imagery employed for Mary herself, who serves as an "icon" of creation and is often compared to the earth, but this final point carries so much contentious baggage that it will not be explored here as an important contribution to ecological theology.[18]

Creation and Incarnation

Creation and Incarnation are linked in a dual fashion in these feasts. On the one hand, Christ's birth as a human being in the Incarnation and his materiality are emphasized. On the other hand, the Incarnation refers back to the Creator and affirms the essential connection between incarnation and creation.

First, the Incarnation, and in particular Mary's role within it, are read as affirmations of matter. Even in the theological tradition Christ's real birth from Mary is often cited as a warning against various sorts of Docetist or Gnostic heresies that do not take seriously Christ's embrace of flesh and matter by becoming incarnate within them. Mary is affirmed to be giving human flesh and created materiality to Christ.[19] She is celebrated primarily for her role as the "Mother of God," and the feasts honoring her employ this language throughout.[20] The essential materiality of the Incarnation is emphasized throughout: "The Word who before was wholly outside matter, in these last times has assumed the material substance of the flesh."[21] Great stress is placed on Mary's "material womb," as in the Feast of her Nativity.[22] The following ode affirms: "It is she who shall bear unto us the Word, appearing in the material substance of the flesh" (121). Mary is consistently depicted as the one who gives flesh to the divine: "and I shall bear Him that is without flesh, who shall borrow flesh from me."[23] Christ's becoming flesh is understood as a kenotic humbling, with frequent reference to diapers: "O Sun, my Son, how shall I wrap Thee in swaddling clothes? How shall I give Thee milk, who givest food to all creation? How shall I hold Thee in my arms who holdest all things?"[24] In the feast of the Nativity, the wise men are affirmed to have been "amazed to see neither sceptre nor throne but only utter poverty. For what is meaner than a cave, what is humbler than swaddling clothes? Yet therein shone forth the wealth of Thy divinity."[25] Christ's incarnation accomplishes salvation by uniting heaven and earth, which had been split apart by the Fall. This is particularly obvious in the liturgy for the feast of the Nativity of Christ: "Heaven and earth are united today, for Christ is born. Today has God come upon the earth, and man gone up to heaven. Today for man's sake is seen in the flesh He who by nature is invisible . . ."[26] That this is indeed put in the context of creation is also supported by the fact that the first reading for the Office of the Nativity (just as for Pascha and Theophany) is Genesis 1.[27]

Second, the language of Incarnation employed in these feasts strongly emphasizes creation. God or the Trinity are consistently referred to as "Creator," and there is much imagery that contrasts the "creation" of Christ's human flesh with his being the Creator. Often this is put in an explicit paradox, as during Vespers for the feast of the Nativity:

Triumph, O Zion; make glad, O Jerusalem, city of Christ our God: receive the Creator who is contained within a cave and a manger. Open unto me the gates, and entering within I shall see as a child wrapped in swaddling clothes Him who upholds the creation in the hollow of His hand, whose praises the angels sing with unceasing voice, the Lord and Giver of Life who saves mankind. (203)

The Sixth Hour on the Feast of the Nativity affirms that "our God and Creator has clothed Himself in created flesh, and He who with His strong arm fashioned the creation reveals Himself in the womb of her that He formed" (238). It is repeatedly said in various of the festal liturgies that the Creator is "fashioned as a creature."[28]

Throughout these texts, the entire Trinity is frequently referred to as "Master of Creation." Yet quite often, Christ is explicitly identified as the Creator: "The Creator, having become a young child without undergoing change, has reshaped according to the form of His divinity our nature, taken from the earth and destined to return to earth once more."[29] At times, Christ as Creator is even placed in contrast to the Father because he identifies more fully with creation through the Incarnation: "The Master, by His coming in the flesh, has cut clean through the harsh enmity of the flesh against Him, and has destroyed the might of the murderer of our souls. Uniting the world to the immaterial essences, He has made the Father merciful to the creation."[30]

Patristic homilies similarly stress the Incarnation and its affirmation of the material world. John of Damascus sees all of creation connected to God through the Incarnation.[31] Gregory Nazianzen makes an explicit link between creation and redemption in an early homily: "This is the origin of the nativity and of the virgin, the origin of the manger and of Bethlehem. The creation explains the nativity; the woman explains the virgin. The rationale for Bethlehem is Eden; the rationale for the manger is paradise. What is great and hidden is shown by what is little and visible."[32] He expresses the condescension or *kenosis* of the Incarnation, which sanctifies the most lowly aspects of nature, in beautiful terms:

> When he teaches on a mountain, when he converses in the plain, when he passes into a boat, when he reprimands the tempests. He accepts sleep without doubt in order to sanctify sleep; he weeps without doubt in order to render tears praiseworthy. He passes from one place to another, he who is contained in no place, he who is outside of time, who has no body, who is not circumscribed by limits.[33]

Christ's condescension in the Incarnation is a full embrace of the material condition. Hesychius of Jerusalem actually refers to the Feast of the Purification (or the Meeting) as the "feast of feasts" or the "most holy feast among the holy feasts" because

> it recapitulates in fact the entire mystery of the Incarnation of Christ, it describes the entire presentation of the only Son. In this feast, Christ was carried as a new-born and confessed as God, the creator of our nature has been offered in the arms as seated on a throne, and he offered a couple of spiritual turtledoves to Symeon and Anna.[34]

He continues in language relying on Isaiah 40:12 and also employed by the liturgical texts: "He carried in his hands him who holds in his hand the inhabited and uninhabited earth, 'he who has measured the water in his hand, the heavens with a span and the entire earth in a measure'" (I.5, 35). For a different Marial feast, Hesychius imagines the Magi asking questions about the paradoxical nature of the miracle of Christ's birth:

> How does he who is perfect become a newborn? How does he who nourishes (the world) suck milk? How is he who embraces the universe enclosed in arms? How is "the Father of the age to come" become a baby? How does he who is on high find himself also below? How can he who is in the heavens be also on earth? . . . How can "he who is in the womb of the Father" be in a crib? (VI.4, 199)

Here the same contrast between mighty creator and creaturely weakness is juxtaposed, as in the Liturgy. Germanos, in a homily on the Annunciation, also draws an explicit connection between creation and redemption:

> Hail, favored one, who caused the Sun that is eternal to arise for the world in flesh, [a Sun] who dazzled the whole of creation with his goodness! Hail, favored one, the all-bright cloud of the life-giving Spirit, which carries the rain of compassion and sprinkles all creation! Hail, favored one, salvation of those born on earth, who transformed grief into joy, and joined the things on earth with those in heaven, and who loosed the dividing walls of enmity![35]

He continues by hailing Mary in various natural imagery by presenting a long dialogue between the angel and the Theotokos, where she only slowly assents (in contrast to Eve, who quickly agrees to eat the fruit), followed by a dialogue between Mary and Joseph. He concludes with another connection between incarnation and paradise, creation and new creation: "This one, the ever flourishing and incorruptible paradise, in which the Tree of life was planted and produced without hindrance the fruit of immortality for everyone! This one, a bringing forth of the new creation in which the water of life gushes!" (245). Ephrem the Syrian, in a homily on the Nativity, employs the same sorts of contrasts: "He who measures the heavens with the span of his hand / lies in a manger a span's breadth; / He whose cupped hands contain the sea / is born in a cave; / His glory fills the heavens / and the manger is filled with His splendor" (lines 28–34, 63).[36] Proclus employs similar language in a homily on the same subject:

> Let me utter the mystery! / Though he is God, "he appeared on earth" (Bar. 3:38), / and came to dwell through the virgin where he was present. / And the birth did not belittle him, / and the birth pains did not change his uncreated nature, / but created form gave a form to the Creator, / and the world contained the uncontainable when he became flesh, / when he became man without sin. (2.4, 73)[37]

In an *Encomium on the Dormition* attributed (probably falsely) to Modestus, Mary is presented as life and spring of the world because the "fountainhead of the universe" was born of her. The homilist concludes that Christ "has, through her, set creation free from slavery, and has brought into reality surpassing joy for the whole cosmos."[38] These themes of joy and liberation of the cosmos are evident also in the liturgical texts themselves.[39]

Creation and Incarnation are, then, closely linked to each other. It is the Creator who becomes incarnate as a creature. This incarnation is an affirmation of the flesh and of matter.[40] Christ has a truly material body, and his birth from a human mother confirms his full identification with the creation. Yet while an emphasis on flesh and materiality is certainly important for a more positive attitude toward nature, it does not yet explicitly affirm that this goes beyond an affirmation of *human* flesh and materiality. What role, if any, do other creatures play in these liturgies?

All Creatures Praise God

Creation actually has a significant role within the Liturgy as participating in the worship of God and the veneration of the Theotokos. In countless repetitions, creation is said to "glorify" or "bring praises" either to God for the miracle of the feast or even to the Theotokos herself. The idea that all of creation rejoices is a constant theme: "Therefore in praise let us sing: Let the whole creation bless the Lord and exalt him above all for ever."[41] The Forefeast of the Nativity similarly exhorts: "Let the creation rejoice exceedingly: for the Creator now makes Himself to be created, and He who was before all things now makes Himself known as God newly revealed."[42] Often, Christ's descending into creation is linked to creation's celebration of this mystery, as is especially the case for the Nativity liturgies: "Thou hast made the whole creation shine with joy. All that hath breath praises Thee, the Image of the glory of the Father."[43] Here it is already implied that Christ's mission extends to all of creation, something that will be explored further below. Yet the participation of all of creation in praise of God is explicit. Some contemporary thinkers seek to dismiss this language as purely metaphorical. Theokritoff has suggested that this would be a mistake and that the participation of non-human creatures in praise of God should be taken more literally.[44]

Indeed, the praise of creation suffuses the liturgical texts. Sometimes the phrase "Let the whole creation bless the Lord and exalt Him above all for ever" is used as a refrain, similar to the way in which it is employed by the Song of the Three Children.[45] Creation joins in praise with the Theotokos, the saints, and the assembled people. The Ikos for Matins on the Synaxis of the Theotokos makes this particularly clear: "Therefore all of creation shares in my joy and cries to me: Hail, thou who art full of grace" (293). The whole world joins together in song: "today all creation greatly rejoices. . . . Today the proud insolence of the serpent is brought low, for the fetters of the curse laid on our forefathers are loosened. Therefore with all the world we cry aloud to thee: Hail, thou who art full of grace."[46] The creation glorifies not merely God but also Mary. She is the one "whose praises all creation sings."[47] The creation rejoices in her birth as it does in that of the Creator because it renews all of creation.[48] Over and over it is affirmed that "the whole creation calls thee blessed."[49]

In some texts one might imagine that "all of creation" stands as a shorthand way of saying "all humans."[50] Yet often that is clearly not the case in these feasts, as various specific beings and parts of creation are explicitly named, such as "the heavens" (referring here to the sky, not the abode of God or angels), "the seas," "mountains, hills, hollows, rivers and seas, and the whole creation," "all the earth," "every creature," and "the depths" (probably including "Sheol," the abode of the dead). Earth and sea rejoice: "Be joyful, all the earth . . . Be glad, O sea . . ."[51] Heaven and earth join equally into song: "Greatly rejoice, O heaven; be glad, O earth."[52] Mountains and rivers celebrate together with human dignitaries: "Let the kings of the whole earth sing rejoicing, and let the companies of the nations be in exceeding joy. Mountains and hills and hollows, rivers and seas, and the whole creation, magnify the Lord who now is born."[53] Various celestial bodies also sing: "the sun sings Thy praises, the moon gives Thee glory, every creature offers its hymn unto Thee, its Author and Creator, for ever."[54] Furthermore, in the Feast of the Nativity, various parts of creation (including humans) are imagined as contributing gifts to celebrate Christ's birth:

What shall we offer Thee, O Christ, who for our sake hast appeared on earth as man? Every creature made by Thee offers Thee thanks. The angels offer Thee a hymn; the heavens a star; the Magi, gifts; the shepherds, their wonder; the earth, its cave; the wilderness, the manger; and we offer Thee a Virgin Mother.[55]

And, indeed, not only does the whole of creation participate in praise, but the manner of this rejoicing is depicted in vivid detail. Creation is portrayed as praising, singing, "leaping with joy," clapping hands, "rejoicing exceedingly and raising its voice," "keeping feast," "blessing the Lord," "being amazed," "rejoicing greatly," even "dancing."[56] This is not just mentioned once or twice but is instead a strong theme in all the texts. Creation clearly plays a role in the Liturgy, and God enjoys its praise. One might even suggest that human praise is guided by this prior praise of nature. "Heaven, earth, and the depths stand in awe of Thee, men bless Thee, fire is Thy servant, all things created obey Thee in fear, O Holy Trinity."[57] Various creatures hence play an active role in the glorification of God accomplished within the liturgy. All creatures join together in the liturgical chorus.

Again, this rejoicing of creation in the liturgical texts is confirmed by many homilies. In fact, this is probably the strongest theme in the Patristic homilies on Mary. In a *Homily on the Nativity* (still called Theophany at the time), Gregory Nazianzen exhorts his audience to join the animals and other figures in the nativity story in gratitude:

> Venerate the manger, at which you, an animal without reason were nourished by the Word. Like an ox, recognize your owner . . . like an ass, know the manger of the Lord himself: whether you are one of the clean beasts, subject to the Law, who chew on the cud of the word and are fit for sacrifice, or whether you are still unclean and unsuited to be food or victim, from the Gentile race. Run with the star; bring gifts, with the Magi, of gold and frankincense and myrrh—gifts for your king, for your God, for the one who became a corpse for your sake! Give glory with the shepherds, sing praise with the angels, dance with the company of archangels! Let there be a common festival for the powers of heaven and earth! For I believe that they, too, are rejoicing and holding festival along with us today, if it is true that they are friends of both humanity and God.[58]

Proclus also imagines the various actors who offer praise in a nativity homily, including explicitly various nonhuman participants together with the human characters in the story. Proclus at times attributes the activity of "offering" certain human characters to the nonhuman ones:

> Today the unsown seed sprouted forth from the field not cultivated,
> and the famished world rejoices.
> Today a birth without intercourse blossomed forth from the womb without birth pains
> and the whole of creation offers gifts to the fatherless child:
> the earth offers the manger;
> the rocks offer the water urns of stone;
> the mountains offer the cavern;
> the cities offer Bethlehem;
> the winds offer obedience,
> the sea offers subjection,
> the waves offer calmness;
> the depths offer the fishes;
> the fishes offer the water;
> the waters offer the Jordan;
> the fountains offer the woman from Samaria;
> the desert offers John;
> the beasts offer the foal;
> the birds offer the dove;
> the magi offer the gifts;
> the women offer Martha;
> the widows offer Anna;
> the barren women offer Elizabeth;
> the virgins offer Mary, the Birthgiver of God;
> the shepherds offer the chanting of hymns;
> the priests offer Symeon;
> the children offer the palm branches;
> the persecutors offer Paul;
> the sinners offer the tax-collector;
> the pagans offer the Canaanite woman;
> the woman with an issue of blood offers faith;
> the harlot offers the perfume;
> the trees offer Zaccheus;
> the wood offers the cross;
> the cross offers the robber;
> the East offers the star;
> the air offers the cloud;
> heaven offers the angels
> Gabriel offers the greeting . . .[59]

In fact, Proclus often refers to the praise of all of creation. In his *Homily* 24 ("On the Nativity of Our Lord Jesus Christ"), he employs the phrase "let heaven rejoice from above" (quoted from Ps. 71:6) as a sort of repeated refrain for a good section of the homily.[60] John of Damascus exhorts earth and mountains to rejoice: "Acclaim the Lord, all the earth, sing, exult, play instruments!" (6.61); "Jump with joy, mountains" (6.61).[61] In fact, John frequently invites creation to join in praise in his Marian homilies.[62] Andrew of Crete also often speaks of the rejoicing of all of creation. In his first *Homily on the Nativity of the Theotokos* he says:

> Let all creation therefore sing and dance and let it introduce with this something of those things worthy of the day! Let there be one common festival today of heavenly and earthly things and let every compound structure[63] that exists both on earth and in a heavenly manner join in the feasting! For today the created precinct of the Creator of all things has been established, and the creature is newly prepared as divine abode for the Creator. Today the nature that was formerly turned to earth takes on the beginning of deification, and the dust that has been exalted is urged to return to the glory that is on high. Today Adam, presenting [her] out of us and on our behalf as firstfruit to God, dedicates Mary, she indeed who was not mixed with the whole dough; through her bread is made for the remodeling of the grace.

In the third homily, he exhorts heaven to be glad and tells the earth to dance, claiming that the earth has been raised by Mary's pregnancy as the water is sanctified by Christ's baptism. He reiterates, "so then, let all creation rejoice and dance and clap its hands!" In his third homily on the Dormition, he similarly invites heaven and earth to join in song.[64] Theodore the Studite, in an *Encomium on the Dormition*, has "the whole of creation jump for joy" and describes Mary as a life-giving spring for the whole creation.[65] John of Thessalonika, in one of the earliest homilies on the Dormition, connects the praise of creation with its renewal in the Incarnation:

> A fitting hymn of honor, praise and glory is always due, from every creature under heaven, to that remarkable, all-glorious and truly great mistress of all the world, the ever-virgin Mother of our Savior and God Jesus Christ. She is truly the God-bearer, and through her all creation has received, by God's saving plan, the great gift of the presence in the flesh of the only Son and Word of God the Father.[66]

Jacob of Serug beautifully imagines the praise of various creatures in a homily on the Dormition:

> The evil demons were disturbed and agitated,
> for they saw the sign which only happened because of our Lord.
> They saw heaven discharging multitudes of hosts
> and the air was utterly sanctified with sweet fragrance.
> New sounds were heard from all the birds;
> where they were chanting in ranks according to their natures.
> All living creatures made a joyful sound of praise in their places;
> all the earth was stirred by their shouts of joy.
> The heavens and the mountains and all the plains which were adorned,
> broke forth in praise when the virginal body was being laid in the grave.
> All living creatures made a joyful sound of praise in their places;
> all the earth was stirred by their shouts of joy.
> All trees with their fruits and produce
> were sprinkled with drew, the sweet fragrance of their gladness.
> All the flowers which were beautiful in their variety, sent forth perfume like sweet spices sending forth fragrance.
> The waters and the fish and all creeping things within the sea,
> were aware of this day and were moved to praise.
> All creatures silent or eloquent,
> according to their natures rendered the praise which was due.[67]

Thus in many Patristic texts individual nonhuman creatures participate in and respond to the events of the Incarnation. The homilists draw on biblical texts to personify various aspects of creation but also elaborate on this imagery creatively. In these homilies, the whole cosmos is painted as actively engaged in God's praise and has a vested interest in the mystery of the Incarnation.[68]

What is this cosmic significance? Kallistos Ware suggests in his introduction to the Festal Liturgies (in regard to the feast of the Nativity of the Theotokos) that it refers to the redemption of all of creation: "In Mary's case, however, the parents' rejoicing is shared by all creation, for her birth foreshadows the universal salvation that is to come."[69] What do the liturgies say about such a cosmic view of redemption?

Cosmic Redemption

The Liturgy does indeed suggest that the Incarnation has an impact on all of creation. Creation is changed by it and restored to full communion with God. Not just humans are redeemed but all of creation. There are several different ways in which this can be said to be the case. First, the Incarnation is seen as a new beginning for all of life. The world has been renewed already in the birth of the Theotokos as it anticipates Christ's birth and redemption: "She is born and with her is the whole world become new again."[70] This eschatological imagery is also present in the Feast of the Annunciation. Although here Christ's becoming flesh is celebrated, Mary is also hailed as the one in whom creation is renewed.[71]

Second, the Incarnation (and the Theotokos in particular) are said to "join earth and heaven." The imagery of a bridge is often used, and heaven is described as "bending down" and touching the earth.[72] This causes "things on earth to be set right" and sanctified. This language is especially strong in the Feast of the Dormition, where the Theotokos is affirmed to be the "firstfruits" of creation having reached the Eschaton in some fashion:

> What spiritual songs shall we now offer thee, O most holy? For by thy deathless Dormition thou hast sanctified the whole world, and then has been translated to the places above the world, there to perceive the beauty of the Almighty and, as His Mother, to rejoice in it exceedingly.[73]

The Dormition transfigures the world and restores it to life.[74] She is the "earthly Heaven" who brings together both earth and heaven:

> Come, O ye people, and gaze in wonder: for the holy Mountain of the Lord, in the sight of all, is exalted above the hills of heaven. The earthly Heaven takes up her dwelling in a heavenly and imperishable land.[75]

At times the connection between praise and redemption is made explicit:

> At thy glorious Dormition the heavens rejoice and the armies of angels exult; the whole earth makes glad, singing a hymn of departure to thee, O Mother of Him who is Lord of all . . . "Hail, thou bearer of the whole divinity: hail, thou who alone by thy childbirth hast brought together earthly things and things on high." . . . By thy holy Dormition, O Virgin Mother and Bride of God, thou who gavest birth to the Life hast been transported into immortal life, attended by angels, principalities, and powers, by apostles, prophets, and the whole creation.[76]

Similar language is used in the Feast of the Annunciation:

> Lo, our restoration is now made manifest to us: God is ineffably united to men. At the words of the Archangel error is laid low; for the Virgin receives joy, and the things of the earth have become heaven. The world

is loosened from the ancient curse. Let the creation rejoice exceedingly and raise its voice to sing: O Lord, our Maker and Deliverer, glory to Thee.[77]

The creation rejoices precisely because earth and heaven have been joined and are again in harmony with each other.

On occasion, it is explicitly affirmed that "the whole creation is made new and godlike," always linked with the earth's rejoicing in this renewal. Mary is made manifest "through whom things on earth are joined with heaven." Consequently (and repeatedly), "today is the beginning of joy for all the world."[78] Although it is Mary who enters into heaven, she takes the whole earth with her in some fashion:

> For today is heaven opened wide as it receives the Mother of Him who cannot be contained. The earth, as it yields up the Source of life, is robed in blessing and majesty. . . . Forget not, O Lady, thy ties of kinship with those who commemorate in faith the feast of thine all-holy Dormition.[79]

This has implications for the fertility of the earth. Given the strongly typological use of characters in the liturgy, this is often represented by Anna's pregnancy with Mary after her long barrenness. Imagery of nature and ground is used to contrast Anna's barrenness with the new fruitfulness made possible in Mary's birth:

> Husbandman of our thoughts and gardener of our souls, Thou hast made the barren earth fertile. Thou hast turned the ground that once was parched into fruitful land, rich in corn and bearing fruit. From holy Ann Thou hast made to blossom an undefiled fruit, the Theotokos.[80]

Here clearly eschatological imagery is implied as a restoration of fruitfulness after the experience of the barren desert.[81]

This newness of creation is envisioned in terms of beauty: "Let the creation now cast off all things old, beholding Thee the Creator made a child. For through Thy birth Thou dost shape all things afresh, making them new once more and leading them back again to their first beauty."[82] "Creation" is not always the term used: at times, the Liturgy speaks of "nature." There is no clear distinction here between "human nature" and the rest of nature. In fact, imagery that speaks of the restoration of nature in terms of a renewed paradise is employed quite often. This clearly has eschatological overtones and is not merely a "recovery" of the pre-Fall Garden, although it is often put in the context of the world being "loosened from the ancient curse." Mary is said to turn the earth again into a paradise: "Going to dwell in the tomb, she made it a paradise. Standing beside this tomb today, we sing with joy: O ye works of the Lord, bless the Lord and exalt Him above all for ever."[83] Mary's tomb in this Feast of the Dormition recalls the cave in Bethlehem, which is repeatedly also said to restore Paradise.[84]

The phrase "bestowing salvation on all who sing thy praises" is also employed repeatedly. For example, the Irmos from the Fifth Canticle during Matins for the Annunciation, "the whole world was amazed at thy divine glory: for thou, O Virgin hast not known wedlock, hast held in thy womb the God of all, and hast given birth to an eternal Son, who rewards with salvation all who sing thy praises" (452), may seem to refer only to human "chanters." Yet, as creation is constantly affirmed to be singing God's praises (as established in the previous section), surely by implication all of creation must be included in salvation as well. One must then conclude that redemption is bestowed on all of creation (especially as the two affirmations occur within lines—or seconds—of each other). Not only does the Incarnation affirm the sanctity and goodness of material flesh as it is embraced by its creation, not only does all of creation (human and otherkind) rejoice in the liturgy and praise the Trinity, but indeed all of creation is redeemed and restored to communion with God in the Eschaton (which is already present within the liturgical celebration).

This is further confirmed by some of the Patristic homilies (although they seldom address this theme explicitly). Leontius in a *Homily on the Nativity* lists its many effects, including the restoration of Paradise and a recreation of the earth:

> Many and innumerable are the God-loving celebrations of the Christians. But what is more worthy of celebration than the present one, because Christ the Master has been born and the world has been reborn? Christ has been born and Adam has been recalled. Christ has been born and Eve has been ransomed from grief. Christ has been born and the snake has disappeared. Christ has been born and paradise has been restored. Christ has been born and the devil has been condemned. Christ has been born and Hades has been changed. Christ has been born and the earth has been recreated. Christ has been born and the air has been purified. Christ has been born and heaven has been gladdened. . . . Christ has been born and the light has been added.[85]

Christ's birth recreates and purifies the natural elements. Even hell is changed by it. Romanos also imagines some impact on the cosmos in his hymns for Nativity: "Savior, save the world: that is why you have come. Restore your whole work: this is why you shine before me, before the wise men and before all of creation."[86] Mary is assured by Christ that she "will see me revive and renew the earth and all the children of the earth."[87] In a homily on the Annunciation, Andrew of Crete speaks of the divine plan, which includes the renewal of the universe:

> Today the Source of all authority, who made all things, brings his plan, which he worked out in advance for the creation of everything in existence, to its goal, in order that he may prevent the plan that was devised for us from the beginning by the founder of evil. For this reason angels dance, human beings rejoice, and the whole universe is renewed and restored to itself.[88]

Since human beings and the universe are here listed separately, one may safely assume that this does indeed refer to the cosmos and not only to humans.

The Dormition renders effects on the earth by far the most explicit. Andrew of Crete, in his first homily on the Dormition, suggests that Christ might renew "the whole of what he had taken from us."[89] In the third homily he describes Mary's body as "the body that has filled all creation with the fragrant myrrh of holiness." It is "the first-fruit of God's communion with his creation, of his identification, as maker of all things, with what he has made."[90] John of Damascus interprets the Dormition as sanctifying the four elements: air, water, earth, and fire (or aether):

> And what happened next? I imagine that the elements of nature were stirred up and altered, that there were sounds, crashes, rumblings, as well as remarkable hymns from angels who flew before her, providing her with an escort and with companions on the way.... The air, the fiery ether, the sky would have been made holy by the ascent of her spirit, as earth was sanctified by the deposition of her body. Even water had its share in the blessing: for she was washed in pure water, which did not so much cleanse her as it was itself consecrated. Then the deaf received perfect hearing again, the feet of the lame had their power to walk restored; sight was renewed in the blind, and the writ of condemnation was torn up for sinners who approached in faith.[91]

Here all the elements are sanctified, purified, made holy, and blessed by Mary's ascent. Theodore the Studite picks up on this theme of blessing and expects concrete results from it:

O, what a radiant, brilliant festival! It is only joy that lets me speak at all! O great sign of your passing, moving us to wonder! O burial of the bearer of light, life and the gift of endless incorruption! As you rise through the clouds on your way to heaven, as you enter the holy of holies with cries of joy and praise, O Mother of God, remember to bless the bounds of this earth. By your intercession temper the air, give us rain in due season, rule over the winds, make the earth fruitful, give peace to the Church, strengthen orthodox faith, defend the Empire, ward off the barbarian tribes, protect the whole Christian people.[92]

Mary's blessing, for him, influences the weather and the fertility of the earth.

Thus the Incarnation, as celebrated in these feasts, is affirmed to have a real impact on the entire cosmos. Not only does Christ hallow human flesh and corporeality by assuming it, but he also sanctifies and renews the whole creation. Materiality and corporeality are assumed and purified by the incarnation. And nonhuman characters participate much more explicitly in these feasts than analyses of the purely human role in worship would lead us to believe. The incarnation serves to bring together earth and heaven. The divine connects itself to the material and unifies the realms of heaven and earth.

A careful analysis of the Liturgy, then, makes it absolutely incumbent upon us to treat creation as a real partner in the redemptive purposes of God. The Liturgy makes possible and works out this task of the church by including the voices of all creatures within the liturgical praise. Within the liturgy, creation is restored and glory rendered to God. The Liturgy works transformation not only for humans but for all creatures. The goodness and integrity of creation is fully affirmed within the liturgical texts. Furthermore, creation plays an active role within worship and the redemption already at work within it. If the Liturgy truly does allow the worshipping community to enter into the restored creation in God's presence and really does transform this community into what it shall be (but is only beginning to become), then care for creation must be an integral, practical, and concrete part of this transformation and mission to the world upon leaving the sacred space of the Liturgy after the celebration.

Traces of Divine Fragrance, Droplets of Divine Love: On the Beauty of Visible Creation

Bruce V. Foltz

> And all of these refer to some slight *trace of the divine fragrance*, which the whole creation, after the manner of a jar for ointments, imitates within itself by the wonders that are seen within it.
> —*St. Gregory of Nyssa*, Homiliae on the Song of Songs

> All things around us are *droplets of the love of God*—both things animate and inanimate, the plants and the animals, the birds and the mountains, the sea and the sunset and the starry sky. They are little loves through which we attain to the great Love that is Christ . . .
> —Elder Porphyrios, Wounded by Love

I

In discussing beauty, which is extraordinary, I want to begin from everyday, ordinary experience, to suggest that ordinariness itself is a constraint we heedlessly impose upon the extraordinary. I want to begin with the small owl unexpectedly encountered, bathing in a pool of water after a rain, whose beauty illumines the remainder of the evening with a certain charm, a spiritual fragrance of enchantment—or with the dusty, late afternoon sky glimpsed momentarily along a country road long ago, whose muted, translucent hues are beautiful in some subtle but deeply satisfying way, giving rise to a distinct sense that this wonderful but inconspicuous beauty, which seemed to come from somewhere else, was connected to an unending source of goodness that could sustain the soul forever.

These ordinary glimpses of beauty that we are granted from time to time are unsought and unexpected—unlike the beauty of the Louvre or the Bernese Alps, which we expectantly seek out. Their ultimate charm, I suspect, lies in their tacit suggestion that our *every* experience of creation has the potential to be extraordinary, beautiful, sublime, if only our souls were prepared for it, if we had the eyes to see.

The ancient Greeks had such eyes. Perhaps to a fault. They saw the extraordinary in the ordinary: in owls and lightning flashes, in the ecstatic exhilaration of the hunt and in the quiet goodness of tender shoots rising up from the earth, they saw the invisible rising up into the visible, they saw the beautiful. And because the beautiful moves and attracts, is *attract-ive*, they were drawn to it so powerfully that they worshiped it everywhere, for they found it all around them. Heraclitus gave expression to this sensibility, saying that "all things are full of gods."

It is this dispersed, fragmented, incoherent worship—and view of nature, upon which it was based—that the early Christians denounced as idolatry—in St. Paul's terms, worshipping and serving the creature rather than the Creator (Rom. 1:35). But for critics from Nietzsche to Lynn White Jr., this denunciation was itself culpable: it was Christianity, they believe, that subverted this laudable veneration of nature, turned its back on the beauty of the visible, and sought instead to escape into another supernatural and otherworldly goodness and beauty, thereby inaugurating a devaluation of nature that would eventually culminate in the environmental crisis of today.

II

The philosophical response to environmental concerns first took shape in the early 1970s, as the search for an environmental ethic. Responses in Christian theology came a few years earlier, and they too were heavily oriented toward moral concerns. But it has by now become evident to many that an exclusively ethical orientation—a narrow focus on concepts of rights and duties, as well as more theologically grounded notions of responsibility and stewardship—is limited and perhaps also distorts something important about nature, something important that eludes the moral outlook. The moral approach is limited first of all because it inevitably leads to conflicts between competing moral demands—for example, concerns for jobs and economic development versus species preservation versus green space and recreation, and so on. But it is also limited because it seems to grant nature no greater status than that of a resource whose value lies in satisfying human needs, whether or not this commodity status is understood to be mediated through a stewardship relation to God. But something is missing when we see the created order only in its usefulness—a sense of its integrity, of its sanctity, of its beauty. Perhaps, then, an aesthetic approach to thinking about the natural environment has something vitally important to add. Moreover, in contrast to the strained application of a modernist lexicon of rights and duties and obligations to environmental problems that they were never meant to address, our native intuitions effortlessly support a respect for nature that is based on admiration for its beauty. Wanton destruction of a natural landscape (or even a single flower) offends our aesthetic sensibilities more than it strikes us as immoral, as would (for example) the ill-treatment of a person. But against the grain of modern philosophy, this aesthetic imperative would need to go beyond such subjective notions as "taste" and "enjoyment," instead deriving its normative power from the ontological standing of beauty itself—from the kind of autonomous and, indeed, commanding being or mode of existence that is specific to beauty in general and more specifically to natural beauty.

But where to look for an aesthetic that would understand the beauty of nature ontologically, as entailing correlative, practical imperatives? Perhaps in some neopaganism, as followers of philosophers such as Nietzsche and to some extent Heidegger have rather ingenuously suggested? Or do we have no other alternative than to look to other cultural traditions—to Taoism or Buddhism, for example? Yet no current of thought, East or West, has displayed a greater proclivity for the beauty of the material world—and more insistently seen it as demanding a practical response—than has Orthodox Christianity, which has always possessed a deep, sacramental orientation not just toward the bread and wine of the Eucharist, the water of baptism, and the oil of creation but toward the material world as a whole. It appears in the beauty of Orthodox temples and iconography, of its chant and liturgy. As Dionysius the Areopagite puts it, the sensuous dimensions of the Liturgy—the fragrance of the incense, the warm luminosity of the candles, the splendors of the iconography, the sonorous loveliness of the chanting, and at its culmination the very taste of the Eucharistic bread and wine on the tongue—are all meant to strike the senses as noetic emanations, as gifts of immaterial light, and ultimately invitations to an ontological participation in the metaphysical locus of Beauty, in Christ Himself, with whom the believer becomes one in the Eucharist (*Celestial Hierarchy* 121c–124a). Moreover, this iconicity extends to the entire cosmos. "The great, all-shining, ever-lighting sun," Dionysius proposes as an example, "is the luminous icon of the Divine Goodness" (*Divine Names* 697c). "Truly," he affirms, "the visible is the manifest icon of the invisible" (*Epistles* 10, 1117B).

The Byzantine predilection for beauty—its *philokalia*, to use a term in currency since the time of St. Basil the Great—its inclination toward the beautiful, extends far beyond temple and monastery and icon corner into an overall orientation toward nature as a whole, a sensibility it has inherited from the Patristic experience of nature—an emended, augmented, transformed, but nevertheless continuous legacy from the sensibilities of the ancient Greeks. For contrary to the romanticized revisionism of Lynn White's claim—based on his reading of the Latin West—that Christianity disrupted a happy pagan love for nature, in fact it was not pagan antiquity at all but early Christianity that first cultivated the very love for nature, the "feel for nature," the appreciation of the beauty of nature for its own sake that not only inspired the romantic movement of the nineteenth century but continues to animate environmentalism today.

This point was argued persuasively by Fr. Pavel Florensky in his *Pillar and Ground of Truth*, perhaps the great neglected work of twentieth-century philosophy, which has only recently been translated into English. Counter to Nietzsche's valorization of the Greek enchantment with surfaces and appearances, Florensky argued that paganism hugged the surfaces, dwelt upon appearances, mostly because of its fear of the demonic realities felt to be lurking beneath and behind the beautiful forms—namely, the gods whom they sensed everywhere, and everywhere feared, and whom they thus strove to "magically control" through sacrifice and ritual.[1] Thales' maxim that all things are full of gods, given Florensky's rendering, would need to be understood less as an expression of misty-eyed veneration and more like a battlefield warning that one step in the wrong direction might trigger a landmine. We would be led to reappraise pagan nature aestheticism with the keen eye of the Septuagint Psalms, which assert that "all the gods of the nations are demons, while the Lord made the heavens" (Ps. 95). In contrast, Florensky maintains that "only Christianity has given birth to an unprecedented being-in-love with creation. . . . If we take the 'sense of nature' to mean a relation to creation itself, not to its [superficial] forms, if we see in this sense more than an external, subjectively aesthetic admiration of 'the beauties of nature,' this sense is then wholly Christian and utterly inconceivable outside of Christianity."[2]

How was this changed relation to creation accomplished, this transition from fear to wonder? Florensky, himself both a scientist and a historian of science, argues that only with Christianity does nature have an inner reality of its own—have its own relationship to the God who has created it—and thus possess an ontological weight, a reality proper to it, as distinct from serving merely as a mask for some shrouded deity—the prerequisite for both the love of nature and later the science of nature. "This relation to nature," he maintains, "became conceivable only when people saw in creation not merely a demonic shell, not some emanation of Divinity, not some illusory appearance of God, like a rainbow in a spray of water, but an independent, autonomous, and responsible creation of God, beloved of God and capable of responding to His love."[3] Only now does nature become fully real, and truly lovable, and ultimately intelligible.

But what about the asceticism—world denying and earth despising—that Nietzsche and his followers have alleged? Florensky helpfully distinguishes between two very different asceticisms. On the one hand, authentic Christian asceticism is in love with God's creation and everywhere encounters the uncorrupted beauty of nature, looking within the outward forms that have become distorted in a fallen world of corruption and death. In contrast, however, are those other asceticisms—ranging from Vedanta to the world weariness of Tolstoy and the Russian intelligentsia—that reject the world altogether, not just its distortions. These truly do represent an "escape" from a world found disgusting and repellent, a repudiation that Florensky argues is a blaspheming of God's creation.

But beyond this, it is precisely in the most perfect forms of Christian asceticism that we find the greatest love for the beauty of creation. Why would this be the case? Above all, because the ability to know and the ability to love both entail spiritual prerequisites that are perfected in monasticism. Nikitas Stithatos writes in the *Philokalia*, "The soul's apprehension of the nature of things changes in accordance with its own inner state."[4] *Changes in accordance with its own inner state.* St. Antony the Great also enjoins, "let us purify our mind [*nous*], for I believe that when the *nous* is completely pure and is in its natural state, it sees more clearly and further . . . since the Lord reveals things to it."[5] And more recently, Elder Porphyrios: "[Not] everyone here sees the light of truth with the same clarity. Each person sees according to the state of his soul."[6] It is the purified, monastic consciousness, always exemplary for ancient Christianity, that sees most deeply the goodness and beauty of nature and hence is most able to love it. "Blessing the universe, the ascetic everywhere and always sees in things God's signs and letters," says Florensky. Thus, it is neither Leonardo nor Galileo who first regards nature as a text but St. Antony: "My book is this created nature. It is always with me, and when I wish I can read in it the words of God."[7] "The higher the Christian ascetic ascends on his path to the heavenly land," writes Florensky, "the brighter his inner eye shines, the deeper the Holy Spirit descends into his heart—the more clearly then will he see the inner, absolutely valuable core of creation. . . . It is precisely among the charismatics and ascetics that we find the most striking examples of a feeling that I can only call the *being-in-love with creation.*"[8]

Florensky's claim—that with Christianity, and especially Christian asceticism, a new sensitivity for the beauty of creation emerges into human awareness—is borne out strikingly in protocols from the great patristic ascetics and their later successors in the Orthodox East, up to the present day. It is, for example, in a letter of St. Basil the Great to his friend St. Gregory of Nazianzus that we find what is likely the first example in antiquity of praise for a natural beauty that is not pastoral but wild and uncultivated.[9] Savoring the beauty of his Cappadocian hermitage overlooking the River Isis, he describes "a lofty mountain covered with thick forest," "cool and transparent" mountain streams, precipices and ravines, and the great river itself with a swifter current than he has ever seen before, cascading dramatically onto rocks and forming deep whirlpools—a far reach from the docile, domesticated beauty of Hesiod or Virgil.[10] And in his *Hexaemeron*, Basil pauses to reflect on how the "beauty and grandeur" of creation—"earth, air, sky, water, day, night, all visible things"—is a "training ground" for the soul to "learn to know God, since by the sight of [these] visible and sensible things the *nous* is led, as by a hand, to the contemplation of invisible things."[11] Later he interrupts his narrative once to address once again his reader directly: "I want creation to penetrate you with so much admiration that everywhere, wherever you may be, the least plant may bring to you the clear remembrance of the Creator."[12] Or we may listen to his brother, St. Gregory of Nyssa, extolling the emergence of springtime from the harsh Cappadocian winters and evoking an image of the Resurrection: "[Springtime here does not] shine forth in its radiant beauty all at once, but as preludes of spring [come] the sunbeam gently warming the earth's frozen surface, and the bud half hidden beneath the clod, and breezes blowing over the earth."[13]

Nor has this love of nature's beauty cooled or diminished in the Orthodox asceticism of modern times. "The holy Athonite Fathers," proclaim the Representatives of the Twenty Monasteries, "have testified to the way in which their communion with supernatural spiritual states led them to feel a special affection and concern for their natural surroundings and to experience a spiritual sense of harmony with the whole of nature."[14] Here are the words of Elder Ephraim, recalling those of St. Gregory: "Now in springtime, when nature is wearing its most beautiful apparel, one feels inexpressible joy when this natural beauty is accompanied by a sublime spiritual state. Truly, our holy God has made all things in wisdom! *The soul cannot get enough of beholding the beauty of nature.*"[15] The Paschal theme is also echoed poignantly by Elder Porphyrios: "I looked at the clear, blue sky, at the sea which stretched out endlessly, at the trees, the birds, the butterflies and all the beauties of nature, and I shouted full of enthusiasm: Christ is Risen!"[16] And who could match the tender aesthetic of the heart expressed by Elder Joseph the Hesychast?

> Listen to the rough crags, those mystical and silent theologians, which expound deep thoughts and guide the heart and *nous* towards the Creator. After spring it is beautiful here [on the Holy Mountain]—from Holy Pascha until the Panagia's day in August.... The beautiful rocks theologize like voiceless theologians, as does all of nature—each creature with its own voice or its silence.[17]

Nor is this love of nature's beauty confined to the Holy Mountain. "Your face," prays St. Nikolai Velimirovich from shores of Lake Ochrid, "pours beauty over all creation. The universe swims in Your beauty as a boat swims in the sea."[18]

"When I began to pray with all my heart," recalls the Russian Pilgrim, "all that surrounded me appeared delightful to me: the trees, the grass, the birds, the earth, the air, and the light."[19] "It is remarkable how the human *nous* sees things differently according to its own light," writes St. Peter of Damascus, "even when these things are unalterable and in themselves remain what they are."[20] For the ascetic who sees most clearly and most deeply, the divine beauty of nature shines forth most vividly, the visible everywhere revealing the invisible. And already by the third century, this "seeing" had been precisely contextualized as the second step in a progression: *katharsis*, the soul's purification; *theoria*, illumination of the soul, by means of which it is able to "see" the extraordinary depths within what has been there unobtrusively all along; and, ultimately, *theosis*, in which we are united to God, divinized by divine grace. His soul now purified by tears of repentance, the young Zosima in Dostoevsky's *Brothers Karamazov* proclaims aloud his new capacity to see the beauty of nature: "look at the divine gifts around us: the clear sky, the fresh air, the tender grass, the birds, nature is beautiful and sinless, and we, we alone, are godless and foolish, and do not understand that life is paradise, for we need only wish to understand, and it will come at once in all its beauty."[21]

Theoria physike, contemplation of nature, enables the purified soul to see the holy beauty of creation. It is central to the ascetic literature of patristic Christianity, which emphasizes that we must first see God in the beauty of creation *before* we can proceed to the ineffable realm of *theosis*. We must begin with the beauty of creation, just as surely as God's self-revelation first began with nature before proceeding to written scripture. Yet this is just the aesthetic of the Orthodox Church itself: in its icons and liturgy, in the fragrance of the incense and the divine beauty of its hymnology: visible and audible and tangible things that abound and overflow with the unseen, the unheard, the intangible. Everywhere the visible becomes saturated with the invisible, spills over with divine fragrance. Nor is it accidental that the icon, intended to be a visible window into invisible orders, to put us in touch with noetic realities, is at the same time invariably beautiful as well: an occasion for wonder, since the icon is neither primarily nor essentially meant to be beautiful at all but simply to present and sustain within the visible what is holy, venerable, invisible. The holy and beautiful arrive together.

Florensky argued that the love of nature, the sense for nature, the susceptibility and vulnerability for—and the appreciation of—its beauty was bound up with the sense that creation was real, existed on its own, possessed a weighty interiority mirroring a unique relation to the creator. And the shining forth of this depth is precisely its beauty. This manifest interiority, accessible to the purified soul, is what St. Maximus called the inner *logos* of each being, every leaf and stone and animal and person reflecting its own relation to God, its own rootedness in the Eternal Logos. And in Byzantine Christianity, this insight is connected historically to a new and radical aesthetic that was to become foundational for the appreciation of nature's beauty and upon which later generations have drawn deeply to the present day, usually without suspecting its origins in ancient Christianity. This new aesthetic was outlined suggestively by Gervase Mathew, a friend of C. S. Lewis and an "Inklings" member, in his *Byzantine Aesthetics*. Mathew argues that Byzantine aesthetics preserved and continued the "surface aesthetics" of antiquity—oriented toward "the intelligibility of nature," carried out through an "essentially mathematical [and ultimately geometrical] approach to beauty [along with] an absorbed interest in optics." But to this, it added a "depth aesthetics" that saw visible beauty (the surface aesthetics) as itself the outer expression of inner, invisible realities.[22] Thus, the beautiful—either in nature or in art—could be contemplated on two levels: either as "beauty rendered visible" or, more deeply, as "the beauty thus reflected."[23]

This depth aesthetic was in part inspired by a broader metaphysical revolution in late antiquity, observable in Middle Platonism, which saw in visible order and symmetry the manifestation of inward life. But to this Byzantine Christianity brought a radical affirmation of the reality of the visible, drawn from three principal sources: First, its perception that the Liturgy itself was the visible, material presentation of spiritual realities, a sacred drama that enacted eternal events unfolding in time—not as a merely semiotic nexus of metaphors or tropes leading away from nature but as divine gifts rendered within material nature, the tangible communion bread just as patently material as the touch of the Savior's hand. Second, its fundamental conviction that the Incarnation had sacralized the material world, lending it an inherent spiritual dimension. And finally, the Alexandrine school of hermeneutics had taught it to see the visible, tangible, concrete events narrated in scripture as manifestations of noetic realities, yet in a way that did not negate their factical, material reality—that is, that did not reduce persons and events in scripture to figures and fables, mere allegories, but esteemed them as concrete, material realities that nevertheless possessed a deeper, inner, mystical dimension. All three factors, then, were richly articulated in the Byzantine East—even as they became diluted in the West, as it gradually lost its taste for sacred art altogether, a process culminating in the merely "religious" art of the Renaissance.

Beauty in nature, both that of *physis* and *techne*, is rather the manifest infusion of material nature with the spiritual reality in which it is rooted, revealing how material nature is both a gift (regarded perceptually) and at the same time a manifestation of the giver (regarded spiritually or noetically). And this view, in turn, provides the basis for the *theoria physike*, the contemplation of noetic realities in created nature, which is articulated in the ascetic tradition from Evagrius to Maximus, where the mystical reading of scripture is presented as analogous to the mystical contemplation of *logoi* in nature—rejecting both a fundamentalism of the senses as well as a fundamentalism of the text—and basing both upon the inherence of nature in an Eternal Logos, whose transformative embodiment has now become not just explicit but the new, true *axis mundi*. And I will here only suggest what I have argued elsewhere, that the modern genre of nature writing (from Thoreau, Emerson, and Muir to the present), which has been critical in shaping environmental sensibilities and which characteristically discerns in the beauty of nature the traces of a hidden holiness that it struggles to articulate, presupposes this spiritual landscape that was first—and far more articulately—developed in ancient Christianity.

III

Are we, then, entitled to conclude that the holy is at the same time the beautiful and that beauty is hence a sign—perhaps the cardinal sign—that it is, in fact, the holy we have encountered? And may we gather as well that authentic Christianity, traditional and patristic Christianity, preserved and perpetuated as a living tradition in Orthodox Christianity, so far from dismissing the beauty of nature is alone able to perceive it adequately, comprehend it, and properly celebrate it? Whatever relevance the criticisms of Nietzsche and his successors may carry toward other modes of religion, in relation to Orthodox spirituality they would be simply misplaced, if not altogether preposterous.

Yet there still remains one final objection to be met. For alongside the celebration of the beauty of nature in the ascetic writings of Byzantine Christianity, one finds at the same time warnings of the *dangers* of this beauty, caveats that seem to lend support to Nietzsche's charges that Christianity denigrates the beauty of creation. Cautions concerning the beauty of creation can be found throughout the literature of Orthodox asceticism, but perhaps their most powerful formulation is one of the earliest. In the fourth chapter of Deuteronomy (15–19), after warning against fabricating idolatrous reproductions of beasts and birds, creeping things on the earth and fish in the water, Moses adds another warning that reveals the true character of idolatry itself: "And *take good heed to your hearts* . . . lest having looked up into the sky, and having seen the sun and the moon and the stars, and all the heavenly bodies, thou shouldest go astray and worship them, and serve them . . ." Don't carve idols, he cautions, but also—and perhaps most importantly—be careful when you look up into the sky and gaze upon a beauty not made by human hands at all, the beauty of the sky that is perhaps the very epitome of all natural beauty.

This suggests that idolatry consists not only, or even primarily, in the making (*techne*) of graven images and their subsequent worship but above all in a certain corruption of the heart that leads to an idolatrous gaze—a gaze that is especially capable of being provoked by the beauty of creation, here exemplified by the beauty of the heavens that wields such power to elevate naturally the heart toward God and to which the Psalmist so often refers us. This beauty sets up a longing, a yearning, an *eros* that moves the soul. It brings the soul into a state of wonder, which for Aristotle was the beginning of all philosophy. But more than this, beauty and the yearning it engenders binds the soul to that for which it longs. The more powerful the beauty, the more powerful the longing, and the more powerful the bonds that are forged. "Beauty summons all things to itself," writes St. Dionysius, "and gathers everything to itself" (*Divine Names* 701D). And the divine beauty that is beyond beings and thus can render *from itself* to beautiful beings the beauty they possess generates a divine longing (*eros*) that leads the soul beyond itself so that it belongs to that for which it longs (*Divine Names* 701C, 712A). Moreover, as St. Gregory of Nyssa points out in his *Commentary on the Song of Songs*, the experience of this divine longing renders the soul insatiable: "Even as now the soul that is joined to God is not satiated by her enjoyment of him, so too the more abundantly she is filled up with his beauty, the more vehemently her longings abound."[24] Nor is this provocative beauty to be found alone in the starry skies, for all around us we can find "some slight trace of the divine perfume, which the whole creation, after the manner of a jar for ointments, imitates within itself by the wonders that are seen within it."[25]

Florensky argues that the pagan worship of many gods was sustained through fear. But does it *originate* in fear as well? How is it that paganism in particular and idolatry as a whole are first generated? The "Wisdom of Solomon," looking out upon the idolatrous worship of the Hellenistic world, provides a negative answer. Seeing "fire, or wind, or the swift air, or the circle of stars, or the violent water, or the lights of heaven," people have foolishly "delighted [in their] beauty," thereby mistaking them for "deities which govern the world." This is folly, the Wisdom Book explains, "for by the greatness and beauty of creatures proportionately the Creator of them is seen (*theōreitai*)." (Wisdom 13:6). *Seen*, it must be emphasized, and not inferred, as proponents of the so-called argument from design presuppose. The divine beauty that is invisible somehow, wonderfully, becomes visible in the beauty of creation. So why does the idolater fail to see what is evident? The Wisdom Book answers this question too: it is because of the corruption of the heart, through which "men have lived dissolutely and unrighteously," that they have attached themselves to the beauty of creation rather than recognizing in the beauty of creation the greater, truer, more fulfilling beauty of the Creator.

"Blessed are the pure in heart, for they shall see God." Conversely, the impure in heart—those who do not "take good heed" (*nepsis*) of their hearts, those whose hearts are corrupted—will to that same extent not see the Creator at all but rather creatures alone and thus attach to created things themselves the soul's longing that creation's beauty evokes. In a text that has been traditionally attributed to St. Theodore the Ascetic, who wrote in seventh-century Syria, and that is included in the *Philokalia*, it is even argued that the Fall itself resulted from a warp, a distortion or deformation of the way that the *protos anthropos*, the first man (Adam) looked upon the perceptual world around him, and most especially upon how he responded to its most engaging feature (its beauty) and how he directed his natural, noetic response (his wonder) to that beauty.[26] Somehow, perversely, Adam's wonder was directed not toward the Creator from whom all this beauty proceeds and to whom it testifies, but rather his wonder and longing became fixated upon the sensuous character of the beauty itself—clinging to the message, ignoring the messenger, and indeed somehow oblivious to the very fact that this wonderful beauty was itself a message at all—a gift and a blessing and not just a source of pleasure with which to satisfy our desires. Rather than his soul (his *nous* or mind, the highest part of his soul) continuing to ascend from the enticingly beautiful character of the visible to the far higher beauty of the Creator, whose icon he found everywhere around him—as he had once done—the first man somehow became disoriented, confusing instead this higher beauty with what he calls its "bastard offspring"—the all-too-familiar enticements of power and wealth, the self-entitled indulgence in the sensual and visible as ends in themselves. This was the primal idolatry, the inner dynamic of the Fall itself, and to one extent or another we are all, like Adam, idolaters, fixedly bedazzled by, obsessively avaricious of, and chronically longing for the purely sensuous beauty of nature rather than freely wondering at where this could possibly have originated and thereby ascending naturally to its source. Virtually all modern marketing (it is worth noting) depends upon the sensual wonder and enticement following from the cheap and facile substitution of the immediately visible for its less obvious—and indeed, invisible—but truly life-giving source.

Thus, in authentic, patristic Christianity we are cautioned about created beauty not in order to deter us from it, nor even less to cultivate contempt for it, but to exhort us to pursue it more deeply, more radically, more authentically to its very source—and thus to warn us against getting sidetracked in the swift currents and swirling eddies of the material world, with its peculiar sorts of back alleys. And this holds true not just for the beauty of nature but for the beauty of icons and chant and liturgies and vestments as well. All these visible beauties are traces of divine fragrance, "droplets of divine love," to which dissolute and unrighteous souls will tend idolatrously to attach themselves but through which instead the original and originating beauty of the Creator can be seen by those who hearts have been purified.

"We shall be like [God]," writes St. John the Evangelist, "for we shall see Him as He is. And everyone who has this hope in [God] purifies himself, just as [God Himself] is pure" (1 John 3:2–3). To see God is to be like God and thus to be likewise purified. The Evangelist, of course, is writing here specifically about "the time when God appears," about "His coming," "when He is revealed" (1 John 2:28, 3:2). It is truly then that "we shall see Him as he is." To see God in nature surely is to see God, but it is also to see Him (as St. Paul put it) "through a glass darkly," not yet "as He is." But at the same time, to see God as He has revealed Himself in the beauty of creation is to see Him as he intended Himself to be seen, to see God through one of the ways that He chose to manifest Himself. Thus it requires of us that even now, through purifying our souls, we must "be like Him" to the same extent that we are able to see him, even becoming "partakers" or participants "of the Divine Nature" in the very act of seeing—in the scent of "divine fragrance," in the savor of the "droplets of divine love," in the long-neglected capacity to hear "the voice of the Lord God walking in the Garden" during the afternoon, and even to sense His "face" or countenance (*prosopon*) "in the midst of the trees of the Garden" (Gen 3:8).

Natural and Supernatural Revelation in Early Irish and Greek Monastic Thought: A Comparative Approach

Chrysostomos Koutloumousianos

Some striking similarities have been traced between Irish and Eastern Christianity in the field of theology and spiritual life, with monasticism being the meeting point of these physically distant traditions. Here we will discuss theological theses expressed in early Irish and Greek religious literature of the first Byzantine period in the context of comparative spirituality, with a view to showing the unity of God's revelation in both nature and history, according to pre-Norman Irish and Greek patristic thought and religious experience, and that testify to a common theological background and a shared insight rooted in the biblical tradition.[1]

The severance of the natural from the historical and of the social from the existential field of reality is one of the main features of modern philosophy and life. This disjunction has its roots in medieval times, when scholastic theology posited natural and supernatural reality as two concurrent and autonomous layers, two kinds of revelation, the physical and the historical, where the latter is understood as a supplement to the former.[2] There is no trace of such a distinction in the early Irish and Greek patristic traditions: nature and history, corporeal and spiritual—everything that is *not* God—constitute an inseparable created reality that is entirely dependent on Him.

For the early Irish Christians, the understanding of the personal and directly functioning omnipresence of God would make any distinction between natural and supernatural reality meaningless. The Celts saw the sovereignty, presence, and glory of God in everything that He created. The Father is the God of the elements, of earth, fire, water, the high winds, the bottomless ocean, the bright stars,[3] not just their distant Maker. As the Cappadocian expresses it, the whole universe is "the magnificent and famed *stoicheion*, in which God is manifested through silent proclamation."[4] Every element, every image or expression of the natural world is conceived as a transparent veil behind which God's power is at work. At the same time, the divine presence is revealed not only in nature but also "in the languages of men throughout the whole world," that is, in culture and history.[5]

An important part of early Irish literature lies in the field of cosmology. Creation functions as a symbol, a sign, of divine things. It is recorded that Columba interpreted the books of Law, studied the mysteries of revelation in the Scriptures, and observed and meditated on the courses of the heavenly bodies and the sea.[6] The great Irish saint observed the stars, but he "discerned the elements according to types." Study arises not from a longing for intellectual occupation but is a product of religious sensitivity. Thus the preface of the *Altus Prosator* announces that the reason for its composition was Columba's desire to praise God.[7] In this same epic one also finds a typological use of cosmology,[8] where everything is seen in the light of the incarnation. The courses and reappearances of Orion and Hesperus in the firmament are understood as types of the second coming of Christ. The theological spirit is inspired by scientific knowledge of the physical and spiritual cosmos, and the veneration of God is the ultimate *desideratum* of scientific toil. The poet's wish is to help his readers understand the life, death, and resurrection of the Lord through observance of the laws of creation, which function as signs.

Furthermore, through conscious participation in the symbolic liturgy, animated creation, physical and noetic, becomes the "angel" of apocryphal knowledge. Even the animal kingdom is familiar with the language of the heavenly ranks, the language all will speak at the Judgment.[9] A typical example is the role of birds in Celtic literature. More than being just a part of the beautiful mosaic of creation, they have a particular relationship with man as well as with the spiritual world. They empathize with men, like the bird who lamented the death of the hermit; they are angels—vehicles of divine messages, they speak all the angelic languages. Their main characteristic is their gift of song, and they participate in the hymns of the angels.[10] We realize that all this poetic inspiration before the miracle and the mysteries of nature, expressed in exaggerated literary schemes or even archaic mythical language, serves the understanding of Christology.

Scientific knowledge of what constitutes a being is not outside the scope and considerations of the Greek Fathers. Basil the Great is acclaimed as the foremost exponent of the scientific-experimental approach. His treatise on the *Hexaemeron* is neither a work of scientific research separated from faith and doxology nor an investigation aimed at proving the truth of the faith.

Insofar as knowledge is an activity of undivided, nondualistic, human existence, it should not be regarded as opposed to mystery; it coexists as a specific facet of a unified life. As St. Basil states, the experience of the mysteries of creation is not undermined by any investigation of the creative processes.[11] His Irish counterparts share in this searching spirit, as is evident in their cosmological treatises, calendar calculations, arithmology, and historical method of biblical exegesis.

For the Greek mind, nature stands as a "school of God's knowledge." The heavenly order and earthly adornments are the guides of faith. "Through the visible we see the invisible" since "the wisdom of the Creator is discernible even in the smallest particles."[12] Divine activities perceived by the noetic capacity of man point to the notion of a Creator as well as to God's goodness and wisdom. The whole of creation, and individually every tiny particle, whether speaking or keeping silence, reveals, proclaims, and gives glory to the Creator.[13] Furthermore, the beauty of creatures is a revelation of the undivided and triadic mode of divine life.[14] Man sees in every created thing an inherent "word" expressed in a symbolic way, a word that informs the human intellect by enlightening the eye of the soul. The nature of the sun conveys a Christological message, the nature of the moon denotes aspects of human beings, the existence of the stars, the natural laws, each and every part of creation become instructors, and to the degree they have not preserved the primordial nobility of their nature, men become students. Creation offers types of things both spiritual and noetic, and every creature teaches a theological or an ethical truth.[15] Consequently, the intellect needs to meditate on God's works, which give pleasure as well as benefit and which delight the senses through physical sight and the soul through comprehension. This physical and spiritual way of seeing all of creation, animate and inanimate, and its inherent *logos* is called "natural contemplation." And in turn, on account of the *logos* that God has implanted in all created things, natural contemplation leads to ethics and theology.[16] The monk is in a state of stillness in the practice of "ethical, natural and theological contemplation."[17] Nature is presented as a reminder of, or as a key to, the divine presence and providence.

Man and his natural environment concelebrate in an everlasting doxology. This is evident in Irish monastic poetry and hymnography, where the monk enters into a continuous concourse with "irrational" creation, by which means he participates in worship that is universal.[18] Thus nature is not only a symbol or a means by which we can ascend: it is a power of influence and maintains an internal, mystical correspondence with the human soul. Accordingly, in the lyrical poetry of St. Gregory Nazianzus, the elements do not function only as vehicles of divine messages but contribute to the formation and expression of the inner state.[19] Breezes, groves, melodious birds, plashing waters, and whatever makes up a paradisiacal picture give sweet tranquility to the saint's despondent soul. In the same way, the Irish calligrapher expresses his gratitude to God for the blessing of exercising his art in the forest to the accompaniment of birdsong. The book, representing knowledge and art, and living creation, which participates in human creativeness, are the two points of reference for the hermit.[20] Eventually, sympathetic affection unites God, nature, and man. It is this compassion, a witness of the paradisiacal state, that is expressed so colorfully in the theological and poetic tradition of Insular Celtic.

It is true that the Greeks differ from the Celts in the stylistic features and the intensity with which this natural theology is articulated. The Greek mode is more philosophical and less naturalistic or mythical. Its language gives the impression that its authors are anxious to extrapolate and lift up the intelligible realities from the sensible, to move from the outer *ad intra*, from creation to the Creator. Creation as things and events, as craftwork and history, offers the starting point. "Walking on this earth, receiving stimuli from visible things, Christians enter novel heavenly visions and glories and mysteries."[21] Comprehending nature is not identical with the vision of God. Yet, as in the Irish narratives, it instigates the ascent "to the vision of the Craftsman."[22]

The Celts never lose sight of the fact that natural contemplation is not identical with the vision of God. They also know that creation does not necessarily lead to the knowledge of God. No hypothesis is ever deduced by logical necessity proceeding from a natural datum. Grandeur in the physical world points to the presence of the Author, but it does not reveal His Person. The *In Tenga Bithnua* narrates how the heavens open and how humans are instructed in all that they were ignorant of, or which before was obscure and confusing to them, by the voice of "the Evernew Tongue."[23] The world remains a mirror, and thus we could say that natural revelation lies within the sphere of supernatural revelation: the book of creation is opened by the multiform experience of God's presence. The Absolute Other is the God of history bound up with the historical drama of a people. The Celts also focus on the workings of God in the history of Israel. And the narrative of God's "struggles" is seen as but a glassful of water from the whole sea or a handful of grain from a rich harvest.[24] As an Irish gloss puts it, "the mystery of the nature of God was seen in His guidance of the people through the Red Sea."[25] Revelation is God's epiphany in creation and history, which culminates in the Incarnation. Seen in this light, natural revelation is an aspect and an unraveling of what is beyond creation.

It should be noted that the Celts cultivated a distinct sense of liminality, in which every place became a boundary between this world and the other world, between the material and the spiritual, even between the created and the uncreated. Such a theology is expressed in the existence of the numerous High Crosses raised over the Irish landscape to signify "cosmic entrance and exit points."[26] This is why the Celt is "a listener among the woods,"[27] attentive and vigilant, seeking immediate links to divine life. It is the fact of the multiform presence of God that makes a place or a person a transcendental point of interaction and union between creation and the Creator. Within this scheme of understanding all the mythical images that delineate the mystical experience of the eternal and unoriginate should be interpreted using the framework and colors of created reality.[28] All created things are receptive to new qualities; through the means of a mystical language they participate in the cosmic doxology and function as vehicles of supernatural revelation, which reached its climactic point at the Incarnation.

Natural and supernatural revelation as a single and undivided reality figures powerfully in the "Odyssey" of the spiritual life, the *Navigatio Sancti Brendani*, in which the sensible, the suprasensible, and the uncreated continuously mingle. In one of its more impressive narratives, Brendan foretells that they shall "see the wonders of the Creator" as soon as their *currach* enters a bright pillar made of a crystal mesh that connects the firmament with the unfathomable sea. Here is delineated a crossing over to the dimension of the divine that penetrates the whole universe, an immediate transition from the natural to the supranatural, a foretaste and experience of divine glory. Within the pillar Brendan and his companions could discern the depths of the sea, which appeared as transparent glass. The light of the sun "was as bright within the water as it was without." Nature is illuminated and reveals its mysteries. But we reach the climactic point when at the end of their enquiry and "measurements" they come upon a chalice and a paten made of the same substance and vivid color as the pillar. The offering of the Holy Gifts, the Eucharist, is the ultimate mystery of divine glory. The world becomes a mirror of the eschatological kingdom.[29]

The Person of Christ is the *pleroma* of every revelation. According to a seventh-century Irish hymn, Christ is "*Universorum fontis iubar luminum/ Aethereorum et orbi lucentium.*"[30] Using this image, the hymnographer enters the central subject of the poem, which is that of the life-giving and redeeming Light. Christ, "as the first-born day, shines from the heavenly arch on the vast world."[31] He is behind everything; He lies at the deepest structure of everything: "When angels carry out their commands, when the stars revolve, when the winds alternate, . . . when vines put forth straight shoots and produce their fruit," it is the Father who "acts in the Son."[32] At the same time, it is a common *locus* in Irish and Greek Patristic theology that the Only-Begotten is the subject of the theophanies that have taken place throughout the whole course of history, from the beginning to the last things.[33] Finally, His Incarnation has a cosmic dimension: God, by becoming one with *terram corporis nostri*, assumes every element into Himself. "For every material substance and every element and every nature which is seen in the world were all combined in the Body with which Christ arose, that is, in the body of every human being." Hence, the whole universe has been redeemed in Christ; nature—*ge, aer, ouranos*—follows man in his eschatological glorification.[34]

Creation participates in the events of the divine economy in a particularly intense manner. Not only do all the elements praise God or arm themselves against God's enemies,[35] but they also display a conscious reaction to the event of Christ's Passion. The sun took back its light when it mourned for the Lord, and it was accompanied by the sky and the sea and the whole of creation. The crucified Christ, whom the elements adore as their Author, is the hero of creation.[36] The river Jordan is personified—as it also is in the Greek *troparion* sung for the feast of Christ's baptism—and recognizes and pays honor to the Creator, throwing three pure waves over His head.[37] The two epicenters of the divine work are Christ's birth and resurrection. Nature alters its behavior on Sunday, the day of Resurrection, and, like Zion's well, which changes its beautiful colors during the Offices of the Hours, participates in the liturgical life of the Church, while during vespers one of the precious stones echoes a melody that has no equal under the sun.[38] At the same time, however, contrary to the pagan tradition, created things remain always within their created order.[39] This feature of rational participation by creation is marked in Byzantine hymnography, but it is also present in the whole corpus of Greek patristic literature.[40] As the *Macarian Homily* says, at the birth of Christ "the angels, the heavens, the stars, the sun, the moon, the earth rejoice . . . because long ago the whole of creation roared at its transition to corruption."[41]

But the above writers go further than making mere metaphors or personifications. Material creation is not just a setting but is rather an attendant or partner in worship, for it has within it "insensible life."[42] This life lies at the core of every being and thing. It will never be extinguished since it was in the Logos of God before the ages of ages. As the *Catechesis Celtica* asserts:

> Neither heaven, nor earth and all that are in them . . . dwells in itself but rather in Him, that is, in God. . . . The life of whatever has been

created is in Him; . . . Thus, the creature always remains in the Creator, and therefore he knew his creatures before he made them. For before they were created, they were life in Him, and that life was not created but is itself Creator . . . because the Word is God, then, the life which is in Him is God, and in that life is the light of men and women.[43]

Each thing does not exist in anything other than in Himself, "in His secret bosom," as a "creative word," a thought conceived by Him above time and space. Even that thing which seems to lack all power of movement has life in the Word. Certainly, this is not identical with the Platonic *idea* that divides the intelligible from the visible, God from the cosmos. Rather it is the "incorporeal principle" that the elements held latent within them at the primal creation.[44] This is clearly, though more subtly, articulated by the Cappadocian Fathers as well as by Cyril of Alexandria, who derives the uncreated nature of the Logos from His uncreated and creative life. Thus, commenting on how "all that came to being was life in him" (John 1:3–4), he says: "There is one single life penetrating all things in a manner that meets each one's premises and capacity of participation," "through an unutterable manner of communion."[45] Their great descendants, Maximus the Confessor and the unknown Areopagite, are in consensus: "The being of all things is the supraessential Deity," the life subsistent in the *hypostasis* of the Logos.[46] No wonder that the array of elements together with the heavenly hosts and the Trinity are invoked by the Irish poet to be His shield, since the cosmos is a carrier of God's vibrant grandeur.[47]

Therefore, God's providential governance is not merely a kind of equitable management: the relationship between God and creation lies not in what is created but in His uncreated life that fills all things and gives everything its appropriate nature. This is "ever since the creation of the world, his eternal power and divine nature" (Rom. 1:20), what the Greek Fathers call divine energy or energies. This energy is God "going out" of Himself; to wit, it is uncreated, since it is the natural "movement" or "radiance" of the unapproachable and incomprehensible Divine essence.[48] The energy-essence distinction, implicit in the Bible, lies not in the sphere of philosophical speculation but in the field of experience, safeguarding both the reality of God's transcendence and the actual participation in His being yet not in His essence. By virtue of that experiential distinction, which was forsaken by Scholastic theology, the Celtic mind was never afraid of pantheism when proclaiming the real presence of the Holy Trinity within every element and every person.[49] That is why the Irish as well as the Greek Fathers express their theology in antinomies: God is seen and invisible, known and imperceptible, within all and beyond all.[50]

A juxtaposition of the apocalyptic *In Tenga Bithnua* and the treatise *De mirabilibus Sacrae Scripturae* by Augustinus Hibernicus[51] indicates the parallel existence of both a mystical and a rational current, which leads us to what on the surface would appear to be a contradiction concerning the Celtic understanding of the divine presence in the world. Yet the main theological and empirical thread in both these works is the belief that God is present in every component of His creation. The Irish Augustine, embarking on a daring investigation of marvels in sacred history, opposes the understanding that the miraculous intervention of God is a sort of supernatural revelation irrelevant or contrary to nature. He attributes the majority of miracles to the first and perfect act of creation, when the Creator endowed the nature of each creature with all these capacities, an act that only subsequently appeared to our reasoning as exceptional divine interventions subverting natural laws. Our perception can grasp and consolidate the usual functioning of creatures, yet God governs them as He wills, and His will is perceived as a *"ratio superior"* recognized in miracles.[52]

The assumption of Augustine is that the whole of creation is a wondrous mystery of divine providence precisely because it is governed.[53] This forms an essential part of the Irish background of Augustine,[54] and for this reason he refutes the existence of any divide between the natural and the supranatural. In the final analysis, everything is regarded as natural since it is attributed to God's creative act. God does not cancel or violate any of the laws He established because creation was perfect. God is not a "changer of natures." Thus the Irish prefer the exegesis that the Holy Spirit appeared to the Magi in the form of a star rather than that the change of the corporeal star's behavior was a result of the alteration of its nature.[55] As for the Cappadocians, they see any progressive formation as having its beginning in the potential that is intrinsic to all nature.[56] That is why Augustine and Basil share the idea of the organic quality of material forms, manifested in their capacity of growing or exerting a living force.[57] But even in St. Basil, the stability of the species is subsumed in a concept of evolution: an olive comes not from a reed but a reed from a reed; everything originates from the relative seed.[58] The ecological repercussions of this thesis are evident: God does not violate nature but unceasingly governs her with unfathomable providential care. Accordingly, God's behavior is reflected in the lives of His imitators. The wondrous deeds of the saints operate for the restoration of nature in its integrity and harmony against the artifice of the evil powers.[59]

This thesis is in accord with the Celtic conception that lies behind the inverted formula of the Eucharist.[60] What happens to the bread and wine of the Eucharist when neither the essential nature nor the external qualities (the accidents of the species) are affected? The Eucharist is presented as a change of Christ Himself into bread and wine rather than the opposite. Eschewing doctrines of transubstantiation, one could easily think that this interpretation invalidates any question concerning the kind of change that happens to these material substances. But in this understanding there is no question of nature changing substance: it is God who is "transfigured"[61] by uniting Himself with His creation in a charismatic and unconfused manner. This concept of God's "embodiments" so that He may be participated in by His creatures is also delineated in Greek texts, the most clear expression being given in the Macarian corpus.[62] The Word becoming flesh was the highest transfiguration. It is for this reason that the theophanic event on Mount Tabor has a catalytic importance in the theology of the Greek Fathers, for it signifies the ultimate disclosure of the Divinity through the incarnate—that is, "transfigured"—*hypostasis* of the Logos, and thus it affirms man's capability of partaking in God's nature.[63]

Returning to Augustinus Hibernicus, we feel that his theology cultivates not only awe before the Creator but also wonder and respect for creation. In the instances that Augustine is unable to give a natural exegesis to a miracle, he posits a phenomenological transmutation of natures that takes place in order that a sign may be given.[64] Yet there are cases that go beyond these norms—theophanic events, like the burning bush and the Lord's transfiguration on Tabor, where an "opening" through the material substance to the invisible inherent Divinity occurs.[65] For Augustine, because the "natural" stems from the ubiquitous creative presence of the Divinity, it acquires a much broader sense. Why should the fact that the divine word sustained Moses during his fast or, hypostatically united with human flesh, nourished Christ's joints and sinews in the desert be labeled supranatural?[66] That something is strange to human experience does not mean that it is unnatural; it might be the manifestation of an invisible and hidden law.[67]

The *fundamentum* of all *mirabilia* is an eternal and immutable act of will. We will not be far from truth if we recognize in the Irish Augustine's thought an identification of divine will with natural laws in the perfection of God's love, as is the case with the Greek Fathers. For the latter, everything is a substantiation of the Word: "in the case of God, the Word is the work."[68] God has set within His creation an infinite fabric of interdependences, without this meaning that His absolute freedom is bound by created nature.

Thus, from the point of view of the relationship of man with creation, the Irish Doctor is moving along the lines of St. Basil. The whole of creation is stable in its holiness, because it is identical with the miracle itself. "The miracle is the structure of creation, since creation is sustained in life and kept in harmony by the creative Word through natural determinacy."[69] For St. Basil, God's intervention is an infinite expansion of the fabric of natural laws. A miracle extends this order to other states of perfection. The present natural order is neither an immutable entity, nor is it known except to a certain degree. Its dimensions are continuously widening, but, in spite of that, they do not fall away from their order, since all is determined and governed "according to the first causes of harmony."[70] The Irish Augustine does not use the evolutionary theory of Basil; after all, he has not the broad cosmological horizon of the Cappadocian. Nevertheless, his thesis is not far from the Basilian assumption, according to which the "instilled power" waits for God's orders.[71] God's operations were carried out "timelessly,"[72] but henceforth the whole of creation is preserved in His power and loving care, which illuminates, nourishes, guides, heals, raises up.[73] These activities are God's *logos*, which "run through creation." Thus natural laws are nothing but the ceaseless outpouring of divine energies, which become the "law of nature."[74]

It is true that the Greeks, although they may have undertaken or encouraged the scientific approach to creation, do not proceed to a similar rationalist method for defining miracles. A miracle escapes all natural regularity and outdoes the plausible arguments of the wise.[75] But even Augustinus Hibernicus is not eager to give final interpretations of reality. His insistence shows a refutation of the magical rather than an attempt to naturalize the supernatural.[76] In other respects he would wholeheartedly embrace the statement of the Irish exegete that God, as Father, Son, and Holy Spirit, works miracles daily, like the miracle of men's conversion.[77] In fact, for the Greek Fathers the new work of God is not the creation of new laws and new natures but the transformation, healing, and deification of man. The "greater work" is Christ's planting of "a new heaven and a new earth" in the soul of man, or, in other words, the implantation of new eyes, new ears, a new tongue, a new mind in the anointing by the Spirit.[78]

Celts and Greeks are not anxious to divide either the world or revelation into a natural and a supernatural part. God's revelation, either on the level of creation or in the realm of sacred history, is a single, transcendent, and ever-present reality. The physical cosmos and human beings are *loci* of theophanies. And theophanies are as natural as they are incomprehensible. In the various wonderful events, we discern the immediate action of immanent divine grace, which is manifested as natural laws. And grace names neither an extraneous instrument of the distant Maker nor some order of entities somewhere between Uncreated-Grace-in-action and the natural order. As "the King shaped every creature . . . without the fair mystery of enchantment,"[79] He also governs the whole of creation, not through what is created but within the infinite matrix of His essential energies. Thus the splendors of heaven and earth, no less than divine interventions, make up sacred history. The bright King of the Mysteries "has revealed to us every wonder, that through them . . . and through the multitude of His miracles, we may understand Him."[80]

God fills everything and surpasses everything.[81] The Celtic and the Greek minds insist on divine immanence without overlooking or relativizing the ontological gap between the created and the uncreated. Or, to put it more accurately, they insist on divine immanence because they recognize the meaning of such an ontological disparity. This radical divide absorbs any other division of existence within created nature or any division of God's revelation in the world and in history. For the whole of material and spiritual reality is utterly dependent on the Uncreated. That is why the supernatural—as a level higher than nature—finds no place in the Irish Augustine's line of thought, not because there is no place for mystery but because the whole of creation abides within the God of mysteries. In this unity, God is revealed either through a created nature or by communicating His radiance in person.[82] He is revealed in the whole of dynamic creation, in every particle of nature moving in history, by a multiplicity of symbols, yet in an immediate and energetic mode. That is why the Irish exegesis of the Lord's Transfiguration follows the interpretative lines of the Greek Fathers, emphasizing the direct disclosure of divinity through the flesh and its transformational power upon creation.

ECOLOGY AND MONASTICISM
Archimandrite Vasileios

I ask for your blessing, because I have nothing to say. I ask for your blessing, but I ask your indulgence as well, because I have nothing to give. I wish to thank all of you because I believe this gathering has been holy and sacred. That we are all working together and have come to some mutual understanding gives me a great deal of satisfaction. Everyone has helped, and I think we have already identified where our topic is to be found.

I believe, then, that the problem is to be found within us; all love and beneficence are found in God, but all wretchedness and loss of dignity are found in man. St. Isaac the Syrian says that God is so great in love that He does not want to infringe upon our freedom, even when our freedom rebels against Him. And Creation itself, which "not of its own will" (Rom. 8:20) has been subjected to corruption, waits for mankind to do something. Thus, we live out the whole drama of the Fall—and there is only one solution: to return to Paradise if we are able and to discover what it means to *cultivate* and *keep* it (Gen. 2:15).[1]

A monk may feel that because he has become a monk, he is at rest.[2] A true monk is truly human. An Orthodox Christian may be at rest because he is truly Orthodox—that is, he has become a true human being; Orthodoxy offers the power and potential for every person to live genuinely. If this were not true, then we could discard Orthodoxy and everything else!

I

And so God placed man within Paradise to "cultivate it and keep it," but we neither cultivated nor kept it as God had wanted. Nonetheless, our nature cannot be changed regardless of whether we believe or not. We have the breath of God within us; we possess something that is great yet causes affliction. St. Symeon the New Theologian says: "I long for something more, and so I am always sighing and groaning"—I am never tranquil nor quiet within. Our calling is to progress toward *theosis* (deification). This never-ending journey and progress toward God is directed, as St. Gregory of Nyssa says, toward the vision of the face of God. We don't just sit somewhere, inactive, looking at things around us, but are on a course toward Someone. "I come to Thee" (John 17:11) says the Lord; we live the vision of the face of God. In Paradise we chose not to live this vision in the way God wanted us to. We decided to do it rebelliously, by our own will and in cooperation with the Devil. Now this is the same devil who, because he knows human nature, made up a "theology." He didn't say: "Now look here, if you want to live well and get away from God do this. . . ." Rather he said: "You should do this, if you wish to become God." For we want to become gods and gain everything. And we have lost it all.

The Son of God came and became the Son of man; He became man to teach us how we must act in order to gain everything. Thus, man was the lord of nature; through his rebellious behavior he lost both himself and his lordship of nature. The Lord came to show what lordship really means. He said to His disciples: "You call Me Teacher and Lord; and you are right, but now see how I act" (John 13:13, 15). And later he says: "You know that those presuming to rule the nations lord it over them and their great ones exercise authority over them. But it is not so among you . . ." (Mark 10:42–43). Note that He does not say "those who rule" but "those who think they rule." It is not to be this way among us because whoever wishes to be great must become the servant of all, and whoever wishes to be first must become the slave of all, for the Son of man did not come "to be served, but to serve, and to give His life as a ransom for many" (Matt. 20:28). In this way everything is turned upside down. It is as if the Lord is saying, "Do you really want to become masters of yourselves and of creation? Is this mankind's mission? You will not accomplish it through your own logic and reasoning nor by the prompting of the evil one. Nor will you accomplish it by the world's logic, but on the contrary, by becoming servants of all and slaves."

So now there is a new mode of being. As it has been said, man is in the image of God because he exists as a person in communion with others, in community. And the Lord, through His behavior, His life, His Passion and Resurrection, taught us the kenotic (self-emptying) mode of existence. We exist—but not to lord it over another. But one might ask, "am I not a lord?"

Very well, this may be attained by becoming a servant to everyone else. One may exist and want to eat so as to live, but not by devouring others. Rather, one should become edible food and drinkable drink for someone else.

This is what the Lord teaches us. I recall another saying from the Gerontikon[3] that relates how the devil once saw a certain monk sitting and doing nothing. He asked him: "Monk, what are you doing here?" The elder replied: "I am keeping this place." The devil said: "Leave him alone; he's a bit mad." But I think that monk's response, "I am keeping this place," has a theological meaning that brings to mind God's command in the Book of Genesis "to keep" Paradise (Gen. 2:15).

II

I recall another incident: A certain man who had come to our monastery went down to the evening service. Afterward he said, "I could never live in a monastery because I can't understand why you stay in church for so many hours doing nothing. I am a man of action, and I like to work." Initially it seemed to me that his assessment was fair, but after a short time a thought came to me as I was entering the church one winter's night. What do monks do inside the church? They don't do anything! They simply dwell[4] in the church. What does an embryo do in its mother's womb? It doesn't do anything, but because it is inside the womb, it grows and develops. Just so, the monk is in his mother's womb; he keeps the place in which he is and is kept by that place. This place has been sanctified, and, consequently, it molds us. One senses in an instant that here a miracle is taking place: here we are entering Paradise, and we don't even realize it! The very thing the Lord said is happening: "Others toiled, and into their rewards you have entered" (John 4:38). We find ourselves within the heart of the communion of the Saints. St. Isaac the Syrian says that the Saints in the kingdom of heaven do not pray but "dwell in the courts of joyful glory." That is to say, they do not pray with prayer because the act of prayer has been *surpassed*; they exist in a state beyond prayer.[5] Now someone may ask: "I pray, and that which appears to be dark may in fact possess much light. A great light may be called a dark cloud because of its 'abundance of illumination.'"[6]

These passages are based on the account of God's appearance to Moses on Mt. Sinai: "Now Mount Sinai was all in smoke because the Lord descended upon it in fire," (Ex. 19:18) and "Moses drew near to the darkness/thick cloud where God was." (Ex. 20:21) The answer then is, "Yes, *you* should pray." "However, the Saints in the Kingdom of Heaven do not—should I not pray?" Often things pray. Instead of prayer, they "dwell in the courts of joyful glory"; they remain in a state of glory.

III

I recall something a certain monk once told me. I had visited this old man, a simple monk, in his hermitage and had asked him: "What do you do, Fr. Timothy?" He replied, "I dwell here." This phrase, "I *dwell* here," says everything. A real monk deeply feels this phrase "here I remain and I dwell." Now someone might say to him: "But what do you *do*?" "Thousands of things are happening, but it isn't necessary to explain and justify everything," the monk might reply. Have you read the verses where the Lord says: "I am the vine and you are the branches" and "my Father is the Vine Dresser" (John 15:5, 1)? The flow of sap from the roots to the branches, this entire process, occurs ceaselessly and silently, without any noise at all. A monk who lives in a monastery such as those on Mt. Athos, in an Orthodox environment, is like a vine or tree planted in its proper climate. As a monk, you feel *at rest* because, what do you do? In that place, in that monastery, you dwell, you live and understand that there is a single essence and purpose for both the soul and the body. You understand that there is a bond between daily life and spiritual life, that daily life is not separated from spiritual life, and that prayer is not separated from work. You sense that others in the past have done much and that you are doing very little or perhaps even nothing at all. And then what happens? Those others, the Saints, force you to be responsible by treating you with leniency when by rights they ought to be upbraiding you. But we upbraid others many times since we are impure, and we even act the teacher toward them. In leaving you free, those who are pure bind you hand and foot. And because you know that they know what you are, you remain at a loss and say: "Fine, okay." What, then, have they accomplished? They have succeeded in achieving union, that is, reconciliation and harmony between God, mankind, and nature; they have brought you into subjection by setting you free; they have enslaved you with their love.

"I *am keeping* this place" (Gen. 2:15), and it *keeps* me. The saints followed the Lord's way of life. This grace was given to them, and they were made holy in soul and body. In other words, they found *rest*, they were freed, they comprehended what man is and entered Paradise, which is freedom from death. Afterward, when over the course of time their soul has been separated from their body, God's grace remains with both their soul and body. Because of this their soul is now seen invisibly; it is manifested and empowers everyone.

Thus St. John of Damascus says that holy relics of the saints, their icons and graves, are full of the grace that their souls and bodies had while they were on earth.[7] Since man is a union of soul and body, both of these have need of deification (*theosis*). This deification was fulfilled by the Lord and has been given as a potentiality to the Church; it has been actualized by the saints. One perceives that by living in the Church and accepting the grace of God through prayer and hymnody, one is strengthened physically. And while one is being nourished bodily at the refectory table as well as by the Garden of the Panagia[8] and her gifts, one feels at the same time spiritually nourished. If this is the case, then the question of "man's relationship to the natural environment" no longer exists as a problem but rather as a physiological and natural relationship. The essence of this relationship is the great wonder and miracle of the Logos (Word) becoming flesh, which "we beheld and our hands handled" (John 1:4 and 1 John 1:1). And by grace that flesh became Logos, so that now, in the words of St. John of Damascus, matter is "replete with divine grace."[9]

IV

In the *Agioreitikos Tomos*, St. Gregory Palamas[10] writes that at the Lord's Transfiguration, His face became radiant, and the uncreated glory of divinity was revealed as the glory of the Lord's body. But the glory of the body is invisible to those "not capable of bearing the things hidden also from the angels." For the glory of the body is the glory of uncreated divinity, which has no beginning; for one to be able to see this glory of the body, one must be worthy—through humility and purification to see the mysteries hidden even to angels. Then one would see that the Lord's created body shines with uncreated grace; His garments shine with the same grace; the Body of the Church shines also with the same grace. In the liturgical texts of the Paschal Resurrection service, we say the Lord is risen, and in rising, He raises up the whole world with Him, "the human world," in the words of the *Synaxarion* for Pascha.[11] In the Orthodox Church, the icon of the Resurrection does not depict Christ smiling above the tomb as if He had accomplished some individualistic feat but rather presents Him with a face so joyful that it appears at the same time sorrowful. He is shown pulling up those "bound in shackles" and drawing out all of the condemned from death into life and from darkness into light. And we sing at Pascha: "Now all things are filled with light—heaven, earth, and the infernal underworld." When one lives within the Orthodox Church, one experiences this as reality, as ontological fact. And when we sing that "all the trees of the forest are rejoicing today; their nature has been sanctified because the Body of Christ was stretched out upon a tree," this too is experienced as reality.

But the question is—how can someone see this glory of the body and the glory of creation? How does one see that "all the trees of the forest rejoice" or that "the universe is today filled with joy" because "Christ is born of the Virgin?" I think that when one lives within the Church in a self-emptying way and perceives that through obedience to the will of God by means of love and humility one can reach true communion and glory, then these things can be understood. In Bergman's film *The Communards*, there is a scene where things are presented realistically as Bergman sees them, which is to say, black and wretched. And at the moment when everything is pitch dark, when Bergman has fully convinced his audience that life is totally black, he brings in the liturgical phrase: "Holy, Holy, Holy is the Lord of hosts, heaven and earth are full of Your glory" (Is. 6:3). He does this to be ironic, but it nonetheless expresses a real subjective pain of mankind. To the contrary, heaven and earth are indeed full of the Lord's glory. Moreover, it is possible for us to see this glory.

V

Now perhaps we should not speak of the lives of Saints who lived in some distant past. Perhaps we should speak of things that affect those of us who live today. St. Isaac the Syrian says that the humble person has put on the same garments that the Lord put on when He became man.[12] All of creation looks on this humble man as God by grace, and while such a person considers himself to be nothing, everyone else honors him. The humble person, who is a man of love, gives position and standing to others. He is, as St. Isaac says, "like a man who has not come into being," as though he were nonexistent. And with his being "nonexistent," he infringes on no one else's space, giving them the possibility and power to live. If someone is an egotist or is constantly boasting about himself, he distances others from him. On the other hand, if one is pure, says St. Isaac, his purity will be manifest in that he sees everyone else as pure. We have all been talking about repentance. St. Isaac asks: "What is repentance?" It is to stop doing what we've been doing up until now and not to repeat it. And what is the next step? The next step is purity. What, then, is purity? St. Isaac does not define purity as not doing this or that, but rather he goes beyond purity to say that it is "a heart merciful to all creation." To say that one is pure means that he sees everyone but himself as pure: no one else appears profane to him. And purity, like fire, consumes the profane, which he considers himself to be. The pure person loves everyone, says St. Isaac. What does mercy mean? It means a heart that burns for all creation, for every person and every animal; it is a heart burning for the enemies of truth and even for the devil. Further on, St. Isaac writes that such a person prays with tears and cannot bear to see even a reptile or the smallest leaf of a plant suffering; such a person acts "according to the likeness of God." Such a person is incapable of not praying, weeping, and suffering out of love for the whole of creation. This is his very breath; it is the presupposition and mode of his existence. Therefore, although he may be standing still, he is in constant motion, and though he does not do anything, everything around him and within him functions on its own; it reveals Him who has existed from the beginning and who will continue to exist when all things have passed away. Everything reveals the eternal meaning, mission, and worth of what is transient and temporal. This man is the new man, the new creation, a theophany and an *anthropophany*, or manifestation of man as he was meant to be. He is an opportunity for the reconciliation of all things into one and the blessing thereof, while at the same time a shining of light and a radiation of love. He expands so as to embrace in himself the whole of creation; by grace he himself becomes the "land of the uncontainable" (*chora tou ahoritou*).

VI

If by chance a person supposes that he loves the creation and, instead of worshipping God, worships creation, he dishonors the creation. If he happens to love certain animals with sentimentality but tortures man at the same time, he dishonors the animals as well. Creation seeks neither worship nor contempt from us; Creation seeks but one thing—for us to be truly human. And this is not a matter of "returning to nature" but of returning to a life lived according to our God-given nature. And to live according to our nature is to become gods by grace. It is then that we shall honor God, worship Him, love our brethren, and perceive that we are of one substance with them. At the same time, we shall perceive that all creation is fashioned by God and that we are ordained to be lords of it. This will be actualized when we become the servants and slaves of creation. According to St. Isaac, the whole problem is within us. He says, "know yourself and you will know everything." "Whoever submits himself to God is close to having everything submitted to him." In other words, if one submits oneself to God, everything will be submitted to him. He goes on to say, "be at peace with yourself, and heaven and earth will be at peace with you." Someone might protest, "but the world today is going through such radical and fundamental changes!" It doesn't matter; it's not important. "But the threat of nuclear war, of nuclear holocaust!" he or she might reply. It doesn't matter; St. Isaac says that if heaven fell and flattened the earth, the humble person would not be perturbed because other kinds of changes have already occurred within him, changes greater and more powerful.

In a meeting, once, a student said to me: "But how can you say such things? Right here we are threatened by a nuclear holocaust that will turn the earth into ashes!" I felt for him and what he was saying. "Certainly," I said, "this is not an impossibility." It was just before Holy Week, and when I later went up to Mount Athos, I attended the liturgy and services of Holy Week and Pascha; I lived, if you like, the "calamity" of Pascha, the Lord's humiliating death on the Cross and His glorious Resurrection. Then I said to myself: "Nothing can happen while this 'calamity' fills everything with light—heaven, earth, and the infernal underworld, then let all the calamities come!" Anyway, a calamity such as a nuclear disaster is perhaps better than living a false and sham way of life. If we wish to acquire everything (and everything is ours to acquire), we will do so by not having anything. We must be "as having nothing yet possessing all things" (2 Cor. 6:10). It is for this reason that in the service in which a monk is tonsured, the Gospel read for the occasion says: "For whoever wishes to save his life shall lose it; but whoever loses it for My sake shall find it" (Matt. 16:25). "All things came into being through Him (Jesus Christ); and apart from Him nothing came into being that has come into being" (John 1:3). If we happen to want to gain these things, we will gain them in Christ Jesus. We will gain everything by giving everything to Christ.

The Prophetic Charisma in Pastoral Theology: Asceticism, Fasting, and the Ecological Crisis

Anestis Keselopoulos

In the Orthodox Church, the core of the prophetic charisma is neither the gift of making apocalyptic statements about impending doom nor the gift of uttering words of encouragement about a resolution to contemporary problems in the future. The heart of prophecy consists of an experience of revelation in which the vision of Christ in glory transfigures the person who beholds Him. Saint John the Theologian explicitly refers to this when he remarks that "these things said Isaiah when He saw His glory, and spoke of Him" (John 12:41). The sixth chapter of Isaiah relates his vision of the Second Person of the Holy Trinity as follows: "I saw also the Lord sitting upon a throne, high and lifted up, and his train filled the temple. Above it stood the seraphim: each one had six wings; with two, he covered his face, and with two, he covered his feet, and with two, he did fly. And one cried unto another, and said, Holy, holy, holy, is the Lord of hosts: the whole earth is full of His glory." This prophetic vision, also understood as a state of *theosis*, brings clarity to human thought, for it equips the prophet with a sure knowledge of the principles underlying the created realm[1] as well as "a partial understanding of the wisdom of God that governs all things."[2] The prophet who has beheld Christ in glory can then offer guidance for the salvation of God's children with the clear-sighted vision of spiritual knowledge.[3]

Of course, the gift of prophecy as the transfiguring vision of Christ is not an experience that is limited to the Bible, but it instead continues to be manifested in the Saints of every age, who behold the glorified Christ in this life and leave their writings as precious guidance for the faithful on their journey toward salvation. In Greek, the word for salvation (*sōteria*) is derived from the word *sōos*, which implies a solid wholeness that commences in this life through man's obedience to God and culminates in the next with the vision of God Himself. Patristic guidance toward salvation not only offers prophetic words about man's restoration to wholeness; it also prophetically reveals in the Holy Spirit all those things that injure the truth and undermine man's future, his quality of life, and his salvation.

Today's world is understandably concerned and anxious about the crisis over man's relationship to his natural environment. Strangely enough, although we find ourselves facing phenomena that testify to man's rape of nature, there is often not even the slightest suspicion that this crisis is not merely scientific or technological but preeminently spiritual. For this reason, the containment solutions, which are proposed from time to time to surmount the crisis, tend to range from the search for some better form of technology to a "return to nature" in the spirit of the romantics. From this perspective, it is highly significant that the prophetic voice of Orthodox theology stresses the spiritual dimension of the ecological crisis and suggests that it can be overcome through an alternative vision of the world and understanding of life.

As early as March 1992, the ruling hierarchs of the Orthodox Churches gathered at the Phanar in Constantinople and concluded their session with an encyclical intended for a worldwide audience and promulgated on the Sunday of Orthodoxy. This message included the following explicit reference to the dangers that threaten the survival of the natural environment:

> Man's unreasonable use of creation in the materialistic pursuit of happiness, in conjunction with scientific and technological progress, has already begun to give rise to irreparable damage to the natural environment. Refusing to remain indifferent in the face of such destruction, the Orthodox Church, through us her bishops, calls all Orthodox Christians to dedicate the first September of each year, the day of the commencement of the ecclesiastical year, to prayer and supplication on behalf of the preservation of God's creation as well as the adoption of a stance towards nature that is consistent with the Divine Eucharist and the ascetic tradition of the Church.

This prophetic remark not only underlines the causes that provoked the ecological crisis but also presents the framework that the Orthodox Church considers a presupposition for surmounting it. If the principal cause of the irreparable damage to the environment lies in man's unreasonable use of creation in the materialistic pursuit of happiness, in conjunction with scientific and technological progress, the adoption of a stance toward nature that is consistent with the Divine Eucharist and the ascetic tradition of the

Church can offset the crisis with an approach whose interpretive tradition spans the ages.

Of course, at this point, we must stress that people a few decades earlier were not speaking about an ecological crisis or even an ecological problem. The ecological crisis is a contemporary phenomenon. From this perspective, one could presume that it is not possible to find in Church tradition an immediately relevant solution or guidance for overcoming it. However, the ecological crisis is not a dissociated independent phenomenon but is rather the most recent development in a continuous series of earlier processes and crises that stem from man's inner crisis. Moreover, this crisis is of special concern not only to the Orthodox Church that has always centered her solicitude on man and his problems but also to the entirety of biblical and patristic theology. It should also be emphasized from the onset that it is not possible to understand correctly the contemporary ecological crisis and to speak decisively about coming to grips with it or solving it unless we take into consideration its origins, which are identified by the prophetic voice of Orthodox pastoral theology.

What is the prophetic word uttered by a patristic interpretation of Holy Scripture and relevant to the ecological problem? At the foundation of the ecological crisis lies the human aspiration to become god without God. Man undertakes any venture and exploits all things in order to fulfill his desire to "be perfected" and to perfect his life. In his initiatives, however, he both ignores the will of God and refuses to shoulder his own personal responsibility for his deeds. Contemporary man lives and acts in a way that is strikingly reminiscent of the Old Testament description of the ancestral sin. Then, man disregarded God's commandment and attributed the responsibility of his actions to others. The same scenario is also repeated today when man acts selfishly and refuses to take his share of the responsibility for the accumulated ills in this world. Moreover, when he ignores God and makes a sharp contrast between himself and everything else apart from himself, he becomes incapable of lovingly embracing both the environment and his fellow man. The separation of man from God lies at the foundation of his estrangement from the rest of humanity, from the natural environment, and from his own self. For this reason, in the final analysis, this sin constitutes the primal cause and very core of the ecological crisis.

Man's responsibility and culpability for this fallen state that encompasses all of creation and today appears as the ecological crisis is highlighted with some emphasis in the New Testament. In particular, Saint Paul notes that the creation is unwillingly subjected to vanity and enslavement: "For the creation was made subject to vanity, not willingly, but by reason of him who subjugated it." In this verse, it is clearly evident not only that man and creation influence and depend on each other in their passage through time and history but also that nature, which is commonly referred to as soulless and considered to be without volition, has been subjected to this condition against her will.

Starting from this biblical foundation, the Church Fathers prophetically note that creation's enslaved state is not a natural development. In their texts, creation appears as a victim since, on man's account, she has lost her cosmic position and pristine form, regardless of whether some consider her present state to be natural. Furthermore, this is why the creation refuses to submit to man, the transgressor. One of the Church Fathers describes creation's relationship with and stance toward man after the Fall as follows:

> Beholding Adam dissociate himself from God and withdraw from paradise, the entire creation, fashioned by God from non-being, no longer wished to subject herself to the transgressor: the sun no longer wished to shine; the moon was unwilling to release her beams; the stars preferred to no longer appear before his eyes; the sources of water had no reason to gush forth. The rivers did not wish to flow, while the air considered receding, so that man who rebelled against God would not be able to breathe. When the beasts and all the animals of the earth saw man stripped of his former glory, they abhorred him en masse and became hardened against him. The sky rightfully made him stir about by threatening to fall upon him and the earth did not consent to carry him on its shoulders.

The patristic interpretation of the Fall furthermore identifies the correct use of creation with fasting. In Orthodox tradition, fasting is characterized as "a commandment stemming from life itself and coeval with human nature." God's first commandment to man is framed as follows: "Of every tree of the garden thou mayest freely eat: But of the tree of the knowledge of good and evil, thou shalt not eat of it: for in the day that thou eatest thereof thou shalt surely die." The central position that fasting holds in the tradition of the Orthodox Church is neither coincidental nor unrelated to the ecological crisis but has unmistakable prophetic significance. Fasting is not some outward conventional act but the voluntary privation of food that heightens man's awareness of his dependency on the outside world. This awareness has decisive importance for ethics. By fasting, man obediently accepts the divine commandment so that he can grow into the likeness of God. In so doing, he recognizes his created nature. In other words, he acknowledges that his "very being is on loan." In the opposite case, the thoughtless use of the fruits of nature, which is associated with disobedience, shows in practice that man doubts that his created nature is borrowed. This has not only led man to his estrangement and alienation from God but has also condemned all of creation that "groaneth and travaileth in pain together until now."

At this point, however, we should make a clarification: true fasting can never be characterized as human disdain or indifference to the physical world. At another level, such a stance would indicate alienation from God and being "conformed to this world," which unfortunately often characterizes certain Christian communities. Despite the abundance of protestations about materialism, society is profoundly idealistic at heart, so much so that it basically hates and despises the world and nature. Man's superiority complex and unjustifiable pride vis-à-vis the rest of creation compel him to look at whatever exists around him merely as means, as utilitarian tools that can assist him in achieving his goals.

This deeply entrenched idealism of contemporary man is precisely what has cut him off from his bodily roots and inevitably causes him to be arbitrary in his dealings with things that indicate his materiality. Truly, he finds himself in a tragic vicious cycle, in which his agonizing struggle to emphasize and promote his material character leads to the destruction of his very materiality, since he devours his very body, which is to say, that extension of his body which is creation. In this way, however, he devours and destroys his very self. Only when man is occasionally roused from his slumber by the very course of events does he become aware that his daily life wreaks havoc on the foundations of his existence, even though he himself severs the branch that he casts aside. Only then does he allow cries of dismay to be heard about the destruction of the environment, the depletion of natural resources, the pollution of the atmosphere, the contamination of rivers and lakes, and so on.

Most tragically, no prophetic voice can be heard broaching the subject of the spiritual basis for this situation or challenging the "theological" criteria that guide a culture that nourishes and then imposes this position on life vis-à-vis the world. From the prophetic vantage point of Orthodox pastoral theology, the ecological crisis is a phenomenon that indisputably testifies to the estrangement of created man from the uncreated God, and this is the result of the severance of living beings and life itself from their ontological Source. This is, moreover, the cause of every human problem, the root of every crisis, and the fountainhead of every ill. Saint Basil the Great notes: "This is evil—alienation from God." This is what puts man in opposition to the world and his very self. And that is not surprising, since man, like the world, was created by God.

Fasting and the ascetic way of life that characterized the Prophets, Apostles, and Saints deeply affect the human approach to creation. Those Saints who lived ascetically were compassionate and sympathetic toward the rest of creation. They had a merciful heart. "And what is a merciful heart?" Saint Isaac the Syrian explains,

> It is a heart's burning for the sake of the entire creation, for men, for birds, for animals . . . and for every created thing; and by the recollection and sight of them the eyes of a merciful man pour forth abundant tears. From the strong and vehement mercy, which grips his heart, and from his great compassion, his heart is humbled and he cannot bear to hear or to see any injury or slight sorrow in creation. For this reason he offers up tearful prayer continually even for irrational beasts, for the enemies of the truth, and for those who harm him, that they be protected and receive mercy. And in like manner he even prays for the family of reptiles because of the great compassion that burns without measure in his heart in the likeness of God.

This same stance toward creation is conveyed by other holy ascetics. Abba Dorotheus not only provides us with the characteristic feature of the correct relationship between man and matter in the form of things; he also defines the boundaries of true materialism, in other words, of the proper human love for material things. He notes, "A good conscience with respect to material objects means not misusing anything and not letting anything be ruined or thrown away." Finally, a Saint of our age, the venerable Silouan of Mount Athos, used to say that the Spirit of God teaches compassion for all of creation, so that not even a leaf from a tree is plucked off without necessity.

Thus, asceticism prophetically throws into high relief the prerequisite of compassion and pity for both nature and the beauty of the world. This is what can impede the downward spiral into barbarism that murders the animal kingdom by genetically mutating animals raised for beef or dairy products into freaks of nature and makes the land infertile with all manner of insecticides and herbicides. If the motive for all these human activities is insatiable greed and the desire for easy profits, then fasting, as a voluntary self-restriction of human needs, can enable man to free himself at least to a certain degree from his desires, so that he can again discover his pristine character, which is to turn toward God, his neighbor, and creation with a genuinely loving disposition. Abstinence from meat, observed by monks all year long and by the rest of Orthodox Christians on the two fasting days during the week and the four Lents of the ecclesiastical year, limits the amount of death we provoke in our relationship to the world. Thus, the institution of fasting is not unrelated to ecology, since it consists of a practical position regarding consumption. Abstinence from certain foods simultaneously aims at protecting, even for a short period of time, animals that in great numbers are so cruelly devoured by man. Obviously for this reason, it has been noted that "the spirit of fasting that we are obliged to preserve today throughout our culture requires that we change course in our relationship to nature from a predatory thirst for blood to that state of gratitude, which is the distinctive mark of the Eucharist."

It is certainly prophetic that, at a time when the subject of an ecological crisis or problem did not exist, ecclesiastical tradition not only ingrained in man a healthy conscience with respect to protecting the environment—as the texts we referred to earlier clearly document—but also identified the spiritual dimension and cause of the problem. Ten centuries before today's ecological stalemate and land-utilization impasse, Saint Symeon the New Theologian considered how man deals with the world and material goods and noted the connection between environmental predicament and the social problem of the unequal distribution of life's necessities. He also stressed that both misfortunes are an outgrowth of one and the same problem, the spiritual plight of mankind. Availing himself of the teachings of the Gospel, he set forth a scathing critique on the social class of his age, a class that for him symbolized both the mistreatment of the world as an unrelated independent entity and a lifestyle of lavish prodigality. The tendency to acquire wealth, to build fences, to appropriate tracts of land, to be greedy, to devour everything with a rapacious insatiability, which have all contributed to the social problem, has today engendered the ecological crisis. In his catechetical homilies, he especially attacks the institution of private property as the source of social injustice and human suffering in both the particular case of the ownership of lands and the more general context of money.

Material goods wield an oppressive tyranny over man because of his efforts, consciously or unconsciously, to detach them utterly from himself and to worship them "instead of the One Who created them." By dealing with nature and man as unrelated independent entities, by rejecting every connection or reference to the cause of their existence, contemporary society makes it difficult not only to identify the real cause of the ecological crisis but also to devise ways of overcoming it. The ecological crisis is usually situated in the context of natural or historical calamities that science and technology attempt to resolve. Since such an approach is derived from the very same principles that led to the crisis, it follows that it will not only fail to rectify the problem but will lead to its further propagation.

From the prophetic vantage point of the Church Fathers, the ecological crisis is primarily a spiritual and ethical crisis that ensues from man's judgment, which is clouded by selfishness, egocentricity, insatiable greed, hedonism, opulence, consumption, waste, and in general a passionate way of life. Man's natural function is to reflect and recapitulate the world, thereby "shaping" all of creation within his being. The truth about man becomes the standard for truth about the world, since man is considered to be a microcosm, "a small world," and the world a *makroanthrōpos*, a massive man. Man as microcosm does not simply stand for the entire world; he also is an entire world not as a mere symbol but in very fact, for he is composed of all the physical, chemical, and spiritual elements of the world. Conversely, the world makes up an extension of man and his wider body. For this reason, the ecological crisis can be seen as man's ethical and social crisis metastasized to the world. It is the manifestation of sin or moral evil in the realm of ecology.

The ecological crisis cannot be understood on its own as an isolated event because it is linked with the totality of man's personal and communal life. It manifests a broader crisis in man's mindset and ethics, science and technology, economy, politics, culture, jurisprudence, and religion. It is the ultimate expression of man's inner crisis as well as of all his patterns of behavior and external displays. It constitutes a complex phenomenon that certainly requires a multifaceted and multidimensional approach. It indisputably calls for the support and structural framework of ethics and the life of society. Above all, however, it presupposes a radical change of ethos, of behavior, of mindset, and way of thinking, which in ecclesiastical terms is called *repentance*, the central message of the prophets to those who had gone astray.

In our days, our position vis-à-vis the environment is clearly that of someone with a split personality. On the one hand, we see certain dangers and take precautions for the protection of the environment, while on the other hand we bury our head in the sand like an ostrich by undermining any positive measures we have taken. It is a pity that not only is interest in the environment not linked to essential purity and true love but that it also walks hand in hand with systematic efforts to pollute the human mind with passionate thoughts and fantasies. The chief ambition that is instilled worldwide is economic gain. For this objective, images of persons and things are associated with various passions and fantasies. For instance, advertising provides a glaring example of the way the imagination can be aroused and polluted by images—images, moreover, under governmental supervision and protection. For example, in spite of the presence of a written warning that smoking "severely harms the health," cigarette advertisements depict attractive and carefree individuals who are the picture of health in the process of relishing and enjoying the act of smoking. In this way, these advertisements associate health, beauty, freedom from cares, and pleasant surroundings with the passion for smoking.

The proper stance toward the world or its mistreatment is no trifle for Orthodox tradition; it is the litmus test that scrutinizes and examines man's entire ethos. The Fathers of the Church tenaciously maintain that man is branded as virtuous or depraved in line with his relationship to the fruits of creation and with his reasonable or irrational use of them, as is manifest in his life. Notwithstanding, it is not possible to have a clean environment when we leave our mind and imagination exposed to multifarious pollutants. At the very least, it is hypocritical to protect the environment from trash while converting our minds into landfills where we bury a mountain of impurities. Unless man is led without delay to a proper relationship with the world and the things of the world, a relationship that is built on the proper relationship with God, there will be no essential change in ecology. This is the prophetic message of Orthodox pastoral theology, and it stems from the tradition of the Orthodox Church not only in its texts but above all in its lived experience of a Eucharistic and anticonsumerist ethos, one that can offer contemporary man guidance for emerging from our present crisis.

THE SPIRIT OF GOD MOVED UPON THE FACE OF THE WATERS: ORTHODOX HOLINESS AND THE NATURAL WORLD

Donald Sheehan

In the *Prima Vita* of the nineteenth-century Russian saint known as Herman of Alaska, this passage occurs:

> In the middle of Spruce Island [a tiny island a few miles out to sea from Kodiak, Alaska] a little river runs from the mountain into the sea. There were always large logs of driftwood at the mouth of this river, continuously brought there by storms. In the springtime when the river fish would appear, the Elder would dig in the sand so that the river could pass by and the fish in the sea would hasten up the river. "It would happen that Apa would say: 'Go and get a fish from the river,'" said Aliaga. Father Herman used to feed birds with dried fish and they in great number would nest near his cell. Under his cell there lived ermines. This little animal, after giving birth to its litter, is unapproachable, yet the Elder would feed them with his own hands. "Wasn't that really a miracle we have seen!" said his disciple Ignatius. Father Herman was also seen feeding the bears. "With the death of the Elder both the birds and the beasts disappeared; even the garden would not give forth crop if someone were to care for it willingly," asserted Ignatius.[1]

Ignatius's final assertion offers us our starting point. When St. Herman died, the birds and beasts suddenly vanished, and the garden became all at once and completely fruitless. What are we to make of this?

In 1922, Fr. Pavel Florensky published in Russia his last theological work, *Iconostasis*. Born in 1882, Fr. Pavel had been, since his ordination in 1911, a leading figure in Russia's extraordinary movement in religious philosophy, a movement whose roots lay in the direct experience of nineteenth-century

Russian monasticism, an experience that had led the novelist Fyodor Dostoevsky in the 1860s and 1870s to create his two final masterpieces, *Demons* and *The Brothers Karamazov*.[2] Thus, the flowering of this movement of Russian religious philosophy can be best understood as an attempt to do two things: to actualize in Orthodox practice the literary images of Orthodox holiness that Dostoevsky in his novels had fashioned, and to shift the whole of Western philosophy and intellectual culture onto a ground of Orthodox practice. Imagine, for a moment, Germany's Kant and Hegel meeting Dostoevsky's Bishop Tikhon and Father Zosima—and becoming all at once Orthodox: following fully all the fasts, attending joyfully all the services, devoutly praying all the prayers. And then imagine what Hegel and Kant—after, say, a dozen years of Orthodox ascetic practice—would then write as works of philosophy. Such works would resemble—just imaginably—what Florensky actually wrote. Thus, between Dostoevsky's death in 1880 and the Bolshevik revolution in 1917, Russian intellectual and spiritual articulation was guided by the voices of religious philosophy—voices to be violently drowned out, of course, by the strident clamor of the triumphant Marxist ones. Only now are their voices once again coming clear to us.

In 1922, Fr. Pavel in his *Iconostasis* explores the significance of the icon: its philosophic depth, its spiritual history, its empirical technique. Late in the book, Fr. Pavel distinguishes in icon painting between the painting of the *face* and the painting of everything else in the icon—"body, garments, rooms, buildings, trees, rocks, and so on."[3] He then says this:

> Painting the face is called *lichnoe* while painting everything else is termed *dolichnoe*; and by *lik* [the Russian root of both words] is understood those secondary organs of expressiveness (i.e., the "little countenances") of hands and feet. In this division of the icon's whole content into the processes of *lichnoe* and *dolichnoe* we can plainly see the Greek patristic understanding of existence being divided into *man* and *nature*; a division wherein each is at once distinct and inseparable from the other; hence, it is a division expressing the primordial paradisiacal harmony of inwardness and outwardness.[4]

The painting of garments is thus entirely distinct from the painting of faces, yet, in the icon, the garments become *secondarily expressive*, he says, and thereby inseparable from the icon's whole content. It is as if the illumined *face* in the icon makes everything else achieve genuine expressiveness in that face's light. In this way, then, the *inseparability* of these two activities in icon painting illustrates what Panayiotis Nellas, in his magnificent book *Deification in Christ*, describes as our paradisiacal beginning: the bringing together of all things into the hands of man in order that man may then give all things back to God. "This," says Nellas, "is man's natural state in the image of God; this is his natural function, his natural work and goal."⁵ We may thus say that, in Florensky's terms, the painting of the world (the *dolichnoe*) manifests the way wherein we see how man restores the world to God in the act of love, while the painting of the face (the *lichnoe*) enacts the way wherein the iconic face illumines the whole of the natural world.

From this perspective, we can return to the passage from St. Herman's *Prima Vita* and now say this: when the Elder feeds the otherwise unapproachable ermine and her newborns, or when he lifts up his hands with bits of dried fish in them and all the birds come, or when his fingers gently touch the bear's mouth, he is expressing the simultaneous inseparability of and distinction between the two realms of man and nature. And just as in the icon, where the trees and rocks are given a secondary expressiveness by the iconic face, so, too, St. Herman here restores to ermine and bear something like a paradisiacal glory—and in this moment the world becomes icon through the light of St. Herman's face.

The question, then, is *how*. How is the natural world made iconic? And how does the iconic face illumine the natural world?

Earlier in *Iconostasis*, Florensky distinguishes between what he calls the human *face* and what he terms the human *countenance*. Once again, here is Fr. Pavel's discussion of the point:

> By face (*litzo*), we mean that which we see in ordinary daylight consciousness, that which we see as the recognizable appearance of the real world; and we can speak . . . of all natural things and creations with whom we are in conscious relation as having a face: as, for example, we speak of the face of nature. Face, we may thus say, is nearly synonymous with the word *appearance*—meaning, however, *appearance to daylight consciousness*. But in saying this, we must not deprive the word *face* of all objective reality; rather, we must see in *face* a boundary between subjectivity and objectivity. . . . On the other hand, the countenance (*lik*) of a thing manifests its ontological reality. In Genesis, *the image of God* is differentiated from *the likeness of God*; and long ago, the Holy Tradition of the Church explained that the *image of God* must be understood as the ontologically actual gift of God, as the spiritual ground of each created person; whereas the *likeness of God* must be understood as the potentiality to achieve spiritual perfection: that is, to construct the *likeness of God* in ourselves from that totality of our empirical personalities called the *image of God*, to incarnate in the flesh of

our personality the hidden inheritance of our sacred likeness to God: and to reveal this incarnation in our *face* (*litzo*):... and our *face* (*litzo*) becomes a *countenance* (*lik*). (51–52)

This is, I submit, an extraordinary understanding. Central to Orthodox asceticism is the work of opening space in ourselves between our desires and our actions. If every desire we have triggers an action we take—if, for example, every time I feel a touch of hunger I put something in my mouth—then two disastrous effects follow. First, our desires soon come to steer all our relations with the natural world, in that the world becomes the materialization of all our desires and all our hungers—and, in that sense, the world is *dematerialized* into these desires and hungers. The second effect that follows when we fail to open space between our desires and our actions is that our selfhood becomes, in time, something like an entirely closed system of autonomous desire and autonomous satisfaction, a system wherein (once again) the natural world is dematerialized and unmade. The results of both effects are fear and depression: the fear born of the fact that our autonomous powers are indeed frail and crumbling; the depression born of the fact that we have willed our own desolation. Dostoevsky's portraits of such fear and depression in his novel *Demons* starkly depict the final goal of such states: suicide. And, in Florensky's terms, when such psychic states are reached, our face becomes not a *countenance* but a *mask* (*lichina*). Florensky writes: "Dostoevsky well understood this process in his character Stavrogin [in *Demons*], whose face had become a stony mask and no longer a real face: such is one of the steps in the disintegration of personality" (56).

Only Orthodox ascetic practice, Florensky holds, can transform our face into our countenance. And when we do so, he says, "all natural things and creations with whom we are in conscious relation" may be spoken of "as having a face." Thus we may say that when St. Herman bent down to feed the mother ermine, his long ascetic practice of distinguishing between his own desires and the natural world had resulted in his face having become a countenance. And when the ermine looked up at St. Herman, her face was illumined by the saint's iconic countenance. All of nature was at that moment achieving a countenance: such is the consequence of all Orthodox asceticism.

In the second century B.C., the Septuagint translators came to the second verse of Genesis: "The spirit of God moved upon the face of the waters." The word they chose for the Hebrew *panéh* (face) was the Greek *prosopon*. This is the same word they used for the divine countenance of God. And a half-millennium later, this is also the word first used to mean the very *Person* of God: so essential is countenance to personhood. In its movement of creatively self-emptying love, the Holy Spirit of God bestows countenance upon the waters. And when we enter into that conscious relation to the created world known as Orthodox ascetic practice, we also—in the likeness of God—bestow countenance upon the created world, and thus we come to experience directly the way wherein the created world is an icon of God. We may thus say that our ascetic practice is (to use Florensky's term) *dolichnoe*.

One further step. Quickened into being by the Holy Spirit of God, the true countenance of the natural world is thus *accomplished* and fulfilled by our exercise of our divinely given sovereignty over it. And our sovereignty over the natural world has, we may say, only one true expression: the action of self-giving love born of holy ascesis, an action by which each of us receives the likeness of God granted by the Holy Spirit. As Vladimir Lossky so beautifully tells us in his *Mystical Theology of the Eastern Church*:

> The Holy Spirit effaces Himself, as Person, before the created persons to whom He will appropriate grace. In Him the will of God is no longer external to ourselves: it confers grace inwardly, manifesting itself within our very person in so far as our human will remains in accord with the divine will and co-operates with it in acquiring grace, in making it *ours*. . . . This divine Person, now unknown, not having His image in another *Hypostasis*, will manifest Himself in deified persons: for the multitude of the saints will be His image.[6]

In the same way, the sanctified human person confers something of grace on the natural world in his or her action of sovereign ascetic love, thereby fulfilling the Divine Image in the natural world and restoring the creation to the Creator.

Lossky further tells us that the "divine Persons do not themselves assert themselves, but one bears witness to another. It is for this reason that St. John Damascene said that 'the Son is the image of the Father, and the Spirit the image of the Son.' It follows that the third *Hypostasis* of the Trinity is the only one not having His image in another Person. The Holy Spirit, as person, remains unmanifested, hidden, concealing Himself in His very appearing" (159–160). That is, until the saints bear witness to Him. What I am suggesting, then, is that in the same way we as persons must somehow, through our ascesis, conceal ourselves, remain hidden, so that the world we have been given to rule may bear witness to the Likeness in us, who are witnessing to the Holy Spirit. The natural world will bear witness to us whether we are trying to be holy or not; far better that we should try to be holy.

Once more, let us return to the final sentence in the passage from St. Herman's *Prima Vita*. When the birds and beasts vanish and the garden becomes fruitless, then we may say (in Florensky's terms) that the face of nature has, for the moment, become a darkened mask. That is, with the disappearance of St. Herman's countenance, the reality of Orthodox asceticism has—in this place, at this moment—vanished. And the effect of such a vanishing is to cease what Nellas calls the bringing together of all things in man so as to return all things to God. For only the human person possesses this capacity to restore the natural world to God because only the human can enter into that Orthodox ascetic practice wherein face (*litzo*) becomes countenance (*lik*).

Such vanishing also touches another issue central to Russian religious philosophy: incorruptibility. Dostoevsky's *The Brothers Karamazov* beautifully explores this issue in the death of Father Zosima. But Dostoevsky is, in turn, drawing from an experience central to all Russian religious history: the death of St. Sergius of Radonezh.

On the morning of September 25, 1392, at the age of seventy-eight, a very frail Father Sergius attended the Liturgy in the Monastery of the Holy Trinity, which he had founded some twenty years earlier. After the Liturgy, he spoke a brief farewell in his cell to his fellow monks. And then he very peacefully died. The fourteenth-century account says that, at the moment of his death, his body gave off an intensely sweet fragrance that filled the cell and the whole hallway beyond. All hearts lifted, the account says, at the sweet intensity of this heavenly odor. Father Sergius was buried next to the Church he had built, some of it with his own hands.

Then the miracles began. Many visiting his grave were healed of all kinds of afflictions and illnesses: the blind could see; the lame walked and danced. Some thirty years passed, and then his body was exhumed by the Church so that his bones might become relics. Then the great miracle was revealed. His body was perfectly preserved, dressed in the clothes he had been buried in, still fresh and intact. His body was then placed in the monastery church, where it remains to this day, still incorrupt. Here is the heart of Orthodox Russia. And here is where, in 1922, Fr. Pavel Florensky wrote *Iconostasis*.

What, then, are we to make of the incorrupt body of St. Sergius?

By way of approaching a response, I want to tell you of my visit, in August 1988, to this place. I traveled to Russia as part of a small Orthodox group on pilgrimage to honor the first thousand years of Orthodoxy in Russia. The Soviet regime would not fall until August 1991. Hence, in the summer of 1988, we were very much in the hands of the Soviet In-tourist Bureau, that branch of the Communist state which firmly controlled the activities of all tourists, especially U.S. citizens—particularly U.S. citizens identified as Eastern Orthodox Christians. Our In-tourist guides thus assumed at every opportunity the right to speak to us about the sunny truths of atheism and the dark lies of religion. Even the tour-bus drivers never missed an opportunity, raising their voices to carry to the back of the bus where I and my tour friend Elizabeth (whose Russian was better than mine) always sat, she quietly translating for me.

So it was that on August 23, 1988, we came by bus to what was then called Zagorsk. For the hour's drive from Moscow, the day's driver had been especially loud in his harsh laughter about the saint "who couldn't even rot right." That's how contemptible St. Sergius was. Our American guide and organizer, Masha Tkachuk, stopped our driver's stream of abuse with a single question: "Have you ever seen the inside of the church where St. Sergius's body lies?" "Well, no, of course not," he spluttered, brought up short. "Come in with us," Masha said quietly. For the final ten miles, he was silent, and as we all got off the bus, he would not look at any of us. Masha spoke to him once more: "Come," she said. He shook his head, a decided "No."

On that hot summer afternoon our little group joined the hundreds of pilgrims crowded in the church. It took me a minute to realize that everyone was silent, and in another minute I identified the faint sound of voices from the front of the church as the voices of Orthodox monks softly chanting words I was still too far away to catch. People in twos and threes were exiting along the walls, so we began to inch slowly forward, toward the point where the monks—and two of them I now could see—were chanting in turns as they faced each other over the ends of a low table. In another few minutes, I would begin to catch the Slavonic forms of biblical names I knew from the Psalms.

Then it became clear. The monks were standing not at a low table but at the head and foot of a coffin, and over the entire coffin was placed a glass dome maybe ten inches high. "Some dozen yards all around the casket there was a field of humming energy that was almost perceptible light," I wrote in my journal that night. Here was the body of St. Sergius of Radonezh.

All the pilgrims were, one by one, going up three steps to the area where St. Sergius lay, kissing the dome above the saint and then saying a brief prayer or petition. After a minute or so, another monk would lightly touch the pilgrim's shoulder or arm, then help him or her to another set of three steps leading back down to the church floor. Already another pilgrim would be at the saint's tomb.

As I came down the exit steps, I was startled to see our tour-bus driver standing against the wall and watching. I could see tears streaming down his face. He was softly shaking his head and saying something. I just caught his words: "I didn't understand, I didn't understand." His eyes were filled with the unshakable joy of beauty.

That evening, in our Moscow hotel, he asked the priest in our group if he would baptize him, and our priest assented. He took the name Sergius as his Orthodox name.

I offer this experience as a tiny narrative icon of incorruptibility. I will remember all my life the depth of the *presence* of St. Sergius. This is what our driver encountered in the monastery church that day. And this presence does not corrupt because—to use Florensky's terms—St. Sergius had, through long ascetic practice of fasting and prayer, so transfigured his body that his face had become iconic countenance and his whole presence therefore had achieved the condition of iconic *dolichnoe*: the condition of unceasing iconic expressiveness. Such a condition brings back an accord between man and nature that makes concrete the original relationship lost in Eden and restored only in ascetic practice: the harmony wherein the human presence ennobles everything and everyone in creation through the action of self-giving love. What Florensky calls the "bad infinity of unrestraint" is "cut at its very root" by ascetic practice, and the ascetic achieves, says Florensky, "an incorruptible body and an incorruptible mind."[7] "And even non-spiritual people," Florensky continues, "receive from this ascetic the strength for a better relation to creation" (*PG*, 200). This is the strength that our tour-bus driver beautifully encountered that day in August 1988.

Christ says in the Gospel: "Let your light so shine before all, that all may see your good works, and glorify your Father who is in heaven" (Mt. 5:16). Florensky notes that the phrase "your good works" is not to be understood as philanthropy and morality but, he says, as "literally, 'the works of your beauty,'" a phrase, he continues, that means, "above all, the illumined face whose beauty arises from the dispersal of inward light into the outward appearance; and the light of this face so overwhelms those who behold it that they glorify the heavenly Father whose image corresponds to this brightness before them" (*PG*, 57). St. Herman's compassionate heart had, through a lifetime of Orthodox ascetic practice, become the beauty of his illumined face—better, his countenance. When St. Herman's ermine and bear beheld this beauty, they were nourished—directly *fed*—by the works of his beauty. And such beauty does not die.

In late August 1994, my wife Xenia, our son Rowan Benedict (then age fourteen), and I traveled to Kodiak, Alaska, to make a tiny pilgrimage to St. Herman's Spruce Island, in honor of the saint's arrival there in the autumn of

1794. Arriving at St. Herman's Orthodox Seminary in Kodiak, where we were to stay, we asked the administrator if there was any way to reach Spruce Island. "Today?" he asked (it was now past noon), shaking his head. "I doubt it, but I'll go see." Mostly silently, we began to unpack our few things and to arrange our icons. We had come six thousand miles. "Perhaps tomorrow we can find a way over," we said.

Then there came a sharp knock on the door. A small but stocky Aleut man stood there. "Do you want to go see Father Herman?" he asked. Our hearts lifted.

Down at the water, two short blocks away, his little craft was beached. Spruce Island was visible some five miles over now calm ocean. Our guide—named Herman, as we might have expected, after the saint—pointed out across the water. "Look at that! Father Herman wants you to come, he's made the water all calm." We clambered into the boat, and Herman shoved us off and then started the motor.

The boat throttled down as we nosed into a small lagoon—Monk's Lagoon, it's called. I looked down. The bottom was rising toward us. Herman said, "I got to drop anchor pretty soon now." A few seconds later, the concrete-block anchor splashed into maybe twenty inches of water. The boat's prow was nearly three yards from the shore.

"We got to jump to shore," said Herman. "From up there on the deck," waving us up.

Our fourteen-year-old son went first, jumping the gap gracefully. Then my wife jumped, going down to her hands and knees as she landed—on dry land. Then I climbed up on the deck. And all at once I felt every one of my fifty-four years and all the gracelessness of my academic life. Then I heard Herman's voice on my left side. He was standing in water above his knees next to the boat. He said, "Come on, get on my back, I'll carry you."

I flushed, embarrassed. "Oh, no, I weigh over 170 pounds."

"Oh, come on," he said. "I carry packs heavier than you."

So I settled myself onto Herman's back. Not since my two sons had, at different points in their childhood, tried to carry me had I been actually carried by someone. Weeks later, as I told my priest of this moment, he smiled, "It's always so. Whenever you visit a holy place, God arranges for a surprise. The real miracle is that you let yourself be carried." I had traveled six thousand miles in order to be carried by someone for the final three yards. It is always so: in every ascetic action we must let go of all our own control.

We made our way up the beach and into the woods toward the church, our son striding ahead, followed by Herman, and my wife and I a little behind them. Then it came to us, to both of us at once: an indescribably sweet odor at once powerful and gentle, an odor like nothing in this world. Our eyes quickly scanned the forest of moss-covered evergreen and found nothing in bloom. We turned to each other. On my wife's face I read perfect joy.

Herman had stopped. "You coming?"

"What's that amazing odor?" I asked, filled with a trembling delight.

"Oh," said Herman, stepping back toward us, his dark-gold face lit in smiling. "That's Father Herman, some folks notice it, that's the land remembering him."

Since that August moment in 1994, Herman's response has come to hold for me much of what the Orthodox Church knows as imperishable joy in the creation: that's the land remembering him. Incorruptibly remembering.

In his remarkable book *Beyond the Shattered Image*, Fr. John Chryssavgis devotes a chapter to a subject very dear to Russian religious philosophy: the subject of Sophia, or Wisdom. Father John offers this luminous definition of the cosmological function of Sophia:

> It is the bridge between God and the World, belonging to and uniting both realities at once. . . . It is also the divine Wisdom whose seeds and traces may be found in the multiplicity of creation. . . . *One in God, she is many in creation*, was the way Florensky described *sophia*.[8]

This mystery of oneness and multiplicity is, of course, the central mystery of creation. And the Orthodox faith calls us to one primary relation to such mystery: attentiveness, watchfulness, alertness.

As an image of such alertness, I offer this marvelous narrative by the nature writer Annie Dillard. She was sitting on a tree trunk by a pond, relaxed, when a bright bird flew from her right to a point behind her, and she swiveled around. "And," she continues, "the next instant, inexplicably, I was looking down at a weasel, who was looking up at me."

> Weasel! I'd never seen one wild before. He was ten inches long, thin as a curve, a muscled ribbon, brown as fruitwood, soft-furred, alert. His face was fierce, small and pointed as a lizard's; he would have made a good arrowhead. There was just a dot of chin, maybe two brown hairs' worth, and then the pure white fur began that spread down his underside. He had two black eyes I didn't see, any more than you see a window.
>
> The weasel was stunned into stillness as he was emerging from beneath an enormous shaggy wild rose bush four feet away. I was stunned

into stillness twisted backward on the tree trunk. Our eyes locked, and someone threw away the key.

Our look was as if two lovers, or deadly enemies, met unexpectedly on an overgrown path when each had been thinking of something else: a clearing blow to the gut. It was also a bright blow to the brain, or a sudden beating of brains, with all the charge and intimate grate of rubbed balloons. It emptied our lungs. It felled the forest, moved the fields, and drained the pond; the world dismantled and tumbled into that black hole of eyes. If you and I looked at each other that way, our skulls would split and drop to our shoulders. But we don't. We keep our skulls. So.

He disappeared. This was only last week, and already I don't remember what shattered the enchantment. I think I blinked, I think I retrieved my brain from the weasel's brain, and tried to memorize what I was seeing, and the weasel felt the yank of separation, the careening splashdown into real life and the urgent current of instinct. He vanished under the wild rose. I waited motionless, my mind suddenly full of data and my spirit with pleadings, but he didn't return.

Please do not tell me about "approach-avoidance conflicts." I tell you I've been in that weasel's brain for sixty seconds, and he was in mine. Brains are private places, muttering through unique and secret tapes—but the weasel and I both plugged into another tape simultaneously, for a sweet and shocking time.[9]

Such a moment of contact—sweet, shocking, and unforgettable—is precisely what every Orthodox liturgy calls us into. The priest chants, "Peace be unto all," and the choir sings "And to your spirit." Then the priest chants: "Let us love one another, that with one mind we may confess"—an incomplete sentence; confess *what*? The choir sings the sentence's completion: "Father, Son, and Holy Spirit, the Trinity, one in essence and undivided." The deacon then intones: "The doors, the doors!"—meaning, keep the doors that are now opening between heaven and earth free from every attack, human or demonic—and the deacon then chants: "In wisdom let us attend." Then we all sing the Creed.

My point is this: What the Orthodox Liturgy is calling us into is precisely the sweet and shocking contact with the mind and countenance of Christ. Our way into that contact is through loving one another so alertly and so entirely that we achieve *one-mindedness*—a condition, to use Dillard's phrase, that has "all the charge and intimate grate of rubbed balloons." But unlike her encounter with the weasel, our contact with Christ doesn't end with His vanishing under the wild rose.

Or perhaps more accurately: our contact with Him *shouldn't* end the moment we turn away from the chalice at communion. For Dillard's weasel vanishing away from us is what St. Herman's mother ermine becomes when our turning away becomes—as Dillard says—a "yank of separation." And there is only one way in the world to sustain the intimate contact that Christ calls us into: the way of Orthodox ascetic practice that St. Herman of Alaska so beautifully shows, the way of giving oneself entirely to and for another, in the sovereign action of ascetic love. And this way is the call into the undying heart of all creation. "Take, eat, this is My body . . . Drink, this is My blood."

Appendixes

APPENDIX

Vespers for the Environment: September 1 (or the First Sunday in September)

Office of supplication to our God and Savior Jesus Christ, who loves humankind, for our environment and for the welfare of the whole creation

I. At Vespers

After the usual opening, at "Lord, I have cried," we chant the following **Prosomia**:

Mode 1. *Joy of the heavenly hosts*

Christ our Savior, Lover of humankind, who brought all things into existence from nothing, and with ineffable [2 Cor. 12:4] wisdom arranged for each one to accomplish unerringly the goal which you laid down in the beginning,[1] as you are powerful, bless the whole creation which you fashioned.

Give peace to all the nations, Lord, and understanding in all things, so that we may lead a tranquil life and always keep your laws, which you laid down for the whole creation for the unalterable maintenance and government of the universe.

Lover of humankind, keep unharmed the environment that clothes the earth, through which, by your will, we who inhabit the earth live and move and have our being,[2] so that we, your unworthy suppliants, may be delivered from destruction and ruin.

Fence round the whole creation, Christ our Savior, with the mighty strength of your love for humankind, and deliver the earth we inhabit from the corruption which threatens it; for we, your servants, have set our hopes on you.

Put an end, O Savior, to the evil designs which are being devised against us with senseless intent, and turn aside from the earth every destructive action of the works of human hands which contrive corruption leading to perdition.

Lord, who wraps creation in clouds,[3] as godly David sang, watch over the environment of the earth, which you created from the beginning for the preservation of mortals, and give us the breath of the winds and the flow of waters.

"Glory to the Father . . ."

Mode 2. Plagal

Almighty Lord, who created all things with wisdom[4] and who watches over and guides them by your all-powerful hand [Wis. 11:17], grant well-being so that the whole creation may prosper and remain unharmed by hostile elements; for you, Master, commanded that the works of your hands should remain unshaken until the end of the age; for you spoke and they came into being[5] and from you they receive mercy for the turning away of all evil, and for the salvation of the human race that glorifies your name which is praised above all.[6]

"Both now and ever . . ."

Theotokion

Who will not call you blessed, All-holy Virgin? Who will not sing the praise of your child-birth without labor? For the only-begotten Son, who shone out from the Father beyond time, came forth from you, pure Maiden, ineffably incarnate. By nature he is God, by nature he became man for our sakes, not divided in a duality of persons, but known without confusion in a duality of natures. O honored and all-blessed, implore him to have mercy on our souls.

Entrance

"O Joyful Light . . ."[7]

The Prokeimenon of the Day

Readings:

The **Reading** is from Genesis[8]
[1:1–13]
In the beginning God made the heaven and the earth. Now the earth was invisible and unformed, and darkness was upon the deep and the Spirit[9] of God was borne upon the water. And God said, "Let there be light," and there was light. And God saw the light, that it was good; and God made a separation between the light and the darkness. And God called the light Day, and the darkness he called Night; and there was evening and there was morning, one day. And God said, "Let there be a firmament in the midst of the water and let there be a separation between the water and the water"; and it was so. And God made the firmament. And God made a separation between the water, which was below the firmament, and between the water which was above the firmament. And God called the firmament Heaven; and God saw that it was good, and there was evening and there was morning, a second day. And God said, "Let the water below heaven be gathered together into one gathering, and let dry land appear"; and it was so. And the water below heaven was gathered together into their gatherings, and the dry land appeared. And God called the dry land Earth, and the accumulations of the waters he called Seas. And God saw that it was good. And God said, "Let the earth sprout herb of grass, sowing seed according to its kind and according to its likeness, and fruiting tree making fruit, whose seed is in it according to its kind upon the earth"; and it was so. And the earth brought forth herb of grass, sowing seed according to its kind and according to its likeness, and fruiting tree making fruit, whose seed was in it according to its kind upon the earth, and God saw that it was good. And there was evening and morning, a third day.

The **Reading** is from Genesis
[1:20–31 and 2:1–3]
And God said: "Let the waters bring forth reptiles of living souls, and winged creatures flying over the earth, under the firmament of heaven"; and it was so. And God made the great whales, and every soul of living reptiles, which the waters brought forth according to their kind, and every winged flying creature according to its kind. And God saw that they were good; and God blessed them and said: "Increase and multiply, and fill the waters in the seas, and let the winged creatures be multiplied upon the earth." And there was evening and there was morning, a fifth day. God said: "Let the earth bring forth living soul according to its kind, quadrupeds, reptiles, and wild

beasts of the earth according to their kind"; and it was so. And God made the wild beasts of the earth according to their kind, and the cattle according to their kind, and all the reptiles of the earth according to their kinds. And God saw that they were good. And God said: "Let us make humanity according to our image and according to our likeness; and let it rule over the fish of the sea and the flying creatures of heaven and the cattle and all the earth and all the reptiles which creep upon the earth." And God made humanity, according to the image of God he made it; male and female he made them. And God blessed them, saying: "Increase and multiply, and fill the earth, and have dominion over it; and rule the fish of the sea and the flying creatures of heaven and all the cattle and all the earth and all the reptiles which creep upon the earth." And God said: "See, I have given you all seed-bearing grass, sowing seed, which is upon the whole earth; and every tree, which has in it fruit of seed-bearing seed, shall be food for you, and for all the wild beasts of the earth and for all the winged creatures of heaven, and for every reptile which creeps upon the earth, which has in itself a soul of life, and every green grass shall be food." And it was so. And God saw everything that he had made; and behold, they were very good. And there was evening and there was morning, a sixth day. [2:1] And the heaven and the earth were accomplished, and all their array. And God accomplished on the sixth day the works which he had made; and he rested on the seventh day from his works which he had made. And God blessed the seventh day and hallowed it; because on it he rested from all his works, which God had begun to make.

The **Reading** is from the Prophecy of Isaias[10]
[63:15–64:5a, 8–9]

Turn,[11] Lord, from heaven and see, from your holy house and your glory. Where is the abundance of your mercy and your acts of pity, that you have withheld yourself from us? For you are our Father, because Abraham has not known us, nor Israel acknowledged us. But do you, Lord, our Father, deliver us; from the beginning your name is upon us. Why have you made us wander from your way, Lord? Why have you hardened our hearts not to fear you? Return for the sake of your servants, for the sake of the tribes that are your heritage, that in a little while we may inherit your holy mountain.[12] Our enemies have trampled down your sanctuary, we have become as at the beginning when you did not rule over us, nor had your name been invoked upon us. If you open the heaven, trembling from you will seize the mountains and they will melt as wax melts before the fire, and fire will burn up your adversaries, and your name will be manifest among your adversaries;

nations will be troubled at your presence. When you do glorious deeds, trembling from you will seize the mountains. From eternity we have not heard, nor have our eyes seen any God but you. And your works are true, and you will perform mercy for those who wait for you. For mercy will meet with those who do right and remember your ways. And now, Lord, you are our Father, while we are clay and you are our Fashioner. We are all the work of your hands. Do not be exceedingly angry with us, Lord, and do not remember our sins for ever. And now, look upon us, Lord, because we are all your people.

At the Liti, Idiomels.

Mode 1

Lord, who created the universe at the beginning[13] and gave to each thing its own rank, do not despise the works of your hands,[14] but with an eye of mercy look from heaven upon this vine and restore it[15] according to your will, turning aside from it every purpose that brings corruption and every destroyer; for you are our Shepherd, Deliverer, and Savior, and from you, Master, we receive help in mercy and acts of compassion, as we glorify you.

Mode 2

Lord and Master, who fenced about the domain of the earth and made it sure with an enveloping layer,[16] deliver its whole structure from harm and disaster; for you are a treasury of strength and the source of life,[17] and all things minister and are subject to your will as your servants, Lord. And so grant us your mercies and turn away from us every disaster, and save our souls, for you love humankind.

Mode 3

Threats and scourges and destruction hang over us, Lord, because of the multitude of our transgressions; for we have sinned and transgressed[18] and gone far from you, and we are affected and afflicted by dire perils; but deliver us, Lord, from the dangers that beset us, and keep the whole structure of the earth unharmed, granting equable breaths of winds and ever-flowing springs of waters for our safe-keeping and salvation, O Lover of humankind.

"Glory to the Father . . ."

Mode 4

Lord, who hold the circle of the earth[19] and make firm its foundations, as the Prophet says, accept our suppliant entreaties, as our guardian, protector, and Savior; for we are your people and the sheep of your pasture,[20] and by your infinite mercy we shall be delivered from anticipated dangers. Do not therefore utterly destroy us, Master, but may your goodness conquer the multitude of our offences, that we may all glorify the ocean of your acts of compassion.

"Both now and ever . . ."

Theotokion[21]

From dangers of every kind protect your servants, blessed Mother of God, that we may glorify you, the hope of our souls.

At the Aposticha, Prosomia

Mode 1 Plagal. *Hail, of ascetic struggles*

Merciful God, who loves humankind, look with an eye of compassion on the works of your hands and set free the expanse of the atmosphere from dread destruction and death-dealing emissions and every poisonous pollution, through which death and danger threaten. Take pity then on what you have fashioned and give to all the prudence not to act senselessly, whose result is corruption, and grant to all pardon, salvation, and your divine mercy.

Verse: With my voice I cried to the Lord, and he heard me from his holy mountain. [Ps. 3:4]

Savior, accept the entreaties of your Mother, which she offers for all creation, and the supplications of all your Saints. Grant to all your mercies, and keep unharmed the firmament which you spread out from the beginning with wisdom, Lord, and brought into being for the benefit of mortals. Keep undamaged from harmful influences, O Word, the whole environment which girds the earth, granting to all pardon and salvation and your great[22] mercy.

Verse: When I called you heard to me, O God of my justice; in affliction you set me at large. [Ps. 4:1]

With humility of soul we all entreat you, Lord, and we fall down before you. At your command deliver the earth on which we dwell from every harm and from harsh ruin, and speedily avert from it and abolish by your will destructive emanations, and pour out the fresh dew of life-sustaining air. With

your mighty power, Master and Savior, fence about the whole enclosure of the environment, granting to all pardon and salvation and your divine mercy.
"Glory to the Father . . ."
"Both now and ever . . ."

Theotokion:

Mode 1 Plagal

Through compassionate pity, O Word, you took another form, refashioned corrupted nature and brought it back to incorruption. Now, we beseech you, yield to the supplications of your most pure Mother and grant stability to the inhabited world and well-being to all creation and deliverance from perils, for the salvation of our souls.

Apolytikia

Mode 1 Plagal. *The Word without beginning*

In wisdom you created all things well, and fashioned humanity in your likeness. Sanctify our time, our Lord and King, for the fulfillment of your commands, that we may sing without ceasing your unbounded mercies for the renewal of the whole cosmos.[23]
"Glory to the Father . . ."

Mode 4. Speedily anticipate

Lord and Savior, who as God brought all things into being by a word, establishing laws and governing them unerringly to your glory, at the prayers of the Mother of God, keep secure and unharmed all the elements which hold the earth together, and save the universe.
"Both now and ever . . ."

Theotokion

The mystery hidden from all eternity and unknown to Angels has been revealed to those on earth through you, O Mother of God: God being made flesh in a union without confusion, and willingly accepting the Cross for us, through which he raised the first-formed man and saved our souls from death.
And Dismissal

II. At Matins

After the 1st Reading from the Psalter, **Kathisma**
Mode 1. The soldiers watching

As God you sustain all things by a word, and keep them all in perfect harmony. Keep unaltered, Lord, the environment which enwraps creation, as you are compassionate, and by your ineffable power turn away from the earth every harm.

Theotokion

All-blameless Virgin, beyond nature you conceived God and gave birth to him in the flesh. Through the abundance of your mercy take pity on those who glorify you in faith and by the streams of your grace cleanse our minds and hearts from sins of many kinds.
After the 2nd Reading, **Kathisma**

Mode 4. *Joseph was amazed*

In the beginning, Savior, universal King, you founded the earth, while the heavens are the works of your hands,[24] and, with the sun, the moon, and the stars. All things proclaim your greatness and your strength. Keep their harmony and majesty untroubled, for all things, O Word, are subject to your almighty will.

Theotokion

Ineffably, Mary, you conceived in your womb without change and without confusion the God who is beyond being; and beyond nature you brought forth for those in the world the One who delivers us from condemnation. Therefore we sing the praise of your many mighty works and glorify with faith your child-bearing beyond understanding. But, O Virgin who bore God, deliver us from every affliction.
After the Polyeleos, Kathisma

Mode 4 Plagal. *The Wisdom and Word*

Lord, lover of humankind, King of all creation, who brings all things into being from nothing, keep unharmed the order which you established and grant your servants every temperate climate. Therefore too, all-powerful

Giver of life, diffusing mild airs, disperse all noxious pollutions from the earth, and grant your peace to all the nations, that we may all sing the praise of your goodness.

Theotokion

The Master and Maker of all things, taking flesh from your immaculate womb, came forth as man, not changed in his Godhead, and granted salvation to all those who worship your ineffable child-bearing. Therefore, all-pure Mother of God, Ever-Virgin Maiden, we have recourse to your fervent protection, and saved we cry: Intercede with your Son and God to grant forgiveness of faults to those who devoutly sing the praise of your many mighty works.

The 1st Antiphon of the Anavathmi in Mode 4 and the Prokeimenon

Lord, our Lord, how wonderful is your name in all the earth. [Ps. 8:1]

Verse: For I will look at the heavens, the works of your fingers, the moon and the stars which you fixed. [Ibid. 3]

The **Reading** is from the Holy Gospel according to Luke [18:2–8]

The Lord spoke this parable, "In a certain city there was a judge who neither feared God nor had respect for people. In that city there was a widow who kept coming to him and saying, 'Grant me justice against my opponent.' For a while he refused; but later he said to himself, 'Though I have no fear of God and no respect for anyone, yet because this widow keeps pestering me, I will grant her justice, so that she may not wear me out by continually coming.'" And the Lord said, "Listen to what the unjust judge says. Will God not grant justice also to his chosen ones who cry to him day and night? Will he delay long in helping them? I tell you, he will quickly grant them justice."

Psalm 50

"Glory to the Father . . ."

At the prayers of the Apostles, O Merciful One, blot out the multitude of my transgressions.

"Both now . . ."

At the prayers of the Mother of God, O Merciful One, blot out the multitude of my transgressions.

Idiomel

Mode 2 Plagal

Have mercy on me, O God, in accordance with your great mercy. According to the fullness of your compassion blot out my offence. [Ps. 50:1]

Lord, who with wisdom keep, maintain and direct all things for our government and sure guidance in the paths of your commandments,[25] accept our suppliant entreaties and rescue us from impending dangers and from all change for the worse of the bounds of nature, and save our souls.

Deacon: O God, save your people . . .

Then the **Canon**, of which the Acrostic is:

O Christ Savior, keep us safe.

Ode 1

Mode 4 Plagal. Irmos. *Crossing the water*

"Crossing the water as on dry land and fleeing from the wickedness of the Egyptians, Israel cried aloud: 'To our Redeemer and our God now let us sing.'"

Troparia

O Word great in mercy, stooping with goodness and compassion, shower down from heaven upon the earth the streams of your divine mercy for our salvation.

Stained with foul passions, Savior, we defile the atmosphere with our dread actions; but grant us, Lord, genuine repentance.

Look on us, Savior, with an eye of mercy, and turn from the earth, we beg, the destruction which comes from poisonous and senseless actions.

Theotokion

Mother of God full of grace,[26] who gave birth to the Word without beginning from your pure blood, save us from dread circumstances.

Ode 3

Irmos. *"You are the firm strength"*

"You are the firm strength, O Lord, of those who have recourse to you. You are the light of those in darkness, and my spirit sings your praise."

Troparia

By the laws which you established, Master, ever keep unshaken and unmoved the works of your hands, which you brought into being of old.

As you possess an inexhaustible ocean of compassion, O All-merciful, dispel the harmful blasts that come against us.

You are Lord of all things, Savior, you the Giver of life. Cleanse from all corruption the elements in which we your servants live.

Theotokion

You appeared as the dwelling of the Maker of all creation, pure Maiden, bearing him ineffably in your womb.

Kathisma

Mode 1 Plagal. *Let us believers praise*

As our Master and Creator, Lover of humankind, we fall before you with faith and we cry out to you, "Keep our atmosphere and the whole earth undamaged by harmful corrupters, and give us repentance and wholeness, O Compassionate, for the salvation of our souls."

Theotokion. Same melody

From your pure blood you bore beyond understanding the Master of all things and remained, as before, a virgin incorrupt, O Mother of God. Keep safe from every evil and corruption of the cunning Deceiver[27] those who with undoubting heart have recourse to your protection.

Ode 4

Irmos. *I have heard, Lord*

I have heard, Lord, of the mystery of your dispensation; I have understood your works and glorified your Godhead.

Troparia

Keep the elements which surround the earth unharmed, Lord, and ever bless us that we may walk in your fear.

We have been estranged, Lord, by transgressing your divine law, and so we beg you: Give us amendment of life.

From pollutions and from destructive blasts deliver the whole earth, O Savior, by your strength, that we may magnify your might.

Theotokion

Mother of God, Ever-Virgin, who gave birth in the body to the Fashioner of the whole creation, deliver us from every calamity.

Ode 5

Irmos. *Enlighten us*

"Enlighten us by your commands, O Lord, and by your upraised arm grant us your peace, O Lover of humankind."

Troparia

Cleanse us from blemishes of soul, O Lover of humankind, and preserve in its own order, we beseech you, the earth's environment.

Empower us, Lord, by your divine fear to accomplish our life without grief in peace and true love.

You founded the heaven and the earth,[28] as David sings, O Creator; guard us then from every affliction.

Theotokion

Accept the voices of those who entreat you with faith, Mother of God, pure and Ever-Virgin, and grant peace to our souls.

Ode 6

Irmos. *I pour out my supplication*

"I pour out my supplication to the Lord, and to him I declare my afflictions, because my soul has been filled with evils and my life has drawn near to Hell; and like Jonas I beg: O God, bring me up from corruption."

Troparia

You established all creation by your mighty strength, O Savior who love humankind; now, therefore, rescue us by your power, Lord, from threatening destruction, and preserve the environment which surrounds the earth.

Keep the upper air undamaged and the flow of the air free from destructive exhalations, pollutions, and the other effects of dangerous activities which bring most painful death.

By a word,[29] Lord, you established the structure of the earth, and wrapped its circumference with a surrounding element as you wished; ever preserve it from corruption and dread influences.

Theotokion

As Mother of the King of glory,[30] Ever-Virgin Maiden, Mother of God, set free my lowly heart from the disgrace of unclean passions, and give me, I beg, sincere and perfect repentance.

Kontakion

Mode 2. With your blood

With your all-powerful strength you framed all things, both visible and invisible;[31] and so keep unharmed, we implore your goodness, **the environment that surrounds the earth.**

Ikos

Loving Savior, we praise the manifestations of your providence and your many saving powers; because with ineffable wisdom and order and harmony you have established for all things laws and unalterable ordinances for the protection of us, your royal fashioning. Keep us unshaken, Lord, from every corrupting activity, change, and destruction, as guardian, protector, and deliverer of all things, keeping in them the essential power unmoved, and especially watching over **the environment that surrounds the earth.**

[The Synaxarion from the Menaion and the following:

On the same day, the beginning of the Indiction, we entreat our God, who loves humankind, for the welfare of the earth on which we live and for the whole creation.

Verses

We fall before you, Master, as we cry:
O Savior, from pollutions free the earth.
To him be glory and might to the ages. Amen.]³²

Ode 7

Irmos. *The Youths from Judea*

"The Youths from Judaea once having come to Babylon, with the faith of the Trinity trampled down the flame of the furnace, as they sang: God of our fathers, blessed are you!"³³

Troparia

You give life to all and conduct all things with ineffable judgments; from harmful pollutions and from every abuse save those who cry out, "God of our fathers, blessed are you!"

By your will, Lord, you adorned the heavens with stars, while you made the whole earth fair with flowers and trees as it sings, "God of our fathers, blessed are you!"

Give pardon and a calm life to us who dwell on the earth, turning away from it corrupting emanations and saving those who sing, "God of our fathers, blessed are you!"

Theotokion

The One born from your womb, pure Maiden, declared you to be the gateway³⁴ of salvation that leads to the glory of the kingdom on high those who cry out to you with faith, "Hail, pure Virgin, the salvation of mortals!"

Ode 8

Irmos. *The King of heaven*

"The King of heaven, whom the hosts of Angels praise, praise and highly exalt to all the ages."³⁵

Troparia

Come, all the inhabitants of earth, let us fall down and cry out to Christ with compunction, "Deliver us, Savior, from just condemnation!"

From pollutions and contaminations rescue the environment, Savior, that we may sing your praise as the only benefactor.

With streams of your vivifying mercy, Compassionate One, quench the flame of bitter passions and grant us well-being and salvation.

Theotokion

Glory of Angels and salvation of mortals, glorious Ever-Virgin Maiden, show us to be partakers in eternal glory.

Ode 9

Irmos. *We who through you*

"We, who have been saved through you, pure Virgin, confess you to be in truth the Mother of God and with the bodiless choirs we magnify you."

Troparia

In your goodness deliver our race from earthquakes and ill fortune, from calamities of many kinds and from soul-destroying pollutions, O Compassionate.

Give strength to the weak, O all-compassionate, and by your power preserve the atmosphere clean from winds that bring death.

From every pollution that breeds death, O Savior, by your power preserve unsullied the air in creation that we breathe.

Make heavenly our hearts, O Compassionate, through a life of virtue and holiness, and deliver us from the grip of uncleanness.

Theotokion

We sing the praise of your child-bearing, through which, O Virgin, we have been delivered from the ancestral curse; for you bore Christ, the Savior of all.
Exapostilarion. Women hear

You once stretched out the heavens[36] at your command, Lord, as the Prophet says, and founded the unformed mass of the earth, Master; preserve the constitution of the universe in harmony and keep every element in creation from contamination.

Theotokion

The Maker of creation through his goodness took human form from you, and was created beyond nature from your pure blood. As his all-pure Mother, O all-immaculate, ask him for us, we beg, that we may find salvation.

At Lauds we insert 4 **Stichera** and sing the following **Prosomia**.

Mode 4. You have given us a sign

With compunction we offer you our praise, Lover of humankind, and with faith we cry out to you: As Creator you hold fast the ends of the earth,[37] and you maintain and govern them. From noxious emanations and from dire pollutions that harbor bitter death, rescue humanity which you fashioned, for you are pitying and compassionate.

By your almighty will you brought all things into being from nothing, Lover of humankind, and all things, Savior, serve your might; therefore we implore you: Keep the environment that enwraps the earth unmoved, for the safe government of your royal fashioning, and for life on earth to be free from strife and destruction.

Let us, the nurselings of true religion, offer to the Lord purity of life and splendor of manners, that we may be delivered from pollutions of many kinds which pollute the whole earth and harbor bitter and painful death for the ends of the earth. From these, Lord, preserve our existence by your almighty power.

You walled the circle of the earth,[38] Lord, as with a wall, with a safe environment. Preserve it always as you established it when you poured out the breaths of winds and vivifying breezes for our preservation, and grant us pardon of sins, Master, and the fulfilling of the commands of your holy will.

"Glory to the Father . . ."

Mode 4 Plagal

As Master of creation do not take from us the treasures of your providence, we beg, Lover of humankind. See our humiliation, Lord, and cleanse creation of polluted winds and noxious contagions and activities, so that, living devoutly and soberly in a pure life, we may be counted worthy of eternal life, as we glorify your great mercy.

"Both now and ever . . ."

Theotokion

Sovereign Lady, accept the entreaties of your servants and rescue us from every constraint and affliction.
Great Doxology and Dismissal

III. At the Liturgy

[The usual. Apostle and Gospel of the 1st of the Indiction, but, if you wish, say also the Gospel according to Mark for the Wednesday of the 17th week of Luke [Mark 13:24–31].]

Prokeimenon

Mode 4 Psalm of David. [Psalm 146]

Great is our God, and great is his strength.

Verse: Praise the Lord, for psalmody is good: let praise be given sweetly to our God.

The **Reading** is from the 1st Epistle of Paul to Timothy[39]
[2:1–7]

Child Timothy, first of all, then, I urge that supplications, prayers, intercessions, and thanksgivings be made for everyone, for kings and all who are in high positions, so that we may lead a quiet and peaceable life in all godliness and dignity. This is right and is acceptable in the sight of God our Savior, who desires all to be saved and to come to the knowledge of the truth. For there is one God; there is also one mediator between God and humanity, a human being, Christ Jesus, who gave himself as a ransom for all; this was attested at the right time. For this I was appointed a herald and an apostle (I am telling the truth in Christ, I am not lying), a teacher of the Gentiles in faith and truth.

[Brethren, submit therefore to God. Resist the devil and he will flee from you. Draw near to God and he will draw near to you. Cleanse your hands, you sinners, and purify your hearts, you double-minded. Be wretched and mourn and weep. Let your laughter be turned to mourning and your joy to dejection. Humble yourselves before the Lord and he will exalt you. Do not speak evil against one another, brethren. One that speaks evil against a brother or judges his brother, speaks evil against the law and judges the law. But if you judge the law, you are not a doer of the law but a judge. There is one lawgiver and judge, he who is able to save and to destroy. But who are you that you judge your neighbor? Come now, you who say, "Today or tomorrow we will go into such and such a town and spend a year there and do business and make a profit"; whereas you do not know about tomorrow. What is your life? For you are a mist that will appear for a little time and then it will vanish. Instead you ought to say, "If the Lord wishes, we will both live and do this or that." As it is, you boast in your arrogance. All such boasting is evil. Anyone who knows what it is right to do and fails to do it, for them it is sin. Come now, you rich, weep and howl for the miseries that are coming upon you. Your riches have rotted and your garments are moth-eaten. Your gold and silver have rusted, and their rust will be evidence against you and will eat your flesh. Like fire you have stored up treasure in the last days. Behold, the wages of the laborers who mowed your fields, which you kept back by fraud, cry out; and the cries of the harvesters have reached the ears of the Lord of hosts. You have lived on the earth in luxury and in pleasure; you have fattened your hearts in a day of slaughter. You have condemned, you have killed the righteous one; he does not resist you. Be patient, therefore, brethren, until the coming of the Lord. Behold, the farmer waits for the precious fruit of the earth, being patient over it until it receives the early and the late rain. You also be patient. Strengthen your hearts, for the coming of the Lord is near. Do not grumble, brethren, against one another, that you may not be judged. See, the Judge is standing at the doors.]

Alleluia

Mode 4 [Psalm 64]

Verse 1: To you, O God, praise is due in Sion; and to you a vow shall be performed.
    Verse 2: We shall be filled with good things of your house.
    The **Reading** is from the holy Gospel according to Luke [4:16–22]
    At that time Jesus came to Nazareth, where he had been brought up, he went to the synagogue on the Sabbath day, as was his custom. He stood up to read, and the scroll of the prophet Isaias was given to him. He unrolled the scroll and found the place where it was written: The Spirit of the Lord is upon me, because he has anointed me to bring good news to the poor. He has sent me to proclaim release to the captives and recovery of sight to the blind, to let the oppressed go free, to proclaim the year of the Lord's favor. And he rolled up the scroll, gave it back to the attendant, and sat down. The eyes of all in the synagogue were fixed on him. Then he began to say to them: "Today this scripture has been fulfilled in your hearing." All spoke

well of him and were amazed at the gracious words that came from his mouth.

The Lord said to his Disciples: "In those days, after that suffering, the sun will be darkened, and the moon will not give its light, and the stars will be falling from heaven, and the powers in the heavens will be shaken. Then they will see the Son of Man coming in clouds with great power and glory. Then he will send out the angels, and gather his elect from the four winds, from the ends of the earth to the ends of heaven. From the fig tree learn its lesson: as soon as its branch becomes tender and puts forth its leaves, you know that summer is near. So also, when you see these things taking place, you know that he is near, at the very doors. Truly I tell you, this generation will not pass away until all these things have taken place. Heaven and earth will pass away, but my words will not pass away."

Communion, with the **Communion** Hymn [repeated]
Praise the Lord from the heavens, praise him in the highest. Alleluia!

Megalynarion

At all times keep unharmed the whole creation we beg you, O Redeemer, and grant us breaths of winds and breezes moist with dew for our safety and salvation, O Lover of humankind.

Distich

Gerasimos, O Master, cries with faith:
    Grant to creation a mild atmosphere.

APPENDIX

B

ENVIRONMENT, NATURE, AND CREATION IN ORTHODOX THOUGHT: A BIBLIOGRAPHY OF TEXTS IN ENGLISH

Compiled by John Chryssavgis and Bruce V. Foltz

Two limitations of this bibliography, which we believe is the most complete so far in English, should be noted. First, it is limited to texts published in the English language. If it were to include works published in Arabic, Greek, Romanian, Russian, Serbian, and so on, its length would be exponentially greater. Second, regarding titles which are not *primarily* devoted to issues concerning nature, environment, and creation, we have had to be very selective, leaving out a host of works that have important things to say about these topics. Indeed, it is part of the task of this volume to show that there are relatively few Orthodox titles that *do not* cast some light on issues of this sort, so central are the cosmic and creational dimensions to the theological concerns of this tradition. The editors also wish to thank a number of the contributors, especially Crina Gschwandtner, Jurretta Jordan Hecksher, and Elizabeth Theokritoff, for their generosity in suggesting important additions to this bibliography.

Books

Ascherson, Neal, and Sarah Hobson, eds. *Danube: River of Life*. Athens: Religion, Science, and the Environment, 2002.

———. *Ecology and Monasticism*. Montreal: Alexander Press, 1996.

Bartholomew, Ecumenical Patriarch. *Conversations with Ecumenical Patriarch Bartholomew I*. By Olivier Clément. Crestwood, N.Y.: St. Vladimir's Seminary Press, 1997.

———. *Encountering the Mystery: Understanding Orthodox Christianity Today*. New York: Doubleday, 2008.

———. *On Earth as in Heaven: Ecological Vision and Initiatives of Ecumenical Patriarch Bartholomew*. Ed. John Chryssavgis. New York: Fordham University Press, 2012.

Bulgakov, Sergei. *Philosophy of Economy: The World as Household*. Trans. Catherine Evtuhov. New Haven, Conn.: Yale University Press, 2000.

Chryssavgis, John. *Beyond the Shattered Image: Orthodox Insights into the Environment*. Minneapolis, Minn.: Light and Life, 1999.

———. *Light Through Darkness: The Orthodox Tradition*. Maryknoll, N.Y.: Orbis, 2004.

Chryssavgis, John, with G. Ferguson. *The Desert Is Alive: Dimensions of Australian Spirituality*. Melbourne: Joint Board of Christian Education, 1990.

The Churches and the Ecological Problem in Europe. The Proceedings of the XIV International Orthodox Postgraduate Conference (1993). Geneva: Foundation of the Orthodox Centre of the Ecumenical Patriarchate, 1993.

Clément, Olivier. *On Human Being: A Spiritual Anthropology*. London: New City, 2000.

The Environment and Religious Education: Proceedings of the Summer 1994 Seminar on Halki. Istanbul: Melitos Editions, 1995.

The Environment and Ethics: Proceedings of the Summer 1995 Seminar on Halki. Istanbul: Melitos Editions, 1996.

Florensky, Pavel. *The Pillar and Ground of Truth: An Essay in Orthodox Theodicy in Twelve Letters*. Trans. Boris Jakim. Princeton, N.J.: Princeton University Press, 1997.

Florovsky, Georges. *The Collected Works*. Vol. 3., *Creation and Redemption*. Belmont, Mass.: Nordland, 1976.

Foltz, Bruce V. *The Noetics of Nature: Environmental Philosophy and the Holy Beauty of Epiphany*. New York: Fordham University Press, 2013.

Gillet, Lev. *The Burning Bush*. London: Fellowship of St. Alban and St. Sergius, 1976.

———. *On the Invocation of the Name of Jesus*. London: Fellowship of St. Alban and St. Sergius, 1950.

Gregorios, Metropolitan Paulos (Verghese). *Cosmic Man: The Divine Presence*. New Delhi: Sophia, 1980. [This book has appeared in other editions, as mentioned below.]

———. *Enlightenment: East and West. Pointers in the Quest for India's Secular Identity*. New Delhi, 1989.

———. *The Freedom of Man*. Philadelphia, 1972.

———. *The Human Presence: An Orthodox View of Nature*. Geneva: WCC, 1978; Park Town: Christian Literature Society, 1980.

———. *The Human Presence: Ecological Spirituality and the Age of the Spirit*. New York, 1987. [A republication of the entry immediately above.]

———. *A Light Too Bright. The Enlightenment Today. An Assessment of the Values of European Enlightenment and a Search for New Foundations*. New York, 1992.

———. *Science for Sane Societies*. Park Town: Christian Literature Society, 1980.
Guroian, Vigen. *Inheriting Paradise: Meditations on Gardening*. Grand Rapids, Mich.: Eerdmans, 1999.
Hart, David Bentley. *The Beauty of the Infinite: The Aesthetics of Christian Truth*. Grand Rapids, Mich.: Eerdmans, 2004.
———. *The Doors of the Sea: Where was God in the Tsunami?* Grand Rapids, Mich.: Eerdmans, 2005.
Hobson, Sarah, and Jane Lubchenko, eds. *Revelation and the Environment* A.D. 95–1995. World Scientific, 1997.
Hobson, Sarah, and Lawrence Mee, eds. *Religion, Science, and the Environment: The Black Sea in Crisis*. World Scientific, 1998.
Keselopoulos, Anestis G. *Man and the Environment: A Study of St. Symeon the New Theologian*. Crestwood, N.Y.: St. Vladimir's Seminary Press, 2001.
Knight, Christopher C. *The God of Nature*. Minneapolis, Minn.: Fortress Press, 2007.
Lang, D. M. *Lives and Legends of the Georgian Saints: Life of St. David of Garesja*. London: Mowbrays, 1976.
Limouris, Metropolitan Gennadios, ed. *Come, Holy Spirit, Renew the Whole Creation*. Brookline, Mass.: Holy Cross Orthodox Press, 1990.
———, ed. *Justice, Peace, and the Integrity of Creation: Insights from Orthodoxy*. Geneva: WCC, 1990.
———, ed. *Orthodox Visions of Ecumenism: Statements, Messages, and Reports on the Ecumenical Movement 1902–1992*. Geneva: WCC, 1994.
Lossky, Vladimir. *The Mystical Theology of the Eastern Church*. Crestwood, N.Y.: St. Vladimir's Seminary Press, 1976.
Louth, Andrew. *Maximus the Confessor*. London: Routledge, 1996.
———. *The Wilderness of God*. London: Darton Longman & Todd, 2003.
Manoussakis, John Panteleimon. *God After Metaphysics: A Theological Aesthetic*. Bloomington: Indiana University Press, 2007.
Muratore, Stephen. *Replenish the Earth: Issues in Christian Environmentalism*. San Francisco: Epiphany Press, 1989.
Nellas, Panayiotis. *Deification in Christ: Orthodox Perspectives on the Nature of the Human Person*. Crestwood, N.Y.: St. Vladimir's Seminary Press, 1987.
Nesteruk, Alexei. *The Universe as Communion: Towards a Neo-Patristic Synthesis of Theology and Science*. London: T&T Clark, 2008.
Nikodemos, Metropolitan, *Service for the Protection of the Environment* [in Greek]. Patras, 1994.
Oleksa, Michael. *Orthodox Alaska: A Theology of Mission*. Crestwood, N.Y.: St. Vladimir's Seminary Press, 1992.
Orthodoxy and the Ecological Crisis. Ecumenical Patriarchate assisted by the World Wide Fund for Nature. Switzerland: WWF International, 1990.
Orthodoxy and Ecology: Resource Book, ed. Alexander Belopopsky and Dimitri Oikonomou. Bialystok, Poland: Syndesmos, 1996.

The Orthodox Church and the Environment. Athens: Ekdotike Athinon; Athens: Ministry of Foreign Affairs, 1992.

Orthodoxy and Ecology: Orthodox Youth Environmental Training Seminar Resource Book. Conference in Neamt, Romania, 1994. World Wide Fund for Nature and Syndesmos, 1994.

Ouspensky, Leonid. *The Theology of the Icon.* Crestwood, N.Y.: St. Vladimir's Seminary Press, 1992.

Ouspensky, Leonid, and Vladimir Lossky. *The Meaning of Icons.* Trans. G. E. H. Palmer and E. Kadloubovsky. Rev. ed. Crestwood, N.Y.: St. Vladimir's Seminary Press, 1982.

The Problem of Ecology Today: The Proceedings of the XIII International Orthodox Postgraduate Conference (1992). Geneva: Foundation of the Orthodox Centre of the Ecumenical Patriarchate, 1992.

Schmemann, Alexander. *For the Life of the World: Sacraments and Orthodoxy.* New York: SVS, 1973.

Sherrard, Philip. *The Eclipse of Man and Nature: An Enquiry into the Origins and Consequences of Modern Science.* West Stockbridge: Lindisfarne, 1987.

———. *Human Image, World Image.* Ipswitch: Golgonooza Press, 1990.

———. *The Sacred in Life and Art.* Ipswitch: Golgonooza Press, 1990.

Siewers, Alfred K. *Strange Beauty: Ecocritical Approaches to Early Medieval Landscape.* New York: Palgrave Macmillan, 2009.

Stefanatos, Joanne. *Animals and Man: A State of Blessedness.* Minneapolis, Minn.: Light and Life, 1992.

Stefanatos, Joanne. *Animals Sanctified: A Spiritual Journey.* Minneapolis, Minn.: Life and Life, 2001.

So That God's Creation Might Live: The Orthodox Church Responds to the Ecological Crisis. Proceedings of the Inter-Orthodox Conference on Environmental Protection, Crete 1991. Bialystok, Poland: Ecumenical Patriarchate assisted by SYNDESMOS, 1991.

Theokritoff, Elizabeth. *Living in God's Creation: Orthodox Perspectives on Ecology.* Crestwood, N.Y.: St. Vladimir's Seminary Press, 2009.

Vasileios, Archimandrite. *Beauty and Hesychia in Athonite Life.* Montreal: Alexander Press, 1996.

Ware, Metropolitan Kallistos (of Diokleia). *Through the Creation to the Creator.* London: Friends of the Centre Papers, 1997.

Woloschak, Gayle E. *Beauty and Unity in Creation: The Evolution of Life.* Minneapolis: Light and Life, 1996.

Articles

Aidan, Rasophoremonk. "Autumn Seeds from Athos." *Friends of Mount Athos Annual Report* (1996).

Alexy II, Patriarch of Moscow. "Nature Is a Friend and Source of God's Wisdom." In *Christianity and Sustainable Development in the Baltic Sea Region.* Stockholm: Christian Council of Sweden, 1997.

Bartholomew, Ecumenical Patriarch. "The Orthodox Faith and the Environment." *Sourozh* 62 (1995).

Bloom, Metropolitan Anthony (of Sourozh). "Body and Matter in Spiritual Life." In *Sacrament and Image.* London: Fellowship of St. Alban and St. Sergius, 1987.

———. "Sacred Materialism in Christianity." In *the Experience of the Incarnation: The Body as the Temple of the Holy Spirit* (Oxford: St. Stephen's Press, n.d.).

Bordeianu, Radu. "Maximus and Ecology: The Relevance of Maximus the Confessor's Theology of Creation for the Present Ecological Crisis." *Downside Review* 127 (2009): 103–126.

Briere [Theokritoff], Elizabeth. "Creation, Incarnation, and Transfiguration: The Material World and Our Understanding of It." *Sobornost/ECR* 11, nos. 1–2 (1989).

Brock, Sebastian. "Humanity and the Natural World in the Syriac Tradition." *Sobornost/ECR* 12, no. 2 (1990).

———. "World and Sacrament in the Writings of the Syrian Fathers." *Sobornost* 6, no. 10 (1974).

Chryssavgis, John. "A Doxological Approach to Creation." *On the Move* 68 (1990).

———. "Essence and Energies: Dynamic Anthropology and Cosmology." In *Human Beings and Nature*, ed. G. Moses and N. Ormerod. Sydney: Sydney College of Divinity, 1992.

———. "Giver of Life, Sustain Your Creation." *WCC Pre-Assembly Report.* 1990.

———. "Reflections on Church and Environment." In *Crosstalk: Topics of Australian Church and Society*, ed. P. Henman. Brisbane: Boolarong, 1991.

———. "Transfigured Creation and Transfigured Persons." In *Come Holy Spirit, Renew the Whole Creation*, ed. G. Lemopoulos. Tertios Publications, Katerini, 1991. In Greek. [Also appeared in English: *The Ecumenical Review* 42 (1990).]

———. "The World of the Icon and Creation: An Orthodox Perspective on Ecology and Pneumatology." In *Christianity and Ecology: Seeking the Well-Being of Earth and Humans*, ed. D. Hessel and R. Radford Ruether. Cambridge, Mass.: Harvard University Press, 1999.

———. "Orthodox Christianity and the Environment." In *Worldviews, Religion, and the Environment: A Global Anthology*, ed. R. Foltz. Thomson: Wadsworth, 2002.

———. "The Cry of the Heart: Environmental Mission." *Bulletin of the Boston Theological Institute* 3, no. 1 (Fall 2003).

———. "The World of the Icon and Creation: An Orthodox Perspective on Ecology and Pneumatology." In *Seeing God Everywhere: Essays on Nature and the Sacred*, ed. Barry Macdonald. Bloomington, Ind.: World Wisdom, 2003.

———. "The Earth as Sacrament: Insights from Orthodox Christian Theology and Spirituality." In *The Oxford Handbook of Religion and Ecology*, ed. Roger S. Gottlieb. Oxford: Oxford University Press, 2006.

Clapsis, E. "Population, Consumption, and the Environment." In *Boston Theological Conference Papers*. Boston, 1996.

Clément, Olivier. "The Glory of God Hidden in His Creatures." In *The Roots of Christian Mysticism*. London: New City, 1993.

Conradie, Ernst M., ed. "Eastern Christian Thought." Chapter 1 of *Creation and Salvation*, vol. 2: *A Companion on Recent Theological Movements*. Zurich, LIT Verlag, 2012.

Constas, Nicholas P. "Commentary on the Patriarchal Message on the Day of the Protection of the Environment." *Greek Orthodox Theological Review* 35, no. 3 (1990): 179–194.

Economou, Elias. "An Orthodox View of the Ecological Crisis." *Theologia* 61, no. 4 (1990): 607–619.

Evdokimov, Paul. "Nature." *Scottish Journal of Theology* 18 (1965).

Foltz, Bruce V., "Discerning the Spirit in Creation: Orthodox Christianity and Environmental Science." In *Science and the Orthodox Church*, ed. D. Buxhoevenden and G. Woloschak. Surrey: Ashgate, 2011.

———. "Ecology." In *The Encyclopedia of Eastern Orthodox Christianity*, ed. J. A. McGuckin, 2:200–205. Oxford: Blackwell, 2011.

———. "Medieval Philosophy." In *The Encyclopedia of Environmental Ethics and Philosophy*, ed. R. Frodeman and B. Callicott. London: Macmillan, 2008.

———. "Nature Godly and Beautiful: The Iconic Earth." *Research in Phenomenology* (2001).

———. "Nature's Other Side: The Demise of Nature and the Phenomenology of Givenness." In *Nature Revisited: New Essays in Environmental Philosophy*, ed. B. V. Foltz and R. Frodeman. Bloomington: Indiana University Press, 2004.

———. "The Resurrection of Nature: Environmental Metaphysics in Sergei Bulgakov's *Philosophy of Economy*." *Philosophy and Theology* 18, no. 1 (2006).

———. "Sailing to Byzantium: Nature and City in the Eastern Empire." In *The Natural City*, ed. S. Scharper and I. Stefanovich. Toronto: University of Toronto Press, 2011.

———. "Seeing God Everywhere: The Philosophy of Nature in Maximus, Florensky, and Ibn 'Arabi." *Sophia: The Journal of Traditional Studies* 13, no. 1 (Spring/Summer 2007).

———. "Shook Foil and Trodden Sod: Nature, Beauty, and the Holy." *Environmental Philosophy* 1, no. 1 (2004).

Gorainoff, Irina. "Holy Men of Patmos." *Sobornost* 6, no. 5 (Spring 1972): 337–344.

Gorodetzky, Nadejda. "The Prayer of Jesus." *Blackfriars* 23, no. 263 (February 1942): 74–78.

Grdzelidze, Tamara. "Creation and Ecology: How Does the Orthodox Church Respond to Ecological Problems?" *Ecumenical Review* 54, no. 3 (2002).

Gregorios, Hieromonk [of Koutloumousiou]. "The Cosmos as Realm of Liturgy." In *Synaxis*, vol. 1: *Environment-Anthropology-Creation*, ed. John Hadjinicolaou, 245–249 (Montreal: Alexander Press, 2006).

Gregorios, Metropolitan Paulos (Verghese). "Christology and Creation." In *Tending the Garden: Essays on the Gospel and the Church*, ed. W. Granberg-Michaelson. Grand Rapids, Mich.: Eerdmans, 1987.

———. "New Testament Foundations for Understanding the Creation." In *Liberating Life: Contemporary Approaches to Ecological Theology*, ed. Charles Birch et al. Maryknoll, N.Y.: Orbis, 1990.

———. "Science and Faith." *Ecumenical Review* 37 (1985). Also appeared in *Church and Society: Ecumenical Perspectives. Essays in Honour of Paul Abrecht*, ed. Emilio Castro. Geneva, 1985.

———. "Science and Faith: Complementary or Contradictory?" In *Faith and Science in an Unjust World*, vol. 1: *Plenary Presentations*, ed. Roger L. Shinn. Geneva, 1980.

———. "Six Bible Studies." In *The New Faith-Science Debate: Probing Cosmology, Technology, and Theology*, ed. John M. Mangum. Geneva, 1989.

———. "Theological Trends. Mastery and Mystery: Spirituality within Humanity's Mediating Role." *The Way: Contemporary Christian Spirituality* (October 1986).

Gschwandtner, Crina. "Orthodox Ecological Theology: Bartholomew I and Orthodox Contributions to the Ecological Debate." *International Journal for the Study of the Christian Church* 10, no. 2–3 (2010): 130–143.

———. "Sabbath and Eighth Day: On the Messianic Dimensions of Ecological Practices." *Sobornost* 33, no. 2 (2011): 56–94.

Guroian, Vigen. "'Cleansers of the Whole Earth': The Ecological Spirituality of the Armenian Church." *Greek Orthodox Theological Review* 36, nos. 3–4 (Fall/Winter 1991): 263–276.

———. "Ecological Ethics: An Ecclesial Event." In *Ethics after Christendom: Towards an Ecclesial Christian Ethic*. Grand Rapids, Mich.: Eerdmans, 1994.

Harakas, Stanley S. "'The Earth Is the Lord's': Orthodox Theology and the Environment." *Greek Orthodox Theological Review* 44, nos. 1–4 (Spring/Winter 1999): 149–162.

———. "Ecological Reflections on Contemporary Orthodox Thought in Greece." *Epiphany Journal* 10, no. 3 (1990): 46–61.

———. "The Ethics of the Energy Crisis." In *Contemporary Moral Issues*. Minneapolis, Minn.: Light and Life, 1982.

Hart, Aidan. "Transfiguring Matter: The Icon as Paradigm of Christian Ecology." http://www.aidanharticons.com.

Horuzhy, Sergey S. "The Process of the Deification of the Human Person and Technology in Eastern-Orthodox Christianity." In *Nature and Technology in the*

World Religions, ed. Peter Koslowski. Dordrecht and Boston: Kluwer Academic Publishers, 2001.
Ignatius IV, Patriarch of Antioch. "Three Sermons on the Environment: A Theology of Creation; A Spirituality of the Creation; The Responsibility of Christians." *Sourozh* 38 (1989).
Khalil, Issa J. "The Ecological Crisis: An Eastern Christian Perspective." *St. Vladimir's Theological Quarterly* 22, no. 4 (1978).
———. "For the Transfiguration of Nature: Ecology and Theology." *Epiphany Journal* 10, no. 3 (1990): 19–36.
Knight, Christopher C. "Theistic Naturalism and the Word Made Flesh: Complementary Approaches to the Debate on Panentheism." In *In Whom We Live and Move and Have Our Being: Panentheistic Reflections on God's Presence in a Scientific World*, ed. Philip Clayton and Arthur Peacocke. Grand Rapids, Mich.: Eerdmans, 2004.
Limouris, Metropolitan Gennadios. "The Church as Mystery." In *Church, Kingdom, World: The Church as Mystery and Prophetic Sign*. Geneva: WCC, 1986.
———. "Creation—Kingdom of God—Eschatology." In *Creation and the Kingdom of God*. Church and Society Documents 5. Geneva, 1988.
———. "New Challenges, Visions, and Signs of Hope: Orthodox Insights on JPIC." In *Between the Flood and the Rainbow*, ed. D. Preman Niles. Geneva: WCC, 1992.
Louth, Andrew. "Between Creation and Transfiguration: The Environment in the Eastern Orthodox Tradition." In *Ecological Hermeneutics: Biblical, Historical, and Theological Perspectives*, ed. D. G. Horrell et al. Edinburgh: T&T Clark, 2012.
———. "The Cosmic Vision of Saint Maximus the Confessor." In *In Whom We Live and Move and Have Our Being: Panentheistic Reflections on God's Presence in a Scientific World*, ed. Philip Clayton and Arthur Peacocke. Grand Rapids, Mich.: Eerdmans, 2004.
Makrides, Vasilios N. "Christianity—Eastern versus Western." In *The Encyclopedia of Religion and Nature*, ed. Bron R. Taylor et al. 2 vols. London: Continuum, 2005, 2008.
Makarios, Monk. "The Monk and Nature in the Orthodox Tradition." In *So That God's Creation Might Live* (see above).
Meyendorff, John. "Creation in the History of Orthodox Theology." *St. Vladimir's Theological Quarterly* 27 (1983).
Morrison, Keith. "Wilderness as the Kingdom of God." *Ecotheology* 6, nos. 1–2 (2001).
Mousalimas, S. A. "The Divine in Nature: Animism or Panetheism?" *Greek Orthodox Theological Review* 35, no. 4 (1990): 367–375.
Mouzelis, Nicos. "Religion, Science, and the Environment: A Synthetic View." *Sourozh* 70 (1997).
Muratore, Stephen. "Earth Stewardship: Radical Deep Ecology of Patristic Christianity." *Epiphany Journal* 3, no. 2 (1992); 3, no. 4 (1993).

Nesteruk, Alexei V. "Ecological Insights on the Anthropic Reasoning in Cosmology: Ecological Imperative versus Cosmological Eschatology." *Proceedings of the First International Conference; Ecology and Democracy—The Challenge of the Twenty-First Century*, ed. Irena Hanousková, Miloslav Lapka, and Eva Cudlinová, 110–113. České Budějovice, 1994.

———. "The Universe as Hypostatic Inherence in the Logos of God." In *In Whom We Live and Move and Have Our Being: Panentheistic Reflections on God's Presence in a Scientific World*, ed. Philip Clayton and Arthur Peacocke. Grand Rapids, Mich.: Eerdmans, 2004.

Oikonomou, Elias. "Holy Scripture and the Natural Environment." In *So That God's Creation Might Live* (see above).

Oleksa, Michael. "Icons and the Cosmos: The Missionary Significance." *Sourozh* 16 (1984); *Sacred Art Journal* 5, no. 1 (1984).

Osborne, Bishop Basil (of Sergievo). "Beauty in the Divine and in Nature." *Sourozh* 70 (1997).

———. "Towards 2000: The Transfiguration of the World." *One in Christ* 3 (1997); *Sourozh* 72 (1998).

Rogich, Daniel. "Ecological Soundings in the Eastern Christian Mystical Tradition." *Epiphany Journal* 10, no. 3 (1990): 62–71.

Rossi, Vincent. "Inspiration: Who Comes out of the Wilderness?" *GreenCross* 2, no. 2 (1996).

Siewers, Alfred K. "The Bluest-Greyest-Greenest Eye: Colours of Martyrdom and Colours of the Winds as Iconographic Landscape." *Cambrian Medieval Celtic Studies* 50 (2005): 31–66.

———. "Cooper's Green World: Adapting Ecosemitics to the Mythic Eastern Woodlands." In *James Fenimore Cooper, His Country and His Art*, ed. Hugh MacDougall, 69–76. Oneonta, N.Y.: SUNY Oneonta and Cooper Society, 2009.

———. "Desert Islands: Europe's Atlantic Archipelago as Ascetic Landscape." In *Studies in the Medieval Atlantic*, ed. Benjamin Hudson. Forthcoming in Palgrave Macmillan's New Middle Ages series, 2012.

———. "The Early Medieval Sublime." In *Beauty and the Beautiful in Eastern Christian Culture*, ed. Natalia Ermolaev. The Sophia Insittute Studies in Orthodox Theology 6, 212–224. New York: Theotokos Press, 2012.

———. "Ecocriticism." In *A Dictionary of Cultural and Critical Theory*, 2nd ed., ed. Michael Payne and Jessica Rae Barbera, 205–210. Malden, Mass.: Wiley-Blackwell, 2010.

———. "Ecopoetics and the Origins of English Literature." In *Environmental Criticism for the Twenty-First Century*, ed. Stephanie LeMenager, Teresa Shewry, and Ken Hiltner, 105–120. Routledge, 2011.

———. "Environmentalist Readings of Tolkien." In *The Tolkien Encyclopedia: Scholarship and Critical Assessment*, ed. Michael D. C. Drout, 166–167. New York: Routledge, 2006.

———. "Eriugena, the Irish Otherworld, and Early Medieval Nature." Invited contribution to *Eriugena and Creation*, ed. W. Otten and M. Allen. Leiden: Brill, forthcoming.

———. "The Green Otherworlds of Early Medieval Literature." In *The Cambridge Companion to Environmental Literature*, ed. Louise Westling. Cambridge: Cambridge University Press, forthcoming.

———. "Landscapes of Conversion: Guthlac's Mound and Grendel's Mere as Expressions of Anglo-Saxon Nation Building." *Viator* 34 (2003): 1–39. Revised and reprinted in *The Postmodern Beowulf: A Critical Casebook*, ed. Eileen A. Joy, Mary K. Ramsey, and Bruce D. Gilchrist. Morgantown: West Virginia University Press, 2006.

———. "Liturgizing the World: Religion, Science, and the Environmental Crisis in Light of the Sacrificial Ethic of Sacred Cosmology." *Ecotheology* 3 (1997).

———. "Pre-Modern Ecosemiotics: The Green World as Literary Ecology." In *Spatiality, Memory, and Visualisation of Culture/Nature Relationships: Theoretical Aspects*, ed. Tiina Peil, 39–68. University of Tartu Press, 2011.

———. "Spenser's Green World." *Early English Studies* 3 (2011). http://www.uta.edu/english/ees/fulltext/siewers3.html.

———. "Tolkien's Cosmic-Christian Ecology." In *Tolkien's Modern Middle Ages*, ed. Jane Chance and Alfred K. Siewers. The New Middle Ages series. New York: Palgrave Macmillan, 2005.

———. "Writing an Icon of the Land: The *Mabinogi* as a Mystagogy of Landscape." *Peritia* 19 (2005): 193–228.

Staniloae, Dimitru. "Christian Responsibility in the World." In *The Tradition of Life*, ed. A. M. Allchin. London: Fellowship of St. Alban and St. Sergius, 1971.

———. "The World as Gift and Sacrament of God's Love." *Sobornost* 5, no. 9 (1969).

Tataryn, Myroslaw. "The Eastern Tradition and the Cosmos." *Sobornost/ECR* 11, nos. 1–2 (1989): 41–52.

Theokritoff, Elizabeth. "The Birth of the Creator and the Wonder of Creation." *Alive in Christ* 17, no. 3 (Winter 2001): 25–28.

———. "Cosmic Priesthood and the Human Animal: Speaking of Man and the Natural World in a Scientific Age." In *Thinking Modernity: Towards a Reconfiguration of the Relationship between Orthodox Theology and Modern Culture*, ed. Assaad E. Kattan and Fadi A. Georgi, 105–131. St. John of Damascus Institute of Theology, University of Balamand/Westphalian Wilhelm's University Center for Religious Studies, 2010.

———. "Creation and Priesthood in Modern Orthodox Thinking." *Ecotheology* 10, no. 3 (December 2005): 344–363.

———. "Creation and Salvation in Orthodox Worship." *Ecotheology* 10 (January 2001).

———. "Creator and Creation." In *Cambridge Companion to Orthodox Christian Theology*, ed. Mary Cunningham and Elizabeth Theokritoff. Cambridge: Cambridge University Press, 2008.

---. "Embodied Word and New Creation: Some Modern Orthodox Insights Concerning the Material World." In *Abba: The Tradition of Orthodoxy in the West. Festschrift for Bishop Kallistos Ware*, ed. John Behr, Andrew Louth, and Dimitri Conomos, 221–238. Crestwood, N.Y.: St Vladimir's Seminary Press, 2003.

---. "Eucharistic and Ascetic Ethos in Parish Life." *Creation's Joy* 1, no. 2 (1996).

---. "A Eucharistic and Ascetic Ethos: Orthodox Christianity and the Environment." In *Shap Working Party on World Religions in Education 2008/2009: The Environment*, 25–27.

---. "From Sacramental Life to Sacramental Living." *Greek Orthodox Theological Review* 44, nos. 1–4 (1999): 505–524.

---. "The High Word's Mystery Play: Creation and Salvation in St. Maximus the Confessor." In *Creation and Salvation*, vol. 1: *A Mosaic of Selected Classic Christian Theologies*, ed. Ernst M. Conradie. Münster: LIT Verlag, 2011.

---. "'Let Them Have Dominion': The Witness of the Saints." *St. Tikhon's Theological Journal* 2 (2004): 51–68.

---. "Natural Symbolism and Creation." *Sourozh* 80 (May 2000).

---. "Orthodoxy and the Environment." *Sourozh* 58 (1994).

---. "Relics and the Transfiguration of the World." *Praxis* 5, no. 2 (Winter 2006): 19–22.

---. "The Salvation of the World and Saving the Earth: An Orthodox Christian Approach." *Worldviews* 14, nos. 2–3 (2010): 141–156.

---. "'Taste and See That the Lord Is Good': Food in Orthodox Christianity." *Shap Working Party on World Religions in Education 2009/2010: Food, Faith, and Community*. http://www.shapworkingparty.org.uk/journals/index_0910.html.

Theokritoff, George. " Evolution and Eastern (Orthodox) Christianity." *Transdisciplinary Studies: Science, Spirituality, Society* 1 (2011): 155–203.

Theoxeni, Sister. "Lifestyle: Orthodox Tradition, and the Protection of the Environment: The Project of the Holy Monastery of Chrysopigi (Chania, Crete)." *Ecotheology* 4 (1998).

---. "The Orthodox Monastic Tradition and Our Relation to the Natural Environment." In *So That God's Creation Might Live* (see above).

Voicu, Constantin. "Orthodox Theology and the Problems of the Environment." *Greek Orthodox Theological Review* 38, nos. 1–4 (1993).

Ware, Metropolitan Kallistos (of Diokleia). "Ecological Crisis, Ecological Hope: The Orthodox Vision of Creation." Orthodoxy in America lecture, Fordham University, Bronx, N.Y., April 5, 2005.

---. "Lent and the Consumer Society." In *Living Orthodoxy in the Modern World*, ed. A. Walker and C. Carras. London: SPCK, 1996.

---. "The Value of Material Creation." *Sobornost* 6, no. 3 (1971).

Woloshak, Gayle. "Ecology, Evolution, and Bulgakov." In *Science and the Orthodox Church*, ed. D. Buxhoevenden and G. Woloschak. London: Ashgate, 2011.

———. "God of Life: Contemplating Evolution, Ecology, Extinction." *Ecumenical Review* 65, no. 2 (2013).

Zizioulas, Metropolitan John (of Pergamon). "The Book of Revelation and the Natural Environment." *Creation's Joy* 1, no. 2–3 (1996).

———. "Ecological Asceticism: A Cultural Revolution." *Our Planet* 7, no. 6 (1995); *Sourozh* 67 (1997).

———. "Ethics Versus Ethos: An Orthodox Approach to the Relation between Ecology and Ethics." In *The Environment and Ethics: Presentations and Reports, Summer Session on Halki '95*, ed. D. Tarasios. Militos Editions, 1997.

———. "The Eucharist and the Kingdom of God." *Sourozh: A Journal of Orthodox Life and Thought* 58 (1994): 1–12; 60 (1995): 32–46.

———. "Man: The Priest of Creation. A Response to the Ecological Problem." In *Living Orthodoxy in the Modern World*, ed. A. Walker and C. Carras. London: SPCK, 1996.

———. "Orthodoxy and Ecological Problems: A Theological Approach." In *The Environment and Religious Education: Presentations and Reports, Summer Session on Halki 1994*, ed. D. Tarasios. Militos Editions, 1997.

———. "Orthodoxy and the Problem of the Protection of the Natural Environment." In *So That God's Creation Might Live* (see above).

———. "Preserving God's Creation: Three Lectures on Theology and Ecology." *King's Theological Review* 12 (1989); *Sourozh* 39–41. Summary in *Christianity and Ecology*, ed. Elizabeth Breuilly and Martin Palmer (London, 1992).

APPENDIX

C

GLOSSARY

Compiled by Nicholas R. Anton

Anakephalaiosis The doctrine of recapitulation developed by St. Irenaeus of Lyons, stating that Christ is the second Adam who came to succeed or correct where Adam had failed, thereby restoring communion between God and humanity and reestablishing the potential for salvation.

Anaphora The part of the Divine Liturgy in the Orthodox Church when the faithful offer the bread and wine to God, who in turn sends down the Holy Spirit to consecrate the holy gifts into the Body and Blood of Christ.

Apokatastasis A controversial doctrine, originated by Origen, according to which in the end all creatures, both good and evil, will share in God's grace of salvation in a particular way; a restoration to the original condition of creation or universal salvation.

Apophaticism Describing God through the use of negations, this teaching underlines the transcendence and incomprehensibility of God while proclaiming the possibility of a face-to-face encounter with the unknowable God, an unmediated union with the inaccessible divinity.

Canon A poem consisting of nine odes praising a biblical event, feast day, or saint. Originating in the seventh century, the *Kanon* flourished after iconoclasm and replaced the *kontakion*.

Docetism The second-century teaching according to which Christ did not actually assume flesh; rather, His physical body was a mere illusion. Docetists do not believe in the death and Resurrection of Christ.

Entelechy A philosophical term meaning the actualization of something which had been potential, contributing to progress in the perfection of the soul.

Gnosticism In the context of the first centuries after Christ's death and resurrection, it teaches that humanity is trapped in the material world by an evil deity, the alleged god of the Old Testament, while the good deity, who is preached by Christ, reveals "special knowledge" to a select few that find salvation in the escape from evil and the material world.

Hyperousiotes Literally translated as "beyond being," this term is used by Dionysius the Areopagite to describe the "otherness" of God from created beings.

Hypostasis A more accurate word than "person" relating to "how" God is and describing the "triune" nature of the Holy Trinity, who is one in essence.

Iconostasis A carved wood or sculpted marble screen with iconic depictions of Christ, the Theotokos, saints, and various biblical scenes, this separates the nave of the church, where the faithful worship, from the sacred altar, where the clergy lead the worship service.

Kataphaticism Describing God using positive terminology, this teaching describes what God is. Since defining God's attributes ultimately limits the limitless, Orthodox Christian theology maintains that kataphatic theology is important as a means toward the less limiting, and therefore superior, apophatic theology.

Kontakion A sermon in poetic form consisting of a number of stanzas, called Oikoi, all of which are structurally and melodically alike. Today, only the leading thematic, melodic hymn remains and is chanted within the Kanon during Matins and the Divine Liturgy.

Logismos Though originally signifying a thought, reckoning, or reasoning, this term is normally understood to have a negative connotation as harmful to the soul or the community.

Logos The Word of God, the second *hypostasis* of the Holy Trinity, namely Christ; the Wisdom, Intellect, and Providence of God, through whom all creation came to be and in whom all creation exists. (For *logoi*, see *theoria physike*.)

Manichaeism The belief in a dualism that combined elements of Gnostic Christianity, Buddhism, Zoroastrianism, and Babylonian folklore. It spread throughout the Far East and Roman Empire between the third and fourteenth centuries. Manichaeans believed in a cosmic battle between good, or light, and evil, or darkness.

Nous St. Paul adopts this term in its original sense of one's rational mind; later the term is used by the Church Fathers to describe the intellectual or spiritual energy realized through prayer to and communion with God. St. Paul also refers to this as one's spirit. *Nous* is often contrasted with *dianoia* or discursive rationality, as a higher faculty of direct experience and immediate knowing rather than an indirect, inferential mode of knowledge

Panagia Literally translated as "all-holy," this term is used in the Orthodox Church as a name or title for the Theotokos or Mother of God. The Theotokos receives this name as she is viewed as the most holy human aside from Christ.

Philokalia A book containing classic spiritual texts on prayer dating from the fourth to the fifteenth centuries compiled by St. Nikodemos of the Holy Mountain and St. Makarios of Corinth in the eighteenth century to provide guidance in the life of silence or *hesychia*.

Pleroma Generally means "fullness"; Christian theology uses this term, starting with St. Paul in his letter to the Colossians, in order to refer to the all-encompassing nature of the divine. It is also used by Gnostics to describe the divinity and the sum of eons emanating therefrom.

Semandron A large wooden or iron plank that produces a resonating sound when struck, it is used in monasteries and churches to call the faithful to worship. This device was first used by Christians under Islamic rule when the use of bells was prohibited.

Spermatikos logos Philosophically, the generative source of cosmic order under which there is a multitude of *logoi*. For Christians, Christ, being the divine Word or Logos, is and always has been this generative source.

Synaxarion A voluminous set of books cataloguing the saints and providing a synopsis of their lives. During Orthodox liturgical services, this book is consulted for the daily commemoration of the saints inasmuch as it is organized in calendar form.

Synaxis A gathering of the faithful for liturgical purposes. Historically, the faithful from various communities assembled in a particular church in order to celebrate a feast. Today, rather than bringing many parishes together on such occasions, each parish celebrates the synaxis individually.

Theanthropocosmic Refers to the view that God, humanity, and all of creation are neither many nor one but rather both. It is the notion of the indestructible union of the three that results when they collaborate positively for the advancement of creation.

Theoria physike "Natural contemplation"; the "contemplation," "illumination," or "spiritual seeing" (*theoria*) of "nature" or "physical creation" (*physike*) that gains insight into its inner relation to the Creator. The term originates from the threefold path of monastic spirituality first articulated by Evagrius of Pontus in the fourth century: *praktike* or ascetic discipline that results in the *katharsis* or purification of the soul, and leads to *theoria physike* or contemplation of the inner essences or *logoi* of creation, and finally to *theologike* or "theology" proper, which Orthodox Christianity understands as union with the divine energies themselves (*theosis*).

Theotokos Literally translated as "God-bearer," a name interchangeable with Mary the Mother of God since she gave birth to Jesus Christ who is fully human and fully divine. There was great debate over this title during the Third Ecumenical Council; Nestorians refused the term, arguing that the uncontainable could not possibly be contained in a woman's body.

Thrice-Holy hymn Having roots in the Book of Isaiah and Christian liturgical foundations in the fourth and fifth centuries, this hymn praises the Holy Trinity by acknowledging the divine with the divine attributes of might and immortality, while ending with a supplication of mercy.

Troparion A brief, single-stanza hymn that makes a theological point. A troparion is written in one of eight modes of Byzantine music.

NOTES

Introduction. "The Sweetness of Heaven Overflows onto the Earth": Orthodox Christianity and Environmental Thought / John Chryssavgis and Bruce V. Foltz

1. Lynn White Jr., *Medieval Technology and Social Change* (Oxford: Oxford University Press, 1974), 134; Lynn White Jr., "The Historical Roots of Our Ecologic Crisis," in *Ecology and Religion in History*, ed. David Spring and Eileen Spring (New York: Harper & Row, 1974), 22–23.

2. Lynn White Jr., "The Historical Roots of Our Ecologic Crisis," 26. Italics added.

3. Cited in Olivier Clément, *The Roots of Christian Mysticism: Texts from the Patristic Era with Commentary* (Hyde Park, N.Y.: New City Press, 1996), 229.

The Logoi of Beings in Greek Patristic Thought / David Bradshaw

1. See Andrew Louth, *The Origins of the Christian Mystical Tradition: From Plato to Denys* (Oxford: Clarendon, 1981), 102–113; Robert E. Sinkewicz, *Evagrius of Pontus: The Greek Ascetic Corpus* (Oxford: Oxford University Press, 2003), xxxiv–xxxvii.

2. Admittedly, Plato specifically mentions only the Forms (*ideas*) of gods and animals (39e–40a). However, since the absolute Living Being is the model for the entire cosmos and all sensible things are images of the Forms (51e–52a), it must include the Forms for other things as well.

3. See Philo *On the Making of the World* 16–20, 34, most conveniently available in volume 1 of the Loeb edition of Philo's works.

4. Nonetheless, Philo does often speak of the Logos as if he were a personality distinct from God. This is apparently just poetic license; see the discussion in John Dillon, *The Middle Platonists, 80 B.C. to A.D. 220* (Ithaca, N.Y.: Cornell University Press, 1977), 155–161.

5. Diogenes Laertius *Lives of Eminent Philosophers* VII.135–136, trans. R. D. Hicks, in the Loeb edition.

6. Origen *Contra Celsum* IV.48.

7. See also *Stoicorum Veterum Fragmenta*, ed. H. von Arnim, 4 vols. (Leipzig: Teubner, 1903–24), vol. 1, numbers 37, 497; vol. 2, numbers 141, 717, 739, 780, 1027; vol. 3, number 141, with discussion in David E. Hahm, *The Origins of Stoic Cosmology* (Columbus: Ohio State University Press, 1977), 60–62, 75–76.

8. Stanley Lombardo, *Sky Signs: Aratus' Phaenomena* (Berkeley, Calif.: North Atlantic Books, n.d.), 1.

9. Origen *Commentary on John* I.19.114. Translations are from Ronald E. Heine, *Origen: Commentary on the Gospel according to John*, 2 vols. (Washington, D.C.: Catholic University of America Press, 1989, 1993). For the Greek, see *Origène: Commentaire sur Saint Jean*, ed. and trans. Cécile Blanc, 4 vols. (Paris: Les Éditions du Cerf, 1966–1982).

10. Ibid., I.34.244.

11. On the identity of the divine Wisdom and Logos, see further *Against Celsus* V.39 and *On First Principles* I.2.2.

12. *Commentary on John* XIII.42.274.

13. Ibid., XIII.42.280, translation modified.

14. This is also the term used in the four-volume translation of the *Philokalia* by G. E. H. Palmer, Philip Sherrard, and Kallistos Ware (London: Faber and Faber, 1979–1995).

15. *Commentary on John* XIX.5.146.

16. Ibid., XIX.5.147.

17. Furthermore, he argues that God could not be almighty unless there were creatures over whom He exercises power, and so (since to be almighty is an essential divine attribute) creatures must have always existed (*On First Principles* I.2.10); cf. n. 40 below.

18. Eusebius *Demonstration of the Gospel* V.5 (PG 22 377A); trans. W. J. Ferrar in Eusebius, *The Proof of the Gospel*, 2 vols. (Grand Rapids, Mich.: Baker, 1981), 1:249.

19. Ibid., IV.13 (PG 22 285A); trans. Ferrar, 1:188.

20. I pass over Plotinus, whose teaching would certainly be important for any full survey of the concept of the *logoi* of beings. For Plotinus, the *logoi* are formative principles found within Intellect, Soul, and bodies, each lower stage being an image or irradiation from the one prior (*Enneads* II.3.16–18, III.2.2, 16, III.5.9, III.8.2, IV.3.10, V.9.3). So far as I can tell, this conception had little influence on Christian authors, who instead understood the *logoi* in terms of the variegated presence of the Logos. Plotinus also does not make the *logoi* objects of vision or give them any significant epistemological function, as do Christian authors. For discussion of the *logoi* in Plotinus, see Deepa Majumdar, *Plotinus on the Appearance of Time and the World of Sense* (Aldershot: Ashgate, 2007), 87–90, and the references there cited.

21. Evagrius *Gnostic Chapters* V.12. For the Syriac text with a French translation, see Antoine Guillaumont, *Les Six Centuries des "Kephalaia Gnostica" d'Évagre le*

Pontique (Paris: Firmin-Didot, 1958) (*Patrologia Orientalia* 28.1). There is an English translation made from the French by Luke Dysinger, O.S.B., available at www.ldysinger.com; I follow it with slight modifications.

22. Ibid., V.42. For other passages on the *logoi* in Evagrius, see I.20, 23; II.35, 36, 45; V.17, 39. Some of these passages refer to the *logoi* only in the alternative Syriac version printed, with a retrotranslation into Greek, by W. Frankenberg, *Evagrius Ponticus* (Berlin: Weidmannsche Buchhandlung, 1912); the Greek is also printed by Dysinger.

23. See Elizabeth Clark, *The Origenist Controversy: The Cultural Construction of an Early Christian Debate* (Princeton, N.J.: Princeton University Press, 1992); or, more briefly, John Meyendorff, *Imperial Unity and Christian Divisions: The Church 450–680* A.D. (Crestwood, N.Y.: St. Vladimir's Seminary Press, 1989), 230–235.

24. Evagrius *On Prayer* 51, trans. Sinkewicz, in *Evagrius of Pontus*, 198, slightly modified. For the Greek text, see *Philokalia tōn Hierōn Nēptikōn* [in Greek] (Athens: Aster, 1974), 1:176–189 (where, however, this is chapter 52).

25. Ibid., 56 (*Philokalia*, chap. 57).

26. This is the famous definition of prayer in *On Prayer* 3.

27. It is surprising how little there is on this subject in the Cappadocian Fathers, who generally were not averse to Origenist ideas. The only reference to the *logoi* I have found is in the *Hexaemeron* of St. Gregory of Nyssa, which affirms that there is "a certain wise and skillful *logos* embedded in each of the things that are, although it may surpass our power to see." *Gregor Nysenni Opera*, vol. 4, pt. 1, ed. Hubertus Drobner (Leiden: Brill, 2009), 21, my translation. But Gregory does little with this idea, using it merely to argue that the speech seemingly attributed to God in Genesis 1 was not that of a literal voice but instead indicates the *logoi* embedded within creation. Gregory returns to the idea that God did not create through literal speech at greater length in *Contra Eunomium* II, where his concern is to combat Eunomius's claim that God gave creatures their original names, but he does not refer there to the *logoi*.

28. Dionysius the Areopagite *Divine Names* V.8 824C, my translation. For the Greek, see *Corpus Dionysiacum*, ed. Beate Regina Suchla, Günter Heil, and Adolf Martin Ritter (Berlin: Walter de Gruyter, 1990).

29. Ibid.

30. Ibid., IV.28 729A.

31. Ibid., VII.3 872A.

32. Dionysius *Celestial Hierarchy* I.3 121C–124A.

33. See, further, Alexander Golitzin, "Liturgy and Mysticism: The Experience of God in Eastern Orthodox Christianity," *Proc Ecclesia* 8 (1999): 159–186; and "Dionysius Areopagita: A Christian Mysticism?," *Pro Ecclesia* 12 (2003): 161–212.

34. For example, Vasilios Karayiannis, *Maxime le Confesseur: essence et energies de Dieu* (Paris: Beauchesne, 1993), 201–206, 215–222; Jean-Claude Larchet, *La divinization de l'homme selon saint Maxime le Confesseur* (Paris: Les Éditions du Cerf, 1996), 112–123; David Bradshaw, *Aristotle East and West: Metaphysics and the Division*

of Christendom (Cambridge: Cambridge University Press, 2004), 201–207; Nikolaos Loudovikos, *A Eucharistic Ontology: Maximus the Confessor's Eschatological Ontology of Being as Dialogical Reciprocity* (Brookline, Mass.: Holy Cross Orthodox Press, 2010), 53–194. I have also written briefly of the *logoi* in "Maximus the Confessor," in *Cambridge History of Philosophy in Late Antiquity*, ed. Lloyd Gerson (Cambridge: Cambridge University Press, 2011), 813–828, from which I borrow in the following.

35. Maximus *Mystagogy* 2 (PG 91 669B–C); trans. G. C. Berthold in *Maximus the Confessor: Selected Writings* (New York: Paulist Press, 1985), 189, modified. The biblical reference is to Ezekiel 1:16, 10:10.

36. Ibid., 5 681B; trans. Berthold, 194.

37. Gregory Nazianzen *Orations* 14.7.

38. Maximus *Ambigua* 7 (PG 91 1077C), my translation. For an English version of this Ambiguum, see *On the Cosmic Mystery of Christ: Selected Writings from St. Maximus the Confessor* (Crestwood, N.Y.: St. Vladimir's Seminary Press, 2003), 45–74.

39. Ibid., 1080A–B. Maximus draws the conclusion only that rational beings are "portions of God," although his argument would seem to imply that the same is true of *all* beings. For more on the distinction between the *logoi* of particulars and universals see *Ambigua* 41, particularly 1312B–1313B; translated in Andrew Louth, *Maximus the Confessor* (London: Routledge, 1996), 156–162.

40. Maximus *Ambigua* 7 1081A–B. I take it that this is Maximus's answer to the argument of Origen that creatures must have always existed since God has always been almighty (*On First Principles* I.2.10; above, n. 17). Interestingly, Maximus's argument takes its cue from Origen's own observation later in *On First Principles* that it may be sufficient merely that creatures preexisted in the Logos "in form and outline" (I.4.4).

41. Maximus *Ambigua* 7 1081B–C.

42. Ibid., 1085A. Note also the discussion of creation in *Centuries on Charity* IV.3–6, which affirms that the creation is not coeternal with God and that God created "when He wished" (*hote eboulēthē*).

43. Maximus *Ambigua* 21 (PG 91 1249B). For a translation of the relevant portion of this treatise, see Panayiotis Nellas, *Deification in Christ: Orthodox Perspectives on the Nature of the Human Person* (Crestwood, N.Y.: St. Vladimir's Seminary Press, 1987), 216–218.

44. Maximus *Ambigua* 21 1248B. The phrase "exemplary image" (*paradigmatikē eikōn*) is a deliberate paradox; presumably it indicates that the faculties of the soul are ontologically prior, so that the senses are images of them, whereas the senses are prior in the order of experience and knowledge. The distinction between *nous* and *logos* is roughly that between intuitive knowledge and discursive reason; see further my "The Mind and the Heart in the Christian East and West," *Faith and Philosophy* 26 (2009): 576–598.

45. Maximus *Ambigua* 21 1248C–D, trans. Nellas, modified.

46. See further Bradshaw, *Aristotle East and West*, 197–201.

47. Maximus *Ambigua* 21 1249C–D, trans. Nellas, modified.

48. Without at all denying the real piety of many early modern scientists, it is worth noting how far the seventeenth-century "Book of Nature" is from its patristic source. The latter is exemplified in an episode recorded of St. Antony the Great by Evagrius: "One of the sages of that time came to Antony the just and said, 'Father, how can you endure being deprived of the comfort of books?' And he said, 'My book, Philosopher, is the nature of beings, and it is present whenever I wish to read the words of God'" (*Praktikos* 92 [PG 40 1249B], trans. Sinkewicz, *Evagrius of Pontus*, 112). Plainly, Antony does not refer here to scientific inquiry but to a direct intuitive vision such as Evagrius went on to describe in his own concept of natural contemplation.

Hierarchy and Love in St. Dionysius the Areopagite / Eric D. Perl

1. M. N. Babu, "Human Cloning: An Ethically Negative Feat in Genetic Engineering," *Philosophy and Social Action* 24 (1998): 47.

2. *Corpus Dionysiacum I. De divinis nominibus*, ed. Beata Regina Suchla (Berlin: Walter de Gruyter, 1990). Henceforth DN.

3. This is, indeed, implied in the Nicene-Constantinopolitan Creed: if God is truly the "maker of all things," it follows that he himself is not one of all things.

4. Dionysius is here citing 1 Cor. 15:28, his principal scriptural justification for attributing to God the names of all things and claiming that all these names are found in the scriptures.

5. Cf. Aristotle *On the Soul* II.4, 415b13: "To be, for a living thing, is to live." So we may say, "To live, for a thinking thing, is to think," and therefore, "To be, for a thinking thing, is to think."

6. *Corpus Dionysiacum II. De Coelesti Hierarchia, De Ecclesiastica Hierarchia, De Mystica Theologia, Epistulae*, ed. Günter Heil and Adolf Martin Ritter (Berlin: Walter de Gruyter, 1991). Henceforth CH.

7. See Jean-Luc Marion, *The Idol and Distance*, trans. Thomas A. Carlson (New York: Fordham University Press, 2001), 166; cf. Louis Bouyer, *Cosmos* (Petersham, Mass.: St. Bede's, 1988), 200: "The various degrees . . . of the Dionysian hierarchies, are simply so many relays for communicating what the higher beings can keep for themselves only by sharing freely with others (as pseudo-Dionysius explicitly asserts). And . . . it is still the gift of God, i.e., not only something he gives, but in the final analysis his very self."

8. In the words of A. H. Armstrong, "That which is utterly beyond us and cannot be expressed or thought is by its very transcendence of distance and difference most intimately present." A. H. Armstrong, "The Hidden and the Open in Hellenic Thought," in *Eranos* 54 (Frankfurt am Main: Insel Verlag, 1987); repr. in *Hellenic and Christian Studies* (Aldershot: Variorum, 1990), 5:103.

The Beauty of the World and Its Significance in St. Gregory the Theologian / John Anthony McGuckin

1. The Platonic epistemological principle of *Homoiosis*. See, further, L. Golden, "Plato's Concept of Mimesis," *British Journal of Aesthetics* 12, no. 2 (1975): 118–131.

2. Why he bans low-level mimetic activity (such as poetry, he thinks) as bound to lead astray from truth. See *Republic* 94e–396a. See, further, Golden, "Plato's Concept of Mimesis."

3. 186–255 A.D. See, further, J. A. McGuckin, ed., *The Westminster Handbook to Origen of Alexandria* (Louisville, Ky.: WJK Press, 2004).

4. The Christian Fathers of the Origenian school consistently understand there to be an ascentive line of triplex awareness in the human: bodily (or somatic) awareness, psychic (epithymic or emotive) awareness, and noetic awareness. The first and some of the second we share with all higher life forms on the planet; the third we share only with the angels. Not all humans manage to experience all three forms fully. The lives of some are lived predominantly in the first two levels of awareness. The attainment of the third, noetic, is only possible after sustained ascesis and is subject to the grace of divine illumination.

5. For the Greek Fathers are quintessentially Eclectics, and to Plato they add large amounts of Aristotelian teleotic theory and stir with a prevailing approach to the Scriptures as numinously revelant text (a practice very similar to methods practiced in the schools of late Pythagoreanism and middle Platonism).

6. One might cite a plethora of examples, but let me take one only here, in terms of appeals to the "unspoiled beauty" of Alaska as a reason to prevent drilling for oil.

7. 186–255 A.D. See, further, John Anthony McGuckin, ed., *The Westminster Handbook to Origen* (Louisville, Ky.: Westminster John Knox Press, 2004).

8. Origen's best intellectual heirs energetically adapt him: Gregory of Nazianzus, Basil of Caesarea, Gregory of Nyssa, Evagrius of Pontus, Didymus of Alexandria, and Maximus the Confessor.

9. *Pace* some recent attempts to drive a wedge of opposition between him and his mentor on the grounds that he did not follow him in certain major aspects of his school's tradition; notwithstanding the fact that by the third century all Christian writers are massively eclectic in one form or another, as was the Platonic *Schola* itself. Porphyry's scorn of Origen as being no Platonist at all comes as an apologetic testimony to the fact that so many of the Christians of the age had adopted him as the proper "fixing" of Plato for the Church.

10. For an account of his life and thought, see J. A. McGuckin, *St. Gregory of Nazianzus: An Intellectual Biography* (Crestwood, N.Y.: SVS Press, 2001); J. A. McGuckin, "Gregory of Nazianzus," in *The Cambridge History of Philosophy in Late Antiquity*, ed. L. Gerson (Cambridge: Cambridge University Press, 2011). Gregory's writings have been abstracted in a modern approachable version in B. E. Daley, ed., *Gregory of Nazianzus* (New York: Routledge, 2006).

11. For a more precise discussion of the texts, see J. A. McGuckin, "Gregory of Nazianzus: The Rhetorician as Poet," in *Gregory of Nazianzus: Images and Reflections*, ed. T. Hagg and J. Bortnes (Copenhagen: Museum Tusculanum Press, 2005), 193–212.

12. One of his most famous and extended prose poems on the beauty of the world comes at the end of *Oration 27* (*First Theological Oration*), where he berates his logician-opponent Eunomius for thinking he can make statements about anything; Gregory tells his readers that many things render one speechless, citing then the beauties of the world order. The irony, of course, is that here we have an extremely well crafted, exceedingly "beautiful" presentation of the glories of the world order, meant to show that the highest appreciation is this apophatic wonderment (reverent awe). In other words—a splendid but extended oratorical advocacy of saying nothing! The priest of the world's beauty is thus, for Gregory, the divinely inspired poet.

13. St. Gregory Nazianzen *Carmina* 1.1.32, in J. P. Migne, ed., *Patrologia Graeca* (PG) 37: 511–514.

14. Also see *Oration* 28.13. "For every rational nature longs for God and for the First Cause, but is unable to grasp Him, for the reasons I have mentioned. Faint therefore with the desire, and as it were restive and impatient of the disability, it tries a second course, either to look at visible things, and out of some of them to make a god . . . (a poor contrivance, for in what respect and to what extent can that which is seen be higher and more godlike than that which sees, that this should worship that?), or else through the beauty and order of visible things to attain to that which is above sight; but not to suffer the loss of God through the magnificence of visible things."

15. See, further, J. A. McGuckin, "Deification in Greek Patristic Thought: The Cappadocian Fathers' Strategic Adaptation of a Tradition," in *Partakers of the Divine Nature: The History and Development of Deification in the Christian Tradition*, ed. M. Christensen and J. Wittung (Teaneck, N.J.: Farleigh Dickinson University Press, 2006).

16. St. Gregory Nazianzen *Carmina* 1.1.29, in J. P. Migne, ed., PG 37: 507–508.
17. St. Gregory Nazianzen *Carmina* 1.1.30, in J. P. Migne, ed., PG 37: 508–510.
18. St. Gregory Nazianzen *Carmina* 1.1.31, in J. P. Migne, ed., PG 37: 510–511.
19. *Orations* 27–31. P. Gallay and M. Jourjon, eds., *Sources Chrétiennes*, vol. 250 (Paris, 1978); J. P. Migne, ed., PG 35.
20. St. Gregory Nazianzen *Oration* 28.21.

Natural Contemplation in St. Maximus the Confessor and St. Isaac the Syrian / Metropolitan Jonah (Paffhausen)

1. Sebastian Brock, *Isaac of Nineveh: "The Second Part"* (Louvain: CSCO, 1995), chaps. IV–XLI.

2. See St. Isaac the Syrian, *The Syriac Fathers on Prayer and the Spiritual Life*, trans. Sebastian Brock (Kalamazoo, Mich.: Cistercian Publications, 1987).

3. See St. Maximus the Confessor, *Philokalia*, vol. 2 (London: Faber & Faber, 1981).

4. *The Ascetic Homilies of Saint Isaac the Syrian* (Boston: Holy Transfiguration Monastery, 1984).

5. See St. Isaac the Syrian, *The Syriac Fathers on Prayer and the Spiritual Life*. See also Brock, *Isaac of Nineveh: "The Second Part,"* chaps. IV–XLI.

Man and Cosmos in St. Maximus the Confessor / Andrew Louth

1. This is a revised version of a paper given at a conference funded by the Templeton Foundation in Windsor in 2001 on Panentheism and published as "The Cosmic Vision of St. Maximos the Confessor," in *In Whom We Live and Move and Have Our Being*, ed. Philip Clayton and Arthur Peacocke (Grand Rapids, Mich.: Eerdmans, 2004), 184–196.

2. For a brief introduction in English with a selection of translated texts, see Andrew Louth, *Maximus the Confessor* (London: Routledge, 1996).

3. Dumitru Stăniloae, *The Experience of God* (Brookline, Mass.: Holy Cross Orthodox Press, 1994), 4–5.

4. On this topic see I. H. Dalmais, "La théorie des 'logoi' des creatures chez S. Maxime le Confesseur," *Revue des Sciences Philosophiques et Théologiques* 36 (1952): 244–249; Joost Van Rossum, "The *Logoi* of Creation and the Divine 'Energies' in Maximus the Confessor and Gregory Palamas," *Studia Patristica* 27 (1993): 213–217; and, most recently, Torstein Theodor Tollefsen, *The Christological Cosmology of St. Maximus the Confessor* (Oxford: Oxford University Press, 2008).

5. See Theodor Haecker, *Hirtengedichte. Vergil: Vater des Abendlandes* (Frankfurt am Main: Fischer Bücherei, 1958), 131–132.

6. Cf. Dionysius *Divine Names* 5.8, quoted by Maximus *Ambigua* 7 (PG 91.1085A).

7. Maximus *Opusc.* 7 (PG 91.80A).

8. *Cap. Theol. et œcon.* II. 60 (PG 90.1149CD). Translation (slightly modified) from *The Philokalia: The Complete Text*, trans. G. E. H. Palmer, Philip Sherrard, and Kallistos Ware (London: Faber & Faber, 1981), 2:151.

9. Gregory Nazianzen *Oratio* 28.3 (ed. Paul Gallay, *Sources Chrétiennes* 250, 1978, p. 106).

10. Maximus *Ambigua* 41 (PG 91.1305BC).

11. Maximus *Ambigua* 41 (PG 91.1305A).

12. The most extensive treatment of St. Maximus's doctrine of deification can be found in Jean-Claude Larchet, *La divinisation de l'homme selon saint Maxime le Confesseur*, Cogitatio Fidei 194 (Paris: Éditions du Cerf, 1996). See also Norman Russell, *The Doctrine of Deification in the Greek Patristic Tradition* (Oxford: Oxford University Press, 2004), esp. 262–295.

13. One way of putting this is to say that the arc of Fall-Redemption (which has dominated Western theology) is in the theology of the Orthodox East subordinated to the arc of Creation-Deification.

14. See, e.g., Maximus *Ambigua* 10.31c (PG 91.1165D).

15. This is, for instance, the only interpretation entertained by St. Gregory of Nyssa in his *On the Making of Man* 1 (PG 44.128–132).

16. B. Pascal, *Pensées*, ed. Philippe Sellier (Paris: Mercure de France, 1976), §233.

17. Ibid., §231.

18. Ibid., §145.

19. See Gregory of Nyssa *On the Making of Man* 2ff., and Nemesios of Emesa *On the Nature of Man* 1.

Ecology, Theology, and the World / Savas Agouridis

1. From an article entitled "Ecology and Theology," *New Ecology* (November 1996): 58–62. Translated (with slight editorial changes in the subtitles) from the Greek by John Chryssavgis; edited by Marilyn Rouvelas. Prof. Agouridis was among the first theologians in Greece to author articles on this subject from as early as 1988; his articles were posthumously published in an anthology entitled *Visions and Realities* [*Oramata kai Pragmata*], 2nd ed. (Athens: Artos Zoes, 2010).

2. In *Science* 155 (1967): 1203–1207.

3. See Gen. 1:1–2:4a, 2:4b–2:7.

4. See Oscar Cullmann, *Christ and Time: The Primitive Christian Conception of Time* (Louisville, Ky.: Westminster John Knox Press, 1964).

5. See, for example, the work by the Roman Catholic theologian H. Paul Santmire, *The Travail of Nature: The Ambiguous Ecological Promise of Creation Theology* (Philadelphia: Fortress, 1985).

6. Idries Shah, *The Sufis* (New York: Anchor, 1970).

7. See E. E. Kellet, *A Short History of Religions* (London: Pelican, 1962), 268.

8. *Oratio ad Graecos* II, 29.

9. *Paedagogus* I, 12.

10. See, for instance, F. Gealy, *The Interpreter's Bible* (Nashville, Tenn.: Abingdon, 1955), 11:450ff.

11. Clearly, however, the passage in 1 Tim. 6:6–10 quickly transitions to the subject of heretics, which is the original reason it is inserted into this context, and it is addressed more generally to the Christian reader. The fact that St. Paul shifts from the context in these verses and writes in a tone that is not particularly Christian seems to imply that this passage is drawn from some Hellenistic instructional material, which he would like either to connect or else adapt to his intention.

12. See Nikodemus of the Holy Mountain, *Unseen Warfare: The Spiritual Combat*, rev. ed. (Scarsdale, N.Y.: St. Vladimir's Seminary Press, 1997).

Through Creation to the Creator / Metropolitan Kallistos (Ware) of Diokleia

1. See Archimandrite Paul Nikitaras, *O Gerontas Amphilochios Makris: mia synchroni morphi tis Patmou (1889–1970)* (Athens, 1984[?]), 47–49; Archimandrite Ignatios Triantis, *O Gerontas tis Patmou Amphilochios Makris (1889–1970)* (Patmos, 1993), 138–140.

2. Markos A. Gkiolas, *O Kosmas Aitolos kai I epochi tou* (Athens, 1972), 434 (para. 96), 93–94.

3. Theophilos Simopoulos, *Kosmas o Aitolos (1714–1779)* (Athens, 1979), 203.

4. Walter de la Mare, *Behold, This Dreamer* (London, 1942), 529.

5. Gregory of Nyssa *The Life of Moses* I, 20; II, 22; trans. Abraham J. Malherbe and Everett Ferguson (New York: Classics of Western Spirituality, 1978), 35, 39.

6. Thomas Traherne, *Centuries of Meditations* III, 2.

7. The title of a book by Philip Sherrard, *For Every Thing That Lives Is Holy* (London: Temenos Academy, 1995).

8. Elizabeth Barrett Browning, *Aurora Leigh* (1856), book 7.

9. Charles Williams, *Seed of Adam*, in *Collected Plays* (London, 1963), 160.

10. *Triads in Defense of the Holy Hesychasts* I, iii, 23.

11. Quoted in John Meyendorff, *Introduction à l'étude de Grégoire Palamas* (Paris, 1959), 294, n. 62.

12. Quoted in ibid., 288, n. 38.

13. *Ambigua* 22, PG91:1257AB. This is an obscure passage, difficult to interpret. See Lars Thunberg, *Man and the Cosmos: The Vision of St. Maximus the Confessor* (New York: St. Vladimir's Seminary Press, 1985), 137–143.

14. *Centuries on Theology* II, 10; trans. Philip Sherrard and Kallistos Ware, *The Philokalia: The Complete Text* (London, 1981), 2:139–140. Compare Matt. 13:31.

15. *The Book of Divine Works* IV, 11; quoted in Fiona Bowie and Oliver Davies, eds., *Hildegard of Bingen: An Anthology* (London, 1990), 33.

16. *The Book of Divine Works* I, 2; in Bowie and Davies, *Hildegard of Bingen*, 91–92. Also cited (in a different translation) by Seyyed Hossein Nasr, *Man and Culture: The Spiritual Crisis of Modern Man* (London: Mandala, 1976), 102–103.

17. Gerard Manley Hopkins, *Poems of Gerard Manley Hopkins*, 3rd ed., ed. Robert Bridges and W. H. Gardner (London, 1948), 95.

18. William Blake, *Poetry and Prose of William Blake*, ed. Geoffrey Keynes (London: Nonesuch, 1948), 860, 862.

19. Martin Buber, *Tales of the Hasidim: The Early Masters* (New York: Schocken, 1968), 97.

20. H. von Arnim, *Stoicorum Veterum Fragmenta* (Leipzig, 1903), 3:95, 390.

21. Aristotle, *Politics* I, i, 9 (1253a).

22. Charles Williams, "The Founding of the Company," in *The Region of the Summer Stars* (London, 1950), 38. Williams puts the phrase in inverted commas, but I do not know whom he is citing here.

23. Charles Williams, "The Redeemed City," in *The Image of the City and Other Essays*, ed. Anne Ridler (London, 1958), 104, 107, 109.

24. Charles Williams, "Anthropotokos," in *The Image of the City and Other Essays*, ed. Anne Ridler (London, 1958), 112.

25. *Oration* xxxviii, 11.

26. Buber, *Tales of the Hasidim*, 317.

27. See Kallistos Ware, "The Unity of the Human Person According to the Greek Fathers," in *Persons and Personality: A Contemporary Inquiry*, ed. Arthur Peacocke and Grant Gillett (Oxford, 1987), 202.

28. See ibid., 201.

29. *For the Life of the World: Sacraments and Orthodoxy* (New York: St. Vladimir's Seminary Press, 1973), 60–61.

30. This point is well made by Metropolitan Paulos Mar Gregorios, *The Human Presence: Ecological Spirituality and the Age of the Spirit* (New York, 1987), chap. 7, "Mastery and Mystery." This book was originally published by the World Council of Churches under the title *The Human Presence: An Orthodox View of Nature* (Geneva: World Council of Churches, 1978).

31. Thomas Merton, *The Way of Chuang Tzu* (New York, 1969), 76.

32. "The World as Gift and Sacrament of God's Love," *Sobornost, the Journal of the Fellowship of St. Alban and St. Sergius* 5, no. 9 (1969): 669.

33. Compare St. Leontius of Cyprus, *In Defense of the Icons of the Saints*, in PG 93:1604AB; cited in Kallistos Ware, *The Orthodox Way*, rev. ed. (New York: St. Vladimir's Seminary Press, 1995), 54–55.

34. Fr. Gervase Matthew, *Byzantine Aesthetics* (London, 1963), 23–24.

35. See Philip Sherrard, *The Rape of Man and Nature: An Enquiry into the Origins and Consequences of Modern Science* (Ipswich: Golgonooza, 1987); and Philip Sherrard, *Human Image: World Image. The Death and Resurrection of Sacred Cosmology* (Ipswich: Golgonooza, 1992).

36. Quoted in full in Vladimir Lossky, *The Mystical Theology of the Eastern Church* (London, 1957), 247–249.

37. *Sermon VI for Holy Week 5*, in PG 59:743–744; cited in Henri de Lubac, *Catholicism: Christ and the Common Destiny of Man* (London: Universe, 1962), 296–297.

38. "Message of His All-Holiness the Ecumenical Patriarch Dimitrios on the Day of the Protection of the Environment" (September 1, 1989), in *Orthodoxy and the Ecological Crisis*, published in 1990 by the Ecumenical Patriarchate and the World Wide Fund for Nature. The present Ecumenical Patriarch Bartholomew, continuing the work of his predecessor, has organized several international symposia on ecology. See in particular *So That God's Creation Might Live: The Orthodox Church Responds to the Ecological Crisis* (Proceedings of the Inter-Orthodox Conference on Environmental Protection, Orthodox Academy of Crete, November 1991), published by the Ecumenical Patriarchate in collaboration with the WWF in 1992.

Creation as Communion in Contemporary Orthodox Theology / Aristotle Papanikolaou

1. Aristotle Papanikolaou, *Being with God: Trinity, Apophaticism, and Divine-Human Communion* (South Bend, Ind.: University of Notre Dame Press, 2006). See also Aristotle Papanikolaou, "Orthodoxy, Postmodernity, and Ecumenism: The Difference That Divine-Human Communion Makes," *Journal of Ecumenical Studies* 42, no. 4 (2007): 527–546.

2. Sergius Bulgakov, *Sophia—The Wisdom of God: An Outline of Sophiology*, rev. ed., trans. Patrick Thompson, O. Fielding Clark, and Xenia Braikevitc (1937; Hudson, N.Y.: Lindisfarne, 1993), 25.

3. Ibid., 39.

4. Sergius Bulgakov, *The Comforter*, trans. Boris Jakim (1936; Grand Rapids, Mich.: Eerdmans, 2004), 359–393.

5. Bulgakov, *Sophia*, 43.

6. Sergius Bulgakov, *The Lamb of God*, trans. Boris Jakim (1933; Grand Rapids, Mich.: Eerdmans, 2008), 111.

7. Bulgakov, *The Comforter*, 63.

8. Bulgakov, *Sophia*, 48–49.

9. Ibid., 41.

10. Ibid., 54.

11. Bulgakov, *The Comforter*, 189.

12. Sergius Bulgakov, *The Bride of the Lamb*, trans. Boris Jakim (1945; Grand Rapids, Mich.: Eerdmans, 2002), 39. Though first published in 1945, this book was finished in 1939.

13. Bulgakov, *The Lamb of God*, 103–104.

14. Bulgakov, *Sophia*, 14.

15. Vladimir Lossky, *The Mystical Theology* (Crestwood, N.Y.: St. Vladimir's Seminary Press, 1974), 96.

16. Vladimir Lossky, *Orthodox Theology: An Introduction*, trans. Ian Kesarcodi-Watson and Ihita Kesarcodi-Watson (Crestwood, N.Y.: St. Vladimir's Seminary Press, 1978), 58.

17. Ibid.; emphasis mine.

18. Lossky, *The Mystical Theology*, 95; see also Vladimir Lossky, "La notion des 'analogies' chez Denys Le Pseudo-Aréopagite," *Archives d'Histoire Doctrinale et Littéraire du Moyen-Age* 5 (1931): 287.

19. Lossky, "La notion des 'analogies,'" 304–305.

20. For the evolution of *eros* as a metaphysical principle in the patristic tradition, see Bernard McGinn, "God as Eros: Metaphysical Foundations of Christian Mysticism," in *New Perspectives on Historical Theology: Essays in Memory of John Meyendorff*, ed. Bradley Nassif (Grand Rapids, Mich.: Eerdmans, 1996), 189–209.

21. "If God appears as light and then as darkness, this means—for Gregory (of Nyssa)—that there is no vision of the divine essence and that union is presented as a path which goes beyond vision, *theoria*, beyond intelligence, to the area where knowl-

edge is suppressed and love alone remains, or rather where gnosis becomes *agape*: *e de gnosis agape ginetai*." Vladimir Lossky, *The Vision of God*, trans. Ashleigh Moorhouse (Crestwood, N.Y.: St. Vladimir's Seminary Press, 1983), 88.

22. For a fuller elaboration of Lossky's theology of the Trinity in comparison with that of John Zizioulas, see my *Being with God*.

23. John Zizioulas, *Communion and Otherness*, ed. Paul McPartlan (London: T&T Clark, 2006), 220.

24. John Zizioulas, "Preserving God's Creation: Lecture Two," *King's Theological Review* 12 (1989): 43.

25. The absence of Sophia is not so curious, since Bulgakov's influence waned after his death.

26. Zizioulas, *Communion and Otherness*, 202.

27. Ibid., 30.

28. For a similar criticism, see Nikolaos Loudovikos, "Person Instead of Grace and Dictated Otherness: John Zizioulas' Final Theological Position," *Heythrop Journal* 48 (2009): 1–16.

29. Zizioulas, *Communion and Otherness*, 202.

30. Lossky, *The Mystical Theology*, 94.

The Theological-Ethical Contributions of Archimandrite Sophrony (Sakharov) to Environmental Issues / Perry T. Hamalis

1. Produced and published jointly by the Ecumenical Patriarchate and the World Wide fund for Nature International (WWF), 1990.

2. See, for example, Kallistos Ware, "'We Must Pray for All': Salvation According to St. Silouan," *Sobornost* 19, no. 1 (1997): 51–53. See also Met. John Zizioulas, "The Theology of St. Silouan the Athonite," [in Greek] in *Saint Silouan of the Oikumene* (New Smyrna: Akritas, 2001), 37; and Jean-Claude Larchet, *Saint Silouane de l'Athos* (Paris: Les Éditions du Cerf, 2001).

3. The reference is to the Stavropegic Monastery of St. John the Baptist in Essex, England, which Fr. Sophrony founded in 1959 and at which he served as spiritual father until his repose on July 11, 1993.

4. See Fr. Sophrony, *We Shall See Him as He Is*, trans. Rosemary Edmonds (Essex: Stavropegic Monastery of St. John the Baptist, 1988), 10–11, 64.

5. Ibid., 37, 195, 211.

6. The book *Staretz Silouan* came out first as a mimeographed edition in 1948 and then was published professionally in 1952. It has since been translated into more than twenty languages. See Nicholas Sakharov, *I Love Therefore I Am* (Crestwood, N.Y.: St. Vladimir's Seminary Press, 2002), 31. Fr. Nicholai's work remains the authoritative account of Fr. Sophrony's biography as well as of the historical influences upon Fr. Sophrony's theology.

7. Several dissertations have been completed and monographs published during the past decade on Fr. Sophrony's thought, including two by members of the community at Essex. The French journal *Buisson Ardent*, which is dedicated to the study

of St. Silouan and Fr. Sophrony, was launched in 1995 and maintains annual publication.

8. Fr. Sophrony, *Saint Silouan the Athonite*, trans. Rosemary Edmonds (Essex: Stavropegic Monastery of St. John the Baptist, 1991), 229.

9. Ibid., 119.

10. Ibid., 229.

11. Fr. Sophrony makes this point in *We Shall See Him as He Is*, "Thanks to [Silouan], year after year I was able to observe at close quarters a truly Christian life, and even become a disciple. I am incomparably more indebted to his prayers than to all my other preceptors, though among them were several outstanding representatives of our Church—grace-endowed ascetics in monasteries and hermitages, bishops and priests; likewise professors in theological schools" (208). Fr. Nicholas Sakharov has provided an authoritative account of the influence of other thinkers upon Fr. Sophrony's thought. See Sakharov, *I Love Therefore I Am*.

12. Fr. Sophrony, *Saint Silouan the Athonite*, 94.

13. Ibid.

14. Ibid., 469.

15. Ibid.

16. See Fr. Sophrony's description of a similar type of weeping in ibid., 151. I will return to this point below in my discussion of hypostatic prayer and the "royal priesthood."

17. Ibid., 95.

18. Ibid., 470.

19. Ibid., 95.

20. For example, St. Silouan writes, "people who attach themselves to animals . . . have forsaken the love of God, and because of this that love between brothers for which Christ died in great suffering gets lost" (ibid., 470).

21. Fr. Sophrony summarizes the point as follows, "[Staretz Silouan] would say that all things were created to serve man, and so, when necessary, everything could be made use of but, at the same time, man was obliged to care for all creation. Therefore harm done unnecessarily to an animal—to plant life, even—gainsays the law of grace. But attachment to animals likewise goes against the Divine commandment, since it diminishes love for God and one's neighbour" (ibid., 96). On the divine commandments as divine energy, see Fr. Sophrony, *We Shall See Him as He Is*, 149–150, 210, 229.

22. See examples in Fr. Sophrony, *We Shall See Him as He Is*, 198, 216; Fr. Sophrony, *Saint Silouan the Athonite*, 47; Fr. Sophrony, *On Prayer*, trans. Rosemary Edmonds (Essex: Stavropegic Monastery of St. John the Baptist, 1996, 132); Fr. Sophrony, *La félicité de connaître la voie*, trans. Hieromonk Symeon (Geneva: Labor et Fides, 1988), 21, 49–50; Fr. Sophrony, *Words of Life*, trans. Sister Magdalen (Essex: Stavropegic Monastery of St. John the Baptist, 1998), 21.

23. Fr. Sophrony, *His Life Is Mine*, trans. Rosemary Edmonds (Crestwood, N.Y.: St. Vladimir's Seminary Press, 1977), 88. Cf. Fr. Sophrony, *La félicité de connaître la voie*, 49–50. It should be noted, as well, that in the refectory at the monastery of St. John the

Baptist, Fr. Sophrony had a mural icon of the "Hospitality of Abraham" painted to which he added the inscription, "Let us make man in our image, after our likeness."

24. See Fr. Sophrony, *On Prayer*, 111, 150; Fr. Sophrony, *Words of Life*, 21, 29.

25. Fr. Sophrony, *Words of Life*, 21.

26. Fr. Sophrony, *Saint Silouan the Athonite*, 47. There is also a similar teaching from St. Antony in the *Sayings of the Desert Fathers*, "Our life and our death is with our neighbor" (no. 9).

27. Fr. Sophrony, *His Life Is Mine*, 77.

28. As he puts it, "Man's personality is indestructible in eternity. 'I AM; I am . . . the truth, and the life.' 'I am the light of the world.' Being, Truth, Light are not abstract concepts, impersonal substances—not 'WHAT' but 'WHO'. Where there is no personal form of being, there is nothing alive either, just as there is neither good nor evil there; neither light nor darkness." Fr. Sophrony, *On Prayer*, 164–165.

29. Fr. Sophrony, *Saint Silouan the Athonite*, 157.

30. Fr. Sophrony, *His Life Is Mine*, 92.

31. Fr. Sophrony, *On Prayer*, 18–19.

32. See *Saint Silouan the Athonite*, 31, 101. Fr. Sophrony's teaching on the fallen condition's ongoing worsening has patristic roots in St. Athanasius, St. Maximus the Confessor, and others. To the best of my knowledge, this theological claim's connection to environmental destruction has not yet been sufficiently explored.

33. Fr. Sophrony, "Trois lettres à Maria," *Buisson Ardent* 5 (1999): 15.

34. Fr. Sophrony, *We Shall See Him as He Is*, 52. For related passages on asceticism, cf. Fr. Sophrony, *La félicité de connaître la voie*, 60; Fr. Sophrony, *On Prayer*, 22; Fr. Sophrony, *Words of Life*, 34.

35. Fr. Sophrony, *We Shall See Him as He Is*, 115.

36. For excellent discussions of this theme in Fr. Sophrony's writings see Nicholas Sakharov, *I Love Therefore I Am*, esp. 105–115. See also Archimandrite Zacharias (Zacharou), *Christ, Our Way and Our Life*, trans. Sr. Magdalen (South Canaan, Penn.: St. Tikhon's Seminary Press, 2003), 233–256; *The Enlargement of the Heart: "Be Ye Also Enlarged" (2 Cor 6:13) in the Theology of Saint Silouan the Athonite and Elder Sophrony of Essex*, ed. C. Veniamin (South Canaan, Penn.: Mount Thabor Publishing, 2006), 114–127, 144–145; and *The Hidden Man of the Heart (1 Pet 3:4): The Cultivation of the Heart in Orthodox Christian Anthropology*, ed. C. Veniamin (South Canaan, Penn.: Mount Thabor Publishing, 2008), 69–90.

37. See Fr. Sophrony, *His Life Is Mine*, 68; Fr. Sophrony, *Saint Silouan the Athonite*, 34.

38. See Archimandrite Sophrony, "L'obéissance, c'est la voie tracée par le Christ," *Buisson Ardent* 7 (2001): 9.

39. Fr. Sophrony, *His Life is Mine*, 110.

40. Ibid., 10. See also the Greek version of *We Shall See Him as He Is*, 351–380, which includes important sections on "Liturgical Prayer" that are not present in the English.

41. See Fr. Sophrony, *Saint Silouan the Athonite*, 116.

The Cosmology of the Eucharist / George Theokritoff

1. St. Ephrem *Hymns on the Table* III. In St. Ephrem the Syrian, *Hymns on Paradise*, trans. Sebastian Brock (Crestwood, N.Y.: St. Vladimir's Seminary Press, 1990); see also St. Irenaeus *Against Heresies* III 11, v. 5; St. John Chrysostom *Homilies on St. John* 22, v. 6, 7.

2. For a discussion in a slightly different context, see Metropolitan Anthony of Sourozh, *Encounter* (London: Darton, Longman, and Todd, 2005), chap. 5, "The Vocation of Man." See also Gregory of Nyssa *The Great Catechism* 37.

3. Leontius of Cyprus *Fifth Homily of Christian Apologetic against the Jews, and on the Icons* PG 93:1604B.

4. See Olivier Clement, "Human Beings and the Cosmos," in *On Human Being: A Spiritual Anthropology* (Hyde Park, N.Y.: New City Press, 2000), 108–125, esp. 109, 116, 118.

5. See Alexander Schmemann, *For the Life of the World: Sacraments and Orthodoxy* (Crestwood, N.Y.: St. Vladimir's Seminary Press, 1973), 26ff.

6. "For these precious gifts, which have been offered and sanctified, let us entreat the Lord . . . that our merciful God, who hath received them at his holy and celestial and invisible altar, unto a breath of spiritual fragrance, send down upon us divine grace and the gift of the Holy Spirit." Litany before the Lord's Prayer, Liturgy of St. John Chrysostom. Similar passages occur in the Liturgies of St. James and St. Basil.

7. John Jillions, "In the Flesh: The Body in Christ's Life and Ministry," in *The Experience of the Incarnation: The Body as the Temple of the Holy Spirit*, Russian Orthodox Diocese of Sourozh, Diocesan Conference, Oxford, May 23–26, 1997, 20–28.

"A 'Tradition' That Never Existed": Orthodox Christianity and the Failures of Environmental History / Jurretta Jordan Heckscher

1. Lynn White Jr., "The Historical Roots of Our Ecologic Crisis," *Science* n.s. 155, no. 3767 (March 10, 1967): 1203–1207.

2. Ibid., 1205–1206.

3. Ibid., 1205–1207.

4. Headnote to White's essay in Thomas R. Detwyler, ed., *Man's Impact on Environment* (New York: McGraw-Hill, 1971), 27; René Dubos, *A God Within* (New York: Charles Scribner's Sons, 1972), 157.

5. Ludwig Feuerbach, *The Essence of Christianity*, trans. George Eliot (New York: Harper & Row, 1957), 287; as cited in H. Paul Santmire, *The Travail of Nature: The Ambiguous Ecological Promise of Christian Theology* (Philadelphia: Fortress, 1985), 3; Max Weber, *The Protestant Ethic and the Spirit of Capitalism* (1904–1905), as cited in the Working Group of the Doctrine Commission of the Church of England, "Report," in *Man and Nature*, ed. Hugh Montefiore (London: Collins, 1975), 24.

6. Comments printed posthumously in Paul Shepard, *Where We Belong: Beyond Abstraction in Perceiving Nature*, ed. Florence Rose Shepard (Athens: University of Georgia Press, 2003), 107–108.

7. Cf. Ian L. McHarg, *Design with Nature* (Garden City, N.Y.: Natural History Press, 1969), 26; and Arnold Toynbee, "The Religious Background to the Present Environmental Crisis," *International Journal of Environmental Studies* 3 (1972): 141–146.

8. Important early counterarguments to White include Yi-Fu Tuan, "Discrepancies between Environmental Attitude and Behaviour: Examples from Europe and China," *Canadian Geographer* 12 (1968): 176–191; Dubos, *A God Within*, 159–161; and A. R. Peacocke, "On 'The Historical Roots of Our Ecological Crisis,'" in *Man and Nature*, ed. Hugh Montefiore (London: Collins, 1975), 155–158. For recent summaries of White's critics' arguments, see David N. Livingstone, "The Historical Roots of Our Ecological Crisis: A Reassessment," *Fides et Historia* 26, no. 1 (Winter/Spring 1994): 38–45; Robert L. Thayer Jr., *Gray World, Green Heart: Technology, Nature, and the Sustainable Landscape* (New York: John Wiley & Sons, 1994), 56–62; Martin Phillips and Tim Mighall, *Society and Exploitation through Nature* (Harlow: Prentice Hall, 2000), 14–15; and Joachim Radkau, *Nature and Power: A Global History of the Environment*, trans. Thomas Dunlap (Cambridge: Cambridge University Press, 2008), 15, 82–84.

9. "Fully half of the 80 or so papers published by Christians during 1970 on Creation-related subjects cited White": Joseph K. Sheldon, *Rediscovery of Creation: A Bibliographical Study of the Church's Response to the Environmental Crisis* (Metuchen, N.J.: Scarecrow, 1992), 27; "by far the greatest volume" of the literature attempting to refute White "develops, in one way or another, the stewardship alternative": J. Baird Callicott, "Genesis Revisited: Murian Musings on the Lynn White, Jr. Debate," *Environmental History Review* 14, no. 1/2, 1989 Conference Papers, part 2 (Spring/Summer 1990): 67.

10. Henryk Skolimowski, *A Sacred Place to Dwell: Living with Reverence upon the Earth* (Rockport, Mass.: Element, 1993), 107–108.

11. Lewis Cass, "Removal of the Indians," *North American Review* 30 (1830): 77; as quoted in Roderick Nash, *Wilderness and the American Mind*, 4th ed. (New Haven, Conn.: Yale University Press, 2001), 31.

12. Cornwall Alliance for the Stewardship of Creation, press release, "Sounding the Alarm about Dangerous Environmental Extremism: Explosive New DVD Series, *Resisting the Green Dragon*, Now Being Distributed Nationally and Abroad," Washington, D.C. (November 10, 2010), http://www.cornwallalliance.org/press/read/sounding-the-alarm-about-dangerous-environmental-extremism; Norman Dennison, quoted in John M. Broder, "Climate Change Doubt Is Tea Party Article of Faith," *New York Times* (October 20, 2010); see also J. Aaron Simmons, "Evangelical Environmentalism: Oxymoron or Opportunity?" *Worldviews* 13 (2009): 40–71; and Jeffrey Goins, "Expendable Creation: Classical Pentecostalism and Environmental Disregard" (MA thesis, University of North Texas, 1997).

13. Peter Hay, *Main Currents in Western Environmental Thought* (Bloomington: Indiana University Press, 2002), 112.

14. Jack Turner, introduction to *Traces of an Omnivore*, by Paul Shepard (Washington, D.C.: Island Press/Shearwater Books, 1996), xix; David Drew, *Man-Environment Processes* (London: George Allen & Unwin, 1983), 2.

15. Gilbert F. LaFrenière, *The Decline of Nature: Environmental History and the Western Worldview* (Palo Alto, Calif.: Academica, 2008), 80 (see also 127); Paul Harrison, *The Third Revolution: Environment, Population, and a Sustainable World* (London: I. B. Tauris, 1992), 34; Roderick Frazier Nash, *The Rights of Nature: A History of Environmental Ethics* (Madison: University of Wisconsin Press, 1989), 92.

16. Val Plumwood, *Environmental Culture: The Ecological Crisis of Reason* (London: Routledge, 2002), 221; David Spangler, "Imagination, Gaia, and the Sacredness of the Earth," in *Earth and Spirit: The Spiritual Dimension of the Environmental Crisis*, ed. Fritz Hull (New York: Continuum, 1993), 79; Frederic L. Bender, *The Culture of Extinction: Toward a Philosophy of Deep Ecology* (Amherst, N.Y.: Humanity, 2003), 206.

17. Stephen Mosley, *The Environment in World History* (London: Routledge, 2010), 41; Charles L. Redman, *Human Impact on Ancient Environments* (Tucson: University of Arizona Press, 1999), 19.

18. Donald Worster, *Nature's Economy: A History of Ecological Ideas*, rev. ed. (Cambridge: Cambridge University Press, 1994), 27, 29; Paul Shepard, "A Post-Historic Primitivism," in *The Wilderness Condition: Essays on Environment and Civilization*, ed. Max Oelschlaeger (Washington, D.C.: Island, 1992), 61.

19. According to the WorldCat (www.worldcat.org) database, which is not comprehensive, as of October 2011, 433 libraries worldwide hold copies of Lossky; 1,552 hold copies of Ware's *The Orthodox Church*; 245 hold copies of the third edition of Zernov; and 608 hold copies of Ware, *The Orthodox Way*.

20. Kallistos (Timothy) Ware, *The Orthodox Way* (Crestwood, N.Y.: St. Vladimir's Orthodox Theological Seminary, 1979), 183 (in 1995 ed., 137).

21. Nicolas Zernov, *The Russians and Their Church*, 3rd ed. (London: SPCK, 1978), 51.

22. Ware, *Orthodox Way*, 158 (1995 ed., 118).

23. Ibid., 58 (1995 ed., 46).

24. Vladimir Lossky, *The Mystical Theology of the Eastern Church*, trans. members of the Fellowship of St. Alban and St. Sergius (London: J. Clarke, 1957; repr. Crestwood, N.Y.: St. Vladimir's Seminary Press, 1976), 101–102.

25. Zernov, *Russians and Their Church*, 105–106.

26. Timothy Ware, *The Orthodox Church* (London: Penguin, 1963), 42 (1997 ed., with insignificant changes, 33–34).

27. Lossky, *Mystical Theology*, 113.

28. Ware, *Orthodox Church*, 239–240 (1997 ed., with insignificant changes, 235).

29. Lossky, *Mystical Theology*, 110–111.

30. Raymond E. Grizzle and Christopher B. Barrett, "The One Body of Christian Environmentalism," *Zygon* 33 (1998): 233–253; Hay, *Main Currents*, 106–113; Max Oelschlaeger, *Caring for Creation: An Ecumenical Approach to the Environmental Crisis* (New Haven, Conn.: Yale University Press, 1994); Ian Ball et al., eds., *The Earth Beneath: A Critical Guide to Green Ecology* (London: SPCK, 1992), as characterized on 1; Douglas Davies, "Christianity," in *Attitudes to Nature*, ed. Jean Holm with John Bowker (London: Pinter, 1994), 28–52; H. Paul Santmire, *Nature Reborn: The Ecological and Cosmic Promise of Christian Theology* (Minneapolis: Fortress, 2000).

31. Michael S. Northcott, *The Environment and Christian Ethics* (Cambridge: Cambridge University Press, 1996).

32. A. M. Allchin, "The Theology of Nature in the Eastern Fathers and among Anglican Theologians," in *Man and Nature*, ed. Hugh Montefiore (London: Collins, 1975), 143–154; Loren Wilkinson et al., *Earthkeeping: Christian Stewardship of Natural Resources* (Grand Rapids, Mich.: Eerdmans, 1980), 221–223; Paulos Mar Gregorios, "New Testament Foundations for Understanding the Creation," in *Liberating Life: Contemporary Approaches to Ecological Theology*, ed. Charles Birch, William Eakin, and Jay B. McDaniel (Maryknoll, N.Y.: Orbis, 1990), 37–45.

33. Charles Cummings, *Eco-Spirituality: Toward a Reverent Life* (Mahwah, N.J.: Paulist Press, 1991); James A. Nash, *Loving Nature: Ecological Integrity and Christian Responsibility* (Nashville: Abingdon, 1991); Duncan Reid, "The End of Matter: Some Ecojustice Principles in the Neo-Patristic Vision," *Ecotheology* 7 (1999): 59–70; Denis Edwards, *Ecology at the Heart of Faith* (Maryknoll, N.Y.: Orbis, 2006); Willis Jenkins, *Ecologies of Grace: Environmental Ethics and Christian Theology* (Oxford: Oxford University Press, 2008); I am indebted to Elizabeth Theokritoff for bringing this last work to my attention.

34. Santmire, *Travail of Nature*; Robin Attfield, "Christian Attitudes to Nature," *Journal of the History of Ideas* 44 (1983): 369–386.

35. Susan Power Bratton, "Oaks, Wolves, and Love: Celtic Monks and Northern Forests," *Journal of Forest History* 33, no. 1 (January 1989): 4.

36. Ecumenical Patriarch Bartholomew I's pioneering statement on the sinfulness of environmental destruction, November 8, 1997, is at http://www.patriarchate.org/documents/santa-barbara-symposium.

37. Santmire, *Nature Reborn*, 17–18; Northcott, *Environment and Christian Ethics*, 124.

38. Garrett De Bell, ed., *The Environmental Handbook. Prepared for the First National Environmental Teach-In, April 1970* (San Francisco: Friends of the Earth, 1970); as characterized in Santmire, *Nature Reborn*, 11.

39. Wendell Berry, "Christianity and the Survival of Creation," *Cross Currents* 43, no. 2 (Summer 1993): 149.

40. See, for example, Edward Goldsmith, *The Way: An Ecological World-View*, rev. ed. (Athens: University of Georgia Press, 1998), 415; Hay, *Main Currents*, 100; Brennan R. Hill, *Christian Faith and the Environment: Making Vital Connections*

(Maryknoll, N.Y.: Orbis, 1998), 2; Northcott, *Environment and Christian Ethics*, 83; Oelschlaeger, *Caring for Creation*, 1; Plumwood, *Environmental Culture*, 218–227; and Irene van Lippe-Biesterfeld with Jessica van Tijn, *Science, Soul, and the Spirit of Nature: Leading Thinkers on the Restoration of Man and Creation* (Rochester, Vt.: Bear, 2005), 61, 66.

41. For ecofeminism, see Carol J. Adams, ed., *Ecofeminism and the Sacred* (New York: Continuum, 1993); Irene Diamond and Gloria Feman Orenstein, eds., *Reweaving the World: The Emergence of Ecofeminism*, rev. ed. (San Francisco: Sierra Club Books, 1990); Heather Eaton, *Introducing Ecofeminist Theologies* (London: T&T Clark, 2005); and Rosemary Radford Ruether, *Gaia and God: An Ecofeminist Theology of Earth Healing* (San Francisco: HarperSanFrancisco, 1992). For contemporary paganisms, see Michael York, *Pagan Theology: Paganism as a World Religion* (New York: New York University Press, 2003), esp. 13–14, 59–67, 159. For Deep Ecology, which is defined in opposition to anthropocentrism, see Bill Devall and George Sessions, *Deep Ecology: Living as If Nature Mattered* (Salt Lake City, Ut.: Gibbs M. Smith/Peregrine Smith Books, 1985); and George Sessions, "The Deep Ecology Movement: A Review," *Environmental Review: ER* 11, no. 2 (Summer 1987): 105–125.

42. Thomas Berry, *The Dream of the Earth* (San Francisco: Sierra Club Books, 1988), 87, 81; Matthew Fox, *Original Blessing: A Primer in Creation Spirituality: Presented in Four Paths, Twenty-Six Themes, and Two Questions* (New York: Jeremy P. Tarcher/Putnam, 2000); Gordon D. Kaufman, "The Theological Structure of Christian Faith and the Feasibility of a Global Ecological Ethic," *Zygon* 38 (2003): 153; Sallie McFague, "An Earthly Theological Agenda," *Christian Century* (January 2–9, 1991): 13–14.

43. For a sampling of these efforts, see the information and links on the Web sites of the Eco-Justice Programmes of the World Council of Churches, http://www.oikoumene.org/en/programmes/justice-diakonia-and-responsibility-for-creation/eco-justice.html; the Eco-Justice Programs of the (American) National Council of Churches of Christ, http://nccecojustice.org; and the Environment section of the Web site of the United States Conference of Catholic Bishops, http://www.usccb.org/issues-and-action/human-life-and-dignity/environment.

44. H. Paul Santmire, *Brother Earth: Nature, God, and Ecology in Time of Crisis* (New York: Thomas Nelson, 1970), 6–7.

45. James A. Nash, "Toward the Ecological Reformation of Christianity," *Interpretation, A Journal of Bible and Theology* 50, no. 1 (January 1996): 7; Lisa V. Bernal, "Embodied Relations and Good Human Action: Bases for a Christian Eco-Justice Ethic of Creation" (Ph.D. diss., Princeton Theological Seminary, 2001), 223–224; John Carmody, *Ecology and Religion: Toward a New Christian Theology of Nature* (New York: Paulist Press, 1983), esp. 2, 130–131; John B. Cobb Jr., *Is It Too Late? A Theology of Ecology*, rev. ed. (Denton, Tex.: Environmental Ethics Books, 1995), 31; Hill, *Christian Faith and the Environment*, 235; John Reader, "Introduction," in *The Earth Beneath: A Critical Guide to Green Ecology*, ed. Ian Ball et al. (London: SPCK, 1992), 5; Santmire, *Nature Reborn*, 15.

46. Daniel M. Cowdin, "Toward an Environmental Ethic," in *Preserving the Creation: Environmental Theology and Ethics*, ed. Kevin W. Irwin et al. (Washington, D.C.: Georgetown University Press, 1994), 112.

47. Radkau, *Nature and Power*, 84; see also Edwin O. Wilson, *The Creation: An Appeal to Save Life on Earth* (New York: Norton, 2006).

48. Quotation from the Orthodox Prayer to the Holy Spirit.

49. John Chryssavgis, ed., *On Earth as in Heaven: Ecological Vision and Initiatives of Ecumenical Patriarch Bartholomew* (New York: Fordham University Publications, 2012); and the "Orthodoxy and the Environment" section of the Patriarchate Web site, http://www.patriarchate.org/environment; "Message for the Day of the Protection of the Environment," September 1, 1989, on the Patriarchate Web site, http://www.patriarchate.org/documents/demetrios.

50. For example, Ignatius IV, Patriarch of Antioch, "Three Sermons: A Theology of Creation; A Spirituality of the Creation; The Responsibility of Christians," *Sourozh: A Journal of Orthodox Life and Thought* 38 (November 1989): 1–15; Alexy II, Patriarch of Moscow, "Nature Is a Friend and Source of God's Wisdom," in *Christianity and Sustainable Development in the Baltic Sea Region* (Stockholm: Christian Council of Sweden, 1997); John (Zizioulas), Metropolitan of Pergamon, "Man the Priest of Creation: A Response to the Ecological Problem," in *Living Orthodoxy in the Modern World: Orthodox Christianity and Society*, ed. Andrew Walker and Costa Carras (Crestwood, N.Y.: St. Vladimir's Seminary Press, 2000), 178–188; John (Zizioulas), Metropolitan of Pergamon, "Preserving God's Creation: Three Lectures on Theology and Ecology," pts. 1–3, *King's Theological Review* 12, no. 1 (Spring 1989): 1–5; 12, no. 2 (Autumn 1989): 41–45; 13, no. 1 (Spring 1990): 1–5; Kallistos (Ware), Metropolitan of Diokleia, "Through the Creation to the Creator," *Ecotheology* 2 (1997): 8–30; and numerous lectures; John Chryssavgis, *Beyond the Shattered Image* (Minneapolis: Light and Life, 1999); and Elizabeth Theokritoff, *Living in God's Creation: Orthodox Perspectives on Ecology* (Crestwood, N.Y.: St. Vladimir's Seminary Press, 2009).

51. E.g., Appendix 2, "Faith Statements on Religion and Ecology," in *Cultural and Spiritual Values of Biodiversity/United Nations Environment Programme: A Complementary Contribution to the Global Biodiversity Assessment*, ed. Darrell Addison Posey et al. (London: Intermediate Technology Publications, 1999), 603–635; William P. Cunningham and Mary Ann Cunningham, *Environmental Science: A Global Concern*, 11th ed. (New York: McGraw-Hill Higher Education, 2010), 31; Judith Fitzgerald and Robert Oren Fitzgerald, comps., *The Sermon of All Creation: Christians on Nature* (Bloomington, Ind.: World Wisdom, 2005); Robert Barry Leal, *Wilderness in the Bible: Toward a Theology of Wilderness* (New York: Peter Lang, 2004), 14, 240; and Michael Northcott, "Christianity," in *Encyclopedia of Environmental Ethics and Philosophy*, ed. J. Baird Callicott and Robert Frodeman (Detroit: Macmillan Reference USA, 2009), 1:148, 151–152.

52. St. Seraphim: Julia de Beausobre, *Flame in the Snow: A Life of St. Serafim of Sarov* (1946; rpt. Springfield, Ill.: Templegate, 1996), 88–89, 95, 106–107, and

iconography; St. Herman: Joanne Stefanatos, *Animals and Man: A State of Blessedness* (Minneapolis: Light and Life, 1992), 186, and iconography; Elder Isidore: Paul Florensky, *Salt of the Earth*, trans. Richard Betts (Platina, Calif.: St. Herman of Alaska Brotherhood, 1987), 71; Fr. Gelasios: personal communications from visitors to Simonopetra during his lifetime, and Philip Sherrard, *Athos: The Holy Mountain* (1982; rpt. Woodstock, N.Y.: Overlook Press, 1985), 168; Elder Amphilochios: Kallistos (Ware), Metropolitan of Diokleia, "Through the Creation to the Creator," 8; St. Silouan: Archimandrite Sophrony, comp., *Wisdom from Mount Athos: The Writings of Staretz Silouan, 1866–1938*, trans. Rosemary Edmonds, rev. ed. (London: Mowbrays, 1974), 32.

53. Metropolitan Tryphon (Turkestanov), "Akathist of Thanksgiving, in Praise of God's Creation," c. 1934, trans. Lydia S. Balashova and Andreas Moran, http://www.monachos.net/content/liturgics/liturgical-texts/237-akathist-of-thanksgiving-in-praise-of-gods-creation.

54. St. Isaac the Syrian, as quoted in Lossky, *Mystical Theology*, 111; "kata panta kai dia panta": "in all things and for all things," the words of offering from the Liturgy of St. John Chrysostom.

Proprietors or Priests of Creation? / Metropolitan John (Zizioulas) of Pergamon

1. Published with kind permission of the author. This article also appears in John D. Zizioulas, *The Eucharistic Communion and the World*, ed. Luke Ben Tallon (London: T&T Clark, 2011), 133–141.

Sedimentation of Meaning in the Concepts of Nature and the Environment / James Carey

1. A particularly insidious instance of sedimentation has taken place with the word "value." It was used by Nietzsche and Marx to imply that the worth of something was projected by the individual will, not necessarily rational, of the evaluating subject and had no necessary relation to an objective order either discernable by reason or revealed by God. It is now widely used not only by relativists and subjectivists of various stripes but even by traditionalists. One hears "family values" touted, "Christian values," and on occasion, alas, even "Orthodox values." Most of the people who speak this way have nothing in common with Nietzsche or Marx or with the social scientists who have persuaded educators to believe that the concepts of good and bad are only subjective projections and bear a necessary relation neither to reality nor to reason. But by thoughtlessly employing the vocabulary of "values" they inadvertently contribute to the reluctance, increasingly conspicuous in young people, to make moral judgments of any sort without qualifications that render them nugatory: "Genocide is wrong according to my values (or my culture's values), but who am I to say that my values are better than Hitler's values?" This question carries some weight *only if* right and wrong, good and evil, are nothing but values.

2. There has undoubtedly been progress in man's understanding of the world, though less in his self-understanding than in his understanding of what is subhuman, for example, the elementary constitution of matter. But progress in man's understanding has proven to be inseparable from regress in man's understanding. In considering what (as we like to put it) "we now know" with what, say, the ancient Greeks knew, it becomes clear that we have lost sight of at least as much as we have caught sight of. A casual comparison of Aristotle's *Physics* with a contemporary physics text will show that the questions that were alive for Aristotle and guided his inquiry have not been answered. They have just been forgotten.

3. The verbal radical is √*mūl*= to take root, to stand fast. It can also mean to grow. Cf. V. S. Apte, *The Practical Sanskrit Dictionary*, rev. and enlarged ed. (Delhi: Motilal Banarsidas, 1978), 769.

4. *Odyssey*, book X, lines 274–329.

5. Aristotle *Metaphysics* 1015 a12.

6. See my "Vedic Tradition and the Origin of Philosophy in Ancient India," *St. John's Review* 49, no. 3 (2007): 5–66.

7. Since the Greek words for both "god" (*theos*) and "intellect" (*nous*) are masculine in gender, Aristotle pairs them with masculine pronouns. When I refer to the first mover as "he," I am simply following Aristotle's usage. The first mover could also be referred to as "it," since he (or it) is impersonal.

8. Aristotle *Metaphysics* 1074a14.

9. Ibid., 1074b34.

10. Ibid., 1074b22–27.

11. Kant, *Critique of Pure Reason*, B 163.

12. Aristotle *Physics* 198b35.

13. Ibid., 192b22, 199b30; Aristotle *Metaphysics* 1014b19.

14. Genesis 1:11. As Robert Sacks points out, this clause employs a very rare verb, "to grass" (דשׁא), in a cognate accusative construction. *A Commentary on the Book of Genesis*, Ancient Near Eastern Texts and Studies 6 (Lewiston, N.Y.: Edwin Mellen, 1990), 7–8. Cf. *A Hebrew and English Lexicon of the Old Testament, Based on the Lexicon of William Gesenius*, trans. Edward Robinson (Oxford: Oxford University Press, 1906; repr. 1951), 205.

15. Wisdom of Solomon 19:7, 15.

16. Ibid. 9:20–21.

17. Ibid. 9:16.

18. Romans 2:14.

19. Aristotle *Metaphysics* 1015a12.

20. Romans 1:26.

21. 2 Peter 1:4.

22. "*Kai eis hen prosōpon kai mian hypostasin.* Latin: *et in unam personam atque subsistentiam.*" See *Enchiridion Symbolorum*, ed. H. Denzinger and A. Schönmetzer, S.J. (Rome: Herder, 1976), 108, on this text, especially on the controvery of the *ek duo physeōn* alternative.

Existential versus Regulative Approaches: The Environmental Issue as an Existential and Not a Canonical Problem / Christos Yannaras

1. Presented during the first ecological symposium of Religion, Science, and the Environment, Patmos, September 25, 1995. First appeared in S. Hobson and J. Lubchenco, eds., *Revelation and the Environment* A.D. 95–1995 (Singapore: World Scientific Publishing Company, 1997). The translation has been slightly modified by J. Chryssavgis.

Nature and Creation: A Comment on the Environmental Problem from a Philosophical and Theological Standpoint / Nikos Nissiotis

1. From *Synaxis* (Montreal: Alexander Press, 2006), 1:233–243. Originally published in ΣΥΝΑΞΗ 14 (April–June 1985): 11–20. Translated from the Greek by Elizabeth Theokritoff. This essay appears here through the kind permission of Dr. John Hadjinicolaou of Alexander Press. The translation is slightly modified by J. Chryssavgis.

2. *Demiourgia* is the classical term for creation; its root meaning of something crafted or fabricated fits well with the "creative" work of the Platonic or Aristotelian god, who essentially shapes preexisting matter. The term *ktisis*, preferred by Scripture, has the root meaning of founding or establishing—that is, creating an entity that previously did not exist. [Translator's note]

3. *Patrologia Graeca* 94: 853.

Physis and *Ktisis*: Two Different Ways of Thinking of the World / John Panteleimon Manoussakis

1. *On Philoponus*; see B. N. Tatakis, *He Byzantine Philosophia* (in Greek) (Athens: 1977), 53–63; in English: *Christian Philosophy in the Patristic and Byzantine Tradition*, trans. George D. Dragas (Rollinsford: Orthodox Research Institute, 2007), 233–238.

2. See, for instance, Aristotle *Physics* B, 192b.

3. See Nikos Nissiotis, "He Physis ōs Ktisis," *Synaxe* 14 (1985): 11–20 (in Greek). Translation appears immediately above, in this volume.

4. This is the tremendous effect that Maximus's reevaluation of motion (*kinesis*) has. See, in particular, his *Ambiguum* VII. The indispensability of the created world for man's salvation is underscored in Dimitru Staniloae's excellent introduction to the Apostoliki Diakonia edition of St. Maximus's *Ambigua* (Athens, 1978), esp. 35.

5. In the liturgy we refer the world to God under the form of the Eucharistic gifts, that is, bread and wine, both of which cannot be found *naturally* in the world and apart from man's labor. The world that is offered as a gift to God, the same world that man will receive back (in communion) as a gift from God, is a world on which man has put his seal.

6. This idea, traced through Gregory of Nyssa (in *De Opificio Hominis*) to Dionysius the Aeropagite and on to Maximus the Confessor, is finally received by John

Scotus Eriugena, who, in his *Periphyseon*, affirms boldly: "In man every creature is established, both visible and invisible. Therefore he is called the workshop of all, seeing that in him all things which came after God are contained. Hence he is also customarily called the Intermediary, for since he consists of soul and body he comprehends within himself and gathers into one, two ultimate extremes of the spiritual and corporeal. That is why the sacred account of the Creation of the Universe introduces him at the end of all, signifying that in him is the consummation of the totality of created nature." *Periphyseon*, V, trans. I. P. Sheldon-Williams, rev. John O'Meara (Montreal: Dumbarton Oaks, 1987), 562–563.

7. See my *God After Metaphysics: A Theological Aesthetic* (Bloomington: Indiana University Press, 2007), 48–50.

8. It is in this sense that we can appreciate the observation made by Fr. John Chryssavgis that in iconography natural entities such as trees, planets, and rivers are depicted with a human face and personified (that is, made personal, hypostatic).

9. On the idea that nothing does not precede creation as something positive but rather is created itself together with the world, see Sergius Bulgakov, *The Bride of the Lamb*, trans. Boris Jakim (Grand Rapids, Mich.: Eerdmans, 2002), 54.

10. Against Lossky, see Zizioulas, *Communion and Otherness*, 30, n. 51, and 138–139, n. 80. There are two different theologies within the Orthodox tradition: one Dionysian that favors some continuity between creation and creator (hierarchies), the other Gregorian that emphasizes the unbridgeable and insurmountable gap (*diastema*) between them. Although the two are not ultimately irreconcilable, Zizioulas clearly favors the latter. The problem with the uncreated energies is that they are unhypostatic (for whose energies are they?). For the differences between Lossky and Zizioulas, see Aristotle Papanikolaou, *Being with God: Trinity, Apophaticism, and Divine-Human Communion* (South Bend, Ind.: University of Notre Dame Press, 2006).

11. We read in 2 Cor. 5:17 that creation (*ktisis*) is renewed in Christ and in Rom. 8:20 that "the creation itself will be liberated from its bondage to decay and brought into the glorious freedom of the children of God."

Human Image, World Image: The Renewal of Sacred Cosmology / Philip Sherrard

1. From Philip Sherrard, *Human Image, World Image: The Death and Resurrection of Sacred Cosmology* (Ipswich: Golgonooza Press, 1992; repr. Limni, Greece: Denise Harvey, 2004). The text in the present volume contains excerpts from the introduction and from chapter 7: "Notes towards the Restitution of Sacred Cosmology."

2. See Henryk Skolimowski, "Worldviews and Values for the Future," *India International Centre Quarterly* (Spring 1989): 159.

3. Implicit in this understanding of things is also the conclusion that it is impossible to conceive of a time in which God's creativity is not engaged and in which therefore He is not present and immanent in the activities and creatures through which He manifests Himself. In effect, to say that the world has a beginning in the

chronological sense involves two further propositions: first, that there was a time when the world did not exist, and, second, that prior to creating the world God either did not possess any creative power or refrained from using it. But both these propositions are nonsensical, for both presuppose a temporal dimension where none exists: for there is no time prior to the creation of the world, and consequently there could not have been a time when the world did not exist, and there is no time *in divinis* such that the words "before" and "after" can be applied to it, and consequently there cannot have been a time prior to which God did not exercise His creative power. We see creation as a temporal act with a beginning in time merely because that corresponds to the restricted mode within which we view things. In reality, since God is not separate from His acts, the act of creation must be an eternal and timeless manifestation of God's eternal and timeless Being. Creation, that is to say, is not an adjunct to God but is eternal in Him, and all things are consequently in their essence eternal because creation is an eternal aspect of the divine nature.

4. For the doctrine of the divine *logoi*, see, e.g., St. Maximus the Confessor, esp. PG 91:1329. A summary of St Maximus's doctrine in this respect, with references to specific texts, is to be found in Lars Thunberg's *Microcosm and Mediator* (Lund, 1965), 76–99. See also St. Dionysius the Areopagite *The Divine Names* PG 3:824.

5. In the Christian tradition the doctrine of the divine Names is chiefly associated with St. Dionysius the Areopagite. See above all his treatise *The Divine Names*. A recent translation of this text into English is to be found in *Pseudo-Dionysius: The Complete Works*, trans. Colm Luibheid (London, 1987). In the perspective of this doctrine, God in His ultimate nature might be described as Universal or Supreme Consciousness, and on that level He does not distinguish Himself from us or from anything else, for were we or anything else on that level we would be wholly transformed into Him. It is from our lower plane of finite being that we distinguish between ourselves and Him. It is because of the limitations of our own consciousness that we perceive such a distinction. Yet in another sense in His ultimate nature God is not conscious at all, for consciousness implies a state in which the conscious subject is aware of himself and so becomes the object of his own perception, and such a state is impossible in the ultimate nature of the Godhead: there, there can be no distinction between conscious subject and the object of consciousness. In fact, there cannot be any distinction at all at this level: the ultimate nature of the Godhead is totally undifferentiated.

Yet if this ultimate unity lies behind, or above, all the manifest diversities of this world, it must contain these diversities in itself in an undifferentiated condition. At the same time, if these diversities are to come into existence at all, it must contain in itself in an undifferentiated state the principle of differentiation that from our level allows us to distinguish between ultimate unity and the whole of plurality. This principle of differentiation is thus contained transcendentally in the Godhead itself, and it is this principle that impels the undifferentiated and unrelated Deity to an eternal act of self-manifestation through which He becomes differentiated and related. The Godhead thus possesses two aspects: that which is beyond all differentiation and relationship and that which embraces a sphere of differentiation and relationship.

It is this latter aspect that constitutes the realm of Being, and it is in this realm that the potentialities not only of creation but also of revelation are first manifest, fused and yet distinct, in the multiple Names of God and even in the Name, God, itself. Some of these Names are as it were titles of that aspect of the Godhead which is beyond differentiation and relationship, or, better stated, they are symbols of this aspect, enshrining as such that of which they are the symbols, and however inadequately they may express its incomprehensible nature, they apply to this nature as a whole and not to any particular element, function, or activity in it. But other Names do connote not the same undifferentiated Deity but certain differentiated elements, functions, or activities. Of these, the Names of the three Persons, or hypostases, of the Trinity have preeminence. But also included among these latter Names are those of all particular things whose destiny it is to proceed beyond the sphere of eternity and into the spatial and temporal world of finite creaturely existence. That is why the ultimate identity of every created being is timeless and eternal and why every created being is potentially divine.

6. For a fuller description of the idea of Image-archetypes, as of the world of the Imagination, or *mundus imaginalis,* which they constitute, see my *The Sacred in Life and Art* (Ipswich: Golgonooza Press, 1990), 136ff.

7. Cf. Psalm 19:1.

8. See my *The Rape of Man and Nature* (Ipswich: Golgonooza Press, 1987), 24ff., for a fuller discussion of this Christological doctrine and its anthropological implications. In effect, Christ's humanity is not something that was assumed in this world at a particular place and moment in historical time. It pertains to Him prior to all manifestation in place and time. Thus in its essence humanity is independent of spatiotemporal (and corporeal in the material sense) restrictions. And since man and God are paradigms of each other, this means that human nature is unseverably rooted in what is uncreated and immortal. See also Meister Eckhart: "For your human nature and that of the divine Logos are not different—it is one and the same," from the sermon "*Sankt Paulus spricht,*" in *Die Deutschen Werke,* ed. J. Quint, I. no. 24.

9. John 1:14.

10. See St. Maximus the Confessor and reference given in note 4 above. A *locus classicus* in this respect in St Maximus's writings is to be found in PG 91:1329. See also Jan van Ruysbroeck, *The Adornment of the Spiritual Marriage,* trans. C. A. Wynschenk Dom (London, 1951), 172–173.

11. 1 Cor. 15:28.

Environment and Security: Toward a Systemic Crisis of Humanity? / Costa Carras

1. This paper is a somewhat free rendering into English by the author of an article written in Greek in January 2008 for a commemorative volume in honor of Professor Theodore Couloumbis, which was published in the volume *International Relations: Contemporary Subjects and Approaches*, ed. D. Triantaphyllou, K. Yfantis, and E. Hatzivassiliou (Athens: Papazisis, 2008).

Church Walls and Wilderness Boundaries: Defining the Spaces of Sanctuary / L. Michael Harrington

1. Reprinted in *The Great New Wilderness Debate*, ed. J. Baird Callicott and Michael P. Nelson (Athens: University of Georgia Press, 1998), 121.

2. Thomas Birch, "The Incarceration of Wilderness: Wilderness Areas as Prisons," *Environmental Ethics* 12 (Spring 1990): 3–26; reprinted in *The Great New Wilderness Debate*, ed. J. Baird Callicott and Michael P. Nelson (Athens: University of Georgia Press, 1998), 443–470.

3. Ibid., 448.

4. Ibid., 445.

5. Although Birch quotes Aldo Leopold approvingly later in his essay (ibid., 465), Leopold holds precisely the position Birch is criticizing here. See his essay on "the land ethic," reprinted in *A Sand County Almanac: With Essays on Conservation from Round River* (New York: Ballantine, 1966), 237–264, esp. 237–239.

6. See Birch, "The Incarceration of Wilderness," 448: "the otherness of wildland is objectified into human resource, or value, categories and allocated by law to specific uses (thus bringing law to the land)."

7. Ibid., 462.

8. Ibid., 464.

9. Libanius *Pro templis* 30.8, as quoted by H. D. Saffrey, "The Piety and Prayers of Ordinary Men and Women in Late Antiquity," in *Classical Mediterranean Spirituality*, ed. A. H. Armstrong (New York: Crossroad, 1986), 200.

10. Martin Heidegger's "The Origin of the Work of Art" is helpful to understanding this aspect of the *temenos*: "the temple, in its standing there, first gives to things their look and to men their outlook on themselves." In *Poetry, Language, Thought*, trans. Albert Hofstadter (New York: Harper and Row, 1971), 43.

11. Lindsay Jones articulates the space of sanctuaries in these terms in *The Hermeneutics of Sacred Architecture* (Cambridge, Mass.: Harvard University Press, 2000), 2:264–293.

12. On the Hellenic relocation of the altar to the interior of the temple, see Barbara Gassowka, "Maternus Cynegius, Praefectus Praetorio Orientis and the Destruction of the Allat Temple in Palmyra," *Archeologia* 33 (1982); see also Frank R. Trombley's summary in *Hellenic Religion and Christianization c. 370–529* (Leiden: Brill, 1993), 1:145–147. On the change in philosophy that accompanied this shift

from an exterior to an interior rite, see L. Michael Harrington, *Sacred Place in Early Medieval Neoplatonism* (New York: Palgrave, 2004), 89–92.

13. Cf. Jonathan Smith, *To Take Place: Toward Theory in Ritual* (Chicago: University of Chicago Press, 1987), 104: "the temple serves as a focusing lens, establishing the possibility of significance by directing attention, by requiring the perception of difference."

14. Dionysius the Areopagite *On the Heavenly Hierarchy*, 11, 13–15 (140A). Page and line numbers refer to the edition of G. Heil and A. M. Ritter, *De Coelestia Hierarchia; De Ecclesiastica Hierarchia; Mystica Theologia; Epistulae* (Berlin: de Gruyter, 1991).

15. Dionysius the Areopagite *On the Ecclesiastical Hierarchy*, 82, 22–83, 2 (429A).

16. Theodore the Studite *Antirrhetikoi*, in *Patrologia Graeca* (PG) 99: 329D–332A.

17. Ibid., PG 99:332B–C.

18. Dionysius the Areopagite *Ep.* 159, 6–10 (1069B).

19. See ibid., 161, 4–5 (1072B): "what is affirmed in the philanthropy of Jesus has the power of a transcendent denial." This includes, as Dionysius notes earlier in the same passage, being born from a virgin and walking on water.

20. Gina Crandell, *Nature Pictorialized: "The View" in Landscape History* (Baltimore, Md.: Johns Hopkins University Press, 1993), 3, makes the more general claim that we have "defined and judged nature on the basis of its conformity with pictures." The pernicious result is that we find geysers and not marshes beautiful, because geysers are more "pictorially satisfying" than marshes, though both are natural. It is crucial, then, to distinguish wilderness, which is pictorially satisfying, from Crandell's "nature" or Birch's "wildness," both of which extend beyond what we frame in our pictures.

21. The vision of wilderness in the original 1964 Wilderness Act has now been shown to have its own theological roots in Puritanism and Calvinism. See J. Baird Callicott, "That Good Old-Time Wilderness Religion," *Environmental Professional* 13 (1991): 378–379; reprinted in *The Great New Wilderness Debate*, ed. J. Baird Callicott and Michael P. Nelson (Athens: University of Georgia Press, 1998), 387–394.

Orthodoxy and Ecopoetics: The Green World in the Desert Sea / Alfred K. Siewers

1. Translated from the early Irish in Séamus Mac Mathúna, ed. and trans., *Immram Brain, Bran's Journey to the Land of the Women: An Edition of the Old Irish Tale with Linguistic Analysis, Notes, and Commentary* (Tübingen: Max Niemeyer Verlag, 1985), 39–40.

2. Translated from Osborn Bergin and R. I. Best, ed. and trans., "Tochmarc Étaíne," *Ériu* 12 (1938): 180–181.

3. Jennifer Neville, *Representations of the Natural World in Old English Poetry* (Cambridge: Cambridge University Press, 1999), 37.

4. Northrop Frye, "The Argument of Comedy," in *English Institute Essays, 1948*, ed. D. A. Robertson Jr. (New York: Columbia University Press, 1949), 58–73.

5. Ecopoetics is defined from its etymology as an environmental-literary "house making," by the literary scholar Jonathan Skinner, a practice that involves "exploring creative-critical edges between writing (with an emphasis on poetry) and ecology (the theory and praxis of deliberate earthlings)." "Editor's Statement," *ecopoetics* 1 (Winter 2001): 5–8. The word *ecopoetics* also relates to the differently spelled term *ecopoiesis* or *ecopoesis*; the former is used in environmental sciences to describe the process of physically shaping ecosystems, as in ecological restoration projects. The philosopher of mind Evan Thompson relates *ecopoiesis* to development of humans fully through empathy. Evan Thompson, *Mind in Life: Biology, Phenomenology, and the Sciences of Mind* (Cambridge, Mass.: Harvard University Press, 2007).

6. Alfred K. Siewers, "Landscapes of Conversion: Guthlac's Mound and Grendel's Mere in Expressions of Anglo-Saxon Nation-Building," in *The Postmodern Beowulf*, ed. Eileen A. Joy and Mary K. Ramsey (Morgantown: West Virginia University Press, 2007), 199–258.

7. Julia Kristeva, "Dostoevsky, the Writing of Suffering, and Forgiveness," in *Black Sun: Depression and Melancholia*, trans. Leon S. Roudiez (New York: Columbia University Press, 1989), 210–211.

8. See Alfred K. Siewers, *Strange Beauty: Ecocritical Approaches to Early Medieval Landscape* (New York: Palgrave Macmillan, 2009); I. P. Sheldon-Williams with John J. O'Meara, trans., *Periphyseon (The Division of Nature)* (Montreal: Éditions Bellarmin/Washington, D.C.: Dumbarton Oaks, 1987).

9. John Carey, *Ireland and the Grail* (Aberystwyth: Celtic Studies Publications, 2008).

10. Marie-Louise Sjoestedt, *Celtic Gods and Heroes*, trans. Myles Dillon (New York: Turtle Island Foundation, 1982), 1.

11. Frye, "The Argument of Comedy," 70.

12. Ibid., 71–72.

13. Dumitru Staniloae, *Orthodox Spirituality: A Practical Guide for the Faithful and a Definitive Manual for the Scholar*, trans. Jerome Newville and Otilia Kloos (South Canaan, Penn.: St. Tikhon's Seminary Press, 2003), 209.

14. Athanasius, *The Life of Antony*, trans. Robert C. Gregg (San Francisco: HarperCollins, 2006), 74.

15. Siewers, *Strange Beauty*, 7.

16. Athanasius, *The Life of Antony*, 46–47, 48.

17. Ibid., 74.

18. Ephrem the Syrian, *Hymns on Paradise*, trans. Sebastian Brock (Crestwood, N.Y.: St. Vladimir's Seminary Press, 1997), 54; Hymn 1.6–7, 79–80.

19. *In Iohannis epistulam ad Parthos Tractatus*, trans. James Innes, in *The Nicene and Post-Nicene Fathers of the Church*, 1st series (Grand Rapids, Mich., 1974), 7:473.

20. Unlike Orthodox tradition, Eriugena most often referred to primordial causes, his version of the *logoi* or energies, as created, yet he also noted that from a divine rather than mortal perspective they could be considered uncreated (*Periphyseon* 3.8, PL 122: 640CD; trans. Sheldon-Williams with O'Meara, 259). Eriugena's description of a spectrum from energies to created theophanies still echoed the dynamic aspect of the energies in Orthodox tradition.

21. See Alfred K. Siewers, "The Bluest-Greyest-Greenest Eye: Colours of Martyrdom and Colours of the Winds as Iconographic Landscape," *Cambrian Medieval Celtic Studies* 50 (Winter 2005): 31–66.

22. Eriugena *Periphyseon* 5.31, 38; *PL* 122: 946A, 998B, 999B, 1000B–C; trans. Sheldon-Williams with O'Meara, *Periphyseon*, 624, 685, 686, 688.

23. Eriugena *Periphyseon* 4.2, trans. Sheldon-Williams and O'Meara, 383; Columbanus *Sancti Columbani Opera*, Scriptores Latini Hiberniae 2, ed. G. S. M. Walker (Dublin: Dublin Institute, 1957), 1.4, 65.

24. Michael J. Oleksa, *Orthodox Alaska: A Theology of Mission* (Crestwood, N.Y.: St. Vladimir's Seminary Press, 1992), 126 and throughout; see also his *Alaskan Missionary Spirituality* (New York: Paulist Press, 1987), 27–28.

25. St. Gregory of Sinai, *Discourse on the Transfiguration*, ed. and trans. David Balfour (Athens: Theologia, 1982), 44–45.

26. Siewers, *Strange Beauty*, chap. 5.

27. Winfried Nöth, "Protosemiotics and Physicosemiosis," *Sign Systems Studies* 29, no. 1 (2001): 13–24.

28. See Kristeva, "Dostoevsky, the Writing of Suffering, and Forgiveness," 173–218.

29. Andrew Louth, "The Body in Western Catholic Christianity" in *Religion and the Body*, ed. Sarah Coakley (Cambridge: Cambridge University Press, 1997), 129–130.

30. Regarding interiorization in Western theology, see Phillip Cary, *Augustine and the Invention of the Inner Self* (Oxford: Oxford University Press, 2000).

31. Alfred K. Siewers, "Writing an Icon of the Land: The *Mabinogi* as a Mystagogy of Landscape," *Peritia* 19 (2005): 193–228.

32. See John Chryssavgis, *Beyond the Shattered Image* (Minneapolis, Minn.: Light and Life, 1999), 139–164. Also, on the feminine associations of double-enfolded landscape, see Edward S. Casey, *The Fate of Place, A Philosophical History* (Berkeley: University of California Press, 1998), 321–330.

33. Christina Harrington, *Women in a Celtic Church, Ireland 450–1150* (Oxford: Oxford University Press, 2002), 280–282.

34. Carey, *Ireland and the Grail*.

35. Andrew Louth, *Greek East and Latin West, The Church* A.D. 681–1071 (Crestwood, N.Y.: St. Vladimir's Seminary Press, 2007), 149.

36. Robert Bartlett, *The Natural and the Supernatural in the Middle Ages* (Cambridge: Cambridge University Press, 2008).

37. Rory McTurk, *Chaucer and the Norse and Celtic Worlds* (London: Ashgate, 2005).

38. Geoffrey Chaucer, *The Canterbury Tales*, ed. Jill Mann (London: Penguin, 2005).

39. This is true, I would argue, even for "The Prioresse's Tale," in which her anti-Semitism is part of a satire of her unspiritual and objectifying ego.

40. A. Kent Hieatt, *Chaucer Spenser Milton, Mythopoeic Continuities and Transformations* (Montreal: McGill-Queen's University Press, 1975), 1–2.

41. Thompson, *Mind in Life*.

42. Harold L. Weatherby, *Mirrors of Celestial Grace: Patristic Theology in Spenser's Allegory* (Toronto: University of Toronto Press, 1994).

43. See Georgios I. Mantzaridis, *Time and Man*, trans. Julian Vulliamy (South Canaan, Penn.: St. Tikhon's Seminary, 1996); and John Romanides, *Patristic Theology: The University Lectures of Fr. John Romanides*, trans. Alexios Trader (Thessalonika: Uncut Mountain Press, 2007), 274–275. To the latter's explication of three modes of patristic time and nontime I have added a fourth based on St. Basil's discussion of the stars in his *Hexaemeron*.

44. The title of Bruce (Seraphim) Foltz's examination of environmental poetics, derived from Heidegger.

45. Jeffrey J. Cohen, *Medieval Identity Machines* (Minneapolis: University of Minnesota Press, 2003), xvi.

46. Gilles Deleuze and Félix Guattari, *A Thousand Plateaus, Capitalism and Schizophrenia 2*, trans. Brian Massumi (Minneapolis: University of Minnesota Press, 1987), throughout and at 40. On ecosemiotics, see Winfried Nöth, "Ecosemiotics," *Sign Systems Studies* 26 (1998): 332–343. On physics and Orthodoxy, see Vlatko Vedral, *Decoding Reality: The Universe as Quantum Information* (Oxford: Oxford University Press, 2010); and Alexei V. Nesteruk, *Universe as Communion: Toward a Neo-Patristic Synthesis of Theology and Science* (London: T&T Clark, 2008).

47. Peter Hallward, *Out of This World: Deleuze and the Philosophy of Creation* (London: Verso, 2006), 2, 4.

48. Eriugena *Periphyseon*, esp. book 5.

49. Gilles Deleuze, "Desert Islands," in *Desert Islands and Other Texts (1953–1974)*, trans. Mike Taormina (Cambridge: Semiotext(e), 2004), 9–14.

50. Ibid., 11.

51. Gilles Deleuze and Félix Guattari, *What Is Philosophy?*, trans. Janis Tomlinson and Graham Burchell III (New York: Columbia University Press, 1996), 105, 169.

52. Adomnán *Vita Columbae* 1.6; Richard Sharpe, trans., *Life of St. Columba* (London: Penguin, 1995), 118.

53. Eriugena *Periphyseon* 4.2, PL122: 744A–B; trans. Sheldon-Williams and O'Meara, 383.

54. I am indebted to Harold Weatherby for pointing this out to me.

55. Weatherby, *Mirrors of Celestial Grace*, 76–94.

56. A. C. Hamilton, Hiroshi Yamashita, Toshiyuki Suzuki, and Shohachi Fukuda, eds., *Spenser: The Faerie Queene*, 2nd ed. (New York: Longman, 2006), 7.7.

57. John McWhorter, *Our Magnificent Bastard Tongue: The Untold History of English* (New York: Gotham, 2008), 61.
58. Lawrence Buell, *The Environmental Imagination: Thoreau, Nature Writing, and the Formation of American Culture* (Cambridge, Mass.: Harvard University Press, 1995), 6–8.
59. Eriugena *Periphyseon* 4.2, PL122: 744A–B; trans. Sheldon-Williams and O'Meara, 383.
60. See J. R. R. Tolkien, "On Fairy-Stories," in *Essays Presented to Charles Williams* (London: Oxford University Press, 1947).
61. St. Nikolai Velimirovich, *Prayers by the Lake*, 13, trans. Todor Mika and Stevan Scott (Grayslake, Ill.: Diocese of New Gracanica and Midwestern America, 2010), 25.
62. St. Maximus the Confessor, *On the Cosmic Mystery of Christ*, trans. Paul M. Blowers and Robert Louis Wilken (Crestwood, N.Y.: St. Vladimir's Seminary Press, 2003), "*Ambiguum* 7: On the Beginning and End of Rational Creatures," 45–74.

Perspectives on Orthodoxy, Evolution, and Ecology / Gayle E. Woloschak

1. Sallie McFague, "An Ecological Christology: Does Christianity Have it?" and Elizabeth A. Johnson, "Losing and Finding Creation in the Christian Tradition," both in *Christianity and Ecology: Seeking the Well-Being of Earth and Humans*, ed. Dieter T. Hessel and Rosemary Radford Ruether (Cambridge, Mass.: Harvard University Press, 2000), 29–45, 3–21.
2. Radu Bordeianu, "Maximus and Ecology: The Relevance of Maximus the Confessor's Theology of Creation for the Present Ecological Crisis," *Downside Review* 127 (2009): 103–126. This synthesis is also described in Hans Urs von Balthasar, *Cosmic Liturgy: The Universe According to Maximus the Confessor* (San Francisco: Ignatius, 2003), 273.
3. L. Thunberg, *Microcosm and Mediator: The Theological Anthropology of Maximus the Confessor*, 2nd ed. (Chicago: Open Court, 1995), 331–332.
4. This idea is expressed well in K. Ware, *Through the Creation to the Creator* (London: Friends of the Centre, 1997). See also the article by Metropolitan Kallistos in this volume.
5. von Balthasar, *Cosmic Liturgy*, 327.
6. See Charles Darwin, *The Descent of Man and Selection in Relation to Sex* (New York: Hurst and Co., 1874); and Charles Darwin, *The Origin of the Species* (Oxford: Oxford University Press, 1996).
7. A. Peacocke, *Paths from Science towards God: The End of All Exploring* (Oxford: Oneworld, 2001).
8. F. Dikötter, *Mao's Great Famine: The History of China's Most Devastating Catastrophe, 1958–62* (New York: Walker and Co., 2010), 333.
9. L. Tolstoy, *War and Peace* (New York: Viking-Penguin, 2006).

10. The lectures are available at www.beyondbelief2006.org.

11. Thomas Aquinas, *Reasons in Proof of the Existence of God*, in his *Summa Theologica*, articles II and II.

12. Sergius Bulgakov, *The Bride of the Lamb* (Grand Rapids, Mich.: Eerdmans, 2002).

13. Ibid.

14. See J. D. Zizioulas, "Preserving God's Creation: Three Lectures on Theology and Ecology," *King's Theological Review* 12 (1989): 1–5, 41–45 and 13 (1990): 1–5; P. Sherrard, *Human Image, World Image: The Death and Resurrection of Sacred Cosmology* (Ipswich: Golgonooza Press, 1992); D. Staniloae, *The Experience of God*, 2 vols. (Brookline, Mass.: Holy Cross Orthodox Press, 1994, 2000); V. Vukanovic, *Science and Faith* (Minneapolis, Minn.: Light and Life, 1995); G. E. Woloschak, *Beauty and Unity in Creation: The Evolution of Life* (Minneapolis, Minn.: Light and Life, 1996); D. B. Hart, *The Beauty of the Infinite: The Aesthetics of Christian Truth* (Grand Rapids, Mich.: Eerdmans, 2003); A. V. Nesteruk, *Light from the East: Theology, Science, and the Eastern Orthodox Tradition* (Minneapolis, Minn.: Fortress, 2003); C. Yannaras, *Postmodern Metaphysics* (Brookline, Mass.: Holy Cross Orthodox Press, 2004); D. B. Hart, *The Doors of the Sea: Where Was God in the Tsunami?* (Grand Rapids, Mich.: Eerdmans, 2005).

15. Sergius Bulgakov, *Sophia: The Wisdom of God* (Hudson, N.Y.: Lindisfarne, 1993).

16. In Bulgakov, *The Bride of the Lamb*.

17. Ibid.

Ecology, Morality, and the Challenges of the Twenty-First Century: The Earth in the Hands of the Sons of Noah / H. Tristram Engelhardt Jr.

1. As an example of the unreliability of large-scale predictions regarding the future, one might consider the predictions of imminent adverse outcomes of uncheckable population growth made by the Club of Rome. See Donella H. Meadows et al., *The Limits to Growth: A Report for the Club of Rome's Project on the Predicament of Mankind*, 2nd ed. (Englewood, N.J.: Universe, 1974). For other examples, see Council on Environmental Quality and the Department of State, *The Global 2000 Report to the President*, 3 vols. (Washington, D.C.: U.S. Government Printing Office, 1980–1981); Intergovernmental Panel on Climate Change, "Climate Change 2007," http://www.ipcc.ch; U.S. Department of Energy, *Technical Guidelines for the Voluntary Reporting of Greenhouse Gas Emissions (1605(b)) Program: Office of Policy and International Affairs* (Washington, D.C.: 2007); U.S. Environmental Protection Agency, *Inventory of U.S. Greenhouse Gas Emissions and Sinks: 1990–2004*, EPA-430-R-06-002 (Washington, D.C.: April 2006).

2. H. T. Engelhardt Jr. and Arthur Caplan, *Scientific Controversies: A Study in the Resolution and Closure of Disputes Concerning Science and Technology* (New York: Cambridge University Press, 1987).

3. For a brief overview of "Climategate," see Eli Kintisch, "Stolen E-mails Turn up Heat on Climate Change Rhetoric," *Science* 326 (December 4, 2009): 1329; Science and Technology Committee, UK Parliament, "The Disclosure of Climate Data from the Climatic Research Unit at the University of East Anglia," Eighth Report of Session 2009–10, HC 387-I (London: Stationery Office, 2010), 3; as well as Fred Pearce, *The Climate Files: The Battle for the Truth about Global Warming* (New York: Random House, 2010).

4. A central source of controversies regarding the future of the environment as we know it has involved the issue of global warming. For an overview of elements of these controversies, see David E. Blockstein and Leo Wiegman, *The Climate Solutions Consensus* (Washington, D.C.: Island, 2010); Anthony Giddens, *The Politics of Climate Change* (Cambridge: Polity, 2009); James Hansen, *Storms of My Grandchildren: The Truth about the Coming Climate Catastrophe and Our Last Chance to Save Humanity* (New York: Bloomsbury, 2009); Mike Hulme, *Why We Disagree about Climate Change* (Cambridge: Cambridge University Press, 2009); Naomi Orestes and Erik M. Conway, *Merchants of Doubt: How a Handful of Scientists Obscured the Truth on Issues from Tobacco Smoke to Global Warming* (New York: Bloomsbury, 2010); Stephen H. Schneider, *Science as a Contact Sport* (Washington, D.C.: National Geographic, 2009); and Stephen H. Schneider et al., eds., *Climate Change Science and Policy* (Washington, D.C.: Island, 2010).

5. John Christy, "Notable & Quotable," *Wall Street Journal* (October 25, 2007).

6. An illustration of the complexity of environmental phenomena is provided by false accounts of the cause for the shrinkage of the glaciers on Kilimanjaro. Although the global shrinkage of glaciers (see J. Oerlemans, "Extracting a Climate Signal from 169 Glacier Records," *Science* 308 [2005]: 675–677) may very well be attributable to global warming, such appears not to be the case with regard to the glaciers on Kilimanjaro. Indeed, global warming may lead to the expansion of the glaciers, not their diminution. See Philip W. Mote and George Kaser, "The Shrinking Glaciers of Kilimanjaro: Can Global Warming Be Blamed?" *American Scientist* 95 (July–August 2007): 318–325.

7. Orthodox Christian theology is substantively different from the theology that emerged in the West in the early second millennium as Roman Catholicism took shape as a recognizable denomination set over and against Orthodox Christianity. Orthodox theology is not set within a framework of governing philosophical assumptions but constitutes the way of coming rightly to know and experience God. Orthodox theology does not rest on a synergy of faith and reason that lies at the basis of a philosophically structured moral theology. In particular, theologians are *sensu stricto* those who know God and not those who merely know about God. Theologians in the strict sense thus need not be academics, and what they know qua theologians is God (or more precisely, they experience His uncreated energies), such that they are not primarily engaged in philosophically elaborating a set of discursive propositions. See H. Tristram Engelhardt Jr., "Critical Reflections on Theology's Handmaiden: Why the Role of Philosophy in Orthodox Christianity Is So Different,"

Philosophy and Theology 18, no. 1 (2006): 53–75; H. Tristram Engelhardt Jr., "Moral Philosophy and Theology: Why Is There So Little Difference for Roman Catholics?" in *Christian Bioethics* 9 (December 2003): 315–330; and H. Tristram Engelhardt Jr., *The Foundations of Christian Bioethics* (Salem, Mass.: Scrivener, 2000).

8. H. T. Engelhardt Jr., *The Foundations of Christian Bioethics* (Salem, Mass.: Scrivener, 2000), chap. 4.

9. Sts. Nikodemus and Agapius, eds., "The 85 Canons," in *The Rudder*, trans. D. Cummings (Chicago: Orthodox Christian Educational Society, 1983), 91.

10. *Homily 27*, 174. See St. John Chrysostom, *Homilies on Genesis 18–45*, in *The Fathers of the Church*, vol. 82, trans. Robert C. Hill (Washington, D.C.: Catholic University of America Press, 1990).

11. As the Apostolic Canon 51 and St. John Chrysostom's *Homily 27 on Genesis* show, the seven laws given by God to Noah are affirmed after the Resurrection, as in the case of the blessing to kill and eat animals (Acts 10:9–16) as well as in the continued Christian prohibition against eating blood (Acts 15:20). See also Apostolic Canon 63 and Canon 67 of the Quinisext Council.

12. A difficulty in assessing current threats to the environment lies in the question of how seriously one should take the arguments of those who are critical of the seemingly widely established thesis that global warming is occurring, primarily because of pollutants contributed by the presence of humans.

13. The argument is that DDT among other things leads to the thinning of the shell of condor eggs, thus threatening their survival. Of course, there appear to be some small risks, too, but many more benefits for humans.

14. Data have accumulated with regard to the adverse effects of adding ethanol to gasoline as part of a project to protect the environment. The findings show the difficulties involved in determining in advance whether particular strategies to protect the environment will cause more harm than benefit. See, for example, David A. Farenthold, "'Green' Fuel May Damage the Bay," *Washington Post* (July 17, 2007); Jerry Taylor and Peter Van Doren, "Ethanol Makes Gasoline Costlier, Dirtier," *Chicago Sun-Times* (January 29, 2007), http://www.cato.org/pub_display.php?pub_id=7308.

15. Olivier Deschênes and Michael Greenstone, "The Economic Impacts of Climate Change: Evidence from Agricultural Output and Random Fluctuations in Weather," *American Economic Review* 97, no. 2 (2007): 354–385.

16. Jerome C. Glenn and Theodore J. Gordon, *2007 State of the Future* (New York: World Federation of UN Associations, 2007).

17. The phrase "consumer culture" is used here in the very narrow sense of a culture that engages in a high level of energy production and energy consumption.

18. For an example of a proposal to remove pollutants, see M. Battle et al., "Global Carbon Sinks and Their Variability Inferred from Atmospheric O_2 and $\delta 13C$," *Science* 287 (2000): 2467–2470; Eileen V. Carey et al., "Are Old Forests Underestimated as Global Carbon Sinks?" *Global Change Biology* 7 (2001): 339–344; and Brandon Scarborough, "Trading Forest Carbon: A Panacea or Pipe Dream to Address Climate Change?" *PERC Policy Series* PS-40 (July 2007): 1–28.

19. Fred C. Iklé and Lowell Wood, "Thinking Big on Global Warming," *Wall Street Journal* (October 15, 2007); Michael Shellenberger and Ted Nordhaus, *Break Through* (Boston: Houghton Mifflin, 2007).

20. St. Basil, "The Long Rules," in *Ascetical Works*, trans. Sister M. Monica Wagner (Washington, D.C.: Catholic University of America Press, 1962), 331: reply to Question 55.

21. J. Baird Callicott and Michael P. Nelson, eds., *The Great New Wilderness Debate* (Athens: University of Georgia Press, 1998); Bill Devall and George Sessions, *Deep Ecology: Living as if Nature Mattered* (Layton, Ut.: Gibbs Smith, 2001).

22. An example of privileging the environment as it would have been without the imprint of man and of rejecting the appropriate dominion of man over nature is provided by ecotheologians such as Thomas Berry. See his *Dream of the Earth* (San Francisco: Sierra Club Books, 2006) and *The Great Work: Our Way into the Future* (New York: Three Rivers, 2000).

23. Author's translation from "Gedächtnis des hl. Bonifatius, Apostel Germaniens," *Das Synaxarion* 2 (Chania, Crete: Monastery of St. John the Forerunner, 2005), 411.

Liturgy, Cosmic Worship, and Christian Cosmology / Elizabeth Theokritoff

1. A good example is Hieromonk Gregorios, "Cosmos as a Realm of Liturgy," in *Synaxis*, vol. 1: *Environment-Anthropology-Creation*, ed. John Hadjinicolaou (Montreal: Alexander Press, 2006), 245–249.

2. Sisters of the Holy Convent of Chrysopigi, eds., *Wounded by Love: The Life and Wisdom of Elder Porphyrios* (Limni Evia: Denise Harvey, 2005), 32.

3. *Apostolic Tradition* of Hippolytus, Latin text; *Hippolyte de Rome, la tradition apostolique*, ed. B. Botte, SC 11bis (Paris: Cerf, 1984), chap. 41, p. 130.

4. *Apostolic Constitutions* VII.35; PG 1:1029B. Ante-Nicene Fathers 7, 473.

5. F. Nau, ed., Anastasius of Sinai, *Récits* III, *Oriens Christianus* II, 61–62.

6. On the inscriptions to the Psalms I.3; W. Jaeger, *Gregorii Nysseni Opera* V, 30–32.

7. Fr. Maximos, "Charisma and Institution at an Athonite Cloister," *Friends of Mount Athos Annual Report 2007*, 17–34. Elder Aimilianos recounts this story about "a certain monk" in "The Prayer of the Holy Mountain": Archimandrite Aimilianos of Simonopetra, *The Church at Prayer* (Athens: Indiktos, 2005), 47–49.

8. We do find instances in patristic writings where the three estates are reduced to two, when someone has reason to be very literal about "praising"—usually when they want to emphasize the necessity of the human contribution. E.g., Leontius of Cyprus's explicit denial that the visible creation glorifies God "directly and by itself" (*Fifth Homily of Christian Apologetic against the Jews, and on the Icons*, PG 93:1604B)—Leontius is making the case for icons.

9. E.g., Liturgy of St. James, Ante-Nicene Fathers 7, 543–544; Alexandrian Liturgy of St. Gregory the Theologian, PG 36:708B–D; Liturgy of St. Basil, Anaphora;

Cyril of Jerusalem, *Mystagogical Catechesis* V.6; Prayer at Blessing of Waters "Great art Thou, O Lord," in Mother Mary and Kallistos Ware, trans., *The Festal Menaion* (London: Faber and Faber, 1969), 356; *Apostolic Constitutions* VIII.12 (Anaphora) and VII.35 (Prayer with thanksgiving).

10. E.g., Liturgy of St. James, Anaphora; *Apostolic Constitutions*, Anaphora and Prayer with Thanksgiving.

11. *Mystagogical Catechesis* V.6.

12. See Hieromonk Gregorios, *The Divine Liturgy: A Commentary in the Light of the Fathers* (Mount Athos: Cell of St. John the Theologian, 2009), 232.

13. Germanos, *Theoria*, PG 98:429D.

14. Paul Meyendorff, ed., *St. Germanus of Constantinople on the Divine Liturgy* (Crestwood, N.Y.: St Vladimir's Seminary Press, 1984), 12.

15. Liturgy of St. Gregory the Theologian, PG 36:708B.

16. See P. Trembelas, ed., *Mikron Evchologion II* (Athens, 1955), 15.

17. Chrysostom, *Comm. on Psalm* 148, PG 55:487–488.

18. Chrysostom, *Comm. on Psalm* 148, PG 55: 489.

19. Fr. Ephrem (Lash), "Biblical Interpretation in Worship," in *The Cambridge Companion to Orthodox Christian Theology*, ed. Mary B. Cunningham and Elizabeth Theokritoff (Cambridge: Cambridge University Press, 2008), 42.

20. *On Psalms*, PG 55:486.

21. Gregory of Nyssa, *Apology on Hexaemeron*, PG 44:73C.

22. St. Basil, *Hom.* 12, *On the Beginning of Proverbs*, 3; PG 31:392AB.

23. Eleventh silent prayer during the Six Psalms; I. F. Hapgood, trans., *Service Book of the Holy Orthodox-Catholic Apostolic Church*, 4th ed. (Brooklyn, N.Y.: Syrian Antiochian Orthodox Archdiocese, 1965), 25.

24. See George Theokritoff, "The Cosmology of the Eucharist," in this volume.

25. Archimandrite Vasileios of Stavronikita, *Hymn of Entry: Liturgy and Life in the Orthodox Church* (Crestwood, N.Y.: St Vladimir's Seminary Press, 1984), 81.

26. *Hymn of Entry*, 67.

27. Ibid.

28. *Mystagogy* 2, PG 91:669CD.

"All Creation Rejoices in You": Creation in the Liturgies for the Feasts of the Theotokos / Christina M. Gschwandtner

1. This eschatological, transfiguring dimension of Eastern Orthodox liturgy is relatively well known and is explicated by many of its contemporary expositors. Alexander Schmemann was one of the earliest and most well known among them; see his *For the Life of the World: Sacraments and Orthodoxy* (Crestwood, N.Y.: St. Vladimir's Seminary Press, 1973). For another exposition, see Kallistos Ware, "The Theology of Worship," in *The Inner Kingdom* (Crestwood, N.Y.: St. Vladimir's Seminary Press, 2004).

2. "Address During the Environmental Symposium in Santa Barbara," November 8, 1997. Bartholomew's various addresses and writings on ecological themes are

collected by Fr. John Chryssavgis in his edited volume *Cosmic Grace and Humble Prayer: The Ecological Vision of the Green Patriarch Bartholomew I* (Grand Rapids, Mich.: Eerdmans, 2003). The above quotation is found on page 219. See also his *Encountering the Mystery: Understanding Orthodox Christianity Today* (New York: Doubleday, 2008), esp. chap. 6, "The Wonder of Creation: Religion and Ecology," 89–119; and a more recent collection of writings also edited by John Chryssavgis, *Speaking the Truth in Love: Theological and Spiritual Exhortations of Ecumenical Patriarch Bartholomew* (New York: Fordham University Press, 2011). There are also interesting comments in Olivier Clément, *Conversations with Ecumenical Patriarch Bartholomew I*, trans. Paul Meyendorff (Crestwood, N.Y.: St. Vladimir's Seminary Press, 1997).

3. For a summary of the main themes in Bartholomew's ecological writings, see my "Orthodox Ecological Theology: Bartholomew I and Orthodox Contributions to the Ecological Debate," *International Journal of the Christian Church* (2010).

4. Some of these reflections are collected in the spring 1990 issue of the *Epiphany Journal*, devoted to the "Symposium on Orthodoxy and Ecology" under the title "For the Transfiguration of Nature." See also John Chryssavgis, "The World of the Icon and Creation: An Orthodox Perspective on Ecology and Pneumatology," in *Christianity and Ecology: Seeking the Well-Being of Earth and Humans*, ed. Dieter T. Hessel and Rosemary Radford Ruether (Cambridge, Mass.: Harvard University Press, 2000), 83–96; John Chryssavgis, *Beyond the Shattered Image* (Minneapolis, Minn.: Light and Life, 1999); Elizabeth Theokritoff, "Orthodoxy and the Environment: Challenges and Opportunities of the Modern Environmental Movement," *Sourozh* 58 (1994): 13–27; Elizabeth Theokritoff, *Living in God's Creation: The Ecological Vision of Orthodox Christianity* (Crestwood, N.Y.: St. Vladimir's Seminary Press, 2009). An older text is Paulos Gregorios, *The Human Presence: An Orthodox View of Nature* (Geneva: WCC, 1978).

5. This is especially strong in John Zizioulas's writings. See his "Man, the Priest of Creation," in *Living Orthodoxy in the Modern World*, ed. Andrew Walker and Costa Carras (London: SPCK, 1996); and "Priest of Creation," in *Environmental Stewardship*, ed. R. J. Berry (Edinburgh: T&T Clark, 2006). See also his keynote address at the fifth symposium of Religion, Science, and the Environment on June 2, 2003, "Proprietors or Priests of Creation?" included in the present volume.

6. Obviously the liturgical texts and rhythms developed in the early centuries do not consciously address our current ecological crises. Yet they can certainly serve as impetus and grounding for our development of such replies in ways that would probably be far more convincing to the average believer than more abstract theological speculation.

7. See, for example, Vigen Guroian, "Ecological Ethics: An Ecclesial Event," in his *Ethics After Christendom: Toward an Ecclesial Christian Ethic* (Grand Rapids, Mich.: Eerdmans, 1994).

8. The feasts of the Theotokos probably developed beginning with the celebration of the *Synaxis of the Theotokos* on the day after Nativity, probably beginning in

the fourth or fifth century. See the more detailed explanation in *The Festal Menaion*, trans. Mother Mary and Archimandrite Kallistos Ware (South Canaan, Penn.: St. Tikhon's Seminary Press, 1998), 535–543. The Menaion contains the liturgical texts for all feast days throughout the year. All quotations from the Orthodox liturgies are taken from this translation, unless indicated otherwise. Although usually liturgical texts are identified by their place within the liturgy, I will provide the page number for the translation in parentheses within the text for easier reference.

9. Jaroslav Pelikan, "Most Generations Shall Call Me Blessed: An Essay in Aid of a Grammar of Liturgy," in *Mary, Mother of God*, ed. Carl E. Braaten and Robert W. Jenson (Grand Rapids, Mich.: Eerdmans, 2004), 1–18.

10. Mgr. Joseph Nasrallah, *Marie dans la sainte et divine liturgie byzantine* (Paris: Nouvelles Éditions Latines, 1954), 45–65.

11. Patriarch Dimitrios, Bartholomew's predecessor as Ecumenical Patriarch, dedicated September 1 as a day of prayer for the environment and celebration of God's creation.

12. Ibid., 65–72.

13. Ibid., 19.

14. P. Paul Doncoeur, "La vierge Marie et la liturgie des anges" in *Maria in Liturgie und Lehrwort*, ed. P. Theodor Bogler (Maria Laach: Verlag Ars Liturgica, 1954), 101.

15. Ibid., 105–109.

16. P. Theodor Strotmann, "Maria in der Lehre und Frömmigkeit der Ostkirche" in *Maria in Liturgie und Lehrwort*, ed. P. Theodor Bogler (Maria Laach: Verlag Ars Liturgica, 1954), 73.

17. These are later developments, and there are no references made to these traditions within the liturgical texts themselves.

18. There is indeed much imagery for the Theotokos that compares her in various ways to other parts of creation. Strotmann discusses the way in which Mary is portrayed as the "new earth," an imagery introduced and popularized by John of Damascus (Strotmann, "Lehre der Ostkirche," 74). For an example of a very typological reading of the Eastern liturgy (by a Roman Catholic thinker), see Joseph Ledit, *Marie dans la liturgie de Byzance* (Paris: Éditions Beauchesne, 1976). Elizabeth Johnson has stressed the danger of much of this imagery in chapters 3 and 4 of her *Truly Our Sister: A Theology of Mary in the Communion of Saints* (New York: Continuum, 2004).

19. Obviously, the language used here makes Aristotelian or generic Greek biological assumptions about human generation, in which "seed" is provided by the Father—in this case assumed to be God—and matter by the mother, Mary. See Aristotle's *On the Generation of Animals*.

20. The mystery of the incarnation is proclaimed in the Aposticha during Vespers at the Synaxis of the Theotokos: "A marvellous wonder has this day come to pass: nature is made new, and God becomes man.... How shall I tell of this great mystery? He who is without flesh becomes incarnate; the Word puts on a body; the

Invisible is seen; He whom no hand can touch is handled; and He who knows no beginning now begins to be" (291).

21. Troparion of the second canon of the third canticle during Matins of the feast of the Nativity, 272.

22. First canon of the seventh canticle during Matins for the feast of the Nativity of the Theotokos, 119.

23. Great Vespers for the feast of the Annunciation, 440. In fact, it is far more often affirmed that God appeared in the flesh or in matter than that he became human.

24. Sticheron during Matins for Forefeast of the Nativity of Christ, 217. Mary's diapers are also worthy of honor: "We venerate thy swaddling clothes, O Theotokos" (Second Canon, Ninth Canticle, Matins for Feast of Nativity of the Theotokos, 124).

25. Ypakoe, Matins, Feast of the Nativity, 272.

26. Litya, Great Compline for Feast of the Nativity, 263.

27. Vespers for Feast of the Nativity, 254.

28. E.g., during the Litya for the Annunciation, 443.

29. Canon, Third Canticle, Matins for the Feast of the Meeting of our Lord, 420.

30. Second Canon, Fifth Canticle, Matins for the Feast of the Nativity, 276.

31. Homily on the Nativity (of the Theotokos) in Mary B. Cunningham, ed. and trans., *Wider Than Heaven: Eight-Century Homilies on the Mother of God* (Crestwood, N.Y.: St. Vladimir's Seminary Press, 2008), 54. Henceforth cited as WTH.

32. Oration 2.24, 121–123. All citations from Gregory Nazianzen refer to *Nicene and Post-Nicene Fathers*, vol. 7 (Peabody, Mass.: Hendrickson, 1994).

33. Oration 37.2, 273–275.

34. *Les Homélies festales d'Hésychius de Jérusalem*, ed. Michel Aubineau (Bruxelles: Société des Bollandistes, 1978), I.1, 25.

35. WTH, 225.

36. He goes on to establish a link between creation and incarnation. See Nativity 23:13; cited in Sebastian Brock, *The Luminous Eye: The Spiritual World of Saint Ephrem the Syrian*, Cistercian Studies Series 124 (Kalamazoo, Mich.: Cistercian Publications, 1992), 85.

37. In a different homily, he inquires about the miracle of the incarnation from various aspects of nature: "For how then will one who is mere grass, clay, earth and ash be able to search/after the mystery of God and the purpose of the Potter? . . ." (36.5, 108).

38. In Brian E. Daley, *On the Dormition of Mary: Early Patristic Homilies* (Crestwood, N.Y.: St. Vladimir's Seminary Press, 1998), 84–85. Henceforth cited as *Dormition*.

39. Bulgakov draws similar connections between creation and Incarnation in a homily on the Annunciation. See Sergius Bulgakov, *Churchly Joy: Orthodox Devotions for the Church Year*, trans. Boris Jakim (Grand Rapids, Mich.: Eerdmans, 2008), 79.

40. Of course, this argument becomes a central component of the later defense of icons, especially in the writings of John of Damascus. See his *Three Treatises on*

the Divine Images, trans. Andrew Louth (Crestwood, N.Y.: St. Vladimir's Theological Press, 2003).

41. Katavasia, Canticle Eight, Matins for Feast of the Entry of the Most Holy Theotokos into the Temple, 190.

42. Canticle Nine, Compline, 209.

43. Sticheron for Vespers, Nativity, 254. Also: "The whole creation leaps with joy, for the Savior and Lord is born in Bethlehem" (Litya, Great Compline, Nativity, 264); "Therefore let all creation sing and dance for joy, for Christ has come to restore it and to save our souls" (Litya, Great Compline, Nativity, 266).

44. After an examination of various liturgical and theological texts to support this, she concludes: "The heavens really are telling the glory of God: it is not something that we read into nature. We proclaim this truth liturgically, and that is a first step towards perceiving its reality in the world around us." Elizabeth Theokritoff, "Liturgy and Cosmology," 12. (This piece is an unpublished conference presentation. I thank Elizabeth for making it available to me.) [Eds.: An edited version of this essay by Elizabeth Theokritoff is included in the present volume. The passage to which Gschwandtner refers is in the last paragraph.]

45. For example, in the first canon of the Eighth Ode during Matins for the Feast of Nativity (280). This occurs fairly often in the eighth ode (of several feasts), since this ode is based on the song of the three children, which employs this phrase (and indeed is full of the praise of creation).

46. Sessional Hymn, Matins, Feast of the Annunciation, 446.

47. Second Canon, Ninth Canticle, Matins, Nativity of Theotokos, 124.

48. See the Sessional Hymn, Matins, Nativity of Theotokos, 108.

49. Second Canon, Third Canticle, Nativity of Theotokos, 113.

50. It is not always clear within the liturgical texts whether the terms "world" (*cosmos*), "earth" (*ge*), "creation" (*ktisis*), and "universe" or "all things" (*ta panta*) designate what we would understand by those terms today or refer primarily (or even exclusively) to humans. This ambivalence is certainly characteristic of many of the Patristic homilies. One must thus give more weight to passages that do actually explicitly list nonhuman creatures.

51. Canticle Eight, Matins, Forefeast of Nativity, 215.

52. Sessional Hymn, Matins, Nativity, 272. For a helpful analysis of the biblical language of heaven and earth, which does not see the two in contrast or opposition to each other (as "natural" and "supernatural"), see Moltmann, *God in Creation*, section 7, "Heaven and Earth," 158–184.

53. Canticle Nine, Matins, Forefeast of Nativity, 216.

54. Second Canon, Canticle Eight, Matins, Nativity of Theotokos, 122.

55. Sticheron, Vespers, Nativity, 254.

56. E.g., Second Canon, Canticle One, Nativity of Theotokos, 111.

57. Second Canon, Canticle Eight, Matins, Nativity of Theotokos, 122.

58. *Oration* 38.17, 126.

59. *Oration* 4.3, 88–90. See also Proclus, Bishop of Constantinople, *Homilies on the Life of Christ*, trans. Jan Harm Barkhuizen, Early Christian Studies 1 (Brisbane: Centre for Early Christian Studies, 2001), 5.2, 93–94.

60. Ibid., 24.2–8, 103–104.

61. He does go on, however, to identify the mountains with "reasonable natures" who should pursue "spiritual contemplation" (6.61).

62. WTH, 58, 61.

63. The editor claims in a footnote, however, that the "compound structure" refers to humans.

64. WTH, 145–146.

65. Theodore the Studite, WTH, 250.

66. WTH, 47.

67. Jacob of Serug, *On the Mother of God*, trans. Mary Hansbury (Crestwood, N.Y.: St. Vladimir's Seminary Press, 1998), *Homily* V, 96.

68. Contemporary authors also occasionally comment on this. Bulgakov in a sermon on nativity suggests that the animals present are significant: "The ox and the ass at the crib, animals toiling with man for the sake of man, in their innocence of sin had deviated less from their primordial purpose than fallen man, their master. The Lord preferred the mute animals to the proud and vain words of the wisdom of this world with its pomp and arrogance." *Churchly Joy*, 26. Relying on the kontakion of the feast, he sees all of nature (earthly, human, and angelic) responding to the nativity of Christ. Theokritoff agrees: "All creation rejoices at the coming of the Savior because it is an event of cosmic significance" (*God's Creation*, 163).

69. Ware, *Festal Menaion*, 46.

70. Aposticha, Great Vespers, Nativity of Theotokos, 107.

71. Ikos, Matins, Annunciation, 454.

72. The ascension traverses the bridge in the opposite direction. While the incarnation brings heaven to earth, the ascension carries earth into heaven. Both serve to link earth and heaven.

73. Sticheron, Small Vespers, *Dormition*, 504.

74. Litya, Great Vespers, *Dormition*, 509.

75. First Canon, Fourth Canticle, Matins, *Dormition*, 517.

76. Sticheron, Matins, *Dormition*, 525.

77. Aposticha, Great Compline, Annunciation, 445.

78. Sticheron, Great Vespers, Birth of Theotokos, 101.

79. Litya, Great Vespers, *Dormition*, 509.

80. Second Canon, Eighth Canticle, Matins, Birth of Theotokos, 122. See also the Fourth Sticheron, Small Vespers, Nativity of Theotokos, 99.

81. See also Litya, Great Vespers, Nativity of Theotokos, 105; Aposticha, Great Vespers, Nativity of Theotokos, 106; Sticheron, Matins, Nativity of Theotokos, 126; and Troparion, Entry of the Theotokos into the Temple, 172.

82. Canticle Four, Matins, Forefeast of Nativity, 212. Obviously this implies a paradisal state here (as is often the case in the liturgy) incongruent with insights of evolution, but these were not available at the time. Vasile Mihoc points out that the paradise or garden of creation "signifies that humanity was in a perfect harmony with the world" (but need not imply finished perfection). "Aspects of the Biblical Theology of Creation," in *Justice, Peace, and the Integrity of Creation: Insights from Orthodoxy*, ed. Gennadios Limouris (Geneva: WCC, 1990), 95.

83. Second Canon, Canticle Eight, Matins, *Dormition*, 523.

84. Ikos, Matins, Nativity, 278.

85. Leontius, Presbyter of Constantinople, *Fourteen Homilies*, trans. Pauline Allen and Cornelis Datema (Brisbane: Australian Association for Byzantine Studies, 1991), XII.1, 172.

86. First Hymn on Nativity, 24, 77.

87. Second Hymn on Nativity, 18, 111.

88. WTH, 198.

89. WTH, 112.

90. Andrew of Crete, "Third Homily on Dormition," *Dormition*, 138–139.

91. WTH, 214–215.

92. WTH, 256.

Traces of Divine Fragrance, Droplets of Divine Love: On the Beauty of Visible Creation / Bruce V. Foltz

1. Pavel Florensky, *The Pillar and Ground of the Truth: An Essay in Orthodox Theodicy in Twelve Letters*, trans. Boris Jakim (Princeton, N.J.: Princeton University Press, 1997), 201.

2. Ibid., 210.

3. Ibid.

4. *The Philokalia: The Complete Text*, comp. St. Nikodemos of the Holy Mountain and St. Makarios of Corinth, trans. G. E. H. Palmer, Philip Sherrard, and Kallistos Ware (London: Faber and Faber, 1995), 4:93.

5. *The Philokalia: The Complete Text*, comp. St. Nikodemos of the Holy Mountain and St. Makarios of Corinth, trans. G. E. H. Palmer, Philip Sherrard, and Kallistos Ware (London: Faber and Faber, 1979), 4:194.

6. Sisters of the Holy Convent of Chrysopigi, *Wounded by Love: The Life and Wisdom of Elder Porphyrios* (Limni, Evia, Greece: Denise Harvey, 2005), 140.

7. Florensky, *Pillar and Ground of Truth*, 200, 527.

8. Ibid., 216; italics added.

9. D. S. Wallace-Hadrill, *The Greek Patristic View of Nature* (Manchester: Manchester University Press, 1968), 87– 91.

10. St. Basil the Great, *Letter* XIV, in *Nicene and Post-Nicene Fathers*, second ser., vol. 8, ed. Philip Schaff and Henry Wace (Peabody, Mass.: Hendrickson, 1999), 124–125.

11. St, Basil the Great, *The Hexaemeron*, in *Nicene and Post-Nicene Fathers*, second ser., vol. 8, ed. Philip Schaff and Henry Wace (Peabody, Mass.: Hendrickson, 1999), 71, 55.

12. Ibid., 76.

13. St. Basil the Great, *Letter* IX, in *Nicene and Post-Nicene Fathers*, second ser., vol. 8, ed. Philip Schaff and Henry Wace (Peabody, Mass.: Hendrickson, 1999), 122–123.

14. *The Natural Beauty of Mt. Athos* (Thessalonika: Hagioritki Hestia, 2003).

15. Elder Ephraim, *Counsels from the Holy Mountain: Selected from the Letters and Homilies of Elder Ephraim* (Florence, Ariz.: St. Anthony's Greek Orthodox Monastery, 1998), 1. Italics added.

16. Sisters of the Holy Convent of Chrysopigi, *Wounded by Love*, 81.

17. Elder Joseph the Hesychast, *Monastic Wisdom: The Letters of Elder Joseph the Hesychast* (Florence, Ariz.: St. Anthony's Greek Orthodox Monastery, 1998), 270.

18. Bishop Nikolai Velimirovich, *Prayers by the Lake* (Grayslake, Ill.: The Serbian Orthodox Metropolitanante of New Gracanica, 1999), 56.

19. *The Pilgrim's Tale*, ed. Aleksei Pentkovsky, trans. T. Allan Smith (New York: Paulist Press, 1999), 77.

20. *The Philokalia: The Complete Text*, comp. St. Nikodemos of the Holy Mountain and St. Makarios of Corinth, trans. G. E. H. Palmer, Philip Sherrard, and Kallistos Ware (London: Faber and Faber, 1984), 3:171.

21. Fyodor Dostoevsky, *The Brothers Karamazov*, trans. Richard Pevear and Larissa Volokhonsky (New York: Vintage, 1993), 299.

22. Gervase Mathew, *Byzantine Aesthetics* (New York: Harper & Row, 1971), 1–6.

23. Ibid., 6.

24. Cited in *The Song of Songs: Interpreted by Early Christian and Medieval Commentator*, ed. Robert Louis Wilken (Grand Rapids, Mich.: Eerdmans, 2003), 22.

25. Ibid, 33.

26. *The Philokalia: The Complete Text*, comp. St. Nikodemos of the Holy Mountain and St. Makarios of Corinth, trans. G. E. H. Palmer, Philip Sherrard, and Kallistos Ware (London: Faber and Faber, 1981), 2:42ff.

Natural and Supernatural Revelation in Early Irish and Greek Monastic Thought: A Comparative Approach / Chrysostomos Koutloumousianos

1. I am indebted to Denise Harvey for her valuable suggestions with regard to the style and language of the text.

2. On the origins of these dichotomies, see Philip Sherrard, "The Desanctification of Nature," in *Sanctity and Secularity: The Church and the World* (Oxford: Blackwell, 1972), 1–20.

3. "Litany of the Trinity," in *Irish Litanies*, ed. C. Plummer (London, 1925), 79; "Catéchèses Celtiques, Analecta Reginensia. Extraits de Manuscripts Latins de la

Reine Christine concervés au Vatican," ed. A. Wilmart, *Studi et Testi* 59 (Vatican City, 1933): 46, 44.

4. S. Gregorii Theologi *Or.* VI, PG 35:740C.

5. *Irish Litanies*, 79.

6. *Amra Choluim Chilli of Dallan Forgaill*, trans. J. O'Beirne Crowe (Dublin, 1871), 5, 10ff.; also, T. O. Clancy and G. Márkus, *Iona: The Earliest Poetry of a Celtic Monastery* (Edinburgh: Edinburgh University Press, 1995), 106–109, 65. On the cosmological system in seventh-century Ireland, see Marina Smyth, *Understanding the Universe in Seventh-Century Ireland* (Woodbridge: Boydell, 1996).

7. John Carey, *King of Mysteries: Early Irish Religious Writings* (Dublin: Four Courts, 2000), 31.

8. "Altus Prosator" U, X, in Clancy and Márkus, *Iona*, 50–52.

9. *In Tenga Bithnua* 10, ed. W. Stokes, *Eriu* 2 (1905): 103.

10. *The Martyrology of Oengus the Culdee*, ed. Whitley Stokes (London, 1905), n. 31, 57; *Navigatio Sancti Brendani Abbatis*, ed. Carl Selmer (South Bend, Ind.: University of Notre Dame Press, 1959), chaps. 11, 15; *In Tenga Bithnua* 90–91, 127–129.

11. See S. Basilii *In Hexaemeron*, PG 29:25A.

12. S. Basilii *In Hexaemeron* 1.6, PG 29:16BC; S. Basilii *In Psalmos*, PG 29:329; S. Nili *Epistolarum Lib.* II.127, PG 79:253C.

13. S. Basilii *Adversus Eunomium, Lib.* I, PG 29:544; S. Gregorii Theologi *Or.* VI, PG 35:740C; S. Basilii *In Psalmos*, PG 29:301; S. Basilii *Ep.* 235, PG 32:872A–C.

14. See S. Maximi Confessoris *Ad Thalassium*, PG 90:296B.

15. S. Nili *Ad Magnam*, PG 79:1052, 1053–1056; Macarius *Hom.* 1, in *Neue Homilien des Makarius/Symeon*, ed. Erich Klostermann and Herinz Berthold (Berlin, 1961), 10.

16. S. Basilii *In Psalmos*, PG 29:285.

17. S. Nili *Ad Magnam*, PG 79:1009C.

18. This is a leitmotif in Irish poetry. The most characteristic example is "Patrick's Hymn," in *Thesaurus Palaeohibernicus: A Collection Old-Irish Glosses, Scholia, Prose, and Verse*, ed. Whitley Stokes and John Strachan (Cambridge: Cambridge University Press, 1901–1903), 2:354–358; see also "The Hermit's Song," ed. K. Meyer, *Eriu* 2 (1905): 55–57. We should also note the central place of "The Song of the Three Children" in the Celtic as well as the Byzantine ritual. See the verses of the eighth canticle in the Orthodox matins and *The Antiphonary of Bangor: An Early Irish Manuscript in the Ambrosian Library at Milan*, ed. F. E. Warren (London, 1893–1895), 2:8–9.

19. See S. Gregorii Theologi *Poemata moralia*, PG 37:755–756.

20. G. Murphy, *Early Irish Lyrics* (Dublin: Four Courts, 1998), 4–5.

21. Macarius *Hom.* 32, in *Die 50 Geistlichen Homilien des Makarios*, ed. H. Dörries, E. Klostermann, and M. Kroeger (Berlin, 1964), 251.

22. S. Basilii *In Psalmos*, PG 29:409.

23. *In Tenga Bithnua* 99–101.

24. James Carney, ed., *The Poems of Blathmac, Son of Cú Brettan, Together with the Irish Gospel of Thomas and a Poem on the Virgin Mary* (Dublin: Educational Company of Ireland, 1964), 26–33; also P. F. Moran, *Acta S. Brendani* (Dublin, 1872), 30ff.; *The Martyrology of Oengus*, epilogue, 284–288; *In Tenga Bithnua* 163, 145–146.

25. *Thesaurus Palaeohibernicus*, 1:328.

26. About the cosmic symbolism of high crosses, see Philip Sheldrake, *Living Between Worlds: Place and Journey in Celtic Spirituality* (London: Darton, Longman & Todd, 1995), 46–50; for their theological meaning, see Helen M. Roe, "The Irish High Cross: Morphology and Iconography," *Journal of the Royal Society of Antiquaries of Ireland* 95 (1965): 213–226.

27. K. Meyer, *The Instructions of King Cormac* (Dublin, 1909), 346b.

28. *In Tenga Bithnua* 54, 119; 88, 127.

29. *Navigatio Sancti Brendani Abbatis*, chap. 22. On *Navigatio* as a presentation of the central dynamic of the monastic life, see Thomas O'Loughlin, "Distant Islands: The Topography of Holiness in the Navigatio Sancti Brendani," in *The Medieval Mystical Tradition—England, Ireland, and Wales*, ed. Marion Glasscoe (Cambridge: D. S. Brewer, 1999), 1–20.

30. "Praecamur Patrem," 3, *The Antiphonary of Bangor*, 5.

31. "Praecamur Patrem," 4, *The Antiphonary of Bangor*, 5.

32. "Catéchèses Celtiques" V.15–20, 59.

33. *Liber de ortu et obitu patriarcharum*, C.C. Series Latina, CVIII E (Turnholti: Brepols, 1996), no. 9, 9–10; 19.2, 18; 42.5, 49–50. Scotti Anonymi, *Comm. in Epist. Cath. I Iohan.* <IV,12>, *Scriptores Hiberniae Minores* I, ed. R. E. McNally (Turnholti: Brepols, 1973–1974), 42–43; Whitley Stokes, "The Tidings of the Resurrection," *Revue Celtique* 25 (1904): 253; *Breviarium in Psalmos*, PL 26:1077C; The Stowe Missal, in F. E. Warren, *The Liturgy and Ritual of the Celtic Church* (Woodbridge: Boydell, 1987), 226–227; S. Athanasii *Contra Arianos* III.14, PG 26:352AB; S. Justini Philosophi *Apologia* I.63, PG 6:424C; S. Irenaei *Contra haereses* IV.v, PG 7:985BC; S. Basilii *Adv. Eunomium* II, PG 30:609–612; Macarius *Hom.* 14, *Neue Homilien*, 74.

34. *In Tenga Bithnua* 11, 13, 103–105. On the theme of cosmic restoration in Irish thought, see John Carey, *A Single Ray of the Sun: Religious Speculation in Early Ireland* (Andover: Celtic Studies Publications, 1999), 75–106. See also *Liber de ordine creaturarum* V.4, ed. Manuel C. Diaz y Diaz (Santiago de Compostela: Universidad de Santiago de Compostela, 1972), 114; "Glosses on the Pauline Epistles," in *Thesaurus Palaeohibernicus*, 1:705; *Breviarium in Psalmos*, PL 26:1213C. For Greek references, see S. Epiphanii *Ancoratus* 61, PG 43:125B–128A; *Adv. Haereses* Lib. II, t.I.xxxi, PG 41:1117D; S. Cyrilli *Ad Romanos*, PG 74:821BC.

35. "Old-Irish Homily," ed. J. Strachan, *Eriu* 3 (1907): 8–10.; Augustinus Hibernicus *De Mirabilibus Sacrae Scripturae* I.19, PL 35:2166.

36. *The Poems of Blathmac* 61–70, 23–25.

37. Ibid., 171, 59.
38. *In Tenga Bithnua* 42, 115; 39, 115; 33, 113; 47, 117.
39. See *The Poems of Blathmac* 191–196, 65–67; *Liber de numeris* 5, PL 83:1296A; Jean Scot, *Homélie sur le prologue de Jean*, VIII, *Sources Chrétiennes* 151 (Paris: Les Editions du Cerf, 1969), 238–240.
40. *Sancti Romani Melodi Cantica*, 6 (*prooemium*), ed. P. Maas and C. A. Trypanis (Oxford: Clarendon, 1963), 20; S. Gregorii Theologi *Or.* 44, PG 36:620; *Or.* 45, PG 36:661D; *The Lenten Triodion*, trans. Mother Mary and Archimandrite Kallistos Ware (London: Faber, 1978), 625, 626, 631, 636, 640.
41. Macarius *Hom.* 52, in *Macarii Anecdota: Seven Unpublished Homilies of Macarius*, ed. G. L. Marriott (Cambridge, 1918), 24.
42. Augustinus Hibernicus *De Mirabilibus* I.29, PL 35:2171.
43. "Catéchèses Celtiques" V, 59–60, trans. Oliver Davies in *Celtic Spirituality* (Mahwah, N.J.: Paulist Press, 1999), 364; *Breviarium in Psalmos*, PL 26.1199A; this thesis is more fully worked out by Eriugena, directly influenced by the Greek Fathers. Jean Scot, *Homélie sur le prologue de Jean*, VIII–X, 236–269; *Iohannis Scotti Eriugenae Carmina*, ed. M. W. Herren (Dublin: Dublin Institute for Advanced Studies, 1993), 76.4; cf. *In Tenga Bithnua* 16, 107.
44. Stokes, *The Tidings of the Resurrection*, 243.
45. See S. Cyrilli *In Joannis Evangelium* Lib. I, PG 73:85–104; S. Gregorii Nyssenis *De professione Christiana*, *PG* 46:248; S. Basilii *In Hexaemeron*, PG 29:164D; S. Basilii *Ad. Eunomium* 1, PG 29:556D–557C.
46. S. Dionysii *De coelesti hierarchia* IV.1, PG 3:177D; *De divinis nominibus* V.8, PG 3:824C; S. Maximi *Ad Thalassium*, PG 90:296CD; *Diversa capita*, PG 90:1208C.
47. See "Patrick's Hymn," in *Thesaurus Palaeohibernicus*, 2:354–358. Also see N. D. O'Donoghue, "St. Patrick's Breastplate," in *An Introduction to Celtic Christianity*, ed. James P. Mackey (Edinburgh: T&T Clark, 1995), 54–56.
48. S. Basilii *Ep.* 234, PG 32:869A; S. Johannis Damasceni *De fide orthodoxa* Lib. I.14, PG 94:860.
49. See, for example, *Sancti Columbani Opera, Instr.* II.1, ed. G. S. M. Walker (Dublin: Dublin Institute for Advanced Studies, 1997), 66.
50. *Sancti Columbani Opera*, Instr.VIII.1, 94; Macarius *Hom.* 16, *Die 50 Geistlichen Homilien*, 160–161.
51. PL 35:2151–2200. For a closer approach to the thought of Augustinus Hibernicus I am indebted to my conversations with Prof. J. P. Mackey.
52. Augustinus Hibernicus *De Mirabilibus* I.18, III.2, III.9.
53. Augustinus Hibernicus *De Mirabilibus* I.1, PL 35:2151. See also "Commentarius in Iohannem," *Scriptores Hiberniae Minores* II, ed. J. F. Kelly, 118, 43–46. Also Macarius *Hom.* 52, *Macarii Anecdota*, 27–28.
54. For example, "Catéchèses Celtiques" V.15–20, 59; VII, 77–78.
55. Augustinus Hibernicus *De Mirabilibus* III.4, PL 35:2194–2195. Cf. Johannes Chrysostomus *In Matthaeum, Hom.* 6.

56. S. Basilii *In Hexaemeron*, PG 29:36B, 149C; S. Gregorii *In Hexaemeron*, PG 44:72AB.

57. S. Basilii *In Hexaemeron*, PG 29:189C–192A; Augustinus Hibernicus *De Mirabilibus* I.29, PL 35:2172.

58. PG 29:97B; 189BC.

59. For example, *Adamnani Vita S. Columbae*, ii.16, 17, 34, ed. J. T. Fowler (Oxford, 1894), 85–86, 102–103; A. J. Festugière, *Vie de Théodore de Sykéon* (Bruxelles: Société des Bollandistes, 1970), chap. 158, 1:132.

60. "Catéchèses Celtiques" I.54–68, 36; 81–2, 37; *Expositio Evangelii Secundum Marcum*, ed. Michael Cahill (Turnholti: Brepols, 1997), 58–59; *Expositio quatuor evangeliorum*, PL 30:580C; *Homiliarium Veronense*, V.333, ed. L. T. Martin (Turnhout: Brepols, 2000); "Un receuil de conferences monastiques Irlandaises du VIIIe siécle. Notes sur le manuscrit 43 de la bibliothèque du chapître de Cracovie," *Revue Benedictine* 49 (1937): 80. M. McNamara detects a similar expression in the *Apophthegmata Patrum* (PG 65.160), but, strangely enough, he conjectures Latin influence. For the historical route of the formula, see Martin McNamara, "The Inverted Eucharistic Formula *Conversio Corporis Christi in Panem et Sanguinis in Vinum*: The Exegetical and Liturgical Background in Irish Usage," *Proceedings of the Royal Irish Academy* 87c (1987): 573–593. A combination of formulas is found in *The Poems of Blathmac* 203, 69.

61. The use of Eucharistic term "transfiguration" was displaced at a later date by "transubstantiation."

62. Macarius Περὶ ὑψώσεως τοῦ νοὸς λόγος, PG 34:896; Macarius *Hom.* 4, *Die 50 Geistlichen Homilien*, 36–37; the "inverted" way is implied in the liturgical prayer read at the preparation of the Eucharistic elements at the Orthodox liturgy.

63. For a comparative approach to the theme of transfiguration, see Chrysostomos Koutloumousianos, *Oi Erastes tis Vassilias. Keltikos kai Byzantinos Monachismos* (Mount Athos: Holy Monastery of Koutloumousiou, 2009), 2:267–297.

64. Augustinus Hibernicus *De Mirabilibus* I.17, PL 35:2164.

65. Ibid., III.11, PL 35:2197–2198.

66. Ibid., I.26; III.6. The same exegesis is given by Macarius *Hom.* 12, *Die 50 Geistlichen Homilien*, 114.

67. Augustine in a way anticipates modern scientific theses that claim the existence of natural laws unknown to the structure of the human mind. See also Stokes, *The Tidings of the Resurrection*, 239.

68. S. Basilii *In Hexaemeron*, PG 29:736C; S. Gregorii Theologi *Or.* 55, 5, PG 36:629.

69. Nikos Matsoukas, *Episteme, Philosophia kai theologia stin Hexaemero tou M. Vasiliou* (Thessalonika: Pournaras, 1990), 68–69.

70. S. Gregorii Theologi *Or.* 6.15, PG 35:741.

71. S. Basilii *In Hexaemeron*, 2.3, PG 29:36B. For the evolutional principles of St. Basil, see Matsoukas, *Episteme*, 98–127.

72. Ibid., 1.6, PG 29:16D–17A. "The teller of the story has divided with his words what God has not divided in the perfecting of the work." Augustinus Hibernicus *De Mirabilibus* I.1, PL 35:2151–2152; also "Dies dominica," in *Scriptores Hiberniae Minores* I, 183–184.

73. S. Basilii *De Spiritu Sancto* 19, PG 32:100D–101B.

74. S. Basilii *In Hexaemeron*, PG 29:96A, 164D, 189BC; S. Basilii *Ad. Eunomium* 1, PG 29:556D–557C; S. Dionysii *De divinis nominibus*, V.8, PG 3:824C; S. Maximi Confessoris *Ad Thalassium*, PG 90:293D–296A.

75. S. Nili *Ad Agathiam*, PG 79:920A; 916D.

76. Most suggestive is his insistence that the wands were changed into serpents not by the spells of the magicians but that the whole episode was an *imago*: PL 35:2164–2165.

77. See *Breviarium in Psalmos*, PL 26:1103D.

78. Macarius *Hom.* 18, *Neue Homilien*, 98; *Hom.* 44, *Die 50 Geistlichen Homilien*, 291.

79. "Saltair na Rann," in Carey, *King of Mysteries*, 99.

80. Ibid., 108.

81. *Sancti Columbani Opera, Instr.* I.3; XII.2, 62, 112.

82. For example, *Homiliarium Veronense, Hom.* XI.133–138, 88; *Hom.* II.213, 29.

Ecology and Monasticism / Archimandrite Vasileios

This article is from Archimandrite Vasileios, *Ecology and Monasticism*, 2nd ed., Mount Athos Series 3 (Montreal: Alexander, 1999), from a talk given at the Orthodox Academy of Crete (Kolymbari Chanion) in November 1991, at the Inter-Orthodox Conference on Environmental Protection, organized by the Ecumenical Patriarchate and the World Wide Fund for Nature International (WWF). Translated from the Greek by Dr. Constantine Kokenes. It appears here thanks to the generous permission of Dr. John Hadjinikolaou of the Alexander Press. The translation has been slightly modified by J. Chryssavgis.

1. "Cultivate," in Greek, *ergazomai*, meaning "to work." "Keep" (*phylasso*), in the sense of "guarding, protecting, watching over, looking after," complements the more active verb *ergazomai* (to work). *Phylasso* (to keep) emphasizes the aspect of *protecting and watching over* what God has given us and in this sense is connected to our receiving, maintaining, and passing on Holy Tradition.

2. "At rest," in Greek, *anapavomai*, meaning "to find a place of comfort." This is an Athonite usage in which a monk might say, on finding the monastery or *obedience* in which he is content, "*anapavomai*." (An obedience is the work, task, or "vocation" a monk is assigned to perform.)

3. *Gerontikon*, the sayings of the Desert Fathers; from the Greek word *geron*, meaning "Elder," the name with which one respectfully addresses a monastic or spiritual father.

4. Dwell: the Greek is *meno*, meaning "to remain, stay, reside, live, stop." From *meno* comes the Greek word for "patience," *hypomone*, which literally means "to accept, stay behind, remain stable."

5. The entire passage is as follows: "Whenever the intellect moves, it is found in the natural realm; but once it enters that other realm, it ceases from prayer. The saints of the age to come do not pray with prayer when their intellects have been swallowed up by the Spirit, but rather, with awestruck wonder, they dwell in that gladdening glory." See St. Isaac the Syrian, *The Ascetical Homilies*, ed. Holy Transfiguration Monastery (Boston, 1984), 119.

6. A reference to St. Dionysius the Areopagite's letter to Dorotheus: "The divine dark cloud is the unapproachable light, wherein it is said God dwells. It is invisible for its exceeding brilliance and unapproachable for its abundance of superessential illumination. Everyone who is worthy to know and to see God comes into this dark cloud." St. Gregory Palamas comments on this passage: "Therefore here he calls the same thing both dark cloud and light, seeing and unseeing, knowing and unknowing. How then, is this both darkness and light? 'For its abundance of illumination,' he writes. So it is mainly light, but it is also darkness, for being more than light, it remains unseen to those trying to approach and see it through the energies of the senses and the mind." See *In Defense of the Holy Hesychasts*, Third Homily, Second Triad, chap. 51.

7. *On the Orthodox Faith* 4, 15.

8. *Panagia*, literally "All Holy" or "Most Blessed One," is an honorific that refers to the Virgin Mary. Mt. Athos itself is often called the Garden of the *Panagia*.

9. *On the Divine Images* 2.14.

10. *Homily on the Transfiguration* 2.13.

11. *Pascha*, from the Hebrew for Passover, is the Orthodox term for Easter, which is the Lord's Passover.

12. *Homily 77*, p. 381.

The Prophetic Charisma in Pastoral Theology: Asceticism, Fasting, and the Ecological Crisis / Anestis Keselopoulos

1. Saint Gregory of Sinai, *Kephalaia di Akrostichidos* 127, PG 150:292A.
2. Saint Maximus the Confessor, *Peri Theologias* 1,70, PG 90:1109A.
3. Saint Nilus the Ascetic, *Logos Askêtikos* 26, PG 79:753C.

The Spirit of God Moved upon the Face of the Waters: Orthodox Holiness and the Natural World / Donald Sheehan

1. *Little Russian Philokalia*, vol. 3, *A Treasury of Saint Herman's Spirituality* (Ouzinkie, Alaska: St. Herman Press/New Valaam Monastery, 1989).

2. These are best read in English in the Orthodox translations by Richard Pevear and Laryssa Volokhonsky. Fyodor Dostoevsky, *The Brothers Karamazov* (San Francisco: North Point, 1990; repr. New York: Vintage, 1991); and Fyodor Dostoevsky, *Demons* (New York: Knopf, 1994).

3. Pavel Florensky, *Iconostasis*, trans. Donald Sheehan and Olga Andrejev, intro. Donald Sheehan (Crestwood, N.Y.: St. Vladimir's Seminary Press, 1996), 135.

4. Ibid., 135–136.

5. Panayiotis Nellas, *Deification in Christ: Orthodox Perspectives on the Nature of the Human Person*, trans. Norman Russell (Crestwood, N.Y.: St. Vladimir's Seminary Press, 1987), 57.

6. Vladimir Lossky, *The Mystical Theology of the Eastern Church* (Crestwood, N.Y.: St. Vladimir's Seminary Press, 1976), 172–173.

7. Pavel Florensky, *The Pillar and Ground of the Truth*, trans. Boris Jakim, intro. Richard F. Gustafson (Princeton, N.J.: Princeton University Press, 1997), 199. Further references will appear in the text as *PG*.

8. John Chryssavgis, *Beyond the Shattered Image* (Minneapolis, Minn.: Light and Life, 1999), 162.

9. Annie Dillard, *Teaching a Stone to Talk* (New York: Harper & Row, 1982), 13–14.

Appendix A: Vespers for the Environment

The original text was commissioned by the Ecumenical Patriarchate in 1990 and produced in 1991 by the foremost hymnographer of Mt. Athos, Monk Gerasimos Mikragiannanitis (d. 1991). The translation that appears here was published in 1991 by Archimandrite Ephrem (Lash) and revised by him in 2011. It is reprinted here, with minor editorial changes, by kind permission of Fr. Ephrem. The endnotes are by Fr. Ephrem.

1. Gen. 1:1.
2. Acts 17:28.
3. Ps. 148:8.
4. Ps. 103:24.
5. Ps. 148:5.
6. Dan. 3:53.

7. This hymn, *Phos Hilaron*, is the most ancient Christian hymn apart from those found in scripture, and it may date to the second century. Since then, it has been sung at the lighting of the candles in the evening. —Eds.

8. The first two readings were quite different in the original text of this office. The former of the new readings is the standard one for the Great Feasts of the Lord; the latter is not a traditional one. These two readings contain the whole account of the creation in the opening of Genesis but omit the fourth day, presumably because human beings can do little to damage the sun, moon, and stars. All six days are covered in the readings at Vespers on the first three days of Lent.

9. A considerable problem for the translator, which I discussed at some length in a review in *Sourozh*. The Fathers themselves are not agreed, St. Basil opting for "Spirit," St. Ephrem for "wind."

10. This is one of the readings for the feast of St. Demetrios on October 26.

11. The Hebrew has "Look." The *Menaion* for October 26 has Ἐπίβλεψον, but this is not the LXX text.

12. The LXX differs noticeably from the Hebrew here. The Greek could also mean "inherit a little of your holy mountain," but in the Hebrew the word for "little" here refers to time. The Sinaiticus, however adds "something" to "little," which suggests that the scribe understood the phrase as "a little of." NETS prefers this interpretation.

13. Psalm 101:26.

14. Ps. 137:8.

15. Ps. 79:14–15. The clause is familiar from the pontifical liturgy.

16. I think this means the "environing atmosphere." διάζωμα is used, rarely, in ancient Greek for a stratum of the atmosphere.

17. Ps. 35:9.

18. Cf. Ps. 105:6; 3 Kingd. 8:47.

19. Is. 40:22.

20. Ps. 78:13.

21. The *Theotokion* is a *troparion* or short hymn to the *Theotokos* or "God-Bearer"—that is, Mary, the Mother of God. —Eds.

22. This seems to be an error for *divine*, since the final phrases of such prosomia tend to be the same. The expression *great mercy* [Ps. 50:1] is far more common than *divine mercy*, and this has probably caused a slip here.

23. This Apolytikion has been added since 1992.

24. Ps. 101:25.

25. Cf. Ps. 118:35.

26. Luke 1:28.

27. Cf. Gen. 3:16.

28. Cf. Ps. 8:3, 101:25, 118:90.

29. Cf. Ps. 32:6.

30. Ps. 23:7–10.

31. Cf. the Nicene Creed.

32. As Fr. Gerasimos wrote a complete office, Vespers, Matins, and Liturgy, I have ventured to add an entry for the Synaxarion, with some Verses, which would normally follow the Kontakion and Ikos.

33. Cf. Dan. 3:52.

34. Cf. Ezek. 44:1–3.

35. Cf. Dan. 3:57–87.

36. Job 9:8.

37. Cf. Ps. 94:4.

38. Isa. 40:22.

39. It is somewhat odd to make provision for two Gospels but not for two Apostles. As a second Apostle I would suggest that for the Thursday of Week 32 [James 4:7–17, 5:1–9]. Unless, of course, where Fr. Gerasimos said "say also the Gospel according to Mark," he meant "say instead."

Contributors

His All-Holiness Bartholomew I, Archbishop of Constantinople–New Rome and Ecumenical Patriarch, is hailed by Robert Kennedy Jr. as "the most forceful of the world's religious leaders in urging that the protection of nature is a primary spiritual duty." A selection of his environmental addresses and texts is found in *On Earth as in Heaven: Ecological Vision and Initiatives of Ecumenical Patriarch Bartholomew*, edited by J. Chryssavgis.

Savas Agouridis (d. 2009) was Professor Emeritus of New Testament Exegesis at the University of Athens. His prolific writing related Orthodox theology to contemporary philosophical and social currents of thought. He was one of the first Greek Orthodox theologians to recognize the critical importance of the ecological crisis.

David Bradshaw, Professor of Philosophy and Department Chair, University of Kentucky, is the author of *Aristotle East and West: Metaphysics and the Division of Christendom*.

Scott Cairns is Professor of English at the University of Missouri and Director of the University of Missouri Writing Workshops in Greece. In addition to his prose and translations, he is one of the most highly respected poets in North America.

James Carey, Distinguished Visiting Professor of Philosophy, U.S. Air Force Academy, holds a joint appointment at St. John's College, Santa Fe, New Mexico, where he served as Dean and as Acting President. He has published widely in the history of philosophy.

Contributors

Costa Carras, among the Orthodox scholars with an early involvement in the environmental movement, co-founded Elliniki Etairia (Society for the Environment and Cultural Heritage) in 1972. He is a Vice President of Europa Nostra, the federation of European conservation organizations, and organized the 1988 meeting on Religion and the Environment in Patmos.

John Chryssavgis, Archdeacon of the Ecumenical Patriarchate and a clergyman of the Greek Orthodox Archdiocese of America, is Theological Advisor to Ecumenical Patriarch Bartholomew on Environmental Issues and author of over twenty books on theology, spirituality, and ecology, including *Beyond the Shattered Image: Insights into an Orthodox Ecological Worldview*.

Chrysostomos Koutloumousianos completed his Ph.D. at the University of Thessalonika and is a monk at Koutloumosiou Monastery on Mt. Athos, Greece. He is the author of several books, in Greek, on Byzantine and Celtic monasticism.

H. Tristram Engelhardt Jr., Professor of Philosophy at Rice University and Emeritus Professor of Medicine at Baylor University, is author or editor of more than thirty books, including *Foundations of Christian Bioethics*.

Bruce V. Foltz, Professor of Philosophy, Eckerd College, Founding President of the International Association for Environmental Philosophy, is author of *Inhabiting the Earth: Heidegger, Environmental Ethics, and the Metaphysics of Nature* and *The Noetics of Nature: Environmental Philosophy and the Holy Beauty of the Visible*.

Christina M. Gschwandtner teaches continental philosophy of religion at Fordham University and is the author of *Reading Jean-Luc Marion: Exceeding Metaphysics* and *Postmodern Apologetics? Arguments for God in Contemporary Philosophy*. She recently completed a second Ph.D. in theology at Durham University on the role of nonhuman creation in the Orthodox feasts.

Perry Hamalis, Cecelia Schneller Mueller Professor of Religion at North Central College, lectures and writes in the fields of ethics, social philosophy, and theology.

L. Michael Harrington, Associate Professor of Philosophy, Duquesne University, is the author of *Sacred Place in Early Medieval Neoplatonism*.

Jurretta Jordan Heckscher is a cultural historian and Research Specialist at the Library of Congress, where she edited the online collection The Evolution of the Conservation Movement, 1850–1920 (http://memory.loc.gov/ammem/amrvhtml/conshome.html).

Anestis Keselopoulos, Professor and Director of the Department of Ethics and Sociology in the School of Theology at the Aristotle University of Thessaloniki, is the author of numerous scholarly works, including *Man and Environment: A Study of St. Symeon the New Theologian*.

Andrew Louth, an Orthodox priest, is Professor Emeritus of Patristic and Byzantine Studies at Durham University, UK, and Visiting Professor of Eastern Orthodox Theology at the Vrije Universiteit, Amsterdam. He is the author of several books on patristics and theology.

The Very Reverend Archimandrite **John Panteleimon Manoussakis** is Assistant Professor of Philosophy at the College of the Holy Cross. He has authored two books (including *God After Metaphysics: A Theological Aesthetic*, 2007), edited five volumes, and published over twenty articles on phenomenology and the philosophy of religion.

John Anthony McGuckin, an Orthodox priest, is the Nielsen Professor in Late Antique and Byzantine Christian History at Union Theological Seminary and Professor of Byzantine Christian Studies at Columbia University. He is the author of many books on patristics and theology and is the Director of the Sophia Institute, New York.

Bill McKibben is an environmentalist, journalist, and author of over fifteen books about the environment, beginning with *The End of Nature*, which is regarded as the first book for a general audience on climate change. He founded the grassroots climate campaign 350.org. In 2012, he was keynote speaker at the Halki Summit.

Nikos Nissiotis (d. 1986) was Professor of Philosophy and Psychology of Religion at the University of Athens and the author of numerous books, including *The Philosophy of Religion* and *Philosophical Theology*. He was a pioneer in relating Orthodox theological doctrines to the modern world and culture, particularly within ecumenical circles.

His Eminence Metropolitan **Jonah (Paffhausen)** of Washington served as the Primate of the Orthodox Church in America from 2008 to 2012. He is the author of *Reflections on a Spiritual Journey*, published in 2011 by St. Vladimir's Seminary Press

Aristotle Papanikolaou, Professor of Theology and Co-Founding Director of the Orthodox Christian Studies Center at Fordham University, is the author most recently of *The Mystical as Political: Democracy and Non-Radical Orthodoxy*. He is also co-editor of *Orthodox Constructions of the West*, published with Fordham University Press in the Orthodox Christianity and Contemporary Thought series.

Eric Perl, Professor of Philosophy at Loyola Marymount University, is the author of *Theophany: The Neoplatonic Philosophy of Dionysius the Areopagite*.

Donald Sheehan (d. 2010), a subdeacon of the Orthodox Church, was Professor of English and Classics at Dartmouth College for many years and the translator of the Psalms in *The Orthodox Study Bible*. He was the first Executive Director of the Frost Place, a center for poetry and the arts.

Philip Sherrard (d. 1995) taught at King's College, London, and was the author, translator, and editor of over thirty books, including the five volumes of *The Philokalia*. The translator of many modern Greek poets, he was the first Orthodox thinker to explore in depth the challenges of the ecological crisis.

Alfred K. Siewers, Associate Professor of Medieval Literature at Bucknell University, is the author of *Strange Beauty: Ecocritical Approaches to Early Medieval Landscape*.

Elizabeth Theokritoff, an independent scholar and occasional visiting lecturer at the Institute of Orthodox Christian Studies in Cambridge, England, is the author of *Living in God's Creation: Orthodox Perspectives on Ecology* as well as numerous articles.

George Theokritoff is retired from the Department of Geological Sciences at Rutgers University. He has published in the earth sciences as well as on the interface between science and Christianity

The Very Reverend **Archimandrite Vasileios** of Iveron, formerly Abbot of Stavronikita and Iviron Monasteries on Mt. Athos, Greece, is the author of *Hymn of Entry: Liturgy and Life in the Orthodox Church*. Influential in the revival of the monastic republic of Mt. Athos, he is a popular speaker among students worldwide.

The Most Reverend **Metropolitan Kallistos (Ware)** of Diokleia, prior to his retirement in 2001, was Spalding Lecturer of Eastern Orthodox Studies at Oxford University. His many publications include *The Orthodox Church* and *The Orthodox Way*. He is also co-translator of *The Philokalia*, The Lenten Triodion, and The Festal Menaion.

Gayle E. Woloschak is Professor in the Department of Radiology and the Department of Cell and Molecular Biology in the Feinberg School of Medicine at Northwestern University. In addition to two books on radiology, she is the author of *Beauty and Unity in Creation: The Evolution of Life*.

Christos Yannaras, Professor Emeritus of Philosophy at the Panteion University of Social and Political Sciences, Athens, is regarded as the most prominent philosopher of contemporary Greece. He is the author of numerous books, many of which are available in English, including *The Freedom of Morality* and *Orthodoxy and the West*.

The Most Reverend **Metropolitan John (Zizioulas)** of Pergamon, Greece, is the author of many essays on ecclesiology and theological ontology, including *Being and Communion* and *Communion and Otherness*. He has served as Chairman of the Academy of Athens and is regarded as the most prominent spokesman for Orthodox Christianity and the environment.

Index of Names (Classical)

Agapius, Saint, 450
Alban, Saint, 399, 402, 407, 425, 432
Anastasius of Sinai, Saint, 298
Andrew of Crete, Saint, 317, 322, 458
Antony the Great, Saint, 328, 419
Aquinas, Thomas, 246, 253, 271, 448
Aristotle, 36, 96, 106, 177–80, 182–84, 205, 333, 417–19, 424, 426, 437–39, 454
Athanasius the Great, Saint, 248, 429, 444
Augustine, Saint, 69, 77, 246, 249, 251, 253, 344–47, 445, 463

Basil the Great, Saint, 3, 104, 286, 300–1, 304–5, 326, 329, 338–39, 344, 346, 360, 406, 420, 430, 446, 451–52, 458–59, 460–64, 466
Brendan, Saint, 249–50, 341
Brigit, Saint, 251

Chaucer, Geoffrey, 247, 252, 254–57, 260, 445–46
Clement of Alexandria, 10, 83
Columba, Saint, 249, 338, 446
Columbanus, Saint, 445
Cyril, Saint, 102, 300, 343, 452, 461–62

Cyril of Alexandria, Saint, 102, 343
Cyril of Jerusalem, Saint, 300, 452

Dante, 245, 255–56
Dionysius the Areopagite, Saint, 16, 23, 63, 112, 238, 411, 419, 440, 443, 462, 464–65
Dorotheus of Gaza, Saint, 361, 465

Eckhart, Meister, 441
Ephrem the Syrian, Saint, 248, 313, 430, 444, 455
Eriugena, John Scotus, 60, 246–51, 253, 258–59, 262, 407, 439, 445–47, 462
Eusebius of Caesarea, 14
Evagrius, 9, 14–16, 35, 53, 332, 412, 415–17, 419–20

Francis of Assisi, Saint, 77, 137, 196

Germanos of Constantinople, Saint, 300, 312, 452
Gregory of Nyssa, Saint, 66, 89, 167, 248, 265, 299, 304, 324, 329, 333, 349, 417, 420, 423–24, 430, 438, 452
Gregory of Sinai, Saint, 445, 465

Indexes prepared by Nicholas R. Anton

Gregory Palamas, Saint, 90–93, 141, 156, 352, 422, 424, 465
Gregory the Dialogist, Saint, 251, 255
Gregory the Theologian (Nazianzen), Saint, 18, 34–35, 37, 97, 301, 311, 315, 329, 418, 420–22, 451–52, 455, 460, 462–63

Heraclitus, 207, 325
Herman of Spruce Island, Saint, 150–51, 365, 367–68, 370, 372–74, 376, 436, 465
Hesychius of Jerusalem, 311
Hildegard of Bingen, Saint, 92, 424
Hippolytus, 297–98, 451
Homer, 176–77, 179, 180, 184, 215

Innocent, Saint, 151, 207, 283, 289
Irenaeus of Lyons, Saint, 131, 134, 145, 157, 410, 430
Isaac the Syrian, Saint, xv, 5, 46, 151, 156–57, 350, 361, 421–22, 436, 465

Jacob of Serug, 318, 457
James, Saint, 145, 175, 260, 295, 300, 406, 430, 433–34, 436, 444, 449, 451–52, 461–62, 467
John Cassian, Saint, 246
John Chrysostom, Saint, 83, 98, 103, 280, 300–1, 304, 430, 436, 450, 452
John Climacus, Saint, 249
John of Damascus, Saint, 150, 200, 259, 317, 322, 352, 369, 407, 455, 462
John of Thessalonika, 317
John the Evangelist, Saint, 335

Kosmas the Aetolian, Saint, 87

Leontius of Cyprus, Saint, 133, 425, 430, 451
Leontius, Presbyter of Constantinople, 312, 458

Macarius, Saint, 460–64
Maximus the Confessor, Saint, 17, 35, 46, 54, 59–60, 113, 157, 167, 265, 343, 400, 402, 405, 408, 418, 421–22, 424, 429, 438, 440–41, 447, 465

Nectarios, Saint, 297
Nikodemus of the Holy Mountain, Saint, 85, 423, 450
Nikolai Velimirovich, Saint, 330, 447, 459
Nilus the Ascetic, Saint, 460, 464–65
Ninian, Saint, 259

Odysseus. *See* Homer
Origen of Alexandria, 10–16, 18–19, 34–36, 145, 416–18, 420

Patrick, Saint, 254, 426, 460, 462
Paul, Saint, 11, 21, 68, 94, 143, 158–59, 170, 181–82, 197, 200–1, 316, 325, 335, 358, 411–12, 423
Peter (disciple), Saint, 182, 297, 437
Peter of Damascus, Saint, 330
Philo of Alexandria, 10–13, 415
Plato, 9–11, 34–37, 39, 63, 66, 194, 215, 415, 420
Plotinus, 10, 416
Proclus, Bishop of Constantinople, Saint, 313, 315–17, 457

Romanos, Saint, 321, 461

Seraphim of Sarov, Saint, 150
Sergius of Radonezh, Saint, 370–71
Silouan (Staretz), Saint, 86, 121–23, 150, 361, 427–29, 436
Stithatos, Nikitas, Saint, 328
Symeon the New Theologian, Saint, 51, 349, 362, 400

Tatian, 83
Theodore the Ascetic, Saint, 334
Theodore the Studite, Saint, 238–39, 317, 322, 443, 457

Virgil, 329

Index of Names (Contemporary)

Alexy II, Patriarch of Moscow, 402, 435
Allchin, A. M., 144, 407, 433
Amphilochios of Patmos, 86, 87, 150, 424, 436
Anthony, Metropolitan of Sourozh, 430

Bartholomew, Ecumenical Patriarch, xii–xiii, 1, 150, 154–55, 159, 162, 227, 307, 398–99, 402, 404, 425, 433, 435, 452–54
Beckett, Thomas, 255
Berdyaev, Nicholas, 122, 215
Berry, Thomas, 148, 434, 451
Berry, Wendell, 140, 147, 433
Blake, William, 90, 424
Boff, Leonardo, 78
Bonhoeffer, Dietrich, 92
Bouyer, Louis, 419
Brock, Sebastian, 402, 421–22, 430, 444
Buber, Martin, 424
Bulgakov, Sergius, 106, 122, 269, 271, 399, 403, 426, 439, 448, 455

Chryssavgis, John, xii, 1, 152, 374, 398–99, 402, 415, 423, 435, 438–39, 445, 453, 464, 466
Clark, Elizabeth, 417
Clément, Oliver, 430
Coakley, Sarah, 445
Cobb, John B., 434

Darwin, Charles, 165, 266–67, 447
Dawkins, Richard, 270, 296
De Beausobre, Julia, 435
De Chardin, Teilhard, 267
De Lubac, Henri, 425
Descartes, René, 1, 96, 163, 179, 188, 194
Dimitrios, Ecumenical Patriarch, 105, 154, 425, 454
Donne, John, 99
Dostoevsky, Fyodor, 156, 330, 366, 368, 370, 444–45, 459, 465

Eliot, George, 430
Emerson, Ralph W., 332

Festugière, André-Jean., 463
Feuerbach, Ludwig, 2–3, 137, 430
Florensky, Pavel, 327–29, 331, 334, 365–70, 372, 374, 399, 403, 436, 458, 466
Florovsky, Georges, 51, 399
Foltz, Bruce (Seraphim), xii, 1, 324, 398–99, 402–3, 446, 458
Fox, Matthew, 148, 434

Galilei, Galileo, 1, 269, 328
Gore, Albert, 277
Gregorios, Mar Paulos, 453
Guillaumont, Antoine, 416
Guroian, Vigen, 400, 404, 453

Index of Names (Contemporary)

Hansen, James, 449
Hapgood, Isabel F., 452
Hawking, Stephen, 270
Hegel, Georg W.F., 2, 187–88, 366
Heidegger, Martin, 190, 326, 442, 446
Hessel, Dieter T., 402, 447, 453
Hopkins, Gerard Manley, 2, 94, 424, 443

Ignatius IV, Patriarch of Antioch, 405, 435
Irwin, Kevin W., 435

John Paul II, Pope of Rome, 162
Johnson, Elizabeth, 263, 454

Kant, Immanuel, 163, 179, 188, 206, 366, 437
Keynes, Geoffrey, 424

Larchet, Jean-Claude, 121, 417, 422, 427
Lash, Ephrem, 302, 452, 466
Lewis, Clive S., 262, 331
Limouris, Gennadios, 400, 405, 458
Lossky, Vladimir, 106, 111–15, 117–20, 122, 141–43, 369, 400–1, 425–27, 432, 436, 439, 466

Mantzaridis, Georgios I., 446
Marx, Karl, 188, 436
Mathew, Gervase, 101, 331, 425, 459
McDaniel, Jay B., 433
McFague, Sallie, 148, 263, 434, 447
McGinn, Bernard, 426
Merton, Thomas, 100, 425
Meyendorff, John, 405, 417, 424, 426, 452–53
Migne, Jacques P., 300, 421
Mikrayiannanites, Monk Gerasimos, 154
Moltmann, Jürgen, 456
Montefiore, Hugh, 430–31, 433
Muir, John, 3, 332

Nash, James A., 139, 145, 431–34
Nasr, Seyyed Hossein, 424
Nellas, Panayiotis, 366–67, 370, 400, 418–19, 466
Newton, Isaac, 94, 267

Nietzsche, Friedrich W., 3
Nissiotis, Nikos, 6, 193, 438

Oleksa, Michael, 250, 400, 406, 445
O'Meara, John J., 439, 444–47

Peacocke, Arthur R., 405–6, 422, 425, 431, 447
Pelikan, Jaroslav, 308, 454
Posey, Darrell Addison, 435
Prince Philip, Duke of Edinburgh, 154

Raine, Kathleen, 100
Romanides, John, 446
Ruether, Rosemary Radford, 402, 434, 447, 453

Sakharov, Sophrony, 121–30, 427–29, 436
Santmire, H. Paul, 77, 145, 148, 423, 430, 433–34
Schmemann, Alexander, 98, 134, 401, 430, 452
Sheldon-Williams, I.P., 439, 444–47
Sheldrake, Philip, 461
Sherrard, Philip, 6, 102, 210, 401, 416, 422, 424–25, 436, 439, 448, 458–59
Spinoza, Baruch, 180–81
Staniloae, Dumitru, 101, 248, 256, 407, 438, 444, 448
Suzuki, Toshiyuki, 446

Tatakis, B. N., 438
Theokritoff, Elizabeth, 131, 295, 314, 398, 401–2, 407–8, 430, 433, 435, 438, 451–53, 456
Thoreau, Henry David, 3, 87, 332, 447
Thunberg, L., 265, 424, 440, 447
Tolkien, John R.R., 101, 250, 260, 262, 406–7, 447
Tolstoy, Leo, 269, 328, 447
Toynbee, Arnold, 431
Traherne, Thomas, 89, 424
Trembelas, P., 452
Twain, Mark, 261

Vasileios, Archimandrite, 348, 401, 452, 464
Von Balthasar, Hans Urs, 265, 295, 447

Ware, Kallistos (Metropolitan of Diokleia), 141, 318, 408, 416, 422, 424–25, 432, 435–36, 452, 454, 458–59, 462
Weber, Max, 2, 137, 164, 430
White, White, 2, 75, 136, 325, 327, 415, 430–31
Whitman, Walt, 87
Wilken, Robert Louis, 447, 459

Wilson, Edwin O., 435
Wittgenstein, Ludwig, 206

Yannaras, Christos, 186, 438, 448
Yeats, William B., 215

Zernov, Nicolas, 141–42, 432
Zizioulas, John (Metropolitan of Pergamon), 106, 115–21, 154, 163, 204, 227, 409, 427, 435–36, 439, 448, 453
Zosima, Elder, 366, 370

General Index

Adam, 57, 64, 76, 95, 98, 100, 125–27, 129–30, 162, 168–69, 196, 243–44, 265, 279–80, 309, 317, 321, 334–35, 359, 410, 424; fall of, 126–27, 168
air, 1, 10, 81, 87, 92, 104, 153, 156, 198, 213, 238, 280–81, 285–86, 316, 318, 321–23, 329–30, 334, 359
anakephalaiosis. See *recapitulation*
anaphora, 295, 299–300, 410, 451–52
angels, 24, 26–27, 31, 42, 104, 133, 162, 298, 300–1, 304, 309, 311, 314–16, 319, 322, 338, 341–42, 352, 420; cherubim, 300, 304; seraphim, 27, 150, 300, 356, 435, 446
animals, 24–26, 32, 57, 64, 81, 87, 89, 95–99, 101, 124–26, 132–33, 141–42, 165–67, 196–98, 207, 210, 212–13, 240, 278–82, 297–98, 315, 324, 354, 359, 361–62, 401, 415, 428, 436, 450, 454, 457
annunciation, 222, 309, 312, 319, 321–22, 455–57
anthropocentrism, 140, 150, 194–95, 205, 263–66, 274, 434; anthropomorphism, 206
apatheia, 20, 54
apocalypse, 87, 105, 186–87, 189–92
apocryphal, 338
apokatastasis, 119, 410

apophatic, 18–19, 40, 44, 49, 109, 111, 411, 421
ascesis, 33, 79, 161, 369, 420
Athos, Mount, 100, 122, 154, 351, 355, 361, 401, 436, 451–52, 459, 463–66
atmosphere, 132, 137, 248, 259, 360, 467

bacteria, 132–33, 270
baptism, 17–18, 81, 103, 150, 155, 160, 168, 203, 250, 303, 317, 326, 342
beauty, xiv, 2, 13, 16, 20, 34–36, 38–45, 61, 63, 68, 92, 95, 99, 105, 108, 110, 142, 151, 156, 158, 185, 190, 195, 198, 206, 218, 222, 224, 244, 304, 307, 319–20, 324–35, 339, 361, 364, 372, 400–1, 403, 406, 420–21, 444–45, 448, 458–59
Bible, xiii, 51, 56, 65, 86, 97, 105, 138–39, 149–50, 166, 179–82, 195, 197–201, 249, 269, 279, 330, 332, 343, 356, 358, 404, 406, 423, 434–35, 438, 466
biology, 165, 266, 273, 444, 450
body, 19, 21, 48–50, 54, 56, 59, 66, 97, 102, 127, 133, 139, 142–44, 150, 156, 159–61, 176, 185, 195–97, 202, 205–6, 219, 221, 223–24, 227, 239–40, 243, 251, 258–59, 311, 313, 318, 322, 342, 351–53, 360, 363, 366, 370–72, 402, 413, 430, 433, 439, 445, 454; of the

church, 75; of experience, 297; of laws, 232; of society, 161; of tradition, 148
Buddhism, 179, 326, 411
byzantine, 6, 59, 68, 90, 101–2, 189, 249–50, 252–53, 258–59, 309, 326, 331–33, 337, 342, 413, 438, 454, 458–60

Catholic (Roman), 77, 149, 267, 269, 308, 423, 454
chrismation, 81, 161
Christ, 17–18, 38–39, 47, 55, 60, 64, 67, 88–89, 91–93, 97–100, 104, 111, 114–20, 128, 130–31, 133–35, 143, 148, 150–51, 155–61, 168–69, 182–84, 200–1, 203, 208–9, 223–24, 238–41, 246, 249, 251–52, 257, 259–60, 264–65, 282, 298, 303–4, 306, 308–15, 317, 319, 321–24, 326, 329, 338, 341–42, 345–46, 352–53, 355–56, 366, 372, 375–76, 400, 406–7, 410–13, 418, 423, 425, 428–30, 439, 447, 455–57, 466; body of , 118, 130–31, 133, 150, 159, 161, 168–69, 203, 222–24, 241, 342, 352–53, 376, 410
Christianity, xiv, 1–5, 11, 23, 34, 37–38, 75–77, 80, 83–84, 98, 100, 111, 121, 130, 136–41, 143–50, 179, 183, 186–87, 189–90, 238, 240–41, 245–46, 252–55, 258, 261, 263–65, 271, 276, 278–82, 287, 325–33, 335, 337, 398, 402–5, 408–9, 411, 413, 415, 417, 430, 433–35, 445, 447, 449, 453, 462
Christology, 208, 223–24, 338, 404, 447
Church Fathers. *See* patristic theology
climate, 235, 266, 277, 351
climate change, 1, 139, 149, 227, 229–30, 232, 431, 48–450; ozone, 227
Climategate, 277, 449
cloning, 23, 419
communion, xi, 15, 35, 47, 50, 52–53, 55, 78, 89–90, 94, 103, 106–7, 110–18, 120, 135, 157, 160–62, 167–68, 191–92, 204, 289, 307, 318, 321–22, 329, 332, 343, 349–50, 353, 376, 400, 410–11, 426–27, 436, 438–39, 446, 454
confession, 41, 44–45, 77, 161

conservation, 102, 121, 128, 164, 184–185, 211, 263, 442
cosmic, 5, 10, 34, 36–37, 44–45, 60–61, 64, 67–68, 71, 85, 88, 91–93, 98, 100, 102–4, 110, 125, 130, 133–34, 141, 143–44, 148, 159, 191, 206, 210, 218, 222, 249–50, 252–53, 258–59, 261, 265, 273, 295–98, 300, 302, 305–6, 308–9, 318, 341–42, 359, 398–99, 405, 407, 411–12, 418, 422, 433, 451, 453, 457, 461; liturgy, 17, 157 , 295, 447
cosmology, 36, 59, 61, 115, 131, 134, 190, 210, 215, 219, 247, 249, 259, 295–96, 338, 402, 404, 406–7, 416, 422, 425, 430, 439, 448, 451–52, 456
cosmos, 10, 13, 36, 39–40, 42, 44, 55, 59–71, 90, 93, 103, 131–34, 141–43, 146, 158, 167, 178, 186–87, 190–91, 206, 213, 239, 245, 249, 251, 253, 262, 271, 289, 295, 302, 304, 309, 313, 318, 321–23, 326, 338, 343, 346, 404, 406–7, 415, 419, 422, 424, 430, 451, 456
Council of Chalcedon. *See* ecumenical councils
creation, xi, xiii–xiv, 1–7, 9–14, 16, 27, 31–32, 34, 36, 40–41, 46–47, 49, 53, 55, 57, 60–64, 66, 68–70, 73, 76–79, 81, 85–86, 88–89, 92–95, 98–102, 104, 106, 109–21, 124, 126, 128–30, 133–35, 138–39, 141–43, 148, 151–54, 156, 158, 160–64, 166–71, 180, 184, 187, 193–205, 207–9, 213–14, 219–20, 222–25, 227, 230, 232, 245–46, 248–49, 252–53, 256, 258–59, 264–66, 269–74, 278–79, 287, 295–331, 333–35, 338–49, 353–54, 357–61, 363–64, 369, 372, 374, 376, 398–412, 417–18, 422–28, 431, 433–36, 438–41, 446–48, 451–58, 466
creator, xi, xiv, 3–5, 9–10, 18, 21, 32, 47, 49, 71, 76, 86, 88–89, 91–95, 97–100, 102, 109, 119, 127, 133, 138, 141, 160–61, 169, 183, 190–91, 196, 198, 200–1, 203, 208, 214, 219, 252, 261, 269, 271–74, 287, 295, 302, 305, 307, 309–14, 317, 320, 325, 329–31, 334–35, 339–45, 369, 401, 407, 412, 424, 435–36, 439, 447

cross, the, 100, 103–4, 133, 158, 161, 168, 259, 312, 316, 341, 355, 433, 461
Crusades, the, 253
crucifixion, 98, 104, 259

David, 298, 300
death, 17–18, 60, 64, 67, 93, 96, 100, 104, 115–16, 119–20, 122, 133–34, 139, 149, 160, 168, 202, 211, 219, 254, 282–83, 305, 328, 338, 351–52, 355, 361, 365–66, 370, 410–11, 425, 427, 429, 439, 448
deification, 19, 21, 40, 56, 65, 67–68, 97, 110, 126, 142, 223–24, 249, 258, 288, 307–8, 317, 330, 346, 349, 352, 356, 366, 400, 404, 413, 417–18, 421–23, 466; *zoon theoumenon*, 97
desert, 78, 80, 145, 157, 162, 243, 246–49, 253, 258–62, 316, 320, 345, 399, 429, 443, 446, 464
diakrisis. *See* discernment
discernment, 37, 188
divinization. *See* deification
domination. *See* dominion
dominion, 24, 31–32, 57, 76, 100, 138, 140, 150, 160, 163, 166, 193, 194, 196, 265, 278, 280, 285–86, 289, 408, 451
doxa. *See* doxology
doxology, 35, 40, 98, 338–39, 341

ecological movement, 75, 82, 264–65
ecology, 169, 402, 444; deep ecology, 78
economy, 79, 164, 169, 188, 233, 284, 342, 363, 399; divine economy, 432
ecumenical councils, 15, 43, 60, 142, 182, 223
Ecumenical Patriarchate, xi, 122, 153–54, 227, 399–401, 425, 427, 464, 466
eikon. *See* icon
energies (divine), 35, 56, 91, 106, 113–14, 118–19, 125, 246–47, 249–50, 256, 258–59, 261, 343, 346, 413, 428
energy, 49, 54, 128, 132, 190–91, 200, 202, 229, 249, 258, 277, 371, 404, 411, 448, 450
enlightenment, 2, 21, 40–41, 49, 163, 187, 399

entelechy, 190, 410
epiphany, 6, 35, 155, 340, 399–400, 404–6, 453
eschatological. *See* eschatology
eschatology, 77, 79–82, 84, 149, 186–87, 191, 306, 319–20, 341–42, 405–6, 418, 452
essence, divine, 3, 16, 92, 108–10, 112–13, 182, 343, 426
ethanol, 283, 450
ethic(s), xii, xiii, 1, 37, 82–84, 121, 127–28, 130, 144, 148–49, 155, 169, 171, 195–96, 201, 276–79, 281–82, 285–87, 289, 325, 339, 359, 363, 399, 403–4, 407, 409, 430, 432–35, 442, 453
ethos, 21, 171, 253, 288, 363–64, 408–9
Eucharist, 17, 81, 98–99, 101, 115, 118, 131–34, 161, 168–70, 191–92, 251, 253, 307, 326, 341, 345, 357, 362, 409, 430, 452
Eve, 39, 44, 57, 76, 98–99, 149, 160, 279–80, 312, 321, 324, 350, 372, 466
evil, 16, 28–29, 54, 102, 137, 140, 189, 194, 202, 246, 253, 287, 318, 322, 344, 349, 359–60, 363, 410–11, 429, 436
evolution (theory of), 165, 198–99, 273
ex nihilo, 112, 115–17, 178, 208
Ezekiel, 17, 81, 89, 251, 418

fasting, 20, 51, 103, 158, 289, 356, 359–62, 372, 465
feminine, 253, 445; feminist, 252
flesh, 12, 50, 65, 84–85, 97, 133, 139, 142–43, 159, 183, 191, 197, 208, 223, 286, 310–11, 313, 317, 319, 321, 323, 345, 347, 352, 367, 405, 410, 430, 454–55
forest, xiv, 1, 62, 86, 153, 259–61, 282, 329, 340, 352–53, 374–75, 450

genetic engineering, 179, 419
global warming, 57, 276, 284–85, 449–51
gnosis, 14, 33, 48, 310, 411, 416, 427; neo-Gnosticism, 185
Gnostic. *See* gnosis

grace, 6, 46, 48–49, 51, 53–56, 65, 97, 102, 143, 145, 157, 161, 203, 246, 252, 274, 288, 301, 314, 317, 330, 346–47, 351–54, 369, 410, 420, 427–28, 430, 433, 446, 453
Green Patriarch, xiii, 150, 307, 453

heart, xv, 5, 13, 42, 45–46, 50, 52, 55, 57, 62, 73, 88, 91, 96, 98, 102, 111, 123, 130, 145–46, 156–57, 161, 211, 281, 296, 299, 328, 330, 333–34, 350, 353–54, 356, 360–61, 370, 372, 376, 402, 418, 429, 431, 433
hermit, 123, 338, 340, 460
hesychast, 51, 330, 459
hierarchy, 16–17, 19, 23–27, 29–32, 161, 219, 252, 326, 417, 419, 443
homoousios, 107, 127
humility, 151–52, 159, 183, 218, 270, 352–53
hypostasis, 10, 12, 16, 53, 109, 116–20, 125, 183, 200, 223, 343, 345, 369, 411

icon, xiv, 4, 6, 17, 31, 34, 40, 95, 150, 156–57, 162, 238–41, 249, 255, 258, 272, 288, 290, 309, 326–27, 331, 335, 352, 366–67, 369, 372, 401–2, 404, 407, 429, 445, 453
image and likeness, 23, 34, 76, 126, 166, 183
image-archetypes, 219–25, 441
incarnation (divine), 156
individualism, 125, 255–57, 352
individualistic. *See* individualism
industrial revolution, 37
industry, 188
intellect. See *nous*
Isaiah, 80, 89, 95, 288, 300, 312, 356, 413
Islam, 78, 227–28, 230, 412

Jacob, 89, 104, 318, 457
Jesus, 17, 37, 47, 84, 88, 104, 110, 117, 128, 155–56, 222, 239, 251, 256, 299, 317, 355, 399, 403, 413, 443
Jordan (river), 155, 303–4, 316, 342
Joseph, 308, 312, 330, 431, 454, 459

Judaism, 98, 144; Hebrews, 38, 161–62, 179, 181, 196, 368, 437, 465, 467; Jewish, 148; Jews, 10, 51, 430, 451

kataphatic, 18, 411
katharsis. See *purification*
kenotic, 100, 108, 310, 349; *kenosis*, 311
kingdom of God, 143, 149, 187, 278, 287–90, 350, 405, 409
kingdom of heaven. *See* kingdom of God
ktisis, 199–201, 204–5, 208, 262, 438–39, 456

liturgy, xii, 4, 17–18, 21, 71, 99, 102, 104, 141, 156–58, 169, 239, 253, 288, 295–301, 306–10, 312–13, 315, 318, 320–21, 323, 326, 330–31, 338, 355, 370, 375, 404, 410–11, 417, 430, 436, 438, 447, 451–52, 454, 456, 458, 461, 463, 467
logikon zoon, 96, 166
logos (logoi), 3, 9, 11–19, 21–22, 35–36, 38, 45, 60, 62–66, 68–71, 90–92, 113, 166–67, 186, 190, 219, 221, 223, 249–50, 256, 262, 265–66, 331–32, 339, 346, 411–12, 415–18, 422, 440, 445; *logismoi*, 54–55
Logos, xiii, 3, 10–16, 18–19, 35–36, 53, 62–66, 71, 89–94, 109–11, 117, 191, 197, 208, 219–25, 250, 259, 262, 331–32, 342–43, 345, 352, 406, 411–12, 415–16, 418, 441, 465
love, xiv–xv, 1, 3, 5, 23–24, 27–32, 48–49, 54, 56–57, 66, 78, 82, 85–87, 94, 96–97, 99–100, 103, 105–15, 117, 119, 123–26, 129–30, 143, 146, 149–51, 157–58, 160, 170, 173, 191, 195–96, 200, 218, 239, 248, 252, 265, 278, 280–81, 285–87, 289, 324, 327–28, 330–31, 335–36, 345, 348, 351, 353–54, 361, 363, 367, 369, 372, 375–76, 407, 419, 425, 427–29, 433, 451, 453, 458–59

macrocosm, 60, 206
Manichean, 33, 189
martyrdom, 103, 249–50, 259, 406, 445

material world, 13–14, 48, 102, 169–70, 193, 202–3, 213, 270, 311, 326, 332, 335, 402, 408, 411
matter, 2, 10–11, 13–14, 16, 19, 23, 25, 38, 40, 48–49, 55, 82, 90, 102, 132–34, 139, 142, 145, 150, 157, 182, 190, 193–203, 207, 217, 223, 306, 310, 313, 352, 361, 402, 404, 433, 437–38, 454–55
mediator, 98, 102, 265, 275, 440, 447
medieval, 32, 40, 77–78, 81, 136, 187–88, 190, 192, 194, 245, 251, 253, 255, 257, 300, 337, 401, 403, 406–7, 415, 443–46, 459, 461; middle ages, 178, 190, 253, 259, 406–7, 445
microcosm, 60–61, 68, 70, 98, 167, 186, 206, 363, 440, 447
minerals, 24, 32, 132
monasticism, 6, 14, 59–60, 82, 87, 100, 103, 121–22, 124, 128, 154, 247–48, 256, 269, 299, 328, 337, 339, 348, 350–51, 355, 366, 371, 373, 398, 405, 451, 464, 466
monk. *See* monasticism
Moses, 88–90, 103, 333, 345, 350, 402, 424
Muslim. *See* Islam

natural contemplation. See *theoria physike*
natural environment, xi, 1, 3, 23, 87, 137, 153–55, 159, 166, 188, 202, 207, 274, 326, 339, 352, 357–58, 406, 408–9
nature, xiv, 2–3, 5–7, 9, 13–17, 20–23, 28–29, 32–33, 41–42, 46, 50, 56–57, 60, 63–64, 66–69, 73, 75–80, 84–85, 89–92, 94–97, 100–1, 104, 108, 110, 116, 119–20, 127, 134, 136–38, 140–46, 148–51, 153, 156–57, 159, 163–65, 167–70, 175–203, 206–8, 211–16, 218, 223, 230–31, 236, 239–40, 245–48, 250, 253–56, 258, 260, 262–65, 269, 271, 273–75, 277, 279–81, 283, 285, 288–90, 296, 301–6, 309–13, 315, 317, 320, 322, 325–33, 335–49, 351, 353–54, 357, 359–62, 366–68, 370, 372, 374, 398–407, 411–12, 418–19, 421, 423, 425, 427, 430–36, 438–41, 443–44, 447, 451, 453–59, 464, 466; *natura naturans, natura naturata*, 215

nature: divine, 97, 110, 182–184, 223, 336, 340, 343, 345, 421, 440; human, 46, 50, 58, 66, 85, 89, 104, 179, 183–185, 199, 208, 214, 223, 239, 320, 349, 359, 423, 441
nepsis, 103, 334
Nicene Creed, 182
Noah, 249, 276, 279–80, 286, 448, 450
noetic. *See nous*
nous, 4, 10, 17, 19–20, 23, 35, 40, 42, 44, 46–50, 53–56, 65–67, 91, 141, 175, 177–78, 193–94, 197, 269, 271, 298, 326, 328–32, 334–35, 338–39, 411, 416, 418, 420, 437, 465
nuclear holocaust. *See* nuclear
nuclear, 82, 355

ousia. *See* essence, divine

paganism, xiv, 38, 71, 87, 140, 184, 208, 302, 327, 334, 342, 434; neopaganism, 147, 326
panentheism, 90, 111, 141, 405, 422
pantheism, 90, 111, 141, 180, 343
Pascha. *See* Passover
passions, 12, 14, 46, 48–51, 53–55, 58–59, 289, 363
Passover, 157, 310, 330, 352, 355, 465
patristic theology, 6, 16, 159, 167, 183–85, 206, 259, 264–66, 274, 342, 358–59, 363, 411, 446
Pentecost, 151, 298, 303
person, 19, 23, 38, 46, 48–49, 51–52, 56, 60–62, 66–67, 90, 92, 97–99, 102–3, 121, 123–30, 157, 161, 166, 181, 183, 190–91, 195–96, 204, 208, 232, 255, 271–74, 283, 297, 307, 326, 328, 331–32, 341, 343, 347–49, 353–56, 363, 367, 369–70, 400, 402, 404, 411, 418, 425, 427, 466; personhood, 97–99, 115–16, 118–20, 208, 369
Philokalia, 6, 15, 103, 326, 328, 334, 412, 416–17, 422, 424, 458–59, 465
philosophy, xii, 4, 9–10, 36, 51, 53, 78–79, 83, 165–66, 175–81, 187, 189, 193–94, 198–99, 205, 207, 215–16, 251, 281, 326–27, 333, 337, 365–66, 370, 374,

399, 403, 418–20, 432, 435, 437–38, 442, 446, 449–50; neoscholasticism, 113; stoicism, 11, 84
physis, 176–78, 180–82, 204–5, 207–8, 332, 438; *physike*, 95
planet, 69–70, 78–79, 82, 102, 104, 132, 153–54, 207, 211, 230, 232–33, 308, 409, 420
plant, 27, 29, 86–87, 121, 123, 128, 132, 176–77, 235, 280, 329, 354, 428; photosynthesis, 132
platonism, 194, 331, 420; middle, 331, 420; neoplatonism, 443
pollution, 1, 82, 97, 153, 155, 199, 202, 280, 284
population, 138, 233, 266, 268, 277, 284–85, 403, 432, 448
poverty, 1, 34, 78–79, 82, 85, 87, 124, 155, 157, 237, , 268, 278, 282–87, 303, 310, 421
praktike, 54, 412
preservation, xi, 29, 77–79, 101, 113, 124, 154–55, 160, 164, 170, 265, 286–89, 325, 357, 362
priest of creation, 39, 42, 44–45, 57, 61, 64, 88, 95, 99, 122, 124, 133, 164–65, 167–71, 227, 250, 265, 275, 305, 372–73, 375, 409, 421, 435, 453; royal priesthood, 129–30, 428
prophet, 13, 39, 92, 95, 356
Protestant, xiii, 75, 163, 252, 256, 260, 430; Calvinist, 163
providence, 19, 50, 63, 77, 91, 181, 339, 344, 411
purification, 49, 53–54, 56, 311, 330, 352, 412; *katharsis*, 3, 330, 412

reason, 10, 14, 16–29, 32, 35, 40, 42, 48, 52–55, 57, 62–64, 67, 70–71, 83, 90, 96, 101–2, 110–12, 141, 149, 153, 163, 165–68, 177, 178–79, 181, 183, 186, 188, 190, 193–96, 202, 208, 214, 217, 229, 231–32, 239, 249, 253, 267, 281, 298, 300–1, 304–5, 315, 322, 338, 342, 344–45, 355, 357–59, 361–63, 369, 411, 418, 420–21, 423, 432, 436–37, 447, 449, 451

recapitulation, 168, 222, 410
recycling, 57, 129, 283, 287
Red Sea, 304, 340
redemption, 4, 29–30, 143, 148, 200–1, 246, 257, 309, 311–12, 318–19, 321, 323, 399, 423
Reformation, 148, 260, 434
renunciation, 53, 79–80, 158–59
repentance, 51, 53, 81, 84, 102, 121, 151, 159–60, 256, 276, 278, 330, 353, 363; *metanoia*, 102–3
resurrection, 17–18, 50, 64, 67, 98, 131, 134, 160, 168, 183–84, 197, 219, 329, 338, 342, 349, 352, 355, 410–11, 425, 439, 448, 450, 461–63
romanticism, 82, 153, 194–195, 202, 245

sacraments, xi, 41, 44–45, 81, 87–88, 90, 94, 103, 135, 152, 157, 160–61, 168, 240, 253, 401–3, 407, 425, 452; unction, 161, 337
salvation, 4, 29–30, 78, 84, 104, 120, 123–24, 126, 128, 138–41, 187, 202, 206, 258, 302, 310, 312, 318, 321, 356–57, 403, 407–8, 410–11, 427, 438; soteriology, 35
science, xii, 2, 21, 59, 69–70, 78–79, 82, 85, 127, 129, 136–37, 163, 165–66, 176, 193, 203, 216–17, 226, 256, 263, 266–67, 269–71, 273–74, 276–77, 282, 327, 362–63, 398, 400–1, 403–5, 407–8, 423, 430, 434–35, 438, 446–50, 453
scripture. *See* Bible
sexuality, 140, 200
sin, xiii, 54, 102, 138, 143, 146, 159, 169, 184, 187, 243–46, 265, 303, 308, 313, 358, 363, 457; original, 157, 246, 274
Sinai, Mount, 298, 350
sobornost, 4, 110, 255, 402–4, 407–8, 425, 427
sophia, 20, 107–10, 117–20, 252, 374, 399, 403, 406, 426–27, 448
sophiology, 111, 113, 426

486   General Index

soul, xiv, 3, 19–21, 35–36, 42, 46–48, 50, 52, 54–56, 66, 71, 77, 84, 87, 98, 104, 110, 123–24, 139, 148, 156, 161, 197, 213, 298, 304, 324, 328–31, 333–35, 339–40, 346, 351–52, 410–412, 416, 418–19, 434, 439

spermatikos logos, 11, 412

stars, xiv, 42, 69–70, 92, 94, 97, 101, 132–33, 157–58, 178, 256, 297–301, 306, 333–34, 337–39, 341–42, 359, 424, 446, 466

steward. *See* stewardship

stewardship, xiii, 100, 130, 138, 148, 163–64, 169, 171, 185, 325, 405, 431, 433, 453; steward, 39, 138, 163–64, 169–70, 198, 264

Sufism, 78, 423

sun, 16, 42, 92, 94, 132, 157, 195, 244, 277, 300–1, 303, 310, 312, 314, 326, 333, 339, 341–42, 359, 444, 450, 461, 466

synergy, 47, 54, 56–57, 131, 246, 249, 258, 449

Tabor, Mount, 156, 345

Taoism, 100, 326

telos, 35–36, 149

theologia, 9, 15, 51, 53–54, 403, 419, 443, 445, 463

theophany, 15, 32, 141, 203, 220, 302–3, 308, 310, 315, 354

theoria, 3, 46–50, 52, 54, 64, 330, 332, 411–12, 426, 452

theoria physike, 3, 46–49, 51–55, 57, 64, 95, 191, 330, 332, 339–40, 411–12, 419, 421

theosis. *See* deification

Theotokos, 252, 307–9, 312–14, 317–20, 406, 411–13, 452–57, 467

transfiguration, 4, 6, 68, 80, 82, 98, 141, 156, 223–24, 256, 307, 345, 347, 352, 402, 405–6, 408, 422, 445, 453, 463, 465

transform, 10, 12, 19, 20, 54, 58, 65, 81–82, 87, 101, 103, 108, 131–34, 138, 143, 146, 148, 170, 179, 187, 214, 222, 224, 286, 288, 306–7, 312, 323, 327, 346, 368, 440

transparency, 94–95, 108, 222

tree of life. *See* cross, the

tree(s), 81, 86–90, 94, 100–1, 103–5, 118, 124–28, 130, 132, 141, 150, 158, 162, 166, 183, 198, 208, 211, 213, 236, 240, 259, 280, 297–98, 312, 316, 318, 329–30, 336, 351–53, 359, 361, 366–67, 374–75, 439; cosmic , 92, 104

Trinitarian. *See* Trinity, Holy (Person)

Trinity, Holy (Person), 11, 14, 16, 62, 71, 91, 106–10, 115–20, 125, 162, 183–84, 190–91, 208, 220, 224, 246, 251, 315, 340–41, 343, 356, 356, 369, 370, 411, 413, 441

uncreated, 3, 19, 63, 66–68, 91, 95, 97, 110, 113–19, 125, 134, 141, 156, 190–92, 205, 208, 219, 246, 248, 256, 260–61, 265, 288, 313, 341, 343, 347, 352, 360, 439, 441, 445, 449

universe, 10–12, 61–62, 67, 69–70, 88, 90, 92–93, 95, 101, 103–4, 141–43, 161, 167, 186–88, 190, 206, 211, 222, 225, 258, 269, 298, 303, 312–13, 322, 328, 330, 337, 341–42, 353, 400, 406, 425, 439, 446–48, 456, 460

Vatican, 150, 460

waste, 129, 157, 363

water(s), 1, 10, 46, 63, 69, 76, 80, 87, 92, 104, 124, 128, 131–33, 141, 150, 153, 156–57, 160, 180, 198, 203, 214, 226, 233, 239, 248–50, 298, 301–4, 312, 316–18, 322, 324, 326, 328–29, 333–34, 337, 340, 359, 365, 368–69, 373, 443, 452, 465; living, 161

wilderness, 88, 122, 210, 235–36, 240–42, 248, 282, 288, 315, 400, 405–6, 431–32, 435, 442–43, 451

wisdom, 10–14, 20, 25–26, 37–38, 40, 42, 44, 59, 71, 91, 98, 113, 122, 131, 135, 149, 181, 200, 214–15, 248, 252, 304–5, 329, 334, 339, 356, 374–75, 402, 416, 426, 435–37, 448, 451, 457–59

World War II, 230, 232
World Wide Fund for Nature International, 154, 400, 425, 427, 464
worship, 17, 20–21, 76, 101, 140, 157, 218, 276, 288–89, 295–303, 305–6, 308–9, 313, 323, 325, 333–34, 339, 342, 354, 362, 407, 411–12, 421, 451–52
WWF. *See* World Wide Fund for Nature International

ORTHODOX CHRISTIANITY AND CONTEMPORARY THOUGHT

SERIES EDITORS
George E. Demacopoulos and Aristotle Papanikolaou

Ecumenical Patriarch Bartholomew, *In the World, Yet Not of the World: Social and Global Initiatives of Ecumenical Patriarch Bartholomew.* Edited by John Chryssavgis. Foreword by José Manuel Barroso.

Ecumenical Patriarch Bartholomew, *Speaking the Truth in Love: Theological and Spiritual Exhortations of Ecumenical Patriarch Bartholomew.* Edited by John Chryssavgis. Foreword by Dr. Rowan Williams, Archbishop of Canterbury.

Ecumenical Patriarch Bartholomew, *On Earth as in Heaven: Ecological Vision and Initiatives of Ecumenical Patriarch Bartholomew.* Edited by John Chryssavgis. Foreword by His Royal Highness the Duke of Edinburgh.

George E. Demacopoulos and Aristotle Papanikolaou (eds.), *Orthodox Constructions of the West.*

John Chryssavgis and Bruce V. Foltz (eds.), *Toward an Ecology of Transfiguration: Orthodox Christian Perspectives on Environment, Nature, and Creation.* Prefatory Letter by Ecumenical Patriarch Bartholomew. Foreword by Bill McKibben.

www.ingramcontent.com/pod-product-compliance
Lightning Source LLC
Chambersburg PA
CBHW031227290426
44109CB00012B/188